W9-BDN-646

College Accounting

Chapters 1–14

College Accounting

Chapters 1–14

John J. Wild
University of Wisconsin at Madison

Vernon J. Richardson
University of Arkansas

Ken W. Shaw
University of Missouri

 **McGraw-Hill Irwin**

Boston   Burr Ridge, IL   Dubuque, IA   Madison, WI   New York
San Francisco   St. Louis   Bangkok   Bogotá   Caracas   Kuala Lumpur
Lisbon   London   Madrid   Mexico City   Milan   Montreal   New Delhi
Santiago   Seoul   Singapore   Sydney   Taipei   Toronto

The McGraw-Hill Companies

McGraw-Hill
Irwin

COLLEGE ACCOUNTING

Published by McGraw-Hill/Irwin, a business unit of The McGraw-Hill Companies, Inc., 1221 Avenue of the Americas, New York, NY, 10020. Copyright © 2008 by The McGraw-Hill Companies, Inc. All rights reserved. No part of this publication may be reproduced or distributed in any form or by any means, or stored in a database or retrieval system, without the prior written consent of The McGraw-Hill Companies, Inc., including, but not limited to, in any network or other electronic storage or transmission, or broadcast for distance learning.

Some ancillaries, including electronic and print components, may not be available to customers outside the United States.

This book is printed on acid-free paper.

1 2 3 4 5 6 7 8 9 0 DOW/DOW 0 9 8 7

ISBN   978-0-07-337944-9 (chapters 1–30)
MHID 0-07-337944-1 (chapters 1–30)
ISBN   978-0-07-333669-5 (chapters 1–14)
MHID 0-07-333669-6 (chapters 1–14)

Editorial director: *Stewart Mattson*
Senior sponsoring editor: *Steve Schuetz*
Developmental editor II: *Christina A. Sanders*
Executive marketing manager: *Krista Bettino*
Senior media producer: *Elizabeth Mavetz*
Project manager: *Kristin Bradley*
Lead production supervisor: *Michael R. McCormick*
Lead designer: *Matthew Baldwin*
Photo research coordinator: *Kathy Shive*
Photo researcher: *Sarah Evertson*
Supplement producer: *Ira C. Roberts*
Lead media project manager: *Cathy L. Tepper*
Cover design: *Matthew Baldwin*
Cover image: *© Corbis Images*
Typeface: *10.5/12 Times Roman*
Compositor: *Techbooks*
Printer: *R. R. Donnelley*

Library of Congress Cataloging-in-Publication Data

Wild, John J.
    College accounting / John J. Wild, Vernon J. Richardson, Ken W. Shaw.
        p. cm.
    Includes index.
    ISBN-13: 978-0-07-337944-9 (chapters 1–30 : alk. paper)
    ISBN-10: 0-07-337944-1 (chapters 1–30 : alk. paper)
    ISBN-13: 978-0-07-333669-5 (chapters 1–14 : alk. paper)
    ISBN-10: 0-07-333669-6 (chapters 1–14 : alk. paper)
    1. Accounting. I. Richardson, Vernon J. II. Shaw, Ken W. III. Title.
HF5636.W67 2008
657—dc22
                                                                2007002396

www.mhhe.com

To my wife **Gail** and children, **Kimberly, Jonathan, Stephanie,** and **Trevor.**

To my wife **Connie** and children, **Alison, Melissa, Hyrum, Joseph, Rebecca, Benjamin, Rachel, Bethany, Matthew, Daniel,** and **David.**

To my wife **Linda** and children, **Erin, Emily,** and **Jacob.**

Dear Friends and Colleagues,

We all struggle with many of the same teaching challenges: motivating students to learn, making accounting relevant to them, integrating technology, and covering crucial material. We wrote this book intending to give our students and us the means to confront each of those challenges.

One problem we find with many college accounting books is that their dated examples and boring companies fail to engage students. As instructors, we are responsible for bringing accounting to life through interesting and contemporary examples of exciting companies and industries. This book's chapter-opening vignettes, and its many examples and marginal notes showcase successful, dynamic entrepreneurs that excite and engage students. Discussions of ethics, fraud, and the Sarbanes-Oxley Act further engage students. We also illustrate many key accounting concepts using the financial statements of Best Buy, Circuit City, and other well-recognized companies.

We all believe that our students must be able to prepare and interpret accounting information to successfully enter the business world. We use short learning sessions, with clear examples and objectives, to ensure student success. To help students transition, we show students where and how business decisions draw on accounting knowledge. An example is the role-playing scenario titled "You Call It" that places students in situations where they must solve business problems.

Students today learn in ways beyond reading chapters and attending classes. Important developments in technology are creating new avenues for learning accounting. Working together, this book's publisher and we developed new tools to reach and sustain students throughout the course. An exciting example of those tools is Homework Manager™ or Homework Manager Plus™ (which includes an interactive eBook). Homework Manager is our application of the accounting adage that "perfect practice makes perfect," and it now includes an algorithmic Test Bank. Other highly successful tools include the book's Online Learning Center and Carol Yacht's General Ledger and Peachtree package.

This is an exciting time to be an accounting instructor. We welcome your thoughts on how we can continue to engage today's accounting students and prepare them for tomorrow's business world.

John Vern Ken

John J. Wild is a professor of accounting and the Robert and Monica Beyer Distinguished Professor at the University of Wisconsin at Madison. He previously held appointments at Michigan State University and the University of Manchester in England. He received his BBA, MS, and PhD from the University of Wisconsin.

Professor Wild teaches accounting courses at both the undergraduate and graduate levels. He has received the Mabel W. Chipman Excellence-in-Teaching Award, the departmental Excellence-in-Teaching Award, and the Teaching Excellence Award from the 2003 and 2005 business graduates at the University of Wisconsin. He also received the Beta Alpha Psi and Roland F. Salmonson Excellence-in-Teaching Award from Michigan State University. Professor Wild is a past KPMG Peat Marwick National Fellow and is a recipient of fellowships from the American Accounting Association and the Ernst and Young Foundation.

Professor Wild is an active member of the American Accounting Association and its sections. He has served on several committees of these organizations, including the Outstanding Accounting Educator Award, Wildman Award, National Program Advisory, Publications, and Research Committees. Professor Wild is author of *Fundamental Accounting Principles, Financial Accounting* and *Financial Statement Analysis*, published by McGraw-Hill/Irwin. His research appears in The Accounting Review, Journal of Accounting Research, Journal of Accounting and Economics, Contemporary Accounting Research, Journal of Accounting, Auditing and Finance, Journal of Accounting and Public Policy, and other journals. He is past associate editor of Contemporary Accounting Research and has served on several editorial boards including The Accounting Review.

Professor Wild, his wife, and four children enjoy travel, music, sports, and community activities.

Vernon J. Richardson is Professor of Accounting and the Ralph L. McQueen Distinguished Chair in the Sam M. Walton College of Business at the University of Arkansas. He received his BS, Masters of Accountancy, and MBA from Brigham Young University and a PhD in accounting from the University of Illinois at Urbana-Champaign. He has taught students at the University of Arkansas, University of Illinois, Brigham Young University, University of Kansas, and the China Europe International Business School (Shanghai).

Professor Richardson is a member of the American Accounting Association. Professor Richardson has published articles in the Journal of Accounting and Economics, Journal of Accounting and Public Policy, Financial Analysts Journal, MIS Quarterly, Journal of Operations Management, Journal of Marketing, and the American Business Law Journal. He is currently an associate editor at MIS Quarterly.

Professor Richardson, his wife, and their eleven children all enjoy music, traveling, sports, and watching movies.

Ken W. Shaw is an associate professor of accounting and the Joseph A. Silvoso Faculty Fellow at the University of Missouri at Columbia. He previously was on the faculty at the University of Maryland at College Park. He received an accounting degree from Bradley University and an MBA and PhD from the University of Wisconsin. He is a Certified Public Accountant with work experience in public accounting.

Professor Shaw teaches financial accounting at the undergraduate and graduate levels. He was voted the "Most Influential Professor" by the 2005 and 2006 School of Accountancy graduating classes and won a College Excellence in Teaching Award in 2003. He is also the faculty advisor to his School's chapter of Beta Alpha Psi, a national accounting fraternity.

Professor Shaw is an active member of the American Accounting Association and its sections. He has served on committees of these organizations and presented his research papers at national and regional meetings. Professor Shaw's research appears in the Journal of Accounting Research; Contemporary Accounting Research; Journal of Financial and Quantitative Analysis; Journal of the American Taxation Association; Journal of Accounting, Auditing, and Finance; Journal of Financial Research; Research in Accounting Regulation; and other journals. He currently serves on the editorial boards of Issues in Accounting Education and the Journal of Business Research.

In his leisure time, Professor Shaw enjoys tennis, cycling, music, and coaching his children's sports teams.

Give your students an Edge!

College Accounting

Help get your students to ride the wave of success. *College Accounting (CA)* will help your students succeed by **giving them an edge** with leading-edge accounting content that engages students, and with state-of-the-art technology.

One of the greatest challenges students confront in a college accounting course is seeing the relevance of materials. *CA* tackles this issue head on with **engaging content** and a **motivating style**. Students are motivated when reading materials that are **clear and relevant**. *CA* stands apart in engaging students. Its chapter-opening vignettes showcase dynamic, successful, entrepreneurial individuals and companies guaranteed to **interest and excite readers**. This text's featured companies–Best Buy and Circuit City–engage students with their annual reports, which are great vehicles for **learning** financial statements. Further, this book's coverage of the accounting cycle is widely praised for its **clarity and effectiveness**.

CA also delivers **cutting-edge technology** to help students succeed. **Homework Manager** provides students with instant grading and feedback for assignments that are completed online. **Homework Manager Plus** integrates an online version of the textbook with our popular Homework Manager system. A new **Algorithmic Test Bank** in Homework Manager offers infinite variations of numerical test bank questions. *CA* also offers accounting students portable **iPod-ready content**.

We're confident you'll agree that **CA gives your students the edge to succeed**.

Cutting-Edge Content

College Accounting by Wild, Richardson and Shaw brings excitement to your College Accounting course in its extensive use of small business examples, integration of computerized learning tools, superior end-of-chapter material, and a highly engaging pedagogical design. *College Accounting* motivates students with real-world applications and examples including engaging chapter openers featuring real entrepreneurs. The text also includes the financial statements of Best Buy and Circuit City to further engage students by applying knowledge learned in the course directly to a familiar company.

Cutting-Edge Technology

College Accounting offers the most advanced and comprehensive technology on the market in a seamless, easy-to-use platform. As students learn in different ways, *CA* provides a technology smorgasbord that helps students learn more effectively and efficiently. Homework Manager, eBook options, and iPod content are some of the options available. Homework Manager Plus takes learning to another level by integrating an online version of the textbook with all the power of Homework Manager. Technology offerings include the following:

- Homework Manager
- Homework Manager Plus
- iPod content
- Algorithmic Test Bank
- Online Learning Center

- Carol Yacht's General Ledger and Peachtree Complete
- ALEKS for the Accounting Cycle
- ALEKS for Financial Accounting

Cutting-Edge Support

McGraw-Hill/Irwin has mobilized a new force of product specialists committed to training and supporting the technology we offer. Our commitment to instructor service and support is top notch and leads the industry. Our new "McGraw-Hill Cares" program provides you with the fastest answers to your questions or solutions to your training needs. Ask your McGraw-Hill sales rep about our Key Media Support Plan and the McGraw-Hill Cares Program.

What Can McGraw-Hill Technology Offer You?

Whether you are just getting started with technology in your course, or you are ready to embrace the latest advances in electronic content delivery and course management, McGraw-Hill/Irwin has the technology you need, and provides training and support that will help you every step of the way.

Our most popular technologies, Homework Manager and Homework Manager Plus, are optional online Homework Management systems that will allow you to assign problems and exercises from the text for your students to work out in an online format. Student results are automatically graded, and the students receive instant feedback on their work. Homework Manager Plus adds an online version of the text for direct access while completing homework within Homework Manager.

Students can also use the Online Learning Center associated with this text on their own to enhance their knowledge of accounting. Plus we now offer iPod content for students who want to study on the go with their iPod.

For instructors, we provide all of the crucial instructor supplements on one easy to use Instructor CD-ROM; we can help build a custom class Website for your course using PageOut; we can deliver a fully developed online course for you to conduct through Blackboard, WebCT, or eCollege; and we have a technical support team that will provide training and support for our key technology products.

How Can Students Study on the Go Using Their iPod?

iPod Content

Harness the power of one of the most popular technology tools students use today–the Apple iPod. Our innovative approach allows students to download audio and video presentations right into their iPod and take learning materials with them wherever they go. Students just need to visit the Online Learning Center at www.mhhe.com/wildCA to download our iPod content. For each chapter of the book they will be able to download audio narrated lecture presentations, financial accounting videos, and even self quizzes designed for use on various versions of iPods.

It makes review and study time as easy as putting in headphones.

How Can My Students Use the Web to Complete Homework?

McGraw-Hill's Homework Manager
is a Web-based supplement that duplicates problem structures directly from the end-of-chapter material in our textbook, using algorithms to provide a limitless supply of online self-graded assignments that can be used for student practice, homework, or testing. Each assignment has a unique solution. Say goodbye to cheating in your classroom; say hello to the power and flexibility you've been waiting for in creating assignments. Quick Studies, Exercises, and Problems are available with Homework Manager.

McGraw-Hill's Homework Manager is also a useful grading tool. All assignments can be delivered over the Web and are graded automatically, with the results stored in your private grade book. Detailed results let you see at a glance how each student does on an assignment or an individual problem—you can even see how many tries it took them to solve it.

> **Jim Shelton**, Freed-Hardeman University
> "Homework Manager is working out really well, and I believe it is significantly contributing to increased performance on exams."

Homework Manager Plus
is an extension of McGraw-Hill's popular Homework Manager System. With Homework Manager Plus you get all of the power of Homework Manager plus an integrated online version of the text. Students simply receive one single access code which provides access to all of the resources available through Homework Manager Plus.

> **Paula Ratliff**, Arkansas State University
> "I like the idea that there are online assignments that change algorithmically so that students can practice with them."

When students find themselves needing to reference the textbook to complete their homework, now they can simply click on hints and link directly to the most relevant materials associated with the problem or exercise they are working on.

How Can Text-Related Web Resources Enhance My Course?

Online Learning Center (OLC)

We offer an Online Learning Center (OLC) that follows *College Accounting* chapter by chapter. It doesn't require any building or maintenance on your part. It's ready to go the moment you and your students type in the URL: www.mhhe.com/wildCA. As students study and learn from *College Accounting*, they can visit the Student Edition of the OLC Website to work with a multitude of helpful tools:

- Generic Template Working Papers
- Chapter Learning Objectives
- Chapter Glossaries
- Key Term Flashcards
- Interactive Chapter Quizzes A & B

- PowerPoint® Presentations
- Narrated PowerPoint® Presentations
- Video Segments
- Excel Template Assignments

A secured Instructor Edition stores essential course materials to save you prep time before class. Everything you need to run a lively classroom and an efficient course is included. All resources available to students, plus . . .

- Sample Syllabi
- General Ledger and Peachtree Solution Files
- Instructor's Manual

- Solutions Manual
- Solutions to Excel Template Assignments

The OLC Website also serves as a doorway to other technology solutions, like course management systems.

Try Our New e-Book Option!

For budget-conscious students, every dollar makes a difference. That's why we offer *College Accounting* in convenient, cost-effective digital formats.

McGraw-Hill's Homework Manager Plus

If you use Homework Manager in your course, your students can purchase McGraw-Hill's Homework Manager Plus for *CA*. Homework Manager Plus gives students direct access to an online edition of the text while working assignments within Homework Manager. If you get stuck working a problem, simply click the "Hint" link and jump directly to relevant content in the online edition of the text.

Visit the Online Learning Center at www.mhhe.com/wildCA
to purchase McGraw-Hill's Homework Manager Plus.

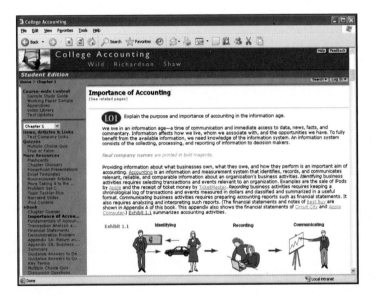

McGraw-Hill/Irwin CARES

At McGraw-Hill/Irwin, we understand that getting the most from new technology can be challenging. That's why our services don't stop after you purchase our product. You can e-mail our Product Specialists 24 hours a day, get product training online, or search our knowledge bank of Frequently Asked Questions on our support Website.

McGraw-Hill/Irwin Customer Care Contact Information

For all Customer Support call **(800) 331-5094**,
Email **hmsupport@mcgraw-hill.com**,
or visit **www.mhhe.com/support**.
One of our Technical Support Analysts will be able to assist you in a timely fashion.

> **Scott Barhight**, Northampton Community College
> "McGraw-Hill gives some of the best customer support, including personal support from John Wild the author of the text."

How Can I Make My Classroom Discussions More Interactive?

CPS Classroom Performance System

This is a revolutionary system that brings ultimate interactivity to the classroom. CPS is a wireless response system that gives you immediate feedback from every student in the class. CPS units include easy-to-use software for creating and delivering questions and assessments to your class. With CPS you can ask subjective and objective questions. Then every student simply responds with his or her individual, wireless response pad, providing instant results. CPS is the perfect tool for engaging students while gathering important assessment data.

How Can McGraw-Hill Help Me Teach My Course Online?

ALEKS®

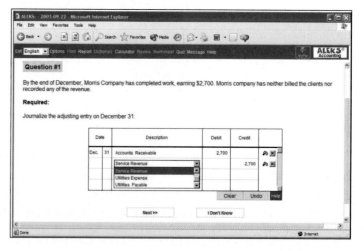

ALEKS® for the Accounting Cycle and ALEKS® for Financial Accounting

Available from McGraw-Hill over the World Wide Web, ALEKS (Assessment and LEarning in Knowledge Spaces) provides precise assessment and individualized instruction in the fundamental skills your students need to succeed in accounting.

ALEKS motivates your students because ALEKS can tell what a student knows, doesn't know, and is most ready to learn next. ALEKS does this using the ALEKS Assessment and Knowledge Space Theory as an artificial intelligence engine to exactly identify a student's knowledge of accounting. When students focus on precisely what they are ready to learn, they build the confidence and learning momentum that fuel success.

To learn more about adding ALEKS to your principles course, visit www.business.aleks.com.

Online Course Management

No matter what online course management system you use (WebCT, BlackBoard, or eCollege), we have a course content ePack available for *CA*. Our new ePacks are specifically designed to make it easy for students to navigate and access content online. They are easier than ever to install on the latest version of the course management system available today.

Don't forget that you can count on the highest level of service from McGraw-Hill. Our online course management specialists are ready to assist you with your online course needs. They provide training and will answer any questions you have throughout the life of your adoption. So try our new ePack for *CA* and make online course content delivery easy and fun.

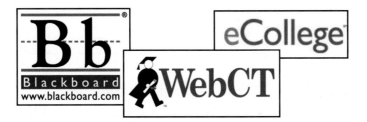

PageOut: McGraw-Hill's Course Management System

PageOut is the easiest way to create a Website for your accounting course. There is no need for HTML coding, graphic design, or a thick how-to book. Just fill in a series of boxes with simple English and click on one of our professional designs. In no time, your course is online with a Website that contains your syllabus!
Should you need assistance in preparing your Website, we can help. Our team of product specialists is ready to take your course materials and build a custom Website to your specifications. You simply need to call a McGraw-Hill/Irwin PageOut specialist to start the process. To learn more, please visit www.pageout.net and see "PageOut & Service" below.

Best of all, PageOut is free when you adopt *College Accounting*!

PageOut Service

Our team of product specialists is happy to help you design your own course Website. Just call 1-800-634-3963, press 0, and ask to speak with a PageOut specialist. You will be asked to send in your course materials and then participate in a brief telephone consultation. Once we have your information, we build your Website for you, from scratch.

What tools bring Accounting to life

Chapter Features

Whether we prepare, analyze, or apply accounting information, one skill remains essential: decision making. To help develop good decision-making habits and to illustrate the relevance of accounting, *College Accounting* uses a unique pedagogical framework comprised of a variety of approaches, giving students insight into every aspect of business decision making. "You Call It" ask students to take the perspective of an accounting user (such as an entrepreneur, small business owner, service provider) and use accounting information to resolve a business problem. Many chapters also include a tool, such as ratio, that uses accounting data to better understand company operations. Answers to You Call It boxes are at the end of each chapter. An "In The News" feature offers information relevant to students entering the business world.

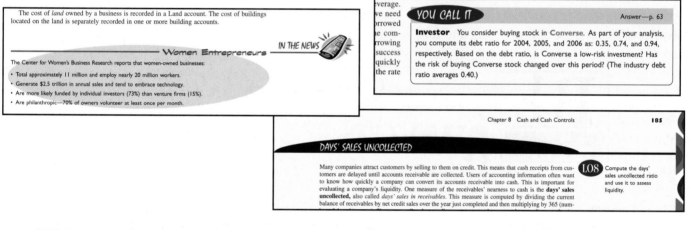

The cost of *land* owned by a business is recorded in a Land account. The cost of buildings located on the land is separately recorded in one or more building accounts.

Women Entrepreneurs — IN THE NEWS

The Center for Women's Business Research reports that women-owned businesses:

- Total approximately 11 million and employ nearly 20 million workers.
- Generate $2.5 trillion in annual sales and tend to embrace technology.
- Are more likely funded by individual investors (73%) than venture firms (15%).
- Are philanthropic—70% of owners volunteer at least once per month.

YOU CALL IT   Answer—p. 63

Investor You consider buying stock in **Converse**. As part of your analysis, you compute its debt ratio for 2004, 2005, and 2006 as: 0.35, 0.74, and 0.94, respectively. Based on the debt ratio, is Converse a low-risk investment? Has the risk of buying Converse stock changed over this period? (The industry debt ratio averages 0.40.)

Chapter 8   Cash and Cash Controls   **185**

DAYS' SALES UNCOLLECTED

Many companies attract customers by selling to them on credit. This means that cash receipts from customers are delayed until accounts receivable are collected. Users of accounting information often want to know how quickly a company can convert its accounts receivable into cash. This is important for evaluating a company's liquidity. One measure of the receivables' nearness to cash is the **days' sales uncollected,** also called *days' sales in receivables.* This measure is computed by dividing the current balance of receivables by net credit sales over the year just completed and then multiplying by 365 (num-

LO8 Compute the days' sales uncollected ratio and use it to assess liquidity.

Chapter Opening

Each chapter opens with Learning Objectives that are highlighted throughout the chapter body and end of chapter materials to help students focus their learning activities. The chapter opener also provides "A Look Back," "A Look at this Chapter," and "A Look Ahead" to inform students where they are, where they were, and where they will be going to help better direct them on their journey through *College Accounting.* Finally, each chapter begins with an opening story of a real entrepreneur that used accounting to help achieve success.

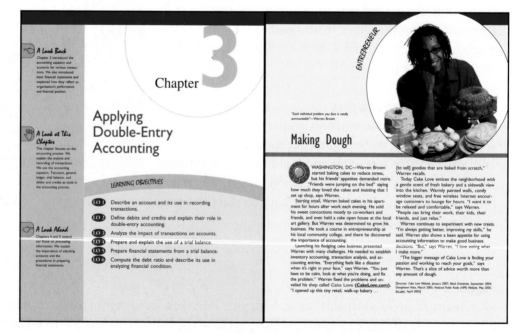

A Look Back
Chapter 2 introduced the accounting equation and accounts for various transactions. We also introduced basic financial statements and explained how they reflect an organization's performance and financial position.

A Look at This Chapter
The chapter focuses on the accounting process. We explain the analysis and recording of transactions. We use the accounting equation, T-account, general ledger, trial balance, and debits and credits as tools in the accounting process.

A Look Ahead
Chapters 4 and 5 extend our focus on processing information. We explain the importance of adjusting accounts and the procedures in preparing financial statements.

Chapter 3

Applying Double-Entry Accounting

LEARNING OBJECTIVES

LO1 Describe an account and its use in recording transactions.

LO2 Define debits and credits and explain their role in double-entry accounting.

LO3 Analyze the impact of transactions on accounts.

LO4 Prepare and explain the use of a trial balance.

LO5 Prepare financial statements from a trial balance.

LO6 Compute the debt ratio and describe its use in analyzing financial condition.

ENTREPRENEUR

"Each individual problem you face is totally surmountable"—Warren Brown

Making Dough

WASHINGTON, DC—Warren Brown started baking cakes to reduce stress, but his friends' appetites demanded more. "Friends were jumping on the bed" saying how much they loved the cakes and insisting that I set up shop, says Warren.

Starting small, Warren baked cakes in his apartment for hours after work each evening. He sold his sweet concoctions mostly to co-workers and friends, and even held a cake open house at the local art gallery. But Warren was determined to grow his business. He took a course in entrepreneurship at his local community college, and there he discovered the importance of accounting.

Launching his fledgling cake business presented Warren with many challenges. He needed to establish inventory accounting, transaction analysis, and accounting entries. "Everything feels like a disaster when it's right in your face," says Warren. "You just have to be calm, look at what you're doing, and fix the problem." Warren fixed the problems and unveiled his shop called Cake Love (**CakeLove.com**). "I opened up this tiny retail, walk-up bakery...

[to sell] goodies that are baked from scratch," Warren recalls.

Today Cake Love entices the neighborhood with a gentle scent of fresh bakery and a sidewalk view into the kitchen. Warmly painted walls, comfy window seats, and free wireless Internet encourage customers to lounge for hours. "I want it to be relaxed and comfortable," says Warren. "People can bring their work, their kids, their friends, and just relax."

Warren continues to experiment with new treats. "I'm always getting better, improving my skills," he said. Warren also shows a keen appetite for using accounting information to make good business decisions. "But," says Warren, "I love eating what I make more."

"The bigger message of Cake Love is finding your passion and working to reach your goals," says Warren. That's a slice of advice worth more than any amount of dough.

[Sources: Cake Love Website, January 2007; Black Enterprise, September 2004; Georgetown Voice, March 2005; National Public Radio (NPR) Website, May 2005; Inc.com, April 2005]

Chapter Preview with Flow Chart

This feature provides a handy textual/visual guide at the start of each chapter. Students can begin their reading with a clear understanding of what they will learn and when, which allows them to stay more focused and organized along the way.

CHAPTER PREVIEW

Merchandising companies purchase inventory to resell to their customers. This chapter introduces the accounting for inventory purchases by merchandising companies and the use of the purchases journal and an accounts payable subsidiary ledger to further enhance this process. This chapter also explains the computation of cost of goods sold and gross profit.

Merchandise Purchases and Accounts Payable

Merchandising Activities	Merchandising Purchases	Journals and Subsidiary Ledgers
• Reporting income • Reporting inventory	• Trade and purchase discounts • Purchase returns and allowances	• Purchases journal • Accounts payable subsidiary ledger

How You Doin'?

These short question/answer features reinforce the material immediately preceding them. They allow the reader to pause and reflect on the topics described, then receive immediate feedback before going on to new topics. Answers are provided at the end of each chapter.

HOW YOU DOIN'?   Answers—p. 188

4. What is a bank statement?
5. What is the meaning of the phrase *to reconcile a bank balance*?
6. Why do we reconcile the bank statement balance of cash and the depositor's book balance of cash?
7. List at least two items affecting the bank balance side of a bank reconciliation and indicate whether the items are added or subtracted.
8. List at least three items affecting the book balance side of a bank reconciliation and indicate whether the items are added or subtracted.

Marginal Student Annotations

These annotations provide students with additional hints, tips, and examples to help them more fully understand the concepts and retain what they have learned.

e invoice date, the invoice shows credit

time allowed before full payment is due **iscount** to encourage buyers to pay ear-rms on the invoice. For example, credit e within a 60-day credit period, but the nt is made within 10 days of the invoice **ount period.** (Sellers sometimes charge the credit period.)

Since both the buyer and seller know the invoice date, this date is used in determining the discount and credit periods.

FastForward

FastForward is a case that takes students through the Accounting Cycle, chapters 2-6. The FastForward icon is placed in the margin whenever this case is discussed.

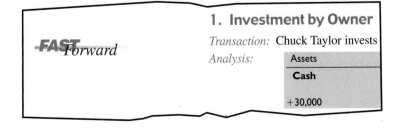

FAST*Forward*

1. Investment by Owner

Transaction: Chuck Taylor invests
Analysis:

Assets
Cash
+30,000

How are chapter concepts

Once a student has finished reading the chapter, how well he or she retains the material can depend greatly on the questions, exercises, and problems that reinforce it. This book leads the way in comprehensive, accurate end-of-chapter assignments.

Demonstration Problems
present both a problem and a complete solution, allowing students to review the entire problem-solving process and achieve success.

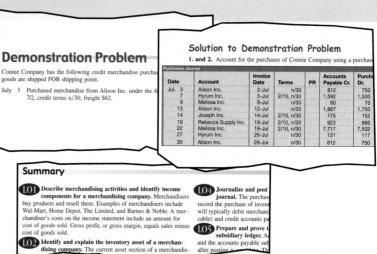

Demonstration Problem

Connie Company has the following credit merchandise purchases; goods are shipped FOB shipping point.

July 3 Purchased merchandise from Alison Inc. under the f 7/2, credit terms n/30, freight $62.

Solution to Demonstration Problem

1. and 2. Account for the purchases of Connie Company using a purchas

Purchases Journal

Date		Account	Invoice Date	Terms	PR	Accounts Payable Cr.	Purch Dr.
Jul.	3	Alison Inc.	2-Jul	n/30		812	750
	7	Hyrum Inc.	5-Jul	2/10, n/30		1,592	1,500
	9	Melissa Inc.	8-Jul	n/30		80	75
	13	Alison Inc.	12-Jul	n/30		1,867	1,750
	14	Joseph Inc.	14-Jul	2/10, n/30		175	152
	19	Rebecca Supply Inc.	19-Jul	2/10, n/30		923	866
	22	Melissa Inc.	19-Jul	2/10, n/30		7,717	7,502
	27	Hyrum Inc.	26-Jul	n/30		131	117
	30	Alison Inc.	28-Jul	n/30		812	750

Chapter Summaries
provide students with a review organized by learning objectives. Chapter Summaries recap each learning objective.

Summary

LO1 Describe merchandising activities and identify income components for a merchandising company. Merchandisers buy products and resell them. Examples of merchandisers include Wal-Mart, Home Depot, The Limited, and Barnes & Noble. A merchandiser's costs on the income statement include an amount for cost of goods sold. Gross profit, or gross margin, equals sales minus cost of goods sold.

LO2 Identify and explain the inventory asset of a merchandising company. The current asset section of a merchandis-

LO4 Journalize and post journal. The purchase record the purchase of invent will typically debit merchand cable) and credit accounts pa

LO5 Prepare and prove t subsidiary ledger. A and the accounts payable sub after posting is

Key Terms
are bolded in the text and repeated at the end of the chapter with definitions and page numbers indicating their location. The book also includes a complete Glossary of Key Terms. Key Terms are also available as online flash cards at the book's Website.

Key Terms

Key Terms are available at the book's Website for learning and testing in an online

Accounts payable ledger (p. 290) Subsidiary ledger listing individual creditor (supplier) accounts.

Cost of goods sold (p. 280) Cost of inventory sold to customers during a period; also called *cost of sales*.

Credit period (p. 283) Time period that can pass before a customer's payment is due.

Credit terms (p. 283) Description of the amounts and timing of

List price (p. 283) Ca discount is deducted.

Merchandise invento expects to sell to custo

Merchandiser (p. 280 selling merchandise.

Net purchases (p. 28

Multiple Choice Quizzes
In response to review and focus group feedback, the authors have created Multiple Choice Quizzes that quickly test chapter knowledge before a student moves on to complete Quick Studies, Exercises, and Problems.

Multiple Choice Quiz   Answers on p. 304

Multiple Choice Quizzes A and B are available at the book's Website.

1. A company has $550,000 in net sales and $193,000 in gross profit. This means its cost of goods sold equals
   a. $743,000
   b. $550,000
   c. $357,000
   d. $193,000
   e. $(193,000)

   c. Includes supplies.
   d. Is classified with investments o
   e. Must be sold within one month.

4. Net purchases includes
   a. Any purchase discounts.
   b. Any returns and allowances.
   c. Any necessary freight in costs.

Quick Study
assignments are short exercises that often focus on one learning objective. All are included in Homework Manager. There are usually 8-10 Quick Study assignments per chapter.

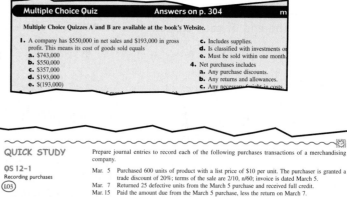

QUICK STUDY

QS 12-1
Recording purchases
LO3

Prepare journal entries to record each of the following purchases transactions of a merchandising company.

Mar. 5   Purchased 600 units of product with a list price of $10 per unit. The purchaser is granted a trade discount of 20%; terms of the sale are 2/10, n/60; invoice is dated March 5.

Mar. 7   Returned 25 defective units from the March 5 purchase and received full credit.

Mar. 15 Paid the amount due from the March 5 purchase, less the return on March 7.

Exercises
are one of this book's many strengths and a competitive advantage. There are about 10-15 per chapter and all are included in Homework Manager.

Prepare journal entries to record the following transactions for a retail store.

Apr. 2   Purchased merchandise from Lyon Company under the following terms: $4,600 price, invoice dated April 2, credit terms of 2/15, n/60, and FOB shipping point.

3   Paid $300 for shipping charges on the April 2 purchase.

4   Returned to Lyon Company unacceptable merchandise that had an invoice price of $600.

17   Sent a check to Lyon Company for the April 2 purchase, net of the discount and the returned merchandise.

18   Purchased merchandise from Frist Corp. under the following terms: $8,500 price, invoice dated April 18, credit terms of 2/10, n/30, and FOB destination.

EXERCISES

Exercise 12-1
Recording entries for merchandise purchases
LO3

Problem Sets A & B
are proven problems that can be assigned as homework or for in-class projects. All problems are coded according to one or more learning objectives, and all are included in Homework Manager.

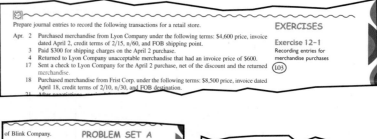

of Blink Company.
r credit terms of 1/15, n/30,
t terms of 2/15, n/60, FOB
return of part of the merchan-
iod.

PROBLEM SET A

Problem 12-1A
Preparing journal entries for merchandising activities
LO3

Check July 16, Cr. Cash $5,940
July 24, Cr. Cash $1,960

PROBLEM SET B

Problem 12-1B
Preparing journal entries for merchandising activities
LO3

Prepare journal ent

May 2   Purchase

5   Paid $25

10   Purchase destinatio

12   Received

Beyond the Numbers exercises ask students to use accounting figures and understand their meaning. Students also learn how accounting applies to a variety of business situations. These creative and fun exercises are divided into 7 sections:

- Reporting in Action
- Comparative Analysis
- Ethics Challenge
- Workplace Communication
- Taking It To The Net
- Teamwork in Action
- Entrepreneurs in Business

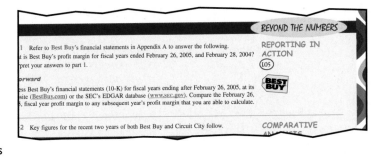

Serial Problems use a continuous running case study to illustrate chapter concepts in a familiar context. Serial Problems can be followed continuously from the first chapter or picked up at any later point in the book; enough information is provided to ensure students can get right to work.

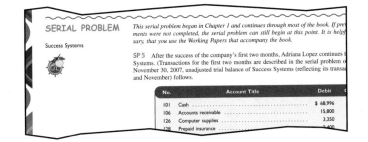

Appendix on Accounting Principles discusses a rules-based versus a principles-based accounting system. It also describes the objectives, characteristics, and assumptions of accounting principles.

The End of the Chapter Is Only the Beginning

Our valuable and proven assignments aren't just confined to the book. From problems that require technological solutions to materials found exclusively online, this book's end-of-chapter material is fully integrated with its technology package.

- Quick Studies, Exercises, and Problems available on Homework Manager (see page xi) are marked with an icon.

- Problems supported by the General Ledger Application Software or Peachtree are marked with an icon.

- The Online Learning Center (OLC) includes Personal Interactive Quizzes and Excel template assignments.

mhhe.com/wildCA

- Problems supported with Microsoft Excel template assignments are marked with an icon.

Put Away Your Red Pen

We pride ourselves on the accuracy of this book's assignment materials. Independent research reports that instructors and reviewers point to the accuracy of this book's assignment materials as one of its key competitive advantages.

The authors extend a special thanks to accuracy checkers Barbara Schnathorst, The Write Solution, Inc. and Beth Woods, CPA, Accuracy Counts.

Instructor's Resource CD-ROM

Chapters 1-14
ISBN: 9780073336923
MHID: 0073336920

CA, Chapters 1-30
ISBN: 9780073336848
MHID: 007333684X

This is your all-in-one resource. It allows you to create custom presentations from your own materials or from the following text-specific materials provided in the CD's asset library:

- Instructor's Resource Manual
- Solutions Manual
- Test Bank, Computerized Test Bank
- PowerPoint® Presentations
  Presentations allow for revision of lecture slides, and include a viewer, allowing screens to be shown with or without the software.
- Excel Template Assignments
- Link to PageOut

Algorithmic Test Bank

ISBN: 9780073336916
MHID: 0073336912

Study Guide and Working Papers

Vol. 1, Chapters 1-14
ISBN: 9780073336855
MHID: 0073336858

Written by John J. Wild, Vernon J. Richardson and Ken W. Shaw.

Electronic Study Guide and Excel Working Papers CD

Chapters 1-30
ISBN: 9780073336701
MHID: 007333670X

Written by John J. Wild, Vernon J. Richardson and Ken W. Shaw.

Study Guide and Working Papers delivered in Excel spreadsheets. Excel Working Papers are available on CD-ROM and can be bundled with the printed Working Papers; see your representative for information. The Study Guide covers each chapter and appendix with reviews of the learning objectives, outlines of the chapters, summaries of chapter materials, and additional problems with solutions.

Carol Yacht's General Ledger & Peachtree Complete 2008 CD-ROM

ISBN: 9780073336824
MHID: 0073336823

GL Software developed by Jack E. Terry, ComSource Associates, Inc.

Peachtree templates prepared by Carol Yacht.

The CD-ROM includes fully functioning versions of McGraw-Hill's own General Ledger Application software as well as Peachtree Complete 2008. Problem templates are included that allow you to assign text problems for working in either Yacht's General Ledger or Peachtree Complete 2008.

We would like to thank the entire McGraw-Hill/Irwin *College Accounting* team, including Stewart Mattson, Steve Schuetz, Christina Sanders, Kristin Bradley, Lori Koetters, Matthew Baldwin, Michael McCormick, Cathy Tepper, and Elizabeth Mavetz. We also thank the great marketing and sales support staff, including Krista Bettino, Dan Silverburg, and Liz Farina. Many talented educators and professionals worked hard to create the supplements for this book, and for their efforts we're grateful. Finally, many more people we either did not meet or whose efforts we did not personally witness nevertheless helped to make this book everything that it is, and we thank them all.

John Wild   Vern Richardson   Ken Shaw

Brief Contents

* Appendixes C and D are available on the book's Website, mhhe.com/wildCA, and as print copy from a McGraw-Hill representative.

Contents

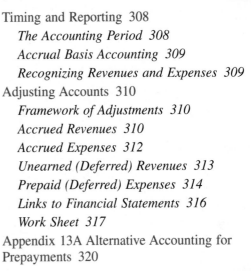

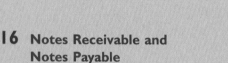

Chapters 15–30 are available in College Accounting, *Chapters 1–30.*

Chapters 15–30 are available in **College Accounting**, *Chapters 1–30.*

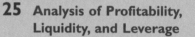

Chapters 15–30 are available in College Accounting, *Chapters 1–30.*

Chapters 15–30 are available in College Accounting, *Chapters 1–30.*

*Appendixes C and D are available on the book's Website, mhhe.com/wildCA, and as print copy from a McGraw-Hill representative.

Chapters 15–30 are available in College Accounting, *Chapters 1–30.*

College Accounting

Chapters 1–14

A Look at This Chapter

Accounting plays a crucial role in the information age. In this chapter, we discuss the importance of accounting to different types of organizations and describe its many users and uses. We explain that ethics are crucial to accounting. We also describe the meaning and source of generally accepted accounting principles.

Chapter

Introduction to Accounting

A Look Ahead

Chapter 2 introduces the accounting equation and how it helps to describe business transactions. Chapters 2 through 6 show (via the accounting cycle) how financial statements reflect business activities.

LEARNING OBJECTIVES

LO 1 Explain the purpose and importance of accounting in the information age.

LO 2 Identify users and uses of accounting.

LO 3 Identify career opportunities in accounting and related fields.

LO 4 Explain why ethics are crucial to accounting.

LO 5 Explain the meaning of generally accepted accounting principles.

LO 6 Identify the groups that establish generally accepted accounting principles.

A *short article* launches each chapter showing the relevance of accounting for a real entrepreneur. An **Entrepreneurs In Business** problem at the end of the assignments returns to this article with a mini-case.

"Ask everyone to give you money… remember, you hold the opportunity for them"
—Shawn Nelson

Love, Peace, and Profits

SALT LAKE CITY—Trying to get comfortable while watching TV, Shawn Nelson thought "a huge beanbag thing" would be far more relaxing than his old couch. So he made one—a big one! Seven feet across and shaped like a baseball, Shawn's creation was the talk of friends and neighbors. Shortly after making and selling a few "huge beanbag things," Shawn knew it needed a better name. Drawing on the 1960s retro spirit of "love and peace," Shawn named his invention the **LoveSac** and his company (**LoveSac.com**) was born.

Yet LoveSac's launch was anything but smooth. Shawn began by working out of his mother's basement. He then set up shop at trade shows and even the local drive-in cinema. He got his first big break when **Limited Too** called after seeing his display at a trade show. "I answered the phone," says Shawn, "Twelve thousand Sacs? Sure, no problem." Who was he kidding?

Shawn's debt swelled to over $50,000 as he worked 19-hour days and slept in the aged building in which he manufactured the Sacs. "It nearly broke me emotionally, physically, mentally," Shawn recalls.

"We finished the order but ate up all our profits." Without profits his business, too, would soon be retro. So Shawn approached furniture retailers to ask if they would carry Sacs. "Shawn can still hear the laughter," states LoveSac's Website.

Just when things seemed bleakest, Shawn's cousin suggested he open a retail location. Desperate, Shawn took a three-month lease in a shopping mall. His goal: sell one SuperSac per day. This would cover rent and pay him and his cousin a $5 hourly wage. Shawn then developed a transaction-based accounting system to get a handle on orders and sales.

Incredibly, customers crowded into his store within days of opening. Four weeks later and just before Christmas, customers were lined up outside the door waiting for Sacs to arrive from the factory. By Christmas Eve, Shawn's store was nearly sold out. Today, Shawn has more than 60 stores projected to generate over $30 million in sales. With results like that we'd all love Sacs!

[Sources: *LoveSac Website*, January 2007; *Entrepreneur*, November 2004; *LA Confidential*, Fall 2004; *Life & Style Weekly*, June 2005.]

*A **Preview** opens each chapter with a summary of topics covered.*

Today's world is one of information—its preparation, communication, analysis, and use. Accounting is at the heart of this information age. Knowledge of accounting provides career opportunities and the insight to take advantage of them. This book introduces concepts, procedures, and analyses that help us make better decisions. In this chapter we describe accounting, the users and uses of accounting information, and career opportunities in accounting. We also emphasize the importance of ethics for accounting.

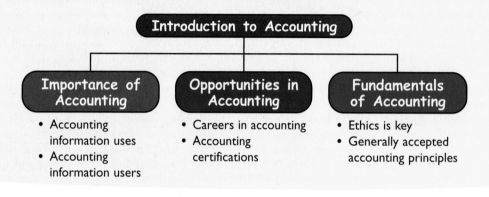

Introduction to Accounting

Importance of Accounting
- Accounting information uses
- Accounting information users

Opportunities in Accounting
- Careers in accounting
- Accounting certifications

Fundamentals of Accounting
- Ethics is key
- Generally accepted accounting principles

Importance of Accounting

LO1 Explain the purpose and importance of accounting in the information age.

We live in an information age—a time of communication and immediate access to data, news, facts, and commentary. Information affects how we live, whom we associate with, and our opportunities. To fully benefit from the available information, we need knowledge of how the information system collects, processes, and reports information to decision makers.

Accounting Information Uses

Providing information about what businesses own, what they owe, and how they perform is an important aim of accounting. **Accounting** is an information and measurement system that identifies, records, and communicates information about an organization's business activities. *Identifying* business activities requires selecting transactions relevant to an organization. Examples are the sale of iPods by **Apple** and the receipt of ticket fees by **TicketMaster**. *Recording* business activities requires keeping a chronological log of transactions measured in dollars and classified and summarized in a useful format. *Communicating* business activities requires preparing accounting reports such as financial statements. It also requires analyzing and interpreting such reports. (The financial statements and notes of **Best Buy** and **Circuit City** are shown in Appendix A of this book.) Exhibit 1.1 summarizes accounting activities.

Real company names are printed in bold magenta.

All aspects of business involve accounting. The most common contact with accounting is through credit approvals, checking accounts, tax forms, and payroll. These experiences tend to focus on the recordkeeping role of accounting. **Recordkeeping,** or **bookkeeping,** is the recording of transactions and events, either manually or electronically. This is just one part of accounting.

Exhibit 1.1

Accounting Activities

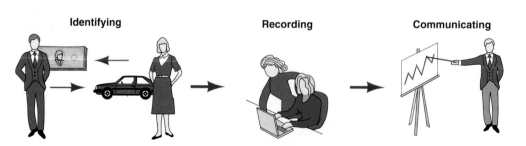

Identifying	Recording	Communicating
Select transactions and events	Input, measure, and classify	Prepare, analyze, and interpret

Accounting also identifies and communicates information on transactions and events, and it includes the crucial processes of analysis and interpretation.

Technology is a key part of modern business and plays a major role in accounting. Accounting software packages reduce the time, effort, and cost of recordkeeping while improving clerical accuracy.

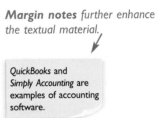

Margin notes further enhance the textual material.

QuickBooks and *Simply Accounting* are examples of accounting software.

Accounting Information Users

Accounting is often called the *language of business* because all organizations set up an accounting information system to communicate information to help people make better decisions. Exhibit 1.2 shows that the accounting information system serves many kinds of users who can be divided into two groups: external users and internal users.

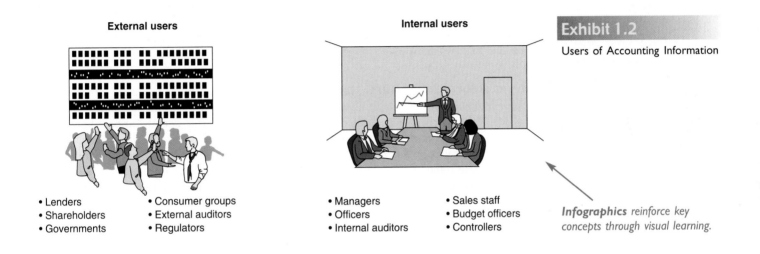

External users

- Lenders
- Shareholders
- Governments
- Consumer groups
- External auditors
- Regulators

Internal users

- Managers
- Officers
- Internal auditors
- Sales staff
- Budget officers
- Controllers

Exhibit 1.2

Users of Accounting Information

Infographics reinforce key concepts through visual learning.

External Information Users   **External users** of accounting information are *not* directly involved in running the organization. They include shareholders (investors), lenders, directors, customers, suppliers, regulators, lawyers, brokers, and the press. External users have limited access to an organization's information. Yet their business decisions depend on information that is reliable, relevant, and comparable.

LO2 Identify users and uses of accounting.

Financial accounting is the area of accounting aimed at serving external users by providing them with financial statements. These statements are known as *general-purpose financial statements*. The term *general-purpose* refers to the broad range of purposes for which external users rely on these statements.

Each external user has special information needs depending on the types of decisions to be made, including the following:

■ *Lenders* (creditors) loan money or other resources to an organization. Banks, savings and loans, and mortgage and finance companies often are lenders. Lenders look for information to help them assess whether an organization is likely to repay its loans with interest.

■ *Shareholders* (investors) are the owners of a corporation. They use accounting reports in deciding whether to buy, hold, or sell stock. Shareholders typically elect a *board of directors* to oversee their interests in an organization. Since directors are responsible to shareholders, their information needs are similar.

Google has more than 400 mil. shares of stock outstanding.

■ *External* (independent) *auditors* examine financial statements to verify that they are prepared according to generally accepted accounting principles.

■ *Labor unions* use financial statements to judge the fairness of wages, assess job prospects, and bargain for better wages.

■ *Regulators* often have legal authority over certain activities of organizations. For example, the Internal Revenue Service (IRS) and other tax authorities require organizations to file accounting reports in computing taxes. Other regulators include utility boards that use accounting information to set utility rates and securities regulators that require reports for companies that sell their stock to the public.

■ *Voters, legislators,* and *government officials* use accounting information to monitor and evaluate government receipts and expenses.

■ *Contributors* to nonprofit organizations use accounting information to evaluate the use and impact of their donations.

■ *Suppliers* use accounting information to judge the soundness of a customer before making sales on credit.

■ *Customers* use financial reports to assess the staying power of potential suppliers.

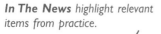

In The News highlight relevant items from practice.

They Fought the Law

Our economic and social welfare depends on reliable accounting information. A few managers in recent years forgot that and are now paying their dues. They include L. Dennis Kozlowski of **Tyco**, convicted of falsifying accounting records; Bernard Ebbers of **WorldCom**, convicted of an $11 billion accounting scandal, and Andrew Fastow of **Enron**, guilty of hiding debt and inflating income.

Internal Information Users   **Internal users** of accounting information are those directly involved in managing and operating an organization. They use the information to help improve the efficiency and effectiveness of an organization. **Managerial accounting** is the area of accounting that serves the decision-making needs of internal users. Internal reports are not subject to the same rules as external reports and instead are designed with the special needs of internal users in mind.

There are several types of internal users that depend on accounting reports, and many are managers of key operating activities including:

■ *Research and development managers* need information about projected costs and revenues of any proposed changes in products and services.

■ *Purchasing managers* need to know what, when, and how much to purchase.

■ *Human resource managers* need information about employees' payroll, benefits, performance, and compensation.

■ *Production managers* depend on information to monitor costs and ensure quality.

■ *Distribution managers* need reports for timely, accurate, and efficient delivery of products and services.

■ *Marketing managers* use reports about sales and costs to target consumers, set prices, and monitor consumer needs, tastes, and price concerns.

■ *Service managers* require information on the costs and benefits of looking after products and services.

■ *Internal auditors* design and test their employer's internal controls. *Internal controls* are procedures designed to protect company property, ensure reliable reports, promote efficiency, and encourage adherence to company policies. Examples are good records, physical controls (locks, passwords, guards), and independent reviews. Both internal and external users rely on internal controls to monitor and control company activities.

Entrepreneurs, particularly in small companies, perform many of the tasks demanded of both external and internal users, and thus rely heavily on accounting information.

How You Doin'? is a chance to stop and reflect on key points.

HOW YOU DOIN'?   Answers—p. 11

1. What is the purpose of accounting?
2. What is the relation between accounting and recordkeeping?
3. Who are the internal and external users of accounting information?
4. Identify at least five types of managers who are internal users of accounting information.
5. What are internal controls and why are they important?

Opportunities in Accounting

Accounting information affects many aspects of our lives. When we earn money, pay taxes, invest savings, budget earnings, and plan for the future, we are influenced by accounting.

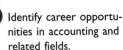

LO3 Identify career opportunities in accounting and related fields.

Career Paths

Accounting has four broad areas of opportunities: financial, managerial, taxation, and accounting-related. Exhibit 1.3 lists selected opportunities in each area.

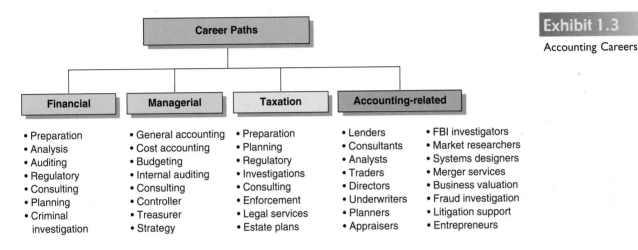

Exhibit 1.3

Accounting Careers

The majority of accounting opportunities are in *private accounting,* as shown in Exhibit 1.4. *Public accounting* offers the next largest number of opportunities. Private accountants are employed by a single manufacturing, merchandising or non-accounting services company. Public accountants provide auditing, tax, and consulting work for other companies for service fees. Still other opportunities exist in government (and not-for-profit) agencies, including business regulation and investigation of law violations.

Certifications

Accounting specialists are highly regarded. Their professional standing often is denoted by a certificate. Certified public accountants (CPAs) must meet education and experience requirements, pass an examination, and exhibit ethical character. Many accounting specialists hold certificates in addition to or instead of the CPA. Three of the most common are the certificate in management accounting (CMA), the certified internal auditor (CIA), and the certified fraud examiner (CFE). Employers also look for specialists with designations such as certified bookkeeper (CB), certified payroll professional (CPP), and personal financial specialist (PFS).

Graphical displays are often used to illustrate key points.

Exhibit 1.4

Accounting Jobs by Area

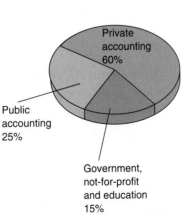

Individuals with accounting knowledge are always in demand as they can help with financial analysis, strategic planning, e-commerce, product feasibility analysis, information technology, and financial management. Benefit packages can include flexible work schedules, telecommuting options, career path alternatives, casual work environments, extended vacation time, and child and elder care.

Demand for accounting specialists is boosting salaries. Exhibit 1.5 reports average annual salaries for several accounting positions. Salary variation depends on location, company size, professional designation, experience, and other factors. For example, salaries for full-charge recordkeepers average $55,000 per year. Salaries for partners in public accounting firms average $181,000. Likewise, annual salaries for bookkeepers range from under $30,000 to more than $80,000.

The Census Bureau reports that for workers 18 and over, higher education yields higher average pay:

Advanced degree	$74,602
Bachelor's degree	51,206
High school degree . . .	27,915
No high school degree	18,734

Exhibit 1.5

Accounting Salaries for Selected Fields

For updated salary data:
www.AICPA.org
Abbott-Langer.com
Kforce.com

Field	Title (experience)	2006 Salary	2011 Estimate*
Public Accounting	Partner	$181,000	$231,000
	Manager (6–8 years)	89,500	114,000
	Senior (3–5 years)	68,500	87,500
	Junior (0–2 years)	49,000	62,500
Private Accounting	Controller/Treasurer	140,000	179,000
	Manager (6–8 years)	83,000	106,000
	Senior (3–5 years)	69,000	88,000
	Junior (0–2 years)	47,000	60,000
Recordkeeping	Full-charge bookkeeper	55,000	70,000
	Accounts manager	48,500	62,000
	Payroll manager	52,000	66,000
	Accounting clerk (0–2 years)	35,500	45,000

*Estimates assume a 5% compounded annual increase over current levels.

HOW YOU DOIN'?
Answers—p. 11

6. What career opportunities exist in the taxation area?

7. What types of certificates are available in accounting?

Fundamentals of Accounting

LO4 Explain why ethics are crucial to accounting.

Sarbanes-Oxley Act requires each issuer of securities to disclose whether it has adopted a code of ethics for its senior officers and the contents of that code.

Accounting is guided by concepts and principles. This section describes two key fundamentals of accounting.

Ethics—A Key Concept

The goal of accounting is to provide useful information for decisions. For information to be useful, it must be trusted. This demands ethics in accounting. **Ethics** are beliefs that distinguish right from wrong. They are accepted standards of good and bad behavior.

Identifying the ethical path is sometimes difficult. The preferred path is a course of action that avoids casting doubt on one's decisions. For example, accounting users are less likely to trust an auditor's report if the auditor's pay depends on the success of the client being audited. To avoid such concerns, ethical rules are often set. For example, external auditors are banned from direct investment in their client and cannot accept pay that depends on figures in the client's reports. Exhibit 1.6 gives guidelines for making ethical decisions.

Exhibit 1.6

Guidelines for Ethical Decision Making

Identify ethical concerns

Use personal ethics to recognize an ethical concern.

Analyze options

Consider all good and bad consequences.

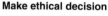

Make ethical decision

Choose best option after weighing all consequences.

Providers of accounting information often face ethical choices as they prepare financial reports. These choices can affect the price a buyer pays and the wages paid to workers. They can even affect the success of products and services. Misleading information can lead to a wrongful closing of a division that harms workers, customers, and suppliers. There is an old saying worth remembering: *Good ethics are good business.*

Some people extend ethics to *social responsibility,* which refers to a concern for the impact of actions on society. An organization's social

YOU CALL IT
Answer—p. 10

Entrepreneur   To get a loan to expand its business, Bob's Auto Body Repair must have its financial statements audited by a certified public accountant (CPA). Bob, the owner, has an old friend and former investor who is a CPA and could perform the audit. Would there be any ethical concerns of having Bob's old friend serve as auditor?

responsibility can include donations to hospitals, colleges, community programs, and law enforcement. It also can include programs to reduce pollution, increase product safety, improve worker conditions, and support continuing education. These programs are not limited to large companies. For example, many small businesses offer discounts to students and senior citizens. Still others help sponsor events such as the Special Olympics and summer reading programs.

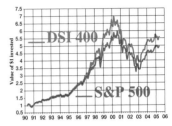

IN THE NEWS

Virtuous Returns

Virtue is not always its own reward. Compare the S&P 500 with the Domini Social Index (DSI), which covers 400 companies that have especially good records of social responsibility. Notice that returns for companies with socially responsible behavior are at least as high as those of the S&P 500.

Copyright © 2005 by KLD Research & Analytics, Inc. The "Domini 400 Social Index" is a service mark of KLD Research & Analytics.

Generally Accepted Accounting Principles

Financial accounting practice is governed by concepts and rules known as **generally accepted accounting principles (GAAP).** To use and interpret financial statements effectively, we need to understand these principles. GAAP aims to make information in financial statements relevant, reliable, and comparable. *Relevant information* affects the decisions of its users. *Reliable information* is trusted by users. *Comparable information* is helpful in contrasting organizations.

L05 Explain the meaning of generally accepted accounting principles.

Setting Accounting Principles   Two main groups establish generally accepted accounting principles in the United States. The **Financial Accounting Standards Board (FASB)** is the private group that sets both broad and specific principles. The **Securities and Exchange Commission (SEC)** is the government group that establishes reporting requirements for companies that issue stock to the public.

L06 Identify the groups that establish generally accepted accounting principles.

In today's global economy, there is increased demand by external users for comparability in accounting reports. This often arises when companies wish to raise money from lenders and investors in different countries. To that end, the **International Accounting Standards Board (IASB)** issues *International Financial Reporting Standards* (*IFRS*) that identify preferred accounting practices. The IASB hopes to create more harmony among accounting practices of different countries. If standards are harmonized, one company can potentially use a single set of financial statements in all financial markets. Many countries' standard setters support the IASB, and differences between U.S. GAAP and IASB's practices are fading. Yet, the IASB does not have authority to impose its standards on companies.

State ethics codes require CPAs who audit financial statements to disclose areas where those statements fail to comply with GAAP. If CPAs fail to report noncompliance, they can lose their licenses and be subject to criminal and civil actions and fines.

Rules-Based versus Principles-Based   U.S. accounting practices are often viewed as *rules-based.* This means that companies apply technical, specific, and detailed rules in preparing financial statements. A *principles-based* approach is sometimes argued as preferable. A principles-based system would develop and apply broad, fundamental concepts for reporting. Companies would have more flexibility in preparing principles-based reports. For example, a broad principle might be that a company must report all debt it might have to repay. Certain executives of **Enron** were able to mislead investors by not reporting some of its debt. While many of Enron's reports technically followed rules-based standards, the reports failed to adequately disclose its debts.

The American Institute of Certified Public Accountants' *Code of Professional Conduct* is available at **www.AICPA.org**.

HOW YOU DOIN'?   Answers—p. 11

8. What three-step guidelines can help people make ethical decisions?

9. Why are ethics and social responsibility valuable to organizations?

10. Why are ethics crucial in accounting?

11. Who sets U.S. accounting rules?

12. How are U.S. companies affected by international accounting standards?

*The **Demonstration Problem** is a review of key chapter content. Planning the Solution offers strategies in solving the problem.*

Demonstration Problem

After months of planning, Polly Guthrie opens SuperSub, a sandwich shop. Because this is her first time running a business, Polly is wondering who will use her financial statements.

Required

List four potential external or internal users of SuperSub's financial statements. Explain how they might use these statements.

Planning the Solution

- Look back at the list of possible external and internal users on pages 5 and 6 and think about how each might use SuperSub's financial statements.
- Consider any user that might use and need SuperSub's financial statements.

Solution to Demonstration Problem

Interested users would include:

1. Polly Guthrie, owner and internal user. Polly will use the financial statements to see where she is earning and spending her money. She can also use her financial statements to predict and budget for future sales and costs.
2. Internal Revenue Service, external user. This regulator will need to see SuperSub's accounting reports to compute and monitor the accurate payment of income tax.
3. Lenders (or a bank), external user. Owners periodically need loans to operate or expand their businesses. The bank often requests financial statements, which it can use to assess whether SuperSub will be able to repay its loans.
4. Suppliers (creditors), external user. Suppliers of the foodstuffs like assurance that they will get paid promptly. They will often ask for financial statements or additional financial information to get the information they need.

*A **Summary** organized by learning objectives concludes each chapter.*

Summary

LO1 **Explain the purpose and importance of accounting in the information age.** Accounting is an information and measurement system that aims to identify, record, and communicate relevant, reliable, and comparable information about business activities. It helps assess opportunities, products, investments, and social and community responsibilities.

LO2 **Identify users and uses of accounting.** Users of accounting are both internal and external. Some users and uses of accounting include (a) managers in controlling, monitoring, and planning; (b) lenders for measuring the risk and repayment of loans; (c) shareholders for assessing the return and risk of stock; (d) directors for overseeing management; and (e) employees for judging employment opportunities.

LO3 **Identify career opportunities in accounting and related fields.** Opportunities in accounting include financial, managerial, and tax accounting. They also include accounting-related fields such as lending, consulting, managing, and planning.

LO4 **Explain why ethics are crucial to accounting.** The goal of accounting is to provide useful information for decision making. For information to be useful, it must be trusted. This demands ethical behavior in accounting.

LO5 **Explain the meaning of generally accepted accounting principles.** Generally accepted accounting principles are a common set of standards applied by accountants. Accounting principles aid in producing relevant, reliable, and comparable information.

LO6 **Identify the groups that establish generally accepted accounting principles.** Generally accepted accounting principles (GAAP) are established by two main groups in the United States: the Financial Accounting Standards Board (FASB) and the Securities and Exchange Commission (SEC). The FASB is a private entity that sets financial accounting principles. The SEC is the governmental entity that establishes financial reporting requirements for companies that issue stock to the public.

Guidance Answer to **YOU CALL IT**

Entrepreneur Ethics rules ban auditors from having a direct investment in their audit clients. Since there currently is no direct investment, there is probably not a conflict of interest. However, since the best course of action is one that avoids any doubt, it is in the best interest of Bob to choose a different auditor, one independent in fact and appearance.

Guidance Answers to *HOW YOU DOIN'?*

1. Accounting is an information and measurement system that identifies, records, and communicates relevant information to help people make better decisions.

2. Recordkeeping, also called *bookkeeping,* is the recording of financial transactions and events, either manually or electronically. Recordkeeping is essential to data reliability; but accounting is this and much more. Accounting includes identifying, measuring, recording, reporting, and analyzing business events and transactions.

3. External users of accounting include lenders, shareholders, directors, customers, suppliers, regulators, lawyers, brokers, and the press. Internal users of accounting include managers, officers, and other internal decision makers involved with strategic and operating decisions.

4. Internal users (managers) include those from research and development, purchasing, human resources, production, distribution, marketing, and servicing.

5. Internal controls are procedures designed to protect assets, ensure reliable accounting reports, promote efficiency, and encourage adherence to company policies. Internal controls are crucial for relevant and reliable information.

6. Tax preparation, tax planning, and tax enforcement are among the various career opportunities in the taxation area.

7. The certificates that exist in accounting include: certified public accountant (CPA), certified management accountant (CMA), certified internal auditor (CIA), certified fraud examiner (CFE), certified bookkeeper (CB), certified payroll professional (CPP), and personal financial specialist (PFS).

8. Ethical guidelines are threefold: (1) identify ethical concerns using personal ethics, (2) analyze options considering all good and bad consequences, and (3) make ethical decisions after weighing all consequences.

9. Ethics and social responsibility yield good behavior, and they often result in higher income and a better working environment.

10. For accounting to provide useful information for decisions, it must be trusted. Trust requires ethics in accounting.

11. Two major participants in setting rules include the SEC and the FASB.

12. Most U.S. companies are not directly affected by international accounting standards. International standards are put forth as preferred accounting practices. However, stock exchanges and other parties are increasing the pressure to narrow differences in worldwide accounting practices. International accounting standards are playing an important role in that process.

A list of key terms with page references concludes each chapter (a complete glossary is at the end of the book and on the book's Website).

Key Terms   mhhe.com/wildCA

Key Terms are available at the book's Website for learning and testing in an online Flashcard Format.

Accounting (p. 4) Information and measurement system that identifies, records, and communicates relevant information about a company's business activities.

Ethics (p. 8) Codes of conduct by which actions are judged as right or wrong, fair or unfair, honest or dishonest.

External users (p. 5) Persons using accounting information who are not directly involved in running the organization.

Financial accounting (p. 5) Area of accounting mainly aimed at serving external users.

Financial Accounting Standards Board (FASB) (p. 9) Independent group of full-time members responsible for setting accounting rules.

Generally Accepted Accounting Principles (GAAP) (p. 9) Rules that specify acceptable accounting principles.

Internal users (p. 6) Persons using accounting information who are directly involved in managing the organization.

International Accounting Standards Board (IASB) (p. 9) Group that identifies preferred accounting practices and encourages global acceptance; issues International Financial Reporting Standards (IFRS).

Managerial accounting (p. 6) Area of accounting mainly aimed at serving the decision-making needs of internal users; also called *management accounting.*

Recordkeeping (p. 4) Part of accounting that involves recording transactions and events, either manually or electronically; also called *bookkeeping.*

Securities and Exchange Commission (SEC) (p. 9) Federal agency Congress has charged to set reporting rules for organizations that sell ownership shares to the public.

Multiple Choice Quiz   Answers on p. 15   mhhe.com/wildCA

Multiple Choice Quizzes A and B are available at the book's Website.

1. Accounting is an information and measurement system that _____ information about an organization's business activities.
   a. Translates
   b. Records
   c. Chooses
   d. Prints out

2. External users of financial information include:
   a. Purchasing managers
   b. Service managers
   c. The chief executive officer
   d. Lenders

3. Typical accounting specialists with designations include all of the following except:
  a. Certified Financial Analyst (CFA)
  b. Certified Public Accountant (CPA)
  c. Certified Bookkeeper (CB)
  d. Certified Payroll Professional (CPP)

4. Generally accepted accounting principles do not aim to make information in financial statements:
  a. Reasonable
  b. Relevant
  c. Reliable
  d. Comparable

5. The Financial Accounting Standards Board is the:
  a. Governmental group that sets financial accounting principles.
  b. International group that identifies preferred international accounting principles.
  c. Private group that sets both broad and specific accounting principles.
  d. Governmental group that sets standards for state and local governmental financial statements.

Discussion Questions

1. What is the purpose of accounting in society?

2. Technology is increasingly used to process accounting data. Why then must we study and understand accounting?

3. Identify at least four kinds of external users and describe how they use accounting information.

4. What are at least three questions business owners and managers might be able to answer by looking at accounting information?

5. Identify three actual businesses that offer services and three actual businesses that offer products.

6. Describe the internal role of accounting for organizations.

7. Identify three types of services typically offered by accounting professionals.

8. What type of accounting information might be useful to the marketing managers of a business?

9. Why is accounting described as a service activity?

10. What are some accounting-related professions?

11. How do ethics rules affect auditors' choice of clients?

12. What work do tax accounting professionals perform in addition to preparing tax returns?

13. Refer to the financial statements of **Best Buy** in Appendix A near the end of the book. Look at the consolidated statements of earnings (income statement). How many years are included and what are their dates?

Quick Study exercises give readers a brief test of key elements.

Homework Manager repeats assignments on the book's Website, which allows instructors to monitor, promote, and assess student learning. It can be used in practice, homework, or exam mode.

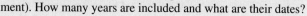

QUICK STUDY

QS 1–1
Identifying accounting terms
(LO5) (LO6)

(a) Define these accounting-related acronyms: GAAP, SEC, FASB and IASB. *(b)* Briefly explain the importance of the knowledge base or organization that is referred to for each of the accounting-related acronyms.

QS 1–2
Identifying accounting users
(LO2)

Identify the following users as either external users (E) or internal users (I).

a. Customers	**d.** Business press	**g.** Shareholders	**j.** FBI and IRS
b. Suppliers	**e.** Managers	**h.** Lenders	**k.** Consumer group
c. Brokers	**f.** District attorney	**i.** Controllers	**l.** Sales staff

---

QS 1–3
Explaining internal control
(LO2)

An important responsibility of many accounting professionals is to design and implement internal control procedures for organizations. Explain the purpose of internal control procedures. Provide two examples of internal controls applied by companies.

QS 1–4
Accounting opportunities
(LO3)

Identify at least three main areas of opportunities for accounting professionals. For each area, identify at least three job possibilities linked to accounting.

QS 1–5
Identifying ethical concerns
(LO4)

Accounting professionals must sometimes choose between two or more acceptable methods of accounting for business transactions and events. Explain why these situations can involve difficult matters of ethical concern.

Many accounting professionals work in one of the following three areas.

A. Financial accounting   **B.** Managerial accounting   **C.** Tax accounting

Identify the area of accounting that is most involved in each of the following responsibilities.

_____ **1.** Internal auditing.
_____ **2.** External auditing.
_____ **3.** Cost accounting.
_____ **4.** Budgeting.

_____ **5.** Investigating violations of tax laws.
_____ **6.** Planning transactions to minimize taxes.
_____ **7.** Preparing external financial statements.
_____ **8.** Reviewing reports for SEC compliance.

Exercise 1–1
Describing accounting responsibilities
(LO2) (LO3)

Much of accounting is directed at serving the information needs of those users that are external to an organization. Identify at least three external users of accounting information and indicate two questions they might seek to answer through their use of accounting information.

Exercise 1–2
Identifying accounting users and uses
(LO2)

Assume the following roles and describe a situation in which ethical considerations play an important part in guiding your decisions and actions.

a. You are a student in an introductory accounting course.
b. You are a manager with responsibility for several employees.
c. You are an accounting professional preparing tax returns for clients.
d. You are an accounting professional with audit clients that are competitors in business.

Exercise 1–3
Identifying ethical concerns
(LO4)

Match each of the numbered descriptions 1 through 7 with the term or phrase it best reflects. Indicate your answer by writing the letter for the term or phrase in the blank provided.

A. Audit   **C.** Ethics   **E.** SEC   **G.** IASB
B. GAAP   **D.** Tax accounting   **F.** Public accountants

_____ **1.** Principles that determine whether an action is right or wrong.
_____ **2.** Accounting professionals who provide services to many clients.
_____ **3.** An accounting area that includes planning future transactions to minimize taxes paid.
_____ **4.** An examination of an organization's accounting system and records that adds credibility to financial statements.
_____ **5.** Government group that establishes reporting requirements for companies that issue stock to the public.
_____ **6.** Concepts and rules that govern financial accounting practice.
_____ **7.** Group that issues preferred international accounting practices.

Exercise 1–4
Learning the language of business
(LO3–LO6)

The following is a list of selected users of accounting information. Match the appropriate user A through E to the following information needs 1 through 5.

A. Suppliers   **C.** Shareholders   **E.** Employees
B. Lenders   **D.** Production managers

_____ **1.** Monitor costs and ensure quality.
_____ **2.** Judge the soundness of a customer before making sales on credit.
_____ **3.** Assessing employment opportunities.
_____ **4.** Assessing whether a loan is likely to be repaid.
_____ **5.** Deciding whether to buy, hold, or sell stock.

Problem 1–1A
Identifying accounting users
(LO2)

The following is a list of broad opportunities in accounting. Match the appropriate opportunity A through D to the specific accounting opportunity 1 through 8.

A. Financial   **C.** Taxation
B. Managerial   **D.** Accounting related

_____ **1.** Appraiser
_____ **2.** Estate planning
_____ **3.** External audit
_____ **4.** Budgeting

_____ **5.** Litigation support
_____ **6.** Internal audit
_____ **7.** Financial statement preparation
_____ **8.** Tax planning

Problem 1–2A
Identify opportunities in accounting
(LO3)

PROBLEM SET B

Problem 1-1B
Identifying accounting users

(LO2)

The following is a list of selected internal users of accounting information. Match the appropriate user A through E to the following information needs 1 through 5.

A. Research and development managers   **C.** Distribution managers   **E.** Service managers
B. Human resource managers   **D.** Purchasing managers

_____ **1.** Assessing when and how much to purchase.

_____ **2.** Judge the costs and benefits of looking after products and services.

_____ **3.** Monitor timely, accurate, and efficient delivery of products and services.

_____ **4.** Assessing employees' payroll, benefits, performance, and compensation.

_____ **5.** Measuring projected costs and revenues of any proposed changes in products and services.

Problem 1-2B
Definition of accounting terms

(LO1) (LO2)

The following is a list of accounting terms. Match the appropriate accounting term A through D to its definition 1 through 4.

A. Accounting   **C.** Managerial accounting
B. Bookkeeping   **D.** Financial accounting

_____ **1.** Area of accounting aimed at serving external users by providing them with financial statements.

_____ **2.** Information and measurement system that identifies, records, and communicates information about an organization's business activities.

_____ **3.** The recording of transactions and events, either manually or electronically.

_____ **4.** Area of accounting that serves the decision-making needs of internal users.

The serial problem starts in this chapter and continues throughout most chapters of the book. It is most readily solved if you use the Working Papers that accompany this book.

SERIAL PROBLEM

Success Systems

SP 1   On October 1, 2007, Adriana Lopez launched a computer services company, **Success Systems,** that is organized as a proprietorship and provides consulting services, computer system installations, and custom program development. Lopez will prepare the company's first set of financial statements on December 31, 2007.

Required

List at least five potential internal and external users of Success Systems' financial statements. Explain why each user would be interested in the financial statements.

Beyond the Numbers (BTN) is a special problem section aimed to refine communication, conceptual, analysis, and research skills. It includes many activities helpful in developing an active learning environment.

BEYOND THE NUMBERS

REPORTING IN ACTION

(LO1)

BEST BUY

BTN 1-1   Find **Best Buy**'s annual report included in Appendix A near the end of the book. In the first footnote to the financial statements, Best Buy reports how it accounts for property and equipment.

Required

1. Describe how Best Buy accounts for property and equipment.

2. List at least three users of Best Buy financial statements and how they would use that information.

COMPARATIVE ANALYSIS

(LO1)

BEST BUY   **circuit city**

BTN 1-2   Key comparative figures ($ millions) for both **Best Buy** and **Circuit City** follow.

Key Figure	Best Buy	Circuit City
Assets	$10,294	$3,789
Net income	984	62
Revenues and sales	27,433	10,472

Required

1. Which company is largest in terms of assets? Which company is largest in terms of sales?

2. Which company earns the higher amount of net income?

3. How might the size differences between these companies be useful to lenders or shareholders?

BTN 1-3   William Shakespeare wrote, *"The evil that men do lives after them; the good is oft interred with their bones."* Business people are oft not remembered for their outstanding ethics, but rather reviled for their ethical lapses. An ethical lapse is defined as behavior that fails to comply with accepted ethical standards.

ETHICS CHALLENGE
(L04)

Required

1. Give an example of an ethical lapse that a prominent figure (business person, politician, or athlete) has made and how he or she will be remembered for it.

2. One way to avoid an ethical lapse is to carefully contemplate whether a decision might violate accepted ethical conduct. What are the guidelines for ethical decision making (consider Exhibit 1.6)? How might those guidelines help us?

BTN 1-4   The Financial Accounting Standards Board (FASB) sets accounting standards. The FASB's mission is described at its Website (**FASB.org**) under the tab "Facts about FASB."

WORKPLACE COMMUNICATION
(L06)

Required

Prepare a half-page report outlining the mission of the FASB. Identify the ways it has set out to accomplish that mission.

BTN 1-5   Find **Best Buy**'s most current financial statements by going to their Website (**BestBuy.com**) and click on the link "For Our Investors" at the bottom of the page. Click on "Annual Reports" in the left column. Click on the most recent annual report.

TAKING IT TO THE NET
(L01)

Required

1. What is the date of this annual report?

2. What are the titles of the financial statements included in this report?

BTN 1-6   Teamwork is important in today's business world. Successful teams schedule convenient meetings, maintain regular communications, and cooperate with and support their members. This assignment aims to establish support/learning teams, initiate discussions, and set meeting times.

TEAMWORK IN ACTION
(L01)

Required

1. Form teams and open a team discussion to determine a regular time and place for your team to meet between each scheduled class meeting. Notify your instructor via a memorandum or e-mail message as to when and where your team will hold regularly scheduled meetings.

2. Develop a list of telephone numbers and/or e-mail addresses of your teammates.

BTN 1-7   Refer to this chapter's opening feature about **LoveSac**. Assume that Shawn Nelson decides to open a new manufacturing facility to meet customer demand. This new company will be called LoveSac Manufacturing. To open the new facility, Shawn would have to get a loan from a bank.

ENTREPRENEURS IN BUSINESS
(L02)

Required

1. Which external users would be interested in reviewing **LoveSac**'s financial statements? Why?

2. What specific information would a loan officer want to review before extending a loan to LoveSac?

~~~~~~

ANSWERS TO MULTIPLE CHOICE QUIZ

1. b

2. d

3. a

4. a

5. c

A Look Back

Chapter 1 explained the importance of accounting to different types of organizations. We also described the use and users of accounting information.

A Look at This Chapter

This chapter explains the accounting equation and how it helps to describe business transactions. We also show how accounting information is reflected in financial statements.

A Look Ahead

Chapter 3 further describes the analysis of business transactions. We also introduce and explore the basics of double-entry accounting.

Chapter 2

Accounting for Business Transactions

LEARNING OBJECTIVES

 LO 1 Define the accounting equation and each of its components.

 LO 2 Analyze business transactions using the accounting equation.

 LO 3 Identify and prepare basic financial statements and explain how they interrelate.

 LO 4 Compute and interpret return on assets.

"This is one of those crazy, quirky ideas, but it just might work ... I've got nothing to lose."
—Alex Tew

A Million Dollar Idea!

LONDON, ENGLAND—One month before attending college, Alex Tew brainstormed about how to avoid student loans and, maybe, actually make money. Then, an epiphany: How about selling 1 million pixels of advertising space on a Website for $1 per pixel. Thus, the **Million Dollar Home Page** (**MillionDollarHomepage.com**) was born.

After selling his first 1,000 pixels to friends and family, his business took on a life of its own. Media, bloggers, online forums, and chat rooms embraced his story. Within two weeks, Alex sold $40,000 worth of pixels, which was enough to pay for college. Within five months, Alex sold the entire $1 million worth of pixel space! In a recent two-week period, Alex counted nearly 4 million unique hits to his Website!

With business growth, Alex faced some problems. First, the server hosting his Website required an upgrade to handle the unexpected traffic. Second, how would he collect fees? PayPal, a method for individuals and businesses to send and receive money online, blocked his account due to the unexpected high transaction volume. Alex needed an alternative collection system. He quickly found a solution, based on an accounting system, to handle collections.

Alex confirms the importance of accounting systems and business plans. "It can be difficult to do cash flow forecasts when you haven't started a business or to write a proper business plan when you don't know how much you're going to make," explains Alex. "But you *have* to lay out in your mind exactly what you're trying to achieve."

So, what's your million dollar idea?

[Sources: MillionDollarHomePage.com *Website,* April 2007, *Entrepreneur,* January 2006; *Wikipedia, June 2006*]

Accounting identifies, records, and communicates information about an organization's business activities. In this chapter, we introduce the accounting equation as a means of identifying and recording business transactions. We also introduce basic financial statements that communicate accounting information about the company's performance and financial position.

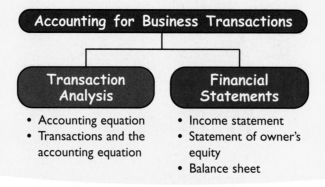

Accounting for Business Transactions

Transaction Analysis
- Accounting equation
- Transactions and the accounting equation

Financial Statements
- Income statement
- Statement of owner's equity
- Balance sheet

Transaction Analysis and the Accounting Equation

LO1 Define the accounting equation and each of its components.

To understand accounting information, we need to know how an accounting system captures relevant data about transactions, and then classifies, records, and reports data. In this section, we introduce the accounting equation and then show how the accounting equation represents each business transaction.

Accounting Equation

The accounting system reflects two basic aspects of a company: what it owns and what it owes. **Assets** are resources with future benefits that are owned or controlled by a company. Examples are cash, supplies, equipment, and land. The claims on a company's assets—what it owes—are separated into owner and nonowner claims. **Liabilities** are what a company owes its nonowners (creditors) in future payments, products, or services. **Equity** (also called owner's equity or capital) refers to the claims of its owner(s). Together, liabilities and equity are the source of funds to acquire assets. The relation of assets, liabilities, and equity is reflected in the following **accounting equation:**

$$\text{Assets} = \text{Liabilities} + \text{Equity}$$

Liabilities are usually shown before equity in this equation because creditors' claims must be paid before the claims of owners. (The terms in this equation can be rearranged; for example, Assets − Liabilities = Equity.) The accounting equation applies to all transactions and events, to all companies and forms of organization, and to all points in time. For example, **Best Buy**'s assets equal $10,294, its liabilities equal $5,845, and its equity equals $4,449 ($ in millions). Let's now look at the accounting equation in more detail.

Assets Assets are resources owned or controlled by a company. These resources are expected to yield future benefits. Examples of assets include Web servers for an online services company, musical instruments for a rock band, land for a vegetable grower, and cash in the company's bank account. The term *receivable* is used to refer to an asset that promises a future inflow of resources. A company that provides a service or product on credit is said to have an account receivable from that customer.

The phrase "on credit" implies that the cash payment will occur at a future date.

Liabilities Liabilities are creditors' claims on assets. These claims reflect obligations to provide assets, products, or services to others. The term *payable* refers to a liability that promises

IN THE NEWS

Web Info

Most organizations maintain Websites that include accounting data—see **Best Buy**'s (**BestBuy.com**) Website as an example. The SEC keeps an online database called EDGAR (**www.sec.gov/edgar.shtml**), which has accounting information for thousands of companies that issue stock to the public.

a future outflow of resources. Examples are wages payable to workers, accounts payable to suppliers, loans (or notes) payable to banks, and taxes payable to the government.

Equity **Equity** is the owner's claim on assets. Equity is equal to assets minus liabilities. This is the reason equity is also called *net assets* or *residual equity*.

Equity for a noncorporate entity—commonly called owner's equity—increases and decreases as follows: owner investments and revenues *increase* equity, whereas owner withdrawals and expenses *decrease* equity. **Owner investments** are assets an owner puts into the company and are included under the generic account **Owner, Capital. Revenues** increase equity and are the assets earned from a company's earnings activities. Examples are consulting services provided, sales of products, facilities rented to others, and commissions from services. **Owner withdrawals** are assets an owner takes from the company for personal use. **Expenses** decrease equity and are the cost of assets or services used to earn revenues. Examples are costs of employee time, use of supplies, and advertising, utilities, and insurance services from others. In sum, equity is the accumulated revenues and owner investments less the accumulated expenses and withdrawals since the company began. This breakdown of equity yields the following **expanded accounting equation.**

> Revenues and owner investments increase equity. Expenses and owner withdrawals decrease equity.

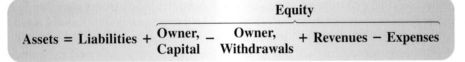

$$\text{Assets} = \text{Liabilities} + \underbrace{\begin{matrix}\text{Owner,} \\ \text{Capital}\end{matrix} - \begin{matrix}\text{Owner,} \\ \text{Withdrawals}\end{matrix} + \text{Revenues} - \text{Expenses}}_{\text{Equity}}$$

Net income occurs when revenues exceed expenses. Net income increases equity. A **net loss** occurs when expenses exceed revenues, which decreases equity.

Transactions and the Accounting Equation

A transaction can be defined as a business activity that affects the accounting equation through specific accounts. An **account** is a record within an accounting system in which increases and decreases are entered and stored. Specific asset, liability, equity, revenue, and expense items are recorded in separate accounts. **External transactions** are exchanges of value between two entities, which yield changes in the accounting equation. An example is a company's payment of its electric bill. **Internal transactions** are exchanges within an entity; they can also affect the accounting equation. An example is a company's use of its supplies, which are reported as expenses when used. **Events** refer to those happenings that affect an entity's accounting equation *and* can be reliably measured. They include business events such as changes in the market value of certain assets and liabilities, and natural events such as floods and fires that destroy assets and create losses. They do not include, for example, the signing of service or product contracts, which by themselves do not impact the accounting equation.

LO2 Analyze business transactions using the accounting equation.

This section uses the accounting equation to analyze 11 selected transactions and events of FastForward, a start-up consulting business, in its first month of operations. Remember that each transaction and event leaves the equation in balance and that assets *always* equal the sum of liabilities and equity.

FastForward

We focus on two questions when analyzing the effects of a transaction on the accounting equation.

1. Which accounts are affected by the transaction?
   a. Identify the affected accounts.
   b. Categorize the affected accounts as assets, liabilities, or equity (including revenues and expenses).

2. How is the accounting equation affected?
   a. Which accounts increase and which decrease as a result of the transaction?
   b. Each transaction leaves the equation in balance; assets always equal the sum of liabilities and equity.

Transaction 1: Investment by Owner   On December 1, Chuck Taylor forms a consulting business, focused on assessing the performance of athletic footwear and accessories, which he names FastForward. He sets it up as a proprietorship, which is a business owned by one person. Taylor owns and manages the business. The marketing plan for the business is to focus primarily on consulting with sports clubs, amateur athletes, and others who place orders for athletic footwear and accessories with manufacturers. Taylor personally invests $30,000 cash in the new company and deposits the cash in a bank account opened under the name of FastForward. After this transaction, the cash (an asset) and the owner's equity each equals $30,000. The source of increase in equity is the owner's investment, which is included in the column titled C. Taylor, Capital. (Owner investments are always included under the title *"Owner name," Capital.*) The effect of this transaction on FastForward is reflected in the accounting equation as follows.

	Assets	=	Liabilities	+	Equity
	Cash	=			**C. Taylor, Capital**
(1)	**+$30,000**	=			**+$30,000**

Transaction 2: Purchase Supplies for Cash   FastForward uses $2,500 of its cash to buy supplies of brand name athletic footwear for performance testing over the next few months. This transaction is an exchange of cash, an asset, for another kind of asset, supplies. It merely changes the form of assets from cash to supplies. The decrease in cash is exactly equal to the increase in supplies. The supplies of athletic footwear are assets because of the expected future benefits from the test results of their performance. This transaction is reflected in the accounting equation as follows:

	Assets			=	Liabilities	+	Equity
	Cash	+	**Supplies**	=			**C. Taylor, Capital**
Old Bal.	$30,000			=			$30,000
(2)	**−2,500**	+	**$2,500**				
New Bal.	$27,500	+	$ 2,500	=			$30,000
		$30,000				$30,000	

> As long as each transaction is entered correctly, the accounting equation remains in balance.

Transaction 3: Purchase Equipment for Cash   FastForward spends $26,000 to acquire equipment for testing athletic footwear. Like transaction 2, transaction 3 is an exchange of one asset, cash, for another asset, equipment. The equipment is an asset because of its expected future benefits from testing athletic footwear. This purchase changes the makeup of assets but does not change the asset total. The accounting equation remains in balance.

	Assets					=	Liabilities	+	Equity
	Cash	+	**Supplies**	+	**Equipment**	=			**C. Taylor, Capital**
Old Bal.	$27,500	+	$2,500			=			$30,000
(3)	**−26,000**			+	**$26,000**				
New Bal.	$ 1,500	+	$2,500	+	$ 26,000	=			$30,000
			$30,000					$30,000	

Transaction 4: Purchase Supplies on Credit   Taylor decides he needs more supplies of athletic footwear and accessories. These additional supplies total $7,100, but as we see from

the accounting equation in transaction 3, FastForward has only $1,500 in cash. Taylor arranges to purchase the supplies on credit from CalTech Supply Company. Thus, FastForward acquires supplies in exchange for a promise to pay for them later. This purchase increases assets by $7,100 in supplies, and liabilities (called *accounts payable*) increase by the same amount. The effects of this purchase follow:

If FastForward pays $500 cash in transaction 4, how does this partial payment affect the liability to CalTech? What would be FastForward's cash balance? *Answers:* The liability to CalTech would be reduced to $6,600 and the cash balance would be reduced to $1,000.

	Assets					=	Liabilities	+	Equity
	Cash	+	Supplies	+	Equipment	=	Accounts Payable	+	C. Taylor, Capital
Old Bal.	$1,500	+	$2,500	+	$26,000	=			$30,000
(4)		+	7,100				+$7,100		
New Bal.	$1,500	+	$9,600	+	$26,000	=	$7,100	+	$30,000
			$37,100					$37,100	

Transaction 5: Provide Services for Cash

FastForward earns revenues by consulting with clients about test results on athletic footwear and accessories. It earns net income only if its revenues are greater than its expenses incurred in earning them. In one of its first jobs, FastForward provides consulting services to an athletic club and immediately collects $4,200 cash. The accounting equation reflects this increase in cash of $4,200 and in equity of $4,200. This increase in equity is identified in the far right column under Revenues because the cash received is earned by providing consulting services.

	Assets					=	Liabilities	+	Equity		
	Cash	+	Supplies	+	Equipment	=	Accounts Payable	+	C. Taylor, Capital	+	Revenues
Old Bal.	$1,500	+	$9,600	+	$26,000	=	$7,100	+	$30,000		
(5)	+4,200									+	$4,200
New Bal.	$5,700	+	$9,600	+	$26,000	=	$7,100	+	$30,000	+	$ 4,200
			$41,300						$41,300		

Transactions 6 and 7: Payment of Expenses in Cash

FastForward pays $1,000 rent to the landlord of the building where its facilities are located. Paying this amount allows FastForward to occupy the space for the month of December. The rental payment is reflected in the following accounting equation as transaction 6. FastForward also pays the biweekly $700 salary of the company's only employee. This is reflected in the accounting equation as transaction 7. Both transactions 6 and 7 are December expenses for FastForward. The costs of both rent and salary are expenses, as opposed to assets, because their benefits are used in December (they have no future benefits after December). These transactions also use up an asset (cash) in carrying out FastForward's operations. The accounting equation shows that both transactions reduce cash and equity. The far right column identifies these decreases as Expenses.

By definition, increases in expenses yield decreases in equity.

	Assets					=	Liabilities	+		Equity			
	Cash	+	Supplies	+	Equipment	=	Accounts Payable	+	C. Taylor, Capital	+	Revenues	−	Expenses
Old Bal.	$5,700	+	$9,600	+	$26,000	=	$7,100	+	$30,000	+	$4,200		
(6)	−1,000											−	$1,000
Bal.	4,700	+	9,600	+	26,000	=	7,100	+	30,000	+	4,200	−	1,000
(7)	− 700											−	700
New Bal.	$4,000	+	$9,600	+	$26,000	=	$7,100	+	$30,000	+	$4,200	−	$ 1,700
			$39,600						$39,600				

Transaction 8: Provide Services and Facilities for Credit   FastForward provides consulting services of $1,600 and rents its test facilities for $300 to an amateur sports club. The rental involves allowing club members to try recommended footwear and accessories at FastForward's testing grounds. The sports club is billed for the $1,900 total. This transaction results in a new asset, called *accounts receivable,* which means the client has not yet paid the $1,900 bill. It also yields an increase in equity from the two revenue components reflected in the Revenues column of the accounting equation:

	Cash	+	Accounts Receivable	+	Supplies	+	Equipment	=	Accounts Payable	+	C. Taylor, Capital	+	Revenues	−	Expenses
	Assets							=	**Liabilities**	+			**Equity**		
Old Bal.	$4,000	+		+	$9,600	+	$26,000	=	$7,100	+	$30,000	+	$4,200	−	$1,700
(8)		+	$1,900									+	1,600		
												+	300		
New Bal.	$4,000	+	$ 1,900	+	$9,600	+	$26,000	=	$7,100	+	$30,000	+	$6,100	−	$1,700
			$41,500										$41,500		

Receipt of cash is not always a revenue. Likewise, payment of cash is not always an expense.

Transaction 9: Receipt of Cash from Accounts Receivable   The client in transaction 8 (the amateur sports club) pays $1,900 to FastForward 10 days after it is billed for consulting services. This transaction 9 does not change the total amount of assets and does not affect liabilities or equity. It converts the receivable (an asset) to cash (another asset). It does not create new revenue. Revenue was recognized when FastForward rendered the services in transaction 8, not when the cash is now collected. The new balances follow:

	Cash	+	Accounts Receivable	+	Supplies	+	Equipment	=	Accounts Payable	+	C. Taylor, Capital	+	Revenues	−	Expenses
	Assets							=	**Liabilities**	+			**Equity**		
Old Bal.	$4,000	+	$1,900	+	$9,600	+	$26,000	=	$7,100	+	$30,000	+	$6,100	−	$1,700
(9)	+1,900	−	1,900												
New Bal.	$5,900	+	$ 0	+	$9,600	+	$26,000	=	$7,100	+	$30,000	+	$6,100	−	$1,700
			$41,500										$41,500		

Transaction 10: Payment of Accounts Payable   FastForward pays CalTech Supply $900 cash as partial payment for its earlier $7,100 purchase of supplies (transaction 4), leaving $6,200 unpaid. The accounting equation shows that this transaction decreases FastForward's cash by $900 and decreases its liability to CalTech Supply by $900. Equity does not change. This event does not create an expense even though cash flows out of FastForward (instead the expense is recorded when FastForward uses the supplies).

	Cash	+	Accounts Receivable	+	Supplies	+	Equipment	=	Accounts Payable	+	C. Taylor, Capital	+	Revenues	−	Expenses
	Assets							=	**Liabilities**	+			**Equity**		
Old Bal.	$5,900	+	$ 0	+	$9,600	+	$26,000	=	$7,100	+	$30,000	+	$6,100	−	$1,700
(10)	− 900								− 900						
New Bal.	$5,000	+	$ 0	+	$9,600	+	$26,000	=	$6,200	+	$30,000	+	$6,100	−	$1,700
			$40,600										$40,600		

Withdrawals are not reported as expenses because they are not part of the company's earning process.

Transaction 11: Withdrawal of Cash by Owner   The owner of FastForward withdraws $200 cash for personal use. Withdrawals are accounted for as a decrease in equity. Since withdrawals are not company expenses, they are not used in computing net income.

By definition, increases in withdrawals yield decreases in equity.

	Assets			=	Liabilities +		Equity			
	Cash +	Accounts Receivable	+ Supplies +	Equipment =	Accounts Payable +	C. Taylor, Capital	− C. Taylor, Withdrawals	+ Revenues	− Expenses
Old Bal.	$5,000 +	$ 0	+ $9,600 +	$26,000 =	$6,200 +	$30,000		+ $6,100	− $1,700
(11)	− 200						− $200		
New Bal.	$4,800 +	$ 0	+ $9,600 +	$26,000 =	$6,200 +	$30,000	− $200	+ $6,100	− $1,700

$40,400 $40,400

Summary of Transactions

We summarize in Exhibit 2.1 the effects of these 11 transactions of FastForward using the accounting equation. Two points should be noted. First, the accounting equation remains in balance after each transaction. Second, transactions can be analyzed by their effects on components of the accounting equation. For example, in transactions 2, 3, and 9, one asset increased while another decreased by equal amounts.

Exhibit 2.1

Summary of Transactions Using the Accounting Equation

	Assets				=	Liabilities +		Equity			
	Cash +	Accounts Receivable	+ Supplies +	Equipment	=	Accounts Payable +	C. Taylor, Capital	− C. Taylor, Withdrawals	+ Revenues	− Expenses
(1)	$30,000				=		$30,000			
(2)	− 2,500		+ $2,500							
Bal.	27,500		+ 2,500		=		30,000			
(3)	−26,000			+ $26,000						
Bal.	1,500		+ 2,500 +	26,000	=		30,000			
(4)			+ 7,100			+$7,100				
Bal.	1,500		+ 9,600 +	26,000	=	7,100 +	30,000			
(5)	+ 4,200								+ $4,200	
Bal.	5,700		+ 9,600 +	26,000	=	7,100 +	30,000		+ 4,200	
(6)	− 1,000									− $1,000
Bal.	4,700		+ 9,600 +	26,000	=	7,100 +	30,000		+ 4,200 −	1,000
(7)	− 700									− 700
Bal.	4,000		+ 9,600 +	26,000	=	7,100 +	30,000		+ 4,200 −	1,700
(8)		+ $1,900							+ 1,600	
									+ 300	
Bal.	4,000 +	1,900	+ 9,600 +	26,000	=	7,100 +	30,000		+ 6,100 −	1,700
(9)	+ 1,900 −	1,900								
Bal.	5,900 +	0	+ 9,600 +	26,000	=	7,100 +	30,000		+ 6,100 −	1,700
(10)	− 900					− 900				
Bal.	5,000 +	0	+ 9,600 +	26,000	=	6,200 +	30,000		+ 6,100 −	1,700
(11)	− 200							− $200		
Bal.	$ 4,800 +	$ 0	+ $ 9,600 +	$ 26,000	=	$ 6,200 +	$ 30,000	− $ 200	+ $6,100 −	$1,700

HOW YOU DOIN'?   Answers—p. 29

1. When is the accounting equation in balance, and what does that mean?
2. How can a transaction not affect any liability and equity accounts?
3. Describe a transaction that increases equity and another transaction that decreases equity.
4. Identify a transaction that decreases both assets and liabilities.

Financial Statements

LO3 Identify and prepare basic financial statements and explain how they interrelate.

This section shows how basic financial statements are prepared from the analysis of business transactions. The financial statements and their purposes are:

1. **Income statement**—describes a company's revenues and expenses along with the resulting net income or loss over a period of time due to earnings activities.
2. **Statement of owner's equity**—explains changes in owner's equity from net income (or loss) and from any owner investments and withdrawals over a period of time.
3. **Balance sheet**—describes a company's financial position (types and amounts of assets, liabilities, and equity) at a point in time.

We prepare these financial statements using the 11 selected transactions of FastForward from Exhibit 2.1.

Income Statement

> Net income is sometimes called *earnings* or *profit.*

The income statement shows the profitability of business operations over a period of time. FastForward's income statement for December is shown at the top of Exhibit 2.2. Information about revenues and expenses is conveniently taken from the Equity columns of Exhibit 2.1. Revenues are reported first on the income statement. They include consulting revenues of $5,800 from transactions 5 and 8 and rental revenue of $300 from transaction 8. Expenses are reported after revenues. (Here we list larger amounts first, but we can sort expenses in different ways.) Rent and salary expenses are from transactions 6 and 7. Expenses reflect the costs to generate the revenues reported. Net income (or loss) is reported at the bottom of the income statement. During the month of December, FastForward had net income, or profit, of $4,400. Owner's investments and withdrawals are *not* part of income.

Statement of Owner's Equity

> The statement of owner's equity is also called the *statement of changes in owner's equity.* Note: Beg. Capital + Net Income − Withdrawals = End. Capital

The statement of owner's equity reports information about how equity changes over the reporting period. This statement shows beginning capital, events that increase it (owner investments and net income), and events that decrease it (withdrawals and net loss). Ending capital is computed in this statement and is carried over and reported on the balance sheet. FastForward's statement of owner's equity is the second report in Exhibit 2.2. The beginning capital balance is measured as of the start of business on December 1. It is zero because FastForward did not exist before then. An existing business reports the beginning balance as of the end of the prior reporting period (such as from November 30). FastForward's statement shows that Taylor's initial investment created $30,000 of equity. It also shows the $4,400 of net income earned during the period. This links the income statement to the statement of owner's equity (see line ①). The statement also reports Taylor's $200 cash withdrawal and FastForward's end-of-period capital balance.

> The statement of cash flows is another financial statement. It is introduced in a later chapter.

Balance Sheet

The balance sheet reports the type and amounts of assets, liabilities, and owner's equity at a point in time. FastForward's balance sheet is the third report in Exhibit 2.2. This statement refers to FastForward's financial condition at the close of business on December 31. The left side of the balance sheet lists FastForward's assets: cash, supplies, and equipment. The upper right side of the balance sheet shows that FastForward owes $6,200 to creditors. Any other liabilities (such as a bank loan) would be listed here. The equity (capital) balance is $34,200. Note the link between the ending balance of the statement of owner's equity and the equity balance here—see line ②.

YOU CALL IT   Answer—p. 29

Retailer You open a wholesale business selling entertainment equipment to retail outlets. You find that most of your customers demand to buy on credit. How can you use the balance sheets of these customers to help you decide which ones to extend credit to?

FASTFORWARD
Income Statement
For Month Ended December 31, 2007

Revenues				
Consulting revenue ($4,200 + $1,600)		$5 8 0 0 00		
Rental revenue		3 0 0 00		
Total revenues			$6 1 0 0 00	
Expenses				
Rent expense		1 0 0 0 00		
Salaries expense		7 0 0 00		
Total expenses			1 7 0 0 00	
Net income			$4 4 0 0 00	

FASTFORWARD
Statement of Owner's Equity
For Month Ended December 31, 2007

C. Taylor, Capital, December 1, 2007			$ 0 00	
Plus: Investments by owner	$30 0 0 0 00			
Net income	4 4 0 0 00	34 4 0 0 00		
		34 4 0 0 00		
Less: Withdrawals by owner		2 0 0 00		
C. Taylor, Capital, December 31, 2007		$34 2 0 0 00		

FASTFORWARD
Balance Sheet
December 31, 2007

Assets		Liabilities		
Cash	$ 4 8 0 0 00	Accounts payable	$ 6 2 0 0 00	
Supplies	9 6 0 0 00	Total liabilities	6 2 0 0 00	
Equipment	26 0 0 0 00			
		Equity		
		C. Taylor, Capital	34 2 0 0 00	
Total assets	$40 4 0 0 00	Total liabilities and equity	$40 4 0 0 00	

Exhibit 2.2

Financial Statements and Their Links

A statement's heading identifies the company, the statement title, and the date or time period.

Arrow lines show how the statements interrelate. ① Net income is used to update equity (capital) ② Ending capital is used to prepare the balance sheet.

The income statement and the statement of owner's equity are prepared for a *period* of time. The balance sheet is prepared as of a *point* in time.

A single ruled line denotes an addition or subtraction. Final totals are double underlined.

HOW YOU DOIN'?

Answers—p. 29

5. Explain the link between the income statement and the statement of owner's equity.

6. Describe the link between the balance sheet and the statement of owner's equity.

RETURN ON ASSETS

An *Analysis* section appears at the end of many chapters. When analyzing ratios and other analysis measures, we need benchmarks to identify good, bad, or average levels. Common benchmarks include the company's prior levels and those of its competitors.

This chapter presents a profitability measure, that of return on assets. Return on assets is useful in evaluating management, analyzing and forecasting profits, and planning activities. **Dell** has its marketing

LO4 Compute and interpret return on assets.

department compute return on assets for *every* order. *Return on assets* (*ROA*), also called *return on investment* (*ROI*), is defined in Exhibit 2.3.

Answer—p. 29

Exhibit 2.3

Return on Assets

$$\text{Return on assets} = \frac{\text{Net income}}{\text{Average total assets}}$$

Net income is from the annual income statement, and average total assets is computed by adding the beginning and ending amounts for that same period and dividing by 2. To illustrate, **Best Buy** reports net income of $984 million in 2005. At the beginning of fiscal 2005, its total assets are $8,652 million and at the end of fiscal 2005, they total $10,294 million. Best Buy's return on assets for 2005 is:

$$\text{Return on assets} = \frac{\$984 \text{ mil.}}{(\$8,652 \text{ mil.} + \$10,294 \text{ mil.})/2} = 10.4\%$$

Is a 10.4% return on assets good or bad for Best Buy? To help answer this question, we compare (benchmark) Best Buy's return with its prior performance, the returns of competitors (such as **Circuit City**, **RadioShack**, and **CompUSA**), and the returns from alternative investments. Best Buy's return for each of the prior five years, from the second column of Exhibit 2.4, ranges from 1.3% to 10.4%. These returns show an increase in its productive use of assets in recent years. We also show Circuit City's returns in the third column of Exhibit 2.4. In four of the five years, Best Buy's return exceeds Circuit City's, and its average return is higher for this period. We also compare Best Buy's return to the normal return for similar merchandisers of electronic products (fourth column). Industry averages are available from services such as **Dun & Bradstreet**'s *Industry Norms and Key Ratios* and **Robert Morris Associates**' *Annual Statement Studies*. When compared to the industry, Best Buy performs well.

YOU CALL IT

Business Owner   You own a small winter ski resort that earns a 21% return on its assets. An opportunity to purchase a winter ski equipment manufacturer is offered to you. This manufacturer earns a 19% return on its assets. The industry return for this manufacturer is 14%. Do you purchase this manufacturer?

Exhibit 2.4

Best Buy, Circuit City, and Industry Returns

| Best Buy Fiscal Year | Return on Assets | | |
	Best Buy	Circuit City	Industry
2005	10.4%	1.6%	3.2%
2004	8.6	(2.3)	3.1
2003	1.3	1.9	3.0
2002	9.3	4.6	3.1
2001	10.1	4.1	6.4

Demonstration Problem

After several months of planning, Jasmine Worthy started a haircutting business called Expressions in August 2008. The following events occurred during its first month.

a. On August 1, Worthy invested $3,000 cash and $15,000 of equipment in Expressions.

b. On August 2, Expressions paid $600 cash for furniture for the shop.

c. On August 3, Expressions paid $500 cash to rent space in a strip mall for August.

d. On August 4, it purchased $1,200 of equipment on credit for the shop (using a long-term note payable).

e. On August 5, Expressions opened for business. Cash received from services provided in the first week and a half of business (ended August 15) is $825.

f. On August 15, it provided $100 of haircutting services on account.

g. On August 17, it received a $100 check for services previously rendered on account on August 15.

h. On August 17, it paid $125 cash to an assistant for working during the grand opening.

i. Cash received from services provided during the second half of August is $930.

j. On August 31, it paid a $400 installment toward principal on the note payable entered into on August 4.

k. On August 31, Worthy made a $900 cash withdrawal for personal use.

Required

1. Arrange the following asset, liability, and equity titles in a table similar to the one in Exhibit 2.1: Cash; Accounts Receivable; Furniture; Store Equipment; Note Payable; J. Worthy, Capital; J. Worthy, Withdrawals; Revenues; and Expenses. Show the effects of each transaction using the accounting equation.

2. Prepare an income statement for August.

3. Prepare a statement of owner's equity for August.

4. Prepare a balance sheet as of August 31.

5. Determine the return on assets ratio for August.

Planning the Solution

- Set up a table like Exhibit 2.1 with the appropriate columns for accounts.
- Analyze each transaction and show its effects as increases or decreases in the appropriate columns. Be sure the accounting equation remains in balance after each transaction.
- Prepare the income statement, and identify revenues and expenses. List those items on the statement, compute the difference, and label the result as *net income* or *net loss*.
- Use information in the Equity columns to prepare the statement of owner's equity.
- Use information in the last row of the transactions table to prepare the balance sheet.
- Calculate return on assets by dividing net income by average assets.

Solution to Demonstration Problem

1.

	Assets							=	Liabilities	+			Equity				
	Cash	+	Accounts Receivable	+	Furniture	+	Store Equipment	=	Note Payable	+	J. Worthy, Capital	−	J. Worthy, Withdrawals	+	Revenues	−	Expenses
a.	$3,000						$15,000				$18,000						
b.	− 600			+	$600												
Bal.	2,400	+		+	600	+	15,000	=			18,000						
c.	− 500															−	$500
Bal.	1,900	+		+	600	+	15,000	=			18,000					−	500
d.						+	1,200		+$1,200								
Bal.	1,900	+		+	600	+	16,200	=	1,200	+	18,000					−	500
e.	+ 825													+	$ 825		
Bal.	2,725	+		+	600	+	16,200	=	1,200	+	18,000			+	825	−	500
f.		+	$100											+	100		
Bal.	2,725	+	100	+	600	+	16,200	=	1,200	+	18,000			+	925	−	500
g.	+ 100	−	100														
Bal.	2,825	+	0	+	600	+	16,200	=	1,200	+	18,000			+	925	−	500
h.	− 125															−	125
Bal.	2,700	+	0	+	600	+	16,200	=	1,200	+	18,000			+	925	−	625
i.	+ 930													+	930		
Bal.	3,630	+	0	+	600	+	16,200	=	1,200	+	18,000			+	1,855	−	625
j.	− 400								− 400								
Bal.	3,230	+	0	+	600	+	16,200	=	800	+	18,000			+	1,855	−	625
k.	− 900											−	$900				
Bal.	$ 2,330	+	$ 0	+	$600	+	$ 16,200	=	$ 800	+	$ 18,000	−	$900	+	$1,855	−	$625

2.

EXPRESSIONS Income Statement For Month Ended August 31, 2008		
Revenues		
Haircutting services revenue		$1 8 5 5 00
Expenses		
Rent expense	$5 0 0 00	
Wages expense	1 2 5 00	
Total expenses		6 2 5 00
Net Income		$1 2 3 0 00

3.

EXPRESSIONS Statement of Owner's Equity For Month Ended August 31, 2008		
J. Worthy, Capital, August 1*		$ 0 00
Plus: Investments by owner	$18 0 0 0 00	
Net income	1 2 3 0 00	19 2 3 0 00
		19 2 3 0 00
Less: Withdrawals by owner		9 0 0 00
J. Worthy, Capital, August 31		$18 3 3 0 00

* If Expressions had been an existing business from a prior period, the beginning capital balance would equal the Capital account balance from the end of the prior period.

4.

EXPRESSIONS Balance Sheet August 31, 2008					
Assets			**Liabilities**		
Cash	$ 2 3 3 0 00		Note payable	$ 8 0 0 00	
Furniture	6 0 0 00		**Equity**		
Store equipment	16 2 0 0 00		J. Worthy, Capital	18 3 3 0 00	
Total assets	$19 1 3 0 00		Total liabilities and equity	$19 1 3 0 00	

5. Return on assets $= \dfrac{\text{Net income}}{\text{Average assets}} = \dfrac{\$1{,}230}{(\$18{,}000^* + \$19{,}130)/2} = \dfrac{\$1{,}230}{\$18{,}565} = \underline{\underline{6.63\%}}$

* Uses the initial $18,000 investment as the beginning balance for the startup period only.

Summary

LO1 **Define the accounting equation and each of its components.** The accounting equation is: Assets = Liabilities + Equity. Assets are resources owned by a company. Liabilities are creditors' claims on assets. Equity is the owner's claim on assets (*the residual*). The expanded accounting equation is: Assets = Liabilities + [Owner Capital − Owner Withdrawals + Revenues − Expenses].

LO2 **Analyze business transactions using the accounting equation.** A *transaction* is an exchange of value between two parties. Examples include exchanges of products, services, money, and rights to collect money. Transactions always have at least two effects on one or more components of the accounting equation. This equation is always in balance.

LO3 **Identify and prepare basic financial statements and explain how they interrelate.** Three basic financial statements report on an organization's activities: balance sheet, income statement, and statement of owner's equity.

LO4 **Compute and interpret return on assets.** Return on assets is computed as net income divided by average assets. For example, if we have an average balance of $100 in a savings account and it earns $5 interest for the year, the return on assets is $5/$100, or 5%.

Guidance Answers to YOU CALL IT

Retailer You can use the accounting equation (Assets = Liabilities + Equity) to help identify risky customers to whom you would likely not want to extend credit. A balance sheet provides amounts for each of these key components. The lower a customer's equity is relative to liabilities, the less likely you would extend credit. A low equity means the business has little value that does not already have creditor claims to it.

Business Owner The 19% return on assets for the manufacturer exceeds the 14% industry return (and many others). This is a positive factor for a potential purchase. Also, the purchase of this manufacturer is an opportunity to spread your risk over two businesses as opposed to one. Still, you should hesitate to purchase a business whose return on assets of 19% is lower than your current resort's return of 21%. You are probably better off directing efforts to increase investment in your resort, assuming you can continue to earn a 21% return on assets.

Guidance Answers to HOW YOU DOIN'?

1. The accounting equation is: Assets = Liabilities + Equity. This equation is always in balance, both before and after each transaction. This means that a company's assets are equal to the claims on those assets.

2. A transaction that changes the makeup of assets would not affect liability and equity accounts. FastForward's transactions 2, 3, and 9 are examples. Each exchanges one asset for another.

3. Earning revenue by performing services, as in FastForward's transaction 5, increases equity (and assets). Incurring expenses while servicing clients, such as in transactions 6 and 7, decreases equity (and assets). Other examples include owner investments that increase equity and owner withdrawals that decrease equity.

4. Paying a liability with an asset reduces both asset and liability totals. One example is FastForward's transaction 10 that reduces a payable by paying cash.

5. An income statement reports a company's revenues and expenses along with the resulting net income or loss. A statement of owner's equity shows changes in equity, including that from net income or loss. Both statements report transactions occurring over a period of time.

6. The balance sheet describes a company's financial position (assets, liabilities, and equity) at a point in time. The equity amount in the balance sheet is obtained from the statement of owner's equity.

Key Terms   mhhe.com/wildCA

Key Terms are available at the book's Website for learning and testing in an online Flashcard Format.

Account (p. 19) Record within an accounting system in which increases and decreases are entered and stored in a specific asset, liability, equity, revenue, or expense.

Accounting equation (p. 18) Equality involving a company's assets, liabilities, and equity; Assets = Liabilities + Equity; also called *balance sheet equation*.

Assets (p. 18) Resources a business owns or controls that are expected to provide current and future benefits to the business.

Balance sheet (p. 24) Financial statement that lists types and dollar amounts of assets, liabilities, and equity at a specific date.

Equity (p. 18) Owner's claim on the assets of a business; equals the residual interest in an entity's assets after deducting liabilities; also called *net assets*.

Expanded accounting equation (p. 19) Assets = Liabilities + Equity; Equity equals [Owner capital − Owner withdrawals + Revenues − Expenses].

Expenses (p. 19) Outflows or using up of assets as part of operations of a business to generate sales.

External transactions (p. 19) Exchanges of value between one entity and another entity.

Income statement (p. 24) Financial statement that subtracts expenses from revenues to yield a net income or loss over a specified period of time; also includes any gains or losses.

Internal transactions (p. 19) Activities within an organization that can affect the accounting equation.

Liabilities (p. 18) Creditors' claims on an organization's assets; involves a probable future payment of assets, products, or services that a company is obliged to make due to past transactions or events.

Net income (p. 19) Amount earned after subtracting all expenses necessary for and matched with sales for a period; also called *income, profit*, or *earnings*.

Net loss (p. 19) Excess over revenues for a period.

Owner, Capital (p. 19) Account showing the owner's claim on company assets; equals owner investments plus net income (or less net losses) minus owner withdrawals since the company's inception; also referred to as *equity*.

Owner investment (p. 19) Assets put into the business by the owner.

Owner withdrawals (p. 19) Payment of cash or other assets from a proprietorship or partnership to its owner or owners.

Return on assets (p. 26) Ratio reflecting operating efficiency; defined as net income divided by average total assets for the period; also called *return on total assets* or *return on investments*.

Revenues (p. 19) Gross increase in equity from a company's business activities that earn income; also called *sales*.

Statement of owner's equity (p. 24) Report of changes in equity over a period; adjusted for increases (owner investment and net income) and for decreases (withdrawals and net losses).

Multiple Choice Quiz   Answers on p. 41   mhhe.com/wildCA

Multiple Choice Quizzes A and B are available at the book's Website.

1. When supplies are paid for with cash, which accounts increase or decrease?
   a. Supplies increase; Cash increases.
   b. Supplies increase; Accounts Payable increases.
   c. Supplies increase; Cash neither increases nor decreases.
   d. Supplies increase; Cash decreases.

2. When supplies are purchased on account, which accounts increase or decrease?
   a. Supplies increase; accounts payable increases.
   b. Supplies increase; accounts receivable increases.
   c. Supplies increase; accounts payable decreases.
   d. Supplies increase; equity decreases.

3. If the assets of a company increase by $100,000 during the year and its liabilities increase by $35,000 during the same year, then the change in equity of the company during the year must have been:
   a. An increase of $135,000.
   b. A decrease of $135,000.
   c. A decrease of $65,000.
   d. An increase of $65,000.
   e. An increase of $100,000.

4. A company borrows $50,000 cash from Third National Bank. How does this transaction affect the accounting equation for this company?

   a. Assets increase by $50,000; liabilities increase by $50,000; no effect on equity.
   b. Assets increase by $50,000; no effect on liabilities; equity increases by $50,000.
   c. Assets increase by $50,000; liabilities decrease by $50,000; no effect on equity.
   d. No effect on assets; liabilities increase by $50,000; equity increases by $50,000.
   e. No effect on assets; liabilities increase by $50,000; equity decreases by $50,000.

5. Geek Squad performs services for a customer and bills the customer for $500. How would Geek Squad record this transaction?
   a. Accounts receivable increase by $500; revenues increase by $500.
   b. Cash increases by $500; revenues increase by $500.
   c. Accounts receivable increase by $500; revenues decrease by $500.
   d. Accounts receivable increase by $500; accounts payable increase by $500.
   e. Accounts payable increase by $500; revenues increase by $500.

Discussion Questions

1. Define (a) *assets,* (b) *liabilities,* (c) *equity*, and (d) *net assets.*
2. What events or transactions change equity?
3. What do accountants mean by the term *revenue?*
4. Define *net income* and explain its computation.
5. Identify the three basic financial statements of a business.
6. What information is reported in an income statement?
7. Give two examples of expenses a business might incur.
8. What is the purpose of the statement of owner's equity?
9. What information is reported in a balance sheet?

10. Define and explain return on assets.
11. Refer to the financial statements of **Best Buy** in Appendix A near the end of the book. To what level are dollar amounts rounded? What time period does its income statement cover?
12. Identify the dollar amounts of **Circuit City**'s 2005 assets, liabilities, and equity shown in its statements in Appendix A near the end of the book.

a. Total assets of Charter Company equal $700,000 and its equity is $420,000. What is the amount of its liabilities?

b. Total assets of Martin Marine equal $500,000 and its liabilities and equity amounts are equal to each other. What is the amount of its liabilities? What is the amount of its equity?

QUICK STUDY

QS 2-1
Applying the accounting equation
(LO1)

Use the accounting equation to compute the missing financial statement amounts (*a*), (*b*), and (*c*).

QS 2-2
Applying the accounting equation
(LO1)

Company	Assets	=	Liabilities	+	Equity
1	$75,000		$ (*a*)		$40,000
2	$ (*b*)		$25,000		$70,000
3	$85,000		$20,000		$ (*c*)

Indicate in which financial statement each item would most likely appear: income statement (I), balance sheet (B), or statement of owner's equity (E).

a. Assets   c. Equipment   e. Liabilities   g. Total liabilities and equity

b. Withdrawals   d. Expenses   f. Revenues

QS 2-3
Identifying items with financial statements
(LO2)

In a recent year's financial statements, **Home Depot** reported the following results. Compute and interpret its return on assets (assume competitors average a 12% return on assets).

Sales	$73,074 million
Net income	5,001 million
Average total assets	36,672 million

QS 2-4
Computing and interpreting return on assets
(LO4)

Determine the missing amount from each of the separate situations a, b, and c below.

EXERCISES

Exercise 2-1
Using the accounting equation
(LO1)

	Assets	=	Liabilities	+	Equity
a.	?	=	$20,000	+	$45,000
b.	$100,000	=	$34,000	+	?
c.	$154,000	=	?	+	$40,000

Classify each of the following accounts as an asset (A), liability (L), or equity (E) account.

_____ **1.** Accounts Payable   _____ **5.** Supplies

_____ **2.** Loan (or Notes) Payable   _____ **6.** Equipment

_____ **3.** Accounts Receivable   _____ **7.** Rod Smith, Capital

_____ **4.** Cash

Exercise 2-2
Classifying accounts
(LO1) (LO2)

Provide an example of a transaction that creates the described effects for the separate cases *a* through *g*.

a. Decreases an asset and decreases equity.   e. Increases an asset and decreases an asset.

b. Increases an asset and increases a liability.   f. Increases a liability and decreases equity.

c. Decreases a liability and increases a liability.   g. Increases an asset and increases equity.

d. Decreases an asset and decreases a liability.

Exercise 2-3
Identifying effects of transactions on the accounting equation
(LO1) (LO2)

Answer the following questions. (*Hint:* Use the accounting equation.)

a. Cadence Office Supplies has assets equal to $123,000 and liabilities equal to $47,000 at year-end. What is the total equity for Cadence at year-end?

Exercise 2-4
Using the accounting equation
(LO1) (LO2)

b. At the beginning of the year, Addison Company's assets are $300,000 and its equity is $100,000. During the year, assets increase $80,000 and liabilities increase $50,000. What is the equity at the end of the year?

Check (c) Beg. equity, $60,000

c. At the beginning of the year, Quasar Company's liabilities equal $70,000. During the year, assets increase by $60,000, and at year-end assets equal $190,000. Liabilities decrease $5,000 during the year. What are the beginning and ending amounts of equity?

Exercise 2–5

Identifying effects of transactions using the accounting equation

(L01) (L02)

Leora Holden began a professional practice on June 1 and plans to prepare financial statements at the end of each month. During June, Holden (the owner) completed these transactions.

a. Owner invested $60,000 cash along with equipment that had a $15,000 market value.

b. Paid $1,500 cash for rent of office space for the month.

c. Purchased $10,000 of additional equipment on credit (payment due within 30 days).

d. Completed work for a client and immediately collected the $2,500 cash earned.

e. Completed work for a client and sent a bill for $8,000 to be received within 30 days.

f. Purchased additional equipment for $6,000 cash.

g. Paid an assistant $3,000 cash as wages for the month.

h. Collected $5,000 cash on the amount owed by the client described in transaction *e.*

i. Paid $10,000 cash to settle the liability created in transaction *c.*

j. Owner withdrew $1,000 cash for personal use.

Required

Check Net income, $6,000

Create a table like the one in Exhibit 2.1, using the following headings for columns: Cash; Accounts Receivable; Equipment; Accounts Payable; Holden, Capital; Holden, Withdrawals; Revenues; and Expenses. Then use additions and subtractions to show the effects of the transactions on individual items of the accounting equation. Show new balances after each transaction.

Exercise 2–6

Identifying effects of transactions on accounting equation

(L01) (L02)

The following table shows the effects of five transactions (*a* through *e*) on the assets, liabilities, and equity of Trista's Boutique. Write short descriptions of the probable nature of each transaction.

	Cash	+	Accounts Receivable	+	Office Supplies	+	Land	=	Accounts Payable	+	Trista, Capital	+	Revenues
	$ 21,000	+	$ 0	+	$3,000	+	$ 19,000	=	$ 0	+	$43,000	+	$ 0
a.	− 4,000					+	4,000						
b.					+	1,000			+1,000				
c.		+	1,900									+	1,900
d.	− 1,000								−1,000				
e.	+ 1,900	−	1,900										
	$ 17,900	+	$ 0	+	$4,000	+	$ 23,000	=	$ 0	+	$43,000	+	$1,900

Column group headers: **Assets** = **Liabilities** + **Equity**

Exercise 2–7

Preparing an income statement

(L03)

On October 1, Keisha King organized Real Answers, a new consulting firm. On October 31, the company's records show the following items and amounts. Use this information to prepare an October income statement for the business.

Check Net income, $2,110

Consulting fees earned	....	14,000	Telephone expense	760
Rent expense	....	3,550	Miscellaneous expenses	580
Salaries expense	....	7,000		

Exercise 2–8

Preparing a statement of owner's equity

(L03)

Jim Hunton starts a systems consulting business on October 1 by investing $35,000 cash in the business. His net income for October is $14,000 and he withdrew $12,000 on October 30. Prepare a statement of owner's equity for the month of October.

Exercise 2–9

Analysis of return on assets

(L04)

Swiss Group reports net income of $40,000 for 2007. At the beginning of 2007, Swiss Group had $200,000 in assets. By the end of 2007, assets had grown to $300,000. What is Swiss Group's 2007 return on assets? How would you assess its performance if competitors average a 10% return on assets?

Problem Set B located at the end of Problem Set A is provided for each problem to reinforce the learning process.

The following financial statement information is from five separate companies.

	Company A	Company B	Company C	Company D	Company E
December 31, 2006					
Assets	$55,000	$34,000	$24,000	$60,000	$119,000
Liabilities	24,500	21,500	9,000	40,000	?
December 31, 2007					
Assets	58,000	40,000	?	85,000	113,000
Liabilities	?	26,500	29,000	24,000	70,000
During year 2007					
Owner investments	6,000	1,400	9,750	?	6,500
Net income	8,500	?	8,000	14,000	20,000
Owner cash withdrawals	3,500	2,000	5,875	0	11,000

Required

1. Answer the following questions about Company A.
   a. What is the amount of equity on December 31, 2006?
   b. What is the amount of equity on December 31, 2007?
   c. What is the amount of liabilities on December 31, 2007?
2. Answer the following questions about Company B.
   a. What is the amount of equity on December 31, 2006?
   b. What is the amount of equity on December 31, 2007?
   c. What is net income for year 2007?
3. Calculate the amount of assets for Company C on December 31, 2007.
4. Calculate the amount of owner investments for Company D during year 2007.
5. Calculate the amount of liabilities for Company E on December 31, 2006.

PROBLEM SET A

Problem 2-1A
Computing missing information using accounting knowledge and the accounting equation
  (L01) (L02)

Check (1*b*) $41,500

(2*c*) $1,600
(3) $55,875

Identify how each of the following separate transactions affects financial statements. For the balance sheet, identify how each transaction affects total assets, total liabilities, and total equity. For the income statement, identify how each transaction affects net income. For increases, place a "+" in the column or columns. For decreases, place a "−" in the column or columns. If both an increase and a decrease occur, place a "+/−" in the column or columns. The first transaction is completed as an example.

Problem 2-2A
Identifying effects of transactions on financial statements
(L01) (L02)

		Balance Sheet			Income Statement
	Transaction	**Total Assets**	**Total Liab.**	**Total Equity**	**Net Income**
1	Owner invests cash in business	+		+	
2	Receives cash for services provided				
3	Pays cash for employee wages				
4	Incurs legal costs on credit				
5	Borrows cash by signing long-term note payable				
6	Owner withdraws cash				
7	Buys land by signing note payable				
8	Provides services on credit				
9	Buys office equipment for cash				
10	Collects cash on receivable from (8)				

Problem 2-3A

Preparing an income statement

(LO3)

The following is selected financial information for Elko Energy Company for the year ended December 31, 2007: revenues, $55,000; expenses, $40,000; net income, $15,000.

Required

Prepare the 2007 income statement for Elko Energy Company.

Problem 2-4A

Preparing a balance sheet

(LO3)

The following is selected financial information for Amity Company as of December 31, 2007: liabilities, $44,000; equity, $46,000; assets, $90,000.

Required

Prepare the balance sheet for Amity Company as of December 31, 2007.

Problem 2-5A

Preparing a statement of owner's equity

(LO3)

Following is selected financial information for Kasio Co. for the year ended December 31, 2007.

K. Kasio, Capital, Dec. 31, 2007	$14,000	K. Kasio, Withdrawals	$1,000
Net income	8,000	K. Kasio, Capital, Dec. 31, 2006	7,000

Required

Prepare the 2007 statement of owner's equity for Kasio.

Problem 2-6A

Analyzing transactions and preparing financial statements

(LO2) (LO3)

e**X**cel

mhhe.com/wildCA

Holden Graham started The Graham Co., a new business that began operations on May 1. Graham Co. completed the following transactions during that first month.

May	1	H. Graham invested $40,000 cash in the business.
	1	Rented a furnished office and paid $2,200 cash for May's rent.
	3	Purchased $1,890 of office equipment on credit.
	5	Paid $750 cash for this month's cleaning services.
	8	Provided consulting services for a client and immediately collected $5,400 cash.
	12	Provided $2,500 of consulting services for a client on credit.
	15	Paid $750 cash for an assistant's salary for the first half of this month.
	20	Received $2,500 cash payment for the services provided on May 12.
	22	Provided $3,200 of consulting services on credit.
	25	Received $3,200 cash payment for the services provided on May 22.
	26	Paid $1,890 cash for the office equipment purchased on May 3.
	27	Purchased $80 of advertising in this month's (May) local paper on credit; cash payment is due June 1.
	28	Paid $750 cash for an assistant's salary for the second half of this month.
	30	Paid $300 cash for this month's telephone bill.
	30	Paid $280 cash for this month's utilities.
	31	Graham withdrew $1,400 cash for personal use.

Required

1. Arrange the following asset, liability, and equity titles in a table like Exhibit 2.1: Cash; Accounts Receivable; Office Equipment; Accounts Payable; H. Graham, Capital; H. Graham, Withdrawals; Revenues; and Expenses.

2. Show effects of the transactions on the accounts of the accounting equation by recording increases and decreases in the appropriate columns. Do not determine new account balances after each transaction. Determine the final total for each account and verify that the equation is in balance.

3. Prepare an income statement for May, a statement of owner's equity for May, and a May 31 balance sheet.

Check (2) Ending balances: Cash, $42,780; Expenses, $5,110

(3) Net income, $5,990; Total assets, $44,670

Problem 2-7A

Analyzing transactions and preparing financial statements

(LO2) (LO3)

e**X**cel

mhhe.com/wildCA

Helga Ander started a new business and completed these transactions during December.

Dec.	1	Helga Ander transferred $65,000 cash from a personal savings account to a checking account in the name of Ander Electric.
	2	Rented office space and paid $1,000 cash for the December rent.
	3	Purchased $13,000 of electrical equipment by paying $4,800 cash and agreeing to pay the $8,200 balance in 30 days.
	5	Purchased office supplies by paying $800 cash.

6 Completed electrical work and immediately collected $1,200 cash for the work.
8 Purchased $2,530 of office equipment on credit.
15 Completed electrical work on credit in the amount of $5,000.
18 Purchased $350 of office supplies on credit.
20 Paid $2,530 cash for the office equipment purchased on December 8.
24 Billed a client $900 for electrical work completed; the balance is due in 30 days.
28 Received $5,000 cash for the work completed on December 15.
29 Paid the assistant's salary of $1,400 cash for this month.
30 Paid $540 cash for this month's utility bill.
31 Ander withdrew $950 cash for personal use.

Required

1. Arrange the following asset, liability, and equity titles in a table like Exhibit 2.1: Cash; Accounts Receivable; Office Supplies; Office Equipment; Electrical Equipment; Accounts Payable; H. Ander, Capital; H. Ander, Withdrawals; Revenues; and Expenses.

2. Use additions and subtractions to show the effects of each transaction on the accounts in the accounting equation. Show new balances after each transaction.

3. Use the increases and decreases in the columns of the table from part 2 to prepare an income statement and a statement of owner's equity for the month. Also prepare a balance sheet as of the end of the month.

Check (2) Ending balances: Cash, $59,180, Accounts Payable, $8,550

(3) Net income, $4,160; Total assets, $76,760

Isabel Lopez started Biz Consulting, a new business, and completed the following transactions during its first year of operations.

a. I. Lopez invests $70,000 cash and office equipment valued at $10,000 in the business.

b. Purchased a $150,000 building to use as an office. Biz paid $20,000 in cash and signed a note payable promising to pay the $130,000 balance over the next ten years.

c. Purchased office equipment for $15,000 cash.

d. Purchased $1,200 of office supplies and $1,700 of office equipment on credit.

e. Paid a local newspaper $500 cash for printing an announcement of the office's opening.

f. Completed a financial plan for a client and billed that client $2,800 for the service.

g. Designed a financial plan for another client and immediately collected a $4,000 cash fee.

h. Lopez withdrew $3,275 cash for personal use.

i. Received a $1,800 cash payment from the client described in transaction *f*.

j. Made a $700 cash payment on the equipment purchased in transaction *d*.

k. Paid $1,800 cash for the office secretary's wages.

Problem 2-8A
Analyzing effects of transactions
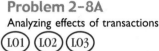

Required

1. Create a table like the one in Exhibit 2.1, using the following headings for the columns: Cash; Accounts Receivable; Office Supplies; Office Equipment; Building; Accounts Payable; Notes Payable; I. Lopez, Capital; I. Lopez, Withdrawals; Revenues; and Expenses.

2. Use additions and subtractions to show the effects of these transactions on individual items of the accounting equation. Show new balances after each transaction.

3. Once you have completed the table, determine the company's net income.

Check (2) Ending balances: Cash, $34,525; Expenses, $2,300; Notes Payable, $130,000

(3) Net income, $4,500

Coca-Cola and PepsiCo both produce and market beverages that are direct competitors. Key financial figures (in $ millions) for these businesses over the past year follow.

Problem 2-9A
Computing and interpreting return on assets
(L04)

Key Figures ($ millions)	Coca-Cola	PepsiCo
Sales	$21,962	$29,261
Net income	4,847	4,212
Average assets	29,335	26,657

Required

1. Compute return on assets for (*a*) Coca-Cola and (*b*) PepsiCo.

2. Which company makes more sales to consumers?

3. Which company is more successful in earning net income from its assets invested?

Check (1*a*) 16.5%; (1*b*) 15.8%

Analysis Component

4. Write a one-paragraph memorandum explaining which company you would invest your money in and why. (Limit your explanation to the information provided.)

Problem 2-10A
Determining expenses, liabilities, equity, and return on assets

(LO1) (LO4)

Kyzera manufactures, markets, and sells cellular telephones. The average total assets for Kyzera is $250,000. In its most recent year, Kyzera reported net income of $65,000 on revenues of $475,000.

Required

1. What is Kyzera's return on assets?

2. Does return on assets seem satisfactory for Kyzera given that its competitors average a 12% return on assets?

3. What are total expenses for Kyzera in its most recent year?

4. What is the average total amount of liabilities plus equity for Kyzera?

Check (3) $410,000
        (4) $250,000

PROBLEM SET B

Problem 2-1B
Computing missing information using accounting knowledge

(LO1) (LO2)

The following financial statement information is from five separate companies.

	Company V	Company W	Company X	Company Y	Company Z
December 31, 2006					
Assets	$54,000	$ 80,000	$141,500	$92,500	$144,000
Liabilities	25,000	60,000	68,500	51,500	?
December 31, 2007					
Assets	59,000	100,000	186,500	?	170,000
Liabilities	36,000	?	65,800	42,000	42,000
During year 2007					
Owner investments	5,000	20,000	?	48,100	60,000
Net income	?	40,000	18,500	24,000	32,000
Owner cash withdrawals	5,500	2,000	0	20,000	8,000

Required

1. Answer the following questions about Company V.
  a. What is the amount of equity on December 31, 2006?
  b. What is the amount of equity on December 31, 2007?
  c. What is the net income or loss for the year 2007?

2. Answer the following questions about Company W.
  a. What is the amount of equity on December 31, 2006?
  b. What is the amount of equity on December 31, 2007?
  c. What is the amount of liabilities on December 31, 2007?

3. Calculate the amount of owner investments for Company X during 2007.

4. Calculate the amount of assets for Company Y on December 31, 2007.

5. Calculate the amount of liabilities for Company Z on December 31, 2006.

Check (1b) $23,000

        (2c) $22,000

        (4) $135,100

Problem 2-2B
Identifying effects of transactions on financial statements

(LO1) (LO2)

Identify how each of the following separate transactions affects financial statements. For the balance sheet, identify how each transaction affects total assets, total liabilities, and total equity. For the income statement, identify how each transaction affects net income. For increases, place a "+" in the column or columns. For decreases, place a "−" in the column or columns. If both an increase and a decrease occur, place "+/−" in the column or columns. The first transaction is completed as an example.

	Transaction	Balance Sheet			Income Statement
		Total Assets	Total Liab.	Total Equity	Net Income
1	Owner invests cash in business	+		+	
2	Buys building by signing note payable				
3	Pays cash for salaries incurred				
4	Provides services for cash				
5	Pays cash for rent incurred				
6	Incurs utilities costs on credit				
7	Buys store equipment for cash				
8	Owner withdraws cash				
9	Provides services on credit				
10	Collects cash on receivable from (9)				

Selected financial information for Offshore Co. for the year ended December 31, 2007, follows:

Problem 2-3B
Preparing an income statement
(LO3)

Revenues	$68,000	Expenses	$40,000	Net income	$28,000

Required

Prepare the 2007 income statement for Offshore Co.

The following is selected financial information for TLC Company as of December 31, 2007.

Problem 2-4B
Preparing a balance sheet
(LO3)

Liabilities	$64,000	Equity	$50,000	Assets	$114,000

Required

Prepare the balance sheet for TLC as of December 31, 2007.

Following is selected financial information of First Act for the year ended December 31, 2007.

Problem 2-5B
Preparing a statement of owner's equity
(LO3)

I. Firstact, Capital, Dec. 31, 2007	$47,000	I. Firstact, Withdrawals	$ 7,000
Net income	5,000	I. Firstact, Capital, Dec. 31, 2006	49,000

Required

Prepare the 2007 calendar-year statement of owner's equity for First Act.

Holly Nikolas launched a new business, Holly's Maintenance Co., that began operations on June 1. The following transactions were completed by the company during that first month.

Problem 2-6B
Analyzing transactions and preparing financial statements
(LO2) (LO3)

June 1   H. Nikolas invested $130,000 cash in the business.
  2   Rented a furnished office and paid $6,000 cash for June's rent.
  4   Purchased $2,400 of equipment on credit.
  6   Paid $1,150 cash for the next week's advertising of the opening of the business.
  8   Completed maintenance services for a customer and immediately collected $850 cash.
  14   Completed $7,500 of maintenance services for City Center on credit.
  16   Paid $800 cash for an assistant's salary for the first half of the month.
  20   Received $7,500 cash payment for services completed for City Center on June 14.
  21   Completed $7,900 of maintenance services for Paula's Beauty Shop on credit.
  24   Completed $675 of maintenance services for Build-It Coop on credit.
  25   Received $7,900 cash payment from Paula's Beauty Shop for the work completed on June 21.
  26   Made payment of $2,400 cash for the equipment purchased on June 4.

28   Paid $800 cash for an assistant's salary for the second half of this month.
29   Nikolas withdrew $4,000 cash for personal use.
30   Paid $150 cash for this month's telephone bill.
30   Paid $890 cash for this month's utilities.

Required

1. Arrange the following asset, liability, and equity titles in a table like Exhibit 2.1: Cash; Accounts Receivable; Equipment; Accounts Payable; H. Nikolas, Capital; H. Nikolas, Withdrawals; Revenues; and Expenses.

2. Show the effects of the transactions on the accounts of the accounting equation by recording increases and decreases in the appropriate columns. Do not determine new account balances after each transaction. Determine the final total for each account and verify that the equation is in balance.

3. Prepare a June income statement, a June statement of owner's equity, and a June 30 balance sheet.

Check   (2) Ending balances: Cash, $130,060; Expenses, $9,790

(3) Net income, $7,135; Total assets, $133,135

Problem 2-7B

Analyzing transactions and preparing financial statements

Truro Excavating Co., owned by Raul Truro, began operations in July and completed the following transactions during that first month.

July 1   R. Truro invested $80,000 cash in the business.
2   Rented office space and paid $700 cash for the July rent.
3   Purchased excavating equipment for $5,000 by paying $1,000 cash and agreeing to pay the $4,000 balance in 30 days.
6   Purchased office supplies for $600 cash.
8   Completed work for a customer and immediately collected $7,600 cash for the work.
10   Purchased $2,300 of office equipment on credit.
15   Completed work for a customer on credit in the amount of $8,200.
17   Purchased $3,100 of office supplies on credit.
23   Paid $2,300 cash for the office equipment purchased on July 10.
25   Billed a customer $5,000 for work completed; the balance is due in 30 days.
28   Received $8,200 cash for the work completed on July 15.
30   Paid an assistant's salary of $1,560 cash for this month.
31   Paid $295 cash for this month's utility bill.
31   Truro withdrew $1,800 cash for personal use.

Required

1. Arrange the following asset, liability, and equity titles in a table like Exhibit 2.1: Cash; Accounts Receivable; Office Supplies; Office Equipment; Excavating Equipment; Accounts Payable; R. Truro, Capital; R. Truro, Withdrawals; Revenues; and Expenses.

2. Use additions and subtractions to show the effects of each transaction on the accounts in the accounting equation. Show new balances after each transaction.

3. Use the increases and decreases in the columns of the table from part 2 to prepare an income statement, and a statement of owner's equity. Also prepare a balance sheet as of the end of the month.

Check   (2) Ending balances: Cash, $87,545; Accounts Payable, $7,100

(3) Net income, $18,245; Total assets, $103,545

Problem 2-8B

Analyzing effects of transactions

Nico Mitchell started a new business, Nico's Solutions, that completed the following transactions during its first year of operations.

a. N. Mitchell invests $70,000 cash and office equipment valued at $10,000 in the business.

b. Purchased a $150,000 building to use as an office. The company paid $20,000 in cash and signed a note payable promising to pay the $130,000 balance over the next ten years.

c. Purchased office equipment for $15,000 cash.

d. Purchased $1,200 of office supplies and $1,700 of office equipment on credit.

e. Paid a local newspaper $500 cash for printing an announcement of the office's opening.

f. Completed a financial plan for a client and billed that client $2,800 for the service.

g. Designed a financial plan for another client and immediately collected a $4,000 cash fee.

h. Mitchell withdrew $3,275 cash for personal use.

i. Received $1,800 cash from the client described in transaction f.

j. Made a $700 cash payment on the equipment purchased in transaction d.

k. Paid $2,300 cash for the office secretary's wages.

Required

1. Create a table like the one in Exhibit 2.1, using the following headings for the columns: Cash; Accounts Receivable; Office Supplies; Office Equipment; Building; Accounts Payable; Notes Payable; N. Mitchell, Capital; N. Mitchell, Withdrawals; Revenues; and Expenses.

2. Use additions and subtractions to show the effects of these transactions on individual items of the accounting equation. Show new balances after each transaction.

3. Once you have completed the table, determine the company's net income.

Check (2) Ending balances: Cash, $34,025; Expenses, $2,800; Notes Payable, $130,000

(3) Net income, $4,000

AT&T and Verizon produce and market telecommunications products and are competitors. Key financial figures (in $ millions) for these businesses over the past year follow.

Problem 2-9B

Computing and interpreting return on assets

(LO4)

Key Figures ($ millions)	AT&T	Verizon
Sales	$34,529	$ 67,468
Net income	1,865	3,077
Average assets	40,396	165,963

Required

1. Compute return on assets for (*a*) AT&T and (*b*) Verizon.

2. Which company is more successful in the total amount of sales to consumers?

3. Which company is more successful in returning net income from its assets invested?

Check (1*a*) 4.6%; (1*b*) 1.9%

Analysis Component

4. Write a one-paragraph memorandum explaining which company you would invest your money in and why. (Limit your explanation to the information provided.)

Carbondale Company manufactures, markets, and sells snowmobile equipment. The average total assets for Carbondale Company is $3,000,000. In its most recent year, Carbondale reported net income of $200,000 on revenues of $1,400,000.

Problem 2-10B

Determining expenses, liabilities, equity, and return on assets

(LO1) (LO4)

Required

1. What is Carbondale Company's return on assets?

2. Does return on assets seem satisfactory for Carbondale given that its competitors average a 9.5% return on assets?

3. What are the total expenses for Carbondale Company in its most recent year?

4. What is the average total amount of liabilities plus equity for Carbondale Company?

Check (3) $1,200,000

(4) $3,000,000

(This serial problem started in Chapter 1 and continues through most of the chapters. If the Chapter 1 segment was not completed, the problem can begin at this point. It is helpful, but not necessary, to use the Working Papers that accompany this book.)

SERIAL PROBLEM

Success Systems

SP 2 On October 1, 2007, Adriana Lopez started a computer services company, **Success Systems,** that provides consulting services, computer system installations, and custom program development. Lopez expects to prepare the company's first set of financial statements on December 31, 2007.

Required

Create a table like the one in Exhibit 2.1 using the following headings for columns: Cash; Accounts Receivable; Computer Supplies; Computer System; Office Equipment; Accounts Payable; A. Lopez, Capital; A. Lopez, Withdrawals; Revenues; and Expenses. Then use additions and subtractions to show the effects of the October transactions for Success Systems on the individual items of the accounting equation. Show new balances after each transaction.

Oct. 1 Adriana Lopez invested $75,000 cash, a $25,000 computer system, and $10,000 of office equipment in the business.

3 Purchased $1,600 of computer supplies on credit from Corvina Office Products.

6 Billed Easy Leasing $6,200 for services performed in installing a new Web server.

8 Paid $1,600 cash for the computer supplies purchased from Corvina Office Products on October 3.

10 Hired Michelle Jones as a part-time assistant for $150 per day, as needed.
12 Billed Easy Leasing another $1,950 for services performed.
15 Received $6,200 cash from Easy Leasing toward its account.
17 Paid $900 cash to repair computer equipment damaged when moving it.
20 Paid $1,790 cash for an advertisement in the local newspaper.
22 Received $1,950 cash from Easy Leasing toward its account.
28 Billed Clark Company $7,300 for services performed.
31 Paid $1,050 cash for Michelle Jones's wages for seven days of work this month.
31 Lopez withdrew $4,000 cash for personal use.

Check Ending balances: Cash, $73,810; Revenues, $15,450; Expenses, $3,740

BEYOND THE NUMBERS

REPORTING IN ACTION

(LO1) (LO4)

Check (2) 10.4%

BTN 2-1 Key financial figures for **Best Buy**'s fiscal year ended February 26, 2005, follow.

Key Figure	In Millions
Liabilities + Equity	$10,294
Net income	984
Revenues	27,433

Required

1. What is the total amount of assets invested in Best Buy?
2. What is Best Buy's return on assets? Its assets at February 28, 2004, equal $8,652 (in millions).
3. How much are total expenses for Best Buy in fiscal year 2005?
4. Does Best Buy's return on assets seem satisfactory if competitors average a 3.2% return?

Fast Forward

5. Access Best Buy's financial statements (Form 10-K) for fiscal years ending after February 26, 2005, from its Website (BestBuy.com) or from the SEC Website (www.sec.gov) and compute its return on assets for those fiscal years. Compare the February 26, 2005, fiscal year-end return on assets to any subsequent years' returns you are able to compute, and interpret the results.

COMPARATIVE ANALYSIS

(LO1) (LO4)

Check (2b) 1.6%

BTN 2-2 Key comparative figures ($ millions) for both **Best Buy** and **Circuit City** follow.

Key Figure	Best Buy	Circuit City
Liabilities + Equity	$10,294	$3,789
Net income	984	62
Revenues	27,433	10,472

Required

1. What is the total amount of assets invested in (*a*) Best Buy and (*b*) Circuit City?
2. What is the return on assets for (*a*) Best Buy and (*b*) Circuit City? Best Buy's beginning-year assets equal $8,652 (in millions) and Circuit City's beginning-year assets equal $3,731 (in millions).
3. How much are expenses for (*a*) Best Buy and (*b*) Circuit City?
4. Is return on assets satisfactory for (*a*) Best Buy and (*b*) Circuit City? (Assume competitors average a 3.2% return.)
5. What can you conclude about Best Buy and Circuit City from these computations?

ETHICS CHALLENGE

(LO1) (LO2)

BTN 2-3 **WorldCom** committed fraud by accounting for some expenses as if they were assets.

Required

1. Using the accounting equation, show the accounting for an expense and the accounting for an asset (assume cash is paid in each instance). Does the accounting equation balance in both instances?
2. What ethical concerns would you have if your business accounted for an expense as if it were an asset?

BTN 2-4   Refer to this chapter's opening feature about **Million Dollar Home Page**. Assume that the founder, Alex Tew, is having difficulty assessing how well his business has performed over the past year. Write Alex Tew a half-page memo to explain which financial statement will provide him the best information on his company's performance and which particular number he should focus on.

WORKPLACE COMMUNICATION
(LO3)

BTN 2-5   Visit the EDGAR database at (www.sec.gov). Access the Form 10-K report of **World Wrestling Entertainment** (ticker WWE) filed on July 13, 2004, covering its 2004 fiscal year.

TAKING IT TO THE NET
(LO3)

Required

1. Item 7 of its 10-K report provides comparative financial highlights of WWE for the years 2000–2004. How would you describe the revenue trend for WWE over this five-year period?

2. Has WWE been profitable (see net income) over this five-year period? Support your answer.

BTN 2-6   Divide the class into teams and play **Monopoly™**. Each team takes ten turns. Each team starts with $1,500 of owners' capital, in cash.

TEAMWORK IN ACTION
(LO1) (LO2)

Required

1. Each team accounts for its first ten transactions using the accounting equation. Use a table like Exhibit 2.1.

2. Each team presents its accounting equation entries to one other team.

BTN 2-7   Refer to this chapter's opening feature about **Million Dollar Home Page**. Assume that Alex Tew decides to open a new Website to meet customer demand. This new company will be called Million Dollar Website.

ENTREPRENEURS IN BUSINESS
(LO2) (LO3)

Required

1. Million Dollar Website obtains a $500,000 loan and Alex contributes $250,000 of his own assets in the new company.

   a. What is the new company's total amount of liabilities plus equity?

   b. What is the new company's total amount of assets?

2. If the new company earns $80,000 in net income in the first year of operation, compute its return on assets (assume average assets equal $750,000). Assess its performance if competitors average an 8% return.

Check   (2) 10.7%

~~~~~~

ANSWERS TO MULTIPLE CHOICE QUIZ

1. d
2. a
3. d;

4. a
5. a

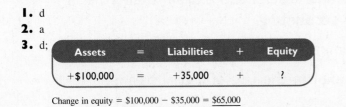

Assets	=	Liabilities	+	Equity
+$100,000	=	+35,000	+	?

Change in equity = $100,000 − $35,000 = $65,000

A Look Back

Chapter 2 introduced the accounting equation and accounts for various transactions. We also introduced basic financial statements and explained how they reflect an organization's performance and financial position.

A Look at This Chapter

This chapter focuses on the accounting process. We explain the analysis and recording of transactions. We use the accounting equation, T-account, general ledger, trial balance, and debits and credits as tools in the accounting process.

A Look Ahead

Chapters 4 and 5 extend our focus on processing information. We explain the importance of adjusting accounts and the procedures in preparing financial statements.

Chapter 3

Applying Double-Entry Accounting

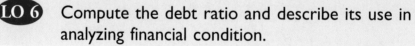

LEARNING OBJECTIVES

 LO 1 Describe an account and its use in recording transactions.

LO 2 Define debits and credits and explain their role in double-entry accounting.

 LO 3 Analyze the impact of transactions on accounts.

LO 4 Prepare and explain the use of a trial balance.

 LO 5 Prepare financial statements from a trial balance.

LO 6 Compute the debt ratio and describe its use in analyzing financial condition.

"Each individual problem you face is totally surmountable"—Warren Brown

Making Dough

WASHINGTON, DC—Warren Brown started baking cakes to reduce stress, but his friends' appetites demanded more. "Friends were jumping on the bed" saying how much they loved the cakes and insisting that I set up shop, says Warren.

Starting small, Warren baked cakes in his apartment for hours after work each evening. He sold his sweet concoctions mostly to co-workers and friends, and even held a cake open house at the local art gallery. But Warren was determined to grow his business. He took a course in entrepreneurship at his local community college, and there he discovered the importance of accounting.

Launching his fledgling cake business presented Warren with many challenges. He needed to establish inventory accounting, transaction analysis, and accounting entries. "Everything feels like a disaster when it's right in your face," says Warren. "You just have to be calm, look at what you're doing, and fix the problem." Warren fixed the problems and unveiled his shop called **Cake Love** (**CakeLove.com**). "I opened up this tiny retail, walk-up bakery . . .

[to sell] goodies that are baked from scratch," Warren recalls.

Today Cake Love entices the neighborhood with a gentle scent of fresh bakery and a sidewalk view into the kitchen. Warmly painted walls, comfy window seats, and free wireless Internet encourage customers to lounge for hours. "I want it to be relaxed and comfortable," says Warren. "People can bring their work, their kids, their friends, and just relax."

Warren continues to experiment with new treats. "I'm always getting better, improving my skills," he said. Warren also shows a keen appetite for using accounting information to make good business decisions. "But," says Warren, "I love eating what I make more."

"The bigger message of Cake Love is finding your passion and working to reach your goals," says Warren. That's a slice of advice worth more than any amount of dough.

[Sources: *Cake Love Website*, January 2007; *Black Enterprise*, September 2004; *Georgetown Voice*, March 2005; *National Public Radio (NPR) Website*, May 2005; *Inc.com*, April 2005]

Financial statements report on the financial performance and condition of an organization. Knowledge of their preparation, organization, and analysis is important. A main goal of this chapter is to illustrate how transactions are recorded and how they are reflected in financial statements. Debits and credits are introduced and identified as a tool in helping analyze and process transactions.

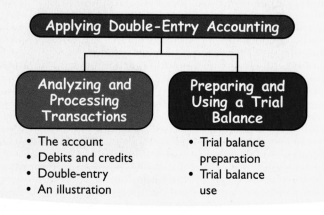

Analyzing and Processing Transactions

In Chapter 2, we introduced the accounting equation, Assets + Liabilities = Equity, as a way to understand what resources the organization owns and who has rights to those resources. However, organizations do not record their transactions in accounting equation form. Instead, they record increases and decreases in individual accounts.

The Account and Its Analysis

LO1 Describe an account and its use in recording transactions.

An **account** is a record of increases and decreases in a specific asset, liability, equity, revenue, or expense item. Information from an account is analyzed, summarized, and presented in reports and financial statements. The **general ledger,** or simply **ledger,** is a record containing all accounts used by a company. The ledger is often in electronic form. While companies' ledgers contain similar accounts, a company often uses one or more unique accounts because of its type of operations. Accounts are arranged into three general categories (based on the accounting equation), as shown in Exhibit 3.1.

Exhibit 3.1

Accounts Organized by the Accounting Equation

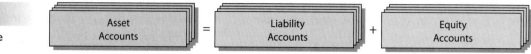

Asset Accounts   Assets are resources owned or controlled by a company and that have expected future benefits. Most accounting systems include (at a minimum) separate accounts for the assets described here.

A *Cash* account reflects a company's cash balance. All increases and decreases in cash are recorded in the Cash account. It includes money and any other medium of exchange that a bank accepts for deposit (checks, money orders, and checking account balances).

Accounts receivable are held by a seller and refer to promises of payment from customers to sellers. These transactions are often called *credit sales* or *sales on account* (or *on credit*). Accounts receivable are increased by credit sales and are decreased by customer payments.

A *note receivable,* or promissory note, is a written promise of another entity to pay a definite sum of money on a specified future date to the holder of the note. A company holding a promissory note signed by another entity has an asset that is recorded in a Note (or Notes) Receivable account.

Customers and others who owe a company are called its **debtors.**

Prepaid accounts (also called *prepaid expenses*) are assets that represent prepayments of future expenses (*not* current expenses). When the expenses are later incurred, the amounts in prepaid accounts are transferred to expense accounts. Common examples of prepaid accounts include prepaid insurance, prepaid rent, and prepaid services (such as club memberships). Prepaid accounts expire with the passage of time (such as with rent) or through use (such as with prepaid meal tickets). When financial statements are prepared, prepaid accounts are adjusted so that (1) all expired and used prepaid accounts are recorded as regular expenses and (2) all unexpired and unused prepaid accounts are recorded as assets (reflecting future use in future periods). To illustrate, when an insurance fee, called a *premium,* is paid in advance, the cost is typically recorded in the asset account Prepaid Insurance. Over time, the expired portion of the insurance cost is removed from this asset account and reported in expenses on the income statement. Any unexpired portion remains in Prepaid Insurance and is reported on the balance sheet as an asset.

> A college parking fee is a prepaid account from the student's standpoint. At the beginning of the term, it represents an asset that entitles a student to park on or near campus. The benefits of the parking fee expire as the term progresses. At term-end, prepaid parking (asset) equals zero as it has been entirely recorded as parking expense.

Supplies are assets until they are used. The costs of unused supplies are recorded in a Supplies asset account. Supplies often include stationery, papers, and pens. When supplies are used, their costs are transferred from the asset accounts to expense accounts.

Equipment is an asset. As equipment is used its cost is gradually reported as an expense (called depreciation). Equipment is often grouped by its purpose—for example, office equipment and store equipment. *Office equipment* includes computers, printers, desks, chairs, shelves, and other office equipment. The Store Equipment account includes the costs of assets used in a store such as counters, showcases, ladders, hoists, and cash registers.

> Some assets are described as *intangible* because they do not have physical existence. A recent balance sheet for **Coca-Cola Company** shows nearly $1 billion in intangible assets.

Buildings such as stores, offices, warehouses, and factories are assets because they provide expected future benefits to those who control or own them. Their costs are recorded in a Buildings asset account. When several buildings are owned, separate accounts are often kept for each.

The cost of *land* owned by a business is recorded in a Land account. The cost of buildings located on the land is separately recorded in one or more building accounts.

— Women Entrepreneurs — IN THE NEWS

The Center for Women's Business Research reports that women-owned businesses:

- Total approximately 11 million and employ nearly 20 million workers.
- Generate $2.5 trillion in annual sales and tend to embrace technology.
- Are more likely funded by individual investors (73%) than venture firms (15%).
- Are philanthropic—70% of owners volunteer at least once per month.

Liability Accounts   Liabilities are claims (by creditors) against assets, which means they are obligations to transfer assets or provide products or services to other entities. **Creditors** are individuals and organizations that own the right to receive payments from a company. If a company fails to pay its obligations, the law gives creditors a right to force the sale of that company's assets to obtain money to meet creditors' claims. When assets are sold under these conditions, creditors are paid first, but only up to the amount of their claims. Any remaining money goes to the owners of the company. Creditors often use a balance sheet to help decide whether to loan money to a company. A loan is less risky if the borrower's liabilities are small in comparison to assets because there are more resources than claims on resources. Common liability accounts are described here.

Accounts payable refer to oral or implied promises to pay later, which commonly arise from purchases of merchandise. Payables can also arise from purchases of supplies, equipment, and services. Accounting systems keep separate records about each creditor.

> Accounts Payable are also called *Trade Payables.*

A *note payable* refers to a formal promise, usually denoted by the signing of a promissory note, to pay a future amount.

Unearned Revenue refers to a liability that is settled in the future when a company delivers its products or services. When customers pay in advance for products or services to be

IN THE NEWS

Revenue Spread

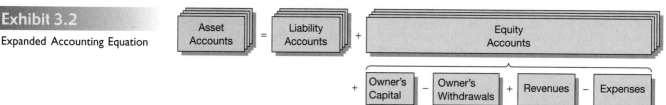

The Philadelphia Eagles have *Unearned Revenues* of about $50 million in advance ticket sales. When the team plays its home games, it settles this liability to its ticket holders and transfers the amount earned to *Ticket Revenues.*

provided later, the seller owes the customer those future products or services. Examples of unearned revenue include magazine subscriptions collected in advance by a publisher, sales of gift certificates by stores, and season ticket sales by sports teams. The seller records these in liability accounts such as Unearned Subscriptions, Unearned Store Sales, and Unearned Ticket Revenue. When products and services are later delivered, the earned portion of the unearned revenue is transferred to revenue accounts such as Subscription Fees, Store Sales, and Ticket Sales.

> If a subscription is cancelled the publisher is expected to refund the unused portion to the subscriber.

Accrued liabilities are amounts owed that are not yet paid. Examples are wages payable, taxes payable, and interest payable. These are often recorded in separate liability accounts by the same title. If they are not large in amount, one or more ledger accounts can be added and reported as a single amount on the balance sheet. (Financial statements often have amounts reported that are a summation of several ledger accounts.)

Equity Accounts   The owner's claim on a company's assets is called *equity* or *owner's equity.* Equity is the owner's *residual interest* in the assets of a business after deducting liabilities. There are four subcategories of equity: owner's capital, owner's withdrawals, revenues, and expenses. We show this visually in Exhibit 3.2 by expanding the accounting equation.

Exhibit 3.2

Expanded Accounting Equation

```
┌──────────┐     ┌──────────┐       ┌─────────────────────────────┐
│  Asset   │  =  │ Liability│   +   │           Equity            │
│ Accounts │     │ Accounts │       │          Accounts           │
└──────────┘     └──────────┘       └─────────────────────────────┘

        ┌────────┐   ┌────────┐       ┌────────┐   ┌────────┐
    +   │ Owner's│ − │ Owner's│   +   │Revenues│ − │Expenses│
        │ Capital│   │Withdraw│       │        │   │        │
        └────────┘   └────────┘       └────────┘   └────────┘
```

> The Owner's Withdrawals account (also called *Drawing* or *Personal* account) is sometimes referred to as a *contra equity* account because it reduces the normal balance of equity.

When an owner invests in a company, the invested amount is recorded in an account titled **Owner, Capital** (where the owner's name is inserted in place of "owner"). The account titled *C. Taylor, Capital* is used for FastForward. Any further owner investments are recorded in this account. When an owner withdraws assets for personal use it decreases both company assets and total equity. Withdrawals are not expenses of the business; they are simply the opposite of owner investments. The **Owner, Withdrawals** account is used to record asset distributions to the owner. The account titled *C. Taylor, Withdrawals* is used for FastForward. (Owners of proprietorships cannot receive company salaries because they are not legally separate from their companies; and they cannot enter into company contracts with themselves.)

> The distribution (withdrawal) of assets to the owners of a corporation is called a *dividend.*

Revenues and expenses are the final two categories of equity. Examples of revenue accounts are Sales, Commissions Earned, Professional Fees Earned, Rent Earned, and Interest Revenue. *Revenues increase equity* and result from products and services provided to customers. Examples of expense accounts are Advertising Expense, Store Supplies Expense, Office Salaries Expense, Office Supplies Expense, Rent Expense, Utilities Expense, and Insurance Expense. *Expenses decrease equity* and result from assets and services used in a company's operations. The variety of revenues and expenses can be seen by looking at the *chart of accounts* that follows the index at the back of this book. (Different companies sometimes use different account titles than those in this book's chart of accounts. For example, some might use Interest Revenue instead of Interest Earned, or Rental Expense instead of Rent Expense. It is important only that an account title describe the item it represents.)

Debits and Credits

LO2   Define debits and credits and explain their role in double-entry accounting.

A **T-account** is a tool used to understand the effects of one or more transactions. Its name comes from its shape like the letter T. The layout of a T-account (shown in Exhibit 3.3) is (1) the account title on top, (2) a left, or **debit,** side, and (3) a right, or **credit,** side.

In Chapter 2, we accounted for the December transactions of FastForward using the accounting equation. As an illustration of the use of the T-account, we show how increases and decreases in cash are accounted for. The T-account for FastForward's Cash account, reflecting its first 11 transactions (from Exhibit 2.1), is shown in Exhibit 3.4. We include descriptions of each transaction for illustration purposes. T-accounts usually include only numbers.

Account Title	
(Left side)	(Right side)
Debit	*Credit*

Exhibit 3.3

The T-Account

Cash			
Investment by owner	30,000	Purchase of supplies	2,500
Consulting services revenue earned	4,200	Purchase of equipment	26,000
Collection of account receivable	1,900	Payment of rent	1,000
		Payment of salary	700
		Payment of account payable	900
		Withdrawal by owner	200
Balance	4,800		

Exhibit 3.4

Computing the Balance for a T-Account

> The ending balance is on the side with the larger dollar amount.

The increases in cash are shown on the left (or debit) side and the decreases in cash are shown on the right (or credit) side. The total increases in its Cash account are $36,100, and the total decreases are $31,300. The difference between total debits and total credits for an account, including any beginning balance, is the **account balance.** When the sum of debits exceeds the sum of credits, the account has a *debit balance*. It has a *credit balance* when the sum of the credits exceeds the sum of debits. When the sum of debits equals the sum of credits, the account has a zero balance. Since the total increases (debits) exceed the total decreases (credits) for FastForward's Cash account, its ending balance in cash is a debit balance of $4,800.

> Think of *debit* and *credit* as accounting directions for left and right.

Double-Entry Accounting

Double-entry accounting requires that each transaction be recorded in at least two accounts. It also means the *total amount debited must equal the total amount credited* for each transaction. Thus, the sum of the debits for all entries must equal the sum of the credits for all entries, and the sum of debit account balances in the ledger must equal the sum of credit account balances. This means the accounting equation is in balance.

The system for recording debits and credits follows from the usual accounting equation—see Exhibit 3.5. Two points are important here. First, like any simple mathematical relation, net increases or decreases on one side of the equation have equal net effects on the other side. For example, a net increase in assets must be accompanied by an identical net increase on the liabilities

"Total debits equal total credits for each entry."

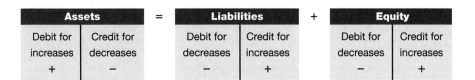

Assets		=	Liabilities		+	Equity	
Debit for increases	Credit for decreases		Debit for decreases	Credit for increases		Debit for decreases	Credit for increases
+	−		−	+		−	+

Exhibit 3.5

Debits and Credits in the Accounting Equation

and equity side. Recall that some transactions affect only one side of the equation, meaning that two or more accounts on one side are affected, but their net effect on this one side is zero. Second, the left side is the *normal balance* side for assets, and the right side of the T-account is the *normal balance* side for liabilities and equity. This matches their layout in the accounting equation where assets are on the left side of this equation, and liabilities and equity are on the right.

Recall that equity increases from revenues and owner investments and it decreases from expenses and owner withdrawals. These important equity relations are conveyed by expanding the accounting equation to include debits and credits in double-entry form as shown in Exhibit 3.6. The abbreviation "Dr." is for debit, and the abbreviation "Cr." is for credit.

> Debits and credits do not mean favorable or unfavorable. A debit to an asset increases it, as does a debit to an expense. A credit to a liability increases it, as does a credit to a revenue.

Exhibit 3.6

Debit and Credit Effects for Expanded Accounting Equation

	Equity										

Assets		=	Liabilities		+	Owner, Capital		–	Owner, Withdrawals		+	Revenues		–	Expenses	
Dr. for increases	Cr. for decreases		Dr. for decreases	Cr. for increases		Dr. for decreases	Cr. for increases		Dr. for increases	Cr. for decreases		Dr. for decreases	Cr. for increases		Dr. for increases	Cr. for decreases
+	–		–	+		–	+		+	–		–	+		+	–
Normal				Normal			Normal		Normal				Normal		Normal	

Increases (credits) to capital and revenues *increase* equity; increases (debits) to withdrawals and expenses *decrease* equity. The normal balance of each account (asset, liability, capital, withdrawals, revenue, or expense) refers to the left or right (debit or credit) side where *increases* are recorded. Understanding debits and credits helps us to prepare, analyze, and interpret financial statements.

HOW YOU DOIN'?

Answers—p. 63

1. Identify each of the following as either an asset, a liability, or equity: (*a*) Prepaid Rent, (*b*) Unearned Fees, (*c*) Building, (*d*) Wages Payable, and (*e*) Office Supplies.

2. What is an account? What is a ledger?

3. Does *debit* always mean increase and *credit* always mean decrease?

Analyzing Transactions—An Illustration

LO3 Analyze the impact of transactions on accounts.

We return to the activities of FastForward to show how double-entry accounting is useful in analyzing and processing transactions. We also show how to record the transactions in T-account form. Study each transaction thoroughly before proceeding to the next. The first 11 transactions are from Chapter 2, and we analyze five additional December transactions of FastForward (numbered 12 through 16) that were omitted earlier.

Here are the steps to follow to record a transaction in T-account form:

1. *Analysis:* Determine which accounts are affected by the transaction.
   a. Identify the affected accounts.
   b. Categorize the affected accounts as either assets, liabilities, or equity (including revenues and expenses).
   c. Determine whether the transaction increases or decreases the account.
   d. Analyze the account using the accounting equation.
2. *Debit-credit rules:* Apply the debit-credit rules for each account affected (using Exhibits 3.5 and 3.6 as aids).
3. *Record in T-accounts:* Record the transaction, using the debit-credit rules, in T-accounts.

1. Investment by Owner

*FAST*Forward

Transaction: Chuck Taylor invests $30,000 cash in FastForward.

Analysis:

Assets	=	Liabilities	+	Equity
Cash				C. Taylor, Capital
+30,000	=	0	+	30,000

Debit-credit rules:

Debit: Increases to an asset account are recorded as a debit. Record a debit of $30,000 to the left side of the Cash T-account.

Credit: Increases to an owner's equity account are recorded as a credit. Record a credit of $30,000 to the right side of the C. Taylor, Capital, T-account.

Record in T-accounts:

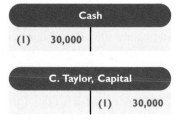

Cash
(1) 30,000

C. Taylor, Capital
(1) 30,000

Total debits equal total credits for each transaction.

2. Purchase Supplies for Cash

Transaction: FastForward pays $2,500 cash for supplies.

Analysis:

Assets		=	Liabilities	+	Equity
Cash	**Supplies**				
−2,500	+2,500	=	0	+	0

Changes the composition of assets but not the total.

Debit-credit rules:

Debit: Increases to an asset account are recorded as a debit. Record a debit of $2,500 to the left side of the Supplies T-account.

Credit: Decreases to an asset account are recorded as a credit. Record a credit of $2,500 to the right side of the Cash T-account.

Record in T-accounts:

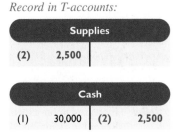

3. Purchase Equipment for Cash

Transaction: FastForward pays $26,000 cash for equipment.

Analysis:

Assets		=	Liabilities	+	Equity
Cash	**Equipment**				
−26,000	+26,000	=	0	+	0

Changes the composition of assets but not the total.

Debit-credit rules:

Debit: Increases to an asset account are recorded as a debit. Record a debit of $26,000 to the left side of the Equipment T-account.

Credit: Decreases to an asset account are recorded as a credit. Record a credit of $26,000 to the right side of the Cash T-account.

Record in T-accounts:

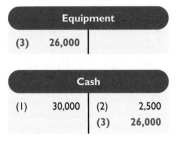

4. Purchase Supplies on Credit

Transaction: FastForward purchases $7,100 of supplies on credit from a supplier.

Analysis:

Assets	=	Liabilities	+	Equity
Supplies		**Accounts Payable**		
+7,100	=	+7,100	+	0

Debit-credit rules:

Debit: Increases to an asset account are recorded as a debit. Record a debit of $7,100 to the left side of the Supplies T-account.

Credit: Increases to a liability account are recorded as a credit. Record a credit of $7,100 to the right side of the Accounts Payable T-account.

Record in T-accounts:

Supplies	
(2) 2,500	
(4) 7,100	

Accounts Payable	
	(4) 7,100

5. Provide Services for Cash

Transaction: FastForward provides consulting services and immediately collects $4,200 cash.

Analysis:

Assets	=	Liabilities	+	Equity
Cash				**Consulting Revenue**
+4,200	=	0		+4,200

Debit-credit rules:

Debit: Increases to an asset account are recorded as a debit. Record a debit of $4,200 to the left side of the Cash T-account.

Credit: Increases to a revenue account are recorded as a credit. Record a credit of $4,200 to the right side of the Consulting Revenue T-account.

Record in T-accounts:

Cash	
(1) 30,000	(2) 2,500
(5) 4,200	(3) 26,000

Consulting Revenue	
	(5) 4,200

6. Payment of Expense in Cash

Transaction: FastForward pays $1,000 cash for December rent.

Analysis:

Assets	=	Liabilities	+	Equity
Cash				**Rent Expense**
−1,000	=	0		−1,000

Debit-credit rules:

Debit: Increases to an expense account are recorded as a debit. Record a debit of $1,000 to the left side of the Rent Expense T-account.

Credit: Decreases to an asset account are recorded as a credit. Record a credit of $1,000 to the right side of the Cash T-account.

Record in T-accounts:

Rent Expense

(6) 1,000	

Cash

(1)	30,000	(2)	2,500
(5)	4,200	(3)	26,000
		(6)	1,000

7. Payment of Expense in Cash

Transaction: FastForward pays $700 cash for employee salaries.

Analysis:

Assets	=	Liabilities	+	Equity
Cash				**Salaries Expense**
−700	=	0		−700

Debit-credit rules:

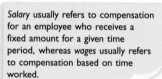

Salary usually refers to compensation for an employee who receives a fixed amount for a given time period, whereas *wages* usually refers to compensation based on time worked.

Debit: Increases to an expense account are recorded as a debit. Record a debit of $700 to the left side of the Salaries Expense T-account.

Credit: Decreases to an asset account are recorded as a credit. Record a credit of $700 to the right side of the Cash T-account.

Record in T-accounts:

Salaries Expense

(7) 700	

Cash

(1)	30,000	(2)	2,500
(5)	4,200	(3)	26,000
		(6)	1,000
		(7)	700

8. Provide Consulting and Rental Services on Credit

Transaction: FastForward provides consulting services of $1,600 and rents its test facilities for $300. The customer is billed $1,900 for these services.

Analysis:

Assets	=	Liabilities	+	Equity	
Accounts Receivable				**Consulting Revenue**	**Rental Revenue**
+1,900	=	0		+1,600	+300

Debit-credit rules:

Debit: Increases to an asset account are recorded as a debit. Record a debit of $1,900 to the left side of the Accounts Receivable T-account.

Credit: Increases to a revenue account are recorded as a credit. Record a credit of $1,600 to the right side of the Consulting Revenue T-account and a credit of $300 to the right side of the Rental Revenue T-account.

Record in T-accounts:

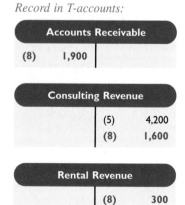

Accounts Receivable

(8) 1,900	

Consulting Revenue

	(5)	4,200
	(8)	1,600

Rental Revenue

	(8)	300

9. Receipt of Cash on Account

Transaction: FastForward receives $1,900 cash from the client billed in transaction 8.

Analysis:

Assets		=	Liabilities	+	Equity
	Accounts				
Cash	**Receivable**				
+1,900	−1,900	=	0	+	0

Changes the composition of assets but not the total.

Debit-credit rules:

Debit: Increases to an asset account are recorded as a debit. Record a debit of $1,900 to the left side of the Cash T-account.

Credit: Decreases to an asset account are recorded as a credit. Record a credit of $1,900 to the right side of the Accounts Receivable T-account.

Record in T-accounts:

Cash			
(1)	30,000	(2)	2,500
(5)	4,200	(3)	26,000
(9)	1,900	(6)	1,000
		(7)	700

Accounts Receivable			
(8)	1,900	(9)	1,900

10. Partial Payment of Accounts Payable

Transaction: FastForward pays the supplier $900 cash toward the account payable from transaction 4.

Analysis:

Assets	=	Liabilities	+	Equity
Cash		**Accounts Payable**		
−900	=	−900	+	0

Debit-credit rules:

Debit: Decreases to a liability account are recorded as a debit. Record a debit of $900 to the left side of the Accounts Payable T-account.

Credit: Decreases to an asset account are recorded as a credit. Record a credit of $900 to the right side of the Cash T-account.

Record in T-accounts:

Accounts Payable			
(10)	900	(4)	7,100

Cash			
(1)	30,000	(2)	2,500
(5)	4,200	(3)	26,000
(9)	1,900	(6)	1,000
		(7)	700
		(10)	900

11. Withdrawal of Cash by Owner

Transaction: Chuck Taylor withdraws $200 cash from FastForward for personal use.

Analysis:

Assets	=	Liabilities	+	Equity
				C. Taylor,
Cash				**Withdrawals**
−200	=	0		−200

Debit-credit rules:

Debit: Decreases to an owner's equity account are recorded as a debit. Record a debit of $200 to the left side of the C. Taylor, Withdrawals T-account.

Credit: Decreases to an asset account are recorded as a credit. Record a credit of $200 to the right side of the Cash T-account.

Record in T-accounts:

C. Taylor, Withdrawals			
(11)	200		

Cash			
(1)	30,000	(2)	2,500
(5)	4,200	(3)	26,000
(9)	1,900	(6)	1,000
		(7)	700
		(10)	900
		(11)	200

12. Receipt of Cash for Future Services

Transaction: FastForward receives $3,000 cash in advance of providing consulting services to a customer.

Analysis:

Assets	=	Liabilities	+	Equity
Cash		**Unearned Consulting Revenue**		
+3,000	=	+3,000	+	0

Accepting $3,000 cash obligates FastForward to perform future services. Unearned revenue is a liability created when customers pay in advance for services (or products). The revenue is earned when the services (or products) are later provided.

Debit-credit rules:

> **Debit:** Increases to an asset account are recorded as a debit. Record a debit of $3,000 to the left side of the Cash T-account.

> **Credit:** Increases to a liability account are recorded as a credit. Record a credit of $3,000 to the right side of the Unearned Consulting Revenue T-account.

Record in T-accounts:

Cash

(1)	30,000	(2)	2,500
(5)	4,200	(3)	26,000
(9)	1,900	(6)	1,000
(12)	3,000	(7)	700
		(10)	900
		(11)	200

Unearned Consulting Revenue

		(12)	3,000

Luca Pacioli, a 15th-century monk, is considered a pioneer in accounting and the first to devise double-entry accounting.

13. Pay Cash for Future Insurance Coverage

Transaction: FastForward pays $2,400 cash (insurance premium) for a 24-month insurance policy. Coverage begins on December 1.

Analysis:

Assets	=	Liabilities	+	Equity
Cash	**Prepaid Insurance**			
−2,400	+2,400	=	0 +	0

Changes the composition of assets from cash to prepaid insurance. Expense is incurred as insurance coverage expires.

Debit-credit rules:

> **Debit:** Increases to an asset account are recorded as a debit. Record a debit of $2,400 to the left side of the Prepaid Insurance T-account.

> **Credit:** Decreases to an asset account are recorded as a credit. Record a credit of $2,400 to the right side of the Cash T-account.

Record in T-accounts:

Prepaid Insurance

(13)	2,400		

Cash

(1)	30,000	(2)	2,500
(5)	4,200	(3)	26,000
(9)	1,900	(6)	1,000
(12)	3,000	(7)	700
		(10)	900
		(11)	200
		(13)	2,400

14. Purchase Supplies for Cash

Transaction: FastForward pays $120 cash for supplies.

Analysis:

Assets	=	Liabilities	+	Equity
Cash	**Supplies**			
−120	+120	=	0 +	0

Debit-credit rules:

> **Debit:** Increases to an asset account are recorded as a debit. Record a debit of $120 to the left side of the Supplies T-account.

> **Credit:** Decreases to an asset account are recorded as a credit. Record a credit of $120 to the right side of the Cash T-account.

Record in T-accounts:

Supplies

(2)	2,500		
(4)	7,100		
(14)	120		

Cash

(1)	30,000	(2)	2,500
(5)	4,200	(3)	26,000
(9)	1,900	(6)	1,000
(12)	3,000	(7)	700
		(10)	900
		(11)	200
		(13)	2,400
		(14)	120

15. Payment of Expense in Cash

Transaction: FastForward pays $230 cash for December utilities expense.

Record in T-accounts:

Analysis:

Assets	=	Liabilities	+	Equity
Cash				**Utilities Expense**
−230	=	0		−230

Utilities Expense

(15) 230	

Debit-credit rules:

Debit: Increases to an expense account are recorded as a debit. Record a debit of $230 to the left side of the Utilities Expense T-account.

Credit: Decreases to an asset account are recorded as a credit. Record a credit of $230 to the right side of the Cash T-account.

Cash

(1)	30,000	(2)	2,500
(5)	4,200	(3)	26,000
(9)	1,900	(6)	1,000
(12)	3,000	(7)	700
		(10)	900
		(11)	200
		(13)	2,400
		(14)	120
		(15)	230

16. Payment of Expense in Cash

Transaction: FastForward pays $700 cash in employee salaries for work performed in the latter part of December.

Record in T-accounts:

Analysis:

Assets	=	Liabilities	+	Equity
Cash				**Salaries Expense**
−700	=	0		−700

Salaries Expense

(7) 700	
(16) 700	

Debit-credit rules:

Debit: Increases to an expense account are recorded as a debit. Record a debit of $700 to the left side of the Salaries Expense T-account.

Credit: Decreases to an asset account are recorded as a credit. Record a credit of $700 to the right side of the Cash T-account.

Cash

(1)	30,000	(2)	2,500
(5)	4,200	(3)	26,000
(9)	1,900	(6)	1,000
(12)	3,000	(7)	700
		(10)	900
		(11)	200
		(13)	2,400
		(14)	120
		(15)	230
		(16)	700

> Accounting software packages do not provide the judgment required to analyze most business transactions. Analysis requires the expertise of skilled and ethical professionals.

Accounting Equation Analysis

Exhibit 3.7 shows the T-accounts of FastForward after all 16 transactions are recorded and ending balances are computed. The accounts are grouped according to the accounting equation: assets, liabilities, and equity. Note several important points. First, as with each transaction, the ending account balances must obey the accounting equation. Specifically, total assets equal $42,470 ($4,350 + $0 + $9,720 + $2,400 + $26,000); total liabilities equal $9,200 ($6,200 + $3,000); and total equity equals $33,270 ($30,000 − $200 + $5,800 + $300 − $1,400 − $1,000 − $230). These numbers prove the accounting equation: Assets of $42,470 = Liabilities of $9,200 + Equity of $33,270. Second, the capital, withdrawals, revenue, and expense accounts reflect the transactions that change equity. Third, the revenue and expense account balances will be summarized and reported in the income statement.

	Debit and Credit Rules	
Accounts	**Increase (normal bal.)**	**Decrease**
Asset	Debit	Credit
Liability	Credit	Debit
Capital	Credit	Debit
Withdrawals	Debit	Credit
Revenue	Credit	Debit
Expense	Debit	Credit

Exhibit 3.7

T-Accounts for FastForward

	Assets		=		Liabilities		+		Equity	

Cash

(1)	30,000	(2)	2,500
(5)	4,200	(3)	26,000
(9)	1,900	(6)	1,000
(12)	3,000	(7)	700
		(10)	900
		(11)	200
		(13)	2,400
		(14)	120
		(15)	230
		(16)	700
Balance	4,350		

Accounts Receivable

(8)	1,900	(9)	1,900
Balance	0		

Supplies

(2)	2,500		
(4)	7,100		
(14)	120		
Balance	9,720		

Prepaid Insurance

(13)	2,400		

Equipment

(3)	26,000		

Accounts Payable

(10)	900	(4)	7,100
		Balance	6,200

Unearned Consulting Revenue

		(12)	3,000

C. Taylor, Capital

		(1)	30,000

C. Taylor, Withdrawals

(11)	200		

Consulting Revenue

		(5)	4,200
		(8)	1,600
		Balance	5,800

Rental Revenue

		(8)	300

Salaries Expense

(7)	700		
(16)	700		
Balance	1,400		

Rent Expense

(6)	1,000		

Utilities Expense

(15)	230		

Accounts in this white area reflect those reported on the income statement.

$42,470	=	$9,200	+	$33,270

HOW YOU DOIN'?

Answers—p. 63

4. What types of transactions increase equity? What types decrease equity?

5. Why are accounting systems called *double entry*?

6. For each transaction, double-entry accounting requires which of the following: (*a*) Debits to asset accounts must create credits to liability or equity accounts, (*b*) a debit to a liability account must create a credit to an asset account, or (*c*) total debits must equal total credits.

7. An owner invests $15,000 cash along with equipment having a market value of $23,000 in a company. Describe the debit-credit rules for this transaction.

8. Matt Waller receives $3,000 cash for his consulting services provided. Describe the debit-credit rules for this transaction.

Trial Balance

Double-entry accounting requires the sum of debit account balances to equal the sum of credit account balances. A trial balance is used to verify this. A **trial balance** is a list of accounts and their balances at a point in time. Account balances are reported in the appropriate debit or credit column of a trial balance. Exhibit 3.8 shows the trial balance for FastForward after its 16 transactions have been recorded in T-accounts. (This is an *unadjusted* trial balance—Chapter 4 explains the necessary adjustments.)

Exhibit 3.8

Trial Balance (unadjusted)

Accounting System: Exhibit 3-8

File Edit Maintain Tasks Analysis Options Reports Window Help

FASTFORWARD
Trial Balance
December 31, 2007

	Debit	Credit
Cash	$ 4,350	
Accounts receivable	0	
Supplies	9,720	
Prepaid insurance	2,400	
Equipment	26,000	
Accounts payable		$ 6,200
Unearned consulting revenue		3,000
C.Taylor, Capital		30,000
C.Taylor, Withdrawals	200	
Consulting revenue		5,800
Rental revenue		300
Salaries expense	1,400	
Rent expense	1,000	
Utilities expense	230	
Totals	$ 45,300	$ 45,300

Sales   Purchases   General Ledger   Payroll   Inventory   Company   Analysis

Accounts in a trial balance are usually ordered according to the accounting equation in Exhibit 3.6.

Preparing a Trial Balance

Preparing a trial balance involves three steps:

1. List each account title and its amount (from the T-accounts) in the trial balance. If an account has a zero balance, list it with a zero in its normal balance column (or omit it entirely).
2. Compute the total of debit balances and the total of credit balances.
3. Verify (*prove*) total debit balances equal total credit balances.

The total of debit balances equals the total of credit balances for the trial balance in Exhibit 3.8. Equality of these two totals does not guarantee that no recording errors were made. For example, the column totals will still be equal when a debit or credit of a correct amount is made to a wrong account. Another error that does not cause unequal column totals is when equal debits and credits of an incorrect amount are recorded.

 L04 Prepare and explain the use of a trial balance.

A trial balance is *not* a financial statement but a mechanism for checking the equality of debits and credits in the ledger. Financial statements do not have debit and credit columns.

IN THE NEWS

Make CEOs Give Back

In the past few years, CEOs of more than 100 companies received bonuses based on income that later was restated to a lesser amount. Although Sarbanes–Oxley requires repayment of bonuses when restatements result from misconduct, most boards don't enforce it.

Searching for and Correcting Errors If the trial balance does not balance (its column totals are not equal), the error (or errors) must be found. Follow these steps to search for an error:

1. Verify that the trial balance columns are correctly added.
2. Verify that account balances are accurately entered from the T-account to the trial balance.
3. Check to see whether a debit (or credit) balance is mistakenly listed in the trial balance as a credit (or debit).
4. Recompute each account balance in the T-accounts.
5. Verify that the debit-credit rules are correctly followed and that the debits equal the credits for each transaction.

At this point the error should be uncovered.[1] An error is corrected with a separate correcting entry to the accounts affected.

Using a Trial Balance to Prepare Financial Statements

LO5 Prepare financial statements from a trial balance.

This section shows how to prepare *financial statements* from the trial balance in Exhibit 3.8 and information on the December transactions of FastForward. The statements differ from those in Chapter 2 because of several additional transactions. These statements are also more precisely called *unadjusted statements* because we need to make some further accounting adjustments (described in Chapters 4 and 5).

Exhibit 3.9

Links between Financial Statements across Time

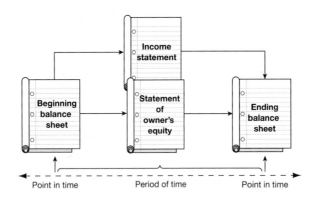

How financial statements are linked in time is illustrated in Exhibit 3.9. A balance sheet reports on an organization's financial position at a *point in time*. The income statement and statement of owner's equity report on financial performance over a *period of time*. The two statements in the middle column of Exhibit 3.9 link balance sheets from the beginning to the end of a reporting period. They explain how financial position changes from one point to another.

A one-year, or annual, reporting period is common, as are semiannual, quarterly, and monthly periods. The one-year reporting period is known as the *accounting,* or *fiscal,* year. Businesses whose accounting year begins on January 1 and ends on December 31 are known as *calendar-year* companies. Many companies choose a fiscal year ending on a date other than December 31. **Best Buy** is a *noncalendar-year* company as reflected in the headings of its February 26 year-end financial statements in Appendix A near the end of the book.

---

[1] *Transposition* occurs when two digits are switched, or transposed, within a number. If transposition is the only error, it yields a difference between the two trial balance totals that is evenly divisible by 9. For example, assume that a $691 debit in an entry is incorrectly posted to the ledger as $619. Total credits are then larger than total debits by $72 ($691 − $619). The $72 error is evenly divisible by 9 (72/9 = 8). The first digit of the quotient (in our example it is 8) equals the difference between the digits of the two transposed numbers (the 9 and the 1).

Income Statement

An income statement reports a company's revenues earned less expenses incurred over a period of time. FastForward's income statement for December is shown at the top of Exhibit 3.10. Information about revenues and expenses is taken from the trial balance in Exhibit 3.8. The income statement reports total revenues ($6,100) and total expenses ($2,630). Net income (revenues minus expenses) of $3,470 is reported at the bottom of the statement. Owner investments and dividends are *not* part of income.

Statement of Owner's Equity

The statement of owner's equity reports information about how equity changes over the reporting period. FastForward's statement of owner's equity is the second report in Exhibit 3.10. It shows the $30,000 owner investment, the $3,470 of net income, the $200 withdrawal, and the $33,270 end-of-period (capital) balance. (The beginning balance in the statement of owner's equity is rarely zero; an exception is for the first period of operations. The beginning capital balance in January 2008 is $33,270, which is December's ending balance.)

"It's been a dismal year, let's issue the shareholders report while everyone's hibernating."

© Edward Smith/artizans.com

Exhibit 3.10

Financial Statements and Their Links

FASTFORWARD
Income Statement
For Month Ended December 31, 2007

Revenues		
Consulting revenue	$5 8 0 0 00	
Rental revenue	3 0 0 00	
Total revenues		$6 1 0 0 00
Expenses		
Rent expense	1 0 0 0 00	
Salaries expense	1 4 0 0 00	
Utilities expense	2 3 0 00	
Total expenses		2 6 3 0 00
Net income		$3 4 7 0 00

FASTFORWARD
Statement of Owner's Equity
For Month Ended December 31, 2007

C. Taylor, Capital, December 1, 2007		$ 0 00
Plus: Investments by owner	$30 0 0 0 00	
Net income	3 4 7 0 00	33 4 7 0 00
		33 4 7 0 00
Less: Withdrawals by owner		2 0 0 00
C. Taylor, Capital, December 31, 2007		$33 2 7 0 00

Arrow lines show how the statements are linked.

FASTFORWARD
Balance Sheet
December 31, 2007

Assets		Liabilities	
Cash	$ 4 3 5 0 00	Accounts payable	$ 6 2 0 0 00
Supplies	9 7 2 0 00	Unearned revenue	3 0 0 00
Prepaid insurance	2 4 0 0 00	Total liabilities	9 2 0 0 00
Equipment	26 0 0 0 00	Equity	
		C. Taylor, Capital	33 2 7 0 00
Total assets	$42 4 7 0 00	Total liabilities and equity	$42 4 7 0 00

A statement's heading lists the 3 W's: **W**ho—name of organization, **W**hat—name of statement, **W**hen—statement's point in time or period of time.

> An income statement is also called an *earnings statement, a statement of operations,* or a *P&L (profit and loss) statement.* A balance sheet is also called a *statement of financial position.*

Balance Sheet   The balance sheet reports the financial position of a company at a point in time, usually at the end of a month, quarter, or year. FastForward's balance sheet is the third report in Exhibit 3.10. This statement refers to financial condition at the close of business on December 31, 2007. The left side of the balance sheet lists FastForward's assets: cash, supplies, prepaid insurance, and equipment. The upper right side of the balance sheet shows that it owes $6,200 to creditors and $3,000 in services to customers who paid in advance. The equity section shows an ending balance of $33,270. Note the link between the ending balance of C. Taylor, on the statement of owner's equity and its disclosure on the balance sheet. This means that FastForward's financial performance for December updates its financial position at the end of December. This updating is a key feature of accounting.

> While revenues increase equity and expenses decrease equity, the amounts are not reported in detail in the statement of owner's equity. Instead, their effects are reflected through net income.

Presentation Issues   Dollar signs are not used in journals and ledgers. They do appear in financial statements and other reports such as trial balances. The usual practice is to put dollar signs beside only the first and last numbers in a column. **Best Buy**'s financial statements in Appendix A show this. Companies also commonly round amounts in reports to the nearest dollar, or even to a higher level. Best Buy is typical of many large companies in that it rounds dollar amounts in its financial statements to the nearest million. This decision is based on the perceived impact of rounding for users' business decisions.

HOW YOU DOIN'?   Answers—p. 63

9. Where are dollar signs typically entered in financial statements?

10. Describe the link between the income statement and the statement of owner's equity.

11. Explain the link between the balance sheet and the statement of owner's equity.

12. Define and describe revenues and expenses.

13. Define and describe assets, liabilities, and equity.

DEBT RATIO

LO6   Compute the debt ratio and describe its use in analyzing financial condition.

An important business objective is gathering information to help assess a company's risk of failing to pay its debts. Companies finance their assets with either liabilities or equity. A company that finances a relatively large portion of its assets with liabilities is said to have a high degree of *financial leverage*. Higher financial leverage involves greater risk because liabilities must be repaid and often require regular interest payments (equity financing does not). The risk that a company might not be able to meet such required payments is higher if it has more liabilities (is more highly leveraged). One way to assess the risk associated with a company's use of liabilities is to compute the **debt ratio** as in Exhibit 3.11.

Exhibit 3.11

Debt Ratio

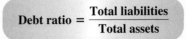
$$\text{Debt ratio} = \frac{\text{Total liabilities}}{\text{Total assets}}$$

> Compare the equity amount to the liability amount to assess the extent of owner versus nonowner financing.

To see how to apply the debt ratio, let's look at **Stride Rite**'s liabilities and assets. Stride Rite makes Keds, Pro-Keds, and other footwear. Exhibit 3.12 computes and reports its debt ratio, and the average debt ratio of companies in its industry, at the end of each year from 2000 to 2004.

Exhibit 3.12

Computation and Analysis of Debt Ratio

	2004	2003	2002	2001	2000
Total liabilities (in mil.)	$ 74	$ 78	$ 82	$100	$110
Total assets (in mil.)	$321	$345	$335	$362	$359
Debt ratio	0.23	0.23	0.25	0.28	0.31
Industry average debt ratio	0.48	0.46	0.45	0.49	0.48

Stride Rite's debt ratio ranges from a low of 0.23 to a high of 0.31. Its ratio is low compared to the industry average ratio. Stride Rite reports that it carries no long-term debt, which is unusual. This analysis implies a low risk from its financial leverage. Is this good or bad? To answer that question we need to compare the company's return on the borrowed money to the rate it is paying creditors. If the company's return is higher, it is successfully borrowing money to make more money. A company's success with making money from borrowed money can quickly turn unprofitable if its own return drops below the rate it is paying creditors.

YOU CALL IT

Answer—p. 63

Investor You consider buying stock in Converse. As part of your analysis, you compute its debt ratio for 2004, 2005, and 2006 as: 0.35, 0.74, and 0.94, respectively. Based on the debt ratio, is Converse a low-risk investment? Has the risk of buying Converse stock changed over this period? (The industry debt ratio averages 0.40.)

Demonstration Problem

(This problem extends the demonstration problem of Chapter 2.) After several months of planning, Jasmine Worthy started a haircutting business called Expressions in August 2007. The following events occurred during its first month.

a. On August 1, Worthy invested $3,000 cash and $15,000 of equipment in Expressions.

b. On August 2, Expressions paid $600 cash for furniture for the shop.

c. On August 3, Expressions paid $500 cash to rent space in a strip mall for August.

d. On August 4, it purchased $1,200 of equipment on credit for the shop (using a long-term note payable).

e. On August 5, Expressions opened for business. Cash received from services provided in the first week and a half of business (ended August 15) is $825.

f. On August 15, it provided $100 of haircutting services on account.

g. On August 17, it received a $100 check for services previously rendered on account.

h. On August 17, it paid $125 to an assistant for working during the grand opening.

i. Cash received from services provided during the second half of August is $930.

j. On August 31, it paid a $400 installment toward principal on the note payable entered into on August 4.

k. On August 31, Worthy withdrew $900 cash for personal use.

Required

1. Apply the debit-credit rules for each transaction.

2. Record each transaction in the appropriate T-account. Open T-accounts for the following accounts: Cash; Accounts Receivable; Furniture; Store Equipment; Note Payable; J. Worthy, Capital; J. Worthy, Withdrawals; Haircutting Services Revenue; Wages Expense; Rent Expense.

3. Prepare a trial balance from the T-accounts as of August 31.

4. Prepare an income statement for August.

5. Prepare a statement of stockholder's equity for August.

6. Prepare a balance sheet as of August 31.

7. Determine the debt ratio as of August 31.

Planning the Solution

- Analyze each transaction and use the debit-credit rules to record each.
- Record each transaction in the appropriate T-accounts.
- Calculate each ending account balance and list the accounts with their balances on a trial balance.
- Verify that the total debits in the trial balance equal the total credits.
- To prepare the income statement, identify revenues and expenses. List those items on the statement, compute the difference between total revenues and total expenses, and label the result as net income or net loss.

- Use information in the T-accounts to prepare the statement of stockholder's equity.
- Use information in the T-accounts to prepare the balance sheet.
- Calculate the debt ratio by dividing total liabilities by total assets.

Solution to Demonstration Problem

1. Apply the debit-credit rules for each transaction.

a.	*Debit:*	Increases to an asset account are recorded as a debit.
		• Record a debit to Cash for $3,000.
		• Record a debit to Store Equipment for $15,000.
	Credit:	Increases to an equity account are recorded as a credit.
		• Record a credit to J. Worthy, Capital for $18,000.
b.	*Debit:*	Increases to an asset account are recorded as a debit.
		• Record a debit to Furniture for $600.
	Credit:	Decreases to an asset account are recorded as a credit.
		• Record a credit to Cash for $600.
c.	*Debit:*	Increases to an expense account are recorded as a debit.
		• Record a debit to Rent Expense $500.
	Credit:	Decreases to an asset account are recorded as a credit.
		• Record a credit to Cash for $500.
d.	*Debit:*	Increases to an asset account are recorded as a debit.
		• Record a debit to Store Equipment for $1,200.
	Credit:	Increases to a liability account are recorded as a credit.
		• Record a credit to Note Payable for $1,200.
e.	*Debit:*	Increases to an asset account are recorded as a debit.
		• Record a debit to Cash for $825.
	Credit:	Increases to a revenue account are recorded as a credit.
		• Record a credit to Haircutting Services Revenue for $825.
f.	*Debit:*	Increases to an asset account are recorded as a debit.
		• Record a debit to Accounts Receivable for $100.
	Credit:	Increases to a revenue account are recorded as a credit.
		• Record a credit to Haircutting Services Revenue $100.
g.	*Debit:*	Increases to an asset account are recorded as a debit.
		• Record a debit to Cash for $100.
	Credit:	Decreases to an asset account are recorded as a credit.
		• Record a credit to Accounts Receivable for $100.
h.	*Debit:*	Increases to an expense account are recorded as a debit.
		• Record a debit to Wage Expense $125.
	Credit:	Decreases to an asset account are recorded as a credit.
		• Record a credit to Cash for $125.
i.	*Debit:*	Increases to an asset account are recorded as a debit.
		• Record a debit to Cash for $930.
	Credit:	Increases to a revenue account are recorded as a credit.
		• Record a credit to Haircutting Services Revenue $930.
j.	*Debit:*	Decreases to a liability account are recorded as a debit.
		• Record a debit to Note Payable for $400.
	Credit:	Decreases to an asset account are recorded as a credit.
		• Record a credit to Cash for $400.
k.	*Debit:*	Decreases to an equity account are recorded as a debit.
		• Record a debit to J. Worthy, Withdrawals for $900.
	Credit:	Decreases to an asset account are recorded as a credit.
		• Record a credit to Cash for $900.

2. Record each transaction in the appropriate T-account.

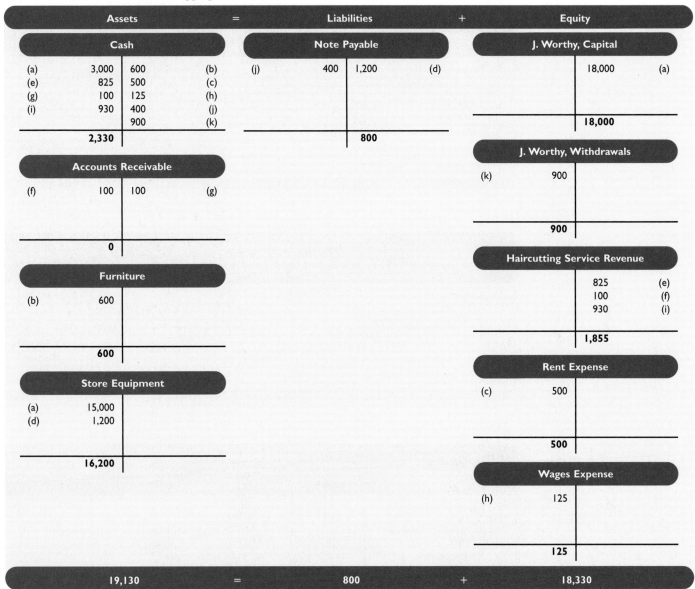

	Assets			=		Liabilities			+		Equity	

Cash

(a)	3,000	600	(b)
(e)	825	500	(c)
(g)	100	125	(h)
(i)	930	400	(j)
		900	(k)
	2,330		

Note Payable

| (j) | 400 | 1,200 | (d) |
| | | **800** | |

J. Worthy, Capital

| | | 18,000 | (a) |
| | | **18,000** | |

Accounts Receivable

| (f) | 100 | 100 | (g) |
| | **0** | | |

J. Worthy, Withdrawals

| (k) | 900 | |
| | **900** | |

Furniture

| (b) | 600 | |
| | **600** | |

Haircutting Service Revenue

		825	(e)
		100	(f)
		930	(i)
		1,855	

Store Equipment

(a)	15,000	
(d)	1,200	
	16,200	

Rent Expense

| (c) | 500 | |
| | **500** | |

Wages Expense

| (h) | 125 | |
| | **125** | |

| 19,130 | = | 800 | + | 18,330 |

3. Prepare a trial balance from the T-accounts.

EXPRESSIONS
Trial Balance
August 31, 2007

	Debit	Credit
Cash	$ 2 3 3 0 00	
Accounts receivable	0 00	
Furniture	6 0 0 00	
Store equipment	16 2 0 0 00	
Note payable		$ 8 0 0 00
J. Worthy, Capital, August 1		18 0 0 0 00
J. Worthy, Withdrawals	9 0 0 00	
Haircutting service revenue		1 8 5 5 00
Wages expense	1 2 5 00	
Rent expense	5 0 0 00	
Totals	$20 6 5 5 00	$20 6 5 5 00

4.

EXPRESSIONS Income Statement For Month Ended August 31, 2007		
Revenues		
Haircutting service revenue		$1 8 5 5 00
Operating expenses		
Rent expense	$ 5 0 0 00	
Wages expense	1 2 5 00	
Total operating expenses		6 2 5 00
Net income		$1 2 3 0 00

5.

EXPRESSIONS Statement of Owner's Equity For Month Ended August 31, 2007		
J. Worthy, Capital, August 1		$ 0 00
Plus: Investments by owner	$18 0 0 0 00	
Net income	1 2 3 0 00	19 2 3 0 00
		19 2 3 0 00
Less: Withdrawals by owner		9 0 0 00
J. Worthy, Capital, August 31		$18 3 3 0 00

6.

EXPRESSIONS Balance Sheet August 31, 2007				
Assets		**Liabilities**		
Cash	$ 2 3 3 0 00	Note payable	$ 8 0 0 00
Furniture	6 0 0 00	**Equity**	
Store equipment	16 2 0 0 00	J. Worthy, Capital, August 31	18 3 3 0 00
Total assets	$19 1 3 0 00	Total liabilities and equity	$19 1 3 0 00

7. Debt ratio $= \dfrac{\text{Total liabilities}}{\text{Total assets}} = \dfrac{\$800}{\$19,130} = 0.0418 = \underline{\textbf{4.18\%}}$

Summary

LO1 **Describe an account and its use in recording transactions.** An account is a detailed record of increases and decreases in a specific asset, liability, equity, revenue, or expense. Information from accounts is analyzed, summarized, and presented in reports and financial statements for decision makers.

LO2 **Define *debits* and *credits* and explain their role in double-entry accounting.** *Debit* refers to left, and *credit* refers to right. Debits increase assets, expenses, and withdrawals while credits decrease them. Credits increase liabilities, owner capital, and revenues; debits decrease them. Double-entry accounting means each transaction affects at least two accounts and has at

least one debit and one credit. The system for recording debits and credits follows from the accounting equation. The left side of an account is the normal balance for assets, withdrawals, and expenses, and the right side is the normal balance for liabilities, capital, and revenues.

LO3 **Analyze the impact of transactions on accounts.** We analyze transactions using concepts of double-entry accounting. This analysis is performed by determining a transaction's effects on accounts.

LO4 **Prepare and explain the use of a trial balance.** A trial balance is a list of accounts, showing their debit or credit balances in separate columns. The trial balance is useful in preparing financial statements and in revealing recordkeeping errors.

LO5 **Prepare financial statements from a trial balance.** The balance sheet, the statement of owner's equity and the income statement, use the trial balance for their preparation.

LO6 **Compute the debt ratio and describe its use in analyzing financial condition.** A company's debt ratio is computed as total liabilities divided by total assets. It reveals how much of the assets are financed by creditor (nonowner) financing. The higher this ratio, the more risk a company faces because liabilities must be repaid at specific dates.

Guidance Answer to   YOU CALL IT

Investor The debt ratio suggests the stock of Converse is of higher risk than normal and that this risk is rising. The average industry ratio of 0.40 further supports this conclusion. The 2006 debt ratio for Converse is twice the industry norm. Also, a debt ratio approaching 1.0 indicates little to no equity.

Guidance Answers to   HOW YOU DOIN'?

1.

Assets	Liabilities	Equity
a,c,e	b,d	—

2. An account is a record in an accounting system that records and stores the increases and decreases in a specific asset, liability, equity, revenue, or expense. The ledger is a collection of all the accounts of a company.

3. No. Debit and credit both can mean increase or decrease. The particular meaning in a circumstance depends on the *type of account*. For example, a debit increases the balance of asset, withdrawals, and expense accounts, but it decreases the balance of liability, capital, and revenue accounts.

4. Equity is increased by revenues and by owner investments. Equity is decreased by expenses and owner withdrawals.

5. The name *double entry* is used because all transactions affect at least two accounts. There must be at least one debit in one account and at least one credit in another account.

6. Answer is (*c*).

7. *Debit:* Increases to an asset account are recorded as a debit.
   - Record a debit to Cash for $15,000.
   - Record a debit to Store Equipment for $23,000.
   Credit: Increases to an equity account are recorded as a credit.
   - Record a credit to Owner, Capital for $38,000.

8. *Debit:* Increases to an asset account are recorded as a debit.
   - Record a debit to Cash for $3,000.

Credit: Increases to a revenue account are recorded as a credit.
   - Record a credit to Consulting Services Revenue for $3,000.

9. At a minimum, dollar signs are placed beside the first and last numbers in a column. It is also common to place dollar signs beside any amount that appears after a ruled line to indicate that an addition or subtraction has occurred.

10. An income statement reports a company's revenues and expenses along with the resulting net income or loss. A statement of owner's equity reports changes in equity, including that from net income or loss. Both statements report transactions occurring over a period of time.

11. The balance sheet describes a company's financial position (assets, liabilities, and equity) at a point in time. The capital amount in the balance sheet is obtained from the statement of owner's equity.

12. Revenues are inflows of assets in exchange for products or services provided to customers as part of the main operations of a business. Expenses are outflows or the using up of assets that result from providing products or services to customers.

13. Assets are the resources a business owns or controls that carry expected future benefits. Liabilities are the obligations of a business, representing the claims of others against the assets of a business. Equity reflects the owner's claims on the assets of the business after deducting liabilities.

Key Terms   mhhe.com/wildCA

Key Terms are available at the book's Website for learning and testing in an online Flashcard Format.

Account (p. 44) Record within an accounting system in which increases and decreases are entered and stored in a specific asset, liability, equity, revenue, or expense.

Account balance (p. 47) Difference between total debits and total credits (including the beginning balance for an account.

Credit (p. 46) Recorded on the right side; an entry that decreases asset and expense accounts, and increases liability, revenue and most equity accounts; abbreviated Cr.

Creditors (p. 45) Individuals or organizations entitled to receive payments.

Debit (p. 46) Recorded on the left side; an entry that increases asset and expense accounts, and decreases liability, revenue, and most equity accounts; abbreviated Dr.

Debt ratio (p. 58) Ratio of total liabilities to total assets; used to reflect risk associated with a company's debts.

Double-entry accounting (p. 47) Accounting system in which each transaction affects at least two accounts and has at least one debit and one credit.

Ledger (p. 44) Record containing all accounts (with amounts) for a business; also called *general ledger*.

Owner, Capital (p. 46) Account showing the owner's claim on company assets; equals owner investments plus net income (or less net losses) minus owner withdrawals since the company's inception; also referred to as *equity*.

Owner, Withdrawals (p. 46) Payment of cash or other assets from a proprietorship or partnership to its owner or owners.

T-account (p. 46) Tool used to show the effects of transactions and events on individual accounts.

Trial balance (p. 55) List of accounts and their balances at a point in time; total debit balances equal total credit balances.

Unearned revenue (p. 45) Liability created when customers pay in advance of products or services to be provided later; earned when the products or services are later delivered.

Multiple Choice Quiz   Answers on p. 73   mhhe.com/wildCA

Multiple Choice Quizzes A and B are available at the book's Website.

1. Asset and expense accounts normally have
  a. Zero balances
  b. Credit balances
  c. Debit balances
  d. Negative balances

2. The accounting equation requires that if assets have a balance of $1 million and equity has a balance of $600,000, then liabilities must equal
  a. $600,000
  b. $1,600,000
  c. $0
  d. $400,000

3. Kirk Hinrich starts a new business by making an investment of $600,000 cash. Using the double-entry method, this increase in cash should be accounted for by
  a. Debiting Cash
  b. Crediting Cash

  c. Debiting Accounts Receivable
  d. Crediting Inventory

4. To record the payment of wages to its employees, Roy Beach Co. would
  a. Debit Wage Expense, debit Cash
  b. Debit Wage Expense, credit Cash
  c. Debit Cash, credit Wage Expense
  d. Credit Cash, credit Wage Expense

5. On May 1, Mattingly Lawn Service collected $2,500 cash from a customer in advance of five months of lawn service. Following the debit-credit rules, Mattingly records this increase in liability as a
  a. Credit to Unearned Lawn Service Fees for $2,500.
  b. Debit to Lawn Service Fees Earned for $2,500.
  c. Credit to Cash for $2,500.
  d. Debit to Unearned Lawn Service Fees for $2,500.
  e. Credit to Capital for $2,500.

Discussion Questions

1. Provide the names of two (*a*) asset accounts, (*b*) liability accounts, and (*c*) equity accounts.

2. What is the difference between a note payable and an account payable?

3. What is an unearned revenue account? Why would customers pay in advance for services (or products) not yet received?

4. If assets are valuable resources and asset accounts have debit balances, why do expense accounts also have debit balances?

5. Why does the recordkeeper prepare a trial balance?

6. Identify the three basic financial statements of a business.

7. What information is reported in an income statement?

8. Why does the user of an income statement need to know the time period that it covers?

9. What information is reported in a balance sheet?

10. Define (*a*) *assets*, (*b*) *liabilities*, (*c*) *equity*, and (*d*) *net assets*.

11. Which financial statement is sometimes called the *statement of financial position*?

12. Review the Best Buy balance sheet in Appendix A. Identify three accounts on its balance sheet that carry debit balances and three accounts on its balance sheet that carry credit balances.

QUICK STUDY

QS 3–1

Identifying financial statement items

(LO1) (LO5)

Identify the financial statement(s) where each of the following items appears. Use I for income statement, E for statement of owner's equity, and B for balance sheet.

  a. Cash withdrawal by owner
  b. Office equipment
  c. Accounts payable

  d. Cash
  e. Utilities expenses
  f. Office supplies

  g. Prepaid rent
  h. Unearned fees
  i. Service fees earned

Using Exhibit 3.6 as a guide, indicate whether a debit or credit *decreases* the normal balance of each of the following accounts.

a. Repair Services Revenue
b. Interest Payable
c. Accounts Receivable
d. Salaries Expense
e. Owner Capital
f. Prepaid Insurance
g. Buildings
h. Interest Revenue
i. Owner Withdrawals
j. Unearned Revenue
k. Accounts Payable
l. Office Supplies

QS 3-2
Linking debit or credit with normal balance
(L02)

Using Exhibit 3.6 as a guide, identify whether a debit or credit yields the indicated change for each of the following accounts.

a. To increase Land   D
b. To decrease Cash   C
c. To increase Utilities Expense D
d. To increase Fees Earned C
e. To decrease Unearned Revenue D
f. To decrease Prepaid Insurance C
g. To increase Notes Payable C
h. To decrease Accounts Receivable C
i. To increase Owner Capital C
j. To increase Store Equipment D

QS 3-3
Analyzing debit or credit by account
(L02)

Identify the normal balance (debit or credit) for each of the following accounts.

a. Office Supplies
b. Owner Withdrawals
c. Fees Earned
d. Wages Expense
e. Cash
f. Prepaid Insurance
g. Wages Payable
h. Building
i. Owner Capital

QS 3-4
Identifying normal balance
(L02)

Apply the debit-credit rules to each of the following selected transactions.

a. On January 13, DeShawn Tyler opens a landscaping business called Elegant Lawns by investing $70,000 cash along with equipment having a $30,000 value.
b. On January 21, Elegant Lawns purchases office supplies on credit for $280.
c. On January 29, Elegant Lawns receives $7,800 cash for performing landscaping services.
d. On January 30, Elegant Lawns receives $1,000 cash in advance of providing landscaping services to a customer.

QS 3-5
Applying debit-credit rules
(L02) (L03)

Indicate the financial statement on which each of the following items appears. Use I for income statement, E for statement of owner's equity, and B for balance sheet.

a. Services Revenue
b. Interest Payable
c. Accounts Receivable
d. Salaries Expense
e. Equipment
f. Prepaid Insurance
g. Buildings
h. Interest Revenue
i. Owner Withdrawals
j. Office Supplies

QS 3-6
Classifying accounts in financial statements
(L01)

Compute the debt ratio for the following companies.

a. Bob's Barbecue had total assets of $370,000, total liabilities of $121,500, and total equity of $248,500.
b. Connie's Christmas Shop had total assets of $250,000, total liabilities of $137,500, and total equity of $112,500.
c. Donna's Donuts had total assets of $125,000, total liabilities of $50,000, and total equity of $75,000.

QS 3-7
Computing the debt ratio
(L06)

For each of the following (1) identify the type of account as an asset, liability, equity, revenue, or expense, (2) enter *debit* (*Dr.*) or *credit* (*Cr.*) to identify the kind of entry that would increase the account balance, and (3) identify the normal balance of the account.

a. Accounts Payable
b. Postage Expense
c. Prepaid Insurance
d. Land
e. Owner Capital
f. Accounts Receivable
g. Owner Withdrawals
h. Cash
i. Equipment
j. Fees Earned
k. Wages Expense
l. Unearned Revenue

EXERCISES

Exercise 3-1
Identifying type and normal balances of accounts
(L01) (L02)

Exercise 3-2
Recording effects of transactions in T-accounts

(LO1) (LO2) (LO3)

Record the transactions below for Amena Company by recording debit and credit amounts directly in the following T-accounts: Cash; Accounts Receivable; Office Supplies; Office Equipment; Accounts Payable; A. Amena, Capital; A. Amena, Withdrawals; Fees Earned; and Rent Expense. Use the letters *a* through *i* to identify transactions in the T-accounts. Determine the ending balance of each T-account.

a. Ahmad Amena, owner, invested $13,325 cash in the business.

b. Purchased office supplies for $475 cash.

c. Purchased $6,235 of office equipment on credit.

d. Received $2,000 cash as fees for services provided to a customer.

e. Paid $6,235 cash to settle the payable for the office equipment purchased in transaction *c*.

f. Billed a customer $3,300 as fees for services provided.

g. Paid $775 cash for the monthly rent.

h. Collected $2,300 cash toward the account receivable created in transaction *f*.

Check　Cash ending balance, $9,340

i. Ahmad Amena withdrew $800 cash for personal use.

Exercise 3-3
Preparing a trial balance

(LO3) (LO4)

After recording the transactions of Exercise 3-2 in T-accounts and calculating the ending balance of each account, prepare a trial balance. Use May 31, 2008, as its report date.

Exercise 3-4
Analyzing revenue transactions

(LO1) (LO2) (LO3)

Examine the following transactions and identify those that create revenues for Valdez Services, a company owned by Brina Valdez. Use debit-credit rules to record the transactions that create revenues. Explain why the other transactions did not create revenues.

a. Brina Valdez invests $39,350 cash in the business.

b. Provided $2,300 of services on credit.

c. Provided services to a client and immediately received $875 cash.

d. Received $10,200 cash from a client in payment for services to be provided next year.

e. Received $3,500 cash from a client in partial payment of an account receivable.

f. Borrowed $120,000 cash from the bank by signing a promissory note.

Exercise 3-5
Analyzing expense transactions

(LO1) (LO2) (LO3)

Examine the following transactions and identify those that create expenses for Valdez Services. Use debit-credit rules to record the transactions that create expenses. Explain why the other transactions did not create expenses.

a. Paid $12,200 cash for office supplies that were purchased on account more than 1 year ago.

b. Paid $1,233 cash for the receptionist's salary for the two weeks just completed.

c. Paid $39,200 cash for equipment.

d. Paid $870 cash for this month's utilities.

e. Owner (B. Valdez) withdrew $4,500 cash for personal use.

Exercise 3-6
Analyzing changes in equity

(LO3)

Compute the missing amount in each of the following separate companies *a* through *d*.

File Edit View Insert Format Tools Data Window Help				
	(a)	**(b)**	**(c)**	**(d)**
Equity, December 31, 2007	$　　0	$　　0	$　　0	$　　0
Owner investments during the year	110,000	?	87,000	210,000
Owner withdrawals during the year	?	(47,000)	(10,000)	(55,000)
Net income (loss) for the year	22,000	90,000	(4,000)	?
Equity, December 31, 2008	104,000	85,000	?	110,000

Exercise 3-7
Interpreting and describing transactions from T-accounts

(LO3)

Assume the following T-accounts reflect Belle Co.'s general ledger and that seven transactions *a* through *g* are posted to them. Provide a short description of each transaction. Include the amounts in your descriptions.

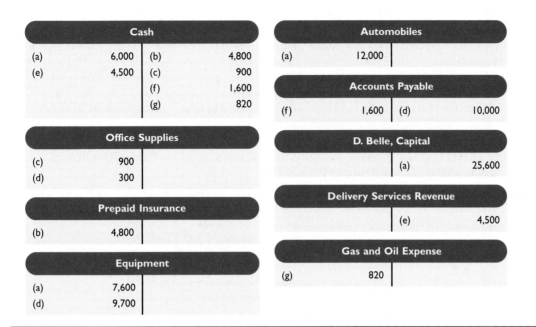

Refer to the T-accounts in Exercise 3-7. Compute ending balances and prepare Belle Company's balance sheet. Assume the balance sheet is dated December 31, 2007. (*Hint:* Its December 31 Capital account balance is $29,280.)

Exercise 3–8
Preparing a balance sheet
(LO5)

a. Compute the debt ratio using year-end information for each of the following six separate companies.

Exercise 3–9
Interpreting the debt ratio
(LO6)

Case	Assets	Liabilities
Company 1	$ 90,500	$ 12,000
Company 2	64,000	47,000
Company 3	32,500	26,500
Company 4	147,000	56,000
Company 5	92,000	31,000
Company 6	104,500	51,500

b. Of the six companies, which relies most heavily on creditor financing?

c. Of the six companies, which relies most heavily on equity financing?

d. Which two companies suggest the greatest risk? Explain.

Denzel Brooks opens a Web consulting business called Venture Consultants and completes the following transactions in March.

March 1 Brooks invested $150,000 cash along with $22,000 of office equipment in the business.

     2 Prepaid $6,000 cash for six months' rent for an office. (*Hint:* Debit Prepaid Rent (an asset) for $6,000.)

     3 Made credit purchases of office equipment for $3,000 and office supplies for $1,200. Payment is due within 10 days.

     6 Completed services for a client and immediately received $4,000 cash.

     9 Completed a $7,500 project for a client, who must pay within 30 days.

   12 Paid $4,200 cash to settle the account payable created on March 3.

   19 Paid $5,000 cash for the premium on a 12-month insurance policy.

   22 Received $3,500 cash as partial payment for the work completed on March 9.

   25 Completed work for another client for $3,820 on credit.

   29 Brooks withdrew $5,100 cash for personal use.

   30 Purchased $600 of additional office supplies on credit.

   31 Paid $500 cash for this month's utility bill.

PROBLEM SET A

Problem 3–1A
Using debit-credit rules;
preparing a trial balance
(LO2) (LO3) (LO4)

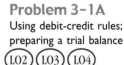

mhhe.com/wildCA

Required

1. Apply the debit-credit rules and explain how to record each transaction (use the account titles listed in part 2).

Check (2) Ending balances: Cash, $136,700; Accounts Receivable, $7,820; Accounts Payable, $600

(3) Total debits, $187,920

2. Open the following T-accounts—Cash; Accounts Receivable; Office Supplies; Prepaid Insurance; Prepaid Rent; Office Equipment; Accounts Payable; D. Brooks, Capital; D. Brooks, Withdrawals; Services Revenue; and Utilities Expense. Record the transactions from part 1 in the T-accounts.

3. Prepare a trial balance as of the end of March.

Problem 3-2A

Applying the debit-credit rules; preparing a trial balance

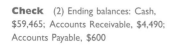

Kendis Lanelle opened a computer consulting business called Viva Consultants and completed the following transactions in the first month of operations.

April	1	Lanelle invested $80,000 cash along with office equipment valued at $26,000 in the business.
	2	Prepaid $9,000 cash for 12 months' rent for office space. (*Hint:* Debit Prepaid Rent (an asset) for $9,000.)
	3	Made credit purchases for $8,000 in office equipment and $3,600 in office supplies. Payment is due within 10 days.
	6	Completed services for a client and immediately received $4,000 cash.
	9	Completed a $6,000 project for a client, who must pay within 30 days.
	13	Paid $11,600 cash to settle the account payable created on April 3.
	19	Paid $2,400 cash for the premium on a 12-month insurance policy. (*Hint:* Debit Prepaid Insurance (an asset) for $2,400.)
	22	Received $4,400 cash as partial payment for the work completed on April 9.
	25	Completed work for another client for $2,890 on credit.
	28	Lanelle withdrew $5,500 cash for personal use.
	29	Purchased $600 of additional office supplies on credit.
	30	Paid $435 cash for this month's utility bill.

Required

1. Apply the debit-credit rules and explain how to record each transaction (use account titles listed in part 2).

Check (2) Ending balances: Cash, $59,465; Accounts Receivable, $4,490; Accounts Payable, $600

(3) Total debits, $119,490

2. Open the following T-accounts—Cash; Accounts Receivable; Office Supplies; Prepaid Insurance; Prepaid Rent; Office Equipment; Accounts Payable; K. Lanelle, Capital; K. Lanelle, Withdrawals; Services Revenue; and Utilities Expense. Record the transactions from part 1 in the T-accounts.

3. Prepare a trial balance as of April 30.

Problem 3-3A

Computing net income from equity analysis, preparing a balance sheet, and computing the debt ratio

mhhe.com/wildCA

The accounting records of Faviana Adriano Shipping show the following assets and liabilities as of December 31, 2007, and 2008.

	December 31	
	2007	**2008**
Cash	$ 64,300	$ 15,640
Accounts receivable	26,240	19,390
Office supplies	3,160	1,960
Office equipment	44,000	44,000
Trucks	148,000	157,000
Building	0	80,000
Land	0	60,000
Accounts payable	3,500	33,500
Note payable	0	40,000

Late in December 2008, the business purchased a small office building and land for $140,000. It paid $100,000 cash toward the purchase and signed a $40,000 note payable for the balance. The owner, Faviana Adriano, had to invest $35,000 cash in the business to enable it to pay the $100,000 cash. The owner withdraws $3,000 cash per month for personal use.

Required

1. Prepare balance sheets for the business as of December 31, 2007, and 2008. (*Hint:* Remember that total equity equals the difference between assets and liabilities.)

Check (2) Net income, $23,290

2. By comparing equity amounts from the balance sheets each year and using the additional information presented in this problem, calculate how much net income the business earned during 2008.

3. Prepare its income statement for the year ended December 31, 2008, using the following ending balances for revenues and expenses: Shipping services revenue of $82,000; Moving services revenue of $4,000; Rent expense of $28,000; Salaries expense of $25,710; Utilities expense of $6,400; and Miscellaneous expenses of $2,600.

Yi Min started an engineering firm called Min Engineering. He began operations and completed seven transactions in May, which included his initial investment of $18,000 cash. After these transactions, the ledger included the following accounts with normal balances.

Cash	$37,641
Office supplies	890
Prepaid insurance	4,600
Office equipment	12,900
Accounts payable	12,900
Y. Min, Capital (May 1)	18,000
Y. Min, Withdrawals	3,329
Engineering fees earned	36,000
Rent expense	7,540

Problem 3–4A

Analyzing account balances and reconstructing transactions

(LO3) (LO4)

Required

1. Prepare a trial balance for this company dated May 31, 2007.

2. Prepare a balance sheet for this company dated May 31, 2007. (*Hint:* Its May 31 Capital account balance is $43,131.)

Check (1) Trial balance totals, $66,900

Diella Management Services opens for business and completes these transactions in November.

Nov. 1 Cicely Diella, the owner, invested $30,000 cash along with $15,000 of office equipment in the business.
  2 Prepaid $4,500 cash for six months' rent for an office. (*Hint:* Debit Prepaid Rent (an asset) for $4,500.)
  4 Made credit purchases of office equipment for $2,500 and of office supplies for $600. Payment is due within 10 days.
  8 Completed work for a client and immediately received $3,400 cash.
  12 Completed a $10,200 project for a client, who must pay within 30 days.
  13 Paid $3,100 cash to settle the payable created on November 4.
  19 Paid $1,800 cash for the premium on a 24-month insurance policy.
  22 Received $5,200 cash as partial payment for the work completed on November 12.
  24 Completed work for another client for $1,750 on credit.
  28 Cicely Diella withdrew $5,300 cash for personal use.
  29 Purchased $249 of additional office supplies on credit.
  30 Paid $831 cash for this month's utility bill.

PROBLEM SET B

Problem 3–1B

Preparing and posting journal entries; preparing a trial balance

(LO2) (LO3) (LO4)

Required

1. Apply the debit-credit rules and explain how to record each transaction (use account titles listed in part 2).

2. Open the following T-accounts—Cash; Accounts Receivable; Office Supplies; Prepaid Insurance; Prepaid Rent; Office Equipment; Accounts Payable; C. Diella, Capital; C. Diella, Withdrawals; Services Revenue; and Utilities Expense. Record the transactions from part 1 in the T-accounts.

3. Prepare a trial balance as of the end of November.

Check (2) Ending balances: Cash, $23,069; Accounts Receivable, $6,750; Accounts Payable, $249

(3) Total debits, $60,599

Johnson Management Services opens for business and completes these transactions in September.

Sept. 1 John Johnson, the owner, invests $38,000 cash along with office equipment valued at $15,000 in the business.
  2 Prepaid $9,000 cash for 12 months' rent for office space. (*Hint:* Debit Prepaid Rent (an asset) for $9,000.)
  4 Made credit purchases for $8,000 in office equipment and $2,400 in office supplies. Payment is due within 10 days.
  8 Completed work for a client and immediately received $3,280 cash.

Problem 3–2B

Preparing and posting journal entries; preparing a trial balance

12   Completed a $15,400 project for a client, who must pay within 30 days.
13   Paid $10,400 cash to settle the payable created on September 4.
19   Paid $1,900 cash for the premium on an 18-month insurance policy. (*Hint:* Debit Prepaid Insurance (an asset) for $1,900.)
22   Received $7,700 cash as partial payment for the work completed on September 12.
24   Completed work for another client for $2,100 on credit.
28   John Johnson withdrew $5,300 cash for personal use.
29   Purchased $550 of additional office supplies on credit.
30   Paid $860 cash for this month's utility bill.

Required

1. Apply the debit-credit rules and explain how to record each transaction (use account titles listed in part 2).

2. Open the following T-accounts—Cash; Accounts Receivable; Office Supplies; Prepaid Insurance; Prepaid Rent; Office Equipment; Accounts Payable; J. Johnson, Capital; J. Johnson, Withdrawals; Service Fees Earned; and Utilities Expense. Record the transactions from part 1 in the T-accounts.

3. Prepare a trial balance as of the end of September.

Check (2) Ending balances: Cash, $21,520; Accounts Receivable, $9,800; Accounts Payable, $550

(3) Total debits, $74,330

Problem 3-3B

Computing net income from equity analysis, preparing a balance sheet, and computing the debt ratio

The accounting records of Tama Co. show the following assets and liabilities as of December 31, 2007, and 2008.

	December 31	
	2007	**2008**
Cash	$20,000	$ 5,000
Accounts receivable	35,000	25,000
Office supplies	8,000	13,500
Office equipment	40,000	40,000
Machinery	28,500	28,500
Building	0	250,000
Land	0	50,000
Accounts payable	4,000	12,000
Note payable	0	250,000

Late in December 2008, the business purchased a small office building and land for $300,000. It paid $50,000 cash toward the purchase and a $250,000 note payable was signed for the balance. J. Tama, the owner, had to invest an additional $15,000 cash to enable it to pay the $50,000 cash. The owner withdraws $250 cash per month for personal use.

Required

1. Prepare balance sheets for the business as of December 31, 2007, and 2008. (*Hint:* Remember that total equity equals the difference between assets and liabilities.)

2. By comparing equity amounts from the balance sheets each year and using the additional information presented in the problem, prepare a calculation to show how much net income was earned by the business during 2008.

3. Prepare its income statement for the year ended December 31, 2008, using the following ending balances for revenues and expenses: Consulting revenue of $46,000; Rental revenue of $3,000; Rent expense of $19,000; Wages expense of $14,300; Utilities expense of $3,200; and Miscellaneous expenses of $2,000.

Check (2) Net income, $10,500

Problem 3-4B

Preparing a trial balance

Roshaun Gould started a Web consulting firm called Gould Solutions. He began operations and completed seven transactions in April that resulted in the following accounts, which all have normal balances.

Cash	$19,982
Office supplies	760
Prepaid rent	1,800
Office equipment	12,250
Accounts payable	12,250
R. Gould, Capital	15,000
R. Gould, Withdrawals	5,200
Consulting fees earned	20,400
Operating expenses	7,658

Required

1. Prepare a trial balance for this company dated April 30, 2007.

2. Prepare a balance sheet for this company dated April 30, 2007. (*Hint:* Its April 30 Capital account balance is $22,542.)

Check (1) Trial balance total, $47,650

(This serial problem started in Chapter 1 and continues through most of the chapters. If the Chapter 1 segment was not completed, the problem can begin at this point. It is helpful, but not necessary, to use the Working Papers that accompany this book.)

SP 3 On October 1, 2007, Adriana Lopez launched a computer services company called Success Systems, which provides consulting services, computer system installations, and custom program development. Lopez adopts the calendar year for reporting purposes and expects to prepare the company's first set of financial statements on December 31, 2007. The company uses the following accounts:

SERIAL PROBLEM

Success Systems

Account	Account
Cash	A. Lopez, Capital
Accounts Receivable	A. Lopez, Withdrawals
Computer Supplies	Computer Services Revenue
Prepaid Insurance	Wages Expense
Prepaid Rent	Advertising Expense
Office Equipment	Mileage Expense
Computer Equipment	Miscellaneous Expenses
Accounts Payable	Repairs Expense—Computer

Required

1. Apply the debit-credit rules to each of the following transactions for Success Systems.

Oct. 1 Lopez invested $75,000 cash, a $25,000 computer system, and $10,000 of office equipment in the business.

2 Paid $3,500 cash for four months' rent. (*Hint:* Debit Prepaid Rent for $3,500.)

3 Purchased $1,600 of computer supplies on credit from Corvina Office Products.

5 Paid $2,400 cash for one year's premium on a property and liability insurance policy. (*Hint:* Debit Prepaid Insurance for $2,400.)

6 Billed Easy Leasing $6,200 for services performed in installing a new Web server.

8 Paid $1,600 cash for the computer supplies purchased from Corvina Office Products on October 3.

10 Hired Michelle Jones as a part-time assistant for $150 per day, as needed.

12 Billed Easy Leasing another $1,950 for services performed.

15 Received $6,200 cash from Easy Leasing on its account.

17 Paid $900 cash to repair computer equipment that was damaged when moving it.

20 Paid $1,790 cash for an advertisement in the local newspaper.

22 Received $1,950 cash from Easy Leasing on its account.

28 Billed Clark Company $7,300 for services performed.

31 Paid $1,050 cash for Michelle Jones's wages for seven days' work.

31 Lopez withdrew $4,000 cash for personal use.

Nov. 1 Reimbursed Lopez in cash for business automobile mileage allowance (Lopez logged 1,200 miles at $0.32 per mile).

2 Received $3,600 cash from Edge Corporation for computer services performed.

5 Purchased computer supplies for $1,750 cash from Corvina Office Products.

8 Billed Gomez Co. $6,500 for services performed.

13 Received notification from Alex's Engineering Co. that Success Systems' bid of $7,000 for an upcoming project is accepted.

18 Received $5,000 cash from Clark Company as partial payment of the October 28 bill.

22 Donated $300 cash to the United Way in the company's name.

24   Completed work for Alex's Engineering Co. and sent it a bill for $7,000.
25   Sent another bill to Clark Company for the past-due amount of $2,300.
28   Reimbursed Lopez in cash for business automobile mileage (1,500 miles at $0.32 per mile).
30   Paid $2,100 cash for Michelle Jones's wages for 14 days' work.
30   Lopez withdrew $2,500 cash for personal use.

2. Record each transaction in the appropriate T-accounts.

3. Prepare a trial balance (dated November 30, 2007) from the ending balances of the T-accounts from part 2.

BEYOND THE NUMBERS

REPORTING IN ACTION
(LO5) (LO6)

BTN 3-1   Refer to **Best Buy**'s financial statements in Appendix A for the following questions.

Required

1. What amount of total liabilities does Best Buy report for each of the fiscal years ended February 28, 2004, and February 26, 2005?

2. What amount of total assets does Best Buy report for each of the fiscal years ended February 28, 2004, and February 26, 2005?

3. Compute Best Buy's debt ratio for each of the fiscal years ended February 28, 2004, and February 26, 2005.

4. In which fiscal year did Best Buy employ more financial leverage (February 28, 2004, or February 26, 2005)? Explain.

COMPARATIVE ANALYSIS
(LO6)

BTN 3-2   Key comparative figures ($ thousands) for both **Best Buy** and **Circuit City** follow.

	Best Buy		Circuit City	
Key Figures	**Current Year**	**Prior Year**	**Current Year**	**Prior Year**
Total liabilities	$ 5,845,000	$5,230,000	$1,701,948	$1,506,565
Total assets	10,294,000	8,652,000	3,789,382	3,730,526

1. What is the debt ratio for Best Buy in the current year and in the prior year?

2. What is the debt ratio for Circuit City in the current year and in the prior year?

3. Which of the two companies has a higher degree of financial leverage? What does this imply?

ETHICS CHALLENGE
(LO5)

BTN 3-3   Craig Thorne works in a public accounting firm and hopes to eventually be a partner. The management of Allnet Company invites Thorne to prepare a bid to audit Allnet's financial statements. In discussing the audit fee, Allnet's management suggests a fee range in which the amount depends on the reported profit of Allnet. The higher its profit, the higher will be the audit fee paid to Thorne's firm.

Required

1. Identify the parties potentially affected by this audit and the fee plan proposed.

2. What are the ethical factors in this situation? Explain.

3. Would you recommend that Thorne accept this audit fee arrangement? Why or why not?

4. Describe some ethical considerations guiding your recommendation.

WORKPLACE COMMUNICATION
(LO5)

BTN 3-4   Lila Corentine is an aspiring entrepreneur and your friend. She is having difficulty understanding the purposes of financial statements and how they fit together across time.

Required

Write a one-page memorandum to Corentine explaining the purposes of the three basic financial statements and how they are linked across time.

BTN 3-5 Access EDGAR online (www.sec.gov) and locate the 2004 fiscal year 10-K report of Amazon.com (ticker AMZN) filed on March 11, 2005. Review its financial statements reported for fiscal years ended 2002, 2003, and 2004 to answer the following questions:

TAKING IT TO THE NET
(L05)

Required

1. What are the amounts of its net income or net loss reported for each of these three years?
2. What are its total assets, total liabilities, and total equity at the end of fiscal 2004?

BTN 3-6 The expanded accounting equation consists of assets, liabilities, capital, withdrawals, revenues, and expenses. It can be used to reveal insights into changes in a company's financial position.

TEAMWORK IN ACTION
(L02) (L03)

Required

1. Form *learning teams* of six (or more) members. Each team member must select one of the six components and each team must have at least one expert on each component: (*a*) assets, (*b*) liabilities, (*c*) capital, (*d*) withdrawals, (*e*) revenues, and (*f*) expenses.
2. Form *expert teams* of individuals who selected the same component in part 1. Expert teams are to draft a report that each expert will present to his or her learning team addressing the following:
   a. Identify for its component the (i) increase and decrease side of the account and (ii) normal balance side of the account.
   b. Describe a transaction, with amounts, that increases its component.
   c. Using the transaction and amounts in (*b*), verify the equality of the accounting equation.
   d. Describe a transaction, with amounts, that decreases its component.
   e. Using the transaction and amounts in (*d*), verify the equality of the accounting equation.
3. Each expert should return to his/her learning team. In rotation, each member presents his/her expert team's report to the learning team. Team discussion is encouraged.

BTN 3-7 Assume Warren Brown of Cake Love wishes to expand but needs a $30,000 loan. The bank requests Warren to prepare a balance sheet and key financial ratios. Warren has not kept formal records but is able to provide the following accounts and their amounts as of December 31, 2008:

ENTREPRENEURS IN BUSINESS
(L06)

Cash	$ 3,600	Accounts Receivable	$ 9,600	Prepaid Insurance	$ 1,500
Prepaid Rent	9,400	Store Supplies	6,600	Equipment	50,000
Accounts Payable	2,200	Unearned Revenues	15,600	Total Equity*	62,900
Annual net income	40,000				

* The total equity amount reflects all owner investments, withdrawals, revenues, and expenses as of December 31, 2008.

Required

1. Prepare a balance sheet as of December 31, 2008, for Cake Love. (You need only report the total equity amount on the balance sheet.)
2. Compute Cake Love's debt ratio and its return on assets (the latter ratio is defined in Chapter 2). Assume average assets equal its ending balance.
3. Do you think the prospects of Cake Love repaying a $30,000 bank loan are good? Why or why not?

ANSWERS TO MULTIPLE CHOICE QUIZ

1. c; Assets and expenses normally have debit balances.
2. d; Assets = Liabilities + Equity.
3. a; The cash investment should be accounted for as a debit to cash (and a credit to K. Hinrich, Capital).
4. b; The accountant would debit Wage Expense and credit Cash.
5. a; Debit Cash for $2,500 and credit Unearned Lawn Service Fees for $2,500.

A Look Back

Chapter 3 explained the analysis and recording of transactions. We showed how to apply and interpret T-accounts, double-entry accounting, and trial balances.

A Look at This Chapter

This chapter continues our focus on the accounting process. We introduce source documents as inputs for analysis and describe a company's chart of accounts. We also explain how transactions are journalized and posted to the general ledger.

A Look Ahead

Chapter 5 explains the need to adjust accounts. We describe the various types of adjustments and the adjusted trial balance and how it is used to prepare financial statements.

Chapter

4

Preparing the General Journal and General Ledger

LEARNING OBJECTIVES

LO 1 Explain the steps in processing transactions.

LO 2 Describe source documents and their purpose.

LO 3 Describe a chart of accounts.

LO 4 Record transactions in a journal and post entries to a ledger.

LO 5 Explain how to correct errors in the journal and ledger.

"You just have to do it. There are no limitations"
—Katrina Markoff

Culinary Adventures

 CHICAGO—"My heritage is Macedonian," says Katrina Markoff, "and my love of cooking has been with me from childhood. I began to think, why not combine international spices and chocolate?" Markoff ultimately created a chocolate confectionary company, **Vosges Haut Chocolat [VosgesChocolate.com],** with an "East-meets-West" feel. "I noticed a lack of creativity in chocolate," says Markoff. "They were all gold boxes with chocolate that tasted lousy and had raspberry and strawberry filling."

With ingredients such as wasabi, balsamic vinegar, jasmine flower, curry, and anise, you won't confuse her chocolate with any others. "When I tell people stories about the ingredients," says Markoff, "they tend to slow down and pay attention to what they're putting in their mouths."

Markoff is also a businessperson. "I couldn't help it," says Markoff, "my mother is an entrepreneur." That business sense mixed with her culinary skills gives her unique insights. This year's sales are projected to exceed $4.5 million. "Best sellers include Naga, Black Pearl, and Absinthe," she explains. Such

results foretell further growth. "I'd like to just keep expanding," Markoff says.

Markoff insists that a timely and reliable accounting system is crucial for Vosges Haut Chocolat's success. This system gives Markoff the financial statement information that has enabled her company to obtain the necessary financing to feed its growth. This chapter focuses on the accounting system underlying financial statements.

The accounting system also gives her information on key expenses. She personally inspects and purchases each spice, flower, and chocolate used. "Right now, I'm trying out a Jamaican-style truffle, flavored with rum and allspice." Once new products meet her culinary standards, they are appropriately priced.

"We want people to experience chocolate through the use of their senses—all six!" exclaims Markoff. One of her newer products is the Aztec collection that combines chocolate with spices of the vanilla bean, ancho chili pepper, Ceylon cinnamon, and cashews. Adds Markoff, both chocolate and spices have a long history as aphrodisiacs. Now we're cooking!

[Sources: *Vosges Haut Chocolat Website,* January 2007; *Inc.* magazine, April 2005; *Entrepreneur,* 2002; Chocomap, January 2007.

Financial statements report on the financial performance and condition of a company. A main goal of this chapter is to illustrate how transactions are recorded, how they are reflected in financial statements, and how they impact analysis of financial statements. Journals and ledgers are introduced as part of a system to record transactions.

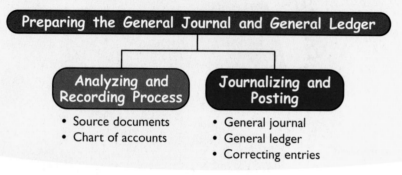

Preparing the General Journal and General Ledger

Analyzing and Recording Process
- Source documents
- Chart of accounts

Journalizing and Posting
- General journal
- General ledger
- Correcting entries

Analyzing and Recording Process

LO1 Explain the steps in processing transactions.

The accounting process identifies business transactions and events, analyzes and records their effects, and summarizes and presents information in reports and financial statements. These reports and statements are used for making investing, lending, and other business decisions. The steps in the accounting process that focus on *analyzing and recording* transactions and events are shown in Exhibit 4.1.

Exhibit 4.1

The Analyzing and Recording Process

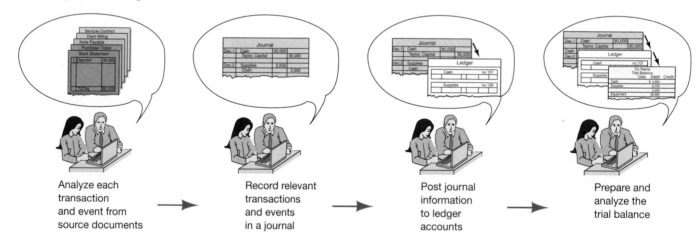

Analyze each transaction and event from source documents → Record relevant transactions and events in a journal → Post journal information to ledger accounts → Prepare and analyze the trial balance

Business transactions and events are the starting points. Relying on source documents, transactions and events are analyzed using the accounting equation to understand how they affect company performance and financial position. These effects are recorded in accounting records, informally referred to as the *accounting books,* or simply the *books.* Additional steps such as posting and then preparing a trial balance help summarize and classify the effects of transactions and events. Ultimately, the accounting process provides information in useful reports or financial statements to decision makers.

Source Documents

LO2 Describe source documents and their purpose.

Source documents identify and describe transactions entering the accounting process. They are the sources of accounting information and can be in either hard copy or electronic form.

Examples are sales invoices, checks, purchase orders, bills from suppliers, employee earnings records, and bank statements (as shown in Exhibit 4.2). To illustrate, when an item is purchased on credit, the seller usually prepares at least two copies of a sales invoice. One copy is given to the buyer. Another copy, often sent electronically, results in an entry in the seller's information system to record the sale. Sellers use invoices for recording sales and for control; buyers use them for recording purchases and for monitoring purchasing activity. Many cash registers record information for each sale on a tape or electronic file locked inside the register. This record can be used as a source document for recording sales in the accounting records. Source documents, especially if obtained from outside the organization, provide objective and reliable evidence about transactions and their amounts.

YOU CALL IT   Answer—p. 87

Cashier   Your manager requires that you, as cashier, immediately enter each sale. Recently, lunch hour traffic has increased and the assistant manager asks you to avoid delays by taking customers' cash and making change without entering sales. The assistant manager says she will add up cash and enter sales after lunch. She says that, in this way, the register will always match the cash amount when the manager arrives at three o'clock. What do you do?

To ensure that all sales are rung up on the register, most sellers require customers to have their receipts to exchange or return purchased items.

Exhibit 4.2

Sampling of Source Documents

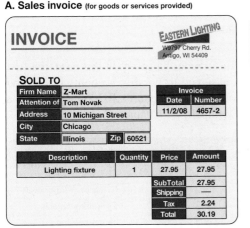

A. Sales invoice (for goods or services provided)

B. Cash register summary (detail of cash receipts)

C. Processed check images (detail of cash payments)

D. Bill from supplier (for goods or services received)

E. Deposit ticket (record of bank deposits)

Chart of Accounts

In Chapter 2, we applied the following two questions to analyze the effects of a transaction on the accounting equation:

 LO3 Describe a chart of accounts.

1. Which accounts are affected by the transaction?
   a. Identify the affected accounts.
   b. Categorize the affected accounts as assets, liabilities, or equity (including revenues and expenses).
2. How is the accounting equation affected?

 IN THE NEWS

Sporting Accounts

The **Miami Heat** have the following major revenue and expense accounts:

Revenues	Expenses
Basketball ticket sales	Team salaries
TV & radio broadcast fees	Game costs
Advertising revenues	NBA franchise costs
Basketball playoff receipts	Promotional costs

To know which account is affected, we must know which accounts a particular company uses. A company's size and diversity of operations affect the number of accounts needed. A small company can get by with as few as 20 or 30 accounts; a large company can require several thousand. The **chart of accounts** is a list of all accounts a company uses and includes an identification number assigned to each account. A small business might use the following numbering system for its accounts:

101–199	Asset accounts
201–299	Liability accounts
301–399	Equity accounts
401–499	Revenue accounts
501–699	Expense accounts

These numbers provide a three-digit code that is useful in recordkeeping. In this case, the first digit assigned to asset accounts is a 1, the first digit assigned to liability accounts is a 2, and so on. The second and third digits relate to the accounts' subcategories. Exhibit 4.3 shows a *partial* chart of accounts for FastForward, the focus company of Chapters 2 and 3.

> Different companies use different account titles. An example of the variety of accounts and their titles can be seen by looking at the chart of accounts located prior to the index at the back of the book.

Exhibit 4.3

Partial Chart of Accounts for FastForward

Account Number	Account Name	Account Number	Account Name
101	Cash	301	C. Taylor, Capital
106	Accounts receivable	302	C. Taylor, Withdrawals
126	Supplies	403	Consulting revenue
128	Prepaid insurance	406	Rental revenue
167	Equipment	622	Salaries expense
201	Accounts payable	637	Insurance expense
236	Unearned consulting revenue	640	Rent expense
		652	Supplies expense
		690	Utilities expense

HOW YOU DOIN'?   Answers—p. 88

1. Identify examples of accounting source documents.
2. Explain the importance of source documents.
3. What determines the number and types of accounts a company uses?
4. Describe a chart of accounts.

Journalizing and Posting Transactions

LO4 Record transactions in a journal and post entries to a ledger.

Processing transactions is a crucial part of accounting. The four usual steps of this process are depicted in Exhibit 4.4. Steps 1 and 2—involving transaction analysis and double-entry accounting—were introduced in Chapters 2 and 3. This section extends that discussion and focuses on steps 3 and 4 of the accounting process. Step 3 is to record each transaction in a journal. A **journal** gives a complete record of each transaction in one place. It also shows debits and credits for each transaction. The process of recording transactions in a journal is called **journalizing.**

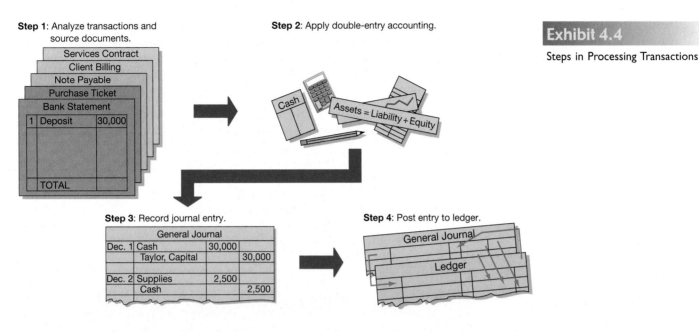

Step 1: Analyze transactions and source documents.

Step 2: Apply double-entry accounting.

Step 3: Record journal entry.

Step 4: Post entry to ledger.

Exhibit 4.4

Steps in Processing Transactions

Step 4 is to transfer (or *post*) entries from the journal to the ledger. The process of transferring journal entry information to the ledger is called **posting.**

Journalizing Transactions   The process of journalizing transactions requires an understanding of a journal. While companies can use various journals, every company uses a **general journal.** It can be used to record any transaction and includes the following information about each transaction: (1) date of transaction, (2) titles of affected accounts, (3) dollar amount of each debit and credit, and (4) explanation of the transaction. Exhibit 4.5 shows how the first two transactions of FastForward are recorded in a general journal. This process is similar for manual and computerized systems. Computerized journals are often designed to look like a manual journal page, and also include error-checking routines that ensure debits equal credits for each entry. Shortcuts allow recordkeepers to select account names and numbers from pull-down menus.

GENERAL JOURNAL				Page 1
Date	**Account Titles and Explanation**	**PR**	**Debit**	**Credit**
2007 Dec. 1	Cash		30,000	
	C.Taylor, Capital			30,000
	Investment by owner.			
Dec. 2	Supplies		2,500	
	Cash			2,500
	Purchased supplies for cash.			

Exhibit 4.5

Partial General Journal for FastForward

To record entries in a general journal, apply these steps; refer to the entries in Exhibit 4.5 when reviewing these steps.

1. Date the transaction: Enter the year at the top of the first column and the month and day on the first line of each journal entry.
2. Enter titles of accounts debited and then enter amounts in the Debit column on the same line. Account titles are taken from the chart of accounts and are aligned with the left margin of the Account Titles and Explanation column.
3. Enter titles of accounts credited and then enter amounts in the Credit column on the same line. Account titles are from the chart of accounts and are indented from the left margin of the Account Titles and Explanation column to distinguish them from debited accounts.

There are no exact rules for writing journal entry explanations. An explanation should be short yet describe why an entry is made.

A journal is often referred to as the *book of original entry.* The ledger is referred to as the *book of final entry* because financial statements are prepared from it.

4. Enter a brief explanation of the transaction on the line below the entry (it often references a source document). This explanation is indented about half as far as the credited account titles to avoid confusing it with accounts. The recordkeeper in a manual system is not likely to write in italics.

A blank line is left between each journal entry for clarity. When a transaction is first recorded, the **posting reference (PR) column** is left blank (in a manual system). Later, when posting entries to the general ledger, the identification numbers of the individual ledger accounts are entered in the PR column.

The general journal gives a complete record of each transaction in one place. To determine the current balance of each specific account, however, information in the journal must be transferred (or posted) to each account. The complete collection of all accounts in an accounting information system is called a **ledger** (or **general ledger**).

Balance Column Account   The T-accounts that were introduced in Chapter 3 are a simple and direct means to show how the accounting process works. However, actual accounting systems need more structure, and therefore use **balance column accounts,** as in Exhibit 4.6.

Exhibit 4.6

Cash Account in Balance Column Format

Cash						Account No. 101
Date	Explanation	PR	Debit	Credit		Balance
2007						
Dec. 1		G1	30,000			30,000
Dec. 2		G1		2,500		27,500
Dec. 3		G1		26,000		1,500
Dec. 10		G1	4,200			5,700

The balance column account format is similar to a T-account in having columns for debits and credits. It differs from a T-account by including transaction date and explanation columns. It also has a column with the running balance of the account after each entry is recorded. To illustrate, FastForward's Cash account in Exhibit 4.6 is debited on December 1 for the $30,000 owner investment, yielding a $30,000 debit balance. The account is credited on December 2 for $2,500, yielding a $27,500 debit balance. On December 3, it is credited again, this time for $26,000, and its debit balance is reduced to $1,500. The Cash account is debited for $4,200 on December 10, and its debit balance increases to $5,700.

The heading of the Balance column does not show whether it is a debit or credit balance. Instead, an account is assumed to have a *normal balance.* Unusual events can sometimes temporarily give an account an abnormal balance. An *abnormal balance* refers to a balance on the side where decreases are recorded. For example, a customer might mistakenly overpay a bill. This gives that customer's account receivable an abnormal (credit) balance. An abnormal balance is often identified by circling it or by entering it in red or some other unusual color in manual systems. An abnormal balance might be shown in brackets in a computerized system. A zero balance for an account is usually shown by writing zeros or a dash in the Balance column to avoid confusion between a zero balance and one omitted in error.

Computerized systems often provide a code beside a balance such as *dr.* or *cr.* to identify its balance.

Posting Journal Entries   Step 4 of processing transactions is to post journal entries to ledger accounts (see Exhibit 4.4). To ensure that the ledger is up-to-date, entries are posted as soon as possible. This might be daily, weekly, or when time permits. All entries must be posted to the ledger before financial statements are prepared to ensure that account balances are up-to-date. When entries are posted to the ledger, the debits in journal entries are transferred into ledger accounts as debits, and credits are transferred into ledger accounts as credits. Exhibit 4.7 shows the four steps to post a journal entry. First, identify the ledger account that is debited in the entry; then, in the ledger, enter the entry date, the journal and page in its PR column, the debit amount, and the new balance of the ledger account. (The letter *G* shows it came from the General Journal; the number 1 indicates it came from page 1 of the General Journal.) Second, enter the ledger account number in the PR column of the journal. Steps three and four repeat the first two steps for credit entries and amounts. The posting process creates a link between the ledger and the journal entry. This link is a useful cross-reference for tracing an amount from one record to another.

Explanations are typically included in ledger accounts only for unusual transactions or events.

Exhibit 4.7

Posting an Entry to the Ledger

Key:
(1) Identify debit account in Ledger: enter date, journal page, amount, and balance.
(2) Enter the debit account number from the Ledger in the PR column of the journal.
(3) Identify credit account in Ledger: enter date, journal page, amount, and balance.
(4) Enter the credit account number from the Ledger in the PR column of the journal.

The fundamental concepts of a manual (pencil-and-paper) system are identical to those of a computerized information system.

Journalizing and Posting Transactions—An Illustration

We return to the activities of FastForward to show how to journalize and post their first 16 transactions. We first show the 16 transactions as journal entries in the general journal (Exhibit 4.8). We then show the results of posting these transactions to ledger accounts (Exhibit 4.9).

GENERAL JOURNAL				Page 1
Transaction	**Account Titles and Explanation**	**PR**	**Debit**	**Credit**
(1)	Cash	101	30 000 00	
	C. Taylor, Capital	301		30 000 00
	Investment by owner.			
(2)	Supplies	126	2 500 00	
	Cash	101		2 500 00
	Purchased supplies for cash.			
(3)	Equipment	167	26 000 00	
	Cash	101		26 000 00
	Purchased equipment for cash.			
(4)	Supplies	126	7 100 00	
	Accounts Payable	201		7 100 00
	Purchased supplies on credit.			

Exhibit 4.8

Journal Entries for FastForward Transactions

[continued on next page]

[continued from previous page]

(5)	Cash	101	4 2 0 0 00	
	Consulting Revenue	403		4 2 0 0 00
	Provide services for cash.			
(6)	Rent Expense	640	1 0 0 0 00	
	Cash	101		1 0 0 0 00
	Payment of rent expense in cash.			
(7)	Salaries Expense	622	7 0 0 00	
	Cash	101		7 0 0 00
	Payment of salaries expense in cash.			
(8)	Accounts Receivable	106	1 9 0 0 00	
	Consulting Revenue	403		1 6 0 0 00
	Rental Revenue	406		3 0 0 00
	Provide rental and consulting services on credit.			
(9)	Cash	101	1 9 0 0 00	
	Accounts Receivable	106		1 9 0 0 00
	Receipt of cash on account.			
(10)	Accounts Payable	201	9 0 0 00	
	Cash	101		9 0 0 00
	Payment of accounts payable (partial).			
(11)	C. Taylor, Withdrawals	302	2 0 0 00	
	Cash	101		2 0 0 00
	Withdrawal of cash by owner.			
(12)	Cash	101	3 0 0 0 00	
	Unearned Consulting Revenue	236		3 0 0 0 00
	Receipt of cash for future services.			
(13)	Prepaid Insurance	128	2 4 0 0 00	
	Cash	101		2 4 0 0 00
	Cash payment for future insurance coverage.			
(14)	Supplies	126	1 2 0 00	
	Cash	101		1 2 0 00
	Purchased supplies for cash.			
(15)	Utilities Expense	690	2 3 0 00	
	Cash	101		2 3 0 00
	Payment of utilities expense in cash.			
(16)	Salaries Expense	622	7 0 0 00	
	Cash	101		7 0 0 00
	Payment of salaries expense in cash.			

Exhibit 4.9

General Ledger for FastForward

Cash Account No. 101

Trans. (or Date)	PR	Debit	Credit	Balance
(1)	G1	30,000		30,000
(2)	G1		2,500	27,500
(3)	G1		26,000	1,500
(5)	G1	4,200		5,700
(6)	G1		1,000	4,700
(7)	G1		700	4,000
(9)	G1	1,900		5,900
(10)	G1		900	5,000
(11)	G1		200	4,800
(12)	G1	3,000		7,800
(13)	G1		2,400	5,400
(14)	G1		120	5,280
(15)	G1		230	5,050
(16)	G1		700	4,350

Accounts Receivable Account No. 106

Trans. (or Date)	PR	Debit	Credit	Balance
(8)	G1	1,900		1,900
(9)	G1		1,900	0

Supplies Account No. 126

Trans. (or Date)	PR	Debit	Credit	Balance
(2)	G1	2,500		2,500
(4)	G1	7,100		9,600
(14)	G1	120		9,720

Prepaid Insurance Account No. 128

Trans. (or Date)	PR	Debit	Credit	Balance
(13)	G1	2,400		2,400

Equipment Account No. 167

Trans. (or Date)	PR	Debit	Credit	Balance
(3)	G1	26,000		26,000

Accounts Payable Account No. 201

Trans. (or Date)	PR	Debit	Credit	Balance
(4)	G1		7,100	7,100
(10)	G1	900		6,200

Unearned Consulting Revenue Account No. 236

Trans. (or Date)	PR	Debit	Credit	Balance
(12)	G1		3,000	3,000

C. Taylor, Capital Account No. 301

Trans. (or Date)	PR	Debit	Credit	Balance
(1)	G1		30,000	30,000

C. Taylor, Withdrawals Account No. 302

Trans. (or Date)	PR	Debit	Credit	Balance
(11)	G1	200		200

Consulting Revenue Account No. 403

Trans. (or Date)	PR	Debit	Credit	Balance
(5)	G1		4,200	4,200
(8)	G1		1,600	5,800

Rental Revenue Account No. 406

Trans. (or Date)	PR	Debit	Credit	Balance
(8)	G1		300	300

Salaries Expense Account No. 622

Trans. (or Date)	PR	Debit	Credit	Balance
(7)	G1	700		700
(16)	G1	700		1,400

Rent Expense Account No. 640

Trans. (or Date)	PR	Debit	Credit	Balance
(6)	G1	1,000		1,000

Utilities Expense Account No. 690

Trans. (or Date)	PR	Debit	Credit	Balance
(15)	G1	230		230

Posting is automatic and immediate with accounting software.

Correcting Errors in the Journal and the Ledger

Errors sometimes occur in journal entries. When they occur, we must correct them. How we correct the error depends on whether it is discovered before or after the journal entry is posted.

If an error in a journal entry is discovered before the error is posted, it can be corrected in a manual system by drawing a line through the incorrect information. The correct information is written above it to create a record of change for the auditor. Many computerized systems allow the operator to replace the incorrect information directly.

LO5 Explain how to correct errors in the journal and ledger

If an error in a journal entry is not discovered until after it is posted, do not strike through both erroneous entries in the journal and ledger. Instead, correct this error by creating a *correcting entry* that removes the amount from the wrong account and records it to the correct account. As an example, suppose a $100 purchase of supplies is journalized with an incorrect debit to Equipment and a correct $100 credit to Cash, and then this incorrect entry is posted to the ledger. The Supplies ledger account balance is understated by $100, and the Equipment ledger account balance is overstated by $100. The correcting entry is: debit Supplies and credit Equipment (both for $100), as illustrated in Exhibits 4.10 and 4.11. The word "Correcting" is entered in the "Trans. (or Date)" column.

Exhibit 4.10

Correcting Journal Entry

GENERAL JOURNAL					
Transaction	**Account Titles and Explanation**	**PR**	**Debit**		**Credit**
2007 July 28	Supplies	126	1 0 0 00		
	Equipment	167			1 0 0 00
	To correct error where equipment was incorrectly debited.				

Exhibit 4.11

Effects of a Correcting Journal Entry on Ledger Accounts

Supplies				Account No. 126
Trans. (or Date)	PR	Debit	Credit	Balance
2007 July 28 Correcting	G1	100		100

Equipment				Account No. 167
Trans. (or Date)	PR	Debit	Credit	Balance
2007 July 15	G1	800		800
22	G1	100		900
28 Correcting	G1		100	800

HOW YOU DOIN'?   Answer—p. 88

5. Assume a $500 purchase of prepaid insurance is journalized with an incorrect debit to Supplies, and this incorrect entry is posted to the ledger. Prepare the correcting journal entry.

Demonstration Problem

(This problem extends the demonstration problem of Chapters 2 and 3.) After several months of planning, Jasmine Worthy started a haircutting business called Expressions. The following events occurred during its first month.

a. On August 1, Worthy invested $3,000 cash and $15,000 of equipment in Expressions.

b. On August 2, Expressions paid $600 cash for furniture for the shop.

c. On August 3, Expressions paid $500 cash to rent space in a strip mall for August.

d. On August 4, it purchased $1,200 of equipment on credit for the shop (using a long-term note payable).

e. On August 5, Expressions opened for business. Cash received from services provided in the first week and a half of business (ended August 15) is $825.

f. On August 15, it provided $100 of haircutting services on account.

g. On August 17, it received a $100 check for services previously rendered on account.

h. On August 17, it paid $125 to an assistant for working during the grand opening.

i. Cash received from services provided during the second half of August is $930.

j. On August 31, it paid a $400 installment toward principal on the note payable entered into on August 4.

k. On August 31, Worthy withdrew $900 cash for personal use.

Required

1. Open the following ledger accounts in balance column format (account numbers are in parentheses): Cash (101); Accounts Receivable (102); Furniture (161); Store Equipment (165); Note Payable (240); J. Worthy, Capital (301); J. Worthy, Withdrawals (302); Haircutting Services Revenue (403); Wages Expense (623); and Rent Expense (640). Prepare general journal entries for the transactions.

2. Post the journal entries from (1) to the ledger accounts.

3. Prepare a trial balance as of August 31.

Extended Analysis

4. In the coming months, Expressions will experience a greater variety of business transactions. Identify which accounts are debited and which are credited for the following transactions. (*Hint:* We must use some accounts not opened in part 1.)

   a. Purchase supplies with cash.

   b. Pay cash for future insurance coverage.

   c. Receive cash for services to be provided in the future.

   d. Purchase supplies on account.

Planning the Solution

- Analyze each transaction and use the debit and credit rules to prepare a journal entry for each.
- Post each debit and each credit from journal entries to their ledger accounts and cross-reference each amount in the posting reference (PR) columns of the journal and ledger.
- Calculate each account balance and list the accounts with their balances on a trial balance.
- Verify that total debits in the trial balance equal total credits.
- Analyze the future transactions to identify the accounts affected and apply debit and credit rules.

Solution to Demonstration Problem

1. General journal entries:

	GENERAL JOURNAL				Page 1
Date	**Account Titles and Explanation**	**PR**	**Debit**		**Credit**
2007 Aug. 1	Cash	101	30 0 0 00		
	Store Equipment	165	15 0 0 0 00		
	J. Worthy, Capital	301			18 0 0 0 00
	Owner's investment.				
2	Furniture	161	6 0 0 00		
	Cash	101			6 0 0 00
	Purchased furniture for cash.				
3	Rent Expense	640	5 0 0 00		
	Cash	101			5 0 0 00
	Paid rent for August.				
4	Store Equipment	165	1 2 0 0 00		
	Note Payable	240			1 2 0 0 00
	Purchased additional equipment on credit.				
15	Cash	101	8 2 5 00		
	Haircutting Services Revenue	403			8 2 5 00
	Cash receipts from first half of August.				
15	Accounts Receivable	102	1 0 0 00		
	Haircutting Services Revenue	403			1 0 0 00
	To record revenue for services provided on account.				

[continued on next page]

[continued from previous page]

	17	Cash		101	1 0 0 00		
		Accounts Receivable		102		1 0 0 00	
		To record cash received as payment on account.					
	17	Wages Expense		623	1 2 5 00		
		Cash		101		1 2 5 00	
		Paid wages to assistant.					
	31	Cash		101	9 3 0 00		
		Haircutting Services Revenue		403		9 3 0 00	
		Cash receipts from second half of August.					
	31	Note Payable		240	4 0 0 00		
		Cash		101		4 0 0 00	
		Paid an installment on the note payable.					
	31	J. Worthy, Withdrawals		302	9 0 0 00		
		Cash		101		9 0 0 00	
		Cash withdrawal by owner.					

2. Post journal entries from part 1 to the ledger accounts:

General Ledger

Cash   Account No. 101

Date	PR	Debit	Credit	Balance
Aug. 1	G1	3,000		3,000
2	G1		600	2,400
3	G1		500	1,900
15	G1	825		2,725
17	G1	100		2,825
17	G1		125	2,700
31	G1	930		3,630
31	G1		400	3,230
31	G1		900	2,330

Accounts Receivable   Account No. 102

Date	PR	Debit	Credit	Balance
Aug. 15	G1	100		100
17	G1		100	0

Furniture   Account No. 161

Date	PR	Debit	Credit	Balance
Aug. 2	G1	600		600

Store Equipment   Account No. 165

Date	PR	Debit	Credit	Balance
Aug. 1	G1	15,000		15,000
4	G1	1,200		16,200

Note Payable   Account No. 240

Date	PR	Debit	Credit	Balance
Aug. 4	G1		1,200	1,200
31	G1	400		800

J. Worthy, Capital   Account No. 301

Date	PR	Debit	Credit	Balance
Aug. 1	G1		18,000	18,000

J. Worthy, Withdrawals   Account No. 302

Date	PR	Debit	Credit	Balance
Aug. 31	G1	900		900

Haircutting Services Revenue   Account No. 403

Date	PR	Debit	Credit	Balance
Aug. 15	G1		825	825
15	G1		100	925
31	G1		930	1,855

Wages Expense   Account No. 623

Date	PR	Debit	Credit	Balance
Aug. 17	G1	125		125

Rent Expense   Account No. 640

Date	PR	Debit	Credit	Balance
Aug. 3	G1	500		500

3. Prepare a trial balance from the ledger:

EXPRESSIONS Trial Balance August 31	Debit	Credit
Cash	$ 2 3 3 0 00	
Accounts receivable	0 00	
Furniture	6 0 0 00	
Store equipment	16 2 0 0 00	
Note payable		$ 8 0 0 00
J. Worthy, Capital		18 0 0 0 00
J. Worthy, Withdrawals	9 0 0 00	
Haircutting services revenue		1 8 5 5 00
Wages expense	1 2 5 00	
Rent expense	5 0 0 00	
Totals	$20 6 5 5 00	$20 6 5 5 00

4a. Supplies *debited*
      Cash *credited*

4b. Prepaid Insurance *debited*
      Cash *credited*

4c. Cash *debited*
      Unearned Services Revenue *credited*

4d. Supplies *debited*
      Accounts Payable *credited*

Summary

LO1 **Explain the steps in processing transactions.** The accounting process identifies business transactions and events, analyzes and records their effects, and summarizes and prepares information useful in making decisions. Transactions and events are the starting points in the accounting process. Source documents help in their analysis. The effects of transactions and events are recorded in journals. Posting along with a trial balance helps summarize and classify these effects.

LO2 **Describe source documents and their purpose.** Source documents identify and describe transactions and events. Examples are sales tickets, checks, purchase orders, bills, and bank statements. Source documents provide objective and reliable evidence, making information more useful.

LO3 **Describe a chart of accounts.** The chart of accounts is a list of all accounts and usually includes an identification number assigned to each account.

LO4 **Record transactions in a journal and post entries to a ledger.** Transactions are recorded in a journal. Each entry in a journal is posted to the accounts in the ledger. This provides information that is used to produce financial statements. Balance column accounts are widely used and include columns for debits, credits, and the account balance.

LO5 **Explain how to correct errors in the journal and ledger.** If an error in a journal entry is discovered before the error is posted, it can be corrected by drawing a line through the incorrect information. If an error in a journal entry is not discovered until after it is posted, correct this error with a *correcting entry* that removes the amount from the erroneous accounts and records it to the correct accounts.

Guidance Answers to *YOU CALL IT*

Cashier The advantages to the process proposed by the assistant manager include improved customer service, fewer delays, and less work for you. However, you should have serious concerns about internal control and the potential for fraud. In particular, the assistant manager could steal cash and simply enter fewer sales to match the remaining cash. You should reject her suggestion without the manager's approval. Moreover, you should have an ethical concern about the assistant manager's suggestion to ignore store policy.

1. Examples of source documents are sales tickets, checks, purchase orders, charges to customers, bills from suppliers, employee earnings records, and bank statements.

2. Source documents serve many purposes, including record-keeping and internal control. Source documents, especially if obtained from outside the organization, provide objective and reliable evidence about transactions and their amounts.

3. A company's size and diversity affect the number of accounts in its accounting system. The types of accounts depend on information the company needs to both effectively operate and report its activities in financial statements.

4. A chart of accounts is a list of all of a company's accounts and their identification numbers.

5. The Supplies ledger account balance is overstated by $500 and the Prepaid Insurance ledger account balance is understated by $500. The correcting journal entry is: debit Prepaid Insurance and credit Supplies (both for $500).

Key Terms   mhhe.com/wildCA

Key Terms are available at the book's Website for learning and testing in an online Flashcard Format.

Balance column account (p. 80) Account with debit and credit columns for recording entries and another column for showing the balance of the account after each entry.

Chart of accounts (p. 78) List of accounts used by a company; includes an identification number for each account.

General journal (p. 79) All-purpose journal for recording the debits and credits of transactions and events.

Journal (p. 78) Record in which transactions are entered before they are posted to ledger accounts; also *book of original entry.*

Journalizing (p. 78) Process of recording transactions in a journal.

Ledger (p. 80) Record containing all accounts (with amounts) for a business; also called *general ledger.*

Posting (p. 79) Process of transferring journal entry information to a ledger; computerized systems automate this process.

Posting reference (PR) column (p. 80) A column in journals in which individual ledger account numbers are entered when entries are posted to those ledger accounts.

Source documents (p. 76) Source of information for accounting entries that can be in either paper or electronic form; also called *business papers.*

Multiple Choice Quiz   Answers on p. 97   mhhe.com/wildCA

Multiple Choice Quizzes A and B are available at the book's Website.

1. The process of transferring debits and credits from the journal to the ledger is called
 a. Transferring
 b. Posting
 c. Journalizing
 d. Referencing

2. Unearned revenue exists when customers pay in advance for products or services and is accounted for as a(n)
 a. Asset
 b. Revenue
 c. Expense
 d. Liability

3. Amalia Company received its utility bill for the current period of $700 and immediately paid it. Its journal entry to record this transaction includes a
 a. Credit to Utility Expense for $700.
 b. Debit to Utility Expense for $700.
 c. Debit to Accounts Payable for $700.
 d. Debit to Cash for $700.
 e. Credit to Capital for $700.

4. Liang Shue contributed $250,000 cash and land worth $500,000 to open his new business, Shue Consulting. Which of the following journal entries does Shue Consulting make to record this transaction?

a. Cash Assets $750,000
    L. Shue, Capital . . . $750,000
b. L. Shue, Capital $750,000
    Assets $750,000
c. Cash $250,000
    Land   500,000
    L. Shue, Capital . . . $750,000
d. L. Shue, Capital $750,000
    Cash $250,000
    Land   500,000

5. A trial balance prepared at year-end shows total credits exceed total debits by $765. This discrepancy could have been caused by
 a. An error in the general journal where a $765 increase in Accounts Payable was recorded as a $765 decrease in Accounts Payable.
 b. The ledger balance for Accounts Payable of $7,650 being entered in the trial balance as $765.
 c. A general journal error where a $765 increase in Accounts Receivable was recorded as a $765 increase in Cash.
 d. The ledger balance of $850 in Accounts Receivable was entered in the trial balance as $85.
 e. An error in recording a $765 increase in Cash as a credit.

Discussion Questions

1. Discuss the steps in processing business transactions.

2. What kinds of transactions can be recorded in a general journal?

3. Are debits or credits typically listed first in general journal entries? Are the debits or the credits indented?

4. Should a transaction be recorded first in a journal or the ledger? Why?

5. If an incorrect amount is journalized and posted to the accounts, how should the error be corrected?

6. Review the **Circuit City** balance sheet in Appendix A. Identify an asset with the word *receivable* in its account title and a liability with the word *payable* in its account title.

Identify the items from the following list that are likely to serve as source documents.

a. Sales ticket

b. Income statement

c. Trial balance

d. Telephone bill

e. Invoice from supplier

f. Company revenue account

g. Balance sheet

h. Prepaid insurance

i. Bank statement

QUICK STUDY

QS 4–1

Identifying source documents

(LO2)

Prepare journal entries for each of the following selected transactions.

a. On January 13, DeShawn Tyler opens a landscaping business called Elegant Lawns by investing $70,000 cash along with equipment having a $30,000 value.

b. On January 21, Elegant Lawns purchases office supplies on credit for $280.

c. On January 29, Elegant Lawns receives $7,800 cash for performing landscaping services.

d. On January 30, Elegant Lawns receives $1,000 cash in advance of providing landscaping services to a customer.

QS 4–2

Preparing journal entries

(LO4)

A trial balance has total debits of $20,000 and total credits of $24,500. Which one of the following errors would create this imbalance? Explain.

a. A $2,250 debit to Rent Expense in a journal entry is incorrectly posted to the ledger as a $2,250 credit, leaving the Rent Expense account with a $3,000 debit balance.

b. A $4,500 debit to Salaries Expense in a journal entry is incorrectly posted to the ledger as a $4,500 credit, leaving the Salaries Expense account with a $750 debit balance.

c. A $2,250 credit to Consulting Fees Earned in a journal entry is incorrectly posted to the ledger as a $2,250 debit, leaving the Consulting Fees Earned account with a $6,300 credit balance.

QS 4–3

Identifying a posting error

(LO4)

On August 4, 2008, a company incorrectly debits Rent Expense instead of Salaries Expense when recording payroll for the month. On August 30, the error is discovered while preparing the trial balance. Propose a correcting journal entry to correct the books. If the error had not been discovered, how would the company's income statement have been affected?

QS 4–4

Preparing a correcting journal entry

(LO5)

Goro Co. bills a client $62,000 for services provided and agrees to accept the following three items in full payment: (1) $10,000 cash, (2) computer equipment worth $80,000, and (3) assume responsibility for a $28,000 note payable related to the computer equipment. What journal entry should Goro make to record this transaction?

EXERCISES

Exercise 4–1

Analyzing effects of transactions on accounts

(LO1) (LO4)

Prepare general journal entries for the following transactions of a new business called Pose-for-Pics.

Aug. 1 Madison Harris, the owner, invested $6,500 cash and $33,500 of photography equipment in the business.

    2 Paid $2,100 cash for an insurance policy covering the next 24 months.

Exercise 4–2

Preparing general journal entries

(LO4)

5   Purchased office supplies for $880 cash.
20   Received $3,331 cash in photography fees earned.
29   Paid $675 cash for August utilities.

Exercise 4–3
Preparing T-accounts (ledger) and a trial balance
(LO4)

Use the information in Exercise 4-2 to prepare an August 31 trial balance for Pose-for-Pics. Open these T-accounts: Cash; Office Supplies; Prepaid Insurance; Photography Equipment; M. Harris, Capital; Photography Fees Earned; and Utilities Expense. Post the general journal entries to these T-accounts (which will serve as the ledger), and prepare a trial balance.

Exercise 4–4
Preparing an income statement
(LO1)

On October 1, Diondre Shabazz organized a new consulting firm called OnTech. On October 31, the company's records show the following items and amounts. Use this information to prepare an October income statement for the business.

Cash	$11,360		D. Shabazz, Withdrawals	$ 2,000
Accounts receivable	14,000		Consulting fees earned	14,000
Office supplies	3,250		Rent expense	3,550
Patents	46,000		Salaries expense	7,000
Office equipment	18,000		Telephone expense	760
Accounts payable	8,500		Miscellaneous expenses	580
D. Shabazz, Capital	84,000			

Check   Net income, $2,110

Exercise 4–5
Preparing a statement of owner's equity
(LO1)

Use the information in Exercise 4-4 to prepare an October statement of owner's equity for OnTech.

Exercise 4–6
Preparing a balance sheet
(LO1)

Use the information in Exercise 4-4 (if completed, you can also use your solution to Exercise 4-5) to prepare an October 31 balance sheet for OnTech.

Exercise 4–7
Preparing general journal entries
(LO4)

Assume the following T-accounts reflect Belle Co.'s general ledger and that seven transactions *a* through *g* are posted to them. Use information from the T-accounts to prepare general journal entries for each of the seven transactions (a) through (g). Provide a short description of each transaction.

Cash			
(a)	6,000	(b)	4,800
(e)	4,500	(c)	900
		(f)	1,600
		(g)	820

Office Supplies	
(c)	900
(d)	300

Prepaid Insurance	
(b)	4,800

Equipment	
(a)	7,600
(d)	9,700

Automobiles	
(a)	12,000

Accounts Payable			
(f)	1,600	(d)	10,000

D. Belle, Capital			
		(a)	25,600

Delivery Services Revenue			
		(e)	4,500

Gas and Oil Expense	
(g)	820

Aracel Engineering completed the following transactions in the month of June.

a. Jenna Aracel, the owner, invested $100,000 cash, office equipment with a value of $5,000, and $60,000 of drafting equipment to launch the business.

b. Purchased land worth $49,000 for an office by paying $6,300 cash and signing a long-term note payable for $42,700.

c. Purchased a portable building with $55,000 cash and moved it onto the land acquired in *b.*

d. Paid $3,000 cash for the premium on an 18-month insurance policy.

e. Completed and delivered a set of plans for a client and collected $6,200 cash.

f. Purchased $20,000 of additional drafting equipment by paying $9,500 cash and signing a long-term note payable for $10,500.

g. Completed $14,000 of engineering services for a client. This amount is to be received in 30 days.

h. Purchased $1,150 of additional office equipment on credit.

i. Completed engineering services for $22,000 on credit.

j. Received a bill for rent of equipment that was used on a recently completed job. The $1,333 rent cost must be paid within 30 days.

k. Collected $7,000 cash in partial payment from the client described in transaction *g.*

l. Paid $1,200 cash for wages to a drafting assistant.

m. Paid $1,150 cash to settle the account payable created in transaction *h.*

n. Paid $925 cash for minor repairs to its drafting equipment.

o. Jenna Aracel withdrew $9,480 cash for personal use.

p. Paid $1,200 cash for wages to a drafting assistant.

q. Paid $2,500 cash for advertisements in the local newspaper during June.

Required

1. Prepare general journal entries to record these transactions (use the account titles listed in part 2).

2. Open the following ledger accounts—their account numbers are in parentheses (use the balance column format): Cash (101); Accounts Receivable (106); Prepaid Insurance (108); Office Equipment (163); Drafting Equipment (164); Building (170); Land (172); Accounts Payable (201); Notes Payable (250); J. Aracel, Capital (301); J. Aracel, Withdrawals (302); Engineering Fees Earned (402); Wages Expense (601); Equipment Rental Expense (602); Advertising Expense (603); and Repairs Expense (604). Post the journal entries from part 1 to the accounts and enter the balance after each posting.

3. Prepare a trial balance as of the end of June.

PROBLEM SET A

Problem 4–1A
Preparing and posting journal entries; preparing a trial balance
(LO3) (LO4)

Check   (2) Ending balances: Cash, $22,945; Accounts Receivable, $29,000; Accounts Payable, $1,333

(3) Trial balance totals, $261,733

Kasey Reese opens a consulting business called Cougar Consulting and completes the following transactions in March.

March 1   Reese invested $150,000 cash along with $22,000 of office equipment in the business.

2   Prepaid $6,000 cash for six months' rent for an office. (*Hint:* Debit Prepaid Rent for $6,000.)

3   Made credit purchases of office equipment for $3,000 and office supplies for $1,200. Payment is due within 10 days.

6   Completed services for a client and immediately received $4,000 cash.

9   Completed a $7,500 project for a client, who must pay within 30 days.

12   Paid $4,200 cash to settle the account payable created on March 3.

19   Paid $5,000 cash for the premium on a 12-month insurance policy.

22   Received $3,500 cash as partial payment for the work completed on March 9.

25   Completed work for another client for $3,820 on credit.

29   Reese withdrew $5,100 cash for personal use.

30   Purchased $600 of additional office supplies on credit.

31   Paid $500 cash for this month's utility bill.

Required

1. Prepare general journal entries to record these transactions (use the account titles listed in part 2).

2. Open the following ledger accounts—their account numbers are in parentheses (use the balance column format): Cash (101); Accounts Receivable (106); Office Supplies (124); Prepaid Insurance (128);

Problem 4–2A
Preparing and posting journal entries; preparing a trial balance
(LO3) (LO4)

mhhe.com/wildCA

Check   (2) Ending balances: Cash, $136,700; Accounts Receivable, $7,820; Accounts Payable, $600

Prepaid Rent (131); Office Equipment (163); Accounts Payable (201); K. Reese, Capital (301); K. Reese, Withdrawals (302); Services Revenue (403); and Utilities Expense (690). Post the journal entries from part 1 to the ledger accounts and enter the balance after each posting.

(3) Total debits, $187,920

3. Prepare a trial balance as of the end of March.

Problem 4-3A

Preparing and posting journal entries; preparing a trial balance

(LO3) (LO4)

Bonnie Stradling opened a computer consulting business called Stradling Consultants and completed the following transactions in the first month of operations.

April 1   Bonnie invested $80,000 cash along with office equipment valued at $26,000 in the business.
      2   Prepaid $9,000 cash for 12 months' rent for office space. (*Hint:* Debit Prepaid Rent for $9,000.)
      3   Made credit purchases for $8,000 in office equipment and $3,600 in office supplies. Payment is due within 10 days.
      6   Completed services for a client and immediately received $4,000 cash.
      9   Completed a $6,000 project for a client, who must pay within 30 days.
   13   Paid $11,600 cash to settle the account payable created on April 3.
   19   Paid $2,400 cash for the premium on a 12-month insurance policy. (*Hint:* Debit Prepaid Insurance for $2,400.)
   22   Received $4,400 cash as partial payment for the work completed on April 9.
   25   Completed work for another client for $2,890 on credit.
   28   Bonnie withdrew $5,500 cash for personal use.
   29   Purchased $600 of additional office supplies on credit.
   30   Paid $435 cash for this month's utility bill.

Required

1. Prepare general journal entries to record these transactions (use the account titles listed in part 2).

Check (2) Ending balances: Cash, $59,465; Accounts Receivable, $4,490; Accounts Payable, $600

2. Open the following ledger accounts—their account numbers are in parentheses (use the balance column format): Cash (101); Accounts Receivable (106); Office Supplies (124); Prepaid Insurance (128); Prepaid Rent (131); Office Equipment (163); Accounts Payable (201); B. Stradling, Capital (301); B. Stradling, Withdrawals (302); Services Revenue (403); and Utilities Expense (690). Post journal entries from part 1 to the ledger accounts and enter the balance after each posting.

(3) Total debits, $119,490

3. Prepare a trial balance as of April 30.

Problem 4-4A

Recording transactions; posting to ledger; preparing a trial balance

(LO3) (LO4)

Business transactions completed by Hannah Venedict during the month of September are as follows.

a. Venedict invested $60,000 cash along with office equipment valued at $25,000 in her startup business named HV Consulting.

b. Purchased land valued at $40,000 and a building valued at $160,000. The purchase is paid with $30,000 cash and a long-term note payable for $170,000.

c. Purchased $2,000 of office supplies on credit.

d. Venedict invested her personal automobile in the business. The automobile has a value of $16,500 and is to be used exclusively in the business.

e. Purchased $5,600 of additional office equipment on credit.

f. Paid $1,800 cash salary to an assistant.

g. Provided services to a client and collected $8,000 cash.

h. Paid $635 cash for this month's utilities.

i. Paid $2,000 cash to settle the account payable created in transaction *c*.

j. Purchased $20,300 of new office equipment by paying $20,300 cash.

k. Completed $6,250 of services for a client, who must pay within 30 days.

l. Paid $1,800 cash salary to an assistant.

m. Received $4,000 cash on the receivable created in transaction *k*.

n. Venedict withdrew $2,800 cash for personal use.

Required

1. Prepare general journal entries to record these transactions (use account titles listed in part 2).

Check (2) Ending balances: Cash, $12,665; Office Equipment, $50,900

2. Open the following ledger accounts—their account numbers are in parentheses (use the balance column format): Cash (101); Accounts Receivable (106); Office Supplies (108); Office Equipment (163); Automobiles (164); Building (170); Land (172); Accounts Payable (201); Notes Payable (250); H. Venedict, Capital (301); H. Venedict, Withdrawals (302); Fees Earned (402); Salaries Expense

(601); and Utilities Expense (602). Post the journal entries from part 1 to the ledger accounts and enter the balance after each posting.

3. Prepare a trial balance as of the end of September.

(3) Trial balance totals, $291,350

After all journal entries have been posted, Levi Hancock finds that errors have been made in recording some company transactions. Help Levi prepare correcting journal entries for each of the following errors.

Problem 4–5A
Correcting errors with journal entries.

1. The following journal entry was made to record the purchase of supplies for $700 cash.

| Equipment | 700 | |
| Cash | | 700 |

2. The following journal entry was made to record the cash payment of $1,850 for prepaid rent.

| Prepaid Insurance | 1,850 | |
| Cash | | 1,850 |

3. The following journal entry was made to record the cash receipt of $2,000 for consulting services.

| Accounts Receivable | 2,000 | |
| Consulting Services Revenue | | 2,000 |

4. The following journal entry was made to record the cash payment of $1,375 for utilities expense.

| Utilities Expense | 1,375 | |
| Accounts Payable | | 1,375 |

~~~~~~

At the beginning of April, Bernadette Grechus launched a custom computer solutions company called Softworks. The company had the following transactions during April.

a. Bernadette Grechus invested $65,000 cash, office equipment with a value of $5,750, and $30,000 of computer equipment in the company.

b. Purchased land worth $22,000 for an office by paying $5,000 cash and signing a long-term note payable for $17,000.

c. Purchased a portable building with $34,500 cash and moved it onto the land acquired in *b*.

d. Paid $5,000 cash for the premium on a two-year insurance policy.

e. Provided services to a client and immediately collected $4,600 cash.

f. Purchased $4,500 of additional computer equipment by paying $800 cash and signing a long-term note payable for $3,700.

g. Completed $4,250 of services for a client. This amount is to be received within 30 days.

h. Purchased $950 of additional office equipment on credit.

i. Completed client services for $10,200 on credit.

j. Received a bill for rent of a computer testing device that was used on a recently completed job. The $580 rent cost must be paid within 30 days.

k. Collected $5,100 cash from the client described in transaction *i*.

l. Paid $1,800 cash for wages to an assistant.

m. Paid $950 cash to settle the payable created in transaction *h*.

n. Paid $608 cash for minor repairs to the company's computer equipment.

o. Grechus withdrew $6,230 cash for personal use.

p. Paid $1,800 cash for wages to an assistant.

q. Paid $750 cash for advertisements in the local newspaper during April.

PROBLEM SET B

Problem 4–1B
Preparing and posting journal entries; preparing a trial balance

Required

1. Prepare general journal entries to record these transactions (use account titles listed in part 2).

2. Open the following ledger accounts—their account numbers are in parentheses (use the balance column format): Cash (101); Accounts Receivable (106); Prepaid Insurance (108); Office Equipment (163); Computer Equipment (164); Building (170); Land (172); Accounts Payable (201); Notes

Check   (2) Ending balances: Cash, $17,262; Accounts Receivable, $9,350; Accounts Payable, $580

Payable (250); B. Grechus, Capital (301); B. Grechus, Withdrawals (302); Fees Earned (402); Wages Expense (601); Computer Rental Expense (602); Advertising Expense (603); and Repairs Expense (604). Post the journal entries from part 1 to the accounts and enter the balance after each posting.

(3) Trial balance totals, $141,080

3. Prepare a trial balance as of the end of April.

Problem 4-2B

Preparing and posting journal entries; preparing a trial balance

(L03) (L04)

Barry Wells Management Group opens for business and completes these transactions in November.

Nov. 1 Barry Wells, the owner, invested $30,000 cash along with $15,000 of office equipment in the business.
    2 Prepaid $4,500 cash for six months' rent for an office. (*Hint:* Debit Prepaid Rent for $4,500.)
    4 Made credit purchases of office equipment for $2,500 and of office supplies for $600. Payment is due within 10 days.
    8 Completed work for a client and immediately received $3,400 cash.
    12 Completed a $10,200 project for a client, who must pay within 30 days.
    13 Paid $3,100 cash to settle the payable created on November 4.
    19 Paid $1,800 cash for the premium on a 24-month insurance policy.
    22 Received $5,200 cash as partial payment for the work completed on November 12.
    24 Completed work for another client for $1,750 on credit.
    28 Barry Wells withdrew $5,300 cash for personal use.
    29 Purchased $249 of additional office supplies on credit.
    30 Paid $831 cash for this month's utility bill.

Required

1. Prepare general journal entries to record these transactions (use account titles listed in part 2).

Check (2) Ending balances: Cash, $23,069; Accounts Receivable, $6,750; Accounts Payable, $249

2. Open the following ledger accounts—their account numbers are in parentheses (use the balance column format): Cash (101); Accounts Receivable (106); Office Supplies (124); Prepaid Insurance (128); Prepaid Rent (131); Office Equipment (163); Accounts Payable (201); B. Wells, Capital (301); B. Wells, Withdrawals (302); Services Revenue (403); and Utilities Expense (690). Post the journal entries from part 1 to the ledger accounts and enter the balance after each posting.

(3) Total debits, $60,599

3. Prepare a trial balance as of the end of November.

Problem 4-3B

Preparing and posting journal entries; preparing a trial balance

(L03) (L04)

Kamilos Management Services opens for business and completes these transactions in September.

Sept. 1 Tom Kamilos, the owner, invests $38,000 cash along with office equipment valued at $15,000 in the business.
    2 Prepaid $9,000 cash for 12 months' rent for office space. (*Hint:* Debit Prepaid Rent for $9,000.)
    4 Made credit purchases for $8,000 in office equipment and $2,400 in office supplies. Payment is due within 10 days.
    8 Completed work for a client and immediately received $3,280 cash.
    12 Completed a $15,400 project for a client, who must pay within 30 days.
    13 Paid $10,400 cash to settle the payable created on September 4.
    19 Paid $1,900 cash for the premium on an 18-month insurance policy. (*Hint:* Debit Prepaid Insurance for $1,900.)
    22 Received $7,700 cash as partial payment for the work completed on September 12.
    24 Completed work for another client for $2,100 on credit.
    28 Tom Kamilos withdrew $5,300 cash for personal use.
    29 Purchased $550 of additional office supplies on credit.
    30 Paid $860 cash for this month's utility bill.

Required

1. Prepare general journal entries to record these transactions (use account titles listed in part 2).

Check (2) Ending balances: Cash, $21,520; Accounts Receivable, $9,800; Accounts Payable, $550

2. Open the following ledger accounts—their account numbers are in parentheses (use the balance column format): Cash (101); Accounts Receivable (106); Office Supplies (124); Prepaid Insurance (128); Prepaid Rent (131); Office Equipment (163); Accounts Payable (201); T. Kamilos, Capital (301); T. Kamilos, Withdrawals (302); Service Fees Earned (401); and Utilities Expense (690). Post journal entries from part 1 to the ledger accounts and enter the balance after each posting.

(3) Total debits, $74,330

3. Prepare a trial balance as of the end of September.

Nuncio Consulting completed the following transactions during June.

a. Armand Nuncio, the owner, invested $35,000 cash along with office equipment valued at $11,000 in the new business.

b. Purchased land valued at $7,500 and a building valued at $40,000. The purchase is paid with $15,000 cash and a long-term note payable for $32,500.

c. Purchased $500 of office supplies on credit.

d. Nuncio invested his personal automobile in the business. The automobile has a value of $8,000 and is to be used exclusively in the business.

e. Purchased $1,200 of additional office equipment on credit.

f. Paid $1,000 cash salary to an assistant.

g. Provided services to a client and collected $3,200 cash.

h. Paid $540 cash for this month's utilities.

i. Paid $500 cash to settle the payable created in transaction *c*.

j. Purchased $3,400 of new office equipment by paying $3,400 cash.

k. Completed $4,200 of services for a client, who must pay within 30 days.

l. Paid $1,000 cash salary to an assistant.

m. Received $2,200 cash on the receivable created in transaction *k*.

n. Armand Nuncio withdrew $1,100 cash for personal use.

Problem 4–4B
Recording transactions; posting to ledger; preparing a trial balance

Required

1. Prepare general journal entries to record these transactions (use account titles listed in part 2).

2. Open the following ledger accounts—their account numbers are in parentheses (use the balance column format): Cash (101); Accounts Receivable (106); Office Supplies (108); Office Equipment (163); Automobiles (164); Building (170); Land (172); Accounts Payable (201); Notes Payable (250); A. Nuncio, Capital (301); A. Nuncio, Withdrawals (302); Fees Earned (402); Salaries Expense (601); and Utilities Expense (602). Post the journal entries from part 1 to the ledger accounts and enter the balance after each posting.

3. Prepare a trial balance as of the end of June.

Check   (2) Ending balances: Cash, $17,860; Office Equipment, $15,600

(3) Trial balance totals, $95,100

After all journal entries have been posted, Kasey Beck finds that errors have been made in recording some company transactions. Help Kasey prepare correcting journal entries for each of the following errors.

1. The following journal entry was made to record the purchase of equipment for $1,450 cash.

| Supplies | 1,450 | |
| Cash | | 1,450 |

2. The following journal entry was made to record the cash purchase of $870 for prepaid rent.

| Rent Expense | 870 | |
| Cash | | 870 |

3. The following journal entry was made to record the cash payment of $1,780 for utilities expense.

| Salaries Expense | 1,780 | |
| Cash | | 1,780 |

4. The following journal entry was made to record $2,000 for consulting services on account.

| Cash | 2,000 | |
| Consulting Services Revenue | | 2,000 |

Problem 4–5B
Correcting errors with journal entries.
(L05)

SERIAL PROBLEM

Success Systems

(LO3)(LO4)

(This serial problem started in Chapter 1 and continues through most of the chapters. If previous chapter segments were not completed, the problem can begin at this point. It is helpful, but not necessary, to use the Working Papers that accompany this book.)

SP 4   On October 1, 2007, Adriana Lopez launched a computer services company called Success Systems, which provides consulting services, computer system installations, and custom program development. Lopez adopts the calendar year for reporting purposes and expects to prepare the company's first set of financial statements on December 31, 2007. The company's initial chart of accounts follows.

Account	No.	Account	No.
Cash	101	A. Lopez, Capital	301
Accounts Receivable	106	A. Lopez, Withdrawals	302
Computer Supplies	126	Computer Services Revenue	403
Prepaid Insurance	128	Wages Expense	623
Prepaid Rent	131	Advertising Expense	655
Office Equipment	163	Mileage Expense	676
Computer Equipment	167	Miscellaneous Expenses	677
Accounts Payable	201	Repairs Expense—Computer	684

Required

1. Prepare journal entries to record each of the following transactions for Success Systems.

Oct. 1   Lopez invested $75,000 cash, a $25,000 computer system, and $10,000 of office equipment in the business.
2   Paid $3,500 cash for four months' rent. (*Hint:* Debit Prepaid Rent for $3,500.)
3   Purchased $1,600 of computer supplies on credit from Corvina Office Products.
5   Paid $2,400 cash for one year's premium on a property and liability insurance policy. (*Hint:* Debit Prepaid Insurance for $2,400.)
6   Billed Easy Leasing $6,200 for services performed in installing a new Web server.
8   Paid $1,600 cash for the computer supplies purchased from Corvina Office Products on October 3.
10   Hired Michelle Jones as a part-time assistant for $150 per day, as needed.
12   Billed Easy Leasing another $1,950 for services performed.
15   Received $6,200 cash from Easy Leasing on its account.
17   Paid $900 cash to repair computer equipment that was damaged when moving it.
20   Paid $1,790 cash for an advertisement in the local newspaper.
22   Received $1,950 cash from Easy Leasing on its account.
28   Billed Clark Company $7,300 for services performed.
31   Paid $1,050 cash for Michelle Jones's wages for seven days' work.
31   Lopez withdrew $4,000 cash for personal use.
Nov. 1   Reimbursed Lopez in cash for business automobile mileage allowance (Lopez logged 1,200 miles at $0.32 per mile).
2   Received $3,600 cash from Edge Corporation for computer services performed.
5   Purchased computer supplies for $1,750 cash from Corvina Office Products.
8   Billed Gomez Co. $6,500 for services performed.
13   Received notification from Alex's Engineering Co. that Success Systems' bid of $7,000 for an upcoming project is accepted.
18   Received $5,000 cash from Clark Company as partial payment of the October 28 bill.
22   Donated $300 cash to the United Way in the company's name.
24   Completed work for Alex's Engineering Co. and sent it a bill for $7,000.
25   Sent another bill to Clark Company for the past-due amount of $2,300.
28   Reimbursed Lopez in cash for business automobile mileage (1,500 miles at $0.32 per mile).
30   Paid $2,100 cash for Michelle Jones's wages for 14 days' work.
30   Lopez withdrew $2,500 cash for personal use.

Check   (2) Cash, Nov. 30 bal., $68,996

(3) Trial bal. totals, $142,550

2. Open ledger accounts (in balance column format) and post the journal entries from part 1 to them.

3. Prepare a trial balance as of the end of November.

BTN 4-1 **Best Buy** sells consumer electronics in its retail outlets and from its online stores.

Required

Based on your understanding of Best Buy, identify at least four types of source documents that Best Buy would likely use in its operations.

REPORTING IN
ACTION
LO2

BTN 4-2 **Best Buy** and **Circuit City** sell consumer electronics in their retail outlets and online stores.

Required

1. Identify the major revenue and expense accounts you would expect to see reported by Best Buy and Circuit City (you might review their financial statements in Appendix A for general categories).
2. Do you expect any differences in major revenue and expense accounts between these two companies? Identify them, if any.

COMPARATIVE
ANALYSIS
LO3

BTN 4-3 Review the *You Call It* case from the first part of this chapter involving the cashier. The guidance answer suggests that you should not comply with the assistant manager's request.

Required

Propose and evaluate two other courses of action that you might consider, and explain why.

ETHICS CHALLENGE
LO2

BTN 4-4 Mark Ellingson is an aspiring entrepreneur and your friend. He is having difficulty understanding the link between the general journal and the general ledger.

Required

Write a half-page memorandum to Ellingson explaining how the general journal and the general ledger are linked to each other.

WORKPLACE
COMMUNICATION
LO4

BTN 4-5 **Quickbooks** is an accounting software program with both a general journal and general ledger. Access Quickbooks' Website (**QuickBooks.com**) and review the various Quickbooks' software programs to answer the following requirements.

Required

1. Which Quickbooks' program would be most appropriate for a small business? Which would be most appropriate for a large business?
2. Many of the examples given in this chapter assumed manual journal entries, where journal entries are recorded and then later posted. How would a computerized program be different? How would the correction of errors differ?

TAKING IT TO
THE NET
LO4 LO5

BTN 4-6 Refer to the chapter's opening feature about Katrina Markoff and her **Vosges Haut Chocolat** company.

Required

Using Exhibit 4.3 as a guide, what are some examples of accounts you would expect to see in the Vosges Haut Chocolat company?

ENTREPRENEURS
IN BUSINESS
LO3

ANSWERS TO MULTIPLE CHOICE QUIZ

1. b
2. d
3. b; debit Utility Expense for $700, and credit Cash for $700.

4. c; debit Cash for $250,000, debit Land for $500,000, and credit L. Shue, Capital for $750,000.
5. d

5

Chapter

A Look Back

Chapters 3 and 4 explained the analysis and recording of transactions. We showed how to apply and interpret company accounts, T-accounts, double-entry accounting, ledgers, postings, and trial balances.

A Look at This Chapter

This chapter introduces the use of a work sheet and the need to adjust accounts. Adjusting accounts is important for recognizing revenues and expenses in the proper period. We describe the adjusted trial balance and how it is used to prepare financial statements.

A Look Ahead

Chapter 6 highlights the completion of the accounting cycle. We explain the important final steps in the accounting process. These include closing procedures and the post-closing trial balance.

Adjusting Accounts and Preparing Financial Statements

LEARNING OBJECTIVES

LO 1 Prepare a work sheet and explain its usefulness.

LO 2 Prepare and explain adjusting entries.

LO 3 Explain and prepare an adjusted trial balance.

LO 4 Prepare financial statements from an adjusted trial balance.

LO 5 Compute profit margin and describe its use in analyzing company performance.

"I'm never content with what we've accomplished"—Nelson Gonzalez
(Alex Aguila on left)

Alienware Aims for Outer Limits

MIAMI—Alex Aguila and Nelson Gonzalez are demanding gamers. Frustrated by the limited power of available PCs, they started **Alienware (alienware.com)** to build computers optimized for game playing. "Everyone told us, 'This is insane,'" recalls Aguila. "We got laughed out of every bank in Miami."

Undaunted, Aguila and Gonzalez scraped together the little cash they had. "Alienware started with $10,000 and a prayer," says Aguila. Building their initial PCs in a garage, the young duo quickly developed a system to account for everything, including cash, inventory, payables, equipment, and sales. They also adopted the unearned revenue model of early PC-makers: First customers pay, and then you build. Thanks to a relentless focus on a neglected niche of hardcore gamers, and positive reviews in gaming magazines, Alienware's sales are soaring.

The unearned revenue model is a blessing for Aguila and Gonzalez. It means no bad debts on customer receivables because cash is received in advance. The model also means little inventory to support because parts are ordered as needed for production.

Although the no-inventory model works well for Alienware, Aguila readily admits, "It takes a strong management team to [run the model] effectively."

Aguila and Gonzalez continue to fine-tune their accounting system by adjusting accounts to correctly reflect company performance. They remain focused on measures of sales, income, assets, and growth. That type of attention allows the company to enjoy profitability and measured growth. But, says Gonzalez, "I have a strong suspicion that there are not too many hardcore gamers in our accounting department!"

Today, Aguila and Gonzalez say Alienware is the largest minority-owned U.S. computer maker. But they expect Alienware to continue to push the outer limits. "For me, running this company is like playing a computer game," says Gonzalez. "It feels great when you win but the next day you're back looking for a higher score, a faster time, more points, better magic."

[Sources: *Alienware Website*, January 2007; *Entrepreneur*, March 2005 and November 2003; *Wired*, August 2004; *Newsweek*, 2005]

The past few chapters showed how companies use accounting systems to collect information about *external* transactions. We also explained how journals, ledgers, and other tools are useful in preparing financial statements. This chapter describes the accounting process for producing useful information involving *internal* transactions. An important part of this process is adjusting account balances so that financial statements at the end of a reporting period reflect the effects of all transactions. We then explain the important steps in preparing financial statements.

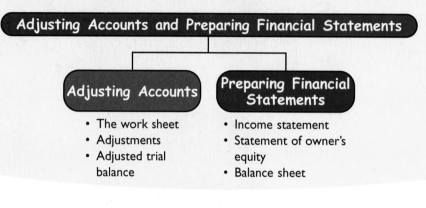

Adjusting Accounts and Preparing Financial Statements

Adjusting Accounts
- The work sheet
- Adjustments
- Adjusted trial balance

Preparing Financial Statements
- Income statement
- Statement of owner's equity
- Balance sheet

Adjusting Accounts

The Work Sheet

LO1 Prepare a work sheet and explain its usefulness.

Information preparers use internal documents to organize information for internal and external decision makers. Internal documents are often called **working papers.** One widely used working paper is the **work sheet.** The work sheet is used to gather all accounting information in one place, to record adjustments, and to aid in the preparation of financial statements. The work sheet also reduces the possibility of errors when working with many accounts.

Exhibit 5.1 presents an example of a work sheet. A typical work sheet has 10 columns for numbers, with two columns each for the unadjusted trial balance, the adjustments, the adjusted trial balance, the income statement, the balance sheet, and the statement of owner's equity. It also includes a column for account titles and account numbers.

To prepare the work sheet, we enter the account numbers and account names in the far left columns. We then get the account balances from the general ledger and check to make sure that the debits equal the credits. This is done by comparing the total debits and credits in the Unadjusted Trial Balance columns. Exhibit 5.1 reflects FastForward's trial balance from Chapter 3 (see also Exhibit 3.8). This work sheet also includes a few account names and balances that we expect to arise from the adjusting entries that will be presented in the next section.

Adjustments

LO2 Prepare and explain adjusting entries.

The process of adjusting accounts involves analyzing each account balance and the transactions that affect it to determine any needed adjustments. Adjustments are considered internal transactions because they do not involve outside parties. An **adjusting entry** is recorded to bring an asset or liability account balance to its proper amount. This entry also updates a related expense or revenue account.

Making adjustments (or adjusting entries) is a three-step process.

1. Determine the current account balance.
2. Determine what the current account balance should be.
3. Record the adjusting journal entry to get from step 1 to step 2.

We highlight two types of adjustments in this chapter: prepaid expenses and accrued expenses.

Exhibit 5.1

Ten-Column Work Sheet with Unadjusted Trial Balance

File Edit View Insert Format Tools Data Window Help

FastForward
Work Sheet
For Month Ended December 31, 2007

No.	Account	Unadjusted Trial Balance Dr.	Cr.	Adjustments Dr.	Cr.	Adjusted Trial Balance Dr.	Cr.	Income Statement Dr.	Cr.	Balance Sheet & Statement of Owner's Equity Dr.	Cr.
101	Cash	4,350									
126	Supplies	9,720									
128	Prepaid insurance	2,400									
167	Equipment	26,000									
168	Accumulated depreciation—Equip.		0								
201	Accounts payable		6,200								
209	Salaries payable		0								
236	Unearned consulting revenue		3,000								
301	C. Taylor, Capital		30,000								
302	C. Taylor, Withdrawals	200									
403	Consulting revenue		5,800								
406	Rental revenue		300								
612	Depreciation expense—Equip.	0									
622	Salaries expense	1,400									
637	Insurance expense	0									
640	Rent expense	1,000									
652	Supplies expense	0									
690	Utilities expense	230									
	Totals	45,300	45,300								

Sheet1 Sheet2 Sheet3

List all accounts from the ledger and those expected to arise from adjusting entries.

Enter all amounts available from ledger accounts. Column totals must be equal.

A work sheet collects and summarizes information used to prepare adjusting entries and financial statements.

Prepaid Expenses

Prepaid expenses refer to items *paid for* in advance of receiving their benefits. Prepaid expenses are assets. When these assets are used, their costs become expenses. Adjusting entries for prepaid items increase expenses and decrease assets as shown in the T-accounts of Exhibit 5.2. Such adjustments reflect transactions and events that use up prepaid expenses (including passage of time). To illustrate the accounting for prepaid expenses, this section focuses on prepaid insurance, supplies, and depreciation.

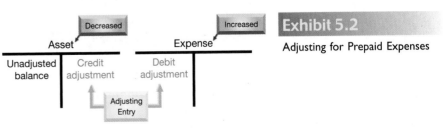

Exhibit 5.2

Adjusting for Prepaid Expenses

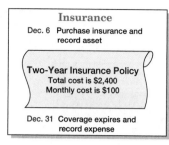

Insurance

Dec. 6 Purchase insurance and record asset

Two-Year Insurance Policy
Total cost is $2,400
Monthly cost is $100

Dec. 31 Coverage expires and record expense

Prepaid Insurance We illustrate prepaid insurance using FastForward's payment of $2,400 for 24 months of insurance benefits beginning on December 1, 2007. With the passage of time, the benefits of the insurance gradually expire and a portion of the Prepaid Insurance asset becomes expense. For instance, one month's insurance coverage expires by December 31, 2007. This expense is $100, computed as ($2,400 ÷ 24 months) × 1 month used. Then, we use our three-step process for adjusting journal entries.

1. Determine current account balances: Prepaid Insurance is $2,400 and Insurance Expense is $0.
2. Determine what the current account balances should be: Since $100 of insurance coverage has elapsed, Insurance Expense should be $100 and Prepaid Insurance should be $2,300.
3. Record the journal entry to get from step 1 to step 2.

The adjusting entry to record this expense and reduce the asset, along with T-account postings, follows:

Assets = Liabilities + Equity
−100   −100

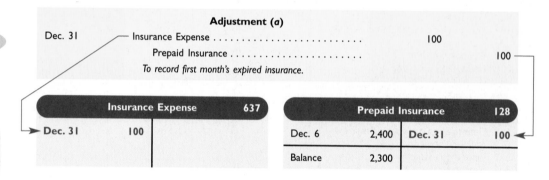

Adjustment (a)

Dec. 31	Insurance Expense	100	
	Prepaid Insurance		100
	To record first month's expired insurance.		

Insurance Expense	637
Dec. 31	100

Prepaid Insurance		128
Dec. 6	2,400	Dec. 31	100
Balance	2,300	

Many companies record adjusting entries only at the end of each year because of the time and cost necessary.

After adjusting and posting, the $100 balance in Insurance Expense and the $2,300 balance in Prepaid Insurance are ready for reporting in financial statements.

Supplies Supplies are a prepaid expense requiring adjustment. To illustrate, FastForward purchased $9,720 of supplies in December and used some of them. When financial statements are prepared at December 31, the cost of supplies used during December must be recognized. When FastForward computes (takes a physical count of) its remaining unused supplies at December 31, it finds $8,670 of supplies remaining of the $9,720 total supplies originally purchased. The $1,050 difference between these two amounts is December's supplies expense. Use our three-step process for adjusting journal entries:

1. Determine the current account balances: Supplies is $9,720 and Supplies Expense is $0.
2. Determine what the current account balances should be: Since $8,670 of supplies remain, the supplies balance should be $8,670. Since $1,050 of supplies have been used up ($9,720 − $8,670), the supplies expense should be $1,050.
3. Record the journal entry to get from step 1 to step 2.

Supplies

Dec. 2,6,26 Purchase supplies and record asset

Dec. 31 Supplies used and record expense

The adjusting entry to record this expense and reduce the Supplies asset account, along with T-account postings, follows:

Assets = Liabilities + Equity
−1,050   −1,050

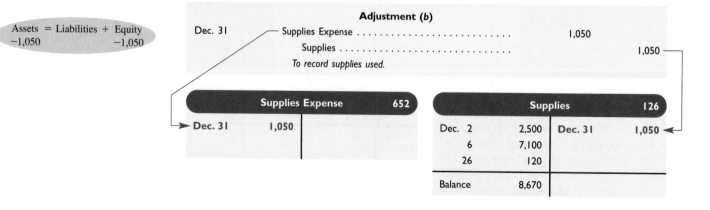

Adjustment (b)

Dec. 31	Supplies Expense	1,050	
	Supplies		1,050
	To record supplies used.		

Supplies Expense	652
Dec. 31	1,050

Supplies		126
Dec. 2	2,500	Dec. 31	1,050
6	7,100		
26	120		
Balance	8,670		

The balance of the Supplies account is $8,670 after posting—equaling the cost of the remaining supplies.

Depreciation A special category of prepaid expenses is **plant assets,** which refers to long-term tangible assets used to produce and sell products and services. Plant assets are expected to provide benefits for more than one period. Examples of plant assets are buildings, machines, vehicles, and fixtures. All plant assets, with the exception of land, eventually wear out or decline in usefulness. The estimated costs of using these assets are gradually reported as expenses in the income statement over the assets' useful lives (benefit periods). **Depreciation** is the process of spreading the costs of these assets over their expected useful lives. Depreciation expense is recorded with an adjusting entry similar to that for other prepaid expenses.

> **YOU CALL IT**   Answer—p. 112
>
> **Investor** A small publishing company signs a well-known athlete to write a book. The company pays the athlete $500,000 to sign plus future book royalties. A note to the company's financial statements says that "prepaid expenses include $500,000 in author signing fees to be matched against future expected sales." Is this accounting for the signing bonus acceptable? How does it affect your analysis?

To illustrate, recall that FastForward purchased equipment for $26,000 in early December to use in earning revenue. This equipment's cost must be depreciated. The equipment is expected to have a useful life (benefit period) of four years and to be worth about $8,000 at the end of four years. This $8,000 is called salvage value. This means the *net* cost of this equipment over its useful life is $18,000 ($26,000 − $8,000). We can use any of several methods to allocate this $18,000 net cost to expense. FastForward uses a method called **straight-line depreciation,** which debits equal amounts of an asset's net cost to depreciation expense during its useful life. Dividing the $18,000 net cost by the 48 months in the asset's useful life gives a monthly cost of $375 ($18,000/48). Use our three-step process for adjusting journal entries:

An asset's expected value at the end of its useful life is called salvage value.

1. Determine current account balances: Depreciation Expense is $0 and Equipment is $26,000.
2. Determine what the current account balances should be: Since the equipment has been used for one month out of an estimated 48 total months of useful life, $375 of the equipment needs to be depreciated. Depreciation Expense should be $375 and Accumulated Depreciation—Equipment (a balance sheet contra account) should be $375.
3. Record the journal entry to get from step 1 to step 2.

The adjusting entry to record monthly depreciation expense, along with T-account postings, follows:

Depreciation
Dec. 3 Purchase equipment and record asset
Dec. 31 Allocate asset cost and record depreciation

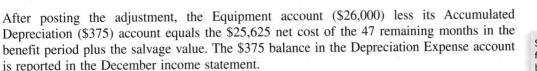

Adjustment (c)

Dec. 31 Depreciation Expense......................... 375
              Accumulated Depreciation—Equipment 375
              To record monthly equipment depreciation.

Assets = Liabilities + Equity
−375   −375

Depreciation Expense—Equipment	612		Equipment	167		Accumulated Depreciation—Equipment	168
Dec. 31 375			Dec. 3 26,000				Dec. 31 375

After posting the adjustment, the Equipment account ($26,000) less its Accumulated Depreciation ($375) account equals the $25,625 net cost of the 47 remaining months in the benefit period plus the salvage value. The $375 balance in the Depreciation Expense account is reported in the December income statement.

Accumulated depreciation is kept in a separate contra account, not in the Equipment account. A **contra account** is an account linked with another account. Its normal balance is opposite of, and it is reported as a subtraction from, that other account's balance.

Source documents provide information for most daily transactions, and in many businesses the recordkeepers record them. Adjustments require more knowledge and are usually handled by senior accounting professionals.

YOU CALL IT   Answer—p. 112

Entrepreneur You are preparing an offer to purchase a family-run restaurant. The depreciation schedule for the restaurant's building and equipment shows costs of $175,000 and accumulated depreciation of $155,000. This leaves a net for building and equipment of $20,000. Is this information useful in helping you decide on a purchase offer?

A contra account allows balance sheet readers to know both the full costs of assets and the total amount of depreciation. By knowing both these amounts, decision makers can better assess a company's capacity and its need to replace assets. For example, FastForward's December 31 balance sheet shows both the $26,000 original cost of equipment and the $375 balance in the accumulated depreciation contra account. This information reveals that the equipment is close to new. If FastForward reports equipment only at its net amount of $25,625, users cannot assess the equipment's age or its need for replacement. The title of the contra account, *Accumulated Depreciation,* indicates that this account includes total depreciation expense for all prior periods for which the asset was used. To illustrate how Accumulated Depreciation increases as the asset's useful life expires, the Equipment and the Accumulated Depreciation accounts appear as in Exhibit 5.3 on February 29, 2008, after three months of adjusting entries.

Exhibit 5.3

Accounts after Three Months of Depreciation Adjustments

Equipment		167
Dec. 3	26,000	

Accumulated Depreciation—Equipment		168
	Dec. 31	375
	Jan. 31	375
	Feb. 29	375
	Balance	1,125

The net cost of equipment is also called the *depreciable basis.*

The $1,125 balance in the accumulated depreciation account is subtracted from its related $26,000 asset cost. The difference ($24,875) between these two balances is the cost of the asset that has not yet been depreciated. This difference is called the **book value,** or *net amount,* which equals the asset's cost less its accumulated depreciation. These account balances are reported in the assets section of FastForward's February 29 balance sheet in Exhibit 5.4.

Exhibit 5.4

Equipment and Accumulated Depreciation on February 29 Balance Sheet

Assets		
Cash		$ ___
⋮		
Equipment	$26,000	
Less accumulated depreciation	1,125	24,875
Total Assets		$ ___

Commonly titled *Equipment, net*

Exhibit 5.5

Adjusting for Accrued Expenses

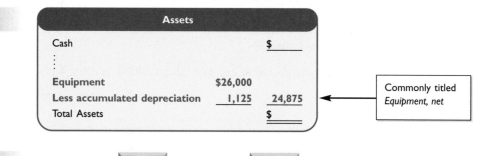

Accrued Expenses

Accrued expenses refer to costs that are incurred in a period but are both unpaid and unrecorded at the end of the period. Accrued expenses must be reported on the income statement of the period when incurred. Adjusting entries for recording accrued expenses involves increasing expenses and increasing liabilities as shown in Exhibit 5.5. This adjustment recognizes expenses incurred in a period but not yet paid. Common examples of accrued expenses are salaries, interest, rent, and taxes. We use salaries and interest to show how to adjust accounts for accrued expenses.

Accrued expenses are also called *accrued liabilities.*

Accrued Salaries Expense FastForward's employee earns $70 per day, or $350 for a five-day workweek beginning on Monday and ending on Friday. This employee is paid every two weeks on Friday. On December 12 and 26, the wages are paid, recorded in the journal, and posted to the ledger. The calendar in Exhibit 5.6 shows three working days occur after the

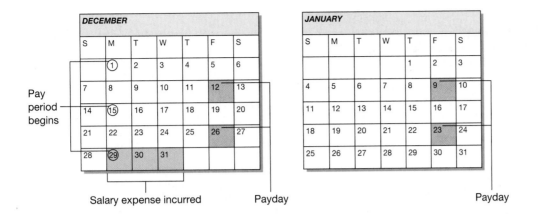

Pay period begins

Salary expense incurred   Payday   Payday

Exhibit 5.6

Salary Accrual and Paydays

December 26 payday (December 29, 30, and 31) and before the end of the month. This means the employee has earned three days' salary by the close of business on Wednesday, December 31, yet this salary cost is not paid or recorded. The financial statements would be incomplete if FastForward fails to report the added expense and liability to the employee for unpaid salary from December 29–31. Use our three-step process for adjusting journal entries:

1. Determine the current account balances: Salaries Expense is currently $1,400 ($70 per day × 20 days) and Salaries Payable is currently $0.
2. Determine what the current account balances should be: Since three days (December 29–31) have been worked by FastForward's employee, Salaries Expense should be $1,610 ($1,400 + $210 additional expense) and Salaries Payable should be $210 to reflect that three days of the salary has not yet been paid.
3. Record the journal entry to get from step 1 to step 2.

The adjusting entry to account for accrued salaries, along with T-account postings, follows:

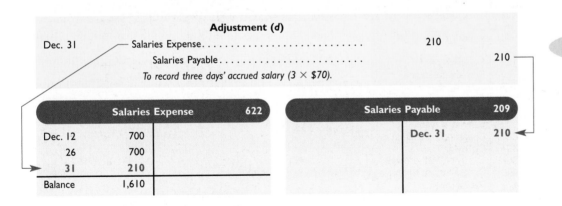

Assets = Liabilities + Equity
        +210   −210

Accrued Interest Expense   Companies commonly have accrued interest expense on notes payable and other long-term liabilities at the end of a period. Interest expense is incurred with the passage of time. Unless interest is paid on the last day of an accounting period, we need to adjust for interest expense incurred but not yet paid. This means we must *accrue* (record) interest cost from the most recent payment date up to the end of the period. The formula for computing accrued interest is:

Principal amount owed × Annual interest rate × Fraction of year since last payment date.

To illustrate, if a company has a $6,000 loan from a bank at 6% annual interest, then 30 days' accrued interest expense is $30—computed as $6,000 × 0.06 × 30/360. The adjusting entry would be to debit Interest Expense for $30 and credit Interest Payable for $30.

Interest computations assume a 360-day year.

 In this chapter, we have considered two types of adjustments: Prepaid Expenses and Accrued Expenses. In Chapter 13 we will also explain two additional types of adjustments: Unearned Revenues and Accrued Revenues.

HOW YOU DOIN'?   Answers—p. 112

1. Why is a work sheet used?

2. What is a contra account? Explain its purpose.

3. What is an accrued expense? Give an example.

4. Describe how a prepaid expense arises. Give an example.

Adjusted Trial Balance

LO3 Explain and prepare an adjusted trial balance.

An **unadjusted trial balance** is a list of accounts and balances prepared *before* adjustments are recorded. An **adjusted trial balance** is a list of accounts and balances prepared *after* adjusting entries have been recorded and posted to the ledger.

Exhibit 5.7 shows both the unadjusted and the adjusted trial balances for FastForward at December 31, 2007. The order of accounts in the trial balance is usually set up to match the order in the chart of accounts. Several new accounts arise from the adjusting entries. Each adjustment (see middle columns) is identified by a letter in parentheses that links it to an adjusting entry explained earlier. Each amount in the Adjusted Trial Balance columns is computed by taking that account's amount from the Unadjusted Trial Balance columns and adding or subtracting any adjustment(s). To illustrate, Supplies has a $9,720 Dr. balance in the unadjusted columns. Subtracting the $1,050 Cr. amount shown in the adjustments columns yields an adjusted $8,670 Dr. balance for Supplies. Not all accounts require adjustment each period, so their accounts have blanks in the adjustments columns.

Exhibit 5.7

Unadjusted and Adjusted Trial Balances

C. Taylor, Capital balance is not updated in the adjusted trial balance.

File Edit View Insert Format Tools Data Accounting Window Help

FASTFORWARD
Trial Balances
December 31, 2007

Acct. No.	Account Title	Unadjusted Trial Balance Dr.	Cr.	Adjustments Dr.	Cr.	Adjusted Trial Balance Dr.	Cr.
101	Cash	$ 4,350				$ 4,350	
126	Supplies	9,720			(b) $1,050	8,670	
128	Prepaid insurance	2,400			(a) 100	2,300	
167	Equipment	26,000				26,000	
168	Accumulated depreciation—Equip.		$ 0		(c) 375		$ 375
201	Accounts payable		6,200				6,200
209	Salaries payable		0		(d) 210		210
236	Unearned consulting revenue		3,000				3,000
301	C. Taylor, Capital		30,000				30,000
302	C. Taylor, Withdrawals	200				200	
403	Consulting revenue		5,800				5,800
406	Rental revenue		300				300
612	Depreciation expense—Equip.	0		(c) 375		375	
622	Salaries expense	1,400		(d) 210		1,610	
637	Insurance expense	0		(a) 100		100	
640	Rent expense	1,000				1,000	
652	Supplies expense	0		(b) 1,050		1,050	
690	Utilities expense	230				230	
	Totals	$45,300	$45,300	$1,735	$1,735	$45,885	$45,885

Sheet1 / Sheet2 / Sheet3 /

Preparing Financial Statements

LO4 Prepare financial statements from an adjusted trial balance.

We prepare financial statements directly from information in the *adjusted* trial balance. An adjusted trial balance (see the right-most columns in Exhibit 5.7) includes all accounts and balances appearing in financial statements and is easier to work from than the entire ledger when preparing financial statements.

Exhibit 5.8 shows how revenue and expense balances are transferred from the adjusted trial balance to the income statement (red lines). The net income and the withdrawals amount are then used to prepare the statement of owner's equity (black lines). Asset and liability balances on the adjusted trial balance are then transferred to the balance sheet (blue lines). The ending capital is determined on the statement of owner's equity and transferred to the balance sheet (green line). The ending capital balance is computed; it *does not* come from the adjusted trial balance.

We usually prepare financial statements in the following order: income statement, statement of owner's equity, and balance sheet. This order makes sense since the balance sheet uses information from the statement of owner's equity, which in turn uses information from the income statement.

Exhibit 5.8

Preparing Financial Statements (Adjusted Trial Balance from Exhibit 5.7)

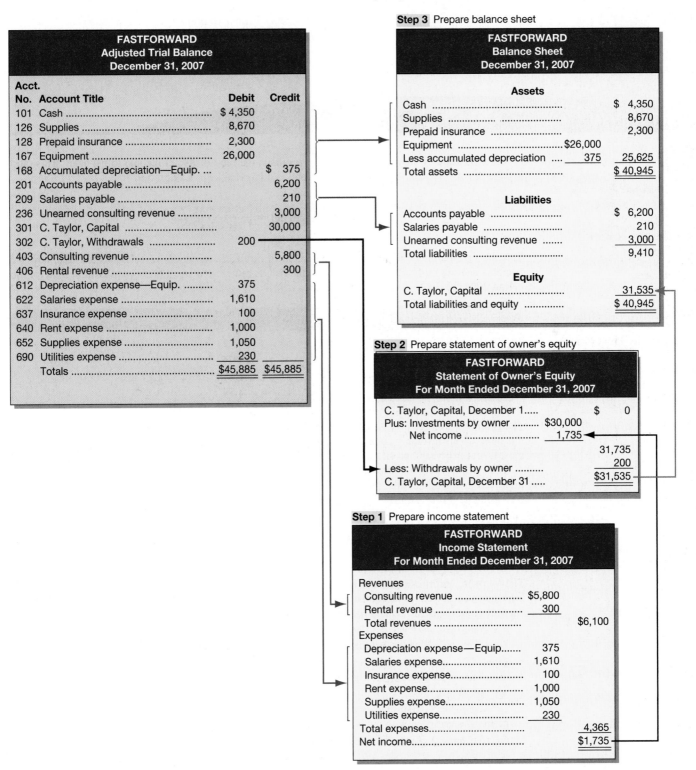

FASTFORWARD
Adjusted Trial Balance
December 31, 2007

Acct. No.	Account Title	Debit	Credit
101	Cash	$ 4,350	
126	Supplies	8,670	
128	Prepaid insurance	2,300	
167	Equipment	26,000	
168	Accumulated depreciation—Equip.		$ 375
201	Accounts payable		6,200
209	Salaries payable		210
236	Unearned consulting revenue		3,000
301	C. Taylor, Capital		30,000
302	C. Taylor, Withdrawals	200	
403	Consulting revenue		5,800
406	Rental revenue		300
612	Depreciation expense—Equip.	375	
622	Salaries expense	1,610	
637	Insurance expense	100	
640	Rent expense	1,000	
652	Supplies expense	1,050	
690	Utilities expense	230	
	Totals	$45,885	$45,885

Step 3 Prepare balance sheet

FASTFORWARD
Balance Sheet
December 31, 2007

Assets

Cash		$ 4,350
Supplies		8,670
Prepaid insurance		2,300
Equipment	$26,000	
Less accumulated depreciation	375	25,625
Total assets		$ 40,945

Liabilities

Accounts payable	$ 6,200
Salaries payable	210
Unearned consulting revenue	3,000
Total liabilities	9,410

Equity

C. Taylor, Capital	31,535
Total liabilities and equity	$ 40,945

Step 2 Prepare statement of owner's equity

FASTFORWARD
Statement of Owner's Equity
For Month Ended December 31, 2007

C. Taylor, Capital, December 1		$ 0
Plus: Investments by owner	$30,000	
Net income	1,735	
		31,735
Less: Withdrawals by owner		200
C. Taylor, Capital, December 31		$31,535

Step 1 Prepare income statement

FASTFORWARD
Income Statement
For Month Ended December 31, 2007

Revenues		
Consulting revenue	$5,800	
Rental revenue	300	
Total revenues		$6,100
Expenses		
Depreciation expense—Equip.	375	
Salaries expense	1,610	
Insurance expense	100	
Rent expense	1,000	
Supplies expense	1,050	
Utilities expense	230	
Total expenses		4,365
Net income		$1,735

Sarbanes-Oxley Act requires that financial statements filed with the SEC be certified by the CEO and CFO, including a declaration that the statements fairly present the issuer's operations and financial condition. Violators can receive a $5,000,000 fine and/or up to 20 years imprisonment.

HOW YOU DOIN'?

Answers—p. 112

5. Jordan Air has the following information in its unadjusted and adjusted trial balances.

	Unadjusted		Adjusted	
	Debit	Credit	Debit	Credit
Prepaid insurance	$6,200		$5,900	
Salaries payable		$ 0		$1,400

What are the adjusting entries that Jordan Air likely recorded?

6. What accounts are taken from the adjusted trial balance to prepare an income statement?

7. In preparing financial statements from an adjusted trial balance, what statement is usually prepared second?

PROFIT MARGIN

LO5 Compute profit margin and describe its use in analyzing company performance.

A useful measure of a company's operating results is the ratio of its net income to net sales. This ratio is called **profit margin**, or *return on sales,* and is computed as in Exhibit 5.9.

$$\text{Profit margin} = \frac{\text{Net income}}{\text{Net sales}}$$

Exhibit 5.9

Profit Margin

This ratio is interpreted as reflecting the percent of profit in each dollar of sales. To illustrate how we compute and use profit margin, let's look at the results of **Limited Brands, Inc.,** in Exhibit 5.10 for the period 2002–2005.

Exhibit 5.10

Limited Brands' Profit Margin

	2005	2004	2003	2002
Net income (in mil.)	$ 705	$ 717	$ 502	$ 519
Net sales (in mil.)	$9,408	$8,934	$8,445	$8,423
Profit margin	7.5%	8.0%	5.9%	6.2%
Industry profit margin	1.4%	1.5%	1.7%	1.5%

The Limited's average profit margin is 6.9%, computed as (7.5% + 8.8% + 5.9% + 6.2%)/4, during this period. This favorably compares to the average industry profit margin of 1.5%. Moreover, Limited's most recent two years' profit margins are markedly better than the earlier two years.

Thus, while 2003 was less successful in generating profits on its sales, Limited's performance has improved in 2004 and 2005. Future success, of course, depends on Limited maintaining and preferably increasing its profit margin.

Demonstration Problem 1

The following information relates to Fanning's Electronics on December 31, 2008. The company, which uses the calendar year as its annual reporting period, initially records prepaid and unearned items in balance sheet accounts (assets and liabilities, respectively).

a. The company's weekly payroll is $8,750, paid each Friday for a five-day workweek. Assume December 31, 2008, falls on a Monday, but the employees will not be paid their wages until Friday, January 4, 2009.

b. Eighteen months earlier, on July 1, 2007, the company purchased equipment that cost $20,000. Its useful life is predicted to be five years, at which time the equipment is expected to be worthless (zero salvage value).

c. On September 1, 2008, the company purchased a 12-month insurance policy for $1,800. The transaction was recorded with an $1,800 debit to Prepaid Insurance.

d. On December 2, 2008, the company receives a $20,000 loan from a bank at 12% annual interest.

Required

1. Prepare any necessary adjusting entries on December 31, 2008, in relation to transactions and events *a* through *d*.
2. Prepare T-accounts for the accounts affected by adjusting entries, and post the adjusting entries. Determine the adjusted balance for the Prepaid Insurance account.

Planning the Solution

- Analyze each situation to determine which accounts need to be updated with an adjustment.
- Use the three-step process to compute the amount of each adjustment and prepare the necessary journal entries.
- Show the amount of each adjustment in the designated accounts and determine the adjusted balance.

Solution to Demonstration Problem 1

1. Adjusting journal entries.

(a)	Dec.	31	Wages Expense	1 7 5 0 00	
			Wages Payable		1 7 5 0 00
			To accrue wages for the last day of the year		
			($8,750 × 1/5).		
(b)	Dec.	31	Depreciation Expense—Equipment	4 0 0 0 00	
			Accumulated Depreciation—Equipment		4 0 0 0 00
			To record depreciation expense for the year		
			($20,000/5 years).		
(c)	Dec.	31	Insurance Expense	6 0 0 00	
			Prepaid Insurance		6 0 0 00
			To adjust for expired portion of insurance		
			($1,800 × 4/12).		
(d)	Dec.	31	Interest Expense	2 0 0 00	
			Interest Payable		2 0 0 00
			To record accrued interest		
			($20,000 × 0.12 × 30/360).		

2. T-accounts for adjusting journal entries *a* through *d*.

Wages Expense			Interest Payable	
(a)	1,750		(d)	200

Depreciation Expense—Equipment			Wages Payable	
(b)	4,000		(a)	1,750

Interest Expense			Accumulated Depreciation—Equipment	
(d)	200		(b)	4,000

Insurance Expense			Prepaid Insurance	
(c)	600		Unadj. Bal.	1,800	(c)	600
			Adj. Bal.	1,200		

Demonstration Problem 2

Use the following adjusted trial balance to answer questions 1 through 3.

CHOI COMPANY Adjusted Trial Balance December 31	Debit	Credit
Cash	$ 3 0 5 0 00	
Accounts receivable	4 0 0 00	
Prepaid insurance	8 3 0 00	
Supplies	8 0 00	
Equipment	217 2 0 0 00	
Accumulated depreciation—Equipment		$ 29 1 0 0 00
Wages payable		8 8 0 00
Interest payable		3 6 0 0 00
Unearned rent		4 6 0 00
Long-term notes payable		150 0 0 0 00
M. Choi, Capital		40 3 4 0 00
M. Choi, Withdrawals	21 0 0 0 00	
Rent earned		57 5 0 0 00
Wages expense	25 0 0 0 00	
Utilities expense	1 9 0 0 00	
Insurance expense	3 2 0 0 00	
Supplies expense	2 5 0 00	
Depreciation expense—Equipment	5 9 7 0 00	
Interest expense	3 0 0 0 00	
Totals	$281 8 8 0 00	$281 8 8 0 00

1. Prepare the annual income statement from the adjusted trial balance of Choi Company.

Answer:

CHOI COMPANY Income Statement For Year Ended December 31			
Revenues			
Rent earned			$57 5 0 0 00
Expenses			
Wages expense	$25 0 0 0 00		
Utilities expense	1 9 0 0 00		
Insurance expense	3 2 0 0 00		
Supplies expense	2 5 0 00		
Depreciation expense—Equipment	5 9 7 0 00		
Interest expense	3 0 0 0 00		
Total expenses			39 3 2 0 00
Net income			$18 1 8 0 00

2. Prepare a statement of owner's equity from the adjusted trial balance and income statement of Choi Company. Choi's capital account balance of $40,340 consists of a $30,340 balance from the prior year-end, plus a $10,000 owner investment during the current year.

Answer:

CHOI COMPANY Statement of Owner's Equity For Year Ended December 31		
M. Choi, Capital, December 31 prior year-end		$30 3 4 0 00
Plus: Owner investments	$10 0 0 0 00	
Net income	18 1 8 0 00	28 1 8 0 00
		58 5 2 0 00
Less: Withdrawals by owner		21 0 0 0 00
M. Choi, Capital, December 31 current year-end		$37 5 2 0 00

3. Prepare a balance sheet from the adjusted trial balance of Choi Company and from its statement of owner's equity prepared in part 2.

Answer:

CHOI COMPANY Balance Sheet December 31		
Assets		
Cash		$ 3 0 5 0 00
Accounts receivable		4 0 0 00
Prepaid insurance		8 3 0 00
Supplies		8 0 00
Equipment	$217 2 0 0 00	
Less accumulated depreciation	29 1 0 0 00	188 1 0 0 00
Total assets		$192 4 6 0 00
Liabilities		
Wages payable		$ 8 8 0 00
Interest payable		3 6 0 0 00
Unearned rent		4 6 0 00
Long-term notes payable		150 0 0 0 00
Total liabilities		154 9 4 0 00
Equity		
M. Choi, Capital		37 5 2 0 00
Total liabilities and equity		$192 4 6 0 00

Summary

LO1 Prepare a work sheet and explain its usefulness. The work sheet is used to gather all accounting information in one place, to record adjustments, and to aid in the preparation of financial statements. The work sheet reduces the possibility of errors when working with many accounts.

LO2 Prepare and explain adjusting entries. *Prepaid expenses* refer to items paid for in advance of receiving their benefits. Prepaid expenses are assets. Adjusting entries for prepaids involve increasing (debiting) expenses and decreasing (crediting) assets. *Accrued expenses* refer to costs incurred in a period that are both unpaid and unrecorded. Adjusting entries for recording accrued expenses involve increasing (debiting) expenses and increasing (crediting) liabilities.

LO3 Explain and prepare an adjusted trial balance. An adjusted trial balance is a list of accounts and balances prepared after recording and posting adjusting entries. Financial statements are often prepared from the adjusted trial balance.

LO4 Prepare financial statements from an adjusted trial balance. Revenue and expense balances are reported on the income statement. Asset, liability, and equity balances are reported on the balance sheet. We usually prepare statements in the following order: income statement, statement of owner's equity, and balance sheet.

LO5 **Compute profit margin and describe its use in analyzing company performance.** *Profit margin* is defined as the reporting period's net income divided by its net sales. Profit margin reflects on a company's earnings activities by showing how much income is in each dollar of sales.

Guidance Answers to *YOU CALL IT*

Investor Prepaid expenses are items paid for in advance of receiving their benefits. They are assets and are expensed as they are used up. The publishing company's treatment of the signing bonus is acceptable provided future book sales can at least match the $500,000 expense. As an investor, you are concerned about the risk of future book sales. The riskier the likelihood of future book sales is, the more likely your analysis is to treat the $500,000, or a portion of it, as an expense, not a prepaid expense (asset).

Entrepreneur Depreciation is a process of cost allocation, not asset valuation. Knowing the depreciation schedule is not especially useful in your estimation of what the building and equipment are currently worth. Your own assessment of the age, quality, and usefulness of the building and equipment is more important.

Guidance Answers to *HOW YOU DOIN'?*

1. A work sheet is used as a tool to record necessary adjustments and to organize the accounting information in a useful way to prepare the financial statements. It helps reduce errors.

2. A contra account is an account that is subtracted from the balance of a related account. Use of a contra account provides more information than simply reporting a net amount.

3. An accrued expense is a cost incurred in a period that is both unpaid and unrecorded prior to adjusting entries. One example is salaries earned but not yet paid at period-end.

4. A prepaid expense arises when items have been paid for in advance of receiving their benefits. Examples are prepaid insurance, prepaid rent, and supplies.

5. The probable adjusting entries of Jordan Air are:

Insurance Expense	300	
Prepaid Insurance		300
To record insurance expired.		
Salaries Expense	1,400	
Salaries Payable		1,400
To record accrued salaries.		

6. Revenue accounts and expense accounts.

7. Statement of owner's equity.

Key Terms

mhhe.com/wildCA

Key Terms are available at the book's Website for learning and testing in an online Flashcard Format.

Accrued expenses (p. 104) Costs incurred in a period that are both unpaid and unrecorded; adjusting entries for recording accrued expenses involve increasing expenses and increasing liabilities.

Adjusted trial balance (p. 106) List of accounts and balances prepared after period-end adjustments are recorded and posted.

Adjusting entry (p. 100) Journal entry at the end of an accounting period to bring an asset or liability account to its proper amount and update the related expense or revenue account.

Book value (p. 104) Asset's acquisition cost less its accumulated depreciation (or depletion, or amortization); also sometimes used synonymously as the *carrying value* of an account.

Contra account (p. 103) Account linked with another account and having an opposite normal balance; reported as a subtraction from the other account's balance.

Depreciation (p. 103) Expense created by allocating the cost of plant and equipment to periods in which the asset is used; represents the expense of using the asset.

Plant assets (p. 103) Tangible long-lived assets used to produce or sell products and services; also called *property, plant and equipment (PP&E)* or *fixed assets.*

Prepaid expenses (p. 101) Items paid for in advance of receiving their benefits; classified as assets.

Profit margin (p. 108) Ratio of a company's net income to its net sales; the percent of income in each dollar of revenue; also called *net profit margin.*

Straight-line depreciation method (p. 103) Method that allocates an equal portion of the depreciable cost of plant asset (cost minus salvage value) to each accounting period in its useful life.

Unadjusted trial balance (p. 106) List of accounts and balances prepared before accounting adjustments are recorded and posted.

Working papers (p. 100) Analyses and other informal reports prepared by accountants and managers when organizing information for formal reports and financial statements.

Work sheet (p. 100) Spreadsheet used to draft an unadjusted trial balance, adjusting entries, adjusted trial balance, and financial statement accounts.

Multiple Choice Quiz   Answers on p. 122   mhhe.com/wildCA

Multiple Choice Quizzes A and B are available at the book's Website.

1. A company forgot to record accrued and unpaid employee wages of $350,000 at period-end. This oversight would
   a. Understate net income by $350,000.
   b. Overstate net income by $350,000.
   c. Have no effect on net income.
   d. Overstate assets by $350,000.
   e. Understate assets by $350,000.

2. Prior to recording adjusting entries, the Office Supplies account has a $450 debit balance. A physical count of supplies shows $125 of unused supplies still available. The required adjusting entry is:
   a. Debit Office Supplies $125; Credit Office Supplies Expense $125.
   b. Debit Office Supplies $325; Credit Office Supplies Expense $325.
   c. Debit Office Supplies Expense $325; Credit Office Supplies $325.
   d. Debit Office Supplies Expense $325; Credit Office Supplies $125.
   e. Debit Office Supplies Expense $125; Credit Office Supplies $125.

3. On May 1, 2008, a two-year insurance policy was purchased for $24,000 with coverage to begin immediately. What is the amount of insurance expense that appears on the company's income statement for the year ended December 31, 2008?
   a. $4,000
   b. $8,000
   c. $12,000
   d. $20,000
   e. $24,000

4. A company purchases a delivery truck for $39,000 on July 1, 2008. The truck is estimated to have a useful life of 6 years and zero salvage value. The company uses the straight-line method of depreciation. How much depreciation expense is recorded on the truck for the year ended December 31, 2008?
   a. $3,500.
   b. $3,250.
   c. $4,000.
   d. $6,500.
   e. $7,000

5. If a company had $15,000 in net income for the year, and its sales were $300,000 for the same year, what is its profit margin?
   a. 20%
   b. 2,000%
   c. $285,000
   d. $315,000
   e. 5%

Discussion Questions

1. What is a prepaid expense and where is it reported in the financial statements?

2. What type of assets require adjusting entries to record depreciation?

3. What contra account is used when recording and reporting the effects of depreciation? Why is it used?

4. Review the balance sheet of **Best Buy** in Appendix A. Identify the asset accounts that require adjustment before annual financial statements can be prepared. What would be the effect on the income statement if these asset accounts were not adjusted?

5. Review the balance sheet of **Circuit City** in Appendix A. In addition to Prepayments, identify two accounts (either assets or liabilities) requiring adjusting entries.

Adjusting entries affect at least one balance sheet account and at least one income statement account. For the following entries, identify the account to be debited and the account to be credited. Indicate which of the accounts is the income statement account and which is the balance sheet account.

a. Entry to record wage expenses incurred but not yet paid (nor recorded).

b. Entry to record expiration of prepaid insurance.

c. Entry to record annual depreciation expense.

QUICK STUDY

QS 5–1
Recording and analyzing adjusting entries
(LO2)

---

a. On July 1, 2008, Lamis Company paid $1,200 for six months of insurance coverage. No adjustments have been made to the Prepaid Insurance account, and it is now December 31, 2008. Prepare the journal entry to reflect expiration of the insurance as of December 31, 2008.

b. Shandi Company has a Supplies account balance of $500 on January 1, 2008. During 2008, it purchased $2,000 of supplies. As of December 31, 2008, $800 of supplies are available. Prepare the adjusting journal entry to correctly report the balance of the Supplies account and the Supplies Expense account as of December 31, 2008.

QS 5–2
Adjusting prepaid expenses
(LO2)

QS 5-3
Adjusting for depreciation
(LO2)

a. Chika Company purchases $20,000 of equipment on January 1, 2008. The equipment is expected to last five years and be worth $2,000 at the end of that time. Prepare the entry to record one year's depreciation expense for the equipment as of December 31, 2008. Use the straight-line method.

b. Madra Company purchases $10,000 of land on January 1, 2008. The land is expected to last indefinitely. What depreciation adjustment, if any, should be made with respect to the Land account as of December 31, 2008?

QS 5-4
Accruing salaries
(LO2)

Lakia Rowa employs one college student every summer in her coffee shop. The student works the five weekdays and is paid on the following Monday. (For example, a student who works Monday through Friday, June 1 through June 5, is paid for that work on Monday, June 8.) Rowa adjusts her books monthly, if needed, to show salaries earned but unpaid at month-end. The student works the last week of July— Friday is August 1. If the student earns $100 per day, what adjusting entry must Rowa make on July 31 to correctly record accrued salaries expense for July?

QS 5-5
Interpreting adjusting entries
(LO2)

The following information is taken from Brooke Company's unadjusted and adjusted trial balances.

	Unadjusted		Adjusted	
	Debit	Credit	Debit	Credit
Prepaid insurance	$4,100		$3,700	
Interest payable		$ 0		$800

Given this information, what were the adjusting entries?

EXERCISES

Exercise 5-1
Classifying adjusting entries
(LO2)

In the blank space beside each adjusting entry, enter the letter of the explanation A through C that most closely describes the entry.

A. To record this period's depreciation expense.
B. To record accrued salaries expense.
C. To record this period's use of a prepaid expense.

_____ 1.	Insurance Expense	3,180	
	Prepaid Insurance		3,180
_____ 2.	Depreciation Expense	38,217	
	Accumulated Depreciation		38,217
_____ 3.	Salaries Expense	13,280	
	Salaries Payable		13,280

Exercise 5-2
Preparing adjusting entries
(LO2)

Check (c) Dr. Office Supplies Expense, $3,882;

(d) Dr. Insurance Expense, $5,800

Prepare adjusting journal entries for the year ended (date of) December 31, 2008, for each of these separate situations.

a. Depreciation on the company's equipment for 2008 is computed to be $18,000.

b. The Prepaid Insurance account had a $6,000 debit balance at December 31, 2008, before adjusting for the costs of any expired coverage. An analysis of the company's insurance policies showed that $1,100 of unexpired insurance coverage remains.

c. The Office Supplies account had a $700 debit balance on December 31, 2007; and $3,480 of office supplies was purchased during the year. The December 31, 2008, physical count showed $298 of supplies available.

d. The Prepaid Insurance account had a $6,800 debit balance at December 31, 2008, before adjusting for the costs of any expired coverage. An analysis of insurance policies showed that $5,800 of coverage had expired.

e. Wage expenses of $3,200 have been incurred but are not paid as of December 31, 2008.

Exercise 5-3
Preparing adjusting entries
(LO2)

For each of the following separate cases, prepare adjusting entries required of financial statements for the year ended (date of) December 31, 2008.

a. Wages of $8,000 are earned by workers but not paid as of December 31, 2008.

b. Depreciation on the company's equipment for 2008 is $18,531.

c. The Office Supplies account had a $240 debit balance on December 31, 2007. During 2008, $5,239 of office supplies is purchased. A physical count of supplies at December 31, 2008, shows $487 of supplies available.

d. The Prepaid Insurance account had a $4,000 balance on December 31, 2007. An analysis of insurance policies shows that $1,200 of unexpired insurance benefits remain at December 31, 2008.

Check   (d) Dr. Insurance Expense, $2,800

Lopez Management has five part-time employees, each of whom earns $250 per day. They are normally paid on Fridays for work completed Monday through Friday of the same week. They were paid in full on Friday, December 28, 2008. The next week, the five employees worked only four days because New Year's Day was an unpaid holiday. Show (*a*) the adjusting entry that would be recorded on Monday, December 31, 2008, and (*b*) the journal entry that would be made to record payment of the employees' wages on Friday, January 4, 2009.

Exercise 5–4
Adjusting and paying accrued wages
(L02)

Determine the missing amounts in each of these four separate situations *a* through *d*.

Exercise 5–5
Determining cost flows through accounts
(L02)

	a	b	c	d
Supplies available—prior year-end	$ 400	$1,200	$1,260	?
Supplies purchased during the current year	2,800	6,500	?	$3,000
Supplies available—current year-end	650	?	1,350	700
Supplies expense for the current year	?	1,200	8,400	4,588

Total weekly salaries expense for all employees is $10,000. This amount is paid at the end of the day on Friday of each five-day workweek. April 30 falls on Tuesday of this year, which means that the employees had worked two days since the last payday. The next payday is May 3.
   What is the required adjusting journal entry as of April 30?

Exercise 5–6
Adjusting and paying accrued expenses
(L02)

Use the following information to compute profit margin for each separate company *a* through *e*.

Exercise 5–7
Computing and interpreting profit margin
(L05)

	Net Income	Net Sales			Net Income	Net Sales
a.	$ 4,390	$ 44,830		**d.**	$65,234	$1,458,999
b.	97,644	398,954		**e.**	80,158	435,925
c.	111,385	257,082				

Which of the five companies is the most profitable according to the profit margin ratio? Interpret that company's profit margin ratio.

Arnez Co. records prepaid expenses in balance sheet accounts. Arnez's annual accounting period ends on December 31, 2008. The following information concerns the adjusting entries to be recorded as of that date.

a. The Office Supplies account started the year with a $4,000 balance. During 2008, the company purchased supplies for $13,400, which was added to the Office Supplies account. The inventory of supplies available at December 31, 2008, totaled $2,554.

b. An analysis of the company's insurance policies provided the following facts.

PROBLEM SET A

Problem 5–1A
Preparing adjusting journal entries
(L02)

Policy	Date of Purchase	Months of Coverage	Cost
A	April 1, 2007	24	$14,400
B	April 1, 2008	36	12,960
C	August 1, 2008	12	2,400

The total premium for each policy was paid in full (for all months) at the purchase date, and the Prepaid Insurance account was debited for the full cost. (Year-end adjusting entries for Prepaid Insurance were properly recorded in all prior years.)

c. The company has 15 employees, who earn a total of $1,960 in salaries each working day. They are paid each Monday for their work in the five-day workweek ending on the previous Friday. Assume that December 31, 2008, is a Tuesday, and all 15 employees worked the first two days of that week.

Because New Year's Day is a paid holiday, they will be paid salaries for five full days on Monday, January 6, 2009.

d. The company purchased a building on January 1, 2008. It cost $960,000 and is expected to have a $45,000 salvage value at the end of its predicted 30-year life. Annual depreciation is $30,500.

Check (1b) Dr. Insurance Expense, $11,440 (1d) Dr. Depreciation Expense, $30,500

Required

Use the information to prepare adjusting entries as of December 31, 2008.

Problem 5-2A

Preparing adjusting entries, adjusted trial balance, and financial statements

(LO2) (LO3) (LO4)

mhhe.com/wildCA

Wells Technical Institute (WTI), a school owned by Tristana Wells, provides training to individuals who pay tuition directly to the school. WTI also offers training to groups in off-site locations. Its unadjusted trial balance as of December 31, 2008, follows. WTI initially records prepaid expenses in balance sheet accounts. Descriptions of items *a* through *f* that require adjusting entries on December 31, 2008, follow.

Additional Information

a. An analysis of the school's insurance policies shows that $2,400 of coverage has expired.

b. An inventory count shows that teaching supplies costing $2,800 are available at year-end 2008.

c. Annual depreciation on the equipment is $13,200.

d. Annual depreciation on the professional library is $7,200.

e. The school's two employees are paid weekly. As of the end of the year, two days' wages have accrued at the rate of $100 per day for each employee.

f. The balance in the Prepaid Rent account represents rent for December.

WELLS TECHNICAL INSTITUTE Unadjusted Trial Balance December 31, 2008	Debit	Credit
Cash	$ 34,000	
Accounts receivable	0	
Teaching supplies	8,000	
Prepaid insurance	12,000	
Prepaid rent	3,000	
Professional library	35,000	
Accumulated depreciation—Professional library		$ 10,000
Equipment	80,000	
Accumulated depreciation—Equipment		15,000
Accounts payable		38,500
Salaries payable		0
T. Wells, Capital		90,000
T. Wells, Withdrawals	50,000	
Tuition fees earned		123,900
Training fees earned		40,000
Depreciation expense—Professional library	0	
Depreciation expense—Equipment	0	
Salaries expense	50,000	
Insurance expense	0	
Rent expense	33,000	
Teaching supplies expense	0	
Advertising expense	6,000	
Utilities expense	6,400	
Totals	$ 317,400	$ 317,400

Required

1. Prepare T-accounts (representing the ledger) with balances from the unadjusted trial balance.

2. Prepare the necessary adjusting journal entries for items *a* through *f* and post them to the T-accounts. Assume that adjusting entries are made only at year-end.

3. Update balances in the T-accounts for the adjusting entries and prepare an adjusted trial balance.

4. Prepare Wells Technical Institute's income statement and statement of owner's equity for the year 2008 and prepare its balance sheet as of December 31, 2008.

Check (3) Adj. Trial balance totals $338,200; (4) Net income, $37,100; Ending T. Wells, Capital $77,100

The adjusted trial balance for Chiara Company as of December 31, 2008, follows.

Problem 5-3A
Preparing financial statements from the adjusted trial balance

(LO4)

	Debit	Credit
Cash	$ 30,000	
Accounts receivable	52,000	
Interest receivable	18,000	
Notes receivable (due in 90 days)	168,000	
Office supplies	16,000	
Automobiles	168,000	
Accumulated depreciation—Automobiles		$ 50,000
Equipment	138,000	
Accumulated depreciation—Equipment		18,000
Land	78,000	
Accounts payable		126,000
Interest payable		20,000
Salaries payable		19,000
Long-term notes payable		138,000
R. Chiara, Capital		255,800
R. Chiara, Withdrawals	46,000	
Fees earned		484,000
Interest earned		24,000
Depreciation expense—Automobiles	26,000	
Depreciation expense—Equipment	18,000	
Salaries expense	188,000	
Wages expense	40,000	
Interest expense	32,000	
Office supplies expense	34,000	
Advertising expense	58,000	
Repairs expense—Automobiles	24,800	
Totals	$1,134,800	$1,134,800

Required

Use the information in the adjusted trial balance to prepare (*a*) the income statement for the year ended December 31, 2008; (*b*) the statement of owner's equity for the year ended December 31, 2008; and (*c*) the balance sheet as of December 31, 2008.

Check (1) Total assets, $600,000

Natsu Co. records prepaid expenses in balance sheet accounts. Natsu's annual accounting period ends on October 31, 2008. The following information concerns the adjusting entries that need to be recorded as of that date.

a. The Office Supplies account started the fiscal year with a $600 balance. During the fiscal year, the company purchased supplies for $4,570, which was added to the Office Supplies account. The supplies available at October 31, 2008, totaled $800.

b. An analysis of the company's insurance policies provided the following facts.

PROBLEM SET B

Problem 5-1B
Preparing adjusting and subsequent journal entries

Policy	Date of Purchase	Months of Coverage	Cost
A	April 1, 2007	24	$6,000
B	April 1, 2008	36	7,200
C	August 1, 2008	12	1,320

The total premium for each policy was paid in full (for all months) at the purchase date, and the Prepaid Insurance account was debited for the full cost. (Year-end adjusting entries for Prepaid Insurance were properly recorded in all prior fiscal years.)

c. The company has four employees, who earn a total of $1,000 for each workday. They are paid each Monday for their work in the five-day workweek ending on the previous Friday. Assume that October 31, 2008, is a Monday, and all five employees worked the first day of that week. They will be paid salaries for five full days on Monday, November 7, 2008.

d. The company purchased a building on November 1, 2007, that cost $175,000 and is expected to have a $40,000 salvage value at the end of its predicted 25-year life. Annual depreciation is $5,400.

Check (1b) Dr. Insurance Expense, $5,350; (1d) Dr. Depreciation Expense, $5,400.

Required

Use the information to prepare adjusting entries as of October 31, 2008.

Problem 5–2B

Preparing adjusting entries, adjusted trial balance, and financial statements

(LO2) (LO3) (LO4)

Following is the unadjusted trial balance for Augustus Institute as of December 31, 2008, which initially records prepaid expenses in balance sheet accounts. The Institute provides one-on-one training to individuals who pay tuition directly to the business and offers extension training to groups in off-site locations. Shown after the trial balance are items *a* through *f* that require adjusting entries as of December 31, 2008.

AUGUSTUS INSTITUTE Unadjusted Trial Balance December 31, 2008		
	Debit	**Credit**
Cash	$ 60,000	
Accounts receivable	0	
Teaching supplies	70,000	
Prepaid insurance	19,000	
Prepaid rent	3,800	
Professional library	12,000	
Accumulated depreciation—Professional library		$ 2,500
Equipment	40,000	
Accumulated depreciation—Equipment		20,000
Accounts payable		39,800
Salaries payable		0
C. Augustus, Capital		71,500
C. Augustus, Withdrawals	20,000	
Tuition fees earned		129,200
Training fees earned		68,000
Depreciation expense—Professional library	0	
Depreciation expense—Equipment	0	
Salaries expense	44,200	
Insurance expense	0	
Rent expense	29,600	
Teaching supplies expense	0	
Advertising expense	19,000	
Utilities expense	13,400	
Totals	$ 331,000	$ 331,000

Additional Information

a. An analysis of the Institute's insurance policies shows that $9,500 of coverage has expired.

b. An inventory count shows that teaching supplies costing $20,000 are available at year-end 2008.

c. Annual depreciation on the equipment is $5,000.

d. Annual depreciation on the professional library is $2,400.

e. The Institute's only employee is paid weekly. As of the end of the year, three days' wages have accrued at the rate of $150 per day.

f. The balance in the Prepaid Rent account represents rent for December.

Required

1. Prepare T-accounts (representing the ledger) with balances from the unadjusted trial balance.

2. Prepare the necessary adjusting journal entries for items *a* through *f*, and post them to the T-accounts. Assume that adjusting entries are made only at year-end.

3. Update balances in the T-accounts for the adjusting entries and prepare an adjusted trial balance.

4. Prepare Augustus Institute's income statement and statement of owner's equity for the year 2008, and prepare its balance sheet as of December 31, 2008.

Check (3) Adj. trial balance totals, $338,850; (4) Net income, $19,850; Ending C. Augustus, Capital, $71,350

The adjusted trial balance for Speedy Courier as of December 31, 2008, follows.

Problem 5–3B
Preparing financial statements from the adjusted trial balance

 LO4

	Debit	Credit
Cash	$ 58,000	
Accounts receivable	120,000	
Interest receivable	7,000	
Notes receivable (due in 90 days)	210,000	
Office supplies	22,000	
Trucks	134,000	
Accumulated depreciation—Trucks		$ 58,000
Equipment	270,000	
Accumulated depreciation—Equipment		200,000
Land	100,000	
Accounts payable		254,000
Interest payable		20,000
Salaries payable		28,000
Long-term notes payable		200,000
L. Horace, Capital		125,000
L. Horace, Withdrawals	50,000	
Delivery fees earned		611,800
Interest earned		34,000
Depreciation expense—Trucks	29,000	
Depreciation expense—Equipment	48,000	
Salaries expense	74,000	
Wages expense	300,000	
Interest expense	15,000	
Office supplies expense	31,000	
Advertising expense	27,200	
Repairs expense—Trucks	35,600	
Totals	$1,530,800	$1,530,800

Required

Use the information in the adjusted trial balance to prepare (*a*) the income statement for the year ended December 31, 2008, (*b*) the statement of owner's equity for the year ended December 31, 2008, and (*c*) the balance sheet as of December 31, 2008.

Check (1) Total assets $663,000

SERIAL PROBLEM

Success Systems

This serial problem began in Chapter 1 and continues through most of the book. If previous chapter segments were not completed, the serial problem can still begin at this point. It is helpful, but not necessary, that you use the Working Papers that accompany the book.

SP 5   After the success of the company's first two months, Adriana Lopez continues to operate Success Systems. (Transactions for the first two months are described in the serial problem of Chapter 4.) The November 30, 2007, unadjusted trial balance of Success Systems (reflecting its transactions for October and November) follows.

No.	Account Title	Debit	Credit
101	Cash	$ 68,996	
106	Accounts receivable	15,800	
126	Computer supplies	3,350	
128	Prepaid insurance	2,400	
131	Prepaid rent	3,500	
163	Office equipment	10,000	
164	Accumulated depreciation—Office equipment		$ 0
167	Computer equipment	25,000	
168	Accumulated depreciation—Computer equipment		0
201	Accounts payable		0
210	Wages payable		0
236	Unearned computer services revenue		0
301	A. Lopez, Capital		110,000
302	A. Lopez, Withdrawals	6,500	
403	Computer services revenue		32,550
612	Depreciation expense—Office equipment	0	
613	Depreciation expense—Computer equipment	0	
623	Wages expense	3,150	
637	Insurance expense	0	
640	Rent expense	0	
652	Computer supplies expense	0	
655	Advertising expense	1,790	
676	Mileage expense	864	
677	Miscellaneous expenses	300	
684	Repairs expense—Computer	900	
	Totals	$142,550	$142,550

Success Systems had the following transactions and events in December 2007.

Dec. 2   Paid $1,200 cash to Hilldale Mall for Success Systems' share of mall advertising costs.
3   Paid $500 cash for minor repairs to the company's computer.
4   Received $7,000 cash from Alex's Engineering Co. for the receivable from November.
10   Paid cash to Michelle Jones for six days of work at the rate of $150 per day.
14   Notified by Alex's Engineering Co. that Success's bid of $9,000 on a proposed project has been accepted. Alex's paid a $2,500 cash advance to Success Systems. (Hint: Debit Cash and Credit Unearned computer services revenue for $2,500.)
15   Purchased $2,100 of computer supplies on credit from Cain Office Products.
16   Sent a reminder to Gomez Co. to pay the fee for services recorded on November 8.
20   Completed a project for Chang Corporation and received $3,620 cash.
22–26   Took the week off for the holidays.
26   Received $3,000 cash from Gomez Co. on its receivable.
26   Reimbursed Lopez's business automobile mileage (800 miles at $0.32 per mile).
27   Lopez withdrew $2,000 cash for personal use.

The following additional facts are collected for use in making adjusting entries prior to preparing financial statements for the company's first three months:

a. The December 31 inventory count of computer supplies shows $775 still available.

b. Three months have expired since the 12-month insurance premium was paid in advance.

c. As of December 31, Michelle Jones has not been paid for four days of work at $150 per day.

d. The company's computer is expected to have a five-year life with no salvage value.

e. The office equipment is expected to have a four-year life with no salvage value.

f. Three of the four months' prepaid rent has expired.

Required

1. Prepare journal entries to record each of the December transactions and events for Success Systems. Post those entries to the accounts in the ledger.

2. Prepare adjusting entries to reflect *a* through *f*. Post those entries to the accounts in the ledger.

3. Prepare an adjusted trial balance as of December 31, 2007.

4. Prepare an income statement for the three months ended December 31, 2007.

5. Prepare a statement of owner's equity for the three months ended December 31, 2007.

6. Prepare a balance sheet as of December 31, 2007.

Check (3) Adjusted trial balance totals, $153,245

(6) Total assets, $122,635

BEYOND THE NUMBERS

BTN 5-1 Refer to **Best Buy**'s financial statements in Appendix A to answer the following.

1. What is Best Buy's profit margin for fiscal years ended February 26, 2005, and February 28, 2004?

2. Interpret your answers to part 1.

Fast Forward

3. Access Best Buy's financial statements (10-K) for fiscal years ending after February 26, 2005, at its Website (**BestBuy.com**) or the SEC's EDGAR database (**www.sec.gov**). Compare the February 26, 2005, fiscal year profit margin to any subsequent year's profit margin that you are able to calculate.

REPORTING IN ACTION

(LO5)

BTN 5-2 Key figures for the recent two years of both Best Buy and Circuit City follow.

Key Figures ($ thousands)	Best Buy Current Year	Best Buy Prior Year	Circuit City Current Year	Circuit City Prior Year
Net income	$ 984,000	$ 705,000	$ 61,658	$ (89,269)
Net sales	27,433,000	24,548,000	10,472,364	9,857,057

COMPARATIVE ANALYSIS

(LO5)

Required

1. Compute profit margins for (*a*) Best Buy and (*b*) Circuit City for the two years of data shown.

2. Which company is more successful on the basis of profit margin? Explain.

BTN 5-3 Jerome Boland works for Sea Biscuit Co. He and Farah Smith, his manager, are preparing adjusting entries for annual financial statements. Boland computes depreciation and records it as

ETHICS CHALLENGE

(LO2)

Depreciation Expense—Equipment	123,000	
Accumulated Depreciation—Equipment		123,000

Smith agrees with his computation but says the credit entry should be directly to the Equipment account. She argues that while accumulated depreciation is technically correct, "it is less hassle not to use a contra account and just credit the Equipment account directly. And besides, the balance sheet shows the same amount for total assets under either method."

Required

1. How should depreciation be recorded? Do you support Boland or Smith?

2. Evaluate the strengths and weaknesses of Smith's reasons for preferring her method.

3. Indicate whether the situation Boland faces is an ethical problem. Explain.

WORKPLACE COMMUNICATIONS
(LO1) (LO2) (LO3) (LO4)

BTN 5-4   Kevin Kobelsky is an aspiring entrepreneur and your friend. He is having difficulty understanding the purpose of the work sheet used to adjust accounts.

Required

Write a half-page memorandum to Kobelsky explaining the purpose of the work sheet and how it facilitates adjusting accounts and preparing financial statements.

TAKING IT TO THE NET
(LO2) (LO5)

BTN 5-5   Access the Gap's Website (gap.com) to answer the following requirements.

Required

1. What are Gap's main brands?
2. Access Gap's annual report either at the company's Website (or at www.sec.gov). What is Gap's fiscal year-end?
3. What is Gap's net sales for the period ended January 29, 2005?
4. What is Gap's net income for the period ended January 29, 2005?
5. Compute Gap's profit margin for the year ended January 29, 2005.
6. Identify at least three accounts that likely require adjustment at period-end for Gap.

TEAMWORK IN ACTION
(LO5)

BTN 5-6   The class should be divided into teams. Teams are to select an industry (such as automobile manufacturing, airlines, defense contractors), and each team member is to select a different company in that industry. Each team member is to acquire the annual report of the company selected. Annual reports can be downloaded from company Websites or from the SEC's EDGAR database (www.sec.gov).

Required

1. Use the annual report to compute the profit margin.
2. Communicate with team members via a meeting, e-mail, or telephone to discuss the meaning of the ratios, how different companies compare to each other, and the industry norm. The team must prepare a single memo reporting the ratio for each company and identifying the conclusions or consensus of opinion reached during the team's discussion. The memo is to be copied and distributed to the instructor and all classmates.

ENTREPRENEURS IN BUSINESS
(LO2) (LO3)

BTN 5-7   Refer to the chapter's opening feature about Alex Aguila and Nelson Gonzalez and their company, Alienware. Assume that Alex and Nelson do not understand the purpose of adjusting journal entries prepared at period-end.

Required

1. Explain why some accounts must be adjusted at period-end.
2. Provide examples of specific accounts that likely require adjustment at Alienware.

ANSWERS TO MULTIPLE CHOICE QUIZ

1. b; the forgotten adjusting entry is: *dr.* Wages Expense, *cr.* Wages Payable.
2. c; Supplies used = $450 − $125 = $325
3. b; Insurance expense = $24,000 × (8/24) = $8,000; adjusting entry is: *dr.* Insurance Expense for $8,000, *cr.* Prepaid Insurance for $8,000.
4. b; $3,250 = [($39,000 − $0)/6 years] × ½ year
5. e; Profit margin = $15,000/$300,000 = 5%

A Look Back

Chapter 5 described why adjusting accounts is important for recognizing revenues and expenses in the proper period. We prepared an adjusted trial balance and used it to prepare financial statements.

A Look at This Chapter

This chapter emphasizes the final steps in the accounting process and reviews the entire accounting cycle. We explain the closing process and the use of a post-closing trial balance. We show how a work sheet aids in preparing financial statements.

A Look Ahead

Chapter 7 considers fraud and controls. We look specifically at how internal controls reduce the likelihood of fraud. We also consider the effect that recent laws, such as Sarbanes-Oxley, have on fraud and internal controls.

Chapter 6

Closing Process and Financial Statements

LEARNING OBJECTIVES

LO 1 Explain how to use a work sheet.

LO 2 Explain why temporary accounts are closed each period.

LO 3 Describe and prepare closing entries.

LO 4 Explain and prepare a post-closing trial balance.

LO 5 Identify steps in the accounting cycle.

LO 6 Compute the current ratio and describe what it reveals about a company's financial condition.

"We really focus on our products . . . we put our all into them"—Janet Freeman

Boarding In Style

PORTLAND—Success did not come easy for Janet Freeman. "I grew up thinking that getting hurt . . . and being cold, wet, and hungry was normal," she says. That background explains Janet's determination and work ethic: Traits that serve her well as owner and founder of **Betty Rides (BettyRides.com),** a snowboard apparel and accessories company.

Her sister's demand that snowboarding clothing show off her figure started Janet along her entrepreneurial path. "She kept bugging me until I did it," says Janet of her initial foray into snowboard fashion. She quickly realized that females were an underserved segment in the snowboarding apparel market.

But for Betty Rides to be successful, it needed to control costs. "I didn't run up huge bills on advertising," says Janet. "When other people were staying in fancy hotels . . . I was staying in cheap places." She controlled materials costs while closely monitoring both revenues and customer needs. She used the accounting system and closing entries to help identify and match costs with revenues for specific time periods. And she worked with a bookkeeper that, says Janet, "helped us simplify our chart of accounts and clarify the payroll entries."

Janet continues to make good business decisions. "We really focus on our product," says Janet. "We don't skimp on our pieces . . . we put our all into them." She adds that women "want fit, function, value, and to look beautiful as well."

The downside of owning a business is that it cuts into Janet's time to snowboard. But, Janet says, she and the team now "do product testing while we ride," and that it still "makes me feel like a teenager." Janet also loves the entrepreneurial ride, noting, "Everyday I wake up and say—'I'm the luckiest person on earth.'"

[Sources: *Betty Rides Website*, January 2007; *Transworld Business*, February 2005; *Transworld Snowboarding*, March 2003; *In Balance Services Website*, July 2005.]

Earlier chapters described how transactions and events are analyzed, journalized, and posted. We also described important adjustments that are often necessary to properly reflect revenues when earned and expenses when incurred. This chapter explains the closing process that readies revenue, expense, and withdrawal accounts for the next reporting period and updates the capital account. A work sheet is shown to be a useful tool for that process and in preparing financial statements.

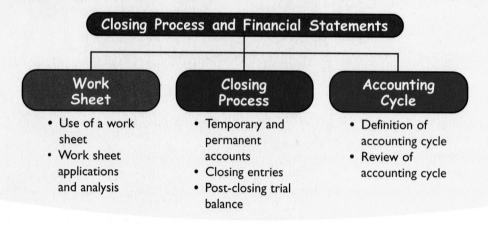

Use of a Work Sheet

LO1 Explain how to use a work sheet

The **accounting cycle** consists of steps taken to prepare the financial statements. It begins with analyzing transactions and ends with closing the accounts for the period. The **work sheet** can be used to help complete the accounting cycle. To describe and interpret the work sheet, we use the information from FastForward. Preparing the work sheet has five important steps. Each step, 1 through 5, is color-coded and explained with reference to Exhibits 6.1 and 6.2.

*FAST*Forward

① Step 1. Enter Unadjusted Trial Balance

Refer to Exhibit 6.1. The first step in preparing a work sheet is to list the title of every account and its account number that is expected to appear on its financial statements. This includes all accounts in the ledger plus any new ones from adjusting entries. Most adjusting entries—including expenses from salaries, supplies, depreciation, and insurance—are predictable and recurring. The unadjusted balance for each account is then entered in the appropriate Debit or Credit column of the unadjusted trial balance columns. The totals of these two columns must be equal. Exhibit 6.1 shows FastForward's work sheet after completing this first step.

A recordkeeper often can complete the procedural task of journalizing and posting adjusting entries by using a work sheet and the guidance that *keying* provides.

② Step 2. Enter Adjustments

Refer to Exhibit 6.1a (turn over first transparency). The second step in preparing a work sheet is to enter adjustments in the Adjustments columns. The adjustments shown are the same ones shown in Exhibit 5.7. An identifying letter links the debit and credit of each adjusting entry. This is called *keying* the adjustments. After preparing a work sheet, adjusting entries must still be entered in the journal and posted to the ledger. The Adjustments columns provide the information for those entries.

③ Step 3. Prepare Adjusted Trial Balance

To avoid omitting the transfer of an account balance, start with the first line (cash) and continue in account order.

Refer to Exhibit 6.1b (turn over second transparency). The adjusted trial balance is prepared by combining the adjustments with the unadjusted balances for each account. As an example, the Prepaid Insurance account has a $2,400 debit balance in the Unadjusted Trial Balance columns. This $2,400 debit is combined with the $100 credit in the Adjustments columns to give Prepaid Insurance a $2,300 debit in the Adjusted Trial Balance columns. The totals of the Adjusted Trial Balance columns confirm the equality of debits and credits.

④ Step 4. Sort Adjusted Trial Balance Amounts to Financial Statements

Refer to Exhibit 6.1c (turn over third transparency). This step involves sorting account balances from the adjusted trial balance to their proper financial statement columns. Expenses go to the Income Statement Debit column and revenues to the Income Statement Credit column. Assets and withdrawals go to the Balance Sheet & Statement of Owner's Equity Debit column. Liabilities and owner's capital go to the Balance Sheet & Statement of Owner's Equity Credit column.

⑤ Step 5. Total Statement Columns, Compute Income or Loss, and Balance Columns

Refer to Exhibit 6.1d (turn over fourth transparency). Each financial statement column (from Step 4) is totaled. The difference between the totals of the Income Statement columns is net income or net loss. This occurs because revenues are entered in the Credit column and expenses in the Debit column. If the Credit total exceeds the Debit total, there is net income. If the Debit total exceeds the Credit total, there is a net loss. For FastForward, the Credit total exceeds the Debit total, giving a $1,735 net income.

The net income from the Income Statement columns is then entered in the Balance Sheet & Statement of Owner's Equity Credit column. Adding net income to the last Credit column implies that it is to be added to owner's capital. If a loss occurs, it is added to the Debit column. This implies that it is to be subtracted from owner's capital. The ending balance of owner's capital does not appear in the last two columns as a single amount, but it is computed in the statement of owner's equity using these account balances. When net income or net loss is added to the proper Balance Sheet & Statement of Owner's Equity column, the totals of the last two columns must balance. If they do not, one or more errors have been made. The error can either be mathematical or involve sorting one or more amounts to incorrect columns.

Accoun-tech  IN THE NEWS

An electronic work sheet using spreadsheet software such as Excel allows us to easily change numbers, assess the impact of alternative strategies, and quickly prepare financial statements at less cost. It can also increase the available time for analysis and interpretation.

Work Sheet Applications and Analysis

A work sheet does not substitute for financial statements. It is a tool we can use at the end of an accounting period to help organize data and prepare financial statements. FastForward's financial statements are shown in Exhibit 6.2. Its income statement amounts are taken from the Income Statement columns of the work sheet. Similarly, amounts for its balance sheet and its statement of owner's equity are taken from the Balance Sheet & Statement of Owner's Equity columns of the work sheet.

A work sheet is also useful to journalize adjusting entries as the information is in the Adjustments columns. It is important to remember that a work sheet is not a journal. This means that even when a work sheet is prepared, it is necessary to both journalize adjustments and post them to the ledger.

YOU CALL IT   Answer—p. 139

Entrepreneur You make a printout of the electronic work sheet used to prepare financial statements. There is no depreciation adjustment, yet you own a large amount of equipment. Does the absence of depreciation adjustment concern you?

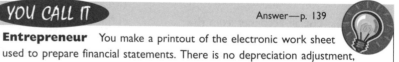

HOW YOU DOIN'?   Answers—p. 139

1. Where do we get the amounts to enter in the Unadjusted Trial Balance columns of a work sheet?
2. What are the advantages of using a work sheet to help prepare adjusting entries?

[text continued on p. 130]

Exhibit 6.1

Work Sheet with Unadjusted Trial Balance

File   Edit   View   Insert   Format   Tools   Data   Window   Help

FastForward
Work Sheet
For Month Ended December 31, 2007

No.	Account	Unadjusted Trial Balance		Adjustments		Adjusted Trial Balance		Income Statement		Balance Sheet & Statement of Owner's Equity	
		Dr.	Cr.	Dr.	Cr.	Dr.	Cr.	Dr.	Cr.	Dr.	Cr.
101	Cash	4,350									
126	Supplies	9,720									
128	Prepaid insurance	2,400									
167	Equipment	26,000									
168	Accumulated depreciation—Equip.		0								
201	Accounts payable		6,200								
209	Salaries payable		0								
236	Unearned consulting revenue		3,000								
301	C. Taylor, Capital		30,000								
302	C. Taylor, Withdrawals	200									
403	Consulting revenue		5,800								
406	Rental revenue		300								
612	Depreciation expense—Equip.	0									
622	Salaries expense	1,400									
637	Insurance expense	0									
640	Rent expense	1,000									
652	Supplies expense	0									
690	Utilities expense	230									
	Totals	45,300	45,300								

Sheet1 / Sheet2 / Sheet3

List all accounts from the ledger and those expected to arise from adjusting entries.

Enter all amounts available from ledger accounts. Column totals must be equal.

A work sheet collects and summarizes information used to prepare adjusting entries, financial statements, and closing entries.

Exhibit 6.2

Financial Statements Prepared from the Work Sheet

FASTFORWARD Income Statement For Month Ended December 31, 2007		
Revenues		
Consulting revenue	$5 8 0 0 00	
Rental revenue	3 0 0 00	
Total revenues		$6 1 0 0 00
Expenses		
Depreciation expense—Equipment	3 7 5 00	
Salaries expense	1 6 1 0 00	
Insurance expense	1 0 0 00	
Rent expense	1 0 0 0 00	
Supplies expense	1 0 5 0 00	
Utilities expense	2 3 0 00	
Total expenses		4 3 6 5 00
Net income		$1 7 3 5 00

FASTFORWARD Statement of Owner's Equity For Month Ended December 31, 2007		
C. Taylor, Capital, December 1		$ 0 00
Add: Investment by owner	$30 0 0 0 00	
Net income	1 7 3 5 00	31 7 3 5 00
		31 7 3 5 00
Less: Withdrawals by owner		2 0 0 00
C. Taylor, Capital, December 31		$31 5 3 5 00

FASTFORWARD Balance Sheet December 31, 2007		
Assets		
Cash		$ 4 3 5 0 00
Supplies		8 6 7 0 00
Prepaid insurance		2 3 0 0 00
Equipment	$26 0 0 0 00	
Less: Accumulated depreciation—Equipment	3 7 5 00	25 6 2 5 00
Total assets		$40 9 4 5 00
Liabilities		
Accounts payable		$ 6 2 0 0 00
Salaries payable		2 1 0 00
Unearned consulting revenue		3 0 0 0 00
Total liabilities		9 4 1 0 00
Equity		
C. Taylor, Capital		31 5 3 5 00
Total liabilities and equity		$40 9 4 5 00

Closing Process

Explain why temporary accounts are closed each period.

The **closing process** is an important step at the end of an accounting period *after* financial statements have been completed. It prepares accounts for recording the transactions and the events of the *next* period. In the closing process we must (1) identify accounts for closing, (2) record and post the closing entries, and (3) prepare a post-closing trial balance. The purpose of the closing process is twofold. First, it resets revenue, expense, and withdrawals account balances to zero at the end of each period. This is done so that these accounts can properly measure income and withdrawals for the next period. Second, it helps in summarizing a period's revenues and expenses. This section explains the closing process.

Temporary Accounts

> Revenues
> Expenses
> Owner Withdrawals
> Income Summary

Permanent Accounts

> Assets
> Liabilities
> Owner Capital

Temporary and Permanent Accounts

Temporary (or *nominal*) **accounts** accumulate data related to one accounting period. They include all income statement accounts, the withdrawals account, and the Income Summary account. They are temporary because the accounts are opened at the beginning of a period, used to record transactions and events for that period, and then closed at the end of the period. *The closing process applies only to temporary accounts.* **Permanent** (or *real*) **accounts** report on activities related to one or more future accounting periods. They carry their ending balances into the next period and generally consist of all balance sheet accounts. These asset, liability, and equity accounts are not closed.

Recording Closing Entries

To record and post **closing entries** is to transfer the end-of-period balances in revenue, expense, and withdrawals accounts to the permanent capital account. Closing entries are necessary at the end of each period after financial statements are prepared because

- Revenue, expense, and withdrawals accounts must begin each period with zero balances.
- Owner's capital must reflect prior periods' revenues, expenses, and withdrawals.

> To understand the closing process, focus on its *outcomes—updating* the capital account balance to its proper ending balance, and getting *temporary accounts* to show *zero balances* for purposes of accumulating data for the next period.

An income statement aims to report revenues and expenses for a *specific accounting period*. The statement of owner's equity reports similar information, including withdrawals. Since revenue, expense, and withdrawals accounts must accumulate information separately for each period, they must start each period with zero balances. To close these accounts, we transfer their balances first to an account called *Income Summary*. **Income Summary** is a temporary account (only used for the closing process) that contains a credit for the sum of all revenues (and gains) and a debit for the sum of all expenses (and losses). Its balance equals net income or net loss and it is transferred to the capital account. Next, the withdrawals account balance is transferred to the capital account. After these closing entries are posted, the revenue, expense, withdrawals, and Income Summary accounts have zero balances. These accounts are then said to be *closed* or *cleared*.

Exhibit 6.3 uses the adjusted account balances of FastForward (from the Adjusted Trial Balance columns of Exhibit 6.4 or from the left side of Exhibit 6.4) to show the four steps necessary to close its temporary accounts. We explain each step.

Describe and prepare closing entries.

Step 1: Close Credit Balances in Revenue Accounts to Income Summary

The first closing entry transfers credit balances in revenue (and gain) accounts to the Income Summary account. We bring accounts with credit balances to zero by debiting them. For FastForward, this journal entry is step 1 in Exhibit 6.4. This entry closes revenue accounts and leaves them with zero balances. The accounts are now ready to record revenues when they occur in the next period. The $6,100 credit entry to Income Summary equals total revenues for the period.

Step 2: Close Debit Balances in Expense Accounts to Income Summary

The second closing entry transfers debit balances in expense (and loss) accounts to the Income Summary account. We bring expense accounts' debit balances to zero by crediting them. With a balance of zero, these accounts are ready to accumulate a record of expenses for the next period. This second closing entry for FastForward is step 2 in Exhibit 6.4. Exhibit 6.3 shows that posting this entry gives each expense account a zero balance.

> It is possible to close revenue and expense accounts directly to owner's capital. Computerized accounting systems do this.

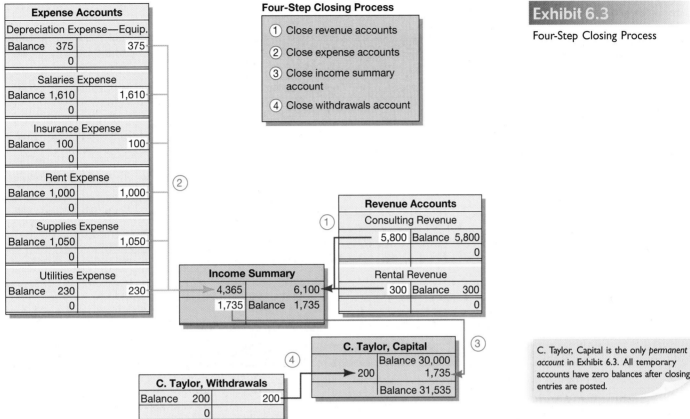

Exhibit 6.3

Four-Step Closing Process

C. Taylor, Capital is the only *permanent account* in Exhibit 6.3. All temporary accounts have zero balances after closing entries are posted.

Exhibit 6.4

Preparing Closing Entries

FASTFORWARD Adjusted Trial Balance December 31, 2007		
	Debit	**Credit**
Cash	$ 4,350	
Supplies	8,670	
Prepaid insurance	2,300	
Equipment	26,000	
Accumulated depreciation—Equip.		$ 375
Accounts payable		6,200
Salaries payable		210
Unearned consulting revenue		3,000
C. Taylor, Capital		30,000
C. Taylor, Withdrawals	200	
Consulting revenue		5,800
Rental revenue		300
Depreciation expense—Equip.	375	
Salaries expense	1,610	
Insurance expense	100	
Rent expense	1,000	
Supplies expense	1,050	
Utilities expense	230	
Totals	$45,885	$45,885

Step 1: **General Journal**

Dec. 31	Consulting Revenue.......... 5,800	
	Rental Revenue.......... 300	
	Income Summary..........	6,100
	To close revenue accounts.	

Step 2:

Dec. 31	Income Summary.......... 4,365	
	Depreciation Expense—Equipment..........	375
	Salaries Expense..........	1,610
	Insurance Expense..........	100
	Rent Expense..........	1,000
	Supplies Expense..........	1,050
	Utilities Expense..........	230
	To close expense accounts.	

Step 3:

Dec. 31	Income Summary.......... 1,735	
	C. Taylor, Capital..........	1,735
	To close the Income Summary account.	

Step 4:

Dec. 31	C. Taylor, Capital.......... 200	
	C. Taylor, Withdrawals..........	200
	To close the withdrawals account.	

Exhibit 6.5

General Ledger after the Closing Process for FastForward

Asset Accounts

Cash   Acct. No. 101

Date	Explan.	PR	Debit	Credit	Balance
2007					
Dec. 1		G1	30,000		30,000
2		G1		2,500	27,500
3		G1		26,000	1,500
5		G1	4,200		5,700
6		G1		2,400	3,300
12		G1		1,000	2,300
12		G1		700	1,600
22		G1	1,900		3,500
24		G1		900	2,600
24		G1		200	2,400
26		G1	3,000		5,400
26		G1		120	5,280
26		G1		230	5,050
26		G1		700	**4,350**

Accounts Receivable   Acct. No. 106

Date	Explan.	PR	Debit	Credit	Balance
2007					
Dec. 12		G1	1,900		1,900
22		G1		1,900	**0**

Supplies   Acct. No. 126

Date	Explan.	PR	Debit	Credit	Balance
2007					
Dec. 2		G1	2,500		2,500
6		G1	7,100		9,600
26		G1	120		9,720
31	Adj.	G1		1,050	**8,670**

Prepaid Insurance   Acct. No. 128

Date	Explan.	PR	Debit	Credit	Balance
2007					
Dec. 6		G1	2,400		2,400
31	Adj.	G1		100	**2,300**

Equipment   Acct. No. 167

Date	Explan.	PR	Debit	Credit	Balance
2007					
Dec. 3		G1	26,000		**26,000**

Accumulated Depreciation— Equipment   Acct. No. 168

Date	Explan.	PR	Debit	Credit	Balance
2007					
Dec. 31	Adj.	G1		375	**375**

Liability and Equity Accounts

Accounts Payable   Acct. No. 201

Date	Explan.	PR	Debit	Credit	Balance
2007					
Dec. 6		G1		7,100	7,100
24		G1	900		**6,200**

Salaries Payable   Acct. No. 209

Date	Explan.	PR	Debit	Credit	Balance
2007					
Dec. 31	Adj	G1		210	**210**

Unearned Consulting Revenue   Acct. No. 236

Date	Explan.	PR	Debit	Credit	Balance
2007					
Dec. 26		G1		3,000	**3,000**

C. Taylor, Capital   Acct. No. 301

Date	Explan.	PR	Debit	Credit	Balance
2007					
Dec. 1		G1		30,000	30,000
31	Closing	G1		1,735	31,535
31	Closing	G1	200		31,535

C. Taylor, Withdrawals   Acct. No. 302

Date	Explan.	PR	Debit	Credit	Balance
2007					
Dec. 24		G1	200		200
31	Closing	G1		200	0

Revenue and Expense Accounts (including Income Summary)

Consulting Revenue   Acct. No. 403

Date	Explan.	PR	Debit	Credit	Balance
2007					
Dec. 5		G1		4,200	4,200
12		G1		1,600	5,800
31	Closing	G1	5,800		0

Rental Revenue   Acct. No. 406

Date	Explan.	PR	Debit	Credit	Balance
2007					
Dec. 12		G1		300	300
31	Closing	G1	300		0

Depreciation Expense— Equipment   Acct. No. 612

Date	Explan.	PR	Debit	Credit	Balance
2007					
Dec. 31	Adj.	G1	375		375
31	Closing	G1		375	0

Salaries Expense   Acct. No. 622

Date	Explan.	PR	Debit	Credit	Balance
2007					
Dec. 12		G1	700		700
26		G1	700		1,400
31	Adj.	G1	210		1,610
31	Closing	G1		1,610	0

Insurance Expense   Acct. No. 637

Date	Explan.	PR	Debit	Credit	Balance
2007					
Dec. 31	Adj.	G1	100		100
31	Closing	G1		100	0

Rent Expense   Acct. No. 640

Date	Explan.	PR	Debit	Credit	Balance
2007					
Dec. 12		G1	1,000		1,000
31	Closing	G1		1,000	0

Supplies Expense   Acct. No. 652

Date	Explan.	PR	Debit	Credit	Balance
2007					
Dec. 31	Adj.	G1	1,050		1,050
31	Closing	G1		1,050	0

Utilities Expense   Acct. No. 690

Date	Explan.	PR	Debit	Credit	Balance
2007					
Dec. 26		G1	230		230
31	Closing	G1		230	0

Income Summary   Acct. No. 901

Date	Explan.	PR	Debit	Credit	Balance
2007					
Dec. 31	Closing	G1		6,100	6,100
31	Closing	G1	4,365		1,735
31	Closing	G1	1,735		0

Step 3: Close Income Summary to Owner's Capital   After steps 1 and 2, the balance of Income Summary is equal to December's net income of $1,735. The third closing entry transfers the balance of the Income Summary account to the capital account. This entry closes the Income Summary account and is step 3 in Exhibit 6.4. The Income Summary account has a zero balance after posting this entry. It continues to have a zero balance until the closing process again occurs at the end of the next period. (If a net loss occurred because expenses exceeded revenues, the third entry is reversed: debit Owner Capital and credit Income Summary.)

> The Income Summary is used only for closing entries.

Step 4: Close Withdrawals Account to Owner's Capital   The fourth closing entry transfers any debit balance in the withdrawals account to the owner's capital account—see step 4 in Exhibit 6.4. This entry gives the withdrawals account a zero balance, and the account is now ready to accumulate next period's withdrawals. This entry also reduces the capital account balance to the $31,535 amount reported on the balance sheet.

We could also have selected the accounts and amounts needing to be closed by identifying individual revenue, expense, and withdrawals accounts in the ledger. This is illustrated in Exhibit 6.4 where we prepare closing entries using the adjusted trial balance. (Information for closing entries is also in the financial statement columns of a work sheet.)

Post-Closing Trial Balance

Exhibit 6.5 shows the entire ledger of FastForward as of December 31 after adjusting and closing entries are posted. (The transaction and adjusting entries are in Chapters 3, 4, and 5.) The temporary accounts (revenues, expenses, and withdrawals) have ending balances equal to zero.

LO4 Explain and prepare a post-closing trial balance.

A **post-closing trial balance** is a list of permanent accounts and their balances from the ledger after all closing entries have been journalized and posted. It lists the balances for all accounts not closed. These accounts comprise a company's assets, liabilities, and equity, which are identical to those in the balance sheet. The aim of a post-closing trial balance is to verify that (1) total debits equal total credits for permanent accounts and (2) all temporary accounts have zero balances. FastForward's post-closing trial balance is shown in Exhibit 6.6. The post-closing trial balance usually is the last step in the accounting process.

FASTFORWARD Post-Closing Trial Balance December 31, 2007	Debit	Credit
Cash	$ 4 3 5 0 00	
Supplies	8 6 7 0 00	
Prepaid insurance	2 3 0 0 00	
Equipment	26 0 0 0 00	
Accumulated depreciation—Equipment		$ 3 7 5 00
Accounts payable		6 2 0 0 00
Salaries payable		2 1 0 00
Unearned consulting revenue		3 0 0 0 00
C. Taylor, Capital		31 5 3 5 00
Totals	$41 3 2 0 00	$41 3 2 0 00

Exhibit 6.6

Post-Closing Trial Balance

Accounting Cycle

Chapters 2 through 6 can be usefully summarized by examining the **accounting cycle.** The term **accounting cycle** refers to the steps in preparing financial statements. It is called a *cycle* because the steps are repeated each reporting period. Exhibit 6.7 shows the 9 steps in the cycle, beginning with analyzing transactions and ending with a post-closing trial balance. Steps 1 through 3 usually occur regularly as a company enters into transactions. Steps 4 through 9 are done at the end of a period.

LO5 Identify steps in the accounting cycle.

Exhibit 6.7

Steps in the Accounting Cycle*

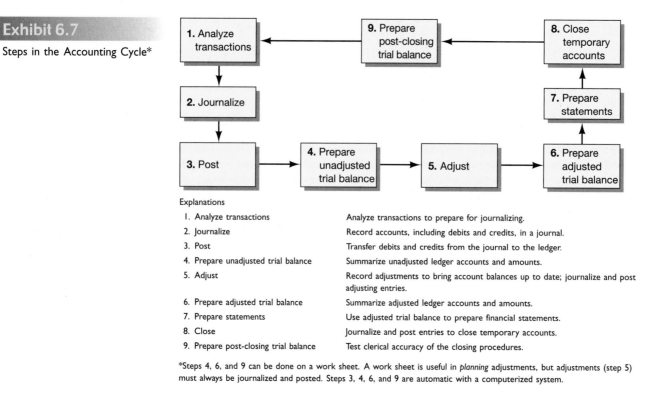

Explanations

1. Analyze transactions — Analyze transactions to prepare for journalizing.
2. Journalize — Record accounts, including debits and credits, in a journal.
3. Post — Transfer debits and credits from the journal to the ledger.
4. Prepare unadjusted trial balance — Summarize unadjusted ledger accounts and amounts.
5. Adjust — Record adjustments to bring account balances up to date; journalize and post adjusting entries.
6. Prepare adjusted trial balance — Summarize adjusted ledger accounts and amounts.
7. Prepare statements — Use adjusted trial balance to prepare financial statements.
8. Close — Journalize and post entries to close temporary accounts.
9. Prepare post-closing trial balance — Test clerical accuracy of the closing procedures.

*Steps 4, 6, and 9 can be done on a work sheet. A work sheet is useful in *planning* adjustments, but adjustments (step 5) must always be journalized and posted. Steps 3, 4, 6, and 9 are automatic with a computerized system.

HOW YOU DOIN'?

Answers—p. 139

3. What are the major steps in preparing closing entries?
4. Why are revenue and expense accounts called *temporary*? Can you identify and list any other temporary accounts?
5. What accounts are listed on the post-closing trial balance?

CURRENT RATIO

LO6 Compute the current ratio and describe what it reveals about a company's financial condition.

An important use of financial statements is to help assess a company's ability to pay its debts in the near future. Such analysis affects decisions by suppliers when allowing a company to buy on credit. It also affects decisions by creditors when lending money to a company, including loan terms such as interest rate, due date, and collateral requirements. It can also affect a manager's decisions about using cash to pay debts when they come due. **Current assets** are cash and other resources that are expected to be sold, collected, or used within one year or the company's operating cycle, whichever is longer. Examples are cash, short-term investments, accounts receivable, short-term notes receivable, goods for sale (called *merchandise* or *inventory*), and prepaid expenses. At this point we can view the operating cycle as starting with the delivery of services (or the purchase of inventory) and ending with the cash receipts from those services or products.

Current liabilities are obligations due to be paid or settled within one year or the operating cycle, whichever is longer. The operating cycle will be defined in later chapters. Examples of current liabilities often include accounts payable, notes payable, wages payable, taxes payable, interest payable, and unearned revenues. The **current ratio** is one measure of a company's ability to pay its short-term obligations. It is defined in Exhibit 6.8 as current assets divided by current liabilities:

$$\text{Current ratio} = \frac{\text{Current assets}}{\text{Current liabilities}}$$

Exhibit 6.8

Current Ratio

Using financial information from **Limited Brands, Inc.**, we compute its current ratio for the recent four-year period. The results are in Exhibit 6.9.

	2005	2004	2003	2002
Current assets (in mil.)	$2,684	$4,433	$3,606	$2,784
Current liabilities (in mil.)	$1,451	$1,388	$1,259	$1,454
Current ratio	1.8	3.2	2.9	1.9
Industry current ratio	2.5	2.7	3.0	2.9

Exhibit 6.9

Limited Brands' Current Ratio

Limited Brands' current ratio averaged 2.5 for 2002–2005. The current ratio for each of these years suggests that the company's short-term obligations can be covered with its short-term assets. However, if its ratio were to approach 1.0, Limited would expect to face challenges in covering liabilities. If the ratio were *less* than 1.0, current liabilities would exceed current assets, and the company's ability to pay short-term obligations could be in doubt.

YOU CALL IT   Answer—p. 139

Analyst You are analyzing the financial condition of a fitness club to assess its ability to meet upcoming loan payments. You compute its current ratio as 1.2. You also find that a major portion of accounts receivable is due from one client who has not made any payments in the past 12 months. Removing this receivable from current assets drops the current ratio to 0.7. What do you conclude?

Demonstration Problem

The partial work sheet of Midtown Repair Company at December 31, 2008, follows.

	Adjusted Trial Balance		Income Statement		Balance Sheet and Statement of Owner's Equity	
	Debit	Credit	Debit	Credit	Debit	Credit
Cash	95,600					
Notes receivable (current)	50,000					
Prepaid insurance	16,000					
Prepaid rent	4,000					
Equipment	170,000					
Accumulated depreciation—Equipment		57,000				
Accounts payable		52,000				
Long-term notes payable		63,000				
C. Trout, Capital		178,500				
C. Trout, Withdrawals	30,000					
Repair services revenue		180,800				
Interest revenue		7,500				
Depreciation expense—Equipment	28,500					
Wages expense	85,000					
Rent expense	48,000					
Insurance expense	6,000					
Interest expense	5,700					
Totals	538,800	538,800				

Required

1. Complete the work sheet by extending the adjusted trial balance totals to the appropriate financial statement columns.
2. Prepare closing entries for Midtown Repair Company.
3. Set up the Income Summary and the C. Trout, Capital account in the general ledger (in balance column format) and post the closing entries to these accounts.
4. Determine the balance of the C. Trout, Capital account to be reported on the December 31, 2008, balance sheet.
5. Prepare an income statement, statement of owner's equity, and balance sheet (in report form) as of December 31, 2008.

Planning the Solution

- Extend the adjusted trial balance account balances to the appropriate financial statement columns.
- Prepare entries to close the revenue accounts to Income Summary, to close the expense accounts to Income Summary, to close Income Summary to the capital account, and to close the withdrawals account to the capital account.
- Post the first and second closing entries to the Income Summary account. Examine the balance of income summary and verify that it agrees with the net income shown on the work sheet.
- Post the third and fourth closing entries to the capital account.
- Use the work sheet's two right-most columns and your answer in part 4 to prepare the balance sheet.

Solution to Demonstration Problem

1. Completing the work sheet.

	Adjusted Trial Balance		Income Statement		Balance Sheet and Statement of Owner's Equity	
	Debit	**Credit**	**Debit**	**Credit**	**Debit**	**Credit**
Cash	95,600				95,600	
Notes receivable (current)	50,000				50,000	
Prepaid insurance	16,000				16,000	
Prepaid rent	4,000				4,000	
Equipment	170,000				170,000	
Accumulated depreciation—Equipment		57,000				57,000
Accounts payable		52,000				52,000
Long-term notes payable		63,000				63,000
C. Trout, Capital		178,500				178,500
C. Trout, Withdrawals	30,000				30,000	
Repair services revenue		180,800		180,800		
Interest revenue		7,500		7,500		
Depreciation expense—Equipment	28,500		28,500			
Wages expense	85,000		85,000			
Rent expense	48,000		48,000			
Insurance expense	6,000		6,000			
Interest expense	5,700		5,700			
Totals	538,800	538,800	173,200	188,300	365,600	350,500
Net Income			15,100			15,100
Totals			188,300	188,300	365,600	365,600

2. Closing entries.

Dec.	31	Repair Services Revenue		180 8 0 0 00	
		Interest Revenue		7 5 0 0 00	
		Income Summary			188 3 0 0 00
		To close revenue accounts.			
Dec.	31	Income Summary		173 2 0 0 00	
		Depreciation Expense—Equipment			28 5 0 0 00
		Wages Expense			85 0 0 0 00
		Rent Expense			48 0 0 0 00
		Insurance Expense			6 0 0 0 00
		Interest Expense			5 7 0 0 00
		To close expense accounts.			
Dec.	31	Income Summary		15 1 0 0 00	
		C. Trout, Capital			15 1 0 0 00
		To close the Income Summary account.			
Dec.	31	C. Trout, Capital		30 0 0 0 00	
		C. Trout, Withdrawals			30 0 0 0 00
		To close the withdrawals account.			

3. Set up the Income Summary and the capital ledger accounts and post the closing entries.

INCOME SUMMARY   Account No. 901

Date		Explanation	PR	Debit	Credit	Balance
2008 Jan.	1	Beginning balance				0 00
Dec.	31	Close revenue accounts			188 3 0 0 00	188 3 0 0 00
	31	Close expense accounts		173 2 0 0 00		15 1 0 0 00
	31	Close income summary		15 1 0 0 00		0 00

C. TROUT, CAPITAL   Account No. 301

Date		Explanation	PR	Debit	Credit	Balance
2008 Jan.	1	Beginning balance				178 5 0 0 00
Dec.	31	Close Income Summary			15 1 0 0 00	193 6 0 0 00
	31	Close C. Trout, Withdrawals		30 0 0 0 00		163 6 0 0 00

4. The final capital balance of $163,600 (from part 3) will be reported on the December 31, 2008, balance sheet. The final capital balance reflects the increase due to the net income earned during the year and the decrease for the owner's withdrawals during the year.

5.

MIDTOWN REPAIR COMPANY Income Statement For Year Ended December 31, 2008			
Revenues			
Repair services revenue	$180 8 0 0 00		
Interest revenue	7 5 0 0 00		
Total revenues		$188 3 0 0 00	
Expenses			
Depreciation expense—Equipment	28 5 0 0 00		
Wages expense	85 0 0 0 00		
Rent expense	48 0 0 0 00		
Insurance expense	6 0 0 0 00		
Interest expense	5 7 0 0 00		
Total expenses		173 2 0 0 00	
Net income		$ 15 1 0 0 00	

MIDTOWN REPAIR COMPANY Statement of Owner's Equity For Year Ended December 31, 2008			
C. Trout, Capital, December 31, 2007			$178 5 0 0 00
Add: Investment by owner	$ 0 00		
Net income	15 1 0 0 00		15 1 0 0 00
			193 6 0 0 00
Less: Withdrawals by owner			30 0 0 0 00
C. Trout, Capital, December 31, 2008			$163 6 0 0 00

MIDTOWN REPAIR COMPANY Balance Sheet December 31, 2008			
Assets			
Cash		$ 95 6 0 0 00	
Notes receivable		50 0 0 0 00	
Prepaid insurance		16 0 0 0 00	
Prepaid rent		4 0 0 0 00	
Equipment	$170 0 0 0 00		
Less: Accumulated depreciation—Equipment	57 0 0 0 00		
Total plant assets		113 0 0 0 00	
Total assets		$278 6 0 0 00	
Liabilities			
Accounts payable		$ 52 0 0 0 00	
Long-term notes payable		63 0 0 0 00	
Total liabilities		115 0 0 0 00	
Equity			
C. Trout, Capital		163 6 0 0 00	
Total liabilities and equity		$278 6 0 0 00	

Summary

LO1 **Explain how to use a work sheet.** A work sheet can be a useful tool in preparing and analyzing financial statements. It is helpful at the end of a period in preparing adjusting entries, an adjusted trial balance, and financial statements. A work sheet usually contains five pairs of columns: Unadjusted Trial Balance, Adjustments, Adjusted Trial Balance, Income Statement, and Balance Sheet & Statement of Owner's Equity.

LO2 **Explain why temporary accounts are closed each period.** Temporary accounts are closed at the end of each accounting period for two main reasons. First, the closing process updates the capital account to include the effects of all transactions and events recorded for the period. Second, it prepares revenue, expense, and withdrawals accounts for the next reporting period by giving them zero balances.

LO3 **Describe and prepare closing entries.** Closing entries involve four steps: (1) close credit balances in revenue (and gain) accounts to Income Summary, (2) close debit balances in expense (and loss) accounts to Income Summary, (3) close Income Summary to the capital account, and (4) close withdrawals account to owner's capital.

LO4 **Explain and prepare a post-closing trial balance.** A post-closing trial balance is a list of permanent accounts and their balances after all closing entries have been journalized and posted. Its purpose is to verify that (1) total debits equal total credits for permanent accounts and (2) all temporary accounts have zero balances.

LO5 **Identify steps in the accounting cycle.** The accounting cycle consists of 9 steps: (1) analyze transactions, (2) journalize, (3) post, (4) prepare an unadjusted trial balance, (5) adjust accounts, (6) prepare an adjusted trial balance, (7) prepare statements, (8) close, and (9) prepare a post-closing trial balance.

LO6 **Compute the current ratio and describe what it reveals about a company's financial condition.** A company's current ratio is defined as current assets divided by current liabilities. We use it to evaluate a company's ability to pay its current liabilities out of current assets.

Guidance Answers to   YOU CALL IT

Entrepreneur   Yes, you are concerned about the absence of a depreciation adjustment. Equipment does depreciate, and financial statements must recognize this occurrence. Its absence suggests an error or a misrepresentation.

Analyst   A current ratio of 1.2 suggests that current assets are sufficient to cover current liabilities, but it implies a minimal buffer in case of errors in measuring current assets or current liabilities. Removing the past due receivable reduces the current ratio to 0.7. Your assessment is that the club will have some difficulty meeting its loan payments.

Guidance Answers to   HOW YOU DOIN'?

1. Amounts in the Unadjusted Trial Balance columns are taken from current account balances in the ledger. The balances for new accounts expected to arise from adjusted entries can be left blank or set at zero.
2. A work sheet offers the advantage of listing on one page all necessary information to make adjusting entries.
3. The major steps in preparing closing entries are to close (1) credit balances in revenue accounts to Income Summary, (2) debit balances in expense accounts to Income Summary, (3) Income Summary to owner's capital, and (4) any withdrawals account to owner's capital.
4. Revenue (and gain) and expense (and loss) accounts are called *temporary* because they are opened and closed each period. The Income Summary and owner's withdrawals accounts are also temporary.
5. Permanent accounts make up the post-closing trial balance, which consist of asset, liability, and equity accounts.

Key Terms   mhhe.com/wildCA

Key Terms are available at the book's Website for learning and testing in an online Flashcard Format.

Accounting cycle (p. 126) Recurring steps performed each accounting period, starting with analyzing transactions and continuing through the post-closing trial balance.

Closing entries (p. 130) Entries recorded at the end of each accounting period to transfer end-of-period balances in revenue, gain, expense, loss, and withdrawal (dividend for a corporation) accounts to the capital account (to retained earnings for a corporation).

Closing process (p. 130) Necessary end-of-period steps to prepare the accounts for recording the transactions of the next period.

Current assets (p. 134) Cash and other assets expected to be sold, collected, or used within one year of the company's operating cycle, whichever is longer.

Current liabilities (p. 134) Obligations due to be paid or settled within one year or the company's operating cycle, whichever is longer.

Current ratio (p. 135) Ratio used to evaluate a company's ability to pay its short-term obligations, calculated by dividing current assets by current liabilities.

Income Summary (p. 130) Temporary account used only in the closing process to which the balances of revenue and expense accounts (including any gains or losses) are transferred; its balance is transferred to the capital account (or retained earnings for a corporation).

Permanent accounts (p. 130) Accounts that reflect activities related to one or more future periods; balance sheet accounts whose balances are not closed; also called *real accounts*.

Post-closing trial balance (p. 133) List of permanent accounts and their balances from the ledger after all closing entries are journalized and posted.

Temporary accounts (p. 130) Accounts used to record revenues, expenses, and withdrawals (dividends for a corporation); they are closed at the end of each period; also called *nominal accounts*.

Work sheet (p. 126) Spreadsheet used to draft an unadjusted trial balance, adjusting entries, adjusted trial balance, and financial statements.

Multiple Choice Quiz   Answers on p. 153   mhhe.com/wildCA

1. G. Venda, owner of Venda Services, withdrew $25,000 from the business during the current year. The entry to close the withdrawals account at the end of the year is:

a.	G. Venda, Withdrawals	25,000
	G. Venda, Capital		25,000
b.	Income Summary	25,000
	G. Venda, Capital		25,000
c.	G. Venda, Withdrawals	25,000
	Cash		25,000
d.	G. Venda, Capital	25,000
	Salary Expense		25,000
e.	G. Venda, Capital	25,000
	G. Venda, Withdrawals		25,000

2. The following information is available for the R. Kandamil Company before closing the accounts. After all of the closing entries are made, what will be the balance in the R. Kandamil, Capital account?

Total revenues	$300,000
Total expenses	195,000
R. Kandamil, Capital	100,000
R. Kandamil, Withdrawals	45,000

   a. $360,000
   b. $250,000
   c. $160,000

   d. $150,000
   e. $60,000

3. Which of the following is a permanent account?
   a. Income Summary
   b. Sales Revenue
   c. Utilities Expense
   d. Rent Expense
   e. Cash

4. Which of the following errors would cause the balance sheet and statement of owner's equity columns of a work sheet to be out of balance?
   a. Entering a revenue amount in the balance sheet and statement of owner's equity debit column.
   b. Entering a liability amount in the balance sheet and statement of owner's equity credit column.
   c. Entering an expense account in the balance sheet and statement of owner's equity debit column.
   d. Entering an asset account in the income statement debit column.
   e. Entering a liability amount in the income statement credit column.

5. The temporary account used only in the closing process to hold the amounts of revenues and expenses before the net difference is added or subtracted from the owner's capital account is called the
   a. Closing account.
   b. Nominal account.
   c. Income Summary account.
   d. Balance Column account.
   e. Contra account.

Discussion Questions

1. What accounts are affected by closing entries? What accounts are not affected?

2. What two purposes are accomplished by recording closing entries?

3. What are the steps in recording closing entries?

4. What is the purpose of the Income Summary account?

5. Explain whether an error has occurred if a post-closing trial balance includes a Depreciation Expense account.

6. What tasks are aided by a work sheet?

7. Why are the debit and credit entries in the Adjustments columns of the work sheet identified with letters?

8. Refer to **Circuit City**'s balance sheet in Appendix A. Identify the accounts listed as current liabilities.

Gloriosa Company began the current period with a $28,000 credit balance in the M. Gloriosa, Capital account. At the end of the period, the company's adjusted account balances include the following temporary accounts with normal balances.

Service fees earned	$45,000	Interest revenue	$6,000
Salaries expense	29,000	M. Gloriosa, Withdrawals	7,200
Depreciation expense	9,000	Utilities expense	3,000

After closing the revenue and expense accounts, what will be the balance of the Income Summary account? After all closing entries are journalized and posted, what will be the balance of the M. Gloriosa, Capital account?

QS 6-1
Determining effects of closing entries
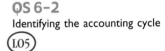
(LO2)(LO3)

List the following steps of the accounting cycle in their proper order.

a. Posting the journal entries.
b. Journalizing and posting adjusting entries.
c. Preparing the adjusted trial balance.
d. Journalizing and posting closing entries.
e. Analyzing transactions and events.
f. Preparing the financial statements.
g. Preparing the unadjusted trial balance.
h. Journalizing transactions and events.
i. Preparing the post-closing trial balance.

QS 6-2
Identifying the accounting cycle
(LO5)

The following information is taken from the work sheet for Warton Company as of December 31, 2008. Using this information, determine the amount for B. Warton, Capital that should be reported on its December 31, 2008, balance sheet.

QS 6-3
Interpreting a work sheet
(LO3)(LO4)

	Income Statement		Balance Sheet and Statement of Owner's Equity	
	Dr.	Cr.	Dr.	Cr.
B. Warton, Capital				72,000
B. Warton, Withdrawals			39,000	
Totals	122,000	181,000		

In preparing a work sheet, indicate the financial statement Debit column to which a normal balance in the following accounts should be extended. Use I for the Income Statement Debit column and B for the Balance Sheet and Statement of Owner's Equity Debit column.

_____ **a.** Equipment
_____ **b.** Owner, Withdrawals
_____ **c.** Prepaid rent
_____ **d.** Depreciation expense—Equipment
_____ **e.** Accounts receivable
_____ **f.** Insurance expense

QS 6-4
Applying a work sheet
(LO1)(LO3)(LO4)

List the following steps in preparing a work sheet in their proper order by writing numbers 1–5 in the blank spaces provided.

a. _____ Total the statement columns, compute net income (loss), and complete work sheet.
b. _____ Extend adjusted balances to appropriate financial statement columns.
c. _____ Prepare an unadjusted trial balance on the work sheet.
d. _____ Prepare an adjusted trial balance on the work sheet.
e. _____ Enter adjustments data on the work sheet.

QS 6-5
Ordering work sheet steps
(LO1)

The ledger of Claudell Company includes the following unadjusted normal balances: Prepaid Rent $1,000 and Wages Expense $25,000. Adjusting entries are required for (a) prepaid rent expense used $200 and (b) accrued wages expense $700. Enter these unadjusted balances and the necessary adjustments on a work sheet and complete the work sheet for these accounts. *Note:* You must include the following accounts: Wages Payable and Rent Expense.

QS 6-6
Preparing a partial work sheet
(LO1)

The ledger of Mai Company includes the following accounts with normal balances: D. Mai, Capital $9,000; D. Mai, Withdrawals $800; Services Revenue $13,000; Wages Expense $8,400; and Rent Expense $1,600. Prepare the necessary closing entries from the available information at December 31.

QS 6-7
Prepare closing entries from the ledger
(LO3)

QS 6-8
Identify post-closing accounts.
(LO4)

Identify the accounts listed in QS 6-7 that would be included in a post-closing trial balance.

EXERCISES

Exercise 6-1
Preparing and posting closing entries
(LO3)

Use the year-end information from the following ledger accounts (assume that all accounts have normal balances) to prepare closing journal entries and then post those entries to the appropriate ledger accounts.

| General Ledger | | | | | | | | | | |

M. Muncel, Capital   Acct. No. 301

Date	PR	Debit	Credit	Balance
Dec. 31	G2			40,000

M. Muncel, Withdrawals   Acct. No. 302

Date	PR	Debit	Credit	Balance
Dec. 31	G2			22,000

Check M. Muncel, Capital (ending balance), $46,200

Services Revenue   Acct. No. 401

Date	PR	Debit	Credit	Balance
Dec. 31	G2			76,000

Depreciation Expense   Acct. No. 603

Date	PR	Debit	Credit	Balance
Dec. 31	G2			15,000

Salaries Expense   Acct. No. 622

Date	PR	Debit	Credit	Balance
Dec. 31	G2			20,000

Insurance Expense   Acct. No. 637

Date	PR	Debit	Credit	Balance
Dec. 31	G2			4,400

Rent Expense   Acct. No. 640

Date	PR	Debit	Credit	Balance
Dec. 31	G2			8,400

Income Summary   Acct. No. 901

Date	PR	Debit	Credit	Balance

Exercise 6-2
Preparing closing entries and a post-closing trial balance
(LO3) (LO4)

The adjusted trial balance for Salonika Marketing Co. follows. Complete the four right-most columns of the table by first entering information for the four closing entries (keyed *1* through *4*) and second by completing the post-closing trial balance.

No.	Account Title	Adjusted Trial Balance		Closing Entry Information		Post-Closing Trial Balance	
		Dr.	Cr.	Dr.	Cr.	Dr.	Cr.
101	Cash	$ 9,200					
106	Accounts receivable	25,000					
153	Equipment	42,000					
154	Accumulated depreciation—Equipment		$ 17,500				
193	Franchise	31,000					
201	Accounts payable		15,000				
209	Salaries payable		4,200				
233	Unearned fees		3,600				
301	E. Salonika, Capital		68,500				
302	E. Salonika, Withdrawals	15,400					
401	Marketing fees earned		80,000				
611	Depreciation expense—Equipment	12,000					
622	Salaries expense	32,500					
640	Rent expense	13,000					
677	Miscellaneous expenses	8,700					
901	Income summary						
	Totals	$188,800	$188,800				

The following adjusted trial balance contains the accounts and balances of Cruz Company as of December 31, 2008, the end of its fiscal year. (1) Prepare the December 31, 2008, closing entries for Cruz Company. (2) Prepare the December 31, 2008, post-closing trial balance for Cruz Company.

Exercise 6-3
Preparing closing entries and a post-closing trial balance
(LO2) (LO3) (LO4)

No.	Account Title	Debit	Credit
101	Cash	$19,000	
126	Supplies	13,000	
128	Prepaid insurance	3,000	
167	Equipment	24,000	
168	Accumulated depreciation—Equipment		$ 7,500
301	T. Cruz, Capital		47,600
302	T. Cruz, Withdrawals	7,000	
404	Services revenue		44,000
612	Depreciation expense—Equipment	3,000	
622	Salaries expense	22,000	
637	Insurance expense	2,500	
640	Rent expense	3,400	
652	Supplies expense	2,200	
	Totals	$99,100	$99,100

Check   (2) T. Cruz, Capital (ending), $51,500; Total debits, $59,000

Use the following December 31, 2008, adjusted trial balance of Wilson Trucking Company to prepare the (1) income statement, (2) statement of owner's equity, and (3) balance sheet for the year ended December 31, 2008. The K. Wilson, Capital account balance is $175,000 at December 31, 2007.

Exercise 6-4
Preparing financial statements
(LO5)

Account Title	Debit	Credit
Cash	$ 8,000	
Accounts receivable	17,500	
Office supplies	3,000	
Trucks	172,000	
Accumulated depreciation—Trucks		$ 36,000
Land	85,000	
Accounts payable		12,000
Interest payable		4,000
Long-term notes payable		53,000
K. Wilson, Capital		175,000
K. Wilson, Withdrawals	20,000	
Trucking fees earned		130,000
Depreciation expense—Trucks	23,500	
Salaries expense	61,000	
Office supplies expense	8,000	
Repairs expense—Trucks	12,000	
Totals	$410,000	$410,000

These 16 accounts are from the Adjusted Trial Balance columns of a company's 10-column work sheet. In the blank space beside each account, write the letter of the appropriate financial statement column (A, B, C, or D) to which a normal account balance is extended.

A. Debit column for the Income Statement columns.

B. Credit column for the Income Statement columns.

C. Debit column for the Balance Sheet and Statement of Owner's Equity columns.

D. Credit column for the Balance Sheet and Statement of Owner's Equity columns.

Exercise 6-5
Extending adjusted account balances on a work sheet
(LO1)

_____	**1.** Interest Revenue		_____	**9.** Accounts Receivable
_____	**2.** Machinery		_____	**10.** Accumulated Depreciation
_____	**3.** Owner, Withdrawals		_____	**11.** Office Supplies
_____	**4.** Depreciation Expense		_____	**12.** Insurance Expense
_____	**5.** Accounts Payable		_____	**13.** Interest Receivable
_____	**6.** Service Fees Revenue		_____	**14.** Cash
_____	**7.** Owner, Capital		_____	**15.** Rent Expense
_____	**8.** Interest Expense		_____	**16.** Wages Payable

Exercise 6-6

Extending accounts in a work sheet

(LO1)

The Adjusted Trial Balance columns of a 10-column work sheet for Planta Company follow. Complete the work sheet by extending the account balances into the appropriate financial statement columns and by entering the amount of net income for the reporting period.

No.	Account Title	Debit	Credit
101	Cash	$ 7,000	
106	Accounts receivable	27,200	
153	Trucks	42,000	
154	Accumulated depreciation—Trucks		$ 17,500
183	Land	32,000	
201	Accounts payable		15,000
209	Salaries payable		4,200
233	Unearned fees		3,600
301	F. Planta, Capital		65,500
302	F. Planta, Withdrawals	15,400	
401	Plumbing fees earned		84,000
611	Depreciation expense—Trucks	6,500	
622	Salaries expense	38,000	
640	Rent expense	13,000	
677	Miscellaneous expenses	8,700	
	Totals	$189,800	$189,800

Check   Net income, $17,800

Exercise 6-7

Completing the income statement columns and preparing closing entries

(LO1) (LO3)

These partially completed Income Statement columns from a 10-column work sheet are for Brown's Bike Rental Company. (1) Use the information to determine the amount that should be entered on the net income line of the work sheet. (2) Prepare the company's closing entries. The owner, H. Brown, did not make any withdrawals this period.

Account Title	Debit	Credit
Rent earned		120,000
Salaries expense	46,300	
Insurance expense	7,400	
Office supplies expense	16,000	
Bike repair expense	4,200	
Depreciation expense—Bikes	20,500	
Totals		
Net income		
Totals		

Check   Net income, $25,600

Exercise 6-8

Preparing a work sheet and recording closing entries

(LO1) (LO3)

The following unadjusted trial balance contains the accounts and balances of Dylan Delivery Company as of December 31, 2008, its first year of operations.

(1) Use the following information about the company's adjustments to complete a 10-column work sheet for Dylan Delivery Company.

a. Unrecorded depreciation on the trucks at the end of the year is $40,000.

b. The total amount of accrued interest expense at year-end is $6,000.

c. The cost of unused office supplies still available at the year-end is $2,000.

(2) Prepare the year-end closing entries for Dylan Delivery Company, and determine the capital amount to be reported on its year-end balance sheet.

Account Title	Debit	Credit
Cash	$ 16,000	
Accounts receivable	34,000	
Office supplies	5,000	
Trucks	350,000	
Accumulated depreciation—Trucks		$ 80,000
Land	160,000	
Accounts payable		24,000
Interest payable		5,000
Long-term notes payable		100,000
S. Dylan, Capital		307,000
S. Dylan, Withdrawals	34,000	
Delivery fees earned		263,000
Depreciation expense—Truck	40,000	
Salaries expense	110,000	
Office supplies expense	15,000	
Interest expense	5,000	
Repairs expense—trucks	10,000	
Totals	$779,000	$779,000

Check Adj. trial balance totals, $820,000; Net income, $39,000

On April 1, 2008, Jiro Nozomi created a new travel agency, Adventure Travel. The following transactions occurred during the company's first month.

PROBLEM SET A

Problem 6-1A
Applying the accounting cycle

mhhe.com/wildCA

(LO2) (LO3) (LO4) (LO5)

April	1	Nozomi invested $30,000 cash and computer equipment worth $20,000 in the business.
	2	Rented furnished office space by paying $1,800 cash for the first month's (April) rent. (Hint: Adventure Travel debited Rent Expense for this payment.)
	3	Purchased $1,000 of office supplies for cash.
	10	Paid $2,400 cash for the premium on a 12-month insurance policy. Coverage begins on April 11.
	14	Paid $1,600 cash for two weeks' salaries earned by employees.
	24	Collected $8,000 cash on commissions from airlines on tickets obtained for customers.
	26	Paid another $1,600 cash for two weeks' salaries earned by employees.
	27	Paid $350 cash for minor repairs to the company's computer.
	27	Paid $750 cash for this month's telephone bill.
	28	Nozomi withdrew $1,500 cash for personal use.

The company's chart of accounts follows:

101	Cash		405	Commissions Earned
106	Accounts Receivable		612	Depreciation Expense—Computer Equip.
124	Office Supplies		622	Salaries Expense
128	Prepaid Insurance		637	Insurance Expense
167	Computer Equipment		640	Rent Expense
168	Accumulated Depreciation—Computer Equip.		650	Office Supplies Expense
209	Salaries Payable		684	Repairs Expense
301	J. Nozomi, Capital		688	Telephone Expense
302	J. Nozomi, Withdrawals		901	Income Summary

Required

1. Use the balance column format to set up each ledger account listed in its chart of accounts.

2. Prepare journal entries to record the transactions for April and post them to the ledger accounts. The company records prepaid and unearned items in balance sheet accounts.

3. Prepare an unadjusted trial balance as of April 30.

4. Use the following information to journalize and post adjusting entries for the month:

   a. Two-thirds of one month's insurance coverage has expired.

   b. At the end of the month, $600 of office supplies are still available.

   c. This month's depreciation on the computer equipment is $500.

   d. Employees earned $420 of unpaid and unrecorded salaries as of month-end.

5. Prepare the income statement and the statement of owner's equity for the month of April and the balance sheet at April 30, 2008.

6. Prepare journal entries to close the temporary accounts and post these entries to the ledger.

7. Prepare a post-closing trial balance.

Check (3) Unadj. trial balance totals, $58,000

(4a) Dr. Insurance Expense, $133

(5) Net income, $447; J. Nozomi, Capital (4/30/2008), $48,947; Total assets, $49,367

(7) P-C trial balance totals, $49,867

Problem 6-2A
Preparing trial balances, closing entries, and financial statements

(LO3) (LO4)

eXcel

mhhe.com/wildCA

The adjusted trial balance of Karise Repairs on December 31, 2008, follows.

No.	Account Title	Debit	Credit
	KARISE REPAIRS		
	Adjusted Trial Balance		
	December 31, 2008		
101	Cash	$ 14 0 0 0 00	
124	Office supplies	1 3 0 0 00	
128	Prepaid insurance	2 0 5 0 00	
167	Equipment	50 0 0 0 00	
168	Accumulated depreciation—Equipment		$ 5 0 0 0 00
201	Accounts payable		14 0 0 0 00
210	Wages payable		6 0 0 00
301	C. Karise, Capital		33 0 0 0 00
302	C. Karise, Withdrawal	16 0 0 0 00	
401	Repair fees earned		90 9 5 0 00
612	Depreciation expense—Equipment	5 0 0 0 00	
623	Wages expense	37 5 0 0 00	
637	Insurance expense	8 0 0 00	
640	Rent expense	10 6 0 0 00	
650	Office supplies expense	3 6 0 0 00	
690	Utilities expense	2 7 0 0 00	
	Totals	$143 5 5 0 00	$143 5 5 0 00

Required

1. Prepare an income statement and a statement of owner's equity for the year 2008, and a balance sheet at December 31, 2008. There are no owner investments in 2008.

2. Enter the adjusted trial balance in the first two columns of a six-column table. Use columns three and four for closing entry information and the last two columns for a post-closing trial balance. Insert an Income Summary account as the last item in the trial balance.

3. Enter closing entry information in the six-column table and prepare journal entries for them.

Check (1) Ending capital balance, $47,750; net income, $30,750

(2) P-C trial balance totals, $67,350

The adjusted trial balance for Tybalt Construction as of December 31, 2008, follows.

Problem 6-3A
Preparing closing entries and
financial statements

(LO3)

TYBALT CONSTRUCTION
Adjusted Trial Balance
December 31, 2008

No.	Account Title	Debit	Credit
101	Cash	$ 5 0 0 0 00	
104	Short-term investments	23 0 0 0 00	
126	Supplies	8 1 0 0 00	
128	Prepaid insurance	7 0 0 0 00	
167	Equipment	40 0 0 0 00	
168	Accumulated depreciation—Equipment		$ 20 0 0 0 00
173	Building	150 0 0 0 00	
174	Accumulated depreciation—Building		50 0 0 0 00
183	Land	55 0 0 0 00	
201	Accounts payable		16 5 0 0 00
203	Interest payable		2 5 0 0 00
208	Rent payable		3 5 0 0 00
210	Wages payable		2 5 0 0 00
213	Property taxes payable		9 0 0 00
233	Unearned professional fees		7 5 0 0 00
251	Long-term notes payable		67 0 0 0 00
301	O. Tybalt, Capital		126 4 0 0 00
302	O. Tybalt, Withdrawals	13 0 0 0 00	
401	Professional fees earned		97 0 0 0 00
406	Rent earned		14 0 0 0 00
407	Dividends earned		2 0 0 0 00
409	Interest earned		2 1 0 0 00
606	Depreciation expense—Building	11 0 0 0 00	
612	Depreciation expense—Equipment	6 0 0 0 00	
623	Wages expense	32 0 0 0 00	
633	Interest expense	5 1 0 0 00	
637	Insurance expense	10 0 0 0 00	
640	Rent expense	13 4 0 0 00	
652	Supplies expense	7 4 0 0 00	
682	Postage expense	4 2 0 0 00	
683	Property taxes expense	5 0 0 0 00	
684	Repairs expense	8 9 0 0 00	
688	Telephone expense	3 2 0 0 00	
690	Utilities expense	4 6 0 0 00	
	Totals	$411 9 0 0 00	$411 9 0 0 00

O. Tybalt invested $5,000 cash in the business during year 2008 (the December 31, 2007, credit balance
of the O. Tybalt, Capital account was $121,400).

Required

1. Prepare the income statement and the statement of owner's equity for the calendar-year 2008, and
the balance sheet at December 31, 2008.

2. Prepare the necessary closing entries at December 31, 2008.

Check   (1) Total assets (12/31/2008),
$218,100; Net income, $4,300

The following unadjusted trial balance is for Ace Construction Co. as of the end of its 2008 fiscal year.
The June 30, 2007, credit balance of the owner's capital account was $53,660, and the owner invested
$35,000 cash in the company during the 2008 fiscal year.

Problem 6-4A
Preparing a work sheet, adjusting
and closing entries, and financial
statements

(LO1) (LO3)

	File Edit View Insert Format Tools Data Window Help			

ACE CONSTRUCTION CO.
Unadjusted Trial Balance
June 30, 2008

No.	Account Title	Debit	Credit
101	Cash	$ 18,500	
126	Supplies	9,900	
128	Prepaid insurance	7,200	
167	Equipment	132,000	
168	Accumulated depreciation—Equipment		$ 26,250
201	Accounts payable		6,800
203	Interest payable		0
208	Rent payable		0
210	Wages payable		0
213	Property taxes payable		0
251	Long-term notes payable		25,000
301	V. Ace, Capital		88,660
302	V. Ace, Withdrawals	33,000	
401	Construction fees earned		132,100
612	Depreciation expense—Equipment	0	
623	Wages expense	46,860	
633	Interest expense	2,750	
637	Insurance expense	0	
640	Rent expense	12,000	
652	Supplies expense	0	
683	Property taxes expense	7,800	
684	Repairs expense	2,910	
690	Utilities expense	5,890	
	Totals	$ 278,810	$ 278,810

Required

1. Prepare a 10-column work sheet for fiscal year 2008, starting with the unadjusted trial balance and including adjustments based on these additional facts.

a. The supplies available at the end of fiscal year 2008 had a cost of $3,300.

b. The cost of expired insurance for the fiscal year is $3,800.

c. Annual depreciation on equipment is $8,400.

d. The June utilities expense of $650 is not included in the unadjusted trial balance because the bill arrived after the trial balance was prepared. The $650 amount owed needs to be recorded.

e. The company's employees have earned $1,800 of accrued wages at fiscal year-end.

f. The rent expense incurred and not yet paid or recorded at fiscal year-end is $500.

g. Additional property taxes of $1,000 have been assessed for this fiscal year but have not been paid or recorded in the accounts.

h. The long-term note payable bears interest at 12% per year. The unadjusted Interest Expense account equals the amount paid for the first 11 months of the 2008 fiscal year. The $250 accrued interest for June has not yet been paid or recorded.

Check (3) Total assets, $122,550;
Current liabilities, $16,000; Net income,
$30,890

2. Use the work sheet to enter the adjusting and closing entries; then journalize them.

3. Prepare the income statement and the statement of owner's equity for the year ended June 30 and the balance sheet at June 30, 2008.

PROBLEM SET B

Problem 6-1B

Applying the accounting cycle

(LO2) (LO3) (LO4) (LO5)

On July 1, 2008, Lula Plume created a new self-storage business, Safe Storage Co. The following transactions occurred during the company's first month.

July 1 Plume invested $30,000 cash and buildings worth $150,000 in the business.
     2 Rented equipment by paying $2,000 cash for the first month's (July) rent. (Hint: Safe Storage debited Rent Expense for this payment.)
     5 Purchased $2,400 of office supplies for cash.
    10 Paid $7,200 cash for the premium on a 12-month insurance policy. Coverage begins on July 11.
    14 Paid an employee $1,000 cash for two weeks' salary earned.
    24 Collected $9,800 cash for storage fees from customers.

26 Paid another $1,000 cash for two weeks' salary earned by an employee.
27 Paid $950 cash for minor repairs to a leaking roof.
27 Paid $400 cash for this month's telephone bill.
28 Plume withdrew $2,000 cash for personal use.

The company's chart of accounts follows:

101	Cash	401	Storage Fees Earned
106	Accounts Receivable	606	Depreciation Expense—Buildings
124	Office Supplies	622	Salaries Expense
128	Prepaid Insurance	637	Insurance Expense
173	Buildings	640	Rent Expense
174	Accumulated Depreciation—Buildings	650	Office Supplies Expense
209	Salaries Payable	684	Repairs Expense
301	L. Plume, Capital	688	Telephone Expense
302	L. Plume, Withdrawals	901	Income Summary

Required

1. Use the balance column format to set up each ledger account listed in its chart of accounts.
2. Prepare journal entries to record the transactions for July and post them to the ledger accounts. Record prepaid and unearned items in balance sheet accounts.
3. Prepare an unadjusted trial balance as of July 31.
4. Use the following information to journalize and post adjusting entries for the month:
   a. Two-thirds of one month's insurance coverage has expired.
   b. At the end of the month, $1,525 of office supplies are still available.
   c. This month's depreciation on the buildings is $1,500.
   d. An employee earned $100 of unpaid and unrecorded salary as of month-end.
5. Prepare the income statement and the statement of owner's equity for the month of July and the balance sheet at July 31, 2008.
6. Prepare journal entries to close the temporary accounts and post these entries to the ledger.
7. Prepare a post-closing trial balance.

Check (3) Unadj. trial balance totals, $189,800

(4a) Dr. Insurance Expense, $400

(5) Net income, $1,575; L. Plume, Capital (7/31/2008), $179,575; Total assets, $179,675

(7) P-C trial balance totals, $181,175

Santo Company's adjusted trial balance on December 31, 2008, follows.

Problem 6–2B
Preparing trial balances, closing entries, and financial statements

(L03) (L04)

SANTO COMPANY
Adjusted Trial Balance
December 31, 2008

No.	Account Title	Debit	Credit
101	Cash	$ 14 4 5 0 00	
125	Store supplies	5 1 4 0 00	
128	Prepaid insurance	1 2 0 0 00	
167	Equipment	31 0 0 0 00	
168	Accumulated depreciation—Equipment		$8 0 0 0 00
201	Accounts payable		1 5 0 0 00
210	Wages payable		2 7 0 0 00
301	P. Holt, Capital		35 6 5 0 00
302	P. Holt, Withdrawals	15 0 0 0 00	
401	Repair fees earned		54 7 0 0 00
612	Depreciation expense—Equipment	2 0 0 0 00	
623	Wages expense	26 4 0 0 00	
637	Insurance expense	6 0 0 00	
640	Rent expense	3 6 0 0 00	
651	Store supplies expense	1 2 0 0 00	
690	Utilities expense	1 9 6 0 00	
	Totals	$102 5 5 0 00	$102 5 5 0 00

Check   (1) Ending capital balance, $39,590

(2) P-C trial balance totals, $51,790

Required

1. Prepare an income statement and a statement of owner's equity for the year 2008, and a balance sheet at December 31, 2008. There are no owner investments in 2008.

2. Enter the adjusted trial balance in the first two columns of a six-column table. Use the middle two columns for closing entry information and the last two columns for a post-closing trial balance. Insert an Income Summary account (No. 901) as the last item in the trial balance.

3. Enter closing entry information in the six-column table and prepare journal entries for them.

Problem 6-3B

Preparing closing entries and financial statements

(LO3)

The adjusted trial balance for Anara Co. as of December 31, 2008, follows.

ANARA CO.
Adjusted Trial Balance
December 31, 2008

No.	Account Title	Debit	Credit
101	Cash	$ 7 4 0 0 00	
104	Short-term investments	11 2 0 0 00	
126	Supplies	4 6 0 0 00	
128	Prepaid insurance	1 0 0 0 00	
167	Equipment	24 0 0 0 00	
168	Accumulated depreciation—Equipment		$ 4 0 0 0 00
173	Building	100 0 0 0 00	
174	Accumulated depreciation—Building		10 0 0 0 00
183	Land	30 5 0 0 00	
201	Accounts payable		3 5 0 0 00
203	Interest payable		1 7 5 0 00
208	Rent payable		4 0 0 00
210	Wages payable		1 2 8 0 00
213	Property taxes payable		3 3 3 0 00
233	Unearned professional fees		7 5 0 00
251	Long-term notes payable		40 0 0 0 00
301	P. Anara, Capital		92 8 0 0 00
302	P. Anara, Withdrawals	8 0 0 0 00	
401	Professional fees earned		59 6 0 0 00
406	Rent earned		4 5 0 0 00
407	Dividends earned		1 0 0 0 00
409	Interest earned		1 3 2 0 00
606	Depreciation expense—Building	2 0 0 0 00	
612	Depreciation expense—Equipment	1 0 0 0 00	
623	Wages expense	18 5 0 0 00	
633	Interest expense	1 5 5 0 00	
637	Insurance expense	1 5 2 5 00	
640	Rent expense	3 6 0 0 00	
652	Supplies expense	1 0 0 0 00	
682	Postage expense	4 1 0 00	
683	Property taxes expense	4 8 2 5 00	
684	Repairs expense	6 7 9 00	
688	Telephone expense	5 2 1 00	
690	Utilities expense	1 9 2 0 00	
	Totals	$224 2 3 0 00	$224 2 3 0 00

P. Anara invested $40,000 cash in the business during year 2008 (the December 31, 2007, credit balance of the P. Anara, Capital account was $52,800).

Required

Check   (1) Total assets (12/31/2008), $164,700; Net income, $28,890

1. Prepare the income statement and the statement of owner's equity for the calendar year 2008 and the balance sheet at December 31, 2008.

2. Prepare the necessary closing entries at December 31, 2008.

The following unadjusted trial balance is for Power Demolition Company as of the end of its April 30, 2008, fiscal year. The April 30, 2007, credit balance of the owner's capital account was $46,900, and the owner invested $40,000 cash in the company during the 2008 fiscal year.

Problem 6–4B

Preparing a work sheet, adjusting and closing entries, and financial statements

(L01) (L03)

File Edit View Insert Format Tools Data Window Help

POWER DEMOLITION COMPANY
Unadjusted Trial Balance
April 30, 2008

No.	Account Title	Debit	Credit
101	Cash	$ 7,000	
126	Supplies	16,000	
128	Prepaid insurance	12,600	
167	Equipment	200,000	
168	Accumulated depreciation—Equipment		$ 14,000
201	Accounts payable		6,800
203	Interest payable		0
208	Rent payable		0
210	Wages payable		0
213	Property taxes payable		0
251	Long-term notes payable		30,000
301	J. Bonair, Capital		86,900
302	J. Bonair, Withdrawals	12,000	
401	Demolition fees earned		187,000
612	Depreciation expense—Equipment	0	
623	Wages expense	41,400	
633	Interest expense	3,300	
637	Insurance expense	0	
640	Rent expense	13,200	
652	Supplies expense	0	
683	Property taxes expense	9,700	
684	Repairs expense	4,700	
690	Utilities expense	4,800	
	Totals	$ 324,700	$ 324,700

Required

1. Prepare a 10-column work sheet for fiscal year 2008, starting with the unadjusted trial balance and including adjustments based on these additional facts.

   a. The supplies available at the end of fiscal year 2008 had a cost of $7,900.

   b. The cost of expired insurance for the fiscal year is $10,600.

   c. Annual depreciation on equipment is $7,000.

   d. The April utilities expense of $800 is not included in the unadjusted trial balance because the bill arrived after the trial balance was prepared. The $800 amount owed needs to be recorded.

   e. The company's employees have earned $2,000 of accrued wages at fiscal year-end.

   f. The rent expense incurred and not yet paid or recorded at fiscal year-end is $3,000.

   g. Additional property taxes of $550 have been assessed for this fiscal year but have not been paid or recorded in the accounts.

   h. The long-term note payable bears interest at 12% per year. The unadjusted Interest Expense account equals the amount paid for the first 11 months of the 2008 fiscal year. The $300 accrued interest for April has not yet been paid or recorded.

2. Enter the adjusting and closing entry information in the work sheet; then journalize them.

3. Prepare the income statement and the statement of owner's equity for the year ended April 30, and the balance sheet at April 30, 2008.

Check (3) Total assets, $195,900; Total liabilities, $43,450; Net income, $77,550

(This serial problem began in Chapter 1 and continues through most of the book. If previous chapter segments were not completed, the serial problem can begin at this point. It is helpful, but not necessary, that you use the Working Papers that accompany the book.)

SERIAL PROBLEM

Success Systems

(L03) (L04)

SP 6 The December 31, 2007, adjusted trial balance of Success Systems (reflecting its transactions from October through December of 2007) follows.

No.	Account Title	Debit	Credit
101	Cash	$ 80,260	
106	Accounts receivable	5,800	
126	Computer supplies	775	
128	Prepaid insurance	1,800	
131	Prepaid rent	875	
163	Office equipment	10,000	
164	Accumulated depreciation—Office equipment		$ 625
167	Computer equipment	25,000	
168	Accumulated depreciation—Computer equipment		1,250
201	Accounts payable		2,100
210	Wages payable		600
236	Unearned computer services revenue		2,500
301	A. Lopez, Capital		110,000
302	A. Lopez, Withdrawals	8,500	
403	Computer services revenue		36,170
612	Depreciation expense—Office equipment	625	
613	Depreciation expense—Computer equipment	1,250	
623	Wages expense	4,650	
637	Insurance expense	600	
640	Rent expense	2,625	
652	Computer supplies expense	4,675	
655	Advertising expense	2,990	
676	Mileage expense	1,120	
677	Miscellaneous expenses	300	
684	Repairs expense—Computer	1,400	
901	Income summary		0
	Totals	$153,245	$153,245

Check Post-closing trial balance
totals, $124,510

Required

1. Record and post the necessary closing entries for Success Systems.

2. Prepare a post-closing trial balance as of December 31, 2007.

BEYOND THE NUMBERS

**REPORTING IN
ACTION**

(LO2) (LO3)

BTN 6-1   Refer to Best Buy's financial statements in Appendix A to answer the following.

Required

1. For the fiscal year ended February 26, 2005, what amount is credited to Income Summary to summarize its revenues earned?

2. For the fiscal year ended February 26, 2005, what amount is debited to Income Summary to summarize its expenses incurred?

3. For the fiscal year ended February 26, 2005, what is the balance of its Income Summary account before it is closed?

Fast Forward

4. Access Best Buy's annual report for fiscal years ending after February 26, 2005, at its Website (BestBuy.com) or the SEC's EDGAR database (www.sec.gov). How has the amount of net income closed to Income Summary changed in the fiscal years ending after February 26, 2005?

BTN 6-2 Key figures for the recent two years of both **Best Buy** and **Circuit City** follow.

Key Figures ($ thousands)	Best Buy		Circuit City	
	Current Year	Prior Year	Current Year	Prior Year
Current assets	$6,903,000	$5,724,000	$2,685,715	$2,919,061
Current liabilities	4,959,000	4,501,000	1,263,846	1,138,198

Required

1. Compute the current ratio for both years and both companies.
2. Which company has the better ability to pay short-term obligations according to the current ratio?
3. Analyze and comment on each company's current ratios for the past two years.
4. How do Best Buy's and Circuit City's current ratios compare to their industry average ratio of 1.6?

BTN 6-3 On January 20, 2008, Tamira Nelson, the accountant for Picton Enterprises, is feeling pressure to complete the annual financial statements. The company president has said he needs up-to-date financial statements to share with the bank on January 21 at a dinner meeting that has been called to discuss Picton's obtaining loan financing for a special building project. Tamira knows that she will not be able to gather all the needed information in the next 24 hours to prepare the entire set of adjusting entries that must be posted before the financial statements accurately portray the company's performance and financial position for the fiscal period ended December 31, 2007. Tamira ultimately decides to estimate several expense accruals at the last minute. When deciding on estimates for the expenses, she uses low estimates because she does not want to make the financial statements look worse than they are. Tamira finishes the financial statements before the deadline and gives them to the president without mentioning that several account balances are estimates that she provided.

Required

1. Identify several courses of action that Tamira could have taken instead of the one she took.
2. If you were in Tamira's situation, what would you have done? Briefly justify your response.

BTN 6-4 Assume that one of your classmates states that a company's books should be ongoing and therefore not closed until that business is terminated. Write a one-half-page memo to this classmate explaining the concept of the closing process by drawing analogies between (1) a scoreboard for an athletic event and the revenue and expense accounts of a business or (2) a sports team's record book and the capital account. (*Hint:* Think about what would happen if the scoreboard is not cleared before the start of a new game.)

BTN 6-5 Access **Motley Fool**'s discussion of the current ratio at www.Fool.com/School/BalanceSheet/ BalanceSheet05.htm. (Note that if the page changed, search the site for the *current ratio*.)

Required

1. What level for the current ratio is generally regarded as sufficient to meet near-term operating needs?
2. Once you have calculated the current ratio for a company, what should you compare it against?
3. What are the implications for a company that has a current ratio that is too high?

BTN 6-6 Review this chapter's opening feature involving Janet Freeman and her company **Betty Rides**.
1. Why was it important for Janet to simplify Betty Rides' chart of accounts?
2. Explain how adjusting and closing entries help Janet make sure the right expenses were charged in the correct period.
3. How can understanding the accounting system for the company help Janet make business decisions?

ANSWERS TO MULTIPLE CHOICE QUIZ

1. e
2. c
3. e

4. a
5. c

A Look Back

Chapter 6 explained the final steps in the accounting cycle. We described the closing process and showed how a work sheet aids in preparing financial statements.

A Look at This Chapter

This chapter extends our study of accounting to fraud and internal control. We explain workplace fraud and describe internal control procedures that can help prevent it.

A Look Ahead

Chapter 8 focuses on cash and control of cash. We discuss control features of banking activities and petty cash systems.

Chapter 7

Fraud, Ethics, and Controls

LEARNING OBJECTIVES

 LO 1 Define workplace fraud and explain the four elements common to all fraud schemes.

 LO 2 Describe the three major types of workplace fraud.

 LO 3 Define internal control and identify its purpose and principles.

 LO 4 Explain how technology impacts an internal control system.

 LO 5 Describe the limitations of internal control.

 LO 6 Explain provisions of the Sarbanes-Oxley Act that are designed to detect and curtail fraud.

 LO 7 *Appendix 7A—Describe the voucher system to control cash disbursements.*

"I'm living my dream every day . . . you have to love it to be successful"—Todd Graves

Fishing for Chicken Fingers

BATON ROUGE, LA—To launch his business, Todd Graves needed to go fishing. "After writing my business plan, buying a cheap suit, and borrowing a briefcase," says Todd, "I went to see every bank in town to fund my first chicken finger restaurant." Not one bank would lend him the money.

Desperate, Todd left for Alaska to work as a salmon fisherman. The pay was great but the job dangerous. "Boats would often ram each other to get better sets for their nets." Having saved enough money to get started, Todd returned to Louisiana and launched **Raising Cane's Chicken Fingers** (**raisingcanes.com**). Today, his restaurants generate millions in annual sales and continue to grow.

Although chicken fingers are key to Raising Cane's success, Todd's internal controls are equally impressive. Several controls keep restaurant activities in check and safeguard assets. These include cash register procedures, inventory controls, and employee management. Todd even safeguards the sauce recipe!

Tight controls boost productivity and cut expenses, but these controls are applied thoughtfully. "We make it a priority to respect, recognize, and reward our crew," says Todd. "It's something we call Cane's Love."

Internal controls are crucial for Todd since on busy days his nearly 30 restaurants attract thousands of customers and their cash. "We have a vision: To be known all over the world," says Todd. "I'm fortunate. I don't have a job; I have a passion. Your passion and culture are what set you apart." So, what is the end game for Raising Cane's? "I don't have an end game," says Todd. "Ray Kroc didn't have an end game. Dave Thomas didn't have an end game." Now that is a winning game plan.

[Sources: *Raising Cane's Chicken Fingers Website*; January 2007; *Entrepreneur*, October 2004 and November 2003; *Business Report*, November 2004; *LSU Reveille*, February 2004]

We all are aware of reports and experiences of theft and fraud. These affect us in several ways: We lock doors, chain bikes, review sales receipts, and buy alarm systems. A company also takes actions to safeguard, control, and manage what it owns. Experience tells us that small companies are most vulnerable, usually due to weak internal controls. This chapter discusses workplace fraud. Management must set up policies and procedures to safeguard a company's assets. To do so, management *and* employees must understand and apply principles of internal control. This chapter describes these principles and how to apply them.

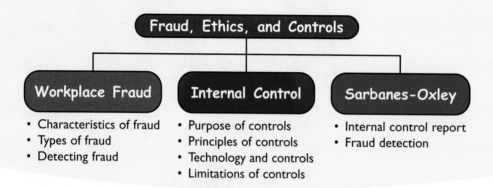

Fraud, Ethics, and Controls		
Workplace Fraud	**Internal Control**	**Sarbanes-Oxley**
• Characteristics of fraud	• Purpose of controls	• Internal control report
• Types of fraud	• Principles of controls	• Fraud detection
• Detecting fraud	• Technology and controls	
	• Limitations of controls	

Workplace Fraud

 LO1 Define workplace fraud and explain the four elements common to all fraud schemes.

Workplace fraud involves the use of one's job for personal gain, through the deliberate misuse of the employer's assets. Such fraud includes, for example, theft of the employer's cash or other assets, overstating reimbursable expenses, payroll schemes, and financial statement frauds. Workplace fraud affects all business and it is costly: A 2006 *Report to the Nation* from the Association of Certified Fraud Examiners estimates the average U.S. business loses 5% of its annual revenues to fraud. Fraud is particularly costly for small businesses because it can lead to the business's demise.

Elements of Workplace Fraud Schemes

While there are many types of fraud schemes, all workplace fraud

- ■ Is secret.
- ■ Violates the employee's duties to his employer.
- ■ Is done to provide direct or indirect benefit to the employee.
- ■ Costs the employer money.

For example, in a billing fraud, an employee sets up a bogus supplier. The employee then secretly prepares bills from the supplier and pays these bills from the employer's checking account. The employee cashes the checks sent to the bogus supplier and uses them for his or her own personal benefit. Later in this chapter we discuss how a system of internal control can help the employer prevent this and other types of fraud schemes.

Major Types of Workplace Fraud

LO2 Describe the three major types of workplace fraud.

According to the Association of Certified Fraud Examiners' *2006 Report to the Nation*, most workplace frauds fall into three broad types:

1. **Asset misappropriation.** This type involves the theft or misuse of the employer's resources. For example, the employee might steal cash or inventory, disburse payroll checks to bogus employees, or pay invoices to fictitious suppliers.
2. **Corruption.** These schemes involve an employee's wrongful use of influence in a business transaction with the result that the employee receives financial gain at the expense of the employer. Bribery is often part of corruption schemes; for example, an employee might bribe another party to take part in a fraudulent invoice scheme.
3. **Fraudulent financial statements.** Falsification of the employer's financial statements commonly includes recording fictitious revenues, overstating certain asset values, and hiding certain liabilities or expenses.

Exhibit 7.1 shows the percentage of reported frauds by type and their related losses. The percentages sum to more than 100 percent as a fraud occurrence might involve more than one type. Asset misappropriation is the most commonly reported fraud, but fraudulent financial statements cause the greatest losses in dollars.

Reported Frauds	Percentage of Reported Frauds	Loss per Occurrence
Asset misappropriation	91.5%	$ 150,000
Corruption	30.8%	$ 538,000
Fraudulent financial statements	10.6%	$2,000,000

Exhibit 7.1

Losses from Fraud

Percentages in this chart sum to more than 100% as several cases involve more than one type of fraud.

Internal Control

This section describes internal control and its fundamental principles. We also discuss how technology impacts internal control and the limitations of control procedures.

Purpose of Internal Control

Managers (or owners) of small businesses often control the entire operation. These managers usually purchase all assets, hire and manage employees, negotiate all contracts, and sign all checks. They know from personal contact and observation whether the business is actually receiving the assets and services paid for. Most companies, however, cannot maintain this close personal supervision. They must use formal procedures to control business activities.

 Define internal control and identify its purpose and principles.

Managers use an internal control system to monitor and control business activities. An **internal control system** is the policies and procedures managers use to:

- Protect assets.
- Ensure reliable accounting.
- Promote efficient operations.
- Urge adherence to company policies.

With company growth comes increased reporting and controls to safeguard assets and manage operations.

Managers like internal control systems because they can prevent avoidable losses, help managers plan operations, and monitor company and employee performance. Internal controls do not provide guarantees against loss, but they lower the company's risk of loss.

What's the Password?
IN THE NEWS

Good internal control prevents unauthorized access to assets and accounting records by requiring passwords. It takes a password, for instance, to boot up most office PCs, log onto a network, and access voice mail, e-mail, and most online services.

Principles of Internal Control

Internal controls vary across companies due to factors like the nature of the business and its size. Certain fundamental internal control principles apply to all companies. The **principles of internal control** are to

1. Establish responsibilities.
2. Maintain adequate records.
3. Insure assets and bond key employees.
4. Separate recordkeeping from custody of assets.
5. Divide responsibility for related transactions.
6. Apply technological controls.
7. Perform regular and independent reviews.

This section explains these seven principles and describes how internal control procedures reduce the risk of workplace fraud and theft. These procedures also increase the reliability and accuracy of accounting records.

Establish Responsibilities

Responsibility for a task should be clearly established and assigned to one person. When a problem occurs in a company where responsibility is not identified, determining who is at fault is difficult. For instance, if two salesclerks share the same cash register and there is a cash shortage, neither clerk can be held accountable. To prevent this problem, one clerk might be given responsibility for handling all cash sales. Alternately, a company can use a register with separate cash drawers for each clerk. Most of us have waited at a retail counter during a shift change while employees swap cash drawers.

Maintain Adequate Records

Good recordkeeping helps protect assets and ensures that employees use prescribed procedures. Reliable records provide information that managers use to monitor company activities. When detailed records are kept, for instance, equipment is unlikely to be lost or stolen without detection. Similarly, transactions are less likely to be entered in wrong accounts if a chart of accounts is set up and carefully used. Preprinted forms and internal documents are also useful. When sales slips are properly designed, for instance, sales personnel can record needed information efficiently with less chance of errors or delays to customers. When sales slips are prenumbered and controlled, each one issued is the responsibility of one salesperson. This prevents the salesperson from pocketing cash by making a sale and destroying the sales slip. Computerized point-of-sale systems achieve the same control results.

Insure Assets and Bond Key Employees

Assets should be adequately insured against loss. Employees handling large amounts of cash and easily transferable assets should be bonded. An employee is *bonded* when a company purchases an insurance policy, or a bond, against losses from theft by that employee. Bonding reduces the risk of loss and discourages theft. Bonded employees know an independent bonding company is unlikely to be sympathetic with an employee involved in theft.

Separate Recordkeeping from Custody of Assets

A person who controls or has access to an asset must not keep that asset's accounting records. This reduces the risk of theft or waste of an asset because the person with control over it knows that another person keeps its records. Also, a recordkeeper who does not have access to the asset has no reason to falsify records. To steal an asset and hide the theft from the records, two or more people must *collude* (agree in secret to commit the fraud).

IN THE NEWS

Tag Control

A novel technique exists for marking physical assets. It involves embedding a less than one-inch-square tag of fibers that creates a unique optical signature recordable by scanners. Manufacturers hope to embed tags in everything from compact discs and credit cards to designer clothes.

Divide Responsibility for Related Transactions

Good internal control divides responsibility for a transaction or a series of related transactions between two or more individuals or departments. This ensures that the work of one individual acts as a check on the other. This *separation of duties* is not a call for duplication of work. Each employee or department should perform unduplicated work. Examples of transactions with divided responsibility are placing purchase orders, receiving merchandise, and paying vendors. These tasks should not be given to one individual or department. Assigning responsibility for two or more of these tasks to one party increases mistakes and perhaps fraud. Having an independent person, for example, check incoming goods for quality and quantity encourages more care and attention to detail than having the person who placed the order do the checking. Added protection can result from having a third person approve payment of the invoice. A company can even designate a fourth person with authority to write checks as another protective measure.

Apply Technological Controls

Cash registers, check protectors, time clocks, and personal identification scanners are examples of devices that can improve internal control. Technology often improves the effectiveness of controls. A cash register with a locked-in tape or electronic file

Many companies have a mandatory vacation policy for employees who handle cash. When another employee must cover for the one on vacation, it is more difficult to hide cash frauds.

The Association of Certified Fraud Examiners (**cfenet.com**) estimates that employee fraud costs small companies more than $100,000 per incident.

makes a record of each cash sale. A check protector perforates the amount of a check into its face and makes it difficult to alter the amount. A time clock registers the exact time an employee both arrives at and leaves from the job. Personal scanners limit access to only authorized individuals. These and other technological controls are an effective part of many internal control systems.

IN THE NEWS

About Face

Face-recognition software snaps a digital picture of a person's face and converts key facial features—say, the distance between the eyes—into a series of numerical values. These can be stored on an ID or ATM card as a simple bar code to prohibit unauthorized access.

Perform Regular and Independent Reviews
Personnel changes, time pressures, and technological advances present risks of errors or fraud. To counter these factors, regular reviews of internal control systems are needed to ensure that procedures are followed. These reviews are preferably done by internal auditors not directly involved in the activities. Many companies also pay for audits by independent, external auditors.

About one-half of frauds detected in small businesses are detected by internal audits. Losses from fraud are lower in businesses with an internal audit department.

Technology and Internal Control

Technology impacts internal control systems in several important ways. Technology allows us quicker access to databases and information. Used effectively, this greatly improves managers' abilities to monitor and control business activities. This section also describes other techno-logical impacts.

 LO4 Explain how technology impacts an internal control system.

Reduced Processing Errors
Technology reduces errors in processing information. If the software and data entry are correct, the risk of mechanical and mathematical errors is nearly eliminated. However, less human involvement in data processing can cause data entry errors to go undiscovered. Also, errors in software can produce consistent but erroneous processing of transactions. Continually checking and monitoring all types of systems are important.

Information on Internet fraud can be found at these Websites: ftc.gov/ftc/consumer.htmsec.gov/ investor/pubs/cyberfraud.htm; www.fraud.org

More Extensive Testing of Records
A company's review and audit of electronic records can include more extensive testing when information is easily and rapidly accessed. When accounting records are kept manually, auditors and others likely select only small samples of data to test. When data are accessible with computer technology, however, auditors can quickly analyze large samples or even the entire database.

IN THE NEWS

Hidden Risks

The basic purposes of paper and electronic documents are similar. However, the internal control system must change to reflect different risks, including confidential and competitive-sensitive information that is at greater risk in electronic systems.

Limited Evidence of Processing
With computers, fewer hard-copy items of documen-tary evidence are available for review. Yet technologically advanced systems can provide new evidence. They can, for instance, record who made the entries, the date and time, the source of the entry, and so on. Technology can also be designed to require the use of passwords or other identification before access to the system is granted. This means that internal control de-pends more on the design and operation of the information system and less on the analysis of its resulting documents.

There's a new security device—a person's ECG (electrocardiogram) reading—that is as unique as a finger-print and a lot harder to lose or steal than a PIN. ECGs can be read through fingertip touches. An ECG also shows that a living person is actually there, whereas fingerprint and facial recognition software can be fooled.

Crucial Separation of Duties
Technology often eliminates or consolidates some jobs. A company with a reduced workforce risks losing its crucial separation of duties. To minimize risk of error and fraud, the person who designs and programs the information system must not be the one who operates it. The company must also separate control over computer programs and files from the activities related to cash receipts and disbursements. For instance, a computer operator should not control check-writing activities. Separation of duties can be especially difficult and costly in small companies with few employees.

Happiest Fraud Victim

Certified Fraud Examiners Website reports the following: Andrew Cameron stole Jacqueline Boanson's credit card. Cameron headed to the racetrack and promptly charged two bets for $150 on the credit card—winning $400. Unfortunately for Cameron the racetrack refused to pay him cash as its policy is to credit winnings from bets made on a credit card to that same card. Cameron was later nabbed, and the racetrack let Ms. Boanson keep the winnings.

"Worst case of identity theft I've ever seen!"

Copyright 2004 by Randy Glasbergen. www.glasbergen.com

Increased E-Commerce Technology has encouraged the growth of e-commerce. Amazon.com and eBay are examples of companies that successfully use e-commerce. Most companies have some e-commerce transactions. All such transactions involve at least three risks. (1) *Credit card number theft* is a risk of using, transmitting, and storing such data online. This increases the cost of e-commerce. (2) *Computer viruses* are harmful programs that attach themselves to innocent files for purposes of infecting other files and programs. (3) *Impersonation* online can result in charges of sales to bogus accounts, purchases of inappropriate materials, and the unknowing release of confidential information to hackers. Companies use both *firewalls* and *encryption* to combat some of these risks—firewalls are points of entry to a system that require passwords to continue, and encryption is a mathematical process to rearrange contents that cannot be read without the process code. Nearly 5% of Americans already report being victims of identity theft, and roughly 10 million say their privacy has been compromised.

Limitations of Internal Control

 Describe the limitations of internal control.

All internal control policies and procedures have limitations which usually arise from either (1) the human element, or (2) the cost-benefit principle.

Internal controls are applied by people. This human element creates several potential limitations that we can categorize as either (1) human error or (2) human fraud. *Human error* can occur from negligence, fatigue, misjudgment, or confusion. *Human fraud* involves intent by people to defeat internal controls, such as *management override,* for personal gain. Fraud also includes collusion to thwart the separation of duties. The human element highlights the importance of establishing an *internal control environment* to convey management's commitment to internal control policies and procedures.

Dollar losses from fraud more than triple when two or more people collude.

Cybercrime.gov pursues computer and intellectual property crimes, including that of e-commerce.

The second major internal control is the *cost-benefit principle.* The costs of internal controls must not exceed their benefits. Analysis of costs and benefits must consider the impact on morale. Most companies, for instance, can legally read employees' e-mails, yet few do unless they have evidence of potential harm to the company. The same holds for drug testing, phone tapping, and hidden cameras. The bottom line is that managers must establish internal control policies and procedures with a net benefit to the company.

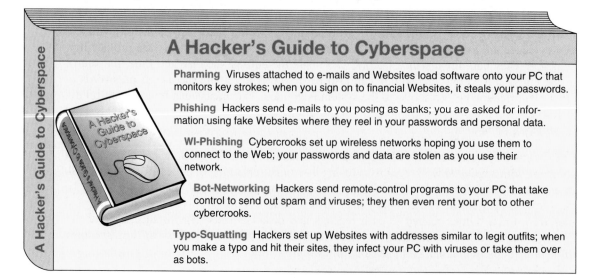

A Hacker's Guide to Cyberspace

Pharming Viruses attached to e-mails and Websites load software onto your PC that monitors key strokes; when you sign on to financial Websites, it steals your passwords.

Phishing Hackers send e-mails to you posing as banks; you are asked for information using fake Websites where they reel in your passwords and personal data.

WI-Phishing Cybercrooks set up wireless networks hoping you use them to connect to the Web; your passwords and data are stolen as you use their network.

Bot-Networking Hackers send remote-control programs to your PC that take control to send out spam and viruses; they then even rent your bot to other cybercrooks.

Typo-Squatting Hackers set up Websites with addresses similar to legit outfits; when you make a typo and hit their sites, they infect your PC with viruses or take them over as bots.

HOW YOU DOIN'?

Answers—p. 166

1. Principles of internal control suggest that (choose one): (*a*) Responsibility for a series of related transactions (such as placing orders, receiving and paying for merchandise) should be assigned to one employee; (*b*) Responsibility for individual tasks should be shared by more than one employee so that one serves as a check on the other; or (*c*) Employees who handle considerable cash and easily transferable assets should be bonded.

2. What are some impacts of computing technology on internal control?

Control of Cash Disbursements

Control of cash disbursements is especially important as most large thefts occur from payment of fictitious invoices. In another disbursement fraud scheme, employees submit fictitious or inflated business expenses for reimbursement. In this section, and in more detail in Appendix 7A, we discuss how a voucher system can help control disbursements. In the next chapter we discuss other important controls for cash disbursements, including payment of most expenditures by check, the use of a petty cash system for small cash expenditures, and bank reconciliations.

Voucher System of Control   A **voucher system** is a set of procedures and approvals designed to control payments and the acceptance of obligations. The voucher system of control establishes procedures for

> A *voucher* is an internal document (or file).

■ Verifying, approving, and recording obligations for eventual cash payment.
■ Issuing checks for payment of verified, approved, and recorded obligations.

A reliable voucher system follows standard procedures for every transaction. This applies even when multiple purchases are made from the same supplier.

Cyber Setup ——— IN THE NEWS

The FTC is on the cutting edge of cybersleuthing. Opportunists in search of easy money are lured to **WeMarket4U.net/netops**. Take the bait and you get warned—and possibly targeted. The top 4 fraud complaints as compiled by the Internet Crime Complaint Center are shown to the right.

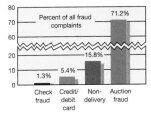

A voucher system often limits the type of obligations that a department or individual can incur. In a large retail store, for instance, only a purchasing department should be authorized to incur obligations for merchandise inventory. Another key factor is that procedures for purchasing, receiving, and paying for merchandise are divided among several departments (or individuals). These departments include the one requesting the purchase, the purchasing department, the receiving department, and the accounting department. To coordinate and control responsibilities of these departments, a company uses several different business documents. Exhibit 7.2 shows how documents are accumulated in a **voucher,** which is an internal file used to accumulate information. This specific example begins with a *purchase requisition* and concludes with a

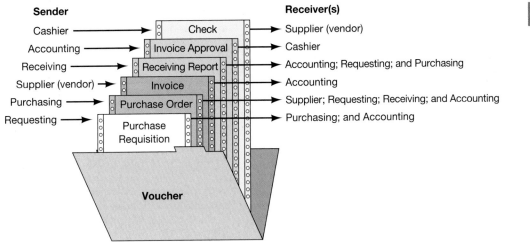

Exhibit 7.2

Document Flow in a Voucher System

External decision makers look to several sources when assessing a company's internal controls. Sources include the auditor's report, management report on controls, management discussion and analysis, and financial press.

check drawn against cash. Appendix 7A describes each document entering and leaving a voucher system. It also describes the internal control objective served by each document.

A voucher system should be applied to all expenditures. To illustrate, when a company receives a monthly telephone bill, it should review and verify the charges, prepare a voucher (file), and insert the bill. This transaction is then recorded with a journal entry. If the amount is currently due, a check is issued. If not, the voucher is filed for payment on its due date. If no voucher is prepared, verifying the invoice and its amount after several days or weeks can be difficult. Also, without records, a dishonest employee could collude with a dishonest supplier to get more than one payment for an obligation, payment for excessive amounts, or payment for goods and services not received. An effective voucher system helps prevent such frauds.

The Sarbanes–Oxley Act

LO6 Explain provisions of the Sarbanes-Oxley Act that are designed to detect and curtail fraud.

Congress passed the Sarbanes-Oxley Act in 2002. This act has several provisions designed to reduce financial fraud. Adherence to the act's provisions is required for U.S. public companies. However, privately held and small businesses can also benefit from many of the control features in the act. Next we discuss some of the act's provisions that might be useful as part of a system of internal control to reduce fraud.

Requirements of the Sarbanes-Oxley Act

The act requires each annual report to include an *internal control* report, which must:

MCI, formerly WorldCom, paid a whopping $500 million in SEC fines for accounting fraud. Among the charges were that it inflated earnings by as much as $10 billion. Its CEO, Bernard Ebbers, was sentenced to 25 years.

■ State managers' responsibility for establishing and maintaining adequate internal controls for financial reporting.
■ Assess the effectiveness of those controls.

In addition, the company's external auditor must test the company's internal control system with respect to financial reporting. This independent review provides an important external check on the company's financial statements.

Each company's chief executive officer (CEO) and chief financial officer (CFO) must certify that the financial statements fairly present the operations and financial condition of the company. This fixes responsibility for the company's financial reports with high-level executives who should have knowledge of the company's accounting.

Of the tips that lead to fraud detection, 64% come from employees, 11% come from customers, and 7% come from vendors.

The act also requires publicly traded companies to establish procedures for "the confidential, anonymous submission by employees of complaints regarding the company's accounting or internal controls." Evidence in the Association of Certified Fraud Examiners 2006 *Report to the Nation* suggests these anonymous tips are a company's best way to detect fraud. About 34% of all detected frauds were detected by tips, leading frauds detected by internal audit (about 20%), and frauds detected by accident (about 25%).

HOW YOU DOIN'?   Answers—p. 166

3. Should all companies require a voucher system? At what point in a company's growth would you recommend a voucher system?

4. What type of company must follow the provisions of the Sarbanes-Oxley Act?

5. What is a company's best way to detect fraud?

Demonstration Problem

Shaw Company applies the following practices for internal control purposes.

1. Each sales clerk uses his or her own cash drawer. The cash drawer can only be opened by swiping an employee identification card.

2. The company's cash registers keep a record of each transaction in an electronic file. The company's manager reviews these files daily.

3. The company's manager issues prenumbered sales slips to salespersons. Salespersons must submit their sales slips to the manager after making a sale. The manager verifies that all sales slips are accounted for each month.

4. The company buys goods for resale from a manufacturer. Each purchase must be approved by a manager. The company's receiving department employees check incoming goods for quantity and quality. The company purchases a bond on each of its receiving department employees. The manager cannot receive goods, and the receiving department employees cannot make purchase orders. Neither the manager nor any of the receiving department employees are allowed to make accounting journal entries.

Required

Identify which of the seven principles of internal control is being applied in each of the above scenarios. More than one principle of internal control might apply to a scenario.

Solution to Demonstration Problem

	Scenario Number			
	1	2	3	4
■ Establish responsibilities	x			
■ Maintain adequate records		x		
■ Insure assets and bond key employees				x
■ Separate recordkeeping from custody of assets				x
■ Divide responsibility for related transactions				x
■ Apply technological controls	x	x		
■ Perform regular and independent reviews		x	x	

APPENDIX
7A

Documents in a Voucher System

This appendix describes the important business documents of a voucher system of control.

L07 Describe the voucher system to control cash disbursements.

Purchase Requisition Department managers are usually not allowed to place orders directly with suppliers. Instead, a department manager prepares and signs a **purchase requisition,** which lists the merchandise needed and requests that it be purchased—see Exhibit 7A.1. Two copies of the purchase requisition are sent to the purchasing department, which then sends one copy to the accounting department. When the accounting department receives a purchase requisition, it creates and maintains a voucher for this transaction. The requesting department keeps the third copy.

Exhibit 7A.1

Purchase Requisition

Purchase Requisition		No. 917
Z-Mart		

From ___Sporting Goods Department___   **Date** _____October 28, 2008_____
To ____Purchasing Department_____   **Preferred Vendor** ___Trex_____

Request purchase of the following item(s):

Model No.	Description	Quantity
CH 015	Challenger X7	1
SD 099	SpeedDemon	1

Reason for Request _____Replenish inventory_____
Approval for Request_____ _TZ_ _____

For Purchasing Department use only: Order Date __10/30/08__   P.O. No. ____P98____

It is important to note that a voucher system is designed to uniquely meet the needs of a specific business. Thus, you should read this appendix as one example of a common voucher system design, but *not* the only design.

Purchase Order A **purchase order** is a document the purchasing department uses to place an order with a **vendor** (seller or supplier). A purchase order authorizes a vendor to ship ordered merchandise at the stated price and terms—see Exhibit 7A.2. When the purchasing department receives a purchase requisition, it prepares at least five copies of a purchase order. The copies are distributed as follows: *copy 1* to the vendor as a purchase request and as authority to ship merchandise; *copy 2,* along with a copy of the purchase requisition, to the accounting department, where it is entered in the voucher and used in approving payment of the invoice; *copy 3* to the requesting department to inform its manager that action is being taken; *copy 4* to the receiving department without order quantity so it can compare with goods received and provide independent count of goods received; and *copy 5* retained on file by the purchasing department.

Exhibit 7A.2

Purchase Order

Purchase Order			No. P98

Z-Mart
10 Michigan Street
Chicago, Illinois 60521

To: Trex
W9797 Cherry Road
Antigo, Wisconsin 54409

Date _____ 10/30/08 _____
FOB _____ Destination _____
Ship by __ As soon as possible __
Terms _____ 2/15, n/30 _____

Request shipment of the following item(s):

Model No.	Description	Quantity	Price	Amount
CH 015	Challenger X7	1	490	490
SD 099	SpeedDemon	1	710	710

All shipments and invoices must include purchase order number

Ordered by
J.W.
_____

Invoice   An **invoice** is an itemized statement of goods prepared by the vendor listing the customer's name, items sold, sales prices, and terms of sale. An invoice is also a bill sent to the buyer from the supplier. From the vendor's point of view, it is a *sales invoice.* The buyer, or **vendee,** treats it as a *purchase invoice.* When receiving a purchase order, the vendor ships the ordered merchandise to the buyer and includes or mails a copy of the invoice covering the shipment to the buyer. The invoice is sent to the buyer's accounting department where it is placed in the voucher.

Receiving Report   Many companies have a separate department to receive all merchandise and purchased assets. When each shipment arrives, this receiving department counts the goods and checks them for damage and agreement with the purchase order. It then prepares four or more copies of a **receiving report,** which is used within the company to notify the appropriate persons that ordered goods have been received and to describe the quantities and condition of the goods. One copy is sent to accounting and placed in the voucher. Copies are also sent to the requesting department and the purchasing department to notify them that the goods have arrived. The receiving department retains a copy in its files.

Invoice Approval   When a receiving report arrives, the accounting department should have copies of the following documents in the voucher: purchase requisition, purchase order, and invoice. With the information in these documents, the accounting department can record the purchase and approve its payment. In approving an invoice for payment, it checks and compares information across all documents. To facilitate this checking and to ensure that no step is omitted, it often uses an **invoice approval,** also called *check authorization*—see Exhibit 7A.3. An invoice approval is a checklist of steps necessary for approving an invoice for recording and payment. It is a separate document either filed in the voucher or preprinted (or stamped) on the voucher.

Exhibit 7A.3

Invoice Approval

Invoice Approval			
Document		By	Date
Purchase requisition	917	72	10/28/08
Purchase order	P98	9w	10/30/08
Receiving report	R85	sk	11/3/08
Invoice:	4657		11/12/08
Price		9k	11/12/08
Calculations		9k	11/12/08
Terms		9k	11/12/08
Approved for payment		8c	

As each step in the checklist is approved, the person initials the invoice approval and records the current date. Final approval implies the following steps have occurred:

1. **Requisition check:** Items on invoice are requested per purchase requisition.
2. **Purchase order check:** Items on invoice are ordered per purchase order.
3. **Receiving report check:** Items on invoice are received, per receiving report.
4. **Invoice check: Price:** Invoice prices are as agreed with the vendor.
   Calculations: Invoice has no mathematical errors.
   Terms: Terms are as agreed with the vendor.

Voucher   Once an invoice has been checked and approved, the voucher is complete. A complete voucher is a record summarizing a transaction. Once the voucher certifies a transaction, it authorizes recording an obligation. A voucher also contains approval for paying the obligation on an appropriate date. The physical form of a voucher varies across companies. Many are designed so that the invoice and other related source documents are placed inside the voucher, which can be a folder.

> Recording a purchase is initiated by an invoice approval, not an invoice. An invoice approval verifies that the amount is consistent with that requested, ordered, and received. This controls and verifies purchases and related liabilities.

Exhibit 7A.4

Inside of a Voucher

	Z-Mart		Voucher No. 4657	
	Chicago, Illinois			

Date ___ Oct. 28, 2008 ___
Pay to ___ Trex ___
City ___ Antigo ___   State ___ Wisconsin ___

For the following: (attach all invoices and supporting documents)

Date of Invoice	Terms	Invoice Number and Other Details	Terms
Nov. 2, 2008	2/15, n/30	Invoice No. 4657	1,200
		Less discount	24
		Net amount payable	1,176

Payment approved

N.O. Neal

Auditor

Completion of a voucher usually requires a person to enter certain information on both the inside and outside of the voucher. Typical information required on the inside of a voucher is shown in Exhibit 7A.4, and that for the outside is shown in Exhibit 7A.5. This information is taken from the invoice and the supporting documents filed in the voucher. A complete voucher is sent to an authorized individual (often called an *auditor*). This person performs a final review, approves the accounts and amounts for debiting (called the *accounting distribution*), and authorizes recording of the voucher.

Exhibit 7A.5

Outside of a Voucher

Voucher No. 4657

Accounting Distribution

Account Debited	Amount
Purchases	1,200
Store Supplies	
Office Supplies	
Sales Salaries	
Other	
Total Vouch. Pay. Cr.	1,200

Due Date ___ November 12, 2008 ___
Pay to ___ Trex ___
City ___ Antigo ___
State ___ Wisconsin ___

Summary of charges:
Total charges ___ 1,200 ___
Discount ___ 24 ___
Net payment ___ 1,176 ___

Record of payment:
Paid ___
Check No. ___

After a voucher is approved and recorded (in a journal called a **voucher register**), it is filed by its due date. A check is then sent on the payment date from the cashier, the voucher is marked "paid", and the voucher is sent to the accounting department and recorded (in a journal called the **check register**). The person issuing checks relies on the approved voucher and its signed supporting documents as proof that an obligation has been incurred and must be paid. The purchase requisition and purchase order confirm the purchase was authorized. The receiving report shows that items have been received, and the invoice approval form verifies that the invoice has been checked for errors. There is little chance for error and even less chance for fraud without collusion unless all the documents and signatures are forged.

Summary

LO1 **Define workplace fraud and explain the four elements common to all fraud schemes.** Workplace fraud involves the use of one's job for personal gain, through deliberate misuse of the employer's assets. All workplace fraud is secret, violates the employee's job duties, provides financial benefit to the employee, and costs the employer money.

LO2 **Describe the three major types of workplace fraud.** Asset misappropriation, corruption, and fraudulent financial statements are the three major types of workplace fraud.

LO3 **Define internal control and identify its purpose and principles.** An internal control system consists of the policies and procedures managers use to protect assets, ensure reliable accounting, promote efficient operations, and urge adherence to company policies. It can prevent avoidable losses and help managers both plan operations and monitor company and human performance. Principles of good internal control include establishing responsibilities, maintaining adequate records, insuring assets and bonding employees, separating recordkeeping from custody of assets, dividing responsibilities for related transactions, applying technological controls, and performing regular independent reviews.

LO4 **Explain how technology impacts an internal control system.** Technology improves managers' abilities to monitor and control business activities. It also allows for more extensive testing of records. However, technological systems often produce less hard-copy evidence to review. Technology often eliminates jobs, making separation of duties more difficult, particularly in small companies.

LO5 **Describe the limitations of internal control.** Internal control systems are limited by the human element and the cost-benefit principle. Human error and/or human fraud, particularly collusion, limit the effectiveness of internal control systems. The cost-benefit principle states that the costs of internal controls must not exceed their benefits. In considering costs the employer must consider the effects of certain controls on employee morale.

LO6 **Explain provisions of the Sarbanes-Oxley Act that are designed to detect and curtail fraud.** The Sarbanes-Oxley Act requires each annual report to include an internal control report that states managers' responsibility for maintaining adequate internal controls for financial reporting. The company must also assess the effectiveness of its internal controls.

LO7 **Describe the voucher system to control cash disbursements.** A voucher system is a set of procedures and approvals designed to control cash disbursements and acceptance of obligations. The voucher system of control relies on several important documents, including the voucher and its supporting files. A key factor in this system is that only approved departments and individuals are authorized to incur certain obligations.

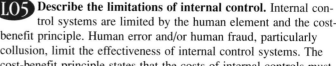
Guidance Answers to   **HOW YOU DOIN'?**

1. (c)

2. Technology reduces processing errors. It also allows more extensive testing of records, limits the amount of hard evidence, and highlights the importance of separation of duties.

3. A voucher system is used when an owner/manager can no longer control purchasing procedures through personal supervision and direct participation.

4. U.S. public companies.

5. Anonymous tips.

Key Terms   mhhe.com/wildCA

Key Terms are available at the book's Website for learning and testing in an online Flashcard Format.

Check register (p. 166) Another name for a cash disbursements journal when the journal has a column for check numbers.

Internal control system (p. 157) All policies and procedures used to protect assets, ensure reliable accounting, promote efficient operations, and urge adherence to company policies.

Invoice (p. 164) Itemized record of goods, prepared by the vendor that lists the customer's name, items sold, sales prices, and terms of sale.

Invoice approval (p. 164) Document containing a checklist of steps necessary for approving the recording and payment of an invoice; also called *check authorization*.

Principles of internal control (p. 157) Principles prescribing management to establish responsibility, maintain records, insure assets, separate recordkeeping from custody of assets, divide responsibility for related transactions, apply technological controls, and perform reviews.

Purchase order (p. 163) Document used by the purchasing department to place an order with a seller (vendor).

Purchase requisition (p. 163) Document listing merchandise needed by a department and requesting it be purchased.

Receiving report (p. 164) Form used to report that ordered goods are received and to describe the quantity and condition.

Vendee (p. 164) Buyer of goods or services.

Vendor (p. 163) Seller of goods or services.

Voucher (p. 161) Internal file used to store documents and information to control cash disbursements and to ensure that a transaction is properly authorized and recorded.

Voucher register (p. 166) Journal (referred to as *book of original entry*) in which all vouchers are recorded after they have been approved.

Voucher system (p. 161) Procedures and approvals designed to control cash disbursements and acceptance of obligations.

Workplace fraud (p. 156) The deliberate misuse of an employer's assets for an employee's personal gain.

Multiple Choice Quiz   Answers on p. 171   mhhe.com/wildCA

Multiple Choice Quizzes A and B are available at the book's Website.

1. When two clerks share the same cash register, it is a violation of which internal control principle?
  a. Establish responsibilities.
  b. Maintain adequate records.
  c. Insure assets.
  d. Bond key employees.
  e. Apply technological controls.

2. The impact of technology on internal controls includes
  a. Reduced processing errors.
  b. Elimination of the need for regular audits.
  c. Elimination of the need to bond employees.
  d. More efficient separation of duties.
  e. Elimination of fraud.

3. The most serious limitation of internal control is
  a. Computer error.
  b. Human fraud or human error.
  c. Cost-benefit principle.

  d. Cybercrime.
  e. Management fraud.

4. A set of procedures and approvals that is designed to control cash disbursements and the acceptance of obligations is referred to as a(n):
  a. Internal cash system.
  b. Petty cash system.
  c. Cash disbursement system.
  d. Voucher system.
  e. Cash control system.

5. The source by which the greatest percentage of workplace fraud schemes is detected is
  a. Tips from customers and vendors.
  b. Internal auditors.
  c. Accident.
  d. Tips from employees.
  e. Independent auditors.

Superscript letter [A] *denotes assignments based on Appendix 7A.*

Discussion Questions

1. List the four common elements of all workplace frauds.

2. List the three major types of workplace frauds.

3. List the seven broad principles of internal control.

4. Internal control procedures are important in every business, but at what stage in the development of a business do they become especially critical?

5. Why should responsibility for related transactions be divided among different departments or individuals?

6. Why should the person who keeps the records of an asset not be the person responsible for its custody?

7. When a store purchases merchandise, why are individual departments not allowed to directly deal with suppliers?

8. What are the limitations of internal controls?

9. What are the three main methods of detecting workplace fraud?

An internal control system consists of all policies and procedures used to protect assets, ensure reliable accounting, promote efficient operations, and urge adherence to company policies.

1. What is the main objective of internal control procedures? How is that objective achieved?

2. Why should recordkeeping for assets be separated from custody over those assets?

3. Why should the responsibility for a transaction be divided between two or more individuals or departments?

QUICK STUDY

QS 7–1
Internal control objectives
(LO3)

A good system of internal control separates the recordkeeping from the control of assets.

1. Explain why this separation of duties can be effective.

2. Which limitation of internal control might limit 'separation of duties' from preventing fraud?

3. How can technology impact a company's ability to separate duties?

QS 7–2
Internal control
(LO3) (LO4) (LO5)

QS 7–3
Internal control procedures

(LO3)

For each of the independent cases below, identify the principle of internal control that is violated, and recommend what should be done to remedy the violation.

1. In order to save money, Regal Company has decided to drop its property insurance on assets and to stop bonding the cashiers who handle less than $10,000 in cash each day.

2. Wang Company records each sale on prenumbered invoices. These invoices are left in an open drawer for any employee to access. No employee at Wang Company examines whether all the invoices are accounted for after employees take them from the open drawer.

3. Gerald McNichols, the owner of McNichols Company, prides himself on hiring only the most competent employees. McNichols believes that since these employees are highly competent and that he trusts them completely and wants to keep employee morale high, there is no need for anyone to review the employees' performance.

QS 7–4^A
Documents in a voucher system

(LO7)

Management uses a voucher system to help control and monitor cash disbursements. Identify at least four key documents that are part of a voucher system of control.

QS 7–5
Sarbanes-Oxley

(LO6)

Identify and explain provisions of the Sarbanes-Oxley Act that are designed to prevent fraud.

EXERCISES

Exercise 7–1
Analyzing internal control

(LO2) (LO3)

Franco Company is a rapidly growing start-up business. Its recordkeeper, who was hired one year ago, left town after the company's manager discovered that a large sum of money had disappeared over the past six months. An audit disclosed that the recordkeeper had written and signed several checks made payable to her fiancé and then recorded the checks as salaries expense. The fiancé, who cashed the checks but never worked for the company, left town with the recordkeeper. As a result, the company incurred an uninsured loss of $184,000. Evaluate Franco's internal control system and indicate which principles of internal control appear to have been ignored. Which type of workplace fraud has been committed?

Exercise 7–2
Principles of internal control

(LO3)

Match each of the following transactions 1 through 10 with the applicable internal control principle A through G (some answers refer to more than one principle).

A. Establish responsibility.

B. Maintain adequate records.

C. Insure assets and bond employees.

D. Separate recordkeeping from custody of assets.

E. Divide responsibility for related transactions.

F. Apply technological controls.

G. Perform regular and independent reviews.

_____ **1.** Cashier does not have access to the cash register recorded tape or file.

_____ **2.** A company uses a voucher system.

_____ **3.** No two clerks share the same cash drawer.

_____ **4.** The bookkeeper prepares and signs checks.

_____ **5.** A company uses a computerized point of sale system.

_____ **6.** A company hires CPAs to perform an audit.

_____ **7.** A company buys an insurance policy to protect against employee theft.

_____ **8.** A company has separate departments for purchasing, receiving, and accounts payable.

_____ **9.** A company has an internal auditor on staff.

_____ **10.** A company uses a check protector.

Exercise 7–3^A
Voucher system

(LO7)

The voucher system of control is designed to control cash disbursements and the acceptance of obligations.

1. The voucher system of control establishes procedures for what two processes?

2. What types of expenditures should be overseen by a voucher system of control?

3. When is the voucher initially prepared? Explain.

Match each document in a voucher system in column one with its description in column two.

Exercise 7–4^A
Documents in a voucher system

Exercise 7–4^A
Documents in a voucher system
(LO7)

Document	Description
1. Purchase requisition	**A.** An itemized statement of goods prepared by the vendor listing the customer's name, items sold, sales prices, and terms of sale.
2. Purchase order	**B.** An internal file used to store documents and information to control cash disbursements and to ensure that a transaction is properly authorized and recorded.
3. Invoice	
4. Receiving report	**C.** A document used to place an order with a vendor that authorizes the vendor to ship ordered merchandise at the stated price and terms.
5. Invoice approval	**D.** A checklist of steps necessary for the approval of an invoice for recording and payment; also known as a check authorization.
6. Voucher	**E.** A document used by department managers to inform the purchasing department to place an order with a vendor.
	F. A document used to notify the appropriate persons that ordered goods have arrived, including a description of the quantities and condition of goods.

Read the article "No Accounting for Being Disorganized" in the March 10, 2004, issue of *BusinessWeek*. (The book's Website provides a free link.)

Exercise 7–5
Workplace fraud and internal controls
(LO1) (LO2) (LO3)

Required

1. Why does Steven Cohen, the author of the article, urge small business owners to be accounting literate?

2. How does Cohen suggest that small business owners "get savvy"?

3. What does Cohen recommend an owner do to stop theft and fraud?

4. What suggestions does Cohen offer for small business owners?

For each of these five separate cases, identify the principle(s) of internal control that is violated. Recommend what the business should do to ensure adherence to principles of internal control.

PROBLEM SET A

Problem 7–1A
Analyzing internal control
(LO3)

1. Halton Company records each sale on a preprinted invoice. Since sometimes invoices are spoiled when they are prepared, the invoices are not prenumbered, but the sales clerk writes the next number onto each invoice.

2. Julia and Justine are cashiers at Tico Company. Justine often processes transactions from Julia's cash drawer when Julia is at lunch.

3. Nori Nozumi posts all patient charges and payments at the Hopeville Medical Clinic. Each night Nori backs up the computerized accounting system to a tape and stores the tape in a locked file at her desk.

4. Benedict Shales prides himself on hiring quality workers who require little supervision. As office manager, Benedict gives his employees full discretion over their tasks and for years has seen no reason to perform independent reviews of their work.

5. Cala Farah's manager has told her to reduce costs. Cala decides to raise the deductible on the plant's property insurance from $5,000 to $10,000. This cuts the property insurance premium in half. In a related move, she decides that bonding the plant's employees is a waste of money since the company has not experienced any losses due to employee theft. Cala saves the entire amount of the bonding insurance premium by dropping the bonding insurance.

It is important that companies assess their risks of workplace fraud. Managers must also possess the skills to identify workplace fraud and the skills to establish internal controls to effectively reduce the risks of such fraud.

Problem 7–2A
Workplace fraud and internal controls
(LO2) (LO3) (LO6)

Required

For each of the following five separate cases, identify which of the three major types of workplace fraud is likely to occur. Recommend internal controls that are effective in reducing the likelihood of such fraud.

1. As part of his computer programming duties, Martin Gomez adds new employees to his company's payroll system. Martin also manages the payroll and signs payroll checks. Martin recently added several fictitious employees to the payroll.

2. Green Oaks Racquet Club uses a manual system to record which member uses its tennis courts. Members often pay for their court times with cash, which is deposited nightly. The manager of Green Oaks notices that several nightly deposits are at unexpectedly low amounts.

3. Haynes Company pays its accountant a bonus based on its financial performance. The accountant overstated the company's revenues in its most recent income statement.

4. An accounts payable clerk has been processing invoices with inflated prices from a certain supplier. In return, the clerk receives 20% of the invoice price as a kickback.

5. Custom Electronics is a major wholesaler of computers, stereos, and other expensive electronic equipment. The inventory is stored in a warehouse that is often left unlocked. Its inventory manager notices that a large number of iPods are missing.

PROBLEM SET B

Problem 7-1B
Analyzing internal control

(LO3)

For each of these five separate cases, identify the principle(s) of internal control that is violated. Recommend what the business should do to ensure adherence to principles of internal control.

1. Latisha Tally is the company's computer specialist and oversees its computerized payroll system. Her boss recently asked her to put password protection on all office computers. Latisha has put a password in place that allows only the boss access to the file where pay rates are changed and personnel are added or deleted from the payroll.

2. Marker Theater has a computerized order-taking system for its tickets. The system is active all week and backed up every Friday night.

3. Sutton Company has two employees handling acquisitions of inventory. One employee places purchase orders and pays vendors. The second employee receives the merchandise.

4. The owner of Super Pharmacy uses a check protector to perforate checks, making it difficult for anyone to alter the amount of the check. The check protector is on the owner's desk in an office that contains company checks and is normally unlocked.

5. Lavina Company is a small business that has separated the duties of cash receipts and cash disbursements. The employee responsible for data base programming and data entry also writes checks to pay for purchases.

Problem 7-2B
Workplace fraud and internal controls

(LO2) (LO3) (LO6)

It is important that companies assess their risks of workplace fraud. Managers must also possess the skills to identify workplace fraud and the skills to establish internal controls to effectively reduce the risks of such fraud.

Required

For each of the following five separate cases, identify which of the three major types of workplace fraud is likely to occur. Recommend internal controls that are effective in reducing the likelihood that such fraud occurs.

1. As part of her computer programming duties, Brandi Marks adds new suppliers to her company's accounts payable system. Brandi also manages accounts payable and signs checks payable to suppliers. Brandi recently added several new suppliers to the accounts payable system.

2. Peña Company has its employees write down their hours worked in a manual ledger. One employee consistently claims more unscheduled overtime hours than any other employee.

3. Gibson Company pays its accountant a bonus based on its financial performance. The accountant understated the company's expenses in its most recent income statement.

4. An employee refuses to buy goods from a potential supplier unless that supplier hires the employee's wife.

5. Ace Electronics is a major wholesaler of electronic equipment. The company's inventory manager is responsible for ordering inventory and paying suppliers. Recently, warehouse employees reported several large shipments of cell phones missing.

BEYOND THE NUMBERS

REPORTING IN
ACTION

(LO2) (LO5) **BEST BUY**

BTN 7-1 Workplace fraud affects **Best Buy**. Refer to Best Buy's financial statements in Appendix A to answer the following:

1. Explain how inventory losses (such as theft) impact how Best Buy reports merchandise inventory on its balance sheet.

2. In which income statement account does Best Buy report inventory losses?

BTN 7-2   The owner of a start-up information services company requires all employees to take at least one week of vacation per year. Why does the employer require this "forced vacation" policy?

ETHICS CHALLENGE
LO2 LO3

BTN 7-3   Assume you are the owner of a small business. You are planning on borrowing money from a local bank. What are some features of the Sarbanes-Oxley Act that you could adopt to help persuade the banker that your financial statements are not fraudulent?

WORKPLACE COMMUNICATION
LO6

BTN 7-4   Visit the Association of Certified Fraud Examiners Website at cfenet.com. Research the fraud facts (refer to the 2006 *Report to the Nation,* see fraud resource center—under publications—*Report to the Nation*) presented at this site and fill in the blanks in the following statements.

TAKING IT TO THE NET
LO1 LO2 LO3

 1. It is estimated that ____% of U.S. organizations' revenues are lost as a result of occupational fraud and abuse. Applied to the U.S. gross domestic product, this translates to losses of approximately $____ billion.
 2. Small businesses are the most vulnerable to occupational fraud and abuse. The average scheme in a small business causes $____ in losses. The average scheme in the largest companies costs $____.
 3. The most common method for detecting occupational fraud is through tips from ____, customers, vendors, and anonymous sources. The second most common method of discovery is ____.
 4. The typical occupational fraud perpetrator is a first-time offender. Only ____% of occupational fraudsters in this study were known to have prior convictions for fraud-related offenses.
 5. All occupational frauds fall into one of three categories: ____, corruption, or ____ statements.
 6. Over ____% of occupational frauds involve asset misappropriations. Cash is the targeted asset ____% of the time.
 7. Corruption schemes account for ____% of all occupational frauds, and they cause over $____ in losses, on average.
 8. Fraudulent statements are the most costly form of occupational fraud with median losses of $____ million per scheme.
 9. Frauds committed by employees cause median losses of $____, while frauds committed by owners cause median losses of $____.
 10. Losses caused by perpetrators older than 60 are ____ times higher than losses caused by employees 25 and younger.

BTN 7-5   Organize the class into teams. Each team must prepare a list of 10 internal controls a consumer could observe in a typical retail department store. When called upon, the team's spokesperson must be prepared to share controls identified by the team that have not been shared by another team's spokesperson.

TEAMWORK IN ACTION
LO1

BTN 7-6   Review the opening feature of this chapter that highlights Todd Graves and his company **Raising Cane's Chicken Fingers**.

ENTREPRENEURS IN BUSINESS
LO3 LO5

Required

 1. List the seven principles of internal control and explain how Graves could implement each of them in his restaurants.
 2. Do you believe that Graves will need to add additional controls as his business expands? Explain.

ANSWERS TO MULTIPLE CHOICE QUIZ

1. a

2. a

3. b

4. d

5. d

A Look Back

Chapter 7 focused on fraud, ethics, and controls. We described control procedures that can reduce fraud.

A Look at This Chapter

This chapter focuses on cash and its control. We explain the control of and accounting for cash receipts and payments. These controls include banking activities, petty cash funds, and bank reconciliations.

A Look Ahead

Chapter 9 focuses on employee payroll. We show how the employer records employee payroll and deductions.

Chapter 8

Cash and Cash Controls

LEARNING OBJECTIVES

LO 1 Define cash and describe three guidelines for control of cash.

LO 2 Describe controls for cash receipts.

LO 3 Describe controls for cash disbursements.

LO 4 Explain and record petty cash fund transactions.

LO 5 Identify banking activities as controls of cash.

LO 6 Describe a bank statement.

LO 7 Prepare and explain a bank reconciliation.

LO 8 Compute the days' sales uncollected ratio and use it to assess liquidity.

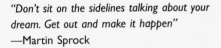

"Don't sit on the sidelines talking about your dream. Get out and make it happen"
—Martin Sprock

Recipe for Growth

 "Welcome to Moe's"! A chorus of welcomes greets each customer at **Moe's Southwest Grill (Moes.com),** a chain of quirky Tex-Mex restaurants. The zaniness continues with menu items such as Art Vandalay, Joey Bag of Donuts, The Full Monty, the Close Talker, and the Billy Barou. They play music from "dead rock stars" like the Beatles, Elvis Presley, and Jimi Hendrix because "Moe wanted to pay tribute to his heroes who have passed on and would never have a chance to taste his food."

Moe's founder Martin Sprock says: "We make a point of having the happiest associates. You feel good visiting our stores, and that means something to me. I'd go so far as to say I'd actually be willing to take a date to them."

But there is more to Moe's than fun. Moe's features burritos, tacos, quesadillas, and salads. To appeal to health-conscious diners, Moe's does not use frozen ingredients, microwaves, or cook with fat; and all its chicken and steak are marinated and grilled. This recipe has resulted in Moe's, founded in 2000, being one of the fastest-growing "fast-casual" restaurant concepts in the country.

With such rapid growth, internal controls are critical. Each Moe's manager earns a degree from "Moe's Training School," where the finer points of cash register operation, hiring staff, and accounting procedures are taught. Each Moe's restaurant applies good cash management, including controls over cash receipts, disbursements, petty cash, and bank reconciliations. Moe's online ordering and payment system is linked with its cash registers to enable managers to better monitor sales and cash receipts.

Martin Sprock's vision is to run a chain of restaurants that treats employees as well as they treat owners. This family-first mentality and service-oriented approach have spurred Moe's dramatic growth. Sprock, a former ski bum, encourages potential entrepreneurs to "Don't sit on the sidelines talking about your dream. Get out and make it happen. I had no money when I started trying to fulfill my ambitions; I just did it."

[Sources: *Moe's Southwest Grill Website*, January 2007; "Raving Brands, A Recipe for Success," article in *Go AirTran Airways* magazine, http://airtranmagazine.com/contents/2005/04/business-martin-sprock/.]

Cash is a necessary asset of every business. Cash is the most liquid of all assets and can be easily hidden or moved. Experience tells us that small businesses are most vulnerable, usually due to weak controls over cash. It is important that the business owner have a system of control over cash. This chapter describes controls to safeguard cash.

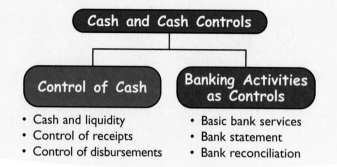

Cash and Cash Controls

Control of Cash
- Cash and liquidity
- Control of receipts
- Control of disbursements

Banking Activities as Controls
- Basic bank services
- Bank statement
- Bank reconciliation

Control of Cash

Cash and Liquidity

LO1 Define cash and describe three guidelines for control of cash.

Good accounting systems help manage cash and control access to it. **Liquidity** refers to a company's ability to pay its near-term obligations. Cash and similar assets are called **liquid assets** because they can be readily used to settle such obligations. A company needs liquid assets to effectively operate.

Cash includes currency and coins along with the amounts on deposit in bank accounts. Cash also includes items that are acceptable for deposit in bank accounts, such as checks and money orders. Cash is a business's most liquid asset. A system of cash control should meet three basic guidelines:

1. Handling cash is separate from recordkeeping of cash.
2. Cash receipts are promptly deposited in a bank.
3. Cash payments are made by check.

> **Google** reports cash and cash equivalents of $186 million in its balance sheet. This amount makes up over 20% of its total assets.

The first guideline separates duties to reduce errors and the potential for fraud. With duties separated, two or more people must work together to steal cash and hide this action in the accounting records. The second and third guidelines produce a timely, independent bank record of cash receipts and payments and reduce the chance of cash theft or loss. Independent bank records of cash receipts and cash payments are useful in controlling cash, as we discuss in the next two sections.

Control of Cash Receipts

LO2 Describe controls for cash receipts.

Control of cash receipts ensures that cash received is properly recorded and deposited. Cash receipts arise from cash sales, collections of customer accounts, receipts of interest earned, bank loans, sales of assets, and owner investments. This section explains control over two important types of cash receipts: over-the-counter and by mail.

> **Day's Cash Expense Coverage:** the ratio of cash (and cash equivalents) to average daily cash expenses indicates the number of days a company can operate without additional cash inflows. It reflects on company liquidity.

Over-the-Counter Cash Receipts Over-the-counter cash sales should be recorded on a cash register at the time of each sale. To help ensure that correct amounts are entered, each register should be located so customers can read the amounts entered. Clerks also should enter each sale before wrapping merchandise and give the customer a receipt for each sale. Each cash register should provide a permanent, locked-in record of each sale (sometimes referred to as a *cash register tape*).

> The most liquid assets are usually reported first on a balance sheet; the least liquid assets are reported last.

Access to cash should be separate from its recordkeeping. For over-the-counter cash receipts, this separation begins with the cash sale. The clerk who has access to cash in the register should not have access to its locked-in record in the register. At the end of the clerk's work period, the clerk should count the cash in the register, record the amount, and turn over the cash and a record of its amount to the company cashier. The cashier, like the clerk, has access to the

IN THE NEWS

Perpetual Accounting

Wal-Mart uses a network of information links with its point-of-sale cash registers to coordinate sales, purchases, and distribution. Its supercenters, for instance, ring up to 15,000 separate sales on heavy days. By using cash register information, the company can fix pricing mistakes quickly and capitalize on sales trends.

cash but should not have access to accounting records (or the cash register tape). A third employee, often a supervisor, compares the record of total register transactions (or the cash register tape) with the cash receipts reported by the cashier. This record is the basis for a journal entry recording over-the-counter cash receipts. The third employee has access to the records for cash but not to the actual cash. The clerk and the cashier have access to cash but not to the accounting records. None of them can make a mistake or divert cash without the difference being revealed—see the following diagram.

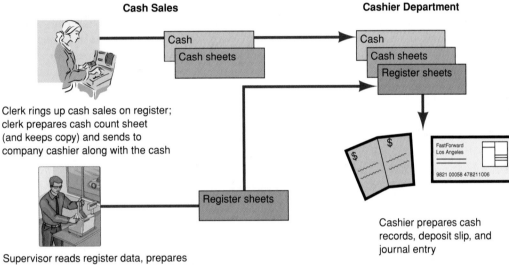

Cash Sales

Clerk rings up cash sales on register; clerk prepares cash count sheet (and keeps copy) and sends to company cashier along with the cash

Supervisor reads register data, prepares register sheet (and keeps copy), and sends both to company cashier

Cashier Department

Cashier prepares cash records, deposit slip, and journal entry

Cash over and short.   Although a clerk is careful, customers can be given the wrong change. This means that at the end of a work period, the cash in a cash register might not equal the record of cash receipts. This difference is reported in the **Cash Over and Short** account, which records the income statement effects of cash overages and cash shortages. A credit entry to Cash Over and Short increases income, while a debit to Cash Over and Short decreases income. To illustrate, if a cash register's record shows $550 but the count of cash in the register is $555, the entry to record cash sales and its overage is

> Retailers often require cashiers to restrictively endorse checks immediately on receipt by stamping them "For deposit only." This endorsement is the safest, since the check can then only be deposited in the company's bank account.

Cash	555	
Cash Over and Short		5
Sales		550
To record cash sales and a cash overage.		

Assets = Liabilities + Equity
+555   + 5
                          +550

Instead, if a cash register's record shows $625 but the count of cash in the register is $621, the entry to record cash sales and its shortage is:

Cash	621	
Cash Over and Short	4	
Sales		625
To record cash sales and a cash shortage.		

Assets = Liabilities + Equity
+621   − 4
                          +625

Since customers more often dispute being shortchanged than being given too much change, the Cash Over and Short account usually has a debit balance at the end of an accounting period. A debit balance reflects an expense.

Cash Receipts by Mail

Control of cash receipts that arrive by mail starts with opening the mail. Two people should be present for opening the mail. If so, theft of cash receipts by mail requires collusion between these two employees. The person(s) opening the mail enters a list (in triplicate) of money received. This list includes a record of each sender's name, the amount, and an explanation of why the money is sent. The first copy is sent with the money to the cashier. A second copy is sent to the recordkeeper. A third copy is kept by the clerks who opened the mail. The cashier deposits the money in a bank, and the recordkeeper records the amounts received in the accounting records.

This process reflects good cash control. When the bank balance is reconciled by another person (explained later in the chapter), errors or acts of fraud by the mail clerks, the cashier, or the recordkeeper are revealed. They are revealed because the bank's record of cash deposited must agree with the records from each of the three. Also, if the mail clerks do not report all receipts correctly, customers will question their account balances. If the cashier does not deposit all receipts, the bank balance does not agree with the recordkeeper's cash balance. The recordkeeper and the person who reconciles the bank balance do not have access to cash and therefore have no opportunity to steal cash. This system makes errors and fraud highly unlikely. The exception is employee collusion.

> Collusion implies that two or more individuals know of or are involved with the activities of the other(s).

IN THE NEWS

Look West

In the annual Small Business Survival Index (**SBEcouncil.org**), the first 4 of the top 5 states ranked as most entrepreneur friendly are west of the Mississippi: (1) South Dakota, (2) Nevada, (3) Wyoming, (4) Washington, and (5) Michigan. Factors considered included taxes, regulations, costs, and crime.

Control of Cash Disbursements

L03 Describe controls for cash disbursements.

Control of cash disbursements is especially important as most large thefts occur from payment of fictitious invoices. One key to controlling cash disbursements is to require all expenditures to be made by check. The only exception is small payments made from petty cash. Another key is to deny access to the accounting records to anyone other than the owner who has the authority to sign checks. A small business owner often signs checks and knows from personal contact that the items being paid for are actually received. This arrangement is impossible in large businesses. Instead, control procedures must be substituted for personal contact. This section describes some of these control procedures.

Petty Cash System of Control

A basic principle for controlling cash disbursements is that all payments must be made by check. An exception is made for **petty cash** disbursements, which are the small payments required for items such as postage, courier fees, minor repairs, and low-cost supplies. To avoid the time and cost of writing checks for small amounts, a company sets up a petty cash fund to make small payments. A petty cash fund is used only for business expenses.

Operating a petty cash fund. Establishing a petty cash fund requires estimating the total amount of small payments likely to be made during a short period such as a week or month. A check is then drawn by the company cashier for an amount slightly in excess of this estimate. This check is recorded with a debit to the Petty Cash account (an asset) and a credit to Cash. The check is cashed, and the cash is given to an employee designated as the *petty cashier*. The petty cashier keeps this cash safe, makes payments from the fund, and keeps records of it in a secure place called the *petty cashbox*.

L04 Explain and record petty cash fund transactions.

When each cash disbursement is made, the person receiving payment should sign a prenumbered *petty cash receipt*—see Exhibit 8.1. The petty cash receipt is then put in the petty cashbox with the remaining money. The sum of all receipts plus the remaining cash always equals the total fund amount. A $100 petty cash fund, for instance, contains any combination of cash and petty cash receipts that totals $100 (examples are $80 cash plus $20 in receipts, or $10 cash plus $90 in receipts). Each disbursement reduces cash and increases the amount of receipts in the petty cashbox.

Exhibit 8.1

Petty Cash Receipt

```
              Petty Cash Receipt              No. 9
                   Z-Mart

  For ____Freight charges____      Date ____11/5/08____

  Charge to __Transportation-In__  Amount ____$6.75____

  Approved by __Jim Gibbs__        Received by __Dick Pitch__
```

Cash should be added to the petty cash fund when the fund nears zero and at the end of an accounting period when financial statements are prepared. The petty cashier sorts the paid receipts by the type of expense and then totals the receipts. The petty cashier gives all paid receipts to the company cashier, who stamps all receipts *paid* so they cannot be reused, files them for recordkeeping, and gives the petty cashier a check for their total. When this check is cashed and the money placed in the petty cashbox, the total money in the petty cashbox equals its original amount. The fund is now ready for a new cycle of petty cash payments.

> Petty cash receipts with either no signature or a forged signature usually indicate misuse of petty cash. Companies respond with surprise petty cash counts for verification.

Illustrating a petty cash fund.   To illustrate, assume Z-Mart establishes a petty cash fund on November 1 and designates one of its office employees as the petty cashier. A $75 check is drawn, cashed, and the cash given to the petty cashier. The entry to record the setup of this petty cash fund is

> Although *individual* petty cash disbursements are not evidenced by a check, the initial petty cash fund is evidenced by a check, and later petty cash expenditures are evidenced by a check to replenish them *in total*.

Nov. 1	Petty Cash................................	75	
	Cash		75
	To establish a petty cash fund.		

> Assets = Liabilities + Equity
> +75
> −75

After the petty cash fund is established, the *Petty Cash account is not debited or credited again unless the amount of the fund is changed.*

Next, assume that Z-Mart's petty cashier makes several November payments from petty cash. Each person who received payment signs a receipt. On November 27, after making a $26.50 cash payment for tile cleaning, only $3.70 cash remains in the fund. The petty cashier summarizes and totals the petty cash receipts as shown in Exhibit 8.2. (This report can also include receipt number and names of those who approved and received cash payment.)

> Reducing or eliminating a petty cash fund would require a credit to Petty Cash.

Exhibit 8.2

Petty Cash Payments Report

Z-MART
Petty Cash Payments Report

Miscellaneous Expenses			
Nov. 2	Washing windows	$20.00	
Nov. 27	Tile cleaning	26.50	$46.50
Freight In			
Nov. 5	Transport of merchandise purchased	6.75	
Nov. 20	Transport of merchandise purchased	8.30	15.05
Delivery Expense			
Nov. 18	Customer's package delivered		5.00
Office Supplies Expense			
Nov. 15	Purchase of office supplies immediately used		4.75
Total			$71.30

Transportation costs for inventory purchases are added to the Transportation-In account. The petty cash payments report and all receipts are given to the company cashier in exchange for a $71.30 check to reimburse the fund. The petty cashier cashes the check and puts the $71.30 cash in the petty cashbox. The recordkeeper makes this entry:

Assets = Liabilities + Equity
−71.30   −46.50
                 −15.05
                 − 5.00
                 − 4.75

Nov. 27	Miscellaneous Expenses	46.50	
	Transportation-In	15.05	
	Delivery Expense	5.00	
	Office Supplies Expense	4.75	
	Cash		71.30
	To reimburse petty cash.		

To avoid errors in recording petty cash reimbursement, follow these steps: (1) prepare payments report, (2) compute cash needed by subtracting cash remaining from total fund amount, (3) record entry, and (4) check "Dr. = Cr." in entry. Any difference is Cash Over and Short.

Increasing or decreasing a petty cash fund.   To illustrate, assume Z-Mart *increases* its petty cash fund from $75 to $100, after making the November 27 entry above. The entry to increase the fund is

Assets = Liabilities + Equity
+25.00
−25.00

Nov. 27	Petty Cash..................................	25	
	Cash		25
	To increase the petty cash fund amount.		

Cash over and short.   Sometimes a petty cashier fails to get a receipt for payment or over-pays for the amount due. When this occurs and the fund is later reimbursed, the petty cash payments report plus the cash remaining will not equal the fund balance. This mistake causes the fund to be *short*. This shortage is recorded as an expense in the reimbursing entry with a debit to the Cash Over and Short account. (An overage in the petty cash fund is recorded with a credit to Cash Over and Short in the reimbursing entry.) To illustrate, the entry to reimburse a $200 petty cash fund when its payments report shows $178 in miscellaneous expenses and $15 cash remains is:

$200 Petty Cash Fund

Petty Cashbox

$15 Cash

$178 Receipts

$7 Short

Miscellaneous Expenses........................	178	
Cash Over and Short......................	7	
Cash..................................		185
To reimburse petty cash.		

YOU CALL IT   Answer—p. 188

Internal Auditor   You make a surprise count of a $300 petty cash fund. You arrive at the petty cashier when she is on the telephone. She politely asks that you return after lunch so that she can finish her business on the telephone. You agree and return after lunch. In the petty cashbox, you find 14 new $20 bills with consecutive serial numbers plus receipts totaling $20. What is your evaluation?

Alternatively, if Z-Mart *decreases* the petty cash fund from $75 to $55 on November 27, the entry is to (1) credit Petty Cash for $20 (decreasing the fund from $75 to $55) and (2) debit Cash for $20 (reflecting the $20 transfer from Petty Cash to Cash).

Event	Petty Cash	Cash	Expenses
Set up fund	Dr.	Cr.	—
Reimburse fund ..	—	Cr.	Dr.
Increase fund ...	Dr.	Cr.	—
Decrease fund ..	Cr.	Dr.	—

HOW YOU DOIN'?   Answers—p. 188

1. Why are some cash payments made from a petty cash fund, and not by check?

2. Why should a petty cash fund be reimbursed at the end of an accounting period?

3. Identify at least two results of reimbursing a petty cash fund.

Banking Activities as Controls

Banks provide many services, including helping companies control cash. Banks safeguard cash, provide detailed and independent records of cash transactions, and provide cash financing. This section describes these services and the banking documents that help control cash.

Basic Bank Services

This section explains basic bank services—such as the bank account, the bank deposit, and checking—that help control cash.

 Identify banking activities as controls of cash.

Bank Account, Deposit, and Check   A *bank account* is a record set up by a bank for a customer. It permits a customer to deposit money for safekeeping and helps control withdrawals. To limit access to a bank account, all persons authorized to write checks on the account must sign a **signature card,** which bank employees use to verify signatures on checks. Many companies have more than one bank account to serve different needs and to handle special transactions such as payroll.

Each bank deposit is supported by a **deposit ticket,** which lists items such as currency, coins, and checks deposited along with their dollar amounts. The bank gives the customer a copy of the deposit ticket or a deposit receipt as proof of the deposit. Exhibit 8.3 shows one type of deposit ticket.

Front

Deposit Ticket

VideoBuster Company
901 Main Street
Hillcrest, NY 11749

Date October 2 20 08
Memo Deposit checks

FN First National
Hillcrest, New York 11750

⑆0124104971⑆ 457923 • 02 75

CHECKS AND OTHER ITEMS ARE RECEIVED FOR DEPOSIT SUBJECT TO THE PROVISIONS OF THE UNIFORM COMMERCIAL CODE OR ANY APPLICABLE COLLECTION AGREEMENT

99-DT/101

CASH	CURRENCY	36	50
	COIN		
LIST CHECKS SINGLY			
TOTAL FROM OTHER SIDE		203	50
TOTAL		240	00
NET DEPOSIT		240	00

USE OTHER SIDE FOR ADDITIONAL LISTINGS

BE SURE EACH ITEM IS PROPERLY ENDORSED

Back

CHECKS	LIST SINGLY	DOLLARS	CENTS
1	14-287/939	90	50
2	82-759/339	82	80
3	76-907/919	30	20
4			
...			
35			
TOTAL		203	50

ENTER TOTAL ON THE FRONT OF THIS TICKET

Exhibit 8.3

Deposit Ticket

A **check** is used to withdraw money from a bank account. A check involves three parties: a *maker* who signs the check, a *payee* who receives the check, and a *bank* (or *payer*) on which the check is drawn. The bank provides a customer checks that are numbered and imprinted

IN THE NEWS

Web-bank

Many companies balance checkbooks and pay bills online. Customers value the convenience of banking services anytime, anywhere. Services include the ability to stop payment on a check, move money between accounts, get up-to-date balances, and identify cleared checks and deposits.

Exhibit 8.4

Check with Remittance Advice

Check
Maker

VideoBuster Company   No. 119
901 Main Street
Hillcrest, NY 11749   *October 3* 20 *08*   99-DT/101

Payee

Pay to the
order of   *Hillcrest Lighting* $ *55.⁰⁰⁄₀₀*

Fifty Five Dollars and ⁰⁰⁄₁₀₀   Dollars

Payer

FN   **First National**
Hillcrest, NY 11750

Memo *Store Lighting Design*   *Jim Hintz*

⑆0124104971⑆ 457923⦁02 438

— — — — — — — — — — — *Detach this portion before cashing* — — — — — — — — — —

Remittance
Advice

Date	Description	Gross Amount	Deductions	Net Amount
10/3/08	Lighting design, Invoice No. 4658	$55.00	—	$55.00

VideoBuster Company, Hillcrest, NY

with the name and address of both the customer and bank. Exhibit 8.4 shows one type of check, accompanied by an optional *remittance advice* explaining the payment. When a remittance advice is unavailable, the *memo* line is often used for a brief explanation.

Electronic Funds Transfer   **Electronic funds transfer (EFT)** is the electronic transfer of cash from one party to another. No paper documents are used. Banks simply transfer cash from one account to another with a journal entry. Companies are increasingly using EFT because it is easy and low cost. For instance, it can cost up to 50 cents to process a check through the banking system, whereas EFT cost is near zero. Items such as payroll, rent, utilities, insurance, and interest payments are commonly handled by EFT. The bank statement lists cash withdrawals by EFT with the checks and other deductions. Cash receipts by EFT are listed with deposits and other additions. A bank statement is sometimes a depositor's only notice of an EFT.

Bank Statement

LO6 Describe a bank statement

Usually once a month, the bank sends each depositor a **bank statement** showing the activity in the account. Different banks use different formats for their bank statements, but all include the following information:

1. Beginning-of-period balance of the depositor's account.
2. Checks and other debits decreasing the account during the period.
3. Deposits and other credits increasing the account during the period.
4. End-of-period balance of the depositor's account.

This information reflects the bank's records. Exhibit 8.5 shows a bank statement. Identify each of these four items in that statement. Part Ⓐ of Exhibit 8.5 summarizes changes in the account. Part Ⓑ lists paid checks along with other debits. Part Ⓒ lists deposits and credits to the account, and part Ⓓ shows the daily account balances.

The depositor's account is a liability on the bank's records. This is because the money belongs to the depositor, not the bank. To increase a depositor's account balance, the bank *credits* that liability account. This means that debit memos from the bank produce *credits* on the depositor's books, and credit memos from the bank produce *debits* on the depositor's books.

Good cash control is to deposit all cash receipts daily and make all payments for goods and services by check. This controls access to cash and creates an independent record of all cash activities.

Exhibit 8.5

Bank Statement

Member FDIC		**FN First National** Hillcrest, NY 11750		Bank Statement	

VideoBuster Company
901 Main Street
Hillcrest, NY 11749

October 31, 2008
Statement Date

494 504 2
Account Number

Ⓐ

Previous Balance	Total Checks and Debits	Total Deposits and Credits	Current Balance
1,609.58	723.00	1,163.42	2,050.00

Ⓑ   Ⓒ   Ⓓ

Checks and Debits			Deposits and Credits		Daily Balance	
Date	No.	Amount	Date	Amount	Date	Amount
10/03	119	55.00	10/02	240.00	10/01	1,609.58
10/09	120	200.00	10/09	180.00	10/02	1,849.58
10/10	121	120.00	10/15	100.00	10/03	1,794.58
10/12		23.00 DM	10/16	150.00	10/09	1,774.58
10/14	122	70.00	10/23	485.00 CM	10/10	1,654.58
10/16	123	25.00	10/31	8.42 IN	10/12	1,631.58
10/23	125	15.00			10/14	1,561.58
10/25		20.00 NSF			10/15	1,661.58
		10.00 DM			10/16	1,786.58
10/26	127	50.00			10/23	2,256.58
10/29	128	135.00			10/25	2,226.58
					10/26	2,176.58
					10/29	2,041.58
					10/31	2,050.00

Symbols:	**CM**–Credit Memo	**EC**–Error Correction	**NSF**–Non-Sufficient Funds	**SC**–Service Charge
	DM–Debit Memo	**IN**–Interest Earned	**OD**–Overdraft	

< Reconcile the account immediately. >

The bank statement includes a list of the depositor's canceled checks (or the actual canceled checks) along with any debit or credit memoranda affecting the account. **Canceled checks** are checks the bank has paid and deducted from the customer's account during the period. Other deductions that can appear on a bank statement include (1) bank service charges and fees, (2) checks deposited that are uncollectible, (3) corrections of previous errors, (4) withdrawals through automated teller machines (ATMs), and (5) periodic payments set up in advance by a depositor. (Most company checking accounts do not allow ATM withdrawals because the company wants to make all disbursements by check.) Except for service charges, the bank notifies the depositor of each deduction with a debit memorandum when the bank reduces the balance. A copy of each debit memorandum is usually sent with the statement.

Transactions that increase the depositor's account include amounts the bank collects on behalf of the depositor and the corrections of previous errors. Credit memoranda notify the depositor of all increases when they are recorded. A copy of each credit memorandum is often sent with the bank statement. Banks that pay interest on checking accounts credit it to the depositor's account each period. In Exhibit 8.5, the bank credits $8.42 of interest to the account.

Bank Reconciliation

LO7 Prepare and explain a bank reconciliation

When a company deposits all cash receipts and makes all cash payments (except petty cash) by check, the bank statement helps prove the accuracy of its cash records. This is done using a **bank reconciliation,** which is a report explaining any differences between the checking account balance according to the depositor's records and the balance reported on the bank statement.

Purpose of Bank Reconciliation   The balance of a checking account reported on the bank statement rarely equals the balance in the depositor's accounting records. This is usually due to information that one party has that the other does not. We must therefore prove the accuracy of both the depositor's records and those of the bank. This means we must *reconcile* the two balances and explain or account for any differences in them. Among the reasons the bank statement balance might differ from the depositor's book balance are these:

■ **Outstanding checks. Outstanding checks** are checks written (or drawn) by the depositor, deducted on the depositor's records, and sent to payees, but not yet received by the bank for payment at the bank statement date.

■ **Deposits in transit** (also called **outstanding deposits**). **Deposits in transit** are deposits made and recorded by the depositor but not yet recorded on the bank statement. For example, companies can make deposits (in the night depository) at the end of a business day after the bank is closed. If such a deposit occurred on a bank statement date, it would not appear on this period's statement. The bank would record such a deposit on the next business day, and it would appear on the next period's bank statement. Deposits mailed to the bank near the end of a period also can be in transit and unrecorded when the statement is prepared.

■ **Deductions for uncollectible items and for services.** A company sometimes deposits another party's check that is uncollectible (usually meaning the balance in the other party's account is not large enough to cover the check). This is called a *non-sufficient funds (NSF)* check. The bank would have initially credited (increased) the depositor's account for the amount of the check. When the bank learns the check is uncollectible, it debits (reduces) the depositor's account for the amount of that check. The bank may also charge the depositor a fee for processing an uncollectible check and notify the depositor of the deduction by sending a debit memorandum. The depositor should record each deduction when a debit memorandum is received, but an entry is sometimes not made until the bank reconciliation is prepared. Other possible bank charges to a depositor's account that are first reported on a bank statement include printing new checks and service fees.

■ **Additions for collections and for interest.** Banks sometimes act as collection agents for their depositors by collecting notes and other items. Banks can also receive electronic funds transfers to the depositor's account. When a bank collects an item, it is added to the depositor's account, less any service fee. The bank also sends a credit memorandum to notify the depositor of the transaction. When the memorandum is received, the depositor should record it; yet it sometimes remains unrecorded until the bank reconciliation is prepared. The bank statement also includes a credit for any interest earned.

■ **Errors.** Both banks and depositors can make errors. Bank errors might not be discovered until the depositor prepares the bank reconciliation. Also, depositor errors can be discovered when the bank balance is reconciled. Error testing includes: (a) comparing deposits on the bank statement with deposits in the accounting records and (b) comparing canceled checks on the bank statement with checks recorded in the accounting records.

Illustration of a Bank Reconciliation   We follow nine steps in preparing the bank reconciliation. It is helpful to refer to the bank reconciliation in Exhibit 8.6 when studying steps ① through ⑨.

Forms of Check Fraud (CkFraud.org)
- Forged signatures—legitimate blank checks with fake payer signature
- Forged endorsements—stolen check that is endorsed and cashed by someone other than the payee
- Counterfeit checks—fraudulent checks with fake payer signature
- Altered checks—legitimate check altered (such as changed payee or amount) to benefit perpetrator
- Check kiting—deposit check from one bank account (without sufficient funds) into a second bank account

Small businesses with few employees often allow recordkeepers to both write checks and keep the general ledger. If this is done, the owner must do the bank reconciliation.

The person preparing the bank reconciliation should not be responsible for processing cash receipts, managing checks, or maintaining cash records.

Exhibit 8.6

Bank Reconciliation

VIDEOBUSTER
Bank Reconciliation
October 31, 2008

①	Bank statement balance		$ 2,050.00	⑤ Book balance		$ 1,404.58
②	Add			⑥ Add		
	Deposit of Oct. 31 in transit		145.00	Collect $500 note less $15 fee	$485.00	
			2,195.00	Interest earned	8.42	493.42
③	Deduct					1,898.00
	Outstanding checks			⑦ Deduct		
	No. 124	$150.00		Check printing charge	23.00	
	No. 126	200.00	350.00	NSF check plus service fee	30.00	53.00
④	**Adjusted bank balance**		**$1,845.00**	⑧ **Adjusted book balance**		**$1,845.00**
			↑	⑨ Balances are equal (reconciled)		↑

① Identify the bank statement balance of the cash account (*balance per bank*). VideoBuster's bank balance is $2,050.

② Identify and list any unrecorded deposits and any bank errors understating the bank balance. Add them to the bank balance. VideoBuster's $145 deposit placed in the bank's night depository on October 31 is not recorded on its bank statement.

③ Identify and list any outstanding checks and any bank errors overstating the bank balance. Deduct them from the bank balance. VideoBuster's comparison of canceled checks with its books shows two checks outstanding: No. 124 for $150 and No. 126 for $200.

④ Compute the *adjusted bank balance,* also called the *corrected* or *reconciled balance.*

⑤ Identify the company's book balance of the cash account (*balance per book*). VideoBuster's book balance is $1,404.58.

⑥ Identify and list any unrecorded credit memoranda from the bank, any interest earned, and errors understating the book balance. Add them to the book balance. Enclosed with VideoBuster's bank statement is a credit memorandum showing the bank collected a note receivable for the company on October 23. The note's proceeds of $500 (minus a $15 collection fee) are credited to the company's account. VideoBuster's bank statement also shows a credit of $8.42 for interest earned on the average cash balance. There was no prior notification of this item, and it is not yet recorded.

⑦ Identify and list any unrecorded debit memoranda from the bank, any service charges, and errors overstating the book balance. Deduct them from the book balance. Debits on VideoBuster's bank statement that are not yet recorded include (a) a $23 charge for check printing and (b) an NSF check for $20 plus a related $10 processing fee. (The NSF check is dated October 16 and was included in the book balance.)

⑧ Compute the *adjusted book balance,* also called *corrected* or *reconciled balance.*

⑨ Verify that the two adjusted balances from steps 4 and 8 are equal. If so, they are reconciled. If not, check for accuracy and missing data until the balances are equal.

> Outstanding checks are identified by comparing canceled checks on the bank statement with checks recorded. This includes identifying any outstanding checks listed on the *previous* period's bank reconciliation that are not included in the canceled checks on this period's bank statement.

Not-So-Free Banking

IN THE NEWS

Fees for bank services are rising—see chart. Bounce protection alone yields $8 billion in annual bank income, or nearly 30% of all bank fees. Regulators are taking notice. Indiana regulators warned that if fees exceeded a 72% annual rate, they would consider it a felony. (*BusinessWeek* 2005)

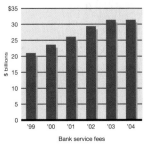

Bank service fees

Adjusting Entries from a Bank Reconciliation A bank reconciliation often identifies unrecorded items that need recording by the company. In VideoBuster's reconciliation, the adjusted balance of $1,845 is the correct balance as of October 31. But the company's accounting records show a $1,404.58 balance. We must prepare journal entries to adjust the book balance to the correct balance. *It is important to remember that only the items reconciling the book balance require adjustment.* A review of Exhibit 8.6 indicates that four entries are required for VideoBuster.

Collection of note. The first entry records the proceeds of its note receivable collected by the bank and the expense of having the bank perform that service. A note receivable is a written promise to pay from a customer.

> Adjusting entries could be combined into one compound entry.

Oct. 31	Cash	485	
	Collection Expense.	15	
	Notes Receivable		500
	To record the collection fee and proceeds		
	for a note collected by the bank.		

Assets = Liabilities + Equity
+485   −15
−500

Interest earned.   The second entry records interest credited to its account by the bank.

Assets = Liabilities + Equity
+8.42   +8.42

Oct. 31	Cash	8.42	
	Interest Revenue		8.42
	To record interest earned on the cash balance in the checking account.		

Check printing.   The third entry records expenses for the check printing charge.

Assets = Liabilities + Equity
−23   −23

Oct. 31	Miscellaneous Expenses	23	
	Cash		23
	Check printing charge.		

NSF check.   The fourth entry records the NSF check that is returned as uncollectible. The $20 check was originally received from T. Woods in payment of his account and then deposited. (The company debited Cash and credited Accounts Receivable.) The bank charged $10 for handling the NSF check and deducted $30 total from VideoBuster's account. The entry must reverse the effects of the original entry made when the check was received and must record (add) the $10 bank fee to the amount owed by T. Woods.

> The company will try to collect the entire NSF amount of $30 from T. Woods.

Assets = Liabilities + Equity
+30
−30

Oct. 31	Accounts Receivable—T. Woods	30	
	Cash		30
	To charge Woods' account for $20 NSF check and $10 bank fee.		

After these four entries are recorded, the book balance of cash is adjusted to the correct amount of $1,845 (computed as $1,404.58 + $485 + $8.42 − $23 − $30). The Cash T-account to the side shows the same computation.

Cash			
Beg. bal.	1,404.58		
⑥	493.42	⑦	23.00
		⑦	30.00
Adj. bal.	1,845.00		

HOW YOU DOIN'?   Answers—p. 188

4. What is a bank statement?

5. What is the meaning of the phrase *to reconcile a bank balance?*

6. Why do we reconcile the bank statement balance of cash and the depositor's book balance of cash?

7. List at least two items affecting the bank balance side of a bank reconciliation and indicate whether the items are added or subtracted.

8. List at least three items affecting the book balance side of a bank reconciliation and indicate whether the items are added or subtracted.

DAYS' SALES UNCOLLECTED

Many companies attract customers by selling to them on credit. This means that cash receipts from customers are delayed until accounts receivable are collected. Users of accounting information often want to know how quickly a company can convert its accounts receivable into cash. This is important for evaluating a company's liquidity. One measure of the receivables' nearness to cash is the **days' sales uncollected,** also called *days' sales in receivables*. This measure is computed by dividing the current balance of receivables by net credit sales over the year just completed and then multiplying by 365 (number of days in a year). Since net credit sales usually are not reported to external users, the net sales (or revenues) figure is commonly used in the computation as in Exhibit 8.7.

LO8 Compute the days' sales uncollected ratio and use it to assess liquidity.

$$\text{Days' sales uncollected} = \frac{\text{Accounts receivable}}{\text{Net sales}} \times 365$$

Exhibit 8.7

Days' Sales Uncollected

We use days' sales uncollected to estimate how much time is likely to pass before the current amount of accounts receivable is received in cash. For evaluation purposes, we need to compare this estimate to that for other companies in the same industry. We also make comparisons between current and prior periods.

To illustrate, we select data from the annual reports of two toy manufacturers, Hasbro and Mattel. Their days' sales uncollected figures are shown in Exhibit 8.8.

Company	Figure ($ millions)	2004	2003	2002	2001
Hasbro	Accounts receivable	$579	$608	$555	$572
	Net sales	$2,998	$3,139	$2,816	$2,856
	Days' sales uncollected	70 days	71 days	72 days	73 days
Mattel	Accounts receivable	$759	$544	$491	$666
	Net sales	$5,103	$4,960	$4,885	$4,688
	Days' sales uncollected	54 days	40 days	37 days	52 days

Exhibit 8.8

Analysis using Days' Sales Uncollected

Days' sales uncollected for Hasbro in 2004 is computed as ($579/$2,998) × 365 days = 70 days. This means that it will take about 70 days to collect cash from ending accounts receivable. This number reflects one or more of the following factors: a company's ability to collect receivables, customer financial health, customer payment strategies, and discount terms. To further assess days' sales uncollected for Hasbro, we compare it to three prior years and to those of Mattel. We see that Hasbro's days' sales uncollected has changed little over the past four years. In comparison, Mattel improved on days' sales uncollected for 2002 (37) and 2003 (40), but then worsened for 2004 (54). Yet, for all years, Mattel is superior to Hasbro on this measure. The less time that money is tied up in receivables often translates into increased profitability.

Demonstration Problem 1

Prepare a bank reconciliation for Jamboree Enterprises for the month ended November 30, 2008. The following information is available to reconcile Jamboree Enterprises' book balance of cash with its bank statement balance as of November 30, 2008:

a. After all posting is complete on November 30, the company's book balance of Cash has a $16,380 debit balance, but its bank statement shows a $38,520 balance.

b. Checks No. 2024 for $4,810 and No. 2026 for $5,000 are outstanding.

c. In comparing the canceled checks on the bank statement with the entries in the accounting records, it is found that Check No. 2025 in payment of rent is correctly drawn for $1,000 but is erroneously entered in the accounting records as $880.

d. The November 30 deposit of $17,150 was placed in the night depository after banking hours on that date, and this amount does not appear on the bank statement.

e. In reviewing the bank statement, a check written by Jumbo Enterprises in the amount of $160 was erroneously drawn against Jamboree's account.

f. A credit memorandum enclosed with the bank statement indicates that the bank collected a $30,000 note and $900 of related interest on Jamboree's behalf. This transaction was not recorded by Jamboree prior to receiving the statement.

g. A debit memorandum for $1,100 lists a $1,100 NSF check received from a customer, Marilyn Welch. Jamboree had not recorded the return of this check before receiving the statement.

h. Bank service charges for November total $40. These charges were not recorded by Jamboree before receiving the statement.

Planning the Solution

- Set up a bank reconciliation with a bank side and a book side (as in Exhibit 8.6). Leave room to both add and deduct items. Each column will result in a reconciled, equal balance.
- Examine each item *a* through *h* to determine whether it affects the book or the bank balance and whether it should be added or deducted from the bank or book balance.
- After all items are analyzed, complete the reconciliation and arrive at a reconciled balance between the bank side and the book side.
- For each reconciling item on the book side, prepare an adjusting entry. Additions to the book side require an adjusting entry that debits Cash. Deductions on the book side require an adjusting entry that credits Cash.

Solution to Demonstration Problem 1

JAMBOREE ENTERPRISES
Bank Reconciliation
November 30, 2008

Bank statement balance		$38 5 2 0 00	Book balance		$16 3 8 0 00
Add			Add		
Deposit of Nov. 30	$17 1 5 0 00		Collection of note	$30 0 0 0 00	
Bank error (Jumbo)	1 6 0 00	17 3 1 0 00	Interest earned	9 0 0 00	30 9 0 0 00
		55 8 3 0 00			47 2 8 0 00
Deduct			Deduct		
Outstanding checks			NSF check (M. Welch)	1 1 0 0 00	
No. 2024	4 8 1 0 00		Recording error (# 2025)	1 2 0 00	
No. 2026	5 0 0 0 00	9 8 1 0 00	Service charge	4 0 00	1 2 6 0 00
Adjusted bank balance		**$46 0 2 0 00**	**Adjusted book balance**		**$46 0 2 0 00**

		REQUIRED ADJUSTING ENTRIES FOR JAMBOREE			
Nov.	30	Cash	30 9 0 0 00		
		Notes Receivable		30 0 0 0 00	
		Interest Earned		9 0 0 00	
		To record collection of note with interest.			
Nov.	30	Accounts Receivable—M. Welch	1 1 0 0 00		
		Cash		1 1 0 0 00	
		To reinstate account due from an NSF check.			
Nov.	30	Rent Expense	1 2 0 00		
		Cash		1 2 0 00	
		To correct recording error on check no. 2025.			
Nov.	30	Bank Service Charges	4 0 00		
		Cash		4 0 00	
		To record bank service charges.			

Demonstration Problem 2

Bacardi Company established a $150 petty cash fund with Dean Martin as the petty cashier. When the fund balance reached $19 cash, Martin prepared a petty cash payments report, which follows.

Petty Cash Payments Report				
Receipt No.	Account Charged		Approved by	Received by
12	Delivery Expense	$ 29	Martin	A. Smirnoff
13	Transportation-In	18	Martin	J. Daniels
15	(Omitted)	32	Martin	C. Carlsberg
16	Miscellaneous Expense	41	(Omitted)	J. Walker
	Total	$120		

Required

1. Identify four internal control weaknesses from the payments report.
2. Prepare general journal entries to record:
   a. Establishment of the petty cash fund.
   b. Reimbursement of the fund. (Assume for this part only that petty cash receipt no. 15 was issued for miscellaneous expenses.)
3. What is the Petty Cash account balance immediately before reimbursement? Immediately after reimbursement?

Solution to Demonstration Problem 2

1. Four internal control weaknesses are
   a. Petty cash ticket no. 14 is missing. Its omission raises questions about the petty cashier's management of the fund.
   b. The $19 cash balance means that $131 has been withdrawn ($150 − $19 = $131). However, the total amount of the petty cash receipts is only $120 ($29 + $18 + $32 + $41). The fund is $11 short of cash ($131 − $120 = $11). Was petty cash receipt no. 14 issued for $11? Management should investigate.
   c. The petty cashier (Martin) did not sign petty cash receipt no. 16. This omission could have been an oversight on his part or he might not have authorized the payment. Management should investigate.
   d. Petty cash receipt no. 15 does not indicate which account to charge. This omission could have been an oversight on the petty cashier's part. Management could check with C. Carlsberg and the petty cashier (Martin) about the transaction. Without further information, debit Miscellaneous Expense.

2. Petty cash general journal entries.
   a. Entry to establish the petty cash fund.   b. Entry to reimburse the fund.

Petty Cash	150	
Cash		150

Delivery Expense	29	
Transportation-In	18	
Miscellaneous Expense ($41 + $32)	73	
Cash Over and Short	11	
Cash		131

3. The Petty Cash account balance *always* equals its fund balance, in this case $150. This account balance does not change unless the fund is increased or decreased.

Summary

 Define cash and describe three guidelines for control of cash. Cash includes currency, coins, amounts on deposit in bank accounts, and checks acceptable for deposit in bank accounts. Guidelines for control of cash include (1) separation of the handling of cash from its recordkeeping, (2) cash receipts should be promptly deposited in a bank, and (3) cash payments should be made by check.

L02 Describe controls for cash receipts. Control of over-the-counter cash receipts includes use of a cash register, customer review, use of receipts, a permanent transaction record locked-in the cash register, and separation of access to cash from its recordkeeping. Control of cash receipts by mail includes at least two people assigned to open mail and a listing of each sender's name, amount paid, and an explanation.

LO3 **Describe controls for cash disbursements.** Except for very small dollar transactions, all expenditures should be made by check. A petty cash system is used to account for small dollar transactions. Employees who sign checks should not have access to accounting records.

LO4 **Explain and record petty cash fund transactions.** Petty cash payments are for amounts for items such as postage, delivery fees, minor repairs, and supplies. A petty fund cashier safeguards the petty cash, makes payments from the petty cash fund, and keeps petty cash receipts and records. A Petty Cash account is debited only when the fund is established or increased in amount. When the fund is replenished, petty cash disbursements are recorded with debits to expense (or asset) accounts and a credit to cash.

LO5 **Identify banking activities as controls of cash.** A bank account is a record set up by a bank, allowing a customer to deposit money for safekeeping and to draw checks on it. A bank deposit ticket proves money was deposited into a bank account. A check tells the bank to pay money from a customer's (*maker*) account to a recipient (*payee*).

LO6 **Describe a bank statement.** A bank statement shows activity in a bank account. Each bank statements lists the beginning-of-period account balance, checks and other debits decreasing the account during the period, deposits and other credits increasing the account during the period, and the end-of-period account balance.

LO7 **Prepare and explain a bank reconciliation.** A bank reconciliation proves the accuracy of the customer's and the bank's records. The bank statement balance is adjusted for items such as outstanding checks and unrecorded deposits made on or before the bank statement date but not reflected on the bank statement. The book balance is adjusted for items like service charges, bank collections for the customer, and interest earned on the account.

LO8 **Compute the days' sales uncollected ratio and use it to assess liquidity.** Many companies attract customers by selling to them on credit. This means that cash receipts from customers are delayed until accounts receivable are collected. Users want to know how quickly a company can convert its accounts receivable into cash. The days' sales uncollected ratio, one measure reflecting company liquidity, is computed by dividing the ending balance of receivables by annual net sales, and then multiplying by 365.

Guidance Answers to YOU CALL IT

Internal Auditor Since you were asked to postpone your count, along with the fact the fund consists of 14 new $20 bills, you have legitimate concerns about whether money is being used for personal use. It is possible the most recent reimbursement of the fund was for $280 (14 × $20) or more. In that case, this reimbursement can leave the fund with sequentially numbered $20 bills. But if the most recent reimbursement was for less than $280, the presence of 14 sequentially numbered $20 bills suggests that the new bills were obtained from a bank as replacement for bills that had been removed. Neither situation shows that the cashier is stealing money, but the second case indicates that the cashier "borrowed" the cash and later replaced it after the auditor showed up. In writing your report, you must not conclude that the cashier is unethical unless other evidence supports it. You should consider additional surprise counts of this petty cashier over the next few weeks.

Guidance Answers to HOW YOU DOIN'?

1. If all cash payments are made by check, numerous checks for small amounts must be written. Since this practice is expensive and time-consuming, a petty cash fund is often established for making small (immaterial) cash payments.

2. If the petty cash fund is not reimbursed at the end of an accounting period, the transactions involving petty cash are not yet recorded and the petty cash asset is overstated.

3. First, petty cash transactions are recorded when the petty cash fund is reimbursed. Second, reimbursement provides cash to allow the fund to continue being used. Third, reimbursement identifies any cash shortage or overage in the fund.

4. A bank statement is a report prepared by the bank describing the activities in a depositor's account.

5. To reconcile a bank balance means to explain the difference between the cash balance in the depositor's accounting records and the cash balance on the bank statement.

6. The purpose of the bank reconciliation is to determine whether the bank or the depositor has made any errors and whether the bank has entered any transactions affecting the account that the depositor has not recorded.

7. Unrecorded deposits—added
Outstanding checks—subtracted

8. Interest earned—added   Debit memos—subtracted
Credit memos—added   NSF checks—subtracted
   Bank service charges—subtracted

Key Terms   mhhe.com/wildCA

Key Terms are available at the book's Website for learning and testing in an online Flashcard Format.

Bank reconciliation (p. 181) Report that explains the difference between the book (company) balance of cash and the cash balance reported on the bank statement.

Bank statement (p. 180) Bank report on the depositor's beginning and ending cash balances, and a listing of its changes, for a period.

Canceled checks (p. 181) Checks that the bank has paid and deducted from the depositor's account.

Cash (p. 174) Includes currency, coins, and amounts on deposit in bank checking or savings accounts.

Cash Over and Short (p. 175) Income statement account used to record cash overages and cash shortages arising from errors in cash receipts or payments.

Check (p. 179) Document signed by a depositor instructing the bank to pay a specific amount to a designated recipient.

Days' sales uncollected (p. 185) Measure of the liquidity of receivables computed by dividing the current balance of receivables by the annual credit (or net) sales and then multiplying by 365; also called *days' sales in receivables*.

Deposits in transit (p. 182) Deposits recorded by the company but not yet recorded by its bank.

Deposit ticket (p. 179) Lists items such as currency, coins, and checks deposited and their corresponding dollar amounts.

Electronic funds transfer (EFT) (p. 180) Use of electronic communication to transfer cash from one party to another.

Liquid assets (p. 174) Resources such as cash that are easily converted into other assets or used to pay for goods, services, or liabilities.

Liquidity (p. 174) Availability of resources to meet short-term cash requirements.

Outstanding checks (p. 182) Checks written and recorded by the depositor but not yet paid by the bank at the bank statement date.

Petty cash (p. 176) Small amount of cash in a fund to pay minor expenses; accounted for using an imprest system.

Signature card (p. 179) Includes the signatures of each person authorized to sign checks on the bank account.

Multiple Choice Quiz   Answers on p. 199   mhhe.com/wildCA

Multiple Choice Quizzes A and B are available at the book's Website.

1. A company needs to replenish its $500 petty cash fund. Its petty cash box has $75 cash and petty cash receipts of $420. The journal entry to replenish the fund includes
  a. A debit to Cash for $75.
  b. A credit to Cash for $75.
  c. A credit to Petty Cash for $420.
  d. A credit to Cash Over and Short for $5.
  e. A debit to Cash Over and Short for $5.

2. The following information is available for Hapley Company:
  • The November 30 bank statement shows a $1,895 balance.
  • The general ledger shows a $1,742 balance at November 30.
  • A $795 deposit placed in the bank's night depository on November 30 does not appear on the November 30 bank statement.
  • Outstanding checks amount to $638 at November 30.
  • A customer's $335 note was collected by the bank in November. A collection fee of $15 was deducted by the bank and the difference deposited in Hapley's account.
  • A bank service charge of $10 is deducted by the bank and appears on the November 30 bank statement.

  How will the customer's note appear on Hapley's November 30 bank reconciliation?
  a. $320 appears as an addition to the book balance of cash.
  b. $320 appears as a deduction from the book balance of cash.
  c. $320 appears as an addition to the bank balance of cash.
  d. $320 appears as a deduction from the bank balance of cash.
  e. $335 appears as an addition to the bank balance of cash.

3. Using the information from question 2, what is the reconciled balance on Hapley's November 30 bank reconciliation?
  a. $2,052
  b. $1,895
  c. $1,742
  d. $2,201
  e. $1,184

4. Using the information from question 2, how will the $10 bank service charge appear on Hapley's November 30 bank reconciliation?
  a. $10 appears as an addition to the book balance of cash.
  b. $10 appears as an addition to the bank balance of cash.
  c. $10 appears as a deduction from the book balance of cash.
  d. $10 appears as a deduction from the bank balance of cash.
  e. The service charge will not appear on the November 30 bank reconciliation.

5. Using the information from question 2, the journal entries to adjust Hapley's book balance of cash to the bank's balance of cash on November 30 will include a
  a. Debit to Cash for the $10 bank service charge.
  b. Credit to Cash for $638 of outstanding checks.
  c. Debit to Cash for $795 of deposits in transit.
  d. Debit to Cash for $320 for collection of note, net of bank collection fees.
  e. Debit to Cash for the $153 difference between the bank's balance of Cash and the book balance of Cash.

Discussion Questions

1. Why should responsibility for related transactions be divided among different individuals?

2. Why should the person who keeps the cash records not have access to cash?

3. Which of the following assets is most liquid? Which is least liquid? Inventory, building, accounts receivable, or cash.

4. What is a petty cash receipt? Who should sign it?

5. Why should cash receipts be deposited on the day of receipt?

6. **Best Buy**'s statement of cash flows in Appendix A **BEST BUY** describes changes in cash and cash equivalents for the year ended February 26, 2005. What amount is provided (used) by investing activities? What amount is provided (used) by financing activities?

7. Refer to **Circuit City**'s balance sheet in Appendix A. **city** How does its cash compare with its other current assets (both in amount and percent) as of February 28, 2005. Compare and assess the cash amount at February 28, 2005, with its amount at February 29, 2004.

QUICK STUDY

QS 8-1

Cash and liquidity

LO1

Good accounting systems help to manage cash and control access to it.

1. What items are included in the category of cash?

2. What does the term *liquidity* refer to?

QS 8-2

Control of cash

LO1 **LO3**

A good system of cash control helps protect both cash receipts and cash disbursements.

1. What are three basic guidelines that help achieve this protection?

2. Identify a control system for cash disbursements.

QS 8-3

Petty cash accounting

LO4

1. The petty cash fund of the Brooks Agency is established at $85. At the end of the current period, the fund contained $14.80 and had the following receipts: film rentals, $21.30, refreshments for meetings, $30.85 (both expenditures to be classified as Entertainment Expense); postage, $8.95; and printing, $9.10. Prepare journal entries to record (*a*) establishment of the fund and (*b*) reimbursement of the fund at the end of the current period.

2. Identify the two events that cause a Petty Cash account to be credited in a journal entry.

QS 8-4

Bank reconciliation

LO7

1. For each of the following items, indicate whether its amount (i) affects the bank or book side of a bank reconciliation and (ii) represents an addition or a subtraction in a bank reconciliation.

   a. Interest on cash balance   **d.** Outstanding checks   **g.** Unrecorded deposits

   b. Bank service charges   **e.** Credit memos

   c. Debit memos   **f.** NSF checks

2. Which of the items in part 1 require an adjusting journal entry in the depositor's books?

QS 8-5

Days' sales uncollected

LO8

The following annual account balances are taken from Armour Sports at December 31.

	2008	2007
Accounts receivable	$ 85,692	$ 80,485
Net sales	2,691,855	2,396,858

What is the change in the number of days' sales uncollected between years 2007 and 2008? According to this analysis, is the company's collection of receivables improving? Explain your answer.

EXERCISES

Exercise 8-1

Analyzing cash control

LO3

Franco Company is a rapidly growing start-up business. Its recordkeeper, who was hired one year ago, left town after the company's manager discovered that a large sum of money had disappeared over the past six months. An audit disclosed that the recordkeeper had written and signed several checks made payable to her fiancé and then recorded the checks as salaries expense. The fiancé, who cashed the checks but never worked for the company, left town with the recordkeeper. As a result, the company incurred an uninsured loss of $184,000. Evaluate Franco's cash control system and indicate which principles of cash control appear to have been ignored.

Some of Crown Company's cash receipts from customers are received by the company with the regular mail. Crown's recordkeeper opens these letters and deposits the cash received each day. (*a*) Identify any internal control problem(s) in this arrangement. (*b*) What changes do you recommend?

Exercise 8–2
Control of cash receipts by mail
(L02)

What control procedures would you recommend in each of the following situations?

1. A concession company has one employee who sells sunscreen, T-shirts, and sunglasses at the beach. Each day, the employee is given enough sunscreen, shirts, and sunglasses to last through the day and enough cash to make change. The money is kept in a box at the stand.

2. An antique store has one employee who is given cash and sent to garage sales each weekend. The employee pays cash for this merchandise that the antique store resells.

Exercise 8–3
Control recommendations
(L01)

Palmona Co. establishes a $200 petty cash fund on January 1. On January 8, the fund shows $38 in cash along with receipts for the following expenditures: postage, $74; photocopy expenses, $29; delivery expenses, $16; and miscellaneous expenses, $43. Prepare journal entries to (1) establish the fund on January 1, (2) reimburse it on January 8, and (3) both reimburse the fund and increase it to $450 on January 8, assuming no entry in part 2. (*Hint:* Make two separate entries for part 3.)

Exercise 8–4
Petty cash fund accounting
(L04)

Check   (2) Cr. Cash $162

Waupaca Company establishes a $350 petty cash fund on September 9. On September 30, the fund shows $104 in cash along with receipts for the following expenditures: printing expenses, $40; postage expenses, $123; and miscellaneous expenses, $80. The petty cashier could not account for a $3 shortage in the fund. Prepare (1) the September 9 entry to establish the fund, (2) the September 30 entry to reimburse the fund, and (3) an October 1 entry to increase the fund to $400.

Exercise 8–5
Petty cash fund with a shortage
(L04)

Check   (2) Cr. Cash $246 and (3) Cr. Cash $50

Prepare a table with the following headings for a monthly bank reconciliation dated September 30.

Exercise 8–6
Bank reconciliation and adjusting entries
(L06) (L07)

Bank Balance		Book Balance			Not Shown on the Reconciliation
Add	Deduct	Add	Deduct	Adjust	

For each item 1 through 12, place an *x* in the appropriate column to indicate whether the item should be added to or deducted from the book or bank balance, or whether it should not appear on the reconciliation. If the book balance is to be adjusted, place a *Dr.* or *Cr.* in the Adjust column to indicate whether the Cash balance should be debited or credited. At the left side of your table, number the items to correspond to the following list.

1. NSF check from customer returned on September 25 but not yet recorded by this company.

2. Interest earned on the September cash balance in the bank.

3. Deposit made on September 5 and processed by the bank on September 6.

4. Checks written by another depositor but charged against this company's account.

5. Bank service charge for September.

6. Checks outstanding on August 31 that cleared the bank in September.

7. Check written against the company's account and cleared by the bank; erroneously not recorded by the company's recordkeeper.

8. Principal and interest on a note receivable to this company is collected by the bank but not yet recorded by the company.

9. Checks written and mailed to payees on October 2.

10. Checks written by the company and mailed to payees on September 30.

11. Night deposit made on September 30 after the bank closed.

12. Special bank charge for collection of note in part 8 on this company's behalf.

Exercise 8-7
Bank reconciliation

(LO7)

Del Gato Clinic deposits all cash receipts on the day they are received and it makes all cash payments by check. At the close of business on June 30, 2008, its Cash account shows an $11,589 debit balance. Del Gato Clinic's June 30 bank statement shows $10,555 on deposit in the bank. Prepare a bank reconciliation for Del Gato Clinic using the following information:

a. Outstanding checks as of June 30 total $1,829.

b. The June 30 bank statement included a $16 debit memorandum for bank services.

c. Check No. 919, listed with the canceled checks, was correctly drawn for $467 in payment of a utility bill on June 15. Del Gato Clinic mistakenly recorded it with a debit to Utilities Expense and a credit to Cash in the amount of $476.

Check Reconciled bal., $11,582

d. The June 30 cash receipts of $2,856 were placed in the bank's night depository after banking hours and were not recorded on the June 30 bank statement.

Exercise 8-8
Adjusting entries from bank reconciliation

(LO7)

Prepare the adjusting journal entries that Del Gato Clinic must record as a result of preparing the bank reconciliation in Exercise 8-7.

Exercise 8-9
Liquid assets and accounts receivable

(LO8)

Deacon Co. reported annual net sales for 2007 and 2008 of $665,000 and $747,000, respectively. Its year-end balances of accounts receivable follow: December 31, 2007, $61,000; and December 31, 2008, $93,000. (*a*) Calculate its days' sales uncollected at the end of each year. (*b*) Evaluate and comment on any changes in the amount of liquid assets tied up in receivables.

PROBLEM SET A

Problem 8-1A
Analyzing cash control

(LO1)

For each of these five separate cases, identify the basic control principle(s) that is violated. Recommend what the business should do for better control.

1. Chi Han records all incoming customer cash receipts for his employer and posts the customer payments to their respective accounts.

2. At Tico Company, Julia and Justine alternate lunch hours. Julia is the petty cash cashier, but if someone needs petty cash when she is at lunch, Justine fills in as cashier.

3. Nori Nozumi personally opens all the mail for Hopeville Medical Clinic and performs monthly bank reconciliations.

4. Benedict Shales prides himself on hiring quality workers who require little supervision. As office manager, Benedict allows his bookkeeper to sign checks for the business.

5. Cala Farah deposits cash receipts for Green Meadows Video once each week.

Problem 8-2A
Establish, reimburse, and increase petty cash

(LO4)

Nakashima Gallery had the following petty cash transactions in February of the current year.

Feb. 2 Wrote a $400 check, cashed it, and gave the proceeds and the petty cashbox to Chloe Addison, the petty cashier.
 5 Purchased bond paper for the copier for $14.15 that is immediately used.
 9 Paid $32.50 COD shipping charges on merchandise purchased for resale, terms FOB shipping point. Nakashima uses the periodic system to account for purchases.
 12 Paid $7.95 postage to express mail a contract to a client.
 14 Reimbursed Adina Sharon, the manager, $68 for business mileage on her car.
 20 Purchased stationery for $67.77 that is immediately used.
 23 Paid a courier $20 to deliver merchandise sold to a customer, terms FOB destination.
 25 Paid $13.10 COD shipping charges on merchandise purchased for resale, terms FOB shipping point.
 27 Paid $54 for postage expenses.
 28 The fund had $120.42 remaining in the petty cash box. Sorted the petty cash receipts by accounts affected and exchanged them for a check to reimburse the fund for expenditures.
 28 The petty cash fund amount is increased by $100 to a total of $500.

Required

1. Prepare the journal entry to establish the petty cash fund.

2. Prepare a petty cash payments report for February with these categories: delivery expense, mileage expense, postage expense, transportation-in, and office supplies expense. Sort the payments into the appropriate categories and total the expenditures in each category.

3. Prepare the journal entries for part 2 to both (*a*) reimburse and (*b*) increase the fund amount.

Check   (3a) Cr. Cash $279.58

Kiona Co. set up a petty cash fund for payments of small amounts. The following transactions involving the petty cash fund occurred in May (the last month of the company's fiscal year).

Problem 8-3A
Establish, reimburse, and adjust petty cash
(LO4)

May 1 Prepared a company check for $300 to establish the petty cash fund.
   15 Prepared a company check to replenish the fund for the following expenditures made since May 1.
       a. Paid $88 for janitorial services.
       b. Paid $53.68 for miscellaneous expenses.
       c. Paid postage expenses of $53.50.
       d. Paid $47.15 to *The County Gazette* (the local newspaper) for an advertisement.
       e. Counted $62.15 remaining in the petty cash box.
   16 Prepared a company check for $200 to increase the fund to $500.
   31 The petty cashier reports that $288.20 cash remains in the fund. A company check is drawn to replenish the fund for the following expenditures made since May 15.
       f. Paid postage expenses of $147.36.
       g. Reimbursed the office manager for business mileage, $23.50.
       h. Paid $34.75 to deliver merchandise to a customer, terms FOB destination.
   31 The company decides that the May 16 increase in the fund was too large. It reduces the fund by $100, leaving a total of $400.

Required

1. Prepare journal entries to establish the fund on May 1, to replenish it on May 15 and on May 31, and to reflect any increase or decrease in the fund balance on May 16 and May 31.

Check   (1) Cr. to Cash: May 15, $237.85; May 16, $200

Analysis Component

2. Explain how the company's financial statements are affected if the petty cash fund is not replenished and no entry is made on May 31.

The following information is available to reconcile Branch Company's book balance of cash with its bank statement cash balance as of July 31, 2008.

Problem 8-4A
Prepare a bank reconciliation and record adjustments
(LO7)

a. After all posting is complete on July 31, the company's Cash account has a $27,497 debit balance, but its July bank statement shows a $27,233 cash balance.

b. Check No. 3031 for $1,482 and Check No. 3040 for $558 were outstanding on the June 30 bank reconciliation. Check No. 3040 is listed with the July canceled checks, but Check No. 3031 is not. Also, Check No. 3065 for $382 and Check No. 3069 for $2,281, both written in July, are not among the canceled checks on the July 31 statement.

c. In comparing the canceled checks on the bank statement with the entries in the accounting records, it is found that Check No. 3056 for July rent was correctly written and drawn for $1,270 but was erroneously entered in the accounting records as $1,250.

d. A credit memorandum enclosed with the July bank statement indicates the bank collected $8,000 cash on a noninterest-bearing note for Branch, deducted a $45 collection fee, and credited the remainder to its account. Branch had not recorded this event before receiving the statement.

e. A debit memorandum for $805 lists a $795 NSF check plus a $10 NSF charge. The check had been received from a customer, Evan Shaw. Branch has not yet recorded this check as NSF.

f. Enclosed with the July statement is a $25 debit memorandum for bank services. It has not yet been recorded because no previous notification had been received.

g. Branch's July 31 daily cash receipts of $11,514 were placed in the bank's night depository on that date, but do not appear on the July 31 bank statement.

Required

1. Prepare the bank reconciliation for this company as of July 31, 2008.
2. Prepare the journal entries necessary to bring the company's book balance of cash into conformity with the reconciled cash balance as of July 31, 2008.

Check   (1) Reconciled balance, $34,602; (2) Cr. Note Receivable $8,000

Analysis Component

3. Assume that the July 31, 2008, bank reconciliation for this company is prepared and some items are treated incorrectly. For each of the following errors, explain the effect of the error on (i) the adjusted bank statement cash balance and (ii) the adjusted cash account book balance.

a. The company's unadjusted cash account balance of $27,497 is listed on the reconciliation as $27,947.

b. The bank's collection of the $8,000 note less the $45 collection fee is added to the bank statement cash balance on the reconciliation.

Problem 8-5A

Prepare a bank reconciliation and record adjustments

eXcel

mhhe.com/wildCA

Chavez Company most recently reconciled its bank statement and book balances of cash on August 31 and it reported two checks outstanding, No. 5888 for $1,028.05 and No. 5893 for $494.25. The following information is available for its September 30, 2008, reconciliation.

From the September 30 Bank Statement

Previous Balance	Total Checks and Debits	Total Deposits and Credits	Current Balance
16,800.45	9,620.05	11,272.85	18,453.25

Checks and Debits			Deposits and Credits		Daily Balance	
Date	No.	Amount	Date	Amount	Date	Amount
09/03	5888	1,028.05	09/05	1,103.75	08/31	16,800.45
09/04	5902	719.90	09/12	2,226.90	09/03	15,772.40
09/07	5901	1,824.25	09/21	4,093.00	09/04	15,052.50
09/17		600.25 NSF	09/25	2,351.70	09/05	16,156.25
09/20	5905	937.00	09/30	12.50 IN	09/07	14,332.00
09/22	5903	399.10	09/30	1,485.00 CM	09/12	16,558.90
09/22	5904	2,090.00			09/17	15,958.65
09/28	5907	213.85			09/20	15,021.65
09/29	5909	1,807.65			09/21	19,114.65
					09/22	16,625.55
					09/25	18,977.25
					09/28	18,763.40
					09/29	16,955.75
					09/30	18,453.25

From Chavez Company's Accounting Records

Cash Receipts Deposited				Cash Disbursements		
Date		Cash Debit		Check No.		Cash Credit
Sept. 5		1,103.75		5901		1,824.25
12		2,226.90		5902		719.90
21		4,093.00		5903		399.10
25		2,351.70		5904		2,060.00
30		1,682.75		5905		937.00
		11,458.10		5906		982.30
				5907		213.85
				5908		388.00
				5909		1,807.65
						9,332.05

Cash						Acct. No. 101
Date		Explanation	PR	Debit	Credit	Balance
Aug.	31	Balance				15,278.15
Sept.	30	Total receipts	R12	11,458.10		26,736.25
	30	Total disbursements	D23		9,332.05	17,404.20

Additional Information

Check No. 5904 is correctly drawn for $2,090 to pay for computer equipment; however, the recordkeeper misread the amount and entered it in the accounting records with a debit to Computer Equipment and a credit to Cash of $2,060. The NSF check shown in the statement was originally received from a customer, S. Nilson, in payment of her account. Its return has not yet been recorded by the company. The credit memorandum is from the collection of a $1,500 note for Chavez Company by the bank. The bank deducted a $15 collection fee. The collection and fee are not yet recorded.

Required

1. Prepare the September 30, 2008, bank reconciliation for this company.

2. Prepare the journal entries to adjust the book balance of cash to the reconciled balance.

Analysis Component

3. The bank statement reveals that some of the prenumbered checks in the sequence are missing. Describe three situations that could explain this.

Check (1) Reconciled balance, $18,271.45 (2) Cr. Note Receivable $1,500

~~~~~~

For each of these five separate cases, identify the basic control principle(s) that is violated. Recommend what the business should do for better control.

1. Lavina Company is a small business that has separated the duties of cash receipts and cash disbursements. The employee responsible for cash disbursements reconciles the bank account monthly.

2. Latisha Tally personally opens all the mail for Professional Systems and performs monthly bank reconciliations.

3. Jim Sutton prides himself on hiring quality workers who require little supervision. As office manager, Jim allows his bookkeeper to sign checks for the business.

4. Victor Vu deposits cash receipts for Quality Lawncare once each week.

5. Gates' Dog Salon uses a petty cash system. Jill is the petty cash cashier, but she allows other employees to access the petty cash drawer if she is away from her desk.

PROBLEM SET B

Problem 8-1B
Analyzing internal control

(L01)

Blues Music Center had the following petty cash transactions in March of the current year.

March 5 Wrote a $250 check, cashed it, and gave the proceeds and the petty cashbox to Jen Rouse, the petty cashier.

6 Paid $12.50 COD shipping charges on merchandise purchased for resale, terms FOB shipping point. Blues uses the periodic system to account for purchases.

11 Paid $10.75 delivery charges on merchandise sold to a customer, terms FOB destination.

12 Purchased file folders for $14.13 that are immediately used.

14 Reimbursed Bob Geldof, the manager, $11.65 for office supplies purchased and used.

18 Purchased printer paper for $20.54 that is immediately used.

27 Paid $45.10 COD shipping charges on merchandise purchased for resale, terms FOB shipping point.

28 Paid postage expenses of $18.

30 Reimbursed Geldof $56.80 for business car mileage.

31 Cash of $61.53 remained in the fund. Sorted the petty cash receipts by accounts affected and exchanged them for a check to reimburse the fund for expenditures.

31 The petty cash fund amount is increased by $50 to a total of $300.

Problem 8-2B
Establish, reimburse, and increase petty cash

(L04)

Required

1. Prepare the journal entry to establish the petty cash fund.

2. Prepare a petty cash payments report for March with these categories: delivery expense, mileage expense, postage expense, transportation-in, and office supplies expense. Sort the payments into the appropriate categories and total the expenses in each category.

3. Prepare the journal entries for part 2 to both (*a*) reimburse and (*b*) increase the fund amount.

Check (2) Total expenses $189.47

(3a) Cr. Cash $188.47

Moya Co. establishes a petty cash fund for payments of small amounts. The following transactions involving the petty cash fund occurred in January (the last month of the company's fiscal year).

Jan. 3 A company check for $150 is written and made payable to the petty cashier to establish the petty cash fund.

14 A company check is written to replenish the fund for the following expenditures made since January 3.

  a. Purchased office supplies for $14.29 that are immediately used up.

  b. Paid $19.60 COD shipping charges on merchandise purchased for resale, terms FOB shipping point. Moya uses the periodic system to account for inventory.

Problem 8-3B
Establishing, reimbursing, and adjusting petty cash

(L04)

    c. Paid \$38.57 to All-Tech for minor repairs to a computer.
    d. Paid \$12.82 for items classified as miscellaneous expenses.
    e. Counted \$62.28 remaining in the petty cash box.
  15 Prepared a company check for \$50 to increase the fund to \$200.
  31 The petty cashier reports that \$17.35 remains in the fund. A company check is written to replenish the fund for the following expenditures made since January 14.
    f. Paid \$50 to *The Smart Shopper* for an advertisement in January's newsletter.
    g. Paid \$48.19 for postage expenses.
    h. Paid \$78 to Smooth Delivery for delivery of merchandise, terms FOB destination.
  31 The company decides that the January 15 increase in the fund was too little. It increases the fund by another \$50, leaving a total of \$250.

Required

Check (1) Cr. to Cash: Jan. 14, \$87.72; Jan. 15, \$50

1. Prepare journal entries to establish the fund on January 3, to replenish it on January 14 and January 31, and to reflect any increase or decrease in the fund balance on January 15 and 31.

Analysis Component

2. Explain how the company's financial statements are affected if the petty cash fund is not replenished and no entry is made on January 31.

Problem 8–4B

Prepare a bank reconciliation and record adjustments

(LO7)

The following information is available to reconcile Severino Co.'s book balance of cash with its bank statement cash balance as of December 31, 2008.

a. After posting is complete, the December 31 cash balance according to the accounting records is \$32,878.30, and the bank statement cash balance for that date is \$46,822.40.

b. Check No. 1273 for \$4,589.30 and Check No. 1282 for \$400.00, both written and entered in the accounting records in December, are not among the canceled checks. Two checks, No. 1231 for \$2,289.00 and No. 1242 for \$410.40, were outstanding on the most recent November 30 reconciliation. Check No. 1231 is listed with the December canceled checks, but Check No. 1242 is not.

c. When the December checks are compared with entries in the accounting records, it is found that Check No. 1267 had been correctly drawn for \$3,456 to pay for office supplies but was erroneously entered in the accounting records as \$3,465.

d. Two debit memoranda are enclosed with the statement and are unrecorded at the time of the reconciliation. One debit memorandum is for \$762.50 and dealt with an NSF check for \$745 received from a customer, Titus Industries, in payment of its account. The bank assessed a \$17.50 fee for processing it. The second debit memorandum is a \$99.00 charge for check printing. Severino did not record these transactions before receiving the statement.

e. A credit memorandum indicates that the bank collected \$19,000 cash on a note receivable for the company, deducted a \$20 collection fee, and credited the balance to the company's Cash account. Severino did not record this transaction before receiving the statement.

f. Severino's December 31 daily cash receipts of \$9,583.10 were placed in the bank's night depository on that date, but do not appear on the December 31 bank statement.

Required

Check (1) Reconciled balance, \$51,005.80; (2) Cr. Note Receivable \$19,000

1. Prepare the bank reconciliation for this company as of December 31, 2008.
2. Prepare the journal entries necessary to bring the company's book balance of cash into conformity with the reconciled cash balance as of December 31, 2008.

Analysis Component

3. Explain the nature of the communications conveyed by a bank when the bank sends the depositor (*a*) a debit memorandum and (*b*) a credit memorandum.

Problem 8–5B

Prepare a bank reconciliation and record adjustments

(LO6)(LO7)

Shamara Systems Co. most recently reconciled its bank balance on April 30 and reported two checks outstanding at that time, No. 1771 for \$781.00 and No. 1780 for \$1,425.90. The following information is available for its May 31, 2008, reconciliation.

From the May 31 Bank Statement

Previous Balance	Total Checks and Debits	Total Deposits and Credits	Current Balance
18,290.70	13,094.80	16,566.80	21,762.70

Checks and Debits			Deposits and Credits		Daily Balance	
Date	No.	Amount	Date	Amount	Date	Amount
05/01	1771	781.00	05/04	2,438.00	04/30	18,290.70
05/02	1783	382.50	05/14	2,898.00	05/01	17,509.70
05/04	1782	1,285.50	05/22	1,801.80	05/02	17,127.20
05/11	1784	1,449.60	05/25	7,350.00 CM	05/04	18,279.70
05/18		431.80 NSF	05/26	2,079.00	05/11	16,830.10
05/25	1787	8,032.50			05/14	19,728.10
05/26	1785	63.90			05/18	19,296.30
05/29	1788	654.00			05/22	21,098.10
05/31		14.00 SC			05/25	20,415.60
					05/26	22,430.70
					05/29	21,776.70
					05/31	21,762.70

From Shamara Systems' Accounting Records

Cash Receipts Deposited

Date		Cash Debit
May	4	2,438.00
	14	2,898.00
	22	1,801.80
	26	2,079.00
	31	2,727.30
		11,944.10

Cash Disbursements

Check No.		Cash Credit
1782		1,285.50
1783		382.50
1784		1,449.60
1785		63.90
1786		353.10
1787		8,032.50
1788		644.00
1789		639.50
		12,850.60

Cash   **Acct. No. 101**

Date		Explanation	PR	Debit	Credit	Balance
Apr.	30	Balance				16,083.80
May	31	Total receipts	R7	11,944.10		28,027.90
	31	Total disbursements	D8		12,850.60	15,177.30

Additional Information

Check No. 1788 is correctly drawn for $654 to pay for May utilities; however, the recordkeeper misread the amount and entered it in the accounting records with a debit to Utilities Expense and a credit to Cash for $644. The bank paid and deducted the correct amount. The NSF check shown in the statement was originally received from a customer, W. Sox, in payment of her account. The company has not yet recorded its return. The credit memorandum is from a $7,400 note that the bank collected for the company. The bank deducted a $50 collection fee and deposited the remainder in the company's account. The collection and fee have not yet been recorded.

Required

1. Prepare the May 31, 2008, bank reconciliation for Shamara Systems.

2. Prepare the journal entries to adjust the book balance of cash to the reconciled balance.

Analysis Component

3. The bank statement reveals that some of the prenumbered checks in the sequence are missing. Describe three possible situations to explain this.

Check (1) Reconciled balance, $22,071.50; (2) Cr. Note Receivable $7,400

SERIAL PROBLEM

Success Systems

(LO7)

(This serial problem began in Chapter 1 and continues through most of the book. If previous chapter segments were not completed, the serial problem can begin at this point. It is helpful, but not necessary, that you use the Working Papers that accompany the book.)

SP 8   Adriana Lopez receives the March bank statement for Success Systems on April 11, 2008. The March 31 bank statement shows an ending cash balance of $86,896. A comparison of the bank statement with the general ledger Cash account, No. 101, reveals the following.

a. Lopez notices that the bank erroneously cleared a $470 check against her account that she did not issue. The check documentation included with the bank statement shows that this check was actually issued by a company named Sierra Systems.

b. On March 25, the bank issued a $50 debit memorandum for the safety deposit box that Success Systems agreed to rent from the bank beginning March 25.

c. On March 26, the bank issued a $75 debit memorandum for printed checks that Success Systems ordered from the bank.

d. On March 31, the bank issued a credit memorandum for $33 interest earned on Success Systems's checking account for the month of March.

e. Lopez notices that the check she issued for $192 on March 31, 2008, has not yet cleared the bank.

f. Lopez verifies that all deposits made in March do appear on the March bank statement.

g. The general ledger Cash account, No. 101, shows an ending cash balance per books as $87,266 (prior to any reconciliation).

Required

1. Prepare a bank reconciliation for Success Systems for the month ended March 31, 2008.

2. Prepare any necessary adjusting entries. Use Miscellaneous Expenses, No. 677, for any bank charges. Use Interest Revenue, No. 404, for any interest earned on the checking account for the month of March.

BEYOND THE NUMBERS

REPORTING IN ACTION

(LO1) (LO8)

BEST BUY

BTN 8-1   Refer to Best Buy's financial statements in Appendix A to answer the following.

1. For both fiscal year-ends February 26, 2005, and February 28, 2004, identify the total amount of cash and cash equivalents. Determine the percent this amount represents of total current assets, total current liabilities, total shareholders' equity, and total assets for both years. Comment on any trends.

2. For fiscal years ended February 26, 2005, and February 28, 2004, use the information in the statement of cash flows to determine the percent change between the beginning and ending year amounts of cash and cash equivalents.

3. Compute the days' sales uncollected as of February 26, 2005, and February 28, 2004. Has the collection of receivables improved? Are accounts receivable an important asset for Best Buy? Explain.

Fast Forward

4. Access Best Buy's financial statements for fiscal years ending after February 26, 2005, from its Website (BestBuy.com) or the SEC's EDGAR database (www.sec.gov). Recompute its days' sales uncollected for fiscal years ending after February 26, 2005. Compare this to the days' sales uncollected for 2005 and 2004.

COMPARATIVE ANALYSIS

(LO8)

BEST BUY **circuit CITY**

BTN 8-2   Key comparative figures ($ millions) for both Best Buy and Circuit City follow.

Key Figures	Best Buy		Circuit City	
	Current Year	Prior Year	Current Year	Prior Year
Accounts receivable	$ 375	$ 343	$ 173	$ 171
Net sales	27,433	24,548	10,472	9,857

Required

Compute days' sales uncollected for both companies for each of the two years shown. Comment on any trends for both companies. Which company has the larger percent change in days' sales uncollected from the prior year to the current year?

BTN 8-3   Harriet Knox, Ralph Patton, and Marcia Diamond work for a family physician, Dr. Gwen Conrad, who is in private practice. Dr. Conrad is knowledgeable about office management practices and has segregated the cash receipt duties as follows. Knox opens the mail and prepares a triplicate list of money received. She sends one copy of the list to Patton, the cashier, who deposits the receipts daily in the bank. Diamond, the recordkeeper, receives a copy of the list and posts payments to patients' accounts. About once a month the office clerks have an expensive lunch they pay for as follows. First, Patton endorses a patient's check in Dr. Conrad's name and cashes it at the bank. Knox then destroys the remittance advice accompanying the check. Finally, Diamond posts payment to the customer's account as a miscellaneous credit. The three justify their actions by their relatively low pay and knowledge that Dr. Conrad will likely never miss the money.

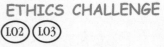
ETHICS CHALLENGE
LO2 LO3

Required

1. Who is the best person in Dr. Conrad's office to reconcile the bank statement?

2. Would a bank reconciliation uncover this office fraud?

3. What are some procedures to detect this type of fraud?

4. Suggest additional controls that Dr. Conrad could implement.

BTN 8-4   Assume you are a salesperson for a small business. The owner of the business informs the sales staff that the days' sales uncollected ratio is too high, and asks you for insight on how to reduce days' sales uncollected.

WORKPLACE
COMMUNICATION
LO8

Required

Explain to the owner strategies the sales staff can employ to reduce days' sales uncollected. Provide a response in memorandum format.

BTN 8-5   Visit the Association of Certified Fraud Examiners Website at **cfenet.com**. Review the cash frauds (refer to the 2006 *Report to the Nation;* see Fraud resource center—under publications—*Report to the Nation*) discussed at this Website and answer the following questions.

TAKING IT TO
THE NET
LO1 LO2 LO3

Required

1. What percentage of asset misappropriation schemes involve cash?

2. What are the three categories of cash frauds? What is the most common type of cash fraud?

3. What are the six types of fraudulent disbursement schemes? What is the most common type of fraudulent disbursement scheme? Which type of fraudulent disbursement scheme has the highest median dollar loss per occurrence?

BTN 8-6   Refer to the chapter opener on **Moe's Southwest Grill**. Identify and describe several cash controls that Moe's likely uses.

ENTREPRENEURS
IN BUSINESS
LO2 LO3

ANSWERS TO MULTIPLE CHOICE QUIZ

1. e; The entry follows.

Debits to expenses (or assets)	420
Cash Over and Short	5
Cash	425

4. c
5. d

2. a; recognizes cash collection of note by bank.

3. a; the bank reconciliation follows.

Bank Reconciliation November 30			
Balance per bank statement	$1,895	Balance per books	$1,742
Add: Deposit in transit	795	Add: Note collected (net fee)	320
Deduct: Outstanding checks	(638)	Deduct: Service charge	(10)
Reconciled balance	$2,052	Reconciled balance	$2,052

A Look Back

Chapter 8 focused on cash. We showed how petty cash systems, bank reconciliations, and banking activities can help the business owner control cash.

A Look at This Chapter

This chapter emphasizes employee payroll. We show how to compute payroll deductions to comply with laws. We also show how the employer uses a payroll register and employee earnings records to record and control its payroll.

A Look Ahead

Chapter 10 explains how the employer pays taxes. It also shows the tax documents the employer must file to comply with laws.

Chapter 9

Employee Earnings, Deductions, and Payroll

LEARNING OBJECTIVES

LO 1 Describe the laws that affect employee payroll.

LO 2 Compute employee gross pay.

LO 3 Compute employee deductions for taxes and net pay.

LO 4 Record employee payroll information in a payroll register.

LO 5 Journalize payroll transactions in a general journal.

LO 6 Prepare an earnings record for each employee.

LO 7 Explain how an employer can control payroll.

LO 8 Compute the sales-per-employee ratio and use it to analyze operating efficiency.

"You must follow through on your promises and do the best work you can"
—Youngsong Martin

Dressing Up for Business

FOUNTAIN VALLEY, CA—Youngsong Martin found the plain, dreary look of most social and business events extremely disappointing. She recalls, "I was too familiar with the institutional look of those metal-rimmed chairs in banquet halls and ballrooms, drab folding chairs at many outdoor events, and the rather ordinary tablecloths and napkins." Martin reacted by launching **Wildflower Linen** (**WildflowerLinens.com**) to provide custom table linens, chair covers, and sashes to dress up banquets, meetings, weddings, and special events of all sorts.

"I derive more pleasure than I had imagined," explains Martin. "It has been a dream come true to 'dress' entire events." Martin also enjoys the service side and getting "to know customers on a more personal level."

But the business side is where Martin needed the most help. "You don't really realize what's involved with running a business until you actually do it," says Martin. "I definitely needed help with the management and financial aspects." Martin needed to attend to many facets of business, including the important task of managing liabilities for payroll, supplies, employee benefits, vacations, training, and taxes. Her effective management of liabilities, especially payroll and employee benefits, was crucial to getting Wildflower where it is today. Martin stresses that if you want to succeed in business, then monitoring and controlling liabilities is a must.

"It's one thing to think you know where your money's going," stresses Martin. "But it's quite another to actually write expenses down and see how they affect your operations." Martin says she must "analyze expenses and determine if they are necessary to help keep my business growing. It's almost like I'm getting an MBA." With nearly 15 employees and growing revenue, Martin has dressed up her business with more than just linens.

[Sources: *Wildflower Linen Website*, January 2007; *SCORE.org Website*, July 2005; *Special Events Business Advisors Website*, July 2005]

In this chapter we discuss the laws that require the employer to withhold amounts from employee pay for taxes. These amounts are additional liabilities in the journal entry to record wages. We also show how the employer can use payroll registers and employee earnings records to comply with laws and control payroll expenses.

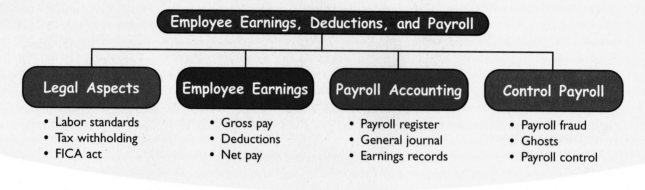

Employee Earnings, Deductions, and Payroll

Legal Aspects	Employee Earnings	Payroll Accounting	Control Payroll
• Labor standards • Tax withholding • FICA act	• Gross pay • Deductions • Net pay	• Payroll register • General journal • Earnings records	• Payroll fraud • Ghosts • Payroll control

Legal Aspects of Employee Payroll

Most employees and employers pay federal and state payroll taxes. Laws require employers to also prepare and submit reports that explain how they computed tax payments. Governments can impose penalties if the employer does not follow payroll tax laws. Law requires employers to withhold amounts from employees' pay for taxes. An **employee** is someone whose work is under the direction of the employer, such as a bookkeeper or secretary. The employer controls what work the employee is to do and how it should be done. For example, employees are typically trained to perform tasks a certain way. An **independent contractor** performs a job for the employer, but decides how to do the work. Independent contractors typically do not receive training from the employer. The employer does not withhold any money for taxes for independent contractors.

> Using independent contractors can help businesses lower their payroll costs. However, the employer must be careful in classifying employees as independent contractors to withstand potential audit by the Internal Revenue Service.

 LO1 Describe the laws that affect employee payroll.

Fair Labor Standards Act

This law applies to firms engaged in business across states. It sets a minimum wage, currently $5.15 per hour, and sets 40 hours as the most an employee can be required to work in a week at the normal pay rate. Employees that work more than 40 hours in a week receive overtime pay. This pay is at least one and one-half times their normal pay rate for those overtime hours.

Federal and State Income Tax Withholding

Each employee fills out an **Employee's Withholding Allowance Certificate (Form W-4)** as shown in Exhibit 9.1. The employer withholds a different amount of federal taxes for each employee. These amounts depend on the employee's marital status, his or her **gross pay,** and the number of withholding allowances the employee claims. Gross pay is the total amount an employee earns before deductions such as taxes. A **withholding allowance** lowers the amount of an employee's gross pay that is taxed. Each employee gets one personal allowance, one for a spouse if they are married, and one for each child or dependent. The more allowances an employee claims, the less tax the employer withholds.

For example, Robert Austin is an employee of Phoenix Sales and Service, a landscape design company. He is single (box 3) and has no dependents. He chooses one withholding allowance (box 5) and elects to have no additional amounts withheld from his paycheck (box 6). Employees who did not pay any taxes in the previous year and do not expect to pay taxes in the current year do not have taxes withheld from their paychecks. They write "Exempt" in box 7 on their W-4.

> Some small business owners use outside payroll services or computerized payroll systems to save time and ensure the business complies with all payroll laws.

Federal Insurance Contributions (FICA) Act

The federal Social Security system pays benefits to qualified workers. Employers usually separate **FICA** taxes into two groups: (1) retirement, disability, and survivors and (2) medical.

Exhibit 9.1

Employee's Withholding
Allowance Certificate (W-4)

Image of Form W-4:

Cut here and give Form W-4 to your employer. Keep the top part for your records.	

Form **W-4**   **Employee's Withholding Allowance Certificate**   OMB No. 1545-0010

Department of the Treasury
Internal Revenue Service
▶ Whether you are entitled to claim a certain number of allowances or exemption from withholding is subject to review by the IRS. Your employer may be required to send a copy of this form to the IRS.

1 Type or print your first name and middle initial   Last name   2 Your social security number
Robert J.   Austin   333 : 22 : 9999

Home address (number and street or rural route)   3 ☑ Single ☐ Married ☐ Married, but withhold at higher Single rate.
18 Roosevelt Blvd., Apt. C   Note. If married, but legally separated, or spouse is a nonresident alien, check the "Single" box.

City or town, state, and ZIP code   4 If your last name differs from that shown on your social security card, check here. You must call 1-800-772-1213 for a new card. ▶ ☐
Tempe, AZ 86322

5 Total number of allowances you are claiming (from line H above or from the applicable worksheet on page 2)   **5** 1
6 Additional amount, if any, you want withheld from each paycheck   **6** $0
7 I claim exemption from withholding for 2005, and I certify that I meet both of the following conditions for exemption.
  • Last year I had a right to a refund of all federal income tax withheld because I had no tax liability and
  • This year I expect a refund of all federal income tax withheld because I expect to have no tax liability.
  If you meet both conditions, write "Exempt" here   ▶ **7**

Under penalties of perjury, I declare that I have examined this certificate and to the best of my knowledge and belief, it is true, correct, and complete.
Employee's signature
(Form is not valid unless you sign it.) ▶ *Robert J. Austin*   Date ▶ 01/01/07

8 Employer's name and address [Employer, Complete lines 8 and 10 only if sending to the IRS.]   9 Office code (optional)   10 Employer identification number (EIN)
Phoenix Sales & Service, 1214 Mill Road, Phoenix, AZ 85621   86 : 3214587

For Privacy Act and Paperwork Reduction Act Notice, see page 2.   Cat. No. 102200   Form **W-4** (2005)

The first group is called *Social Security benefits* and it is paid for with *Social Security taxes.* The second group is called *Medicare benefits* and it is paid for with *Medicare taxes.*

Law requires employers to withhold FICA taxes from employees to pay for this system. For the year 2006, the amount withheld from each employee's pay for Social Security taxes is 6.2% of the first $94,200 the employee earns during the year. The most an individual employee could pay for Social Security tax in 2006 is $5,840.40 (0.062 × $94,200). The Medicare tax for 2006 is 1.45% of *all* amounts the employee earns. There is no upper limit on the amount of Medicare tax an employee could pay. For any changes in tax rates or maximum earnings levels, check the IRS Website at **www.IRS.gov** or the Social Security Administration Website at **www.SSA.gov**.

Self-Employment Tax   A person who operates their own business as a sole proprietor or independent contractor pays **self-employment tax.** A self-employed person must pay both the employee and employer FICA taxes. The self-employment tax rates are 12.4% (6.2% × 2) for Social Security and 2.9% (1.45% × 2) for Medicare. So, the most a self-employed person could pay for Social Security taxes in 2006 is $11,680.80 (2 × 0.062 × $94,200). There is no upper limit on the amount of Medicare tax a self-employed person could pay.

> Currently, people who earn $400 or more from self-employment must pay self-employment tax. This also applies to individuals who operate a part-time business in addition to a regular job.

Employee Earnings

This section explains how we compute employee gross pay and net pay, and how withholdings impact employee pay.

Computing Employee Gross Pay

Many employers pay wages for each hour worked. The employer must keep records of the number of hours each employee works on each day during a pay period. This can be done with a time sheet or a time clock. For example, see Exhibit 9.2 for Robert Austin's time sheet for the week ending January 7, 2007.

If Robert Austin earns a wage of $10 per hour worked, his gross pay for the week of January 7, 2007, is $400 (40 × $10). John Diaz, another employee of Phoenix Sales and Service, turns in a time card for the week of January 7, 2007, that shows he worked 40 regular hours and 2 overtime hours. If John Diaz's normal pay rate is $14 per hour, and he is paid one and one-half

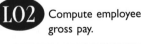

LO2 Compute employee gross pay.

> Time card frauds can be very costly. Employers are increasingly using biometrics, or body measurements, to uniquely identify people. Fingerprint readers can help the employer control time card scams.

Exhibit 9.2

Employee Time Sheet

Time Sheet

EMPLOYEE ID No.	EMPLOYEE NAME	WEEK ENDING
AR101	Robert Austin	January 7, 2007

	TIME		TIME		HOURS WORKED	
DAY	IN	OUT	IN	OUT	REGULAR	OVERTIME
Mon	7:30	11:30	12:30	4:30	8	
Tues	8:05	12:00	1:00	5:05	8	
Wed	8:00	12:00	12:30	4:30	8	
Thurs	7:45	11:45	12:45	4:45	8	
Fri	7:15	12:15	12:45	3:45	8	
				Total Hours	40	

Enter your time in HH:MM format

times his normal pay rate for overtime, his gross pay for the week ending January 7, 2007, is computed as:

Regular pay:	40 hours × $14 per hour =	$560
Overtime premium:	2 hours × $21 per hour =	42
Total gross pay		$602

Computing Withholdings from Employee Gross Pay

LO3 Compute employee deductions for taxes and net pay.

Payroll deductions, commonly called *withholdings,* are amounts withheld from an employee's gross pay. Required deductions result from law and include income taxes and Social Security taxes. Voluntary deductions, at an employee's option, include pension and health contributions, union dues, and charitable giving. Exhibit 9.3 summarizes the typical employee payroll deductions.

Exhibit 9.3

Payroll Deductions

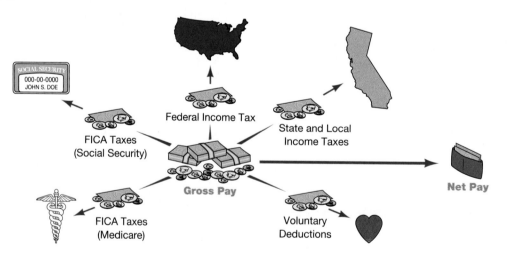

Federal Income Tax Withholding   The employer uses a withholding table (called **Circular E**) from the IRS to compute the amount of federal taxes to withhold. Circular E is available for free from www.IRS.gov. Separate withholding tables are provided for single or married persons, and for different pay periods (for example weekly or monthly). Exhibit 9.4 provides a part of a Circular E **withholding table** for single persons paid weekly. Exhibits 9.5, 9.6, and 9.7 show additional excerpts from the withholding table.

IRS withholding tables are based on projecting weekly (or other period) pay into an annual amount.

From his W-4 form, Robert Austin is a single employee who claims one withholding allowance. He is paid each week. Robert's gross pay was $400 for the week ending January 7, 2007. To determine Robert's federal tax withholding, scan the "If wages are" columns until "at least $400 but less than $410" is found. This range includes the $400 of income Robert earned this week. Then find the column for 1 withholding allowance and scan down the table to the row found earlier. Based on Robert's gross pay of $400 and his one withholding allowance, Phoenix Sales and Service will withhold $37 for federal taxes from Robert's gross pay for the week of January 7, 2007.

Exhibit 9.4

Withholding Table Example—
Single Persons Paid Weekly

SINGLE Persons—WEEKLY Payroll Period
(For Wages Paid in 2006)

At least	But less than	0	1	2	3	4	5	6	7	8	9	10
$400	$410	$46	$37	$27	$17	$10	$4	$0	$0	$0	$0	$0
410	420	48	38	29	19	11	5	0	0	0	0	0
420	430	49	40	30	20	12	6	0	0	0	0	0
430	440	51	41	32	22	13	7	0	0	0	0	0
440	450	52	43	33	23	14	8	1	0	0	0	0
450	460	54	44	35	25	15	9	2	0	0	0	0
460	470	55	46	36	26	17	10	3	0	0	0	0
470	480	57	47	38	28	18	11	4	0	0	0	0
480	490	58	49	39	29	20	12	5	0	0	0	0
490	500	60	50	41	31	21	13	6	0	0	0	0
500	510	61	52	42	32	23	14	7	1	0	0	0
510	520	63	53	44	34	24	15	8	2	0	0	0
520	530	64	55	45	35	26	16	9	3	0	0	0
530	540	66	56	47	37	27	18	10	4	0	0	0
540	550	67	58	48	38	29	19	11	5	0	0	0
550	560	69	59	50	40	30	21	12	6	0	0	0
560	570	70	61	51	41	32	22	13	7	1	0	0
570	580	72	62	53	43	33	24	14	8	2	0	0
580	590	73	64	54	44	35	25	16	9	3	0	0
590	600	75	65	56	46	36	27	17	10	4	0	0
600	610	76	67	57	47	38	28	19	11	5	0	0
610	620	78	68	59	49	39	30	20	12	6	0	0
620	630	80	70	60	50	41	31	22	13	7	0	0
630	640	82	71	62	52	42	33	23	14	8	1	0
640	650	85	73	63	53	44	34	25	15	9	2	0
650	660	87	74	65	55	45	36	26	17	10	3	0
660	670	90	76	66	56	47	37	28	18	11	4	0
670	680	92	77	68	58	48	39	29	20	12	5	0
680	690	95	79	69	59	50	40	31	21	13	6	0
690	700	97	81	71	61	51	42	32	23	14	7	1
700	710	100	84	72	62	53	43	34	24	15	8	2
710	720	102	86	74	64	54	45	35	26	16	9	3
720	730	105	89	75	65	56	46	37	27	18	10	4
730	740	107	91	77	67	57	48	38	29	19	11	5
740	750	110	94	78	68	59	49	40	30	21	12	6
800	810	125	109	93	77	68	58	49	39	30	20	12
810	820	127	111	95	79	69	60	50	41	31	22	13
820	830	130	114	98	82	71	61	52	42	33	23	14
830	840	132	116	100	84	72	63	53	44	34	25	15
840	850	135	119	103	87	74	64	55	45	35	26	17
900	910	150	134	118	102	86	73	64	54	45	35	26
910	920	152	136	120	104	89	75	65	56	46	37	27
920	930	155	139	123	107	91	76	67	57	48	38	29
930	940	157	141	125	109	94	78	68	59	49	40	30
940	950	160	144	128	112	96	80	70	60	51	41	32
950	960	162	146	130	114	99	83	71	62	52	43	33
960	970	165	149	133	117	101	85	73	63	54	44	35
970	980	167	151	135	119	104	88	74	65	55	46	36
980	990	170	154	138	122	106	90	76	66	57	47	38
990	1,000	172	156	140	124	109	93	77	68	58	49	39
1,100	1,110	200	184	168	152	136	120	104	88	75	65	56
1,110	1,120	202	186	170	154	139	123	107	91	76	67	57
1,120	1,130	205	189	173	157	141	125	109	93	78	68	59
1,130	1,140	207	191	175	159	144	128	112	96	80	70	60
1,140	1,150	210	194	178	162	146	130	114	98	83	71	62
1,150	1,160	212	196	180	164	149	133	117	101	85	73	63
1,160	1,170	215	199	183	167	151	135	119	103	88	74	65
1,170	1,180	217	201	185	169	154	138	122	106	90	76	66
1,180	1,190	220	204	188	172	156	140	124	108	93	77	68
1,190	1,200	222	206	190	174	159	143	127	111	95	79	69
1,200	1,210	225	209	193	177	161	145	129	113	98	82	71
1,210	1,220	227	211	195	179	164	148	132	116	100	84	72
1,220	1,230	230	214	198	182	166	150	134	118	103	87	74
1,230	1,240	232	216	200	184	169	153	137	121	105	89	75
1,240	1,250	235	219	203	187	171	155	139	123	108	92	77

Exhibit 9.5

Withholding Table Example—
Married Persons Paid Weekly

MARRIED Persons—WEEKLY Payroll Period
(For Wages Paid in 2006)

At least	But less than	0	1	2	3	4	5	6	7	8	9	10
		The amount of income tax to be withheld is—										
$440	$450	$29	$23	$16	$10	$4	$0	$0	$0	$0	$0	$0
450	460	31	24	17	11	5	0	0	0	0	0	0
460	470	32	25	18	12	6	0	0	0	0	0	0
470	480	34	26	19	13	7	0	0	0	0	0	0
480	490	35	27	20	14	8	1	0	0	0	0	0
490	500	37	28	21	15	9	2	0	0	0	0	0
500	510	38	29	22	16	10	3	0	0	0	0	0
510	520	40	30	23	17	11	4	0	0	0	0	0
520	530	41	32	24	18	12	5	0	0	0	0	0
530	540	43	33	25	19	13	6	0	0	0	0	0
540	550	44	35	26	20	14	7	1	0	0	0	0
550	560	46	36	27	21	15	8	2	0	0	0	0
560	570	47	38	28	22	16	9	3	0	0	0	0
570	580	49	39	30	23	17	10	4	0	0	0	0
580	590	50	41	31	24	18	11	5	0	0	0	0
590	600	52	42	33	25	19	12	6	0	0	0	0
600	610	53	44	34	26	20	13	7	1	0	0	0
610	620	55	45	36	27	21	14	8	2	0	0	0
620	630	56	47	37	28	22	15	9	3	0	0	0
630	640	58	48	39	29	23	16	10	4	0	0	0
740	750	74	65	55	46	36	27	21	15	8	2	0
750	760	76	66	57	47	38	28	22	16	9	3	0
760	770	77	68	58	49	39	30	23	17	10	4	0
770	780	79	69	60	50	41	31	24	18	11	5	0
780	790	80	71	61	52	42	33	25	19	12	6	0
790	800	82	72	63	53	44	34	26	20	13	7	1
800	810	83	74	64	55	45	36	27	21	14	8	2
810	820	85	75	66	56	47	37	28	22	15	9	3
820	830	86	77	67	58	48	39	29	23	16	10	4
830	840	88	78	69	59	50	40	31	24	17	11	5
840	850	89	80	70	61	51	42	32	25	18	12	6
850	860	91	81	72	62	53	43	34	26	19	13	7
860	870	92	83	73	64	54	45	35	27	20	14	8
870	880	94	84	75	65	56	46	37	28	21	15	9
880	890	95	86	76	67	57	48	38	29	22	16	10
890	900	97	87	78	68	59	49	40	30	23	17	11
900	910	98	89	79	70	60	51	41	32	24	18	12
910	920	100	90	81	71	62	52	43	33	25	19	13
920	930	101	92	82	73	63	54	44	35	26	20	14
930	940	103	93	84	74	65	55	46	36	27	21	15
940	950	104	95	85	76	66	57	47	38	28	22	16
950	960	106	96	87	77	68	58	49	39	30	23	17
960	970	107	98	88	79	69	60	50	41	31	24	18
970	980	109	99	90	80	71	61	52	42	33	25	19
980	990	110	101	91	82	72	63	53	44	34	26	20
990	1,000	112	102	93	83	74	64	55	45	36	27	21
1,000	1,010	113	104	94	85	75	66	56	47	37	28	22
1,010	1,020	115	105	96	86	77	67	58	48	39	29	23
1,020	1,030	116	107	97	88	78	69	59	50	40	31	24
1,030	1,040	118	108	99	89	80	70	61	51	42	32	25
1,190	1,200	142	132	123	113	104	94	85	75	66	56	47
1,200	1,210	143	134	124	115	105	96	86	77	67	58	48
1,210	1,220	145	135	126	116	107	97	88	78	69	59	50
1,220	1,230	146	137	127	118	108	99	89	80	70	61	51
1,230	1,240	148	138	129	119	110	100	91	81	72	62	53

Exhibit 9.6

Withholding Table Example—
Single Persons Paid Monthly

SINGLE Persons—MONTHLY Payroll Period
(For Wages Paid in 2006)

At least	But less than	0	1	2	3	4	5	6	7	8	9	10
		The amount of income tax to be withheld is—										
1,840	1,880	215	174	133	92	54	26	0	0	0	0	0
1,880	1,920	221	180	139	98	58	30	3	0	0	0	0
1,920	1,960	227	186	145	104	62	34	7	0	0	0	0
1,960	2,000	233	192	151	110	68	38	11	0	0	0	0
2,000	2,040	239	198	157	116	74	42	15	0	0	0	0
2,040	2,080	245	204	163	122	80	46	19	0	0	0	0
2,080	2,120	251	210	169	128	86	50	23	0	0	0	0
2,120	2,160	257	216	175	134	92	54	27	0	0	0	0
2,160	2,200	263	222	181	140	98	58	31	3	0	0	0
2,200	2,240	269	228	187	146	104	63	35	7	0	0	0
2,240	2,280	275	234	193	152	110	69	39	11	0	0	0
2,280	2,320	281	240	199	158	116	75	43	15	0	0	0
2,320	2,360	287	246	205	164	122	81	47	19	0	0	0
2,360	2,400	293	252	211	170	128	87	51	23	0	0	0
2,400	2,440	299	258	217	176	134	93	55	27	0	0	0

Exhibit 9.7

Withholding Table Example—
Married Persons Paid Monthly

MARRIED Persons—**MONTHLY** Payroll Period
(For Wages Paid in 2006)

If the wages are—		And the number of withholding allowances claimed is—										
At least	But less than	0	1	2	3	4	5	6	7	8	9	10
		The amount of income tax to be withheld is—										
840	880	19	0	0	0	0	0	0	0	0	0	0
880	920	23	0	0	0	0	0	0	0	0	0	0
920	960	27	0	0	0	0	0	0	0	0	0	0
960	1,000	31	4	0	0	0	0	0	0	0	0	0
1,000	1,040	35	8	0	0	0	0	0	0	0	0	0
1,040	1,080	39	12	0	0	0	0	0	0	0	0	0
1,080	1,120	43	16	0	0	0	0	0	0	0	0	0
1,120	1,160	47	20	0	0	0	0	0	0	0	0	0
1,160	1,200	51	24	0	0	0	0	0	0	0	0	0
1,200	1,240	55	28	0	0	0	0	0	0	0	0	0
4,840	4,880	567	526	484	443	402	361	319	278	237	196	154
4,880	4,920	573	532	490	449	408	367	325	284	243	202	160
4,920	4,960	579	538	496	455	414	373	331	290	249	208	166
4,960	5,000	585	544	502	461	420	379	337	296	255	214	172
5,000	5,040	591	550	508	467	426	385	343	302	261	220	178
5,040	5,080	597	556	514	473	432	391	349	308	267	226	184
5,080	5,120	603	562	520	479	438	397	355	314	273	232	190
5,120	5,160	609	568	526	485	444	403	361	320	279	238	196
5,160	5,200	615	574	532	491	450	409	367	326	285	244	202
5,200	5,240	621	580	538	497	456	415	373	332	291	250	208

State Income Tax Withholding   States withhold income taxes based on either withholding tables or a percentage of the amount withheld for federal taxes. In our examples we assume the state income tax withholding is 8 percent of the dollar amount withheld for federal income tax. Phoenix Sales and Service will withhold $2.96 (0.08 × $37) from Robert's pay for Arizona state income tax.

FICA Withholding   As of January 7, 2007 Robert Austin has earned less than the $94,200 annual maximum for Social Security taxes. Phoenix Sales and Service will withhold $24.80 (0.062 × $400) from his gross pay for FICA Social Security taxes. Phoenix Sales and Service will also withhold $5.80 (0.0145 × $400) from his gross pay for Medicare taxes.

Voluntary Deductions   The required deductions above result from laws. Employees can choose to have other amounts withheld from their pay. These voluntary deductions can include contributions for retirement and health plans, union dues, and gifts to charity. In this example Robert Austin has not chosen any voluntary deductions.

Many companies provide employee benefits beyond salaries and wages. An employer might pay all or part of medical, dental, life, and disability insurance and might contribute to employee pension plans. Payroll cost often exceeds employee gross earnings by 25% or more after these benefits are included.

Computing Net Pay

An employee's **net pay,** also called *take-home pay,* is gross pay minus all deductions. For the week of January 7, 2007, Robert Austin's net pay is computed as

Gross pay	$400.00
Minus deductions for:	
Federal income tax withholding	(37.00)
State income tax withholding	(2.96)
FICA—Social Security	(24.80)
FICA—Medicare	(5.80)
Net pay	$329.44

IN THE NEWS

A growing number of companies let employees collect their pay in "payroll cards." These cards are like debit cards and allow the employee to withdraw cash from ATMs or make purchases. They are particularly useful for employees who do not have bank accounts or whose small bank account balances would generate high fees. The use of "paperless" payroll can lower payroll processing costs by up to 75%.

HOW YOU DOIN'?   Answers—p. 215

1. A company pays its one employee $3,000 per month. This company's Social Security tax rate is 6.2% of the first $94,200; and its Medicare tax rate is 1.45% of all amounts earned. The company's March payroll will include what amount for employee Social Security and Medicare taxes?

2. Identify whether the employer or employee or both incur each of the following: (a) FICA taxes, and (b) withheld income taxes.

3. An employee worked 45 hours in a pay period. She earns $16 per hour and one and one-half her normal hourly wage for all overtime hours. What is her gross pay?

Payroll Accounting

This section describes payroll accounting, including the purpose and importance of a payroll register, the recording of payroll, and the use of banking services in dispensing payroll.

Payroll Register

LO4 Record employee payroll information in a payroll register.

A **payroll register** is often used to keep a record of pay period dates, hours worked, gross pay, deductions, and net pay of each employee for each pay period. Exhibit 9.8 shows the payroll register for Phoenix Sales and Service as of January 7, 2007. For each employee, the register includes whether they are single (S) or married (M) and the number of withholding allowances they chose on their Form W-4. This information is used with each employee's gross pay, and the withholding tables from Circular E, to determine the correct amount of tax to withhold for federal income taxes. This amount is reported in the "Federal Income Tax" column. In our example, withholdings for state purposes are 8% of the amount withheld for federal income tax; the amount is shown in the "State Income Tax" column in the payroll register.

Exhibit 9.8

Phoenix Sales and Service Payroll Register for Week Ended January 7, 2007

Payroll Register

Employee Name	Marital Status and Allowances	Beginning Cumulative Gross Earnings	Hours Worked This Pay Period	Hourly Wage	EARNINGS THIS PERIOD			Ending Cumulative Gross Earnings
					Regular	Overtime	Gross	
Austin, Robert	S-1	0.00	40	10.00	400.00	00.00	400.00	400.00
Cross, Judy	S-2	0.00	41	14.00	560.00	21.00	581.00	581.00
Diaz John	M-0	0.00	42	14.00	560.00	42.00	602.00	602.00
Kiefe, Kay	M-2	0.00	40	14.00	560.00	00.00	560.00	560.00
Miller, Lee	M-0	0.00	40	14.00	560.00	00.00	560.00	560.00
Sears, Dale	S-0	0.00	40	14.00	560.00	00.00	560.00	560.00
Total					3,200.00	63.00	3,263.00	3,263.00

TAXABLE EARNINGS FOR			EMPLOYEE DEDUCTIONS FOR				PAYMENT INFORMATION	
Social Security	Medicare	Unemployment	Social Security	Medicare	Federal Income Tax	State Income Tax	Net Pay	Check Number
400.00	400.00	400.00	24.80	5.80	37.00	2.96	329.44	9001
581.00	581.00	581.00	36.02	8.42	54.00	4.32	478.24	9002
602.00	602.00	602.00	37.32	8.73	53.00	4.24	498.71	9003
560.00	560.00	560.00	34.72	8.12	28.00	2.24	486.92	9004
560.00	560.00	560.00	34.72	8.12	47.00	3.76	466.40	9005
560.00	560.00	560.00	34.72	8.12	69.00	5.52	442.64	9006
3,263.00	3,263.00	3,263.00	202.30	47.31	288.00	23.04	2,702.35	

Phoenix Sales and Service collects time sheets from each of its employees, verifies their accuracy, and records the number of hours worked in the "Hours Worked This Pay Period" column. Each employee's hourly wage is entered into the "Hourly Wage" column, and employee gross earnings (regular and overtime) are computed as we showed earlier for Robert Austin and John Diaz.

The payroll register also reports the gross pay used to compute Social Security, Medicare, and the employer's unemployment taxes (in the "Taxable Earnings For" columns). These amounts can be different. For example, once an employee has earned at least $7,000 during a year, the employer stops paying unemployment tax for that employee. (We discuss employer payroll taxes, including unemployment, in the next chapter.) The employer also stops withholding Social Security tax for any employee who has earned at least $94,200 during the year.

Only employers pay unemployment taxes.

Since this is the first pay period of the year for Phoenix Sales and Service, none of its employees has reached these income maximums. Social Security taxes are entered for each employee in the "Social Security" column. Medicare taxes are entered for each employee in the "Medicare" column. Finally, each employee's net pay (gross pay minus all deductions) is computed and reported in the "Net Pay" column.

Recording and Settling Payroll

The payroll register provides the data to prepare the journal entry to record the payroll in the general ledger accounts. For the pay period ending January 7, 2007, Phoenix Sales and Service records the following journal entry in the general journal.

LO5 Journalize payroll transactions in a general journal.

Jan.	07	Wage Expense	3 2 6 3 00					
		FICA—Social Security Taxes Payable (6.2%)				2 0 2 30	
		FICA—Medicare Taxes Payable (1.45%)				4 7 31	
		Employee Federal Income Taxes Payable				2 8 8 00	
		Employee State Income Taxes Payable				2 3 04	
		Accrued Wages Payable				2 7 0 2 35	
		To record payroll for week ending January 7.					

Assets = Liabilities + Equity
+202.30   −3,263.00
+47.31
+288.00
+23.04
+2,702.35

Paying Employees   To safeguard its cash, Phoenix Sales and Service should pay its employees by check or electronic funds transfer. Exhibit 9.9 shows the *payroll check* for Robert Austin. Included with the check is a detachable *statement of earnings* that shows Robert's gross pay, deductions, and net pay. Robert Austin should keep this statement of earnings for his

Exhibit 9.9

Payroll Check and Statement of Earnings

EMPLOYEE NO.	EMPLOYEE NAME		SOCIAL SECURITY NO.	PAY PERIOD END	CHECK DATE
AR101	Robert Austin		333-22-9999	1/7/07	1/7/07

ITEM	RATE	HOURS	TOTAL	ITEM	THIS CHECK	YEAR TO DATE
Regular	10.00	40.00	400.00	Gross	400.00	400.00
				Fed. Income tax	-37.00	-37.00
				FICA-Soc. Sec.	-24.80	-24.80
				FICA-Medicare	-5.80	-5.80
				State Income tax	-2.96	-2.96

HOURS WORKED	GROSS THIS PERIOD	GROSS YEAR TO DATE	NET CHECK	CHECK No.
40.00	400.00	400.00	$329.44	9001
		(Detach and retain for your records)		

PHOENIX SALES & SERVICE
1214 Mill Road
Phoenix, AZ 85621
602-555-8900

Phoenix Bank and Trust
Phoenix, AZ 85621
3312-87044

9001

CHECK NO.	DATE	AMOUNT
9001	Jan 7, 2007	**************$329.44*

Three Hundred Twenty–Nine and 44/100 Dollars

PAY TO THE ORDER OF

Robert Austin
18 Roosevelt Blvd., Apt C
Tempe, AZ 86322

Mary Wills
AUTHORIZED SIGNATURE

records and deposit his paycheck in a bank. The payroll clerk enters the check number (9001) in the payroll register.

Companies with few employees often pay them with checks drawn on the company's regular bank account. Companies with many employees often use a special **payroll bank account** to pay employees. The payroll bank account is only used to pay employee payroll. If a payroll bank account is used, the company either (1) draws one check for the total payroll on the regular bank account and deposits it in the payroll bank account or (2) electronically transfers funds to the payroll bank account. Individual employee payroll checks are then drawn on the payroll bank account. This helps control the company's cash and helps in reconciling the regular bank account.

Paying Employees From the Regular Bank Account Each Phoenix Sales and Service employee will receive a check for net pay. If the employees are paid from the company's regular checking account, the company makes the following entry in the general journal.

Assets = Liabilities + Equity
−329.44   −2,702.35
−478.24
−498.71
−486.92
−466.40
−442.64

Jan.	07	Accrued Wages Payable	2 7 0 2 35	
		Cash—R. Austin		3 2 9 44
		Cash—J. Cross		4 7 8 24
		Cash—J. Diaz		4 9 8 71
		Cash—K. Kiefe		4 8 6 92
		Cash—L. Miller		4 6 6 40
		Cash—D. Sears		4 4 2 64
		To pay payroll for pay period ending January 7, 2007.		

Paying Employees From a Special Payroll Bank Account If instead Phoenix Sales and Service uses a special payroll bank account, the following journal entries will be made in the general journal.

Assets = Liabilities + Equity
+2,702.35
−2,702.35

Assets = Liabilities + Equity
−2,702.35   −2,702.35

Jan.	07	Cash—Payroll Bank Account	2 7 0 2 35	
		Cash		2 7 0 2 35
		To transfer cash to the payroll bank account.		
Jan.	07	Accrued Wages Payable	2 7 0 2 35	
		Cash—Payroll Bank Account		2 7 0 2 35
		To pay payroll for pay period ending January 7, 2007.		

HOW YOU DOIN'?   Answers—p. 215

4. What two items determine the amount deducted from an employee's wages for federal income taxes?

5. What amount of income tax is withheld from the salary of an employee who is single with three withholding allowances and earnings of $645 in a week? (*Hint:* Use the wage bracket withholding table from Exhibit 9.4.)

6. Which of the following steps are executed when a company draws one check for total payroll and deposits it in a special payroll bank account? (*a*) Write a check to the payroll bank account for the total payroll and record it with a debit to Accrued Payroll Payable and a credit to Cash. (*b*) Deposit a check (or transfer funds) for the total payroll in the payroll bank account. (*c*) Issue individual payroll checks drawn on the payroll bank account. (*d*) All of the above.

Employee Earnings Records

LO6 Prepare an earnings record for each employee.

Law requires employers to maintain **employee earnings records.** These records summarize each employee's earnings, deductions, net pay, and total earnings during each calendar year. Information in these records is used to prepare quarterly and annual tax reports (discussed in the next chapter). Exhibit 9.10 provides an employee earnings record for Robert Austin for the month ended March 31, 2007. For this exhibit we assume Robert Austin works 40 hours in each of the 8 weeks from January 1, 2007, through February 24, 2007, and then works 40 hours in each of the four weeks in March. This means his gross pay is $400 each week. The next pay period ends on Sunday, April 1, 2007.

Exhibit 9.10

Employee Earnings Report

PHOENIX SALES AND SERVICE
Employee Earnings Report
For Month Ended March 31, 2007

EMPLOYEE ID No.	EMPLOYEE NAME	EMPLOYEE SS No.
AR101	Austin, Robert	333-22-9999

		EMPLOYEE DEDUCTIONS				
Date	Gross Pay	Federal Income Tax	State Income Tax	FICA-Social Security	FICA-Medicare	Net Pay
Beg. balance	3,200.00	296.00	23.68	198.40	46.40	2,635.52
3/4/2007	400.00	37.00	2.96	24.80	5.80	329.44
3/11/2007	400.00	37.00	2.96	24.80	5.80	329.44
3/18/2007	400.00	37.00	2.96	24.80	5.80	329.44
3/25/2007	400.00	37.00	2.96	24.80	5.80	329.44
Total: 3/4/07 through 3/25/07	1,600.00	148.00	11.84	99.20	23.20	1,317.76
Year-to-date total for Robert Austin	4,800.00	444.00	35.52	297.60	69.60	3,953.28

The amount in the year-to-date gross pay column in each individual employee earnings report is entered into the "Beginning Cumulative Gross Earnings" column of the payroll register in Exhibit 9.8 at the beginning of each pay period. This alerts the accountant of those employees with year-to-date income higher than the maximum amounts for Social Security or unemployment taxes. For example, $4,800 would be entered into the payroll register for the week ending April 1, 2007, for Robert Austin.

Control Over Payroll

Payroll activities present important risks for the business owner. First, there are often fines and penalties for not following the many laws impacting payroll. For example, a 100% penalty can be levied, with interest, on any unpaid employee withholding taxes. The government can even close a company, take its assets, and pursue legal actions against those involved. Second, the employer must maintain confidential and sensitive data on employees; for example, their Social Security numbers. Employees can become victims of identity theft if this information falls into the wrong hands. Third, the employer must be careful not to pay employees for hours not worked or to pay fictitious employees. For example, poor controls led the United States Army to pay nearly $10 million to deserters, fictitious soldiers, and other unauthorized entities.

 Explain how an employer can control payroll.

Payroll Fraud

Employee fraud is costly. The Association of Certified Fraud Examiners (www.acfe.com) estimates that employee fraud costs small companies more than $190,000 per incident. Many employee frauds involve payroll schemes. Joseph Wells discusses three common types of payroll fraud (*Occupational Fraud and Abuse,* Austin, TX (Obsidian Publishing Co., Inc., 1997) and "Keep Ghosts Off the Payroll," 2002 article at www.acfe.com.):

Ghost Employees   A ghost employee is a reference to a name of an individual included on the payroll register who is not an employee of the company. The ghost might be a former employee or a fictitious employee created by a payroll clerk. Wells estimates that the average loss to an employer victimized by a ghost employee payroll fraud is $275,000.

Overstated Hours Worked and Salary Rates   Employees might overstate the number of hours they worked on their time cards. Dishonest payroll clerks might inflate their own or other employees' pay rates. Wells estimates that the average loss to an employer victimized by a false hours or pay rate fraud is $30,000.

Overstated Salespersons' Commissions   Salespeople might overstate the amount of sales they made. Wells estimates that the average loss to an employer victimized by a commission payroll fraud is $200,000.

Payroll Control

Several procedures can help the employer reduce payroll risks. First, the employer must be careful in employee hiring and assign only the most-trusted employees to payroll activities. Second, the employer should review and verify all time sheets. Third, all employee payroll data should be kept in locked files. Only the payroll clerk and the employer should have access to these files. Fourth, any changes to employees' withholdings or voluntary deductions must be supported by authorization forms signed by the employee. The employer must keep these forms in locked files.

The employer also must separate certain payroll duties. The signer of the payroll checks should verify the data for each employee in the payroll register. Payroll checks should not be distributed by the payroll clerk who prepared them. The payroll clerk should not reconcile the bank account.

HOW YOU DOIN'?   Answer—p. 215

7. What type of payroll fraud has the highest average dollar loss?

SALES-PER-EMPLOYEE

LO8 Compute the sales-per-employee ratio and use it to analyze operating efficiency.

Employee productivity is important to a business's success. One measure of employee productivity is the **sales-per-employee** *ratio,* computed as:

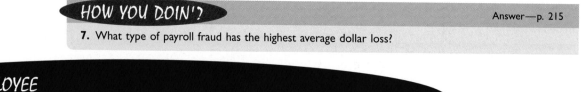

$$\text{Sales-per-employee ratio} = \frac{\text{Net sales}}{\text{Average number of employees}}$$

Both numbers in this ratio are obtained from a company's financial reports. The net sales figure is reported on the income statement, and the number of employees at year-end is typically disclosed in the footnotes to the financial statements. The average number of employees is computed as the number of employees at the prior year-end, plus the number of employees at the current year-end, all divided by two.

A high sales-per-employee ratio implies the company is operating more efficiently, as compared to companies with lower ratios. It is particularly useful when analyzing the productivity of businesses where employees deal directly with customers—for example, banks and retailers.

To illustrate, consider Exhibit 9.11, which reports data for **Abercrombie and Fitch**, a retail clothing store.

Exhibit 9.11

Abercrombie and Fitch Sales and Employee Data

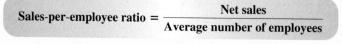

($ thousands)	2005	2004	2003
Net sales	$2,784,711	$2,021,253	$1,707,810
Average number of employees	69,100	48,500	30,200

Based on these data, Abercrombie and Fitch's sales per employee are $47,359 in 2005 and $51,366 in 2004. While the company's sales increased in 2005, the sales-per-employee ratio suggests Abercrombie and Fitch's efficiency of operations has declined. Of course, the sales-per-employee ratio is but one piece of our analysis of the company.

Demonstration Problem

A1 Lawns reports the information below related to its employees for the week ending June 7, 2008. A1 pays its employees one and one-half times their normal hourly wage for all hours worked beyond 40 hours per week. Each of A1 Lawns' employees is single.

Employee	Hours Worked	Hourly Wage	Withholding Allowances
S. House	40	$14.25	2
E. James	46	$15.00	2
R. Johnson	44	$12.13	1

Required

1. Compute each employee's gross pay for the week.
2. Compute the amounts A1 Lawns must withhold from its employees' pay for the week ending June 7, 2008, for
   a. Federal income taxes (use wage bracket withholding tables in Exhibit 9.4).
   b. State income taxes (assume A1 Lawns withholds 8% of the amount of federal income taxes withheld).
   c. Social Security taxes.
   d. Medicare taxes.
3. Compute net pay for the week for each employee.
4. Prepare the journal entry to record the payroll for the week.
5. Prepare the journal entry to pay the payroll assuming two separate scenarios:
   a. A1 Lawns does not use a special payroll bank account, and
   b. A1 Lawns uses a special payroll bank account.

Planning the Solution

- For 1, multiply hours worked (up to 40) by the employee's hourly wage, and add to that the product of any hours worked over 40 multiplied by one and one-half times the employee's hourly wage.
- For 2, use wage bracket withholding tables and tax rules to compute each employee's deductions.
- For part 3, for each employee, subtract your answer in part 2 from your answer in part 1.
- For 4 and 5 determine the accounts affected and then record the entries.

Solution to Demonstration Problem

1. Gross pay for each employee is computed as:

S. House	40 × $14.25	= $570.00
E. James	(40 × $15.00) + (6 × $22.50)	= $735.00
R. Johnson	(40 × $12.13) + (4 × $18.20)	= $558.00

2. Employee deductions:
   a. Withholdings

	Federal Income Tax[a]	State Income Tax[b]	Social Security[c]	Medicare[d]	Total
S. House	$53.00	$4.24	$35.34	$ 8.27	$100.85
E. James	77.00	6.16	45.57	10.66	139.39
R. Johnson	59.00	4.72	34.60	8.09	106.41

[a] From federal wage bracket withholding tables in Exhibit 9.4.

[b] Dollar amount withheld for federal income tax × 8%.

[c] Gross pay × 6.2%.

[d] Gross pay × 1.45%.

3. Net pay = Gross pay minus total deductions; computations follow:

S. House	$570.00 − $100.85	= $469.15
E. James	$735.00 − $139.39	= $595.61
R. Johnson	$558.00 − $106.41	= $451.59

4.

June	7	Wage Expense	1 8 6 3 00		
		FICA—Social Security Taxes Payable (6.2%)			1 1 5 51
		FICA—Medicare Taxes Payable (1.45%)			2 7 02
		Employee Federal Income Taxes Payable			1 8 9 00
		Employee State Income Taxes Payable			1 5 12
		Accrued Wages Payable			1 5 1 6 35
		To record payroll for week ending June 7.			

5. a. Payroll paid from general bank account.

June	7	Accrued Wages Payable	1 5 1 6 35		
		Cash—S. House			4 6 9 15
		Cash—E. James			5 9 5 61
		Cash—R. Johnson			4 5 1 59
		To pay payroll for pay period ending June 7, 2008.			

b. Payroll paid from special payroll bank account.

June	7	Cash—Payroll Bank Account	1 5 1 6 35		
		Cash			1 5 1 6 35
		To transfer cash to the payroll bank account.			
June	7	Accrued Wages Payable	1 5 1 6 35		
		Cash—Payroll Bank Account.			1 5 1 6 35
		To pay payroll for pay period ending June 7, 2008.			

Summary

LO1 **Describe the laws that affect employee payroll.** Law requires employers to withhold amounts from employee pay for Social Security taxes, Medicare taxes, and for federal and state income taxes.

LO2 **Compute employee gross pay.** Gross pay is the amount of compensation the employee earned during the period before deductions for items like taxes. It is commonly computed as the employee's hourly wage rate multiplied by the number of hours the employee worked during the pay period.

LO3 **Compute employee deductions for taxes and net pay.** Employees pay 6.2% of their gross pay (up to $94,200) for Social Security taxes and 1.45% of their income for Medicare taxes. Based on the number of withholding allowances the employee choses, the employer computes federal and state income tax withholdings from tax tables.

LO4 **Record employee payroll information in a payroll register.** A payroll register is often used to keep a record of pay period dates, hours worked, gross pay, deductions, and net pay of each employee for each pay period. The payroll register provides information the accountant can use to make journal entries and prepare tax documents.

LO5 **Journalize payroll transactions in a general journal.** The accountant debits Wage Expense for the total gross pay and credits tax liability accounts for amounts owed, and Accrued Wages Payable for employees' net pay. Paying the payroll results in a debit to Accrued Wages Payable and a credit to Cash.

LO6 **Prepare an earnings record for each employee.** Employee earnings records summarize each employee's earnings, deductions, net pay, and total earnings during each calendar year. This information is used in computing taxes and in preparing tax documents required by law.

LO7 **Explain how an employer can control payroll.** The employer can control payroll by hiring trustworthy employees, maintaining confidential records in locked files, and by separating important payroll duties.

LO8 **Compute the sales-per-employee ratio and use it to analyze operating efficiency.** The sales-per-employee ratio is computed as annual net sales divided by the average number of employees. A higher ratio indicates a company is operating more efficiently.

1. $(0.062 \times \$3,000) + (0.0145 \times \$3,000) = \underline{\$229.50}$

2. (a) FICA taxes are incurred by both employee and employer. (b) Withheld income taxes are incurred by the employee.

3. $(40 \times \$16) + (5 \times \$24) = \$760.$

4. An employee's gross earnings and number of withholding allowances determine the deduction for federal income taxes.

5. $53

6. (d)

7. The ghost employee scheme, with an average loss of $275,000.

Key Terms

mhhe.com/wildCA

Key Terms are available at the book's Website for learning and testing in an online Flashcard Format.

Circular E (p. 204) IRS federal income tax withholding tables.

Employee (p. 202) Someone whose work is under the direction of an employer.

Employee benefits (p. 207) Additional compensation paid to or on behalf of employees, such as premiums for medical, dental, life, and disability insurance, and contributions to pension plans.

Employee earnings records (p. 211) Record of an employee's net pay, gross pay, deductions, and year-to-date payroll information.

Employee's Withholding Allowance Certificate (Form W-4) (p. 202) A form which shows an employee's withholding allowances.

Federal Insurance Contributions Act (FICA) Taxes (p. 203) Taxes assessed on both employers and employees; for Social Security and Medicare programs.

Gross pay (p. 202) Total compensation earned by an employee.

Independent contractor (p. 202) Someone who does a job for an employer, but decides how to do the work.

Individual employee earnings records (p. 211) Records that summarize each employee's earnings, deductions, and net pay during each calendar year.

Net pay (p. 207) Gross pay less all deductions; also called *take-home pay*.

Payroll bank account (p. 210) Bank account used solely for paying employees; each pay period an amount equal to the total employees' net pay is deposited in it and the payroll checks are drawn on it.

Payroll deductions (p. 204) Amounts withheld from an employee's gross pay; also called *withholdings*.

Payroll register (p. 208) Record for a pay period that shows the pay period dates, regular and overtime hours worked, gross pay, net pay, and deductions.

Sales-per-employee ratio (p. 212) Net sales divided by the average number of employees; it is a measure of employee productivity.

Self-employment tax (p. 203) Social Security and Medicare taxes for persons who operate their own businesses. Currently, the self-employment tax rates are 12.4% on the first $94,200 of income for Social Security and 2.9% on all income for Medicare.

Wage bracket withholding table (p. 204) Table of the amounts of income tax withheld from employees' wages.

Withholding allowance (p. 202) This determines the amount of federal income taxes to withhold from an employee's pay.

Multiple Choice Quiz   Answers on p. 225   mhhe.com/wildCA

Multiple Choice Quizzes A and B are available at the book's Website.

1. An employee earned $50,000 during the year. FICA tax for social security is 6.2% and FICA tax for Medicare is 1.45%. The employee's share of FICA taxes is
   a. Zero, since the employee's pay exceeds the FICA limit.
   b. Zero, since FICA is not an employee tax.
   c. $3,100
   d. $725
   e. $3,825

2. Which of the following taxes is not withheld from employee's pay?
   a. Social security taxes.
   b. Unemployment taxes.
   c. Federal income taxes.
   d. State income taxes.
   e. Medicare taxes.

3. An employee worked 48 hours in the last weekly pay period. She is paid a normal wage of $12 per hour and is paid one and one-half times her normal hourly wage for all hours worked beyond 40 hours. For this pay period her *gross pay* is
   a. $480
   b. $576
   c. $624
   d. $720
   e. $864

4. A single employee claiming 4 withholding allowances earns $710 per week. If she is paid weekly, what amount will be withheld from her pay for federal income tax withholdings? (Use the withholding table in Exhibit 9.4).
   a. $64
   b. $102
   c. $54
   d. $53
   e. $56

5. A company uses a special bank account to pay its payroll. If total gross pay for a pay period was $3,500 and total net pay for the same period was $2,750, the journal entry to pay the payroll will include a

   a. credit to Cash for $3,500.

   b. credit to Cash—Payroll Bank Account for $3,500.

   c. debit to Cash—Payroll Bank Account for $2,750 and a credit to Cash for $2,750.

   d. credit to Cash—Payroll Bank Account for $2,750.

   e. debit to Wage Expense for $2,750 and a credit to Cash for $2,750.

Discussion Questions

1. What is the combined amount (in percent) of the employee and employer Social Security tax rate?

2. What is the current maximum annual level of salary used to compute an employee's Social Security taxes?

3. What is the current Medicare tax rate? This rate is applied to what maximum level of salary and wages?

4. What determines the amount deducted from an employee's wages for federal income taxes?

5. Which payroll taxes are the employee's responsibility and which are the employer's responsibility?

6. What are examples of items employees might voluntarily choose to have deducted from their pay?

7. What is a wage bracket withholding table?

8. What amount of income tax is withheld from the salary of an employee who is single with two withholding allowances and earns $725 per week? What if the employee earned $625 and has no withholding allowances? (Use Exhibit 9.4)

9. What are employee earnings records? Why do employers maintain employee earnings records?

10. What risks do payroll activities pose for employers?

11. Give three examples of common payroll fraud schemes that are costly to employers.

12. What procedures can an employer use to control payroll fraud?

QUICK STUDY

QS 9-1
Computing gross pay

(LO2)

Compute *gross pay* for each of the following employees. An overtime rate of one and one-half times the normal hourly wage is paid for each hour worked beyond 40 hours.

	Hourly Rate	No. of Hours Worked
Mike Mura	$11	42
Pedro Chavez	$14	50

QS 9-2
Computing tax withholdings

(LO3)

Nouri Hitzu's cumulative earnings before this pay period were $45,000. Nouri's gross pay for this weekly pay period was $845. What amounts will be withheld from Nouri's pay for this period for federal income taxes? Nouri is married and claims a total of two withholding allowances. Nouri is paid weekly. (Use the tax withholding table in Exhibit 9.5).

QS 9-3
Computing FICA taxes

(LO3)

Refer to QS 9-2. What amount must Nouri's employer withhold from Nouri's pay for Social Security (6.2%) taxes and Medicare (1.45%) taxes?

QS 9-4
Computing FICA taxes

(LO3)

An employee earned $3,450 for the current period. Calculate the total and individual amounts to be withheld for Social Security (6.2%), Medicare (1.45%), and federal income tax (15%) assuming the entire employee's pay is subject to FICA taxes.

QS 9-5
Computing withholdings

(LO3)

Dextra Computing's payroll register reports that Ramesh Jain's cumulative earnings before this pay period were $98,000. Ramesh earned $1,240 this pay period. Ramesh is single and claims one withholding allowance. How much should be withheld from Ramesh's pay for federal income tax withholdings, Social Security taxes, and Medicare taxes?

QS 9-6
Record employer payroll taxes

(LO2) (LO3) (LO5)

Major Co. has five employees, each of whom earns $2,500 per month and has been employed since January 1. FICA Social Security taxes are 6.2% of the first $94,200 paid to each employee, and FICA Medicare taxes are 1.45% of gross pay. Federal income tax withholding is 15% of gross pay. State income tax withholding is 8% of the dollar amount withheld for federal income tax purposes. Prepare the March 31 journal entry to record the March wage expense and related liabilities.

Refer to QS 9-6. Prepare the journal entries to pay the March 31 payroll, assuming Major Co. uses a special payroll bank account.

QS 9-7

Journalize payroll transactions

(LO5)

A self-employed worker earned $47,000 during the year. The FICA tax for Social Security is 6.2% and the FICA tax for Medicare is 1.45%. How much should this worker pay for FICA taxes?

QS 9-8

Computing FICA taxes

(LO3)

BMX Co. has one employee, Keesha Parks, and the company is subject to the following taxes:

EXERCISES

Exercise 9-1

Computing payroll taxes and income tax withholdings

(LO2)

Tax	Rate	Applied To
FICA—Social Security	6.20%	First $94,200
FICA—Medicare	1.45	All gross pay

Compute BMX's amounts for FICA taxes and federal income tax withholdings as applied to Keesha's gross earnings for September under each of three separate situations (*a*), (*b*), and (*c*). (Use the withholding tables in Exhibit 9.6 and Exhibit 9.7.).

	Gross Pay through August	Gross Pay for September	Marital Status	Withholding Allowances
a.	$ 6,800	$ 900	M	2
b.	19,200	2,200	S	1
c.	92,200	5,000	M	4

Using the data in situation *b* of Exercise 9-1, prepare the employer's September 30 journal entries to record (1) salary expense and its related payroll liabilities for this employee and (2) payment of the payroll. BMX does not use a special payroll bank account.

Exercise 9-2

Payroll-related journal entries

(LO5)

Use withholding tables from Exhibits 9.4 and 9.5 to compute the amount of federal tax withheld from the weekly pay of the following employees:

Exercise 9-3

Computing federal tax withholdings

(LO3)

Name	Gross Pay	Withholding Allowances	Marital Status
Keisha	$520	1	Single
James	600	3	Single
Tyrell	476	4	Married
Emily	817	2	Married

The payroll records of One Click Software show the following information about Keisha LeShon, an employee, for the weekly pay period ending September 30, 2008. LeShon is single and claims one allowance. Compute her Social Security tax (6.2%), Medicare tax (1.45%), federal income tax withholding, state income tax (0.5%), and net pay for the current pay period. The state income tax is 0.5 percent on the first $9,000 earned. (Use the wage bracket withholding table in Exhibit 9.4 for the amount of federal income tax to withhold.)

Exercise 9-4

Net pay and tax computations

(LO3)

Total (gross) earnings for current pay period	$ 725
Cumulative earnings of previous pay periods	9,600

Check Net pay, $580.54

Lucinda Florita, an unmarried employee, works 48 hours in the week ended January 12. Her pay rate is $14 per hour, and her wages are subject to no deductions other than FICA—Social Security, FICA—Medicare, and federal income taxes. She claims two withholding allowances. Compute her regular pay, overtime pay (overtime premium is 50% of the regular rate for hours in excess of 40 per week), and gross pay. Then compute her FICA tax deduction (use 6.2% for the Social Security portion and 1.45%

Exercise 9-5

Gross and net pay computation

(LO2) (LO3)

Check Net Pay, $597.30

for the Medicare portion), income tax deduction (use the wage bracket withholding table in Exhibit 9.4), total deductions, and net pay.

Exercise 9-6
Computing net pay

(LO3)

Phildell Phoenix is paid monthly. For the month of January of the current year, he earned gross pay of $8,288. FICA tax for Social Security is 6.2% and the FICA tax for Medicare is 1.45%. The amount of federal income tax withheld from his earnings was $1,375.17. Phildell contributes $125 of his monthly pay to a retirement plan and has $25 of union dues deducted from his monthly pay. Compute Phildell's net pay for the month.

Exercise 9-7
Payroll terms

Match each of the following terms A through G with the appropriate definitions 1 through 7.

A. FICA taxes
B. Payroll register
C. Withholding allowance
D. Gross pay
E. Wage bracket withholding table
F. Net pay
G. Payroll bank account

_____ **1.** A record for a pay period that shows the pay period dates, regular and overtime hours worked, gross pay, net pay, and deductions.

_____ **2.** A special bank account used solely for paying employees; each pay period an amount equal to the total employees' net pay is deposited and the employees' payroll checks are drawn on that account.

_____ **3.** Total compensation earned by an employee.

_____ **4.** Gross pay less all deductions.

_____ **5.** A number that is used to reduce the amount of federal income tax withheld from an employee's pay.

_____ **6.** A table of amounts of income tax to be withheld from employees' wages.

_____ **7.** Taxes assessed on both employer and employees under the Federal Insurance Contributions Act. These taxes fund Social Security and Medicare.

PROBLEM SET A

Problem 9-1A
Payroll expenses, withholdings, and taxes

(LO2) (LO3)

Paloma Co. pays its employees each week. Its employees' gross pay is subject to these taxes:

Tax	Rate	Applied To
FICA—Social Security	6.20%	First $94,200
FICA—Medicare	1.45	All gross pay

The company is preparing its payroll calculations for the week ended August 25. Payroll records show the following information for the company's four employees.

Name	Gross Pay through 8/18	Current Week Gross Pay	Current Week Income Tax Withholding
Dahlia	$93,400	$2,800	$284
Trey	31,700	1,000	145
Kiesha	6,850	550	39
Chee	1,250	500	30

In addition to gross pay, each employee must pay one-half of the $34 per employee weekly health insurance premium. Dahlia contributes 5% of her weekly gross pay to a retirement plan. Trey and Chee each contribute $25 per week to the local United Way.

Required

Compute the following for the week ended August 25 (round amounts to the nearest cent):

1. Each employee's FICA withholdings for Social Security.

2. Each employee's FICA withholdings for Medicare.

3. Each employee's health insurance premium deduction.

4. Each employee's other voluntary deductions.

5. Each employee's net (take-home) pay.

Check (5) Total net pay, $3,846.97

On January 8, the end of the first weekly pay period of the year, Regis Company's payroll register showed that its employees earned $22,760 of office salaries and $65,840 of sales salaries. Withholdings from the employees' salaries include FICA Social Security taxes at the rate of 6.2%, FICA Medicare taxes at the rate of 1.45%, $12,860 of federal income taxes, $1,340 of medical insurance deductions, and $840 of union dues.

Problem 9–2A
Entries for payroll transactions
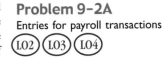

Required

1. Calculate FICA Social Security taxes payable and FICA Medicare taxes payable. Prepare the journal entry to record Regis Company's January 8 employee payroll expenses and liabilities.

2. Prepare the journal entry to pay the January 8 payroll. Regis uses a special payroll bank account.

Check (1) Cr. Accrued Payroll
Payable, $66,782.10

The payroll records of Swift Company provided the following data for the weekly pay period ended December 7:

Problem 9–3A
Payroll entries, deductions, and net pay
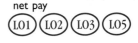

Employee	Earnings to End of Previous Week	Gross Pay	Marital Status	No. of Allowances	Medical Insurance Deduction	Union Dues	United Way
Ronald Arthur ..	$54,000	$1,200	Married	3	$125	$15	$15
John Baines	40,500	900	Single	2	135	15	30
Ted Carter	45,000	1,000	Married	2	150	–0–	20

The FICA Social Security tax rate is 6.2% and the FICA Medicare tax rate is 1.45% on all of this week's wages paid to each employee. The state income tax equals 8 percent of the amount withheld for federal income tax purposes. (Use the withholding tables in Exhibits 9.4 and 9.5.)

Required

1. Prepare a payroll register similar to that in Exhibit 9.8 for Swift Company for the pay period ending December 7. Your payroll register should have columns for employee name, gross pay, federal income tax withheld, state income tax withheld, Social Security tax, Medicare tax, and deductions for medical insurance, union dues, and United Way contributions, and net pay.

2. Prepare the journal entry to record the December 7 payroll.

3. Prepare the journal entry to pay the December 7 payroll. Swift Company does not use a special payroll bank account.

Mackenzie Price operates Downtown Salon and Spa. Information on her three employees for the payroll period (week) ending June 1, 2007, is provided below. Each employee receives one and one-half times the normal hourly pay rate for any hour worked beyond 40 in a week. The FICA Social Security tax rate is 6.2% on the first $94,200 of each employee's gross pay and the FICA Medicare tax rate is 1.45% on all of this week's wages paid to each employee. Federal income tax withholdings are computed from withholding tables and state income tax withholdings are assumed to be 8% of the amount withheld for federal income tax. (Use the withholding tables in Exhibits 9.4 and 9.5.)

Problem 9–4A
Payroll deductions, net pay, payroll register

Employee	Earnings to End of Previous Week	Hours Worked	Regular Hourly Rate	Marital Status	No. of Allowances
Emily Jacobs	$20,800	46	$20.00	S	1
Shu Ming	14,560	40	14.00	M	5
Carter Johns	16,120	48	15.50	M	2

Required

1. Enter each employee's name, year-to-date earnings before this pay period, marital status, regular hourly rate, hours worked, and number of withholding allowances in a payroll register. Hours worked beyond 40 are considered overtime hours.

2. Compute the regular, overtime, and total gross pay for each employee for this pay period. Enter these amounts in the payroll register.

3. Compute the amounts of FICA taxes to be withheld from each employee's pay and enter these amounts in the payroll register.

4. Determine the amount of federal income tax to withhold from each employee's gross pay. Use the withholding tables in Exhibits 9.4 and 9.5. Enter these amounts in the payroll register.

5. Determine the amount of state income tax to withhold from each employee's gross pay. Enter these amounts in the payroll register.

6. Compute each employee's net pay and enter it into the payroll register.

7. Total the payroll register.

Problem 9–5A

Payroll deductions, employee earnings records

Refer to Problem 9-4A. Before the pay period ending June 1, 2007, the individual employee earnings record for Emily Jacobs reports the following:

DOWNTOWN SALON AND SPA
Employee Earnings Report
For Month Ended May 25, 2007

Employee
Name   Jacobs, Emily
SS No.   344-88-9999

Reference	Date	Gross Pay	Federal Income Tax	State Income Tax	FICA— Social Security	FICA— Medicare	Net Pay
Beg. Balance		20 800 00	2 834 00	2 26 72	1 289 60	3 01 60	16 148 08
	6/01/2007						
	6/08/2007						
	6/15/2007						
	6/22/2007						
	6/29/2007						
Total of 6/01/2007 through 6/29/2007							
Year-to-date total for Emily Jacobs							

Social Security taxes of 6.2% and Medicare taxes of 1.45% are deducted from each employee's gross pay. Tax withholding tables are used to compute amounts to withhold for federal income taxes. State income tax withheld equals 8% of the dollar amount of federal income taxes withheld.

Required

1. Refer to Problem 9-4A and enter the payroll information for the pay period ending June 1, 2007, in an individual employee earnings record for Emily Jacobs.

2. Assume that Emily Jacobs works exactly 40 hours in each of the payroll periods ending June 8, June 15, June 22, and June 29 of 2007. Compute the amounts to withhold from Emily's weekly net pay

for Social Security taxes, Medicare taxes, federal income tax withholdings, and state income tax withholdings.

3. Enter the amounts computed in requirement 2 in Emily Jacobs's individual employee earnings record.

4. Compute the total amounts of gross pay, federal income tax withholdings, state income tax withholdings, Social Security taxes, Medicare taxes, and net pay for Emily Jacobs for the month of June 1 through June 29, 2007. Enter these amounts in Emily Jacobs's individual employee earnings record.

5. Update the year-to-date totals of gross pay, federal income tax withholdings, state income tax withholdings, Social Security taxes, Medicare taxes, and net pay on Emily Jacobs's individual employee earnings record through June 29, 2007.

Fishing Guides Co. pays its employees each week. Employees' gross pay is subject to these taxes.

Tax	Rate	Applied To
FICA—Social Security	6.20%	First $94,200
FICA—Medicare	1.45%	All gross pay

PROBLEM SET B

Problem 9-1B
Payroll expenses, withholdings, and taxes
(LO2) (LO3)

The company is preparing its payroll calculations for the week ended September 30. Payroll records show the following information for the company's four employees.

Name	Gross Pay through 9/23	Current Week Gross Pay	Current Week Income Tax Withholding
Ahmed	$92,600	$2,700	$250
Carlos	58,700	1,245	190
Jun	5,350	525	51
Marie	24,300	700	64

In addition to gross pay, each employee must pay one-half of the $40 per employee weekly health insurance premium. Ahmed contributes 5% of his weekly gross pay to a retirement plan. Carlos contributes $15 per week to charity. Jun pays $5 per week in union dues.

Required

Compute the following for the week ended September 30 (round amounts to the nearest cent):

1. Each employee's FICA withholdings for Social Security.

2. Each employee's FICA withholdings for Medicare.

3. Each employee's health insurance premium deduction.

4. Each employee's other voluntary deductions.

5. Each employee's net (take-home) pay.

Check (5) Total net pay $4,052.70

Tavella Company's first weekly pay period of the year ends on January 8. On that date, the column totals in Tavella's payroll register indicate its sales employees earned $34,745, its office employees earned $21,225, and its delivery employees earned $1,030. The employees are to have withheld from their wages FICA Social Security taxes at the rate of 6.2%, FICA Medicare taxes at the rate of 1.45%, $8,625 of federal income taxes, $1,160 of medical insurance deductions, and $138 of union dues.

Problem 9-2B
Entries for payroll transactions
(LO3) (LO5)

Required

1. Calculate FICA Social Security taxes payable and FICA Medicare taxes payable. Prepare the journal entry to record Tavella Company's January 8 employee payroll expenses and liabilities.

2. Prepare the journal entry to pay the January 8 payroll. Tavella uses a special payroll bank account.

Check (1) Cr. Accrued Payroll Payable, $42,716.50

Problem 9–3B
Payroll entries, deductions, net pay

(LO2) (LO3) (LO5)

The payroll records of JK Landscape Design provided the following data for the weekly pay period ended October 7:

Employee	Earnings to End of Previous Week	Gross Pay	Marital Status	No. of Allowances	Medical Insurance Deduction	Union Dues	United Way
Roland Ames ..	$44,000	$1,100	Single	3	$ 85	$10	$25
Jan Barnes	30,500	780	Married	1	150	–0–	20
Todd Crane	35,000	985	Married	5	150	–0–	30

The FICA Social Security tax rate is 6.2% and the FICA Medicare tax rate is 1.45% on all of this week's wages paid to each employee. Use withholding tables in Exhibits 9.4 and 9.5 to find the amount of federal income tax to withhold and assume state income tax is 8% of the dollar amount of federal income tax withheld.

Required

1. Prepare a payroll register similar to that in Exhibit 9.8 for JK Landscape Design for the pay period ending October 7. Your payroll register should have columns for employee name, gross pay, federal income tax withheld, state income tax withheld, Social Security tax, Medicare tax, and deductions for medical insurance, union dues, and United Way contributions, and net pay.
2. Prepare the journal entry to record the October 7 payroll.
3. Prepare the journal entry to pay the October 7 payroll. JK Landscape Design does not use a special payroll bank account.

Problem 9–4B
Payroll deductions, net pay, payroll register

(LO2) (LO3) (LO4)

Merle Perkins operates A1 Auto Repair. Information on his three employees for the payroll period (week) ending June 1, 2007, is provided below. Each employee receives one and one-half times the normal hourly pay rate for any hour worked beyond 40 in a week. The FICA Social Security tax rate is 6.2% on the first $94,200 of each employee's gross pay and the FICA Medicare tax rate is 1.45% on all of this week's wages paid to each employee. Federal income tax withholdings are computed from withholding tables and state income tax withholdings are assumed to be 8% of the amount withheld for federal income tax. (Use the withholding tables in Exhibits 9.4 and 9.5.)

Employee	Earnings to End of Previous Week	Hours Worked	Regular Hourly Rate	Marital Status	No. of Allowances
Andre Jones	$21,600	42	$21.00	S	2
Xiu Yi	12,480	35	15.00	M	3
Duane Wells	19,320	46	17.50	M	4

Required

1. Enter each employee's name, year-to-date earnings before this pay period, marital status, regular hourly rate, hours worked, and number of withholding allowances in a payroll register. Hours worked beyond 40 are considered overtime hours.
2. Compute the regular, overtime, and total gross pay for each employee for this pay period. Enter these amounts in the payroll register.
3. Compute the amounts of FICA taxes to be withheld from each employee's pay and enter these amounts in the payroll register.
4. Determine the amount of federal income tax to withhold from each employee's gross pay. Use the withholding tables in Exhibits 9.4 and 9.5. Enter these amounts in the payroll register.
5. Determine the amount of state income tax to withhold from each employee's gross pay. Enter these amounts in the payroll register.
6. Compute each employee's net pay and enter it into the payroll register.
7. Total the payroll register.

Refer to Problem 9-4B. Before the pay period ending June 1, 2007, the individual employee earnings record for Andre Jones reports the following:

A1 AUTO REPAIR								
Employee Earnings Report								
For Month Ended May 25, 2007								

Employee
Name   Jones, Andre
SS No.   333-55-9999

			Employee Deductions					
Reference	**Date**	**Gross Pay**	**Federal Income Tax**	**State Income Tax**	**FICA—Social Security**	**FICA—Medicare**	**Net Pay**	
Beg. Balance		21 600 00	2 943 00	235 44	1 339 20	313 20	16 769 16	
	6/01/2007							
	6/08/2007							
	6/15/2007							
	6/22/2007							
	6/29/2007							
Total of 6/01/2007								
through 6/29/2007								
Year-to-date total								
for Andre Jones								

Social Security taxes of 6.2% and Medicare taxes of 1.45% are deducted from each employee's gross pay. Tax withholding tables are used to compute amounts to withhold for federal income taxes. State income tax withheld equals 8% of the dollar amount of federal income taxes withheld.

Required

1. Refer to Problem 9–4B and enter the payroll information for the pay period ending June 1, 2007, in an individual employee earnings record for Andre Jones.

2. Assume that Andre Jones works exactly 40 hours in each of the payroll periods ending June 8, June 15, June 22, and June 29 of 2007. Compute the amounts to withhold from Andre's weekly net pay for Social Security taxes, Medicare taxes, federal income tax withholdings, and state income tax withholdings.

3. Enter the amounts computed in requirement 2 in Andre Jones's individual employee earnings record.

4. Compute the total amounts of gross pay, federal income tax withholdings, state income tax withholdings, Social Security taxes, Medicare taxes, and net pay for Andre Jones for the month of June 1 through June 29, 2007. Enter these amounts in Andre Jones's individual employee earnings record.

5. Update the year-to-date totals of gross pay, federal income tax withholdings, state income tax withholdings, Social Security taxes, Medicare taxes, and net pay on Andre Jones's individual employee earnings record through June 29, 2007.

(This serial problem began in Chapter 1 and continues through most of the book. If previous chapter segments were not completed, the serial problem can begin at this point. It is helpful, but not necessary, for you to use the Working Papers that accompany the book.)

SERIAL PROBLEM

Success Systems

SP 9   Michelle Jones earned $150 per day for the 8 days in the most recent pay period ending on February 26.

Required

1. Assume that Michelle Jones is an unmarried employee. Her wages are subject to no deductions other than FICA Social Security taxes, FICA Medicare taxes, and federal income taxes. Her federal income taxes for this pay period total $189. Compute her gross pay and net pay for the eight days' work paid on February 26.

2. Record the journal entry to reflect the payroll payment to Michelle Jones as computed in part 1. Success Systems does not use a payroll bank account.

BEYOND THE NUMBERS

REPORTING IN ACTION
(L05)

BEST BUY

BTN 9-1   Refer to the financial statements of Best Buy in Appendix A to answer the following:

Required

1. What payroll-related liability does Best Buy report at February 26, 2005?
2. In what income statement accounts does Best Buy report its payroll and benefit costs?

Fast Forward

3. Access Best Buy's financial statements for fiscal years ending after February 26, 2005, at its Website (www.BestBuy.com) or the SEC's EDGAR database (www.SEC.gov). What payroll-related liability does Best Buy report for years ending after February 26, 2005?

COMPARATIVE ANALYSIS
(L08)

BEST BUY

circuit city

BTN 9-2   Key comparative figures for both Best Buy and Circuit City follow.

	Best Buy			Circuit City		
	2005	**2004**	**2003**	**2005**	**2004**	**2003**
Net sales ($ millions)	$ 27,433	$ 24,548	$20,943	$10,472	$ 9,857	$10,055
Number of employees	109,000	100,000	98,000	45,946	43,211	38,849

Required

1. Compute sales-per-employee for 2005 and 2004 for each company.
2. Comment on each company's operating efficiency based on the sales-per-employee ratio. Assume an industry average of $200,000 for each year.

ETHICS CHALLENGE
(L01)

BTN 9-3   You take a summer job working for a family friend as a Web page designer for a small information technology service. On your first payday, the owner slaps you on the back, gives you full payment in cash, winks, and adds: "No need to pay those high taxes, eh."

Required

What action, if any, do you take? Explain.

WORKPLACE COMMUNICATION
(L07)

BTN 9-4   An owner of a growing business hires you as a consultant. He is concerned about rising payroll costs, and also concerned about payroll fraud. Currently, his payroll clerk collects time sheets and computes gross pay and deductions. The payroll clerk also adds new employees to the payroll system and makes all changes to employees' withholdings and voluntary deductions. Once the payroll is processed, the payroll clerk signs and distributes the payroll checks.

Required

Prepare a set of written recommendations to the business owner to strengthen the owner's control over payroll procedures. Your answer should be in a memorandum format.

BTN 9–5 Access the February 27, 2006, filing of the December 31, 2005, annual 10-K report of McDonald's Corporation (Ticker: MCD), which is available from www.sec.gov.

TAKING IT TO THE NET

(L08)

Required

1. Identify the amount of accrued payroll and other liabilities on McDonald's balance sheet as of December 31, 2005.

2. Compute sales-per-employee for McDonald's for 2005. Use sales by company-operated restaurants. Assume McDonald's had the same number of employees in 2004 as it had in 2005.

3. What amount does McDonald's report for payroll and other benefits costs for its company-operated restaurants on its 2005 income statement? Expressed as a percentage of sales, discuss how payroll and benefit costs for company-operated restaurants changed from the year ending 2004 to the year ending 2005.

BTN 9–6 Each team should select an industry for analysis. Each team member selects a firm within that industry and collects net sales and number of employee data for the current year, one year prior, and two years prior, from annual reports. Each team member computes the sales-per-employee for the current year and one year prior. Each team should also collect average sales per employee data for its industry; see www.bizstats.com—Employee Productivity—for industry data. Finally, each team prepares a written analysis of the operating efficiency of its selected firms, based on sales-per-employee.

TEAMWORK IN ACTION

(L08)

BTN 9–7 Review the chapter's opening feature about Youngsong Martin and Wildflower Linens.

ENTREPRENEURS IN BUSINESS

(L07)

Required

Martin stresses that controlling payroll liabilities is a must to succeed in business. What are some procedures Martin can use to reduce the chance that Wildflower Linens is hurt by a payroll fraud scheme?

ANSWERS TO MULTIPLE CHOICE QUIZ

1. e; $50,000 \times (.062 + .0145) = \$3,825$

2. b

3. c; $(40 \times \$12) + (8 \times \$18) = \$624$

4. c

5. d

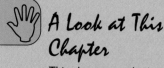

A Look Back

Chapter 9 focused on employee payroll and deductions. We showed how to compute employee tax deductions to comply with laws. We also showed how the employer records and controls its payroll.

A Look at This Chapter

This chapter emphasizes the employer's payroll reporting. We show how the employer computes and pays its payroll taxes and prepares tax documents to comply with laws.

A Look Ahead

Chapter 11 explains the accounting for merchandise sales and accounts receivable. We analyze and record merchandise sales transactions and explain the use of a sales journal.

Chapter

10

Employer Payroll Tax Reporting

LEARNING OBJECTIVES

LO 1 Describe laws that impact employer's payroll obligations.

LO 2 Compute employer's FICA taxes and record them in a general journal.

LO 3 Journalize employer's deposit of federal income taxes and FICA taxes withheld, and prepare a deposit coupon.

LO 4 Prepare Form 941, Employer's Quarterly Federal Tax Return.

LO 5 Prepare Form W-2, Employee's Wage and Tax Statement, and Form W-3, Transmittal of Wage and Tax Statements.

LO 6 Compute employer's state and federal unemployment taxes and record them in a general journal.

LO 7 Prepare unemployment tax returns.

LO 8 Compute and record workers' compensation insurance premiums for employers.

"1-800-GOT-JUNK brings together great people to build a business that we can all be proud of"
—CEO, Brian Scudamore

One Man's Junk

Brian Scudamore was waiting in a McDonald's drive-thru when he realized his future was junk. With his last $700, Brian bought a used pickup truck and began hauling junk—old couches, appliances, household clutter—any nonhazardous material that two people can lift. "With a vision of creating the 'FedEx' of junk removal, I became a fulltime JUNKMAN," explains Brian. "My father was not impressed in the least."

He is now. Brian's vision resulted in him starting **1-800-GOT-JUNK (1800gotjunk.com),** the world's largest junk removal service. The company's approach is simple: Use clean, shiny trucks that serve as mobile billboards and employ professional, courteous drivers who are always on time. Develop a culture that is young, fun, and focused on employee growth, and "build a business that we can be proud of." With revenues of over $66 million in 2005, multiple "Best Company to Work For" awards, and a presence in 47 of North America's 50 top cities, the company has much to be proud of.

Unlike many entrepreneurs who attempt to minimize risk by outsourcing to independent contractors, Scudamore took a different approach. "I hired my first employee, a good friend of mine, a week after I started. I always believed in hiring people versus contract or consultants. I felt that if I wasn't willing to make the investment then I was questioning my own faith in the business."

Brian's investments in his employees include five weeks of vacation per year, full health benefits, flex time, and a generous profit-sharing program that pays out 25% of company profits. While these employer-provided benefits are costly, Brian believes they help drive his company's success. "I've always said a great company is all about people."

Brian's goal is $100 million in revenues by the end of 2006. Not bad for his initial investment of $700.

[Sources: *1-800-GOT-JUNK Website,* January 2007; <u>About.com</u>, December 2006; <u>bcbusinessmagazine.com</u>, December 2004]

Keeping accurate payroll records and reports is essential to a company's success. Many laws impact the employer's payroll obligations. The employer can be assessed large penalties for not complying with these laws. This chapter shows how the employer computes its tax liabilities and prepares necessary tax documents to comply with laws.

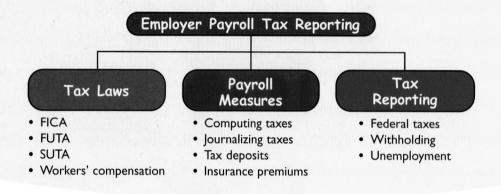

Laws Impacting Employer's Payroll Tax

Employer Identification Number

Each employee of a business has a unique Social Security number. Likewise, each business has its own **employer identification number (EIN).** The business uses its EIN for reporting its income and taxes. The business obtains its EIN by completing **Form SS-4,** available from **www.IRS.gov**. Form SS-4 is an Internal Revenue Service form that asks for general information about the business, including its name, location, main activity, and estimated number of employees.

Employer FICA Tax

LO1 Describe laws that impact employer's payroll obligations.

Under the **Federal Insurance Contributions Act (FICA),** the employer must pay the same amounts as its employees do for Social Security and Medicare taxes. For 2006 the employer pays 6.2% of each employee's annual gross pay, up to a maximum annual gross pay of $94,200, for Social Security taxes. The employer also pays 1.45% of each employee's annual gross pay for Medicare taxes. There is no limit on Medicare taxes. Remember that self-employed persons pay both the employee and employer FICA taxes. This means the total FICA tax rate for self-employed individuals is 15.3%.

Federal and State Unemployment Tax Acts

The federal government works with states to provide a joint federal and state unemployment insurance program. These programs pay unemployment benefits to qualified workers. Each state runs its own program. The employer pays for the cost of this program. No amounts are withheld from employees.

Federal Unemployment Taxes (FUTA) For 2006, employers pay FUTA taxes of as much as 6.2% of the first $7,000 earned by each employee in that year. This amount can be reduced by a credit of up to 5.4% of unemployment taxes paid to a state program. So, the net federal unemployment tax is often only 0.8% of the first $7,000 of each employee's annual gross pay.

Sources of U.S. tax receipts are roughly as follows:
10%	Corporate income tax
50	Personal income tax
35	FICA and FUTA taxes
5	Other taxes

State Unemployment Taxes (SUTA) In most states, the base rate for SUTA taxes is 5.4% of the first $7,000 paid to each employee during the year. For example, an employer with 50 employees who each earns more than $7,000 per year will pay $18,900 (0.054 × 50 × $7,000) of SUTA taxes. This base rate is adjusted for the employer's **merit rating.** The state assigns a merit rating that reflects the company's stability in employing workers. A company with low employee turnover receives a high merit rating and pays less than 5.4%. For example, the company with the same 50 employees from above might get a high merit rating and pay SUTA taxes of only 1%. This company would pay a total of only $3,500 (0.01 × 50 × $7,000) for SUTA taxes. This unemployment tax savings of $15,400 ($18,900 − $3,500) results from having a stable workforce with low employee turnover.

Workers' Compensation Insurance

Most states require employers to provide **workers' compensation insurance** for their employees. Workers' compensation provides benefits for employees who are injured on the job. The employer pays a premium, either to the state or to private insurance companies. The premium depends on the type of work the employees perform. Since construction work is considered more risky than secretarial work, an employer would pay a higher premium on its construction workers than on its secretaries. For example, the employer might pay a premium of $0.15 per each $100 of wages for a secretary, but pay $4 per each $100 of wages for a construction worker.

Employers with a small number of employees pay an estimated premium at the beginning of the year. This estimated premium is based on the company's estimated total wages for the upcoming year. At the end of the year, the actual premium is computed based on that year's total wages. The employer then either receives a refund or pays an additional premium.

HOW YOU DOIN'?
Answers—p. 243

1. What are the limits on an employee's annual pay for computing the employer's *(a)* Social Security tax; *(b)* Medicare tax; *(c)* federal unemployment tax; and *(d)* state unemployment tax?

2. Indicate whether the employer or employee or both incur each of the following: *(a)* FICA taxes; *(b)* FUTA taxes; *(c)* SUTA taxes; and *(d)* withheld income taxes.

3. A company pays its one employee $3,000 per month. The company's FUTA rate is 0.8% on the first $7,000 earned; its SUTA rate is 4.0% on the first $7,000; its Social Security tax rate is 6.2% of the first $94,200; and its Medicare tax rate is 1.45% of all amounts earned. What is the employer's total payroll tax expense for March?

Employer's Payroll Taxes

Computing Employer's FICA Tax

We return to our example of Phoenix Sales and Service, begun in Chapter 9. Phoenix Sales and Service must pay the same FICA tax amount it withholds from its employees' pay. For Robert Austin, and the week ending January 7, 2007, Phoenix Sales and Service must pay $24.80 for Social Security taxes and $5.80 for Medicare taxes. A partial payroll register for Phoenix Sales and Service is shown in Exhibit 10.1. From its payroll register, the total amounts Phoenix Sales and Service owes for FICA taxes for all of its employees for the period ending January 7, 2007, are $202.31 (Social Security) and $47.31 (Medicare).

 Compute employer's FICA taxes and record them in a general journal.

General Journal Entry to Record Employer FICA Tax

The general journal entry to record Phoenix Sales and Service Social Security and Medicare payroll taxes for the week ending January 7, 2007, is:

Jan.	07	Payroll Tax Expense	2 4 9 62		
		Employer FICA—Social Security Taxes Payable		2 0 2 31	
		Employer FICA—Medicare Taxes Payable		4 7 31	
		To record employer Social Security and Medicare payroll taxes.			

Assets = Liabilities + Equity
+202.31   −249.62
+47.31

Exhibit 10.1

Phoenix Sales and Service Partial Payroll Register

(continued across top of next page)

Partial Payroll Register

Employee Name	Marital Status and Allowances	Beginning Cumulative Gross Earnings	Hours Worked This Pay Period	Hourly Wage	EARNINGS			Ending Cumulative Gross Earnings
					Regular	Overtime	Gross	
Austin, Robert	S-1	0.00	40	10.00	400.00	00.00	400.00	400.00
Cross, Judy	S-2	0.00	41	14.00	560.00	21.00	581.00	581.00
Diaz, John	M-0	0.00	42	14.00	560.00	42.00	602.00	602.00
Keife, Kay	M-2	0.00	40	14.00	560.00	00.00	560.00	560.00
Miller, Lee	M-1	0.00	40	14.00	560.00	00.00	560.00	560.00
Sears, Dale	S-0	0.00	40	14.00	560.00	00.00	560.00	560.00
Total	Week of January 7, 2007				3,200.00	63.00	3,263.00	3,263.00
Total	Month of January 2007				12,800.00	252.00	13,052.00	13,052.00
Total	First Quarter of 2007				41,600.00	819.00	42,419.00	42,419.00
Total	Year Ending December 31, 2007				166,400.00	3,276.00	169,676.00	169,676.00

Payroll Tax Deposits

If the employers' total tax liability is less than $2,500 in a quarter, no deposit is required for that quarter. In this case the employer includes a check for its tax liabilities with its tax returns.

Timing of Payroll Tax Deposits   The Internal Revenue Service (IRS) requires employers to deposit payroll taxes either monthly or semiweekly (once or twice each week). New companies deposit monthly. For other companies, the IRS has a **look-back rule** to classify depositors. The IRS looks back to a one-year period that begins on July 1 and ends on June 30. To determine an employer's status for 2007, the IRS looks back to find the total amount of Social Security, Medicare, and federal income taxes the business paid from July 1, 2005, through June 30, 2006. If this amount is less than $50,000, the IRS classifies the business as a monthly depositor. If this amount is more than $50,000, the IRS classifies the business as a semiweekly depositor. A company's depositor status is reevaluated every year. In our example, Phoenix Sales and Service is classified as a monthly depositor. A monthly depositor must deposit its employee and employer FICA taxes and employees' federal income tax withholdings by the 15th of the next month.

IN THE NEWS

A company's delay or failure to pay withholding taxes to the government has severe consequences. For example, a 100% penalty can be levied, with interest, on the unpaid balance. The government can even close a company, take its assets, and pursue legal action against those involved.

Computing and Recording Payroll Tax Deposits

Federal tax withholdings   By law, the employer must deposit federal tax withholdings on a timely basis in a **federal depository bank.** A federal depository bank is authorized to accept deposits of amounts payable to the federal government. These banks can either be **Federal Reserve Banks** or **authorized depositories.** A Federal Reserve Bank can accept payroll deposits from any business. An authorized depository can accept payroll deposits from its own checking account customers.

The company uses information from its payroll register to make tax deposits. Assume that Phoenix Sales and Service employee wages and deductions for the remaining three weekly

TAXABLE EARNINGS FOR			EMPLOYEE DEDUCTIONS FOR				PAYMENT INFORMATION	
Social Security	Medicare	Unemployment	Social Security	Medicare	Federal Income Tax	State Income Tax	Net Pay	Check Number
400.00	400.00	400.00	24.80	5.80	37.00	2.96	329.44	9001
581.00	581.00	581.00	36.02	8.42	54.00	4.32	478.23	9002
602.00	602.00	602.00	37.33	8.73	53.00	4.24	498.71	9003
560.00	560.00	560.00	34.72	8.12	28.00	2.24	486.92	9004
560.00	560.00	560.00	34.72	8.12	47.00	3.76	466.40	9005
560.00	560.00	560.00	34.72	8.12	69.00	5.52	442.64	9006
3,263.00	3,263.00	3,263.00	202.31	47.31	288.00	23.04	2,702.34	
13,052.00	13,052.00	13,052.00	809.24	189.24	1,152.00	92.16	10,809.36	
42,419.00	42,419.00	40,200.00	2,630.03	615.03	3,744.00	299.52	35,130.42	
169,676.00	169,676.00	42,000.00	10,520.12	2,460.12	14,976.00	1,198.08	140,521.68	

payroll periods in January are exactly the same as those for the week of January 7, 2007. The "Total Month of January 2007" row in Exhibit 10.1 reports the following withholdings:

Employees' federal income taxes	$1,152.00
Employee FICA—Social Security taxes	809.24
Employee FICA—Medicare taxes	189.24
Employer FICA—Social Security taxes (match employee amount)	809.24
Employer FICA—Medicare taxes (match employee amount)	189.24
Total	$3,148.96

Form 8109 The total of $3,148.96 must be deposited in a federal depository bank. The company can make the tax payment either by electronic funds transfer or by check. Companies with annual federal tax deposits above $200,000 must use electronic funds transfers. If the tax payment is made by check, the accountant prepares a **Form 8109,** Federal Tax Deposit Coupon. These preprinted deposit coupons are obtained from the Internal Revenue Service.

If the company does not have a current supply of Forms 8109 or is a new entity, it completes **Form 8109-B.** Exhibit 10.2 presents Form 8109-B for Phoenix Sales and Service for

Exhibit 10.2

Form 8109-B, Federal Tax Deposit Coupon

LO3 Journalize employer's deposit of federal income taxes and FICA taxes withheld, and prepare a deposit coupon.

the month of January. The company has a calendar year-end, so the accountant writes "12" in the "Month Tax Year Ends" box. The accountant also enters the company's EIN and the dollar amount ($3,148.96) of the tax deposit. Finally, the accountant darkens the "941" and "1st quarter" ovals, since the company is depositing Federal taxes it will report on Form 941 (see below) and the deposit is for a month in the first quarter of the year.

General Journal Entry to Record Payroll Tax Deposit   Phoenix Sales and Service's accountant then makes the following entry in its general journal.

Assets = Liabilities + Equity
-3,148.96   -1,152.00
             -809.24
             -189.24
             -809.24
             -189.24

Jan.	31	Employee Federal Income Taxes Payable	1 1 5 2 00	
		Employee FICA—Social Security Taxes Payable	8 0 9 24	
		Employee FICA—Medicare Taxes Payable	1 8 9 24	
		Employer FICA—Social Security Taxes Payable	8 0 9 24	
		Employer FICA—Medicare Taxes Payable	1 8 9 24	
		Cash		3 1 4 8 96
		Deposit January payroll tax withholdings.		

February and March Payroll Records   Assume that February has four weekly payroll periods and March has five weekly payroll periods. Also assume that employee wages and deductions for each weekly payroll period in February and March are exactly the same as those reported in the payroll register for the week ending January 7, 2007. The accountant for Phoenix Sales and Service has updated the company's payroll register and individual employee earnings records and made all the necessary journal entries for payroll. Then, the "Total First Quarter of 2007" row in Exhibit 10.1 reports the following withholdings:

Employees' federal income taxes	$ 3,744.00
Employee FICA—Social Security taxes	2,630.03
Employee FICA—Medicare taxes	615.03
Employer FICA—Social Security taxes (match employee amount)	2,630.03
Employer FICA—Medicare taxes (match employee amount)	615.03
Total	$10,234.12

Employer's Payroll Tax Reporting

Employer's Quarterly Federal Tax Return

LO4 Prepare Form 941, Employer's Quarterly Federal Tax Return.

Each calendar quarter the employer must file **Form 941, Employer's Quarterly Federal Tax Return,** with the Internal Revenue Service. This form reports the employer's federal income tax withholdings, Social Security taxes (employee plus employer portions), and Medicare taxes (employee plus employer portions) for the quarter just ended. Form 941 is due by the end of the next month after the end of the calendar quarter.

    The accountant for Phoenix Sales and Service, Mary Wills, uses this quarterly information to prepare the Form 941, shown in Exhibit 10.3. Due to rounding, the dollar amount ($10,234.11) in the "Total taxes before adjustment" column does not agree with the total federal tax withholdings in the payroll register ($10,234.12). This difference is adjusted by adding $0.01 in box 7a of Form 941.

Form **941**	**Employer's Quarterly Federal Tax Return**	9901
	Department of the Treasury — Internal Revenue Service	OMB No. 1545-0029

Employer identification number   8 6 – 3 2 1 4 5 8 7

Name *(not your trade name)*   Mary Wills

Trade name *(if any)*   Phoenix Sales & Service

Address   1214   Mill Road
           Number   Street   Suite or room number

           Phoenix   AZ   85621
           City   State   ZIP code

Report for this Quarter ...
(Check one.)

[✓] **1:** January, February, March

[ ] **2:** April, May, June

[ ] **3:** July, August, September

[ ] **4:** October, November, December

Read the seperate instructions before you fill out this form. Please type or print within the boxes.

Part 1: Answer these questions for this quarter.

1	Number of employees who received wages, tips, or other compensation for the pay period including: *Mar. 12* (Quarter 1), *June 12* (Quarter 2), *Sept. 12* (Quarter 3), *Dec. 12* (Quarter 4) **1**	6
2	Wages, tips, and other compensation **2**	42,419.00
3	Total income tax withheld from wages, tips, and other compensation **3**	3,744.00
4	If no wages, tips, and other compensation are subject to social security or Medicare tax . . [ ] Check and go to line 6.	
5	Taxable social security and Medicare wages and tips:	

	Column 1		Column 2
5a Taxable social security wages	42,419.00	× .124 =	5,259.96
5b Taxable social security tips	0.00	× .124 =	0.00
5c Taxable Medicare wages & tips	42,419.00	× .029 =	1,230.15

5d	Total social security and Medicare taxes (*Column 2*, lines 5a + 5b + 5c = line 5d) . **5d**	6,490.11
6	Total taxes before adjustments (lines 3 + 5d = line 6) **6**	10,234.11
7	Tax adjustments (If your answer is a negative number, write it in brackets.):	

7a	Current quarter's fractions of cents	.01
7b	Current quarter's sick pay	.
7c	Current quarter's adjustments for tips and group-term life insurance	.
7d	Current year's income tax withholding (Attach Form 941c) . .	.
7e	Prior quarters' social security and Medicare taxes (Attach Form 941c)	.
7f	Special additions to federal income tax (reserved use) . . .	.
7g	Special additions to social security and Medicare (reserved use)	.

7h	Total adjustments (Combine all amounts: lines 7a through 7g.) **7h**	.01
8	Total taxes after adjustments (Combine lines 6 and 7h.) **8**	10,234.12
9	Advance earned income credit (EIC) payments made to employees **9**	0.00
10	Total taxes after adjustment for advance EIC (lines 8 – 9 = line 10) **10**	10,234.12
11	Total deposits for this quarter, including overpayment applied from a prior quarter . . **11**	10,234.12
12	Balance due (lines 10 – 11 = line 12) Make checks payable to the *United States Treasury* . **12**	0.00
13	Overpayment (If line 11 is more than line 10, write the difference here.) 0.00 Check one [ ] Apply to next return. [ ] Send a refund.	

Next →

(continued)

Exhibit 10.3

Form 941, Employer's Quarterly Federal Tax Return

Refer to www.irs.gov for revised versions of this form.

Exhibit 10.3

(concluded)

9902

Name *(not your trade name)*
Mary Wills

Employer identification number
86-3214587

Part 2: Tell us about your deposit schedule for this quarter.

If you are unsure about whether you are a monthly schedule depositor or a semiweekly schedule depositor, see *Pub. 15 (Circular E)*, section 11.

14 [A] [Z]   Write the state abbreviation for the state where you made your deposits OR write "MU" if you made your deposits in *multiple* states.

15   Check one: ☐   Line 10 is less than $2,500. Go to Part 3.

☑   You were a monthly schedule depositor for the entire quarter. Fill out your tax liability for each month. Then go to Part 3.

Tax liability:	Month 1	3,148.94
	Month 2	3,148.94
	Month 3	3,936.24
	Total	10,234.12	Total must equal line 10.

☐   You were a semiweekly schedule depositor for any part of this quarter. Fill out *Schedule B (Form 941): Report of Tax Liability for Semiweekly Schedule Depositors*, and attach it to this form.

Part 3: Tell us about your business. If a question does NOT apply to your business, leave it blank.

16   If your business has closed and you do not have to file returns in the future . . . . ☐ Check here, and

enter the final date you paid wages   [/   /] .

17   If you are a seasonal employer and you do not have to file a return for every quarter of the year . . ☐ Check here.

Part 4: May we contact your third-party designee?

Do you want to allow an employee, a paid tax preparer, or another person to discuss this return with the IRS? See the instructions for details.

☐ Yes. Designee's name [   ]

Phone ( ) –   Personal Identification Number (PIN) ☐ ☐ ☐ ☐ ☐

☑ No.

Part 5: Sign here

Under penalties of perjury, I declare that I have examined this return, including accompanying schedules and statements, and to the best of my knowledge and belief, it is true, correct, and complete.

✗ Sign your name here   *Mary Wills*

Print name and title   Mary Wills, Accountant

Date   04 / 30 /2007   Phone (602) 555 – 8900

Part 6: For paid preparers only *(optional)*

Preparer's signature [   ]

Firm's name [   ]

Address [   ]   EIN [   ]

[   ]   ZIP Code [   ]

Date   [/   /]   Phone ( ) –   SSN/PTIN [   ]

☐ Check if you are self-employed.

Employer's Annual Withholding Reporting

L05   Prepare Form W-2, Employee's Wage and Tax Statement, and Form W-3, Transmittal of Wage and Tax Statements

Form W–2   The employer must provide a **Form W-2, Wage and Tax Statement,** to each employee by January 31 after the calendar year ends. Form W-2 reports each employee's total earnings and deductions for the year just ended. This information comes from each employee's individual earnings record, shown in Chapter 9.

Exhibit 10.4 shows a Form W-2 for 2007 for Robert Austin. The amounts in Exhibit 10.4 assume Robert Austin's payroll information is exactly the same for each of the 52 weeks in 2007. For example, his total "wages, tips, and other compensation" of $20,800 (box 1) equals

$400 (his weekly wage from Exhibit 10.1) times 52 weeks. The employer prepares several copies of Form W-2 for each employee. The employer sends one copy of Form W-2 for each employee to the Social Security Administration, one copy to the state tax department, and several copies to the employee for his or her federal and state tax returns. The employer also keeps a copy of Form W-2 for each employee.

Exhibit 10.4

Form W-2, Wage and Tax Statement

a Control number: AR101 | 22222 | OMB No. 1545-0008

b Employer identification number (EIN): 86-3214587

c Employer's name, address, and ZIP code: Phoenix Sales & Service, 1214 Mill Road, Phoenix, AZ 85621

1 Wages, tips, other compensation: 20,800.00
2 Federal income tax withheld: 1,924.00
3 Social security wages: 20,800.00
4 Social security tax withheld: 1,289.60
5 Medicare wages and tips: 20,800.00
6 Medicare tax withheld: 301.60
7 Social security tips
8 Allocated tips
9 Advance EIC payment
10 Dependent care benefits
11 Nonqualified plans
12a
13 Statutory employee / Retirement plan / Third-party sick pay
12b
14 Other
12c
12d

d Employee's social security number: 333-22-9999

e Employee's first name and initial: Robert J. Last name: Austin

18 Roosevelt Blvd., Apt. C, Tempe, AZ 86322

f Employee's address and ZIP code

15 State	Employer's state ID number	16 State wages, tips, etc.	17 State income tax	18 Local wages, tips, etc.	19 Local income tax	20 Locality name
AZ	13-902319	20,800.00	153.92			

Form **W-2** Wage and Tax Statement

Copy 1—For State, City, or Local Tax Department

Department of the Treasury—Internal Revenue Service

Form W-3 The employer also submits **Form W-3, Transmittal of Wage and Tax Statements,** with the W-2 Forms it sends to the Social Security Administration. Form W-3 reports the total wage and withholding information for all of the company's employees. Form W-3 is due by the last day of February after each calendar year-end. Exhibit 10.5 presents the Form W-3 for Phoenix Sales and Service for 2007.

Some employees will quit or be fired during the year. These employees must be sent their Forms W-2 by either their last paycheck or within 30 days of their request.

Exhibit 10.5

Form W-3, Transmittal of Wage and Tax Statements

DO NOT STAPLE OR FOLD

a Control number | 33333 | For Official Use Only ▶ OMB No. 1545-0008

b Kind of Payer: 941 ☑ Military ☐ 943 ☐ CT-1 ☐ Hshld. emp. ☐ Medicare govt. emp. ☐ Third-party sick pay ☐

c Total number of Forms W-2: 6 | d Establishment number

e Employer identification number (EIN): 86-3214587

f Employer's name: Phoenix Sales & Service

1214 Mill Road, Phoenix, AZ 85621

g Employer's address and ZIP code

h Other EIN used this year

1 Wages, tips, other compensation: 169,676.00
2 Federal income tax withheld: 14,976.00
3 Social security wages: 169,676.00
4 Social security tax withheld: 10,520.12
5 Medicare wages and tips: 169,676.00
6 Medicare tax withheld: 2,460.12
7 Social security tips
8 Allocated tips
9 Advance EIC payments
10 Dependent care benefits
11 Nonqualified plans
12 Deferred compensation
13 For third-party sick pay use only
14 Income tax withheld by payer of third-party sick pay

15 State: AZ | Employer's state ID number: 12-345678
16 State wages, tips, etc.: 169,676.00
17 State income tax: 1,198.08
18 Local wages, tips, etc.
19 Local income tax

Contact person: Mary Wills
Telephone number: (602) 555-8900
For Official Use Only
Email address: MWills@pss.com
Fax number: (602) 555-8901

Under penalties of perjury, I declare that I have examined this return and accompanying documents, and, to the best of my knowledge and belief, they are true, correct, and complete.

HOW YOU DOIN'?

Answers—p. 243

4. For each of the following separate cases determine how frequently (monthly or semiweekly) the employer must deposit payroll taxes for 2008: (*a*) a new business expects to pay $55,000 in payroll taxes during 2008; (*b*) a business had payroll taxes of $42,000 during the period July 1, 2006, through June 30, 2007; (*c*) a business had payroll taxes of $91,500 during the period July 1, 2006, through June 30, 2007.

5. How frequently does the employer report federal payroll taxes? What tax form is used?

6. What is a Form W-2? A Form W-3?

Federal (FUTA) and State (SUTA) Unemployment Taxes

Federal and state unemployment taxes are computed at the end of each quarter. Deposits for FUTA taxes are due on the last day of the next month after the end of a quarter. The company uses either electronic funds transfer or prepares a Form 8109, Federal Tax Deposit coupon.

It is important to remember three points regarding unemployment taxes. First, unemployment taxes usually apply to only the first $7,000 of each employee's earnings during a year. The payroll clerk must keep individual employee earnings records up-to-date and be alert to employees' earnings passing this limit. Second, companies with a relatively stable employment history can pay a lower SUTA tax rate. Third, the employer receives a credit for SUTA taxes paid, and this lowers the employer's FUTA tax rate.

Computing Employer's Unemployment Taxes

LO6 Compute employer's state and federal unemployment taxes and record them in a general journal.

Phoenix Sales and Service has a good merit rating, so it pays 2.7% of the first $7,000 earned by each employee for SUTA taxes. It receives a credit for these payments and so pays only 0.8% of the first $7,000 earned by each employee for FUTA taxes. Note that the company's FUTA tax rate is reduced by the full credit of 5.4%, even though its actual SUTA rate was only 2.7%.

For the first quarter of 2007, Phoenix Sales and Service payroll register in Exhibit 10.1 reports total earnings subject to unemployment taxes of $40,200. Each employee's total pay for FUTA and SUTA taxes is the lesser of their gross pay or $7,000. Assuming each employee earns the same gross pay in the remaining 12 weekly pay periods as he or she did for the week of January 7, 2007, this amount is computed as follows:

Employee	Weekly Gross Pay	× 13 =	Total Quarterly Gross Pay	Total Pay for FUTA and SUTA
Austin, Robert	$400.00		$5,200.00	$ 5,200.00
Cross, Judy	581.00		7,553.00	7,000.00
Diaz, John	602.00		7,826.00	7,000.00
Keife, Kay	560.00		7,280.00	7,000.00
Miller, Lee	560.00		7,280.00	7,000.00
Sears, Dale	560.00		7,280.00	7,000.00
				$40,200.00

Phoenix Sales and Service computes the total amounts it owes for FUTA and SUTA taxes for the first quarter of 2007 as:

Federal Unemployment Taxes: 0.008 × $40,200.00 =	$ 321.60
State Unemployment Taxes: 0.027 × $40,200.00 =	1,085.40
Total Unemployment Tax Expense	$1,407.00

General Journal Entry to Record Unemployment Taxes   The accountant then makes the following general entry in the general journal.

Apr.	10	Payroll Tax Expense	1 4 0 7 00		
		Federal Unemployment Taxes Payable		3 2 1 60	
		State Unemployment Taxes Payable		1 0 8 5 40	
		Employer's unemployment taxes for first quarter.			

Assets = Liabilities + Equity
+321.60   −1,407.00
+1,085.40

Reporting Employer's Unemployment Taxes

FUTA and SUTA taxes are typically due by the end of the next month following the end of the quarter.

LO7 Prepare unemployment tax returns.

Reporting State Unemployment Taxes   Phoenix Sales and Service must now do two things to meet the SUTA deadline. First, it files an **Employer's Quarterly Unemployment Tax Report** for unemployment taxes owed the state of Arizona and includes a check for $1,085.40. This report is shown in Exhibit 10.6. The dollar amounts in boxes 1, 3, and 4 all agree with amounts in the company's payroll register and individual employee earnings records. Phoenix Sales and Service did not owe any additional amounts for interest, penalties, or job training taxes. Second, it deposits $321.60 in a federal depository bank, as we showed earlier.

Reporting Federal Unemployment Taxes   The employer files **Form 940,** or **Form 940-EZ, Employer's Annual Federal Unemployment Tax Return** by January 31 after the year ends. This deadline is extended to February 10 if the employer has made all tax deposits during the year on time. The employer uses Form 940-EZ if it pays unemployment taxes to only one state.

The employer files *quarterly* reports for state unemployment taxes and *annual* reports for federal unemployment taxes.

Exhibit 10.6

Employer's Quarterly
Unemployment Tax Report

Exhibit 10.6

Employer's Quarterly Unemployment Tax Report

ARIZONA DEPARTMENT OF ECONOMIC SECURITY
PO BOX 52027
PHOENIX, AZ 85072-2027
Telephone (602) 248-9354

ARIZONA ACCOUNT NUMBER
CALENDAR QUARTER ENDING
TO AVOID PENALTY MAIL BY
FEDERAL ID NO.

For Online Filling: **www.azui.com**

USE BLACK INK ONLY

PLEASE RETURN ORIGINAL

UNEMPLOYMENT TAX AND WAGE REPORT

A. NUMBER OF EMPLOYEES -
Report for each month, the number of full and part-time covered workers who worked during or received pay subject to UI Taxes for the payroll period which includes the 12th of the month.

6

6

6

B. WAGES - List all employees in Social Security Number order, or alphabetically by last name. Please use white paper in the same format for additional employees. If you have six or more employees, consider reporting via magnetic media. Ask for "Arizona Magnetic Media Reporting" (PAU-430). We support diskette and cartridge media. Or consider online reporting at **www.azui.com.**

C. WAGE SUMMARY - See Reverse For Instructions

1. **TOTAL WAGES PAID IN QUARTER** From Section B. Wage Listing	42,419	00
2. **SUBTRACT EXCESS WAGES** Cannot exceed Line 1 - see instructions	2,219	00
3. **TAXABLE WAGES PAID** Up to $7000 per Employee - Line 1 minus line 2	40,200	00
4. **TAX DUE** Line 3 × Tax Rate of The decimal equivalant = .027	1,085	40
5. **ADD INTEREST DUE** 1% of Tax Due for each month payment is late	0	00
6. **ADD PENALTY FOR LATE REPORT** 0.10% of Line 1 ($35 min / $200 max)	0	00
7. **ADD JOB TRAINING TAX DUE** 0.10% of Line 3	0	00
8. **TOTAL PAYMENT DUE** If the sum of lines 4 & 7 is equal to or less than $9.99, payment of the taxes due is not required.	1,085	40
9. **SUBTRACT ANY CREDIT BALANCE** If a balance is listed, subtract from Line 8.		
10. **AMOUNT PAID** Make check Payable to DES-Unemployment Tax	1,085	40

LIEN MAY BE FILED WITHOUT FURTHER NOTICE ON DELINQUENT TAXES.

1. Employee Social Security Number	2. Employee Name (*Last, First*)	3. Total Wages Paid in Quarter
333 - 22 - 9999	Austin, Robert	5,200.00
299 - 11 - 9201	Cross, Judy	7,553.00
444 - 11 - 9090	Diaz, John	7,826.00
909 - 11 - 3344	Keife, Kay	7,280.00
444 - 56 - 3211	Miller, Lee	7,280.00
	TOTAL WAGES THIS PAGE	35,139.00
Signature *Mary Wills*	TOTAL WAGES ALL PAGES	42,419.00*

Title: Accountant

Prepared by: Mary Wills

Date: 04/10/2007

Telephone: (602) 555-8900

PHOTO COPY FOR YOUR RECORDS

*Dale Sears' wages of $7,280.00 would be reported on a separate page.

Assume that Phoenix Sales and Service hires no new workers during 2007. As we illustrated earlier, five of the company's six employees' gross pay exceeds the $7,000 annual limit by the end of the first quarter of 2007. Robert Austin's gross pay also passes this limit during 2007. So, for 2007 Phoenix Sales and Service has total wages subject to FUTA tax of $42,000 (6 × $7,000). The company pays a total of $336 in FUTA taxes for the year ($42,000 × 0.008). The company pays a total of $1,134 in SUTA taxes for the year ($42,000 × 0.027). By no later than January 31, 2008, the accountant files the Form 940-EZ shown in Exhibit 10.7.

General Journal Entry to Record Employer's Payment of Unemployment

Taxes After these tasks are done, the following entry is made in Phoenix Sales and Service's general journal. The employer does not file quarterly tax reports for FUTA taxes. These taxes are reported only annually. We show an example for Phoenix Sales and Service for 2007 next.

Apr.	10	Federal Unemployment Taxes Payable	321 60		
		State Unemployment Taxes Payable	1085 40		
		Cash		1407 00	
		Remit employer's unemployment taxes for first quarter.			

Assets = Liabilities + Equity
−1,407.00   −321.60
           −1,085.40

HOW YOU DOIN'?

Answers—p. 243

7. A company has 10 employees. This company's FUTA rate is 0.8% on the first $7,000 earned; its SUTA rate is 2.5% on the first $7,000. Each employee earns over $7,000 in 2008, and the employer's total gross pay is $200,000. What amount of (a) FUTA taxes and (b) SUTA taxes will the employer pay in 2008?

8. How frequently does an employer report state and federal unemployment taxes?

Exhibit 10.7

Form 940-EZ, Employer's Annual Federal Unemployment (FUTA) Tax Return

Refer to www.irs.gov for revised versions of this form.

Form **940-EZ**
Department of the Treasury
Internal Revenue Service

Employer's Annual Federal Unemployment (FUTA) Tax Return

▶ See the separate Instructions for Form 940-EZ for information on completing this form.

OMB No. 1545-1110

T	
FF	
FD	
FP	
I	
T	

You must complete this section. ▶

Name (as distinguished from trade name)
Mary Wills

Trade name, if any
Phoenix Sales & Service

Address (number and street)
1214 Mill Road

Calendar year
2007

Employer identification number (EIN)
86-3214587

City, state, and ZIP code
Phoenix, AZ 85621

*Answer the questions under **Who May Use Form 940-EZ** on page 2. If you cannot use Form 940-EZ, you must use Form 940.*

A Enter the amount of contributions paid to your state unemployment fund (see the separate instructions) . . ▶ $ _____1,134 | 00

B (1) Enter the name of the state where you have to pay contributions . . . . ▶ Arizona
    (2) Enter your state reporting number as shown on your state unemployment tax return. ▶ 12-345678

If you will not have to file returns in the future, check here (see **Who Must File** in separate instructions) **and complete and sign the return.** ▶ ☐

If this is an Amended Return, check here (see **Amended Returns** in the separate instructions) . . . . ▶ ☐

Part I   **Taxable Wages and FUTA Tax**

1	Total payments (including payments shown on lines 2 and 3) during the calendar year for services of employees	**1**	169,676	00
2	Exempt payments. (Explain all exempt payments, attaching additional sheets if necessary.) ▶ _____	**2**		
3	Payments of more than $7,000 for services. Enter only amounts over the first $7,000 paid to each employee **(see the separate instructions)**	**3**	127,676	00
4	Add lines 2 and 3 . . . . ▶	**4**	127,676	00
5	**Total taxable wages** (subtract line 4 from line 1) . . . . ▶	**5**	42,000	00
6	**FUTA tax.** Multiply the wages on line 5 by .008 and enter here. **(If the result is over $500, also complete Part II.)**	**6**	336	00
7	Total FUTA tax deposited for the year, including any overpayment applied from a prior year . . .	**7**	336	00
8	**Balance due** (subtract line 7 from line 6). Pay to the "United States Treasury." . . . . ▶	**8**	0	00
	If you owe more than $500, see **Depositing FUTA tax** in the separate instructions.			
9	**Overpayment** (subtract line 6 from line 7). Check if it is to be: ☐ **Applied to next return** or ☐ **Refunded** ▶	**9**		

Part II   **Record of Quarterly Federal Unemployment Tax Liability** (Do not include state liability.) **Complete only if line 6 is over $500.**

Quarter	First (Jan. 1 – Mar. 31)	Second (Apr. 1 – June 30)	Third (July 1 – Sept. 30)	Fourth (Oct. 1 – Dec. 31)	Total for year
Liability for quarter	321.60	14.40			336.00

Third–Party Designee

Do you want to allow another person to discuss this return with the IRS (see the separate instructions)?   ☐ **Yes.** Complete the following.   ☑ **No**

Designee's name ▶

Phone no. ▶ ( )

Personal identification number (PIN) ▶ ☐☐☐☐☐

Under penalties of perjury, I declare that I have examined this return, including accompanying schedules and statements, and, to the best of my knowledge and belief, it is true, correct, and complete, and that no part of any payment made to a state unemployment fund claimed as a credit was, or is to be, deducted from the payments to employees.

Signature ▶ *Mary Wills*   Title (Owner, etc.) ▶ Accountant   Date ▶ 01/14/2008

For Privacy Act and Paperwork Reduction Act Notice, see the separate instructions.   ▼ **DETACH HERE** ▼   Cat. No. 10983G   Form **940-EZ**

Workers' Compensation Insurance

Computing Estimated Workers' Compensation Insurance Premium

Compute and record workers' compensation insurance premiums for employers.

Phoenix Sales and Service has two types of workers: office workers and landscapers. The company pays a workers' compensation premium of $0.30 per $100 of office worker wages and $2.50 per $100 of landscapers' wages. Based on previous experience at the beginning of 2007, Phoenix Sales and Service estimates its total wages in 2007 will be $160,000. The company also estimates $53,000 of its total wages will be paid to office workers, and $107,000 will be paid to landscapers. It computes estimated workers' compensation insurance premiums for 2007 as follows:

> Office workers ($53,000/100) × $0.30 = $ 159.00
> Landscapers ($107,000/100) × $2.50 =   2,675.00
> Total $2,834.00

General Journal Entry to Record Estimated Workers' Compensation Insurance Premium   Phoenix Sales and Service pays this premium in January 2007. The company makes the following entry in the general journal.

Assets = Liabilities + Equity
−2,834.00   −2,834.00

Jan.	14	Workers' Compensation Insurance Expense		2 8 3 4 00	
		Cash			2 8 3 4 00
		Estimated workers' compensation insurance premium for 2007.			

Computing Actual Workers' Compensation Insurance Premium

After the end of 2007, the payroll clerk updates the individual employee earnings records, as we showed in Chapter 9. Assume that these records show the following actual total wages for Phoenix Sales and Service employees for the year ending December 31, 2007.

> Office workers . . . . $ 49,920
> Landscapers   119,756

The actual workers' compensation insurance premium for Phoenix Sales and Service for 2007 is

> Office workers ($49,920/100) × $0.30 = $ 149.76
> Landscapers ($119,756/100) × $2.50 =   2,993.90
> Total $3,143.66

If instead the company had overpaid its workers' compensation insurance premium, it would receive a refund. The company would debit Workers' Compensation Insurance Refund Receivable and credit Workers' Compensation Insurance Expense.

General Journal Entry to Adjust Workers' Compensation Insurance Premium for Actual Wages   The company's estimated workers' compensation insurance premium for 2007 ($2,834.00) was too low. It pays the difference of $309.66 ($3,143.66 − $2,834.00) and makes the following journal entry.

Assets = Liabilities + Equity
−309.66   −309.66

Dec.	31	Workers' Compensation Insurance Expense		3 0 9 66	
		Cash			3 0 9 66
		Pay additional workers' compensation insurance premium			
		based on actual wages paid in 2007.			

HOW YOU DOIN'?

9. A company has office staff and construction workers. The company pays workers' compensation insurance premiums of $0.20 per $100 of office staff wages and $3.00 per $100 of construction worker wages. The company estimates it will pay $65,000 in total pay to office workers and $218,000 in total pay to construction workers in 2008. What amount of estimated workers' compensation insurance premium will the company pay at the beginning of 2008?

10. What journal entry will the company in question 9 make to record the payment of its estimated workers' compensation insurance premium at the beginning of 2008?

11. Assume the company in question 9 actually pays $66,000 in total pay to office staff and $209,400 in total pay to construction workers during 2008. What journal entry will the company make to adjust its 2008 workers' compensation expense for actual 2008 wages?

> Many payroll services now compute unemployment premiums based on actual payroll. These "pay-as-you-go" systems eliminate large upfront payments at the start of the insurance policy period and large end of year surprises from actual wages differing from expected wages.

Demonstration Problem

The Cutting Edge hair salon pays its employees monthly. Employees' gross pay is subject to the following taxes.

Tax	Rate	Applied to
FICA—Social Security	6.20%	First $94,200
FICA—Medicare	1.45	All gross pay
FUTA	0.80	First $7,000
SUTA	2.00	First $7,000

The company reports the following in its payroll register for its three employees for the month ending September 30, 2008.

	Gross Pay through 8/31	Current Month Gross Pay	Federal Income Tax Withholding
Brianna	$17,940	$1,840	$298
Juan	4,625	1,500	243
Shi	5,600	1,680	272
Total	$28,165	$5,020	$813

Required

1. Compute the following employer payroll taxes for the month ending September 30, 2008: (a) FICA—Social Security, (b) FICA—Medicare, (c) FUTA, and (d) SUTA.

2. Prepare the journal entries to record The Cutting Edge's payroll taxes for the month ending September 30, 2008. Assume $813 of federal income tax withheld has already been recorded with a debit to Payroll Taxes Expense and a credit to Employee Federal Income Taxes Payable.

3. The Cutting Edge deposits its payroll taxes monthly. Prepare the journal entry to record the company's payroll tax deposit for September.

4. Assume The Cutting Edge pays its FUTA and SUTA taxes monthly. Prepare the journal entry to record the payment of the company's FUTA and SUTA taxes for September.

Planning the Solution

- For 1, determine if any employee's gross pay through 8/31 is above the annual limits for any of the payroll taxes. Determine the amount of total income for the month subject to each tax. Multiply this income amount by the appropriate tax rate.
- For parts 2, 3, and 4, determine the accounts affected and then record the entries.

Solution to Demonstration Problem

1. No employee's gross pay through 8/31 exceeds the limit ($94,200) for FICA—Social Security tax. Brianna's gross pay through 8/31 does exceed the limit for FUTA and SUTA taxes, so The Cutting Edge does not owe FUTA or SUTA taxes on her pay for September. Shi's gross pay for September, when added to her gross pay through 8/31, causes her to exceed the FUTA and SUTA limit. The Cutting Edge pays FUTA and SUTA taxes on only $1,400 of Shi's September gross pay. The September payroll taxes are:

   a. FICA—Social Security $5,020 × 6.2% = $311.24
   b. FICA—Medicare $5,020 × 1.45% = $72.79
   c. FUTA $2,900* × 0.8% = $23.20
   d. SUTA $2,900 × 2.0% = $58.00

   *Juan's gross pay of $1,500 + $1,400 of Shi's gross pay.

2.

Payroll Tax Expense	465.23	
Employer FICA—Social Security Taxes Payable . .		311.24
Employer FICA—Medicare Taxes Payable		72.79
Federal Unemployment Taxes Payable.		23.20
State Unemployment Taxes Payable		58.00

3.

Employee Federal Income Taxes Payable	813.00	
Employer FICA—Social Security Taxes Payable	311.24	
Employer FICA—Medicare Taxes Payable.	72.79	
Cash		1,197.03

4.

Federal Unemployment Taxes Payable	23.20	
State Unemployment Taxes Payable	58.00	
Cash		81.20

Summary

LO1 **Describe laws that impact employer's payroll obligations.** Law requires employers to match their employees' Social Security and Medicare taxes. Employers must also pay federal and state unemployment taxes and workers' compensation insurance premiums.

LO2 **Compute employer's FICA taxes and record them in a general journal.** The employer pays 6.2% of each employee's annual gross pay (up to $94,200) for Social Security taxes and 1.45% of their annual gross pay for Medicare taxes. The accountant debits Payroll Tax Expense and credits Employer FICA—Social Security Tax Payable and Employer—FICA Medicare Tax Payable.

LO3 **Journalize employer's deposit of federal income taxes and FICA taxes withheld and prepare a deposit coupon.** The employer must periodically deposit amounts withheld from employee pay in a federal depository. This is done by either electronic funds transfer or by completing a Form 8109. The accountant debits Employer FICA—Social Security Tax Payable and Employer FICA—Medicare Tax Payable and credits Cash.

LO4 **Prepare Form 941, Employer's Quarterly Federal Tax Return.** The accountant files this federal tax form within one month after each quarter ends. It reports on the employer's Federal Unemployment Taxes for the quarter.

LO5 **Prepare Form W-2, Employee's Wage and Tax Statement, and Form W-3, Transmittal of Wage and Tax Statements.**

After each calendar year-end the employer sends each employee a Form W-2, which summarizes the employee's wages and deductions for the year just ended. The employer transmits copies of these W-2's to the Social Security Administration and includes a Form W-3 that summarizes all the individual W-2's.

LO6 **Compute employer's state and federal unemployment taxes and record them in a general journal.** The employer pays unemployment taxes of up to 6.2% of employee gross pay. Employers with stable employment histories and low turnover typically pay lower SUTA rates. Employers also receive credits for SUTA taxes and often pay FUTA taxes of only 0.8% of their employee's annual gross pay. The accountant debits Payroll Tax Expense and credits Federal Unemployment Taxes Payable and State Unemployment Taxes Payable.

LO7 **Prepare unemployment tax returns.** The employer files a quarterly state unemployment tax return. Federal unemployment taxes are reported annually on Form 940, the Employer's Federal Unemployment Tax Return.

LO8 **Compute and record workers' compensation insurance premiums for employers.** Most states require the employer to provide benefits or pay insurance premiums for employees injured while on the job. Premium amounts are based on total estimated salary amounts and how hazardous the job is.

1. The annual limits are: (a) $94,200, (b) none, (c) $7,000, and (d) $7,000.

2. (a) FICA taxes are incurred by both employee and employer. (b) FUTA taxes are incurred by the employer. (c) SUTA taxes are incurred by the employer. (d) Withheld income taxes are incurred by the employee.

3. ($1,000 × 0.8%) + ($1,000 × 4%) + ($3,000 × 6.2%) + ($3,000 × 1.45%) = $277.50. $1,000 of the $3,000 March pay is subject to FUTA and SUTA—the entire $6,000 pay from January and February was subject to them.

4. (a) New businesses make monthly payroll tax deposits. (b) The company had less than $50,000 in payroll taxes in the "look-back" period (July 1, 2006, through June 30, 2007), so it makes monthly payroll tax deposits. (c) The company had more than $50,000 in payroll taxes in the "look-back" period (July 1, 2006, through June 30, 2007), so it makes semiweekly payroll tax deposits.

5. Federal payroll taxes are reported quarterly on Form 941.

6. A W-2 is an annual statement sent to each employee that reports the employee's total earnings and deductions for the year just ended. Form W-3 reports the total wage and withholding information for all of the company's employees.

7. (a) FUTA = 10 × $7,000 × 0.8% = $560. (b) SUTA = 10 × $7,000 × 2.5% = $1,750.

8. The employer files *quarterly* reports for state unemployment taxes and *annual* reports for federal unemployment taxes.

9. [($65,000 / $100) × $0.20] + [($218,000 / $100) × $3.00] = $6,670.

10.

Workers' Compensation Insurance Expense . . .	6,670	
Cash		6,670

11. The company's actual workers' compensation insurance premium for 2008 is: [($66,000 / $100) × $0.20] + [($209,400 / $100) × $3.00] = $6,414. The company is entitled to a refund of $256 ($6,670 − $6,414), which is recorded as:

Workers' Compensation Insurance		
Refund Receivable	256	
Workers' Compensation Insurance Expense . .		256

Key Terms

Key Terms are available at the book's Website for learning and testing in an online Flashcard Format.

Authorized depository (p. 230) A bank that can accept payroll deposits from its own checking account customers.

Employer identification number (EIN) (p. 228) A number issued by the federal government that uniquely identifies a business.

Employer Quarterly Unemployment Tax Report (p. 237) A report filed with the state that shows an employer's unemployment taxes owed.

Federal depository bank (p. 230) Bank authorized to accept deposits of amounts payable to the federal government.

Federal Insurance Contributions Act (FICA) taxes (p. 228) Taxes assessed on both employers and employees; for Social Security and Medicare programs.

Federal Reserve Bank (p. 230) A bank that can accept payroll deposits from any business.

Federal unemployment taxes (FUTA) (p. 228) Payroll taxes on employers assessed by the federal government to support its unemployment insurance program.

Form 940 (p. 237) IRS form used to report an employer's federal unemployment taxes (FUTA) on an annual filing basis.

Form 940-EZ (p. 237) The Employer's Annual Federal Unemployment Tax Return. This shows the amount of FUTA tax the employer owes for the year.

Form 941 (p. 232) IRS form filed to report FICA taxes owed and remitted.

Form 8109 (p. 231) A preprinted Federal Tax Deposit Coupon. It is used when an employer deposits money into a federal depository bank.

Form 8109-B (p. 231) A Federal Tax Deposit Coupon used by new businesses or when the business does not have a supply of preprinted Forms 8109.

Form SS-4 (p. 228) An Internal Revenue Service form filed by a business in order to receive an employer identification number.

Form W-2 (p. 234) Annual report by an employer to each employee showing the employee's wages subject to FICA and federal income taxes along with amounts withheld.

Form W-3 (p. 235) The Transmittal of Wage and Tax Statements form. This form reports the total wages and tax withholding information for all the employer's employees for the year.

Look-back rule (p. 230) A rule used to classify business as monthly or semiweekly depositors.

Merit rating (p. 228) Rating assigned to an employer by a state based on the employer's record of employment.

State unemployment taxes (SUTA) (p. 228) State payroll taxes on employers to support its unemployment programs.

Workers' compensation insurance (p. 229) An insurance program that provides benefits to workers who are injured on the job.

Multiple Choice Quiz   Answers on p. 255   mhhe.com/wildCA

Multiple Choice Quizzes A and B are available at the book's Website.

1. An employee earned $50,000 during the year. FICA tax for social security is 6.2% and FICA tax for Medicare is 1.45%. The employer's share of FICA taxes is
   a. Zero, since the employee's pay exceeds the FICA limit.
   b. Zero, since FICA is not an employer tax.
   c. $3,100
   d. $725
   e. $3,825

2. Assume the FUTA tax rate is 0.8% and the SUTA tax rate is 5.4%. Both taxes are applied to the first $7,000 of an employee's pay. What is the total unemployment tax an employer must pay on an employee's annual wages of $40,000?
   a. $2,480
   b. $434
   c. $56
   d. $378
   e. Zero; the employee's wages exceed the $7,000 maximum.

3. A company estimates that its office employees will earn $70,000 next year and its construction employees will earn $145,000 next year. The company pays for workers' compensation insurance for all of its employees. The rates for this insurance are $0.40 per $100 of wages for office employees and $6.00 per $100 of wages for construction workers. The company's estimated workers' compensation insurance premium for the year is
   a. $4,780
   b. $8,980

   c. $898
   d. Zero; the company pays based on actual, not estimated, wages
   e. $13,760

4. A company's payroll register reports total employee gross pay of $16,200 for a recent pay period. A total of $14,000 of this amount is subject to Social Security tax. Only one of the company's employees has total gross pay for the year less than $7,000; this employee earned gross pay of $1,150 during the recent pay period. Assume a Social Security tax rate of 6.2%, a Medicare tax rate of 1.45%, a SUTA rate of 1.5%, and a FUTA rate of 0.8%. The employer's payroll tax expense for this pay period is
   a. $113.85
   b. $1,088.45
   c. $1,611.90
   d. $1,129.35
   e. $1,256.75

5. The Federal Insurance Contributions Act (FICA) requires that each employer file a
   a. W-4.
   b. Form 941.
   c. Form 1040.
   d. Form 1099.
   e. All of the above.

Discussion Questions

1. What is the combined amount (in percent) of the employee and employer Social Security tax rate?

2. What is the current Medicare tax rate? This rate is applied to what maximum level of salary and wages?

3. Which payroll taxes are the employee's responsibility and which are the employer's responsibility?

4. What is an employer's unemployment merit rating? How are these ratings assigned to employers?

5. What is a federal depository bank?

6. What is a Form W-2? To whom is Form W-2 sent?

7. What is a Form W-3? To whom is a Form W-3 sent?

8. How does an employer report its state and federal unemployment taxes?

9. When does an employer typically pay premiums for workers' compensation insurance?

10. How often must an employer deposit federal income tax withholdings?

11. How does an employer make federal income tax withholding deposits?

QUICK STUDY

QS 10–1

Employer's payroll obligations

(LO1)

Match each of the following terms A through H with the appropriate definitions 1 through 8.

A. EFTPS   D. FICA taxes   G. FUTA taxes
B. Form 941   E. Form 940   H. Federal depository bank
C. Merit rating   F. Form W-2

_____ 1. A rating assigned to an employer by a state based on the employer's past record regarding stable employment.

_____ 2. Taxes assessed on both employer and employees under the Federal Insurance Contributions Act. These taxes fund Social Security and Medicare.

_____ 3. Payroll taxes on employers assessed by the federal government to support the federal unemployment insurance program.

_____ **4.** A bank authorized to accept deposits of amounts payable to the federal government, including payroll taxes.

_____ **5.** A system for depositing payroll taxes via computer or telephone.

_____ **6.** A statement that reports an individual employee's total earnings and deductions for the year.

_____ **7.** A form that reports an employer's federal tax withholdings for a quarter.

_____ **8.** A form that reports an employer's annual federal unemployment taxes.

Major Co. has five employees, each of whom earns $2,500 per month and has been employed since January 1. FICA Social Security taxes are 6.2% of the first $94,200 paid to each employee, and FICA Medicare taxes are 1.45% of gross pay. FUTA taxes are 0.8% and SUTA taxes are 2.8% of the first $7,000 paid to each employee. Prepare the March 31 journal entry to record the March payroll tax expense.

QS 10-2
Record employer payroll taxes
(LO2) (LO6)

A company's employees had the following earnings records at the close of the weekly payroll period ending August 7, 2007.

QS 10-3
Employer's payroll tax expenses
(LO2) (LO6)

Employees	Earnings through Prior Pay Period	Earnings This Pay Period
D. Adams	$11,300	$3,900
J. Hess	6,100	2,500
R. Lui	9,500	3,100
T. Morales	4,800	1,400
L. Vang	10,000	3,000

The company's payroll taxes expense on each employee's earnings includes: FICA Social Security taxes of 6.2% on the first $94,200 plus 1.45% FICA Medicare on all wages; 0.8% federal unemployment taxes on the first $7,000; and 2.5% state unemployment taxes on the first $7,000. Compute the employer's total payroll tax expense for the current pay period.

Refer to QS 10-3. Prepare the August 7, 2007, entry in the company's general journal to record the employer's payroll taxes for the current pay period.

QS 10-4
Recording employer payroll taxes
(LO2)

A company's employer payroll taxes are 0.8% for federal unemployment taxes, 5.4% for state unemployment taxes, 6.2% for FICA Social Security taxes on earnings up to $94,200, and 1.45% for FICA Medicare taxes on all earnings. Compute the Form W-2 Wage and Tax Statement information required below for the following employees:

QS 10-5
Preparing Form W-2
(LO5)

Employee	Gross Earnings	Federal Income Taxes Withheld
A. Baker	$84,000	$17,600
C. Dirkson	52,000	8,200

W-2 Information	A. Baker	C. Dirkson
Federal income tax withheld	_____	_____
Wages, tips, other compensation	_____	_____
Social Security tax withheld	_____	_____
Social Security wages	_____	_____
Medicare tax withheld	_____	_____
Medicare wages	_____	_____

QS 10-6
Preparing Form W-3
(LO6)

Refer to the data in QS 10-5. Compute the company's Form W-3 Transmittal of Wage and Tax Statements information required below.

W-3 Information	
Federal Income Tax Withheld	_____
Wages, Tips, Other Compensation	_____
Social Security Tax Withheld	_____
Social Security Wages	_____
Medicare Tax Withheld	_____
Medicare Wages	_____

QS 10-7
Employer's payroll taxes
(LO2) (LO6)

A company's payroll information for the month of May follows:

Administrative salaries	$2,000
Sales salaries	3,500
Shop wages	4,000
FICA taxes withheld	700
Federal income taxes withheld	1,300
Medical insurance premiums withheld	415
Union dues withheld	205

On May 31 the company issued Check No. 335 payable to the Payroll Bank Account to pay for the May payroll. It issued payroll checks to the employees after depositing the check. (1) Prepare the journal entry to record (accrue) the employer's payroll for May. (2) Prepare the journal entry to pay the May payroll. The federal and state unemployment tax rates are 0.8% and 5.4%, respectively, on the first $7,000 paid to each employee; the wages and salaries subject to these taxes were $6,000. (3) Prepare the journal entry to record the employer's payroll taxes. (Refer to Chapter 9 if necessary in answering questions 1 and 2.)

QS 10-8
Computing employer taxes
(LO1) (LO2) (LO6)

An employee earned $62,500 during the year working for an employer. The FICA tax for Social Security is 6.2% and the FICA tax for Medicare is 1.45%. The current FUTA tax rate is 0.8%, and the SUTA tax rate is 5.4%. Both unemployment taxes are applied to the first $7,000 of an employee's pay. What is the amount of total unemployment taxes the employer will pay for this employee?

EXERCISES

Exercise 10-1
Computing payroll taxes
(LO2) (LO6)

BMX Co. has one employee, and the company is subject to the following taxes:

Tax	Rate	Applied to
FICA—Social Security	6.20%	First $94,200
FICA—Medicare	1.45	All gross pay
FUTA	0.80	First $7,000
SUTA	2.90	First $7,000

Compute BMX's amounts for each of these four taxes as applied to the employee's gross earnings for September under each of three separate situations (*a*), (*b*), and (*c*).

	Gross Pay through August	Gross Pay for September
a.	$ 6,800	$ 900
b.	19,200	2,200
c.	89,200	8,000

Check   (a) FUTA, $1.60; SUTA, $5.80

Using the data in situation *a* of Exercise 10-1, prepare the employer's September 30 journal entries to record (1) the employer's payroll tax expense and its related liabilities and (2) its tax deposits. In preparing the tax deposit entry assume that the employer has already recorded liabilities for employee payroll taxes and withholdings. The employee's federal income taxes withheld by the employer are $150 for this pay period.

Exercise 10-2
Payroll-related journal entries
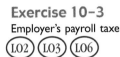

Metro Express has five sales employees, each of whom earns $4,000 per month and is paid on the last working day of the month. Each employee's wages are subject to FICA Social Security taxes of 6.2% and Medicare taxes of 1.45% on all wages. Withholding for each employee also includes federal income tax of 16%. Metro Express pays one-half of each employees' monthly medical insurance premiums of $110. Metro Express also pays federal unemployment taxes of 0.8% of the first $7,000 paid each employee, and state unemployment taxes of 4.0% of the first $7,000 paid to each employee.

   Prepare the journal entries to record (1) the employee's payroll taxes at January 31, (2) the employer's payroll taxes at January 31, and (3) payment of the employer's payroll tax liabilities at January 31 for Metro Express. Metro Express deposits taxes monthly.

Exercise 10-3
Employer's payroll taxes
LO2 LO3 LO6

Premier Landscaping reports the following in its payroll register for August. The company makes monthly tax deposits.

Exercise 10-4
Employer's tax deposits
LO3

Pay Period End	Employee Deductions for		
	Federal Income Tax	Social Security	Medicare
Aug. 7	$1,530.00	$632.40	$147.90
Aug. 14	1,447.50	598.30	139.93
Aug. 21	1,563.00	646.04	151.09
Aug. 28	1,620.00	669.60	156.60

Prepare the general journal entry to record Premier Landscaping's deposit of its federal income tax withholdings and FICA taxes (employee and employer portions) for August.

Ideal Systems' employees had the following earnings records at the close of the first quarter:

Exercise 10-5
Computing and reporting unemployment taxes
LO6 LO7

Employee	Gross Pay for First Quarter
A. Poe	$8,200
B. Rye	7,450
C. Sims	6,770

The state unemployment tax is 5.4%, but Ideal Systems pays only 2% due to its high merit rating. Ideal Systems also pays 0.8% for federal unemployment taxes. Unemployment taxes are based on the first $7,000 of each employee's earnings during the year.

1. Compute Ideal Systems' SUTA and FUTA tax liabilities for the first quarter.
2. Prepare the general journal entry to record Ideal Systems' SUTA and FUTA tax liabilities for the first quarter.
3. Prepare the general journal entry to record Ideal Systems' payment of its SUTA and FUTA tax liabilities for the first quarter.
4. Explain how Ideal Systems will report its unemployment taxes to the state and federal governments.

A1 Construction began operations on January 1, 2007. The company pays workers' compensation insurance premiums for its employees. The company's accountant assembled the data below for 2007:

Exercise 10-6
Computing workers' compensation insurance premiums

Classification	Estimated Wages	Rate per $100 of Wages
Office workers	$ 60,000	0.25
Construction	320,000	4.20

1. Compute A1 Construction's estimated workers' compensation insurance premium for 2007.
2. Prepare the general journal entry to record A1 Construction's payment of its 2007 workers' compensation insurance premium on January 9, 2007.

PROBLEM SET A

Problem 10-1A
Payroll expenses, withholdings, and taxes

(LO2) (LO6)

eXcel
mhhe.com/wildCA

Paloma Co. pays its employees each week. Its employees' gross pay is subject to these taxes:

Tax	Rate	Applied to
FICA—Social Security	6.20%	First $94,200
FICA—Medicare	1.45	All gross pay
FUTA	0.80	First $7,000
SUTA	2.15	First $7,000

The company is preparing its payroll calculations for the week ended August 25. Payroll records show the following information for the company's four employees.

		Gross Pay	Current Week	
	Name	through 8/18	Gross Pay	Income Tax Withholding
3	Dahlia	$93,400	$2,800	$284
4	Trey	31,700	1,000	145
5	Kiesha	6,850	550	39
6	Chee	1,250	500	30

In addition to gross pay, the company must pay one-half of the $34 per employee weekly health insurance; each employee pays the remaining one-half. The company also contributes an extra 8% of each employee's gross pay (at no cost to employees) to a pension fund.

Required

Compute the following for the week ended August 25 (round amounts to the nearest cent):

Check (1) $176.70
(2) $70.33
(3) $5.20

1. Employer's FICA taxes for Social Security.
2. Employer's FICA taxes for Medicare.
3. Employer's FUTA taxes.
4. Employer's SUTA taxes.
5. Employer's total payroll-related expense for each employee.

Problem 10-2A
Entries for payroll transactions

(LO2) (LO6)

On January 8, the end of the first weekly pay period of the year, Regis Company's payroll register showed that its employees earned $22,760 of office salaries and $65,840 of sales salaries. Withholdings from the employees' salaries include FICA Social Security taxes at the rate of 6.2%, FICA Medicare taxes at the rate of 1.45%, $12,860 of federal income taxes, $1,340 of medical insurance deductions, and $840 of union dues. No employee earned more than $7,000 in this pay period. Regis Company does not pay for its employees' medical insurance premiums or union dues.

Required

Check (1) Cr. Social Security Taxes
Payable, $5,493.20
(2) Dr. Payroll Taxes Expense,
$4,252.80

1. Calculate Regis Company's FICA Social Security taxes payable and FICA Medicare taxes payable (employer portion). Prepare the journal entry to record Regis Company's January 8 (employer) payroll expenses and liabilities.
2. Prepare the journal entry to record Regis's (employer) unemployment taxes resulting from the January 8 payroll. Regis's merit rating reduces its state unemployment tax rate to 4.0% of the first $7,000 paid each employee. The federal unemployment tax rate is 0.8%.

Francisco Company has 10 employees, each of whom earns $2,800 per month and is paid on the last day of each month. All 10 have been employed continuously at this amount since January 1. Francisco uses a payroll bank account and special payroll checks to pay its employees. On March 1, the following accounts and balances exist in its general ledger:

a. FICA—Social Security Taxes Payable, $3,472; FICA—Medicare Taxes Payable, $812. (The balances of these accounts represent total liabilities for *both* the employer's and employees' FICA taxes for the February payroll only.)

b. Employees' Federal Income Taxes Payable, $4,000 (liability for February only).

c. Federal Unemployment Taxes Payable, $448 (liability for January and February together).

d. State Unemployment Taxes Payable, $2,240 (liability for January and February together).

During March and April, the company had the following payroll transactions.

Mar. 15   Issued check payable to Swift Bank, a federal depository bank authorized to accept employers' payments of FICA taxes and employee income tax withholdings. The $8,284 check is in payment of the February FICA and employee income taxes.

31   Recorded the March payroll and transferred funds from the regular bank account to the payroll bank account. Issued checks payable to each employee in payment of the March payroll. The payroll register shows the following summary totals for the March pay period.

Salaries and Wages					
Office Salaries	Shop Wages	Gross Pay	FICA Taxes*	Federal Income Taxes	Net Pay
$11,200	$16,800	$28,000	$1,736 $ 406	$4,000	$21,858

*FICA taxes are Social Security and Medicare, respectively.

31   Recorded the employer's payroll taxes resulting from the March payroll. The company has a merit rating that reduces its state unemployment tax rate to 4.0% of the first $7,000 paid each employee. The federal rate is 0.8%.

Apr. 15   Issued check to Swift Bank in payment of the March FICA and employee income taxes.

15   Issued check to the State Tax Commission for the January, February, and March state unemployment taxes. Mailed the check and the first quarter tax return to the Commission.

30   Issued check payable to Swift Bank in payment of the employer's FUTA taxes for the first quarter of the year.

30   Mailed Form 941 to the IRS, reporting the FICA taxes and the employees' federal income tax withholdings for the first quarter.

Required

Prepare journal entries to record the transactions and events for both March and April.

Refer to Problem 10-3A. Francisco Company's tax year ends on December 31 and its Employer Identification Number is 851435867. It is located at 12 Round Rock Road, Santa Fe, New Mexico 87501.

Required

1. Prepare a Form 8109 for Francisco Company's April 15 deposit of its March FICA and employee income taxes.

2. Prepare Francisco Company's Form 941 for the first quarter.

Warner Co. pays state unemployment tax of 2.0% of each employee's first $7,000 of annual gross pay. It also pays federal unemployment tax of 0.8% of each employee's first $7,000 of annual gross pay. Warner Co.'s Employer Identification Number is 778125398, its state taxpayer identification number is 13-458232, and it is located at 605 Main Street, Dallas, Texas 75201. Warner Co. reports the following summary information in its payroll register for 2007.

Problem 10-3A
Entries for payroll transactions
(LO2) (LO3) (LO6)

Check   March 31: Cr. Accrued Payroll Payable, $21,858

March 31: Dr. Payroll Taxes Expenses, $2,814

April 15: Cr. Cash, $8,284

Problem 10-4A
Preparing deposit coupons and Form 941
(LO3) (LO4)

Problem 10-5A
Employer's payroll taxes, unemployment tax returns
(LO3) (LO6) (LO7)

Quarter Ended	Total Gross Pay	Total Gross Pay for FUTA and SUTA
March 31	$32,310.00	31,340.70
June 30	29,675.00	24,333.50
September 30	31,274.00	7,818.50
December 31	27,420.00	1,096.80

Required

1. Compute the amounts of FUTA and SUTA taxes Warner Co. owes for each quarter in 2007.

2. Prepare the general journal entry to record Warner Co.'s FUTA and SUTA taxes for the second quarter (ending on June 30) of 2007. This journal entry is made on June 30, 2007.

3. Prepare the general journal entry to record Warner Co.'s deposit of its second quarter FUTA and SUTA taxes. This journal entry is made on June 30, 2007.

4. Prepare a Form 940-EZ for Warner Co. for the year 2007.

Problem 10-6A
Workers' compensation insurance premiums
(LO8)

Precision Tool began operations on January 1, 2007. Precision Tool pays workers' compensation insurance premiums for its employees. The company's accountant assembled the data below for Precision Tool for 2007:

Classification	Estimated Wages	Rate per $100 of Wages
Office workers	$ 90,000	0.15
Machine operators	292,500	3.20
Warehouse workers	67,500	1.75

Classification	Actual Wages Situation A	Actual Wages Situation B
Office workers	$ 86,469	$ 99,834
Machine operators	281,024	294,748
Warehouse workers	64,852	80,818

Required

1. Prepare the general journal entry to record Precision Tool's payment of its estimated 2007 workers' compensation insurance premium on January 5, 2007.

2. For each of the two separate situations (A) and (B) prepare the general journal entry to adjust Precision Tool's 2007 workers' compensation insurance premium for its actual wages during 2007. Assume this entry is made on January 15, 2008.

PROBLEM SET B

Problem 10-1B
Payroll expenses, withholdings, and taxes
(LO2) (LO6)

Fishing Guides Co. pays its employees each week. Employees' gross pay is subject to these taxes.

Tax	Rate	Applied to
FICA—Social Security	6.20%	First $94,200
FICA—Medicare	1.45	All gross pay
FUTA	0.80	First $7,000
SUTA	1.75	First $7,000

The company is preparing its payroll calculations for the week ended September 30. Payroll records show the following information for the company's four employees.

		File Edit View Insert Format Tools Data Accounting Window Help		
		Gross Pay	Current Week	
	Name	through 9/23	Gross Pay	Income Tax Withholding
3	Ahmed	$92,600	$2,700	$250
4	Carlos	58,700	1,245	190
5	Jun	5,350	525	51
6	Marie	24,300	700	64

Sheet1 / Sheet2 / Sheet3

In addition to gross pay, the company must pay one-half of the $40 per employee weekly health insurance; each employee pays the remaining one-half. The company also contributes an extra 5% of each employee's gross pay (at no cost to employees) to a pension fund.

Required

Compute the following for the week ended September 30 (round amounts to the nearest cent):

1. Employer's FICA taxes for Social Security.

2. Employer's FICA taxes for Medicare.

3. Employer's FUTA taxes.

4. Employer's SUTA taxes.

5. Employer's total payroll-related expense for each employee.

Check (1) $252.34
(2) $74.96
(3) $4.20

Tavella Company's first weekly pay period of the year ends on January 8. On that date, the column totals in Tavella's payroll register indicate its sales employees earned $34,745, its office employees earned $21,225, and its delivery employees earned $1,030. The employees are to have withheld from their wages FICA Social Security taxes at the rate of 6.2%, FICA Medicare taxes at the rate of 1.45%, $8,625 of federal income taxes, $1,160 of medical insurance deductions, and $138 of union dues. No employee earned more than $7,000 in the first pay period. Tavella Company does not pay medical insurance premiums or union dues for its employees.

Required

1. Compute Tavella Company's FICA Social Security taxes payable and FICA Medicare taxes payable. Prepare the journal entry to record Tavella Company's January 8 (employer) payroll expenses and liabilities.

2. Prepare the journal entry to record Tavella's (employer) unemployment taxes resulting from the January 8 payroll. Tavella's merit rating reduces its state unemployment tax rate to 3.4% of the first $7,000 paid each employee. The federal unemployment tax rate is 0.8%.

Problem 10–2B
Entries for payroll transactions
(LO2) (LO6)

Check (1) Cr. FICA—Social Security
Taxes Payable, $3,534
(2) Dr. Payroll Taxes Expense,
$2,394

MLS Company has five employees, each of whom earns $1,600 per month and is paid on the last day of each month. All five have been employed continuously at this amount since January 1. MLS uses a payroll bank account and special payroll checks to pay its employees. On June 1, the following accounts and balances exist in its general ledger:

a. FICA—Social Security Taxes Payable, $992; FICA—Medicare Taxes Payable, $232. (The balances of these accounts represent total liabilities for *both* the employer's and employees' FICA taxes for the May payroll only.)

b. Employees' Federal Income Taxes Payable, $1,050 (liability for May only).

c. Federal Unemployment Taxes Payable, $88 (liability for April and May together).

d. State Unemployment Taxes Payable, $440 (liability for April and May together).

During June and July, the company had the following payroll transactions.

June 15 Issued check payable to Security Bank, a federal depository bank authorized to accept employers' payments of FICA taxes and employee income tax withholdings. The $2,274 check is in payment of the May FICA and employee income taxes.

30 Recorded the June payroll and transferred funds from the regular bank account to the payroll bank account. Issued checks payable to each employee in payment of the June payroll. The payroll register shows the following summary totals for the June pay period.

Problem 10–3B
Entries for payroll transactions
(LO2) (LO3) (LO6)

Check June 30: Cr. Accrued Payroll
Payable, $6,338

| Salaries and Wages | | | | Federal | |
Office Salaries	Shop Wages	Gross Pay	FICA Taxes*	Income Taxes	Net Pay
$3,800	$4,200	$8,000	$496	$1,050	$6,338
			$116		

*FICA taxes are Social Security and Medicare, respectively.

Check June 30: Dr. Payroll Taxes Expenses, $612

July 15: Cr. Cash $2,274

30   Recorded the employer's payroll taxes resulting from the June payroll. The company has a merit rating that reduces its state unemployment tax rate to 4.0% of the first $7,000 paid each employee. The federal rate is 0.8%.

July 15   Issued check payable to Security Bank in payment of the June FICA and employee income taxes.

15   Issued check to the State Tax Commission for the April, May, and June state unemployment taxes. Mailed the check and the second quarter tax return to the State Tax Commission.

31   Issued check payable to Security Bank in payment of the employer's FUTA taxes for the second quarter of the year.

31   Mailed Form 941 to the IRS, reporting the FICA taxes and the employees' federal income tax withholdings for the second quarter.

Required

Prepare journal entries to record the transactions and events for both June and July.

Problem 10-4B

Preparing deposit coupons and Form 941

(LO3) (LO4)

Refer to Problem 10-3B. MLS Company's tax year ends on December 31 and its federal Employer Identification Number is 548932154. It is located at 102 Grindstone Way, Columbus, Ohio 43085.

Required

1. Prepare a Form 8109 for MLS Company's April 15 deposit of its March FICA and employee income taxes.

2. Prepare MLS Company's Form 941 for the first quarter.

Problem 10-5B

Employer's payroll taxes, unemployment tax returns

(LO3) (LO6) (LO7)

Prestige Travel reports the following summary information in its payroll register for 2007. Prestige Travel pays state unemployment tax of 2.0% of each employee's first $7,000 of annual gross pay. Prestige Travel also pays federal unemployment tax of 0.8% of each employee's first $7,000 of annual gross pay. Prestige Travel's Employer Identification Number is 845699482. It is located at 11 Coral Lane, Miami, Florida 33101.

Quarter Ended	Total Gross Pay	Total Gross Pay for FUTA and SUTA
March 31	35,310.00	31,900.00
June 30	39,675.00	31,344.50
September 30	41,274.00	3,714.66
December 31	37,420.00	1,683.90

Required

1. Compute the amounts of FUTA and SUTA taxes Prestige Travel owes for each quarter in 2007.

2. Prepare the general journal entry to record Prestige Travel's FUTA and SUTA taxes for the third quarter (ending on September 30) of 2007. This journal entry is made on September 30, 2007.

3. Prepare the general entry to record Prestige Travel's deposit of its fourth quarter FUTA and SUTA taxes. This journal entry is made on September 30, 2007.

4. Prepare a Form 940-EZ for Prestige Travel for the year 2007.

Landmark Homes began operations on January 1, 2007. The company pays workers' compensation insurance premiums for its employees. The company's accountant assembled the data below for Landmark Homes for 2007:

Problem 10-6B
Workers' compensation insurance premiums
(LO8)

Classification	Estimated Wages	Rate per $100 of Wages
Clerical office	$ 65,000	0.21
Carpentry	175,000	5.82
Electricians	100,000	3.07

Classification	Actual Wages Situation A	Actual Wages Situation B
Clerical office	$ 66,262	$ 59,834
Carpentry	186,410	171,211
Electricians	97,312	98,247

Required

1. Prepare the general journal entry to record Landmark Homes' payment of its estimated 2007 workers' compensation insurance premium on January 5, 2007.

2. For each of the two separate situations (A) and (B) prepare the general journal entry to adjust Landmark Homes' 2007 workers' compensation insurance premium for its actual wages during 2007.

(This serial problem began in Chapter 1 and continues through most of the book. If previous chapter segments were not completed, the serial problem can begin at this point. It is helpful, but not necessary, for you to use the Working Papers that accompany the book.)

SERIAL PROBLEM

Success Systems

SP 10 Refer to the serial problem from Chapter 9. Michelle Jones' gross pay for the February 26 payroll equals $1,200.

1. Record the journal entry to reflect the employer payroll tax expenses for the February 26 payroll payment. Assume Michelle Jones has not met earnings limits for FUTA and SUTA—the FUTA rate is 0.8% and the SUTA rate is 4% for Success Systems. FICA taxes are 6.2% and 1.45% for Social Security and Medicare, respectively.

BEYOND THE NUMBERS

BTN 10-1 Refer to the financial statements of Best Buy in Appendix A to answer the following:

REPORTING IN ACTION
(LO1)

Required

1. In what income statement account(s) does Best Buy report its payroll and benefit costs?

2. Does Best Buy sponsor any retirement savings plans? (*Hint:* See footnote 8 on page A-17 of Appendix A.) If so, what dollar amounts did Best Buy contribute to these plans during 2005? What amounts did Best Buy's employees contribute to these plans in 2005?

Fast Forward

3. Access Best Buy's financial statements for fiscal years ending after February 26, 2005, at its Website (www.BestBuy.com) or the SEC's EDGAR database (www.SEC.gov). What dollar amounts did Best Buy and its employees contribute to retirement savings plans for years ending after February 26, 2005?

BTN 10-2 As ZTech's accountant you make payroll tax deposits. Recently ZTech has experienced financial distress. Your boss suggests that the company skip its upcoming quarterly tax deposit, and make the amount up at the end of the year "after business improves."

ETHICS CHALLENGE
(LO3) (LO4)

Required

1. Is your boss's suggestion ethical?

2. Is it a sound business decision?

**WORKPLACE
COMMUNICATIONS**
(LO8)

BTN 10-3   As the accountant for Prestige Home Construction you record your employer's workers' compensation costs. At a meeting discussing the year-end financial statements, your boss, Dusty Haynes, says, "We paid over $15,000 for workers' compensation insurance at the beginning of the year. We didn't file any workers' compensation claims this year, so we should get a refund this year. But you tell me we have to pay another $2,000 to our insurer. What is going on here?"

Required

Write a one-page memorandum to your boss explaining this situation.

**TAKING IT TO
THE NET**
(LO1)

BTN 10-4   Many employers are switching to payroll cards instead of issuing paper payroll checks to employees. Go to the **American Payroll Association** Website (**www.americanpayroll.org**) and select "PaycardPortal" and then select "Advantages."

Required

1. Discuss at least three cost savings an employer can expect from using payroll cards instead of paper paychecks.
2. How do payroll cards help minimize the employer's risk of paycheck fraud?
3. How do payroll cards reduce employees' chances of being harmed by identity theft?

**TEAMWORK IN
ACTION**
(LO2) (LO6) (LO8)

BTN 10-5   Form learning teams of three members each. Each team member is to become an expert on one of the types of employer payroll tax listed below:

a. FICA (Social Security and Medicare)

b. Unemployment (State and Federal)

c. Worker's Compensation

Using the following data, teams are to develop a presentation answering requirements 1 through 4.

Background

Superior Stone Company designs and installs stone walls for homes and businesses. At the beginning of the year it employed two office workers and seven stone installers. During 2007 one office worker quit and was not replaced. Due to strong demand Superior Stone's stone installers worked a lot of overtime during 2007. It reports the following data for 2007 (the state unemployment tax rate is 1%; the federal unemployment tax rate is 0.8%).

Type of Employee	Estimated 2007 Wages	Actual 2007 Wages	Workers' Compensation Rate per $100 of Wages	2007 Wages Subject to FICA, FUTA, and SUTA Estimated	2007 Wages Subject to FICA, FUTA, and SUTA Actual
Office worker	$ 77,500	$ 46,500	$0.20	$14,000	$14,000
Stone installer	232,500	263,500	2.50	49,000	49,000
Total	$310,000	$310,000		$63,000	$63,000

Required

1. Each team member computes the estimated amount of one employer payroll tax for 2007.
2. Each team member computes the actual amount of one employer payroll tax for 2007.
3. Team members share their computations and compute the total estimated and actual payroll tax amounts for 2007.
4. Team members discuss differences between estimated and actual payroll tax amounts for 2007.
   Round calculations to the nearest dollar.

BTN 10-6   Review the chapter's opening feature about Brian Scudamore and **1-800-GOT-JUNK**. Scudamore had to attend to payroll, employee benefits, and taxes, among other issues, in getting his company where it is today.

ENTREPRENEURS IN BUSINESS

(L01)

Required

Prepare a one-page memorandum that summarizes the types of employer payroll taxes and how they are reported. To the extent possible, reference the form to be filed for each tax.

ANSWERS TO MULTIPLE CHOICE QUIZ

1. e; $50,000 × (.062 + .0145) = $3,825

2. b; $7,000 × (.054 + .008) = $434

3. b; (($70,000/100) × $0.40) + (($145,000/100) × $6.00) = $8,980

4. d; ($14,000 × 0.062) + ($16,200 × 0.0145) + ($1,150 × 0.015) + ($1,150 × 0.008) = $1,129.35

5. b

A Look Back

Chapter 10 focused on employer payroll taxes and reporting. We showed how payroll taxes are computed and paid. We also showed how to account for workers' compensation programs.

A Look at This Chapter

This chapter emphasizes merchandise activities. We analyze merchandise sales transactions, sales discounts, and sales returns and allowances. We show how special journals, sales journals, and accounts receivable subsidiary ledgers help in accounting for merchandise activities.

A Look Ahead

Chapter 12 extends our coverage of merchandising activities, with emphasis on accounting for merchandise purchases and inventory.

Chapter

Merchandise Sales and Accounts Receivable

LEARNING OBJECTIVES

 LO 1 Analyze and record transactions for merchandise sales.

 LO 2 Describe how to compute and record sales discounts.

LO 3 Explain how to record sales returns and allowances.

 LO 4 Describe the use of special journals and subsidiary ledgers.

 LO 5 Journalize and post transactions using a sales journal.

 LO 6 Prepare and prove the accuracy of the accounts receivable subsidiary ledger.

LO 7 Compute the acid-test ratio and explain its use to assess liquidity.

"*Celebrate today, don't wait until tomorrow*"
—Bert and John Jacobs

The Good Life!

HUDSON, NEW HAMPSHIRE—For five years, brothers Bert and John Jacobs, owners of **Life is good** (**Lifeisgood.com**), hawked tee shirts door-to-door at college dorms up and down the east coast. They lived on peanut butter and jelly and slept in their van. After heading home from a long, less-than-fruitful road trip, they brainstormed how to keep their dreams alive. The result was "Jake," a new logo with an optimistic message. They began by printing up 48 Jake tee shirts for a street fair and all 48 tee shirts sold within hours. Once Jake was introduced to local retailers, the market embraced his positive message and the company took off.

As a wholesaler, Life is good must ensure that its distributors have the right product mix (colors, styles and sizes), with the right volume at the right price. Bert and John use accounting and inventory systems to set the sales price, monitor costs, and establish inventory levels to avoid costs of out-of-stock and excess inventory. When told by consultants that they could make $3 more on every tee shirt by skimping on quality, John countered, "We want this to be people's favorite shirt and we want it to still be their favorite shirt 10 years from now. It won't be if it's got holes and the collar's stretched out." The inventory system captures merchandising sales information to help with these and other business decisions.

Life is good's optimism is contagious as they now sell a full range of clothing for men, women and children, in addition to jewelry, bags and headwear. Despite the challenges from competition, copycats, and knock-off products, Life is good continues to look at the cup as half full. Bert and John Jacobs suggest that we "appreciate everything." They add, "Celebrate today, don't wait until tomorrow."

[Sources: *LifeisGood.com Website*, April 2007; *Inc.*, October 2006; *Wikipedia*, October 2006; *Worthwhile Magazine*, 2005]

Merchandising activities are a major part of modern business. Consumers expect a wealth of products, discount prices, and inventory on demand. This chapter introduces the business and accounting practices used by companies engaged in merchandising activities. We show how to account for merchandise sales, sales discounts, and sales returns. We also show how to use special journals and subsidiary ledgers to make the accounting more efficient.

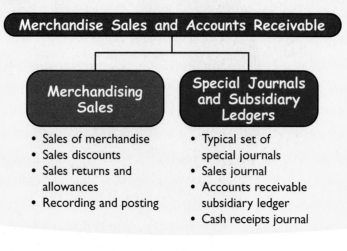

Merchandise Sales and Accounts Receivable

Merchandising Sales
- Sales of merchandise
- Sales discounts
- Sales returns and allowances
- Recording and posting

Special Journals and Subsidiary Ledgers
- Typical set of special journals
- Sales journal
- Accounts receivable subsidiary ledger
- Cash receipts journal

Merchandising Sales

LO1 Analyze and record transactions for merchandise sales.

Previous chapters emphasized the accounting and reporting activities of service companies. The company described in Chapters 2 through 6, FastForward, is an example of a service business. A merchandising company's activities differ from those of a service company. **Merchandise** consists of products, also called *goods,* that a company acquires to resell to customers. A **merchandiser** earns net income by buying and selling merchandise. Merchandisers are often identified as either wholesalers or retailers. A **wholesaler** is an *intermediary* that buys products from manufacturers or other wholesalers and sells them to retailers or other wholesalers. A **retailer** is an intermediary that buys products from manufacturers or wholesalers and sells them to consumers. Many retailers sell both products and services.

Fleming, SuperValu, and **SYSCO** are wholesalers. **Gap, Oakley,** and **Wal-Mart** are retailers.

In this chapter we show how to account for merchandise sales. In the next chapter, we will show how to account for merchandise purchases, inventory, and costs of goods sold. To illustrate, we use the transactions of Z-Mart, a merchandiser. Merchandising companies must account for sales, sales discounts, and sales returns and allowances.

Sales of Merchandise

Merchandisers can have credit sales (sales on account) and cash sales. To illustrate the accounting for credit sales, the following general journal entry records Z-Mart's $2,400 sale of merchandise on credit on November 3.

Assets = Liabilities + Equity
+2,400   +2,400

Nov.	3	Accounts Receivable	2 4 0 0 00	
		Sales		2 4 0 0 00
		Sold merchandise on credit.		

This entry reflects an increase in Z-Mart's assets in the form of an account receivable. It also shows the increase in revenue (Sales). If the sale is for cash, the debit is to Cash instead of Accounts Receivable.

IN THE NEWS

Suppliers and Demands

Merchandising companies often bombard suppliers with demands. These include discounts for bar coding and technology support systems, and fines for shipping errors. Merchandisers' goals are to reduce inventories, shorten lead times, and eliminate errors.

Sales Discounts

To encourage timely payment from its customers that buy merchandise on credit, companies often offer **sales (or cash) discounts.** Sales discounts on credit sales can benefit a seller by decreasing the delay in receiving cash and reducing future collection efforts and default.

LO2 Describe how to compute and record sales discounts.

Credit Terms   **Credit terms** for a sale include the amounts and timing of payments from a buyer to a seller. Credit terms usually reflect an industry's practices. To illustrate, when sellers require payment within 10 days after the end of the month of the invoice date, the invoice will show credit terms as "n/10 EOM," which stands for net 10 days after end of month (**EOM**). When sellers require payment within 30 days after the invoice date, the invoice shows credit terms of "n/30," which stands for *net 30 days.*

Exhibit 11.1 portrays credit terms. The amount of time allowed before full payment is due is called the **credit period.** Sellers can grant a **cash discount** to encourage buyers to pay earlier. Any cash discounts are described in the credit terms on the invoice. For example, credit terms of "2/10, n/60" mean that full payment is due within a 60-day credit period, but the buyer can deduct 2% of the invoice amount if payment is made within 10 days of the invoice date. This reduced payment applies only for the **discount period.** (Sellers sometimes charge fees if the full invoice price is not paid by the end of the credit period.)

> Since both the buyer and seller know the invoice date, this date is used in determining the discount and credit periods.

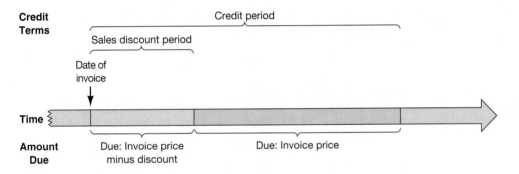

Exhibit 11.1

Credit Terms

Credit Sales Entries   At the time of a credit sale, a seller does not know whether a customer will pay within the discount period and take advantage of a purchases discount. This means the seller usually does not record a sales discount until a customer actually pays within the discount period. To illustrate, Z-Mart completes a credit sale for $1,000 on November 12 with terms of 2/10, n/60. The following entry records this sale.

Nov.	12	Accounts Receivable	1000 00	
		Sales		1000 00
		Sold merchandise under terms of 2/10, n/60.		

Assets = Liabilities + Equity
+1,000   +1,000

This entry records the receivable and the revenue as if the customer will pay the full amount. The customer has two options, however. One option is to wait 60 days until January 11 and pay the full $1,000. In this case, Z-Mart records that payment as:

Jan.	11	Cash	1000 00	
		Accounts Receivable		1000 00
		Received payment for Nov. 12 sale		

Assets = Liabilities + Equity
+1,000
−1,000

The customer's other option is to pay within the 10-day discount period ending November 22 and receive the cash discount. The cash discount is computed by multiplying the sales price by the discount percentage. In this case, the discount is $20, computed as the $1,000 sales price multiplied by 2%. If the customer pays on (or before) November 22, Z-Mart records the payment as:

Assets = Liabilities + Equity
+980   −20
−1,000

Nov.	22	Cash		9 8 0 00	
		Sales Discounts		2 0 00	
		Accounts Receivable			1 0 0 0 00
		Received payment for Nov. 12 sale less discount.			

Sales Discounts is a contra revenue account, meaning it is deducted from the Sales account when computing a company's net sales (see Exhibit 11.2). Management monitors Sales Discounts to assess the effectiveness and cost of its discount policy.

Exhibit 11.2

Net Sales Computation

Z-MART Computation of Net Sales For Year Ended December 31, 2008		
Sales		$321 0 0 0 00
Less: Sales discounts	$4 3 0 0 00	
Sales returns and allowances	2 0 0 0 00	6 3 0 0 00
Net sales		314 7 0 0 00

IN THE NEWS

Return to Sender

Book merchandisers such as **Barnes & Noble** and **Borders Books** can return unsold books to publishers at their purchase price. Publishers say returns of new hardcover books run between 35% and 50% of sales.

Sales Returns and Allowances

LO3 Explain how to record sales returns and allowances.

Sales returns refer to merchandise that customers return to the seller after a sale. Many companies allow customers to return merchandise for a full refund. *Sales allowances* refer to reductions in the selling price of merchandise sold to customers. This can occur with damaged or defective merchandise that a customer is willing to purchase with a reduction in selling price. Sales returns and allowances usually involve dissatisfied customers and the possibility of lost future sales, and managers need information about returns and allowances to monitor these problems.

Sales Returns   To illustrate, recall Z-Mart's sale of merchandise on November 3 for $2,400. Assume that the customer returns $800 of this merchandise on November 6. The journal entry for this transaction must reflect the decrease in sales and accounts receivable from the customer's return of merchandise as follows:

Assets = Liabilities + Equity
−800   −800

Nov.	6	Sales Returns and Allowances		8 0 0 00	
		Accounts Receivable			8 0 0 00
		Customer returns merchandise from Nov. 3 sale.			

Sales Returns and Allowance is also a contra revenue account, meaning it is deducted from the Sales account when computing net sales (see Exhibit 11.2). The Sales Returns and Allowances account is kept separate from the Sales account so the company can monitor the extent of sales returns and allowances.

Sales Allowances   To illustrate sales allowances, assume that $800 of the merchandise Z-Mart sold on November 3 is defective but the buyer decides to keep it because Z-Mart offers a $100 price reduction. Z-Mart records this transaction as:

Assets = Liabilities + Equity
−100   −100

Nov.	6	Sales Returns and Allowances		1 0 0 00	
		Accounts Receivable			1 0 0 00
		To record sales allowance on Nov. 3 sale.			

The seller usually prepares a credit memorandum to confirm a buyer's return or allowance. A seller's **credit memorandum** informs a buyer of the seller's credit to the buyer's Account Receivable (on the seller's books).

> The sender (maker) of a credit memorandum will *credit* the account of the receiver. The receiver of a credit memorandum will *debit* the account of the sender.

HOW YOU DOIN'?

Answers—p. 269

1. Why are sales discounts and sales returns and allowances recorded in contra revenue accounts instead of directly in the Sales account?
2. When merchandise is sold on credit and the seller notifies the buyer of a price allowance, does the seller create and send a credit memorandum or a debit memorandum?

Recording and Posting Merchandise Sales

Companies also must collect state and local government sales tax on retail sales of certain goods and services and send them to the government on a regular basis. When goods or services are sold on credit, the sales tax is recorded as sales tax payable even though the cash has not yet been collected. Sales Tax Payable is a liability account.

To illustrate the accounting (both journal entries and posting to the general ledger) for sales and sales taxes, we consider Z-Mart's following transactions during November.

Nov. 3   Sold merchandise on credit to Bradford Inc.; Sales Invoice No. 145 for $2,400 plus $144 sales tax

5   Sold merchandise on credit to Smith Inc.; Sales Invoice No. 146 for $1,050 plus $63 sales tax

8   Sold merchandise on credit to Cluff Inc.; Sales Invoice No. 147 for $250 plus $15 sales tax

11   Sold merchandise on credit to Dobson Inc.; Sales Invoice No. 148 for $550 plus $33 sales tax

The general journal entries are in Exhibit 11.3. The journal entries are then posted to the general ledger as shown in Exhibit 11.4.

GENERAL JOURNAL				Page 17	
Date	Description	PR	Debit	Credit	
Nov 3	Accounts Receivable	106	2 5 4 4 00		
	Sales Tax Payable	232		1 4 4 00	
	Sales	401		2 4 0 0 00	
	Sold merchandise on credit to Bradford Inc.; Invoice No. 145				
5	Accounts Receivable	106	1 1 1 3 00		
	Sales Tax Payable	232		6 3 00	
	Sales	401		1 0 5 0 00	
	Sold merchandise on credit to Smith Inc.; Invoice No. 146				
8	Accounts Receivable	106	2 6 5 00		
	Sales Tax Payable	232		1 5 00	
	Sales	401		2 5 0 00	
	Sold merchandise on credit to Cluff Inc.; Invoice No. 147				
11	Accounts Receivable	106	5 8 3 00		
	Sales Tax Payable	232		3 3 00	
	Sales	401		5 5 0 00	
	Sold merchandise on credit to Dobson Inc.; Invoice No. 148				

Exhibit 11.3

General Journal Entries of November Sales for Z-Mart

Assets = Liabilities + Equity
+2,544   +144   +2,400

Assets = Liabilities + Equity
+1,113   +63   +1,050

Assets = Liabilities + Equity
+265   +15   +250

Assets = Liabilities + Equity
+583   +33   +550

Exhibit 11.4

Posting of Journal Entries for
November Sales of Z-Mart

General Ledger

Accounts Receivable   **Acct. No. 106**

Date	Item	PR	Debit	Credit	Balance
Nov. 1	Balance	✓			3,152
3		G17	2,544		5,696
5		G17	1,113		6,809
8		G17	265		7,074
11		G17	583		7,657

Sales   **Acct. No. 401**

Date	Item	PR	Debit	Credit	Balance
Nov. 3		G17		2,400	2,400
5		G17		1,050	3,450
8		G17		250	3,700
11		G17		550	4,250

Sales Tax Payable   **Acct. No. 232**

Date	Item	PR	Debit	Credit	Balance
Nov. 1	Balance	✓			967
3		G17		144	1,111
5		G17		63	1,174
8		G17		15	1,189
11		G17		33	1,222

Special Journals and Subsidiary Ledgers

LO4 Describe the use of special journals and subsidiary ledgers.

Exhibit 11.3 shows that entering a journal entry each time there is a credit sale is a tedious, repetitive task. Writing descriptions of each sale and posting each transaction to the general ledger takes considerable effort. To make this process more efficient, special journals are used. While a **general journal** is an all-purpose journal where we can record any transaction, a **special journal** is used to record and post transactions of a similar type. Most transactions of a merchandiser, for instance, can be categorized into the journals shown below. Special journals are efficient tools in helping journalize and post transactions. This is done by accumulating debits and credits of similar transactions.

A specific transaction is recorded in only *one* journal.

Sales Journal	Cash Receipts Journal	Purchases Journal	Cash Disbursement Journal	General Journal
For recording credit sales	For recording cash receipts	For recording credit purchases	For recording cash payments	For transactions not in special journals

Sales Journal

A typical **sales journal** is used to record sales of inventory *on credit*. Sales of inventory for cash are not recorded in a sales journal but in a cash receipts journal. Sales of noninventory assets on credit are recorded in the general journal.

LO5 Journalize and post transactions using a sales journal.

Journalizing   Credit sale transactions are recorded with information about each sale entered separately in a sales journal. This information is often taken from a copy of the sales ticket or invoice prepared at the time of sale (as shown in Exhibit 11.5). Exhibit 11.6 shows a typical sales journal from a merchandiser. It has columns for recording the date, customer's name, invoice number, posting reference, and the amount of each credit sale. The sales journal in this exhibit is called a **columnar journal,** which is any journal with more than one column. Each transaction recorded in the sales journal yields an entry in the Accounts Receivable, Sales Tax Payable, and Sales columns. Exhibit 11.6 shows the credit sales transactions that Z-Mart experienced in November.

Exhibit 11.5

Sales Invoice

① **Z-Mart**

10 Michigan Street
Chicago, IL 60521

Sold to

| Firm Name _Bradford Inc._ ③ |
| Attention of _Tom Novak, Purchasing Agent_ |
| Address _710 Dickson Street_ |
| _Fayetteville   Arkansas   72701_ |
| City   State   Zip |

	Invoice
Date ②	Number
11/3/08	145

④   ⑤   ⑥

P.O. Date 10/30/08	Salesperson #141	Terms 2/10, n/30	Freight FOB Destination	Ship Via FedEx
Model No.	Description		Quantity Price	Amount
⑦ CH015	_Challenger X7_		1 2,400	2,400

See reverse for terms of sale and returns.

SubTotal	2,400
Shipping	—
Tax	144
⑧ Total	2,544

Key: ① Seller   ② Invoice date   ③ Purchaser   ④ Order date   ⑤ Credit terms
⑥ Freight terms   ⑦ Goods   ⑧ Total invoice amount

Exhibit 11.6

Sales Journal Example

Sales Journal   Page 3 _ □ ×

Date	Account Debited	Invoice Number	PR	Accounts Receivable Dr.	Sales Tax Payable Cr.	Sales Cr.
Nov. 3	Bradford Inc.	145		2,544	144	2,400
5	Smith Inc.	146		1,113	63	1,050
8	Cluff Inc.	147		265	15	250
11	Dobson Inc.	148		583	33	550
12	Taylor Inc.	149		1,431	81	1,350
15	Burns Inc.	150		636	36	600
17	Smith Inc.	151		1,484	84	1,400
23	Dobson Inc.	152		1,272	72	1,200
27	Taylor Inc.	153		318	18	300

Accounts Receivable Subsidiary Ledger

A **subsidiary ledger** contains detailed information on a specific account in the general ledger. Many general ledger accounts have subsidiary ledgers. The **accounts receivable ledger** stores transaction data of individual customers. (The accounts payable ledger is presented in the next chapter.) The accounts receivable ledger shows how much each customer purchased, paid, and has yet to pay. Usually, the general ledger has a single Accounts Receivable account and the accounts receivable ledger keeps a separate account for each customer.

Controlling Account and Subsidiary Ledger   Exhibit 11.7 shows the relation between the Accounts Receivable general ledger account and the individual customer accounts in the subsidiary ledger. After all items are posted, the balance in the Accounts Receivable account must equal the sum of all balances of its customers' accounts. The Accounts Receivable account is said to control the accounts receivable ledger and is called a **controlling account.** Since the accounts receivable ledger is a supplementary record controlled by an account in the general ledger, it is called a *subsidiary* ledger.

L06 Prepare and prove the accuracy of the accounts receivable subsidiary ledger.

When a general ledger account has a subsidiary ledger, any transaction that impacts one of them also impacts the other—some refer to this as *general and subsidiary ledgers kept in tandem.*

Exhibit 11.7

Accounts Receivable Controlling Account and Its Subsidiary Ledger

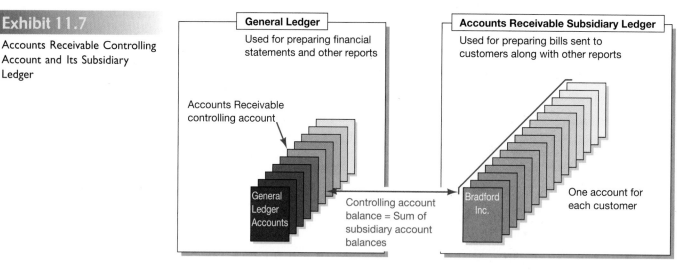

Posting

A sales journal is posted as reflected in the arrow lines of Exhibit 11.8. Two types of posting are shown: (1) posting to the subsidiary ledger(s) and (2) posting to the general ledger.

> Postings are automatic in a computerized system, which are done when an entry is made.

Posting to subsidiary ledger.   Individual transactions in the sales journal are posted regularly to customer accounts in the accounts receivable ledger. These postings keep customer accounts up-to-date, which is important for the person granting credit to customers. When sales recorded in the sales journal are individually posted to customer accounts in the accounts receivable ledger, check marks are entered in the sales journal's PR column. Check marks are used rather than account numbers because customer accounts usually are arranged alphabetically in the accounts receivable ledger. Note that posting debits to Accounts Receivable twice—once to Accounts Receivable and once to the customer's subsidiary ledger account—does not violate the accounting equation of debits equal credits. The equality of debits and credits is always maintained in the general ledger.

> PR column is only checked *after* the amount(s) is posted.

YOU CALL IT

Answer—p. 269

Entrepreneur   You want to know how promptly customers are paying their bills. This information can help you plan your cash payments and decide whether to extend credit. Where do you find this information?

Posting to general ledger.   The sales journal's account columns are totaled at the end of each period (the month of November in this case). In this example, the total accounts receivable from credit sales for the month of November of $9,646 is posted to the general ledger. The total sales tax payable for the month of $546 is also posted to the general ledger. The total sales for the month of $9,100 is posted to the general ledger. When totals are posted to accounts in the general ledger, the account numbers are entered below the column total in the sales journal for cross referencing. For example, we enter (106) below the account receivable column, (232) below the sales tax payable, and (401) below the sales column in the sales journal.

A company identifies in the PR column of its subsidiary ledgers the journal and page number from which an amount is taken. We identify a journal by using an initial. Items posted from the sales journal carry the initial *S* before their journal page numbers in a PR column.

LO6   Prepare and prove the accuracy of the accounts receivable subsidiary ledger.

Proving the Ledgers

Account balances in the general ledger and subsidiary ledgers are periodically proved (or reviewed) for accuracy after posting. To do this we first prepare a trial balance of the general ledger to confirm that debits equal credits. Second, we test a subsidiary ledger by preparing a *schedule* of individual accounts and amounts. A **schedule of accounts receivable** lists each customer and the balance owed. If this total equals the balance of the Accounts Receivable controlling account, the accounts in the accounts receivable ledger are assumed correct. Exhibit 11.9 shows a schedule of accounts receivable drawn from the accounts receivable ledger of Exhibit 11.8.

> In accounting, the word *schedule* generally means a list.

Exhibit 11.8

Sales Journal with Posting

File Edit Maintain Tasks Analysis Options Reports Window Help

Sales Journal   Page 3 □ ×

Date	Account Debited	Invoice Number	PR	Accounts Receivable Dr.	Sales Tax Payable Cr.	Sales Cr.
Nov. 3	Bradford Inc.	145	✓	2,544	144	2,400
5	Smith Inc.	146	✓	1,113	63	1,050
8	Cluff Inc.	147	✓	265	15	250
11	Dobson Inc.	148	✓	583	33	550
12	Taylor Inc.	149	✓	1,431	81	1,350
15	Burns Co.	150	✓	636	36	600
17	Smith Inc.	151	✓	1,484	84	1,400
23	Dobson Inc.	152	✓	1,272	72	1,200
27	Taylor Inc.	153	✓	318	18	300
30	Totals			9,646	546	9,100
				(106)	(232)	(401)

Totals are posted at the end of the period to General Ledger accounts.

Individual line item amounts in the Accounts Receivable column are posted immediately to the subsidiary ledger.

Accounts Receivable Ledger   □ ×

Bradford Inc.

Date	PR	Debit	Credit	Balance
Nov. 3	S3	2,544		2,544

Smith Inc.

Date	PR	Debit	Credit	Balance
Nov. 5	S3	1,113		1,113
17	S3	1,484		2,597

Cluff Inc.

Date	PR	Debit	Credit	Balance
Nov. 8	S3	265		265

Customer accounts are in a subsidiary ledger and the financial statement accounts are in the General Ledger.

Dobson Inc.

Date	PR	Debit	Credit	Balance
Nov. 11	S3	583		583
23	S3	1,272		1,855

Taylor Inc.

Date	PR	Debit	Credit	Balance
Nov. 12	S3	1,431		1,431
27	S3	318		1,749

Burns Co.

Date	PR	Debit	Credit	Balance
Nov. 15	S3	636		636

Rytting Co.

Date	PR	Debit	Credit	Balance
Nov. 1	Bal.			3,152

General Ledger   □ ×

Account: Accounts Receivable No. 106

Date	PR	Debit	Credit	Balance
Nov. 1	Bal.			3,152
30	S3	9,646		12,798

Account: Sales Tax Payable No. 232

Date	PR	Debit	Credit	Balance
Nov. 1	Bal.			967
30	S3		546	1,513

Account: Sales No. 401

Date	PR	Debit	Credit	Balance
Nov. 30	S3		9,100	9,100

Sales   Purchases   General Ledger   Payroll   Inventory   Company   Analysis

Exhibit 11.9

Schedule of Accounts Receivable

Schedule of Accounts Receivable November 30	
Bradford Inc.	$2,544
Smith Inc.	2,597
Cluff Inc.	265
Dobson Inc.	1,855
Taylor Inc.	1,749
Burns Co.	636
Rytting Co. (outstanding balance from pre-November sales)	3,152
Total accounts receivable	$12,798

Cash Receipts Journal

The **cash receipts journal** is typically used to record all receipts of cash including (1) cash from credit customers in payment of their accounts, (2) cash from cash sales, and (3) cash from other sources. Exhibit 11.10 shows a common form of the cash receipts journal. (Cash sales are usually journalized daily or at point of sale, but are journalized weekly in Exhibit 11.10 for brevity.) Column totals are posted to their respective general ledger accounts at the end of the period. Individual line item amounts in the Other Accounts column and the Accounts Receivable column are posted immediately. **Appendix 11A, available on the book's Website, shows further details of this posting process along with an illustration.**

Exhibit 11.10

Cash Receipts Journal

Cash Receipts Journal — Page 2

Date	Account Credited	Explanation	PR	Cash Dr.	Sales Discount Dr.	Accounts Receivable Cr.	Sales Cr.	Other Accounts Cr.
Feb. 7	Sales	Cash sales		4,450			4,450	
12	Jason Henry	Invoice 307, 2/2		441	9	450		
14	Sales	Cash sales		3,925			3,925	
17	Albert Co.	Invoice 308, 2/7		490	10	500		
20	Notes Payable	Note to bank		750				750
21	Sales	Cash sales		4,700			4,700	
22	Interest revenue	Bank account		250				250
23	Kam Moore	Invoice 309, 2/13		343	7	350		
25	Paul Roth	Invoice 310, 2/15		196	4	200		
28	Sales	Cash sales		4,225			4,225	
28	Totals			19,770	30	1,500	17,300	1,000

HOW YOU DOIN'?

Answers—p. 269

3. How do debits and credits remain equal when credit sales are posted twice (once to Accounts Receivable and once to the customer's subsidiary account)?

4. How do we identify the journal from which an amount in a ledger account was posted?

5. How are sales taxes recorded in the context of special journals?

ACID-TEST RATIO

LO7 Compute the acid-test ratio and explain its use to assess liquidity.

For many merchandisers, inventory makes up a large portion of current assets. Inventory must be sold and any resulting accounts receivable must be collected before cash is available. Chapter 4 explained that the current ratio, defined as current assets divided by current liabilities, is useful in assessing a company's ability to pay current liabilities. Since it is sometimes unreasonable to assume that inventories are a source of payment for current liabilities, we look to other measures.

One measure of a merchandiser's ability to pay its current liabilities (referred to as its *liquidity*) is the acid-test ratio. It differs from the current ratio by excluding less liquid current assets such as inventory and prepaid expenses that take longer to be converted to cash. The **acid-test ratio,** also called *quick* *ratio,* is defined as *quick assets* (cash, short-term investments, and current receivables) divided by current liabilities—see Exhibit 11.11.

Exhibit 11.11

Acid-Test (Quick) Ratio

$$\text{Acid-test ratio} = \frac{\text{Cash and equivalents} + \text{Short-term Investments} + \text{Current receivables}}{\text{Current liabilities}}$$

Exhibit 11.12 shows both the acid-test and current ratios of retailer **JCPenney** for fiscal years 2002 through 2005. JCPenney's acid-test ratio reveals a general increase from 2002–2005 that exceeds the average for the retailing industry. Further, JCPenney's current ratio (never less than 1.7) suggests that its short-term obligations can be confidently covered with short-term assets.

Exhibit 11.12

JCPenney's Acid-Test and Current Ratios

($ millions)	2005	2004	2003	2002
Total quick assets	$5,091	$3,227	$2,698	$3,538
Total current assets	$8,427	$6,590	$5,758	$8,677
Total current liabilities	$3,447	$3,754	$2,563	$4,499
Acid-test ratio	1.48	0.86	1.05	0.79
Current ratio	2.44	1.76	2.25	1.93
Industry acid-test ratio	0.6	0.5	0.6	0.5
Industry current ratio	2.7	2.7	2.5	2.6

An acid-test ratio less than 1.0 means that current liabilities exceed quick assets. A rule of thumb is that the acid-test ratio should have a value near or higher than 1.0 to conclude that a company is unlikely to face near-term liquidity problems. A value much less than 1.0 raises liquidity concerns unless a company can generate enough cash from inventory sales or if much of its liabilities are not due until late in the next period. Similarly, a value slightly larger than 1.0 can hide a liquidity problem if payables are due shortly and receivables are not collected until late in the next period. Analysis of JCPenney reveals a slight concern with its liquidity in 2002 and 2004, especially when benchmarked against the industry. However, in other years, JCPenney's acid-test ratios exceed the industry average.

> Successful use of a just-in-time inventory system can reduce inventory and narrow the gap between the acid-test ratio and the current ratio.

YOU CALL IT   Answer—p. 269

Supplier   A retailer requests to purchase supplies on credit from your company. You have no prior experience with this retailer. The retailer's current ratio is 2.1, its acid-test ratio is 0.5, and inventory makes up most of its current assets. Do you extend credit?

Demonstration Problem

Perry Company has the following credit sales transactions for January.

Jan. 4   Sold merchandise on credit to Hinckley Inc., Invoice No. 1123 for $2,015, plus $161 sales tax.
Jan. 7   Sold merchandise on credit to Bednar Co., Invoice No. 1124 for $1,616, plus $129 sales tax.
Jan. 9   Sold merchandise on credit to Packer Enterprises, Invoice No. 1125 for $222, plus $18 sales tax.
Jan. 13   Sold merchandise on credit to Nelson Inc., Invoice No. 1126 for $456, plus $36 sales tax.
Jan. 14   Sold merchandise on credit to Packer Enterprises, Invoice No. 1127 for $16, plus $1 sales tax.
Jan. 19   Sold merchandise on credit to Hinckley Inc., Invoice No. 1128 for $1,732, plus $139 sales tax.
Jan. 22   Sold merchandise on credit to Uchtdorf Co., Invoice No. 1129 for $1,819, plus $145 sales tax.
Jan. 27   Sold merchandise on credit to Nelson Inc., Invoice No. 1130 for $152, plus $12 sales tax.
Jan. 30   Sold merchandise on credit to Ballard Corp., Invoice No. 1131 for $157, plus $13 sales tax.

Required

1. Record these sales in a sales journal using Accounts Receivable (#106), Sales Tax Payable (#232), and Sales (#401). Assume these accounts have zero balances at the beginning of January.
2. Post these sales to the general ledger and post the references.
3. Post these sales to the accounts receivable subsidiary ledger.

Planning the Solution

- Set up the sales journal using the template from Exhibit 11.6 or Exhibit 11.8 with a debit entry column for Accounts Receivable and credit entry columns for Sales Tax Payable and Sales.
- Record each sale, with each transaction taking one line in the sales journal.
- Sum the columns in the special journal to prepare to post totals to the general ledger accounts.
- Post each transaction to the appropriate account in the Accounts Receivable subsidiary ledger.

Solution to Demonstration Problem

1.

Sales Journal						Page 1 _ □ ✕
Date	**Account Debited**	**Invoice Number**	**PR**	**Accounts Receivable Dr.**	**Sales Tax Payable Cr.**	**Sales Cr.**
Jan. 4	Hinckley Inc.	1123		2,176	161	2,015
7	Bednar Co.	1124		1,745	129	1,616
9	Packer Enterprises	1125		240	18	222
13	Nelson Inc.	1126		492	36	456
14	Packer Enterprises	1127		17	1	16
19	Hinckley Inc.	1128		1,871	139	1,732
22	Uchtdorf Co.	1129		1,964	145	1,819
27	Nelson Inc.	1130		164	12	152
30	Ballard Corp.	1131		170	13	157

2. and **3.**

File Edit Maintain Tasks Analysis Options Reports Window Help

Sales Journal						Page 1 _ □ ✕
Date	**Account Debited**	**Invoice Number**	**PR**	**Accounts Receivable Dr.**	**Sales Tax Payable Cr.**	**Sales Cr.**
Jan. 4	Hinckley Inc.	1123	✓	2,176	161	2,015
7	Bednar Co.	1124	✓	1,745	129	1,616
9	Packer Enterprises	1125	✓	240	18	222
13	Nelson Inc.	1126	✓	492	36	456
14	Packer Enterprises	1127	✓	17	1	16
19	Hinckley Inc.	1128	✓	1,871	139	1,732
22	Uchtdorf Co.	1129	✓	1,964	145	1,819
27	Nelson Inc.	1130	✓	164	12	152
30	Ballard Corp.	1131	✓	170	13	157
30	Totals			8,839	654	8,185
				(106)	(232)	(401)

Accounts Receivable Subsidiary Ledger _ □ ✕

Hinckley Inc.

Date	PR	Debit	Credit	Balance
Jan. 4	S1	2,176		2,176
19	S1	1,871		4,047

Bednar Co.

Date	PR	Debit	Credit	Balance
Jan. 7	S1	1,745		1,745

Packer Enterprises

Date	PR	Debit	Credit	Balance
Jan. 9	S1	240		240
14	S1	17		257

Nelson Inc.

Date	PR	Debit	Credit	Balance
Jan. 13	S1	492		492
27	S1	164		656

Uchtdorf Co.

Date	PR	Debit	Credit	Balance
Jan. 22	S1	1,964		1,964

Ballard Corp.

Date	PR	Debit	Credit	Balance
Jan. 30	S1	170		170

General Ledger _ □ ✕

Account: Accounts Receivable No. 106

Date	PR	Debit	Credit	Balance
Jan. 30	S1	8,839		8,839

Account: Sales Tax Payable No. 232

Date	PR	Debit	Credit	Balance
Jan. 30	S1		654	654

Account: Sales No. 401

Date	PR	Debit	Credit	Balance
Jan. 30	S1		8,185	8,185

Sales   Purchases   General Ledger   Payroll   Inventory   Company   Analysis

Summary

LO1 **Analyze and record transactions for merchandise sales.** A merchandiser records sales at the invoice price of the sale. The sale may be for cash or on credit.

LO2 **Describe how to compute and record sales discounts.** When cash discounts from the sales price are offered and customers pay within the discount period, the seller debits Sales Discounts, a contra account to Sales.

LO3 **Explain how to record sales returns and allowances.** Refunds or credits given to customers for unsatisfactory merchandise are recorded as debits to Sales Returns and Allowances, a contra account to Sales.

LO4 **Describe the use of special journals and subsidiary ledgers.** Special journals are used for recording transactions of similar type, each meant to cover one kind of transaction. Four of the most common special journals are the sales journal, cash receipts journal, purchases journal, and cash disbursements journal. Special journals are efficient and cost-effective tools in the journalizing and posting process.

LO5 **Journalize and post transactions using a sales journal.** The sales journal is an efficient means to record sales of inventory on credit. The sales journal will typically debit Accounts Receivable and credit Sales and Sales Tax Payable (if applicable).

LO6 **Prepare and prove the accuracy of the accounts receivable subsidiary ledger.** Account balances in the general ledger and the accounts receivable subsidiary ledger are tested for accuracy after posting is complete. This procedure is twofold: (1) prepare a trial balance of the general ledger to confirm that debits equal credits and (2) prepare a schedule of accounts receivable to confirm that the controlling account's balance equals the subsidiary ledger's balance.

LO7 **Compute the acid-test ratio and explain its use to assess liquidity.** The acid-test ratio is computed as quick assets (cash, short-term investments, and current receivables) divided by current liabilities. It indicates a company's ability to pay its current liabilities with its existing quick assets. An acid-test ratio equal to or greater than 1.0 is often adequate.

Guidance Answers to YOU CALL IT

Entrepreneur The accounts receivable subsidiary ledger has much of the information you need. It lists detailed information for each customer's account, including the amounts, dates for transactions, and dates of payments. It can be reorganized into an "aging schedule" to show how long customers wait before paying their bills.

Supplier A current ratio of 2.1 suggests sufficient current assets to cover current liabilities. An acid-test ratio of 0.5 suggests, however, that quick assets can cover only about one-half of current liabilities. This implies that the retailer depends on money from sales of inventory to pay current liabilities. If sales of inventory decline or profit margins decrease, the likelihood that this retailer will default on its payments increases. Your decision is probably not to extend credit. If you do extend credit, you are likely to closely monitor the retailer's financial condition. (It is better to hold unsold inventory than uncollectible receivables.)

Guidance Answers to HOW YOU DOIN'?

1. Recording sales discounts and sales returns and allowances separately from sales gives useful information to managers for internal monitoring and decision making.

2. Credit memorandum—seller credits accounts receivable from buyer.

3. The equality of debits and credits is kept within the general ledger. The subsidiary ledger keeps the customer's individual account and is used only for supplementary information.

4. An initial and the page number of the journal from which the amount was posted are entered in the PR column next to the amount.

5. A separate column for Sales Taxes Payable can be included in the sales journal.

Key Terms

mhhe.com/wildCA

Key Terms are available at the book's Website for learning and testing in an online Flashcard Format.

Accounts receivable ledger (p. 263) Subsidiary ledger listing individual customer accounts.

Acid-test ratio (p. 266) Ratio used to assess a company's ability to settle its current debts with its most liquid assets; defined as quick assets (cash, short-term investments, and current receivables) divided by current liabilities.

Cash discount (p. 259) Reduction in the price of merchandise granted by a seller to a buyer when payment is made within the discount period.

Columnar journal (p. 262) Journal with more than one column.

Controlling account (p. 263) General ledger account, the balance of which (after posting) equals the sum of the balances in its related subsidiary ledger.

Credit memorandum (p. 261) Notification that the sender has credited the recipient's account in the sender's records.

Credit period (p. 259) Time period that can pass before a customer's payment is due.

Credit terms (p. 259) Description of the amounts and timing of payments that a buyer (debtor) agrees to make in the future.

Discount period (p. 259) Time period in which a cash discount is available and the buyer can make a reduced payment.

EOM (p. 259) Abbreviation for *end of month;* used to describe credit terms for credit transactions.

General journal (p. 262) All-purpose journal for recording the debits and credits of transactions and events.

Merchandise (p. 258) Goods that a company owns and expects to sell to customers; also called *merchandise inventory.*

Merchandiser (p. 258) Entity that earns net income by buying and selling merchandise.

Retailer (p. 258) Intermediary that buys products from manufacturers or wholesalers and sells them to consumers.

Sales discount (p. 259) Term used by a seller to describe a cash discount granted to buyers who pay within the discount period.

Sales journal (p. 262) Journal normally used to record sales of goods on credit.

Schedule of accounts receivable (p. 264) List of the balances for all accounts in the accounts receivable ledger and their total.

Special journal (p. 262) Any journal used for recording and posting transactions of a similar type.

Subsidiary ledger (p. 263) List of individual sub-accounts and amounts with a common characteristic; linked to a controlling account in the general ledger.

Wholesaler (p. 258) Intermediary that buys products from manufacturers or other wholesalers and sells them to retailers or other wholesalers.

Multiple Choice Quiz   Answers on p. 276   mhhe.com/wildCA

Multiple Choice Quizzes A and B are available at the book's Website.

1. A company has cash sales of $75,000, credit sales of $320,000, sales returns and allowances of $13,700, and sales discounts of $6,000. Its net sales equal
   a. $395,000
   b. $375,300
   c. $300,300
   d. $339,700
   e. $414,700

2. The sales journal is used to record
   a. Credit sales
   b. Cash sales
   c. Cash receipts
   d. Cash purchases
   e. Credit purchases

3. The ledger that contains the financial statement accounts of a company is the
   a. General journal
   b. Column balance journal

   c. Special ledger
   d. General ledger
   e. Special journal

4. A subsidiary ledger that contains a separate account for each customer to the company is the
   a. Controlling account
   b. Accounts payable ledger
   c. Accounts receivable ledger
   d. General ledger
   e. Special journal

5. A company sells $1,000 worth of goods to a customer on July 19 with credit terms of 2/10 net 30. If the customer pays on July 28, they would pay:
   a. $1,000
   b. $1,020
   c. $983
   d. $980
   e. Cannot be determined

Discussion Questions

1. Why do companies offer cash discounts?

2. How is net sales computed?

3. What account is used to show that a company has collected sales tax but has not yet remitted it to the state or local government? Is this account an asset, a liability, or an equity account?

4. Why do businesses monitor the amount of sales returns and allowances?

5. Why would one merchandising company use a sales journal, but another merchandising company would not?

6. Why does a company maintain an accounts receivable subsidiary ledger?

7. What type of account is Sales Discounts? What is its normal balance?

8. When a company uses an accounts receivable subsidiary ledger, it must make one entry into the individual account of the subsidiary ledger and another entry into the accounts receivable account of the general ledger. If two entries are made, will the debits equal the credits in the trial balance? Why or why not?

9. Refer to the income statement for **Best Buy** in Appendix A. How does Best Buy title its net sales revenue account? Does it disclose sales returns and allowances separately?

10. Refer to the income statement for **Circuit City** in Appendix A. How does Circuit City title its net sales revenue account?

Show the general journal entries for the following sale transactions for Martindale Company from June 2009. Sales tax equals 8% of sales price.

June 2 Sold merchandise on credit to A. Fullmer, $3,300 plus tax.
    9 Sold merchandise on credit to B. Olson, $2,600 plus tax.
  13 Sold merchandise on credit to P. Bleak, $1,200 plus tax.
  27 Sold merchandise on credit to B. Taysom, $4,100 plus tax.

QS 11-1
Journalizing credit sales
(LO1)

Interpret the meaning of the following credit terms.
a. 2/10, n/60   **c.** 3/10, n/30
b. 2/EOM, n/60   **d.** 2/10, n/30

QS 11-2
Interpreting credit terms
(LO2)

Steele Manufacturing uses special journals in its accounting system. Indicate the journal that would be used for each of the following transactions. (*Hint:* Use Exhibit 11.4 as a guide)

A. Sales Journal   **C.** Cash Receipt Journal   **E.** Purchases Journal
B. Cash Disbursement Journal   **D.** General Journal

_____ **1.** Purchased merchandise for cash.
_____ **2.** Sold merchandise for cash.
_____ **3.** Purchased merchandise on credit.
_____ **4.** Gave $700 credit for returned merchandise.
_____ **5.** Sold merchandise on credit.
_____ **6.** Paid cash for merchandise previously purchased on credit.
_____ **7.** Purchased merchandise on credit.
_____ **8.** Sold merchandise for cash.

QS 11-3
Identifying special journals
(LO4)

Refer to the transactions in QS 11-1. Show how these transactions would be entered in a sales journal. (*Hint:* Use Exhibit 11.6 as a guide.)

QS 11-4
Journalizing credit sales in a sales journal
(LO5)

Compute net sales for 2007 for Snedigar Company given the following information.

Sales (Gross)	43,251
Sales Discounts	757
Sales Returns and Allowances	2,253

QS 11-5
Computing net sales
(LO1) (LO2) (LO3)

Use the following information on current assets and current liabilities to compute and interpret the acid-test ratio. Explain what the acid-test ratio of a company measures.

Cash	$1,500	Prepaid expenses	$ 700
Accounts receivable	2,800	Accounts payable	5,750
Inventory	6,000	Other current liabilities	850

QS 11-6
Computing and interpreting acid-test ratio
(LO7)

Allied Parts, a wholesaler, was organized on May 1, 2008, and made its first purchase of merchandise on May 3. The purchase was for 2,000 units at a price of $10 per unit. On May 5, Allied Parts sold 1,500 of the units for $14 per unit to Baker Co. Terms of the sale were 2/10, n/60. Ignore sales taxes. Prepare entries for Allied Parts to record the May 5 sale and each of the following separate transactions *a* through *c*.
a. On May 7, Baker returns 200 units because they did not fit its customer's needs.
b. On May 8, Baker discovers that 300 units are damaged but are still of some use and, therefore, keeps the units. Allied Parts sends Baker a credit memorandum for $600 to compensate for the damage.

Exercise 11-1
Recording sales returns and allowances
(LO3)

Check (c) Dr. Sales Returns and
Allowances $680

c. On May 15, Baker discovers that 100 units are the wrong color. Baker keeps 60 of these units because Allied sends a $120 credit memorandum to compensate. However, Baker returns the remaining 40 units to Allied.

Exercise 11-2
Sales returns and allowances
(LO3)

Business decision makers desire information on sales returns and allowances. (1) Explain why a company's manager wants the accounting system to record customers' returns of unsatisfactory goods in the Sales Returns and Allowances account instead of the Sales account. (2) Explain whether this information would be useful for external decision makers.

Exercise 11-3
Identifying the special journal of entry
(LO4)

Wilcox Electronics uses a sales journal, a purchases journal, a cash receipts journal, a cash disbursements journal, and a general journal as illustrated in Exhibit 11.4. Wilcox recently completed the following transactions *a* through *h*. Identify the journal in which each transaction should be recorded.

a. Sold merchandise on credit.
b. Purchased shop supplies on credit.
c. Paid an employee's salary in cash.
d. Borrowed cash from the bank.

e. Sold merchandise for cash.
f. Purchased merchandise on credit.
g. Purchased inventory for cash.
h. Paid cash to a creditor.

Exercise 11-4
Posting to subsidiary ledger accounts; preparing a schedule of accounts receivable
(LO4)

At the end of May, the sales journal of Mountain View appears as follows. (There are no sales taxes on Mountain View's sales.)

Sales Journal					
Date	**Account Debited**	**Invoice Number**	**PR**	**Accounts Receivable Dr.**	**Sales Cr.**
May 6	Aaron Reckers	190		3,880	3,880
10	Sara Reed	191		2,940	2,940
17	Anna Page	192		1,850	1,850
25	Sara Reed	193		1,340	1,340
31	Totals			10,010	10,010

Mountain View also recorded the return of defective merchandise with the following entry.

May	20	Sales Returns and Allowances	3 5 0 00	
		Accounts Receivable—Anna Page		3 5 0 00
		Customer returned (worthless) merchandise.		

Required

1. Open an accounts receivable subsidiary ledger that has a T-account for each customer listed in the sales journal. Post to the customer accounts the entries in the sales journal and any portion of the general journal entry that affects a customer's account. Ignore sales tax. Assume that these accounts have zero balances at the beginning of May.

2. Open a general ledger that has T-accounts for Accounts Receivable, Sales, and Sales Returns and Allowances. Assume that these accounts have zero balances at the beginning of May. Post the sales journal and any portion of the general journal entry that affects these accounts.

Check (3) Accounts Receivable, $9,660

3. Prepare a schedule of accounts receivable as of May 31 and prove that its total equals the balance in the Accounts Receivable controlling account at May 31.

Exercise 11-5
Accounts receivable ledger; posting from sales journal
(LO4)

Keeler Company had the following credit sales to its customers during June.

Date	Customer	Sales Price
June 2	Joe Mack	$ 4,600
8	Eric Horner	7,100
10	Tess Cox	14,400
14	Hong Jiang	21,500
20	Tess Cox	12,200
29	Joe Mack	8,300
	Total credit sales	$68,100

Required

1. Open an accounts receivable subsidiary ledger having a T-account for each customer. Post the invoices to the subsidiary ledger. Ignore sales tax.

2. Open an Accounts Receivable controlling T-account and a Sales T-account to reflect general ledger accounts. The Accounts Receivable controlling account has a zero balance on June 1. Post the end-of-month total from the sales journal to these accounts.

3. Prepare a schedule of accounts receivable as of June 30 and prove that its total equals the Accounts Receivable controlling account balance on June 30.

Assume the transactions in Exercise 11-5 involve cash sales instead of credit sales. Also assume that the Keeler company receives interest revenue on June 17 of $350 from the bank and receives a loan of $2,000 on June 23 from the bank. Prepare headings for a cash receipts journal like the one in Exhibit 11.10. Prepare a cash receipts journal for these cash receipts during the month of June.

Exercise 11-6
Cash receipts journal
(LO4)

Wiset Company completes the following transactions during April, its first month of operations. A tax rate of 8% applies to all sales.

PROBLEM SET A

Problem 11-1A
Sales journal and accounts receivable subsidiary ledger
(LO5) (LO6)

Apr.	3	Sold $4,000 of merchandise on credit to Page Alistair, Invoice No. 760.
	5	Sold $8,000 of merchandise on credit to Paula Kohr, Invoice No. 761.
	11	Sold $10,500 of merchandise on credit to Nic Nelson, Invoice No. 762.
	13	Sold $5,100 of merchandise on credit to Page Alistair, Invoice No. 763.
	27	Sold $3,170 of merchandise on credit to Paula Kohr, Invoice No. 764.
	27	Sold $6,700 of merchandise on credit to Nic Nelson, Invoice No. 765.

Required

1. Prepare a sales journal like that in Exhibit 11.6. Number the sales journal page as page 3. Enter the transactions in the sales journal.

2. Open the following general ledger accounts: Accounts Receivable, Sales Tax Payable, and Sales. Also open accounts receivable subsidiary ledger accounts for Paula Kohr, Page Alistair, and Nic Nelson. Post the transactions to the subsidiary ledger accounts. Prepare the month-end postings to the general ledger accounts.

Using your solution to Problem 11-1A, prove the accuracy of the accounts receivable subsidiary ledger by preparing a schedule of accounts receivable as of April 30.

Problem 11-2A
Schedule of Accounts Receivable
(LO6)

Church Company completes the following transactions during March, its first month of operations (terms for all its credit sales are 2/10, n/30).

Mar.	2	Sold merchandise on credit to Min Cho, Invoice No. 854, for $16,800 plus sales tax of $1,176.
	3	Sold merchandise on credit to Linda Witt, Invoice No. 855, for $10,200 plus sales tax of $714.
	10	Sold merchandise on credit to Jovita Albany, Invoice No. 856, for $5,600 plus sales tax of $392.
	27	Sold merchandise on credit to Jovita Albany, Invoice No. 857, for $14,910 plus sales tax of $1,044.
	28	Sold merchandise on credit to Linda Witt, Invoice No. 858, for $4,315 plus sales tax of $302.

Problem 11-3A
Sales journal, subsidiary ledger, and schedule of accounts receivable
(LO5) (LO6)
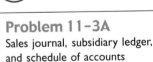
mhhe.com/wildCA

Required

1. Open the following general ledger accounts: Accounts Receivable, Sales, and Sales Tax Payable. Open the following accounts receivable subsidiary ledger accounts: Jovita Albany, Min Cho, and Linda Witt.

2. Enter the transactions in a sales journal like Exhibit 11.6. Number all journal pages as page 2.

3. Post all transactions to the accounts receivable subsidiary ledger and its month-end totals to the general ledger.

4. Prove the accuracy of the subsidiary ledger by preparing a schedule of accounts receivable as of March 31.

Check (4) Total accounts receivable, $55,453

The March sales transactions of Church Company are described in Problem 11-3A. In addition to those transactions, Church has the following nonsales transactions.

Mar.	12	Received cash payment from Min Cho for the March 2 sale less the 2% cash discount.
	13	Received cash payment from Linda Witt for the March 3 sale less the 2% cash discount.
	20	Received cash payment from Jovita Albany for the March 10 sale less the 2% cash discount.
	30	Issued a credit memorandum of $500 (plus a $35 sales tax refund) for damaged goods from the sale to Linda Witt made on March 28.

Problem 11-4A
Journal entries for cash receipts, sales discounts, and sales returns and allowances
(LO1) (LO2) (LO3)

Required

Record each cash receipt (less any cash discount) as a general journal entry. Also, record any sales return as a general journal entry.

PROBLEM SET B

Problem 11-1B

Sales journal and accounts receivable subsidiary ledger

(L05) (L06)

Acorn Industries completes the following transactions during July, its first month of operations (the terms of all its credit sales are 2/10, n/30). A tax rate of 10% applies to all sales.

July 5   Sold merchandise on credit to Kim Nettle, Invoice No. 918, for $19,200.
      6   Sold merchandise on credit to Ruth Blake, Invoice No. 919, for $7,500.
     13   Sold merchandise on credit to Ashton Moore, Invoice No. 920, for $8,550.
     14   Sold merchandise on credit to Kim Nettle, Invoice No. 921, for $5,100.
     29   Sold merchandise on credit to Ruth Blake, Invoice No. 922, for $17,500.
     30   Sold merchandise on credit to Ashton Moore, Invoice No. 923, for $16,820.

Required

1. Prepare a sales journal like that in Exhibit 11.6. Number the sales journal as page 3.
2. Open the following general ledger accounts: Accounts Receivable, Sales Tax Payable, and Sales. Also open accounts receivable subsidiary ledger accounts for Kim Nettle, Ashton Moore, and Ruth Blake. Post the transactions to the subsidiary ledger accounts. Prepare the month-end postings to the general ledger accounts.

Problem 11-2B

Schedule of Accounts Receivable

(L06)

Using your solution to 11-1B, prove the accuracy of the accounts receivable subsidiary ledger by preparing a schedule of accounts receivable as of July 31.

Problem 11-3B

Sales journal, subsidiary ledger, and schedule of accounts receivable

(L05) (L06)

Grassley Company completes the following transactions during November, its first month of operations (terms for all its credit sales are 2/10, n/30).

Nov. 8   Sold merchandise on credit to Cyd Rounder, Invoice No. 439, for $6,550 plus sales tax of $524.
     10   Sold merchandise on credit to Carlos Mantel, Invoice No. 440, for $13,500 plus sales tax of $1,080.
     15   Sold merchandise on credit to Tori Tripp, Invoice No. 441, for $5,250 plus sales tax of $420.
     22   Sold merchandise on credit to Carlos Mantel, Invoice No. 442, for $3,695 plus sales tax of $296.
     24   Sold merchandise on credit to Tori Tripp, Invoice No. 443, for $4,280 plus sales tax of $342.

Required

1. Open the following general ledger accounts: Accounts Receivable, Sales, and Sales Tax Payable. Open the following accounts receivable subsidiary ledger accounts: Carlos Mantel, Tori Tripp, and Cyd Rounder.
2. Enter the transactions in a sales journal like that in Exhibit 11.6. Number the journal page as page 2.
3. Post all transactions to the accounts receivable subsidiary ledger and its month-end totals to the general ledger.

Check   (4) Total accounts receivable, $35,937

4. Prove the accuracy of the subsidiary ledger by preparing a schedule of accounts receivable as of November 30.

Problem 11-4B

Journal entries for sales discounts and sales returns and allowances

(L01) (L02) (L03)

The November sales transactions of Grassley Company are described in Problem 11-3B. In addition to those transactions, Grassley has the following nonsales transactions.

Nov. 18   Received cash payment from Cyd Rounder for the November 8 sale less the 2% cash discount.
     19   Received cash payment from Carlos Mantel for the November 10 sale less the 2% cash discount.

25 Received cash payment from Tori Tripp for the November 15 sale less the 2% cash discount.
29 Issued a credit memorandum of $675 (plus a $54 sales tax refund) for damaged goods from
the sale to Carlos Mantel made on November 22.

Required

Record each cash receipt (less any cash discount) as a general journal entry. Also, record any sales return
as a general journal entry.

BEYOND THE NUMBERS

BTN 11-1 Refer to **Best Buy**'s financial statements in Appendix A to answer the following.

Required

1. Identify and total the quick assets (cash, short-term investments, and current receivables) as of February
26, 2005, and February 28, 2004, for Best Buy. Compute the percentage of quick assets relative to both
current assets and total assets.

2. Compute the current ratio and acid-test ratio as of February 26, 2005, and February 28, 2004. Interpret
and comment on the ratio results. How does Best Buy compare to the industry average of 1.6 for the
current ratio and 0.7 for the acid-test ratio?

Fast Forward

3. Access Best Buy's financial statements (form 10-K) for fiscal years ending after February 26, 2005,
from its Website (BestBuy.com) or the SEC's EDGAR database (www.sec.gov). Recompute and interpret the current ratio and acid-test ratio for these current fiscal years.

REPORTING IN
ACTION

(L07)

BTN 11-2 Key comparative figures ($ millions) for both **Best Buy** and **Circuit City** follow.

Key Figures	Best Buy		Circuit City	
	Current Year	Prior Year	Current Year	Prior Year
Quick assets	$4,238	$3,723	$1,056	$1,178
Current liabilities	6,056	4,959	1,622	1,263

COMPARATIVE
ANALYSIS

(L07)

Required

1. Compute the acid-test ratio for the two years shown for both companies.

2. Drawing on results from part 1, which company is better able to pay its current liabilities?

3. Did the acid-test ratio improve or decline for each of these companies?

BTN 11-3 Amy Martin is a student who plans to attend approximately four professional events a year
at her college. Each event necessitates a financial outlay of $100–$200 for a new suit and accessories.
After incurring a major hit to her savings for the first event, Amy developed a different approach. She
buys the suit on credit the week before the event, wears it to the event, and returns it the next week to
the store for a full refund on her charge card.

ETHICS CHALLENGE

(L01) (L03)

Required

1. Comment on the ethics exhibited by Amy and possible consequences of her actions.

2. How does the merchandising company account for the suits that Amy returns?

3. How can an accounts receivable subsidiary ledger alert the store's manager to Amy's behavior?

WORKPLACE COMMUNICATION

(LO4) (LO5) (LO6)

BTN 11–4   Your friend, Wendy Geiger, owns a small retail store that sells candies and nuts. Geiger acquires her goods from a few select vendors. She generally makes purchase orders by phone and on credit. Sales are primarily for cash. Geiger keeps her own manual accounting system using a general journal and a general ledger. At the end of each business day, she records one summary entry for cash sales. Geiger recently began offering items in creative gift packages. This has increased sales substantially, and she is now receiving orders from corporate and other clients who order large quantities and prefer to buy on credit. As a result of increased credit transactions in both purchases and sales, keeping the accounting records has become extremely time consuming. Geiger wants to continue to maintain her own manual system and calls you for advice. Write a memo to her advising how she might modify her current manual accounting system to accommodate the expanded business activities. Geiger is accustomed to checking her ledger by using a trial balance. Your memo should explain the advantages of what you propose and of any other verification techniques you recommend.

TAKING IT TO THE NET

(LO7)

BTN 11–5   Access the SEC's EDGAR database (www.sec.gov) and obtain the April 25, 2006, filing of its fiscal 2005 10-K report (for year ended January 28, 2006) for **J. Crew Group, Inc.**

Required

Prepare a table that reports the acid-test ratios for J. Crew using the quick assets and current liabilities data from J. Crew's balance sheet for 2005 and 2006. Analyze and comment on any trend in its acid-test ratio.

TEAMWORK IN ACTION

(LO1) (LO5)

BTN 11–6   William Fuerst Company completes the following transactions during July of the current year. A tax rate of 8% applies to all sales.

July	3	Sold $6,000 of merchandise on credit to Susan Scholz, Invoice No. 1060.
	7	Sold $4,500 of merchandise on credit to Mike Ettredge, Invoice No. 1061.
	9	Sold $7,700 of merchandise on credit to Mark Hirschey, Invoice No. 1062.
	13	Sold $1,600 of merchandise on credit to Susan Scholz, Invoice No. 1063.
	24	Sold $5,300 of merchandise on credit to Gilbert Karuga, Invoice No. 1064.
	29	Sold $7,100 of merchandise on credit to Mark Hirschey, Invoice No. 1065.

Required

Divide your team into two groups. Have one group prepare the general journal entries for each sale. Have the other group prepare a sales journal like that in Exhibit 11.6. Compare and contrast the advantages and disadvantages of each approach.

ENTREPRENEURS IN BUSINESS

(LO4)

BTN 11–7   Refer to the opening feature about Bert and John Jacobs and their **Life is good** company.

Required

1. Identify the special journals that Life is good would likely use in its operations.

2. Identify any subsidiary ledgers that Life is good would likely use.

ANSWERS TO MULTIPLE CHOICE QUIZ

1. b; Net sales = $75,000 + $320,000 − $13,700 − $6,000 = $375,300

2. a

3. d

4. c

5. d; $1,000 less $20 (.02 × $1,000) discount

A Look Back

Chapter 11 emphasized merchandise sales transactions, sales discounts, and sales returns and allowances. We also explained the use of a sales journal and an accounts receivable subsidiary ledger.

A Look at This Chapter

Chapter 12 extends our coverage of merchandising activities, with emphasis on accounting for merchandise purchases and accounts payable.

A Look Ahead

Chapter 13 provides a summary of accrual accounting. We emphasize the matching of expenses with the revenues generated.

Chapter 12

Merchandise Purchases and Accounts Payable

LEARNING OBJECTIVES

 Describe merchandising activities and identify income components for a merchandising company.

 Identify and explain the inventory asset of a merchandising company.

 Analyze and record transactions for merchandise purchases.

Journalize and post transactions using a purchases journal.

 Prepare and prove the accuracy of an accounts payable subsidiary ledger.

 Compute the gross margin ratio and explain its use to assess profitability.

"We're selling a feeling to the consumer"
—Renee Pepys Lowe

CoCaLo Creates Sweet Dreams

COSTA MESA, CA—"I always had my mother to lean on," admits Renee Pepys Lowe. But when her mother decided to sell her small business in which Renee worked, Renee lost her job. "That was a big change," recalls Renee. "I did a lot of soul-searching."

Renee rebounded by starting an infant bedding and nursery accessories company, CoCaLo (**CoCaLo.com**)—named after her daughters, Courtenay and Catherine Lowe. Renee envisioned a company with fashionable, high-quality products at affordable prices. Fortunately, she says her designers have "a remarkable talent for seeing what fabrics, colors, and textures can look like in combination."

Although CoCaLo is now profiting in the infant bedding industry, the early days were not easy. "You really have to take a lot of risks," says Renee. "It's all about allowing everyone to have a bedding collection with style, without having to spend a thousand dollars to get it." Adds Renee, "The scariest part for me is that I'm responsible for . . . finances, loans [and all aspects of accounting]."

To succeed, Renee needed to make smart business decisions. She set up an accounting system to capture and communicate costs and sales information. Effectively tracking merchandising activities is needed to set prices and create policies for discounts and allowances, returns on sales, and purchases. An inventory system enabled CoCaLo to stock the right type and amount of merchandise and to avoid the costs of out-of-stock and excess inventory.

Mastering accounting for merchandising is a means to an end for Renee. "I love this business," she says. "There's something about giving new parents the tools to create a room they can feel proud of." Judging by CoCaLo's sales, there are plenty of proud parents out there.

[Sources: *CoCaLo Website*, January 2007; *Entrepreneur*, November 2003; *Kids Today*, July 2004]

Merchandising companies purchase inventory to resell to their customers. This chapter introduces the accounting for inventory purchases by merchandising companies and the use of the purchases journal and an accounts payable subsidiary ledger to further enhance this process. This chapter also explains the computation of cost of goods sold and gross profit.

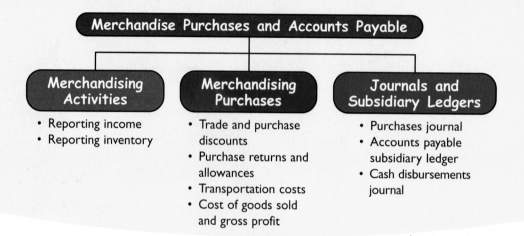

Merchandise Purchases and Accounts Payable

Merchandising Activities
- Reporting income
- Reporting inventory

Merchandising Purchases
- Trade and purchase discounts
- Purchase returns and allowances
- Transportation costs
- Cost of goods sold and gross profit

Journals and Subsidiary Ledgers
- Purchases journal
- Accounts payable subsidiary ledger
- Cash disbursements journal

Merchandising Activities

Reporting Income for a Merchandiser

LO1 Describe merchandising activities and identify income components for a merchandising company.

A **merchandiser** buys and sells products. Net income to a merchandiser equals revenues from selling merchandise minus both the cost of merchandise sold to customers and the cost of other expenses for the period (see Exhibit 12.1). The usual accounting term for revenues from selling merchandise is *sales,* and the term used for the expense of buying and preparing that merchandise is **cost of goods sold** (also called *cost of sales*). Cost of goods sold is often the largest single expense on a merchandiser's income statement. (Many service companies use the term *sales* instead of revenues.)

Exhibit 12.1

Computing Income for a Merchandising Company versus a Service Company

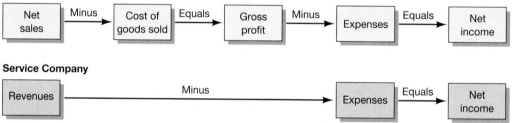

Merchandiser

Net sales → Minus → Cost of goods sold → Equals → Gross profit → Minus → Expenses → Equals → Net income

Service Company

Revenues → Minus → Expenses → Equals → Net income

Analysis of gross profit is important to effective business decisions, and is described later in the chapter.

The income statement for Z-Mart in Exhibit 12.2 illustrates these key components of a merchandiser's net income. The first two lines show that products are acquired at a cost of $230,400 and sold for $314,700. The third line shows an $84,300 **gross profit,** also called **gross margin.** This equals net sales less cost of goods sold. Other expenses of $71,400 are reported, which leaves $12,900 in net income.

Exhibit 12.2

Merchandiser's Income Statement

Z-MART Income Statement For Year Ended December 31, 2008	
Net sales	$314 7 0 0 00
Cost of goods sold	230 4 0 0 00
Gross profit	84 3 0 0 00
Expenses	71 4 0 0 00
Net income	$ 12 9 0 0 00

Reporting Inventory for a Merchandiser

A merchandiser's balance sheet includes a current asset called *merchandise inventory*. This item is not on a service company's balance sheet. **Merchandise inventory,** or simply **inventory,** refers to products that a company owns and intends to sell. The cost of this asset includes the cost incurred to buy the goods, ship them to the store, and make them ready for sale.

Exhibit 12.3 shows that a company's *merchandise available for sale* consists of what it begins with (beginning inventory) and what it purchases (net cost of purchases). The merchandise available is either sold (cost of goods sold) or kept for future sales (ending inventory).

 Identify and explain the inventory asset of a merchandising company.

Exhibit 12.3

Merchandiser's Cost Flow for a Single Time Period

Answers—p. 294

HOW YOU DOIN'?

1. Describe a merchandiser's cost of goods sold.
2. What is gross profit for a merchandising company?
3. A merchandiser had $20,000 of beginning inventory. Its net purchases cost $115,000. If it has $17,000 of ending inventory, compute (*a*) merchandise available for sale and (*b*) cost of goods sold.

Accounting for Merchandise Purchases

Merchandising companies must account for purchases, trade and purchase discounts, and purchase returns and allowances.

Purchasing Procedures

Most merchandisers need inventory in their stores or warehouses to sell to customers. For a large firm, a central purchasing department will locate potential suppliers and negotiate prices and credit terms and ultimately place orders for inventory. In a small retail store, the owner or manager of the store will perform all of these purchasing tasks.

When a department needs products to sell, the department (or sales) manager will prepare and sign a **purchase requisition** listing the merchandise needed (see Exhibit 12.4) and send it to the purchasing department.

LO3 Analyze and record transactions for merchandise purchases.

Exhibit 12.4

Purchase Requisition

Purchase Requisition		No. 917
Z-Mart		

From Sporting Goods Department **Date** October 28, 2008
To Purchasing Department **Preferred Vendor** Trex

Request purchase of the following item(s):

Model No.	Description	Quantity
CH 015	Challenger X7	1
SD 099	SpeedDemon	1

Reason for Request Replenish inventory
Approval for Request *T.Z.*

For Purchasing Department use only: Order Date 10/30/08 P.O. No. P98

The purchasing department then selects a **vendor** (also called a supplier) that can supply the goods, and places a **purchase order.** A purchase order authorizes a vendor to ship ordered merchandise at the stated price and credit terms (see Exhibit 12.5). Someone with authority to approve purchases signs the purchase order (sometimes abbreviated as P.O.) and sends it to the vendor.

Exhibit 12.5

Purchase Order

Purchase Order	No. P98

Z-Mart
10 Michigan Street
Chicago, Illinois 60521

To: Trex
W9797 Cherry Road
Antigo, Wisconsin 54409

Date 10/30/08
FOB Destination
Ship by As soon as possible
Terms 2/15, n/30

Request shipment of the following item(s):

Model No.	Description	Quantity	Price	Amount
CH 015	Challenger X7	1	490	490
SD 099	SpeedDemon	1	710	710

All shipments and invoices must include purchase order number

Ordered by

T. N.

Upon receipt of the purchase order, the vendor ships the ordered merchandise to the buyer. Many companies maintain a separate department to receive all merchandise and purchased assets. When each shipment arrives, a receiving department employee counts the goods and checks them for damage and agreement with the purchase order. This person then prepares a **receiving report,** which is used within the company to notify the appropriate persons that ordered goods have been received and to describe the quantities and condition of the goods.

The seller sends an invoice when the ordered merchandise is shipped. The **invoice** is an itemized statement of goods sent by the vendor listing the customer's name, items sold, sales prices, and terms of sale. As shown in Exhibit 12.6, an invoice is also a bill sent to the buyer from the vendor. From the vendor's point of view, it is a *sales invoice*. The buyer treats it as a *purchase invoice*.

Accounting for Purchases and Freight Charges

Shortly before the invoice (or bill) is due, the accounting department will make payment. Under the periodic system of inventory accounting, the cost of merchandise purchased for resale is recorded in the Purchases account. The Purchases account is a temporary account that is closed to Cost of Goods Sold at the end of the accounting period. The normal balance for the Purchases account is a debit.

The cost of shipping the goods from the vendor to the buyer is called **Transportation-In.** This freight charge is accounted for separately from the purchases account as a debit. To illustrate, Z-Mart purchases $1,200 of merchandise on credit and incurs $96 of freight charges. The journal entry to record this credit purchase is:

Assets = Liabilities + Equity
+1,296   −1,200
−96

Nov.	2	Purchases		1 2 0 0 00	
		Transportation-In		9 6 00	
		Accounts Payable			1 2 9 6 00

Trade Discounts

When a manufacturer or wholesaler prepares a catalog of items it has for sale, it usually gives each item a **list price,** also called a *catalog price*. However, an item's intended *selling price*

Exhibit 12.6

Invoice

	TREX				
①	W9797 Cherry Rd. Antigo, WI 54409				

Sold to

Firm Name *Z-Mart* ③
Attention of *Tom Novak,* Purchasing Agent
Address   *10 Michigan Street*
Chicago   *Illinois*   *60521*
City   State   Zip

Invoice	
Date	Number
11/2/08 ②	4657-2

④	⑤		⑥		
P.O. Date 10/30/08	Salesperson #141	Terms 2/10, n/30	Freight FOB Destination		Ship Via FedEx
Model No.	Description		Quantity	Price	Amount
⑦ CH015	*Challenger X7*		1	490	490
SD099	*Speed Demon*		1	710	710

See reverse for terms of sale and returns.

	SubTotal	1,200
	Shipping	—
	Tax	—
⑧	Total	1,200

Key: ① Seller ② Invoice date ③ Purchaser ④ Order date ⑤ Credit terms
    ⑥ Freight terms ⑦ Goods ⑧ Total invoice amount

equals list price minus a given percent called a **trade discount.** The amount of trade discount usually depends on whether a buyer is a wholesaler, retailer, or final consumer. A wholesaler buying in large quantities is often granted a larger discount than a retailer buying in smaller quantities. A buyer records the net amount of list price minus trade discount. For example, in the November 2 purchase of merchandise by Z-Mart, the merchandise was listed in the seller's catalog at $2,000 and Z-Mart received a 40% trade discount. This meant that Z-Mart's purchase price was $1,200, computed as $2,000 − (40% × $2,000).

Purchase Discounts

A buyer can receive a **purchase discount** if timely payment is made. Any purchase (cash) discount is described in the **credit terms** on the invoice. Exhibit 12.7 portrays the credit

Since both the buyer and seller know the invoice date, this date is used in determining the discount and credit periods.

Exhibit 12.7

Credit Terms

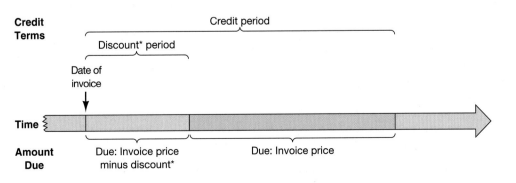

*Discount refers to a purchase discount for a buyer and a sales discount for a seller.

terms. Recall from Chapter 11, credit terms of "2/10, n/30" mean that full payment is due within a 30-day **credit period,** but the buyer can deduct 2% of the invoice amount if payment is made within 10 days of the invoice date. This reduced payment applies only in the **discount period.**

Purchase discounts are recorded in a contra-purchases account that normally carries a credit balance. The entry to record the merchandise purchase under a periodic inventory system is

Assets = Liabilities + Equity
     +1,200   −1,200

Nov.	2	Purchases	1 2 0 0 00	
		Accounts Payable		1 2 0 0 00
		Purchased merchandise on credit, invoice		
		dated Nov. 2, terms 2/10, n/30.		

If Z-Mart pays the amount due on (or before) November 12, the entry is

Assets = Liabilities + Equity
−1,176   −1,200   +24

Nov.	12	Accounts Payable	1 2 0 0 00	
		Purchase Discounts		2 4 00
		Cash		1 1 7 6 00
		Paid for the $1,200 purchase of Nov. 2 less the		
		discount of $24 (2% × $1,200).		

> These entries illustrate what is called the *gross method* of accounting for purchases with discount terms.

After these entries are posted, the net cost of merchandise purchased is reflected in Purchases minus Purchase Discounts. The Accounts Payable account shows a zero balance. The ledger accounts, in T-account form, follow:

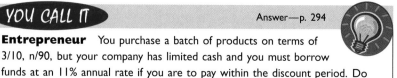

Purchases		
Nov. 2	1,200	
Balance	1,200	

Accounts Payable			
Nov. 12	1,200	Nov. 2	1,200
		Balance	0

Purchase Discounts		
	Nov. 12	24
	Balance	24

YOU CALL IT   Answer—p. 294

Entrepreneur   You purchase a batch of products on terms of 3/10, n/90, but your company has limited cash and you must borrow funds at an 11% annual rate if you are to pay within the discount period. Do you take advantage of the purchase discount?

A buyer's failure to pay within a discount period can be expensive. To illustrate, if Z-Mart does not pay within the 10-day 2% discount period, it can delay payment by 20 more days. This delay costs Z-Mart $24, computed as 2% × $1,200. Most buyers take advantage of a purchase discount because of the usually high interest rate implied from not taking it.[1] Also, good cash management means that no invoice is paid until the last day of the discount or credit period.

---

[1] The *implied annual interest rate* formula is:

$$(365 \text{ days} \div [\text{Credit period} - \text{Discount period}]) \times \text{Cash discount rate.}$$

For terms of 2/10, n/30, missing the 2% discount for an additional 20 days is equal to an annual interest rate of 36.5%, computed as (365 days/[30 days − 10 days]) × 2% discount rate. *Favorable purchase discounts* are those with implied annual interest rates that exceed the purchaser's annual rate for borrowing money.

Purchase Returns and Allowances

Purchase returns refer to merchandise a buyer acquires but then returns to the seller. A *purchase allowance* is a reduction in the cost of defective or unacceptable merchandise that a buyer acquires. Buyers often keep defective but still marketable merchandise if the seller grants an acceptable allowance.

When a buyer returns or takes an allowance on merchandise, the buyer issues a **debit memorandum** to inform the seller of a debit made to the seller's account in the buyer's records. To illustrate, on November 15 Z-Mart (buyer) issues a $300 debit memorandum for an allowance from Trex for defective merchandise. Z-Mart's November 15 entry to record the purchase allowance is

> The sender (maker) of a *debit memorandum* will debit the account of the memo's receiver. The memo's receiver will credit the account of the sender.

Nov.	15	Accounts Payable	3 0 0 00	
		Purchase Returns and Allowances		3 0 0 00
		Allowance for defective merchandise.		

Assets = Liabilities + Equity
−300   +300

If this had been a return, then the total *recorded cost* (all costs less any discounts) of the defective merchandise would be entered. The buyer's cost of returned and defective merchandise is usually offset against the buyer's current account payable balance to the seller. When cash is refunded, the Cash account is debited instead of Accounts Payable.

YOU CALL IT

Answer—p. 294

Credit Manager As the new credit manager, you are being trained by the outgoing manager. She explains that the system prepares checks for amounts net of favorable cash discounts, and the checks are dated the last day of the discount period. She also tells you that checks are not mailed until five days later, adding that "the company gets free use of cash for an extra five days, and our department looks better. When a supplier complains, we blame the computer system and the mailroom." Do you continue this payment policy?

Transportation Costs and Ownership Transfer

The buyer and seller must agree on who is responsible for paying any freight costs and who bears the risk of loss during transit for merchandising transactions. This determines the point when ownership transfers from the seller to the buyer. The point of transfer is called the **FOB** (*free on board*) point, which determines who pays transportation costs (and often other incidental costs of transit such as insurance).

Exhibit 12.8 identifies two alternative points of transfer. (1) *FOB shipping point,* also called *FOB factory,* means the buyer accepts ownership when the goods leave the seller's place of

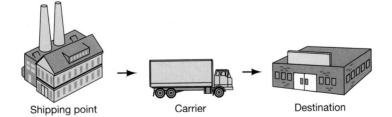

Shipping point — Carrier — Destination

	Ownership Transfers When Goods Passed to	Transportation Costs Paid by
FOB shipping point	Carrier	Buyer
FOB destination	Buyer	Seller

Exhibit 12.8

Ownership Transfer and Transportation Costs

business. The buyer is then responsible for paying shipping costs and bearing the risk of damage or loss when goods are in transit. The goods are part of the buyer's inventory when they are in transit since ownership has transferred to the buyer. **Cannondale**, a major bike manufacturer, uses FOB shipping point. (2) *FOB destination* means ownership of goods transfers to the buyer when the goods arrive at the buyer's place of business. The seller is responsible for paying shipping charges and bears the risk of damage or loss in transit. The seller does not record revenue from this sale until the goods arrive at the destination because this transaction is not complete before that point. The buyer does not record the purchase until the goods arrive at the buyer's place of business.

Z-Mart's $1,200 purchase on November 2 is on terms of FOB destination. This means Z-Mart does not pay transportation costs. When a buyer is responsible for paying transportation costs, the payment is made to a carrier or directly to the seller depending on the agreement. The cost principle requires that any necessary transportation costs of a buyer (often called *transportation-in* or *freight-in*) be included as part of the cost of purchased merchandise. To illustrate, Z-Mart's entry to record a $75 freight charge from an independent carrier for merchandise purchased FOB shipping point is

Assets = Liabilities + Equity
−75   −75

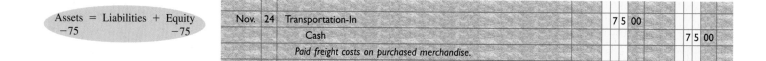

Nov.	24	Transportation-In	7 5 00	
		Cash		7 5 00
		Paid freight costs on purchased merchandise.		

A seller records the costs of shipping goods to customers in a Delivery Expense account when the seller is responsible for these costs. Delivery Expense, also called *transportation-out* or *freight-out,* is reported as a selling expense in the seller's income statement.

In sum, purchases are recorded as debits to the Purchases account. Any purchase discounts or returns and allowances are credited to the Purchase Discounts and Purchases Returns and Allowances accounts, respectively. Freight charges are debited to Transportation-In. These items are used to compute **net purchases.** Z-mart's itemized cost of net merchandise purchases for year 2008 are shown in Exhibit 12.9.

Exhibit 12.9

Itemized Costs of Net Merchandise Purchases

Z-MART	
Itemized Costs of Net Merchandise Purchases	
For Year Ended December 31, 2008	
Purchases	$235 8 0 0 00
Less: Purchase discounts	(4 2 0 0 00)
Purchase returns and allowances	(1 5 0 0 00)
Add: Transportation-In	2 3 0 0 00
Net purchases	$232 4 0 0 00

Computing Cost of Goods Sold and Gross Profit

Before we can determine net income for a merchandising business, we must compute cost of goods sold and gross profit (gross margin). We illustrate these computations by examining Z-Mart's merchandise sales and purchases from Chapters 11 and 12. Beginning inventory is $68,000, and ending inventory is $70,000.

There are three steps for computing gross profit.

1. Compute *net sales* (from Chapter 11, Exhibit 11.2).

Net sales = Sales − Sales discounts − Sales returns and allowances

Sales		$ 321,000
Less: Sales discounts	$4,300	
Sales returns and allowances	2,000	6,300
Net sales		**$314,700**

2. Compute *cost of goods available for sale* and *cost of goods sold.*

Cost of goods available for sale = Beginning inventory + Net purchases (from Exhibit 12.9)

Cost of goods sold = Cost of goods available for sale − Ending inventory

Purchases		$235,800	
Less: Purchase discounts	$4,200		
Purchase returns and allowances	1,500	5,700	
Add: Cost of transportation-in		2,300	
Net purchases			$ 232,400
Add: Beginning inventory			68,000
Cost of goods available for sale			300,400
Less: Ending inventory			70,000
Cost of goods sold			**$230,400**

3. Compute *gross profit.*

Gross profit = Net sales − Cost of goods sold

Net sales	$314,700
Less: Cost of goods sold	230,400
Gross profit	**$ 84,300**

Answers—p. 294

HOW YOU DOIN'?

4. How long are the credit and discount periods when credit terms are 2/10, n/60?

5. Identify which items are subtracted from the *list* amount and not recorded when computing purchase price: (*a*) transportation-in; (*b*) trade discount; (*c*) purchase discount; (*d*) purchase return.

6. What does *FOB* mean? What does *FOB destination* mean?

Purchases Journal and Accounts Payable Subsidiary Ledger

Exhibit 12.10 illustrates the accounting for several February merchandise purchases on credit by Z-Mart. The journal entries are entered in the general journal and then posted to the general ledger. As you can see from Exhibit 12.10, entering a journal entry each time there is a credit purchase is a tedious, repetitive task. Writing descriptions of each purchase and posting each transaction to the general ledger represent significant effort. To make this process more efficient, a purchases journal is used.

Exhibit 12.10

General Journal Entries and
Posting of February Purchases
for Z-Mart

GENERAL JOURNAL   Page 1

Date		Description	PR	Debit	Credit
Feb.	3	Purchases	502	325 00	
		Transportation-In	503	25 00	
		Accounts Payable	207		350 00
		Purchased Merchandise from Horning Supply Co.,			
		Invoice 337, terms n/30			
	5	Purchases	502	177 00	
		Transportation-In	503	23 00	
		Accounts Payable	207		200 00
		Purchased Merchandise from Ace Mfg Co.,			
		Invoice 4242, terms 2/10, n/30			
	13	Purchases	502	135 00	
		Transportation-In	503	15 00	
		Accounts Payable	207		150 00
		Purchased Merchandise from Wynet & Co.,			
		Invoice 667, terms 2/10, n/30			
	20	Purchases	502	283 00	
		Transportation-In	503	17 00	
		Accounts Payable	207		300 00
		Purchased Merchandise from Smite Co.,			
		Invoice 2333, terms 2/10, n/30			
	25	Purchases	502	92 00	
		Transportation-In	503	8 00	
		Accounts Payable	207		100 00
		Purchased Merchandise from Ace Mfg. Co.,			
		Invoice 4295, terms 2/10, n/30			
	28	Purchases	502	207 00	
		Transportation-In	503	18 00	
		Accounts Payable	207		225 00
		Purchased Merchandise from ITT Co.,			
		Invoice 3367, terms n/30			

Account

Accounts Payable   Account No. 207

Date		Item	PR	Debit	Credit	Balance
Feb.	1	Balance				0
	3		G1		350	350
	5		G1		200	550
	13		G1		150	700
	20		G1		300	1,000
	25		G1		100	1,100
	28		G1		225	1,325

Purchases   Account No. 502

Date		Item	PR	Debit	Credit	Balance
Feb.	3		G1	325		325
	5		G1	177		502
	13		G1	135		637
	20		G1	283		920
	25		G1	92		1,012
	28		G1	207		1,219

[continued on next page]

[continued from previous page]

Transportation-In   **Account No. 503**

Date	Item	PR	Debit	Credit	Balance
Feb. 3		G1	25		25
5		G1	23		48
13		G1	15		63
20		G1	17		80
25		G1	8		88
28		G1	18		106

Purchases Journal

A **purchases journal** is typically used to record all credit purchases. Cash purchases are typically recorded in the cash disbursements journal or general journal. We illustrate all credit merchandise purchases for Z-Mart in the month of February in Exhibit 12.11. To record transactions in a purchases journal, use the information on the purchase invoice.

LO4 Journalize and post transactions using a purchases journal.

1. Enter the date of the journal entry, the invoice date, and credit terms.
2. In the Accounts Payable Credit column, enter the total owed to the supplier.
3. In the Purchases Debit column, enter the total amount of purchases bought.
4. In the Transportation-In Debit column, enter the freight charges.

Once the journal entries are entered in the purchases journal, totals are posted to the general ledger. As illustrated in Exhibit 12.11, compute totals for the Accounts Payable Credit column ($1,325) and for the Purchases Debit ($1,219) and Transportation-In Debit ($106) columns. Before posting, we must ensure the debits (Purchases and Transportation-In) equal the credits (Accounts Payable). Then we post the column totals from the Purchases journal to the general ledger as follows:

1. Locate the general ledger accounts needed: Accounts Payable (207), Purchases (502), and Transportation-In (503).
2. Enter the date of the posting.
3. Post the reference. In this case, we post P2. **P** is for purchases journal. The number **2** denotes the second page of the purchases journal.
4. Post the total from the Accounts Payable Credit column. Compute the new balance.
5. Post the total from the Purchases Debit column. Compute the new balance.
6. Post the total from the Transportation-In Debit column. Compute the new balance.

Posting to the Accounts Payable Subsidiary Ledger

Once the purchases journal is posted to the general ledger, the ledger accounts are up to date. To keep accurate information on the amounts, timing, and credit terms for the money owed to creditors, an accounts payable subsidiary ledger is often kept. The **accounts payable ledger** is a listing of individual supplier (creditor) accounts. Exhibit 12.11 provides an illustration of posting the accounts payable to the individual supplier accounts. We suggest the following steps:

1. Locate the accounts payable account for the first supplier in the purchases journal, Horning Supply Company.
2. Enter the date the first transaction with this supplier was posted to the purchases journal.
3. Post the reference. In this case, we post P2. **P** is for purchases journal. The number **2** denotes the second page of the purchases journal.
4. Enter the amount owed from the Accounts Payable Credit column.
5. Enter a checkmark in the Post Reference column in the Purchases journal to indicate that the purchase has been posted in the accounts payable ledger.
6. Repeat these steps for each transaction in the purchases journal.

Exhibit 12.11

Purchases Journal with Posting

File Edit Maintain Tasks Analysis Options Reports Window Help

Purchases Journal   Page 2

Date	Account	Invoice Date	Terms	PR	Accounts Payable Cr.	Purchases Dr.	Transportation- In Dr.
Feb. 3	Horning Supply Co.	02/02/08	n/30	✓	350	325	25
5	Ace Mfg. Co.	02/05/08	2/10, n/30	✓	200	177	23
13	Wynet & Co.	02/10/08	2/10, n/30	✓	150	135	15
20	Smite Co.	02/18/08	2/10, n/30	✓	300	283	17
25	Ace Mfg. Co.	02/24/08	2/10, n/30	✓	100	92	8
28	ITT Co.	02/28/08	n/30	✓	225	207	18
28	Totals				1,325	1,219	106
					(207)	(502)	(503)

Accounts Payable Subsidiary Ledger

Ace Mfg. Co.

Date	PR	Debit	Credit	Balance
Feb. 5	P2		200	200
25	P2		100	300

Horning Supply Co.

Date	PR	Debit	Credit	Balance
Feb. 3	P2		350	350

ITT Co.

Date	PR	Debit	Credit	Balance
Feb. 28	P2		225	225

Smite Co.

Date	PR	Debit	Credit	Balance
Feb. 20	P2		300	300

Wynet & Co.

Date	PR	Debit	Credit	Balance
Feb. 13	P2		150	150

General Ledger

Account: Accounts Payable   No. 207

Date	PR	Debit	Credit	Balance
Feb. 1	Balance			0
28	P2		1,325	1,325

Account: Purchases   No. 502

Date	PR	Debit	Credit	Balance
Feb. 28	P2	1,219		1,219

Account: Transportation-In   No. 503

Date	PR	Debit	Credit	Balance
Feb. 28	P2	106		106

Sales   Purchases   General Ledger   Payroll   Inventory   Company   Analysis

LO5 Prepare and prove the accuracy of an accounts payable subsidiary ledger

Exhibit 12.12

Schedule of Accounts Payable

Proving the Ledger   Accounts payable balances in the subsidiary ledger are proved after posting the purchases journal. We prove the subsidiary ledger by preparing a **schedule of accounts payable,** which is a list of accounts from the accounts payable ledger with their balances and the total. If this total equals the balance of the Accounts Payable controlling account, the accounts in the accounts payable ledger are assumed correct (proved). Exhibit 12.12 shows a schedule of accounts payable drawn from the accounts payable ledger of Exhibit 12.11. Its total ($1,325) equals the balance of Accounts Payable in the general ledger.

Schedule of Accounts Payable February 28	
Ace Mfg. Company	$ 300
Horning Supply Company	350
ITT Company	225
Smite Company	300
Wynet & Company	150
Total accounts payable	$1,325

Cash Disbursements Journal

The **cash disbursements journal,** also called a cash payments journal, is typically used to record all cash payments. The cash disbursements journal shown in Exhibit 12.13 illustrates the repetitive entries to the Cash Cr. Column of this journal (reflecting cash payments). Column totals, except for the Other Accounts column, are posted at the end of the period. Individual amounts in the Other Accounts column and the Accounts Payable column are posted immediately. **Appendix 12A, available on the book's Website, shows further details of this posting process along with an illustration.**

Exhibit 12.13

Cash Disbursements Journal

Cash Disbursements Journal | | | | | | | | Page 2

Date	Ck. No.	Payee	Account Debited	PR	Cash Cr.	Purchases Discounts Cr.	Other Accounts Dr.	Accounts Payable Dr.
Feb. 3	105	L. and N. Railroad	Purchases		15		15	
12	106	East Sales Co.	Purchases		25		25	
15	107	Ace Mfg. Co.	Ace Mfg. Co.		196	4		200
15	108	Jerry Hale	Salaries Expense		250		250	
20	109	Wynet and Co.	Wynet and Co.		147	3		150
28	110	Smite Co.	Smite Co.		294	6		300
28		Totals			927	13	290	650

HOW YOU DOIN'?

Answers—p. 294

7. What are the normal recording and posting procedures when using special journals and controlling accounts with subsidiary ledgers?

8. What is the process for posting to a subsidiary ledger and its controlling account?

9. How do we prove the accuracy of account balances in the general ledger and subsidiary ledgers after posting?

GROSS MARGIN RATIO

The cost of goods sold makes up much of a merchandiser's expenses. Without sufficient gross profit, a merchandiser will likely fail. Users often compute the gross margin ratio to analyze a merchandiser's operations. It differs from the profit margin ratio in that it excludes all costs except cost of goods sold. The **gross margin ratio** is defined as *gross margin* (net sales minus cost of goods sold) divided by net sales—see Exhibit 12.14.

LO6 Compute the gross margin ratio and explain its use to assess profitability.

$$\text{Gross margin ratio} = \frac{\text{Net sales} - \text{Cost of goods sold}}{\text{Net sales}}$$

Exhibit 12.14

Gross Margin Ratio

Exhibit 12.15 shows the gross margin ratio of **JCPenney** for fiscal years 2002–2005. For JCPenney, each $1 of sales in 2005 yielded about 39¢ in gross margin to cover all other expenses and still produce a profit. This 39¢ margin is up from 34¢ in 2002. This increase is an important (and positive) development. Success for merchandisers such as JCPenney depends on adequate gross margin. Overall, the gross margin ratio suggests that the financial condition and performance of JCPenney has markedly improved over the past four years. Of course, gross margin is just one part of the analysis of a company.

YOU CALL IT

Answer—p. 294

Financial Officer Your company has a 36% gross margin ratio and a 17% net profit margin ratio. Industry averages are 44% for gross margin and 16% for net profit margin. Do these comparative results concern you?

($ millions)	2005	2004	2003	2002
Gross margin	$ 7,139	$ 6,620	$ 6,334	$ 6,082
Net sales	$18,424	$17,786	$17,633	$18,092
Gross margin ratio	38.7%	37.2%	35.9%	33.6%

Exhibit 12.15

JCPenney's Gross Margin Ratio

Demonstration Problem

Connie Company has the following credit merchandise purchase transactions in the month of July. All goods are shipped FOB shipping point.

July 3   Purchased merchandise from Alison Inc. under the following terms: $750 price, invoice date 7/2, credit terms n/30, freight $62.

      7   Purchased merchandise from Hyrum Inc. under the following terms: $1,500 price, invoice date 7/5, credit terms 2/10, n/30, freight $92.

      9   Purchased merchandise from Melissa Inc. under the following terms: $75 price, invoice date 7/8, credit terms n/30, freight $5.

   13   Purchased merchandise from Alison Inc. under the following terms: $1,750 price, invoice date 7/12, credit terms n/30, freight $117.

   14   Purchased merchandise from Joseph Inc. under the following terms: $152 price, invoice date 7/14, credit terms 2/10, n/30, freight $23.

   19   Purchased merchandise from Rebecca Supply Inc. under the following terms: $866 price, invoice date 7/19, credit terms 2/10, n/30, freight $57.

   22   Purchased merchandise from Melissa Inc. under the following terms: $7,502 price, invoice date 7/19, credit terms n/30, freight $215.

   27   Purchased merchandise from Hyrum Inc. under the following terms: $117 price, invoice date 7/26, credit terms 2/10, n/30, freight $14.

   30   Purchased merchandise from Alison Inc. under the following terms: $750 price, invoice date 7/28, credit terms n/30, freight $62.

Required

1. Account for these purchases in a purchases journal using Accounts Payable (acct. #207), Purchases (acct. #502), and Transportation-In (acct. #503). The purchase journal page is page 3. Remember to include the invoice date and credit terms.

2. Post these accounts to the general ledger and post the references.

3. Post these transactions to the accounts payable subsidiary ledger.

Planning the Solution

1. Set up the purchases journal using the template from Exhibit 12.11 with a credit column for Accounts Payable and debit entry columns for Purchases and Transportation-In.

2. Record each credit purchase, with each transaction taking one line in the purchases journal.

3. When complete, sum the columns in the purchase journal to prepare to post totals to the general ledger accounts.

4. Post the column totals in Accounts Payable Credit, Purchases Debit, and Transportation-In Debit to their general ledger accounts.

5. Post each transaction from the purchases journal to the appropriate account in the accounts payable subsidiary ledger.

Solution to Demonstration Problem

1. and 2. Account for the purchases of Connie Company using a purchases journal.

Purchases Journal							Page 3 _ □ X
Date	Account	Invoice Date	Terms	PR	Accounts Payable Cr.	Purchases Dr.	Transportation-In Dr.
Jul. 3	Alison Inc.	2-Jul	n/30		812	750	62
7	Hyrum Inc.	5-Jul	2/10, n/30		1,592	1,500	92
9	Melissa Inc.	8-Jul	n/30		80	75	5
13	Alison Inc.	12-Jul	n/30		1,867	1,750	117
14	Joseph Inc.	14-Jul	2/10, n/30		175	152	23
19	Rebecca Supply Inc.	19-Jul	2/10, n/30		923	866	57
22	Melissa Inc.	19-Jul	n/30		7,717	7,502	215
27	Hyrum Inc.	26-Jul	2/10, n/30		131	117	14
30	Alison Inc.	28-Jul	n/30		812	750	62

3. and 4. Post the totals from the purchases journal to the general ledger.

File Edit Maintain Tasks Analysis Options Reports Window Help

Purchases Journal

Page 3

Date	Account	Invoice Date	Terms	PR	Accounts Payable	Purchases Dr.	Transportation-In Dr.
Jul. 3	Alison Inc.	2-Jul	n/30	✓	812	750	62
7	Hyrum Inc.	5-Jul	2/10, n/30	✓	1,592	1,500	92
9	Melissa Inc.	8-Jul	n/30	✓	80	75	5
13	Alison Inc.	12-Jul	n/30	✓	1,867	1,750	117
14	Joseph Inc.	14-Jul	2/10, n/30	✓	175	152	23
19	Rebecca Supply Inc.	19-Jul	2/10, n/30	✓	923	866	57
22	Melissa Inc.	19-Jul	n/30	✓	7,717	7,502	215
27	Hyrum Inc.	26-Jul	2/10, n/30	✓	131	117	14
30	Alison Inc.	28-Jul	n/30	✓	812	750	62
31	Total				14,109	13,462	647
					(207)	(502)	(503)

General Ledger

Account: Accounts Payable — No. 207

Date	PR	Debit	Credit	Balance
July 1				0
31	P3		14,109	14,109

Account: Purchases — No. 502

Date	PR	Debit	Credit	Balance
July 31	P3	13,462		13,462

Account: Transportation-In — No. 503

Date	PR	Debit	Credit	Balance
July 31	P3	647		647

Sales   Purchases   General Ledger   Payroll   Inventory   Company   Analysis

5. Posting the accounts payable balances to the accounts payable subsidiary ledger.

Accounts Payable Subsidiary Ledger

Alison Inc.

Date	PR	Debit	Credit	Balance
Jul. 3	P3		812	812
13	P3		1,867	2,679
30	P3		812	3,491

Hyrum Inc.

Date	PR	Debit	Credit	Balance
Jul. 7	P3		1,592	1,592
27	P3		131	1,723

Melissa Inc.

Date	PR	Debit	Credit	Balance
Jul. 9	P3		80	80
22	P3		7,717	7,797

Joseph Inc.

Date	PR	Debit	Credit	Balance
Jul. 14	P3		175	175

Rebecca Supply Inc.

Date	PR	Debit	Credit	Balance
Jul. 19	P3		923	923

Summary

LO1 **Describe merchandising activities and identify income components for a merchandising company.** Merchandisers buy products and resell them. Examples of merchandisers include Wal-Mart, Home Depot, The Limited, and Barnes & Noble. A merchandiser's costs on the income statement include an amount for cost of goods sold. Gross profit, or gross margin, equals sales minus cost of goods sold.

LO2 **Identify and explain the inventory asset of a merchandising company.** The current asset section of a merchandising company's balance sheet includes *merchandise inventory,* which refers to the products a merchandiser sells and that are available for sale at the balance sheet date.

LO3 **Analyze and record transactions for merchandise purchases.** A merchandiser records sales at list price less any trade discounts. The merchandiser records applicable purchase discounts for cash payment within the discount period as well as applicable purchase returns and freight charges.

LO4 **Journalize and post transactions using a purchases journal.** The purchases journal is an efficient means to record the purchase of inventory on credit. The purchases journal will typically debit merchandise inventory (and transportation-in if applicable) and credit accounts payable.

LO5 **Prepare and prove the accuracy of an accounts payable subsidiary ledger.** Account balances in the general ledger and the accounts payable subsidiary ledger are tested for accuracy after posting is complete. This procedure is twofold: (1) prepare a trial balance of the general ledger to confirm that debits equal credits and (2) prepare a schedule to confirm that the controlling account's balance equals the subsidiary ledger's balance.

LO6 **Compute the gross margin ratio and explain its use to assess profitability.** The gross margin ratio is computed as gross margin (net sales minus cost of goods sold) divided by net sales. It indicates a company's profitability before considering other expenses.

Guidance Answers to **YOU CALL IT**

Entrepreneur   For terms of 3/10, n/90, missing the 3% discount for an additional 80 days equals an implied annual interest rate of 13.69%, computed as (365 days ÷ 80 days) × 3%. Since you can borrow funds at 11% (assuming no other processing costs), it is better to borrow and pay within the discount period. You save 2.69% (13.69% − 11%) in interest costs by paying early.

Credit Manager   Your decision is whether to comply with prior policy or to create a new policy and not abuse discounts offered by suppliers. Your first step should be to meet with your superior to find out if the late payment policy is the actual policy and, if so, its rationale. If it is the policy to pay late, you must apply your own sense of ethics. One point of view is that the late payment policy is unethical. A deliberate plan to make late payments means the company lies when it pretends to make payment within the discount period. Another view is that the late payment policy is acceptable. In some markets, attempts to take discounts through late payments are accepted as a

continued phase of "price negotiation." Also, your company's suppliers can respond by billing your company for the discounts not accepted because of late payments. However, this is a dubious viewpoint, especially since the prior manager proposes that you dishonestly explain late payments as computer or mail problems and since some suppliers have complained.

Financial Officer   Your company's net profit margin is about equal to the industry average and suggests typical industry performance. However, gross margin reveals that your company is paying far more in cost of goods sold or receiving far less in sales price than competitors. Your attention must be directed to finding the problem with cost of goods sold, sales, or both. One positive note is that your company's expenses make up 19% of sales (36% − 17%). This favorably compares with competitors' expenses that make up 28% of sales (44% − 16%).

Guidance Answers to **HOW YOU DOIN'?**

1. Cost of goods sold is the cost of merchandise purchased from a supplier that is sold to customers during a specific period.

2. Gross profit (or gross margin) is the difference between net sales and cost of goods sold.

3. Merchandise available equals $135,000 ($20,000 + $115,000). Cost of goods sold equals $118,000 ($135,000 − $17,000).

4. Under credit terms of 2/10, n/60, the credit period is 60 days and the discount period is 10 days.

5. (*b*) trade discount.

6. *FOB* means "free on board." It is used in identifying the point when ownership transfers from seller to buyer. *FOB destination* means that the seller transfers ownership of goods to the buyer when they arrive at the buyer's place of business. It also means that the seller is responsible for paying shipping charges and bears the risk of damage or loss during shipment.

7. The normal recording and posting procedures are threefold. First, transactions are entered in a special journal if applicable. Second, individual amounts are posted to any subsidiary ledger accounts. Third, column totals are posted to general ledger accounts if not already individually posted.

8. Controlling accounts are debited periodically for an amount or amounts equal to the sum of their respective debits in the subsidiary ledgers (equals journal column totals), and they are credited periodically for an amount or amounts equal to the sum of their respective credits in the subsidiary ledgers (from journal column totals).

9. Tests for accuracy of account balances in the general ledger and subsidiary ledgers are twofold. First, we prepare a trial balance of the general ledger to confirm that debits equal credits. Second, we prove the subsidiary ledgers by preparing schedules of accounts receivable and accounts payable.

Key Terms

mhhe.com/wildCA

Key Terms are available at the book's Website for learning and testing in an online Flashcard Format.

Accounts payable ledger (p. 289) Subsidiary ledger listing individual creditor (supplier) accounts.

Cost of goods sold (p. 280) Cost of inventory sold to customers during a period; also called *cost of sales*.

Credit period (p. 284) Time period that can pass before a customer's payment is due.

Credit terms (p. 283) Description of the amounts and timing of payments that a buyer (debtor) agrees to make in the future.

Debit memorandum (p. 285) Notification that the sender has debited the recipient's account in the sender's records.

Discount period (p. 284) Time period in which a cash discount is available and the buyer can make a reduced payment.

FOB (p. 285) Abbreviation for *free on board;* the point when ownership of goods passes to the buyer; *FOB shipping point* (or *factory*) means the buyer pays shipping costs and accepts ownership of goods when the seller transfers goods to carrier; *FOB destination* means the seller pays shipping costs and buyer accepts ownership of goods at the buyer's place of business.

Gross margin (p. 280) (See *gross profit.*)

Gross margin ratio (p. 291) Gross margin (net sales minus cost of goods sold) divided by net sales; also called *gross profit ratio*.

Gross profit (p. 280) Net sales minus cost of goods sold; also called *gross margin*.

Inventory (p. 281) Goods a company owns and expects to sell in its normal operations.

Invoice (p. 282) Itemized record of goods prepared by the vendor that lists the customer's name, items sold, sales prices, and terms of sale.

List price (p. 282) Catalog (full) price of an item before any trade discount is deducted.

Merchandise inventory (p. 281) Goods that a company owns and expects to sell to customers; also called *merchandise* or *inventory*.

Merchandiser (p. 280) Entity that earns net income by buying and selling merchandise.

Net purchases (p. 286) Net cost of merchandise purchased; computed as Purchases minus Purchase Discounts, minus Purchase Returns and Allowances, plus Transportation-In.

Purchase discount (p. 283) Term used by a purchaser to describe a cash discount granted to the purchaser for paying within the discount period.

Purchase order (p. 282) Document used by the purchasing department to place an order with a seller (vendor).

Purchase requisition (p. 281) Document listing merchandise needed by a department and requesting it be purchased.

Purchases journal (p. 289) Journal normally used to record all purchases on credit.

Receiving report (p. 282) Form used to report that ordered goods are received and to describe their quantity and condition.

Schedule of accounts payable (p. 290) List of the balances of all accounts in the accounts payable ledger and their total.

Trade discount (p. 283) Reduction from a list or catalog price that can vary for wholesalers, retailers, and consumers.

Transportation-In (p. 282) Freight costs paid by the buyer.

Vendor (p. 282) Seller of goods or services.

Multiple Choice Quiz   Answers on p. 304   mhhe.com/wildCA

Multiple Choice Quizzes A and B are available at the book's Website.

1. A company has $550,000 in net sales and $193,000 in gross profit. This means its cost of goods sold equals
   a. $743,000
   b. $550,000
   c. $357,000
   d. $193,000
   e. ($193,000)

2. A company purchased $4,500 of merchandise on May 1 with terms of 2/10, n/30. On May 6, it returned $250 of that merchandise. On May 8, it paid the balance owed for merchandise, taking any discount it is entitled to. The cash paid on May 8 is
   a. $4,500
   b. $4,250
   c. $4,160
   d. $4,165
   e. $4,410

3. Merchandise inventory
   a. Is a long-term asset account.
   b. Is a current asset account.
   c. Includes supplies.
   d. Is classified with investments on the balance sheet.
   e. Must be sold within one month.

4. Net purchases includes
   a. Any purchase discounts.
   b. Any returns and allowances.
   c. Any necessary transportation-in costs.
   d. Any trade discounts.
   e. All of the above.

5. A company's net sales are $675,000, its costs of goods sold are $459,000, and its net income is $74,250. Its gross margin ratio equals
   a. 32%
   b. 68%
   c. 47%
   d. 11%
   e. 34%

Discussion Questions

1. In comparing the accounts of a merchandising company with those of a service company, what additional accounts would the merchandising company likely use?

2. What items appear in financial statements of merchandising companies but not in the statements of service companies?

3. Explain how a business can earn a positive gross profit on its sales and still have a net loss.

4. Why do companies offer cash discounts?

5. Distinguish between cash discounts and trade discounts. Is the amount of a trade discount on purchased merchandise recorded in the accounts?

6. What is the difference between a sales discount and a purchase discount?

7. Why would a company's manager be concerned about the quantity of its purchase returns if its suppliers allow unlimited returns?

8. Refer to the balance sheet and income statement for **Best Buy** in Appendix A. What does the company title its inventory account? Does the company present a detailed calculation of its cost of goods sold?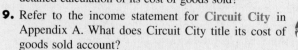

9. Refer to the income statement for **Circuit City** in Appendix A. What does Circuit City title its cost of goods sold account?

QUICK STUDY

Prepare journal entries to record each of the following purchases transactions of a merchandising company.

QS 12–1
Recording purchases
(LO3)

Mar. 5   Purchased 600 units of product with a list price of $10 per unit. The purchaser is granted a trade discount of 20%; terms of the sale are 2/10, n/60; invoice is dated March 5.

Mar. 7   Returned 25 defective units from the March 5 purchase and received full credit.

Mar. 15   Paid the amount due from the March 5 purchase, less the return on March 7.

QS 12–2
Computing cost of goods sold and gross margin
(LO2) (LO3) (LO6)

Following are financial figures for five companies. Compute net purchases, cost of goods available for sale, cost of goods sold, gross margin, and the gross margin ratio.

	Company a	Company b	Company c	Company d	Company e
Beginning inventory	50,000	75,000	18,000	25,000	117,000
Ending inventory	42,000	98,000	16,000	28,000	120,000
Purchases	143,000	177,000	86,000	110,000	263,000
Purchase discounts	18,000	23,000	16,000	0	24,000
Purchase returns	16,000	12,000	7,000	8,000	12,000
Net sales	200,000	188,000	119,000	152,000	313,000

QS 12–3
Computing and analyzing gross margin
(LO6)

Compute net sales, gross profit, and the gross margin ratio for each separate case *a* through *d*. Interpret the gross margin ratio for case *a*.

	a	b	c	d
Sales	$150,000	$550,000	$38,700	$255,700
Sales discounts	5,200	17,500	600	4,200
Sales returns and allowances	20,000	6,000	5,300	900
Cost of goods sold	79,600	329,700	24,300	126,900

Following are financial figures for five companies. Solve for the missing items a through e.

QS 12–4
Computing cost of goods sold
and gross margin

	Company 1	Company 2	Company 3	Company 4	Company 5
Beginning inventory	57,000	63,000	97,000	30,000	e
Purchases	150,000	173,000	92,000	115,000	255,000
Purchase discounts	17,000	21,000	15,000	12,000	23,000
Purchase returns	17,000	13,000	8,000	7,000	15,000
Cost of goods available for sale	a	202,000	166,000	126,000	329,000
Ending inventory	56,000	69,000	72,000	d	130,000
Cost of goods sold	117,000	133,000	c	110,000	199,000
Sales	200,000	b	119,000	152,000	313,000
Gross profit	83,000	55,000	25,000	42,000	114,000

Account for the following purchases in a purchases journal using Accounts Payable (acct. #207), Purchases (acct. #502), and Transportation-In (acct. #503). (*Hint:* Use the chapter demonstration problem as a guide.)

Dec. 3   Purchase $850 in merchandise from Camille Inc., credit terms n/30; invoice date 12/2, freight $72.
Dec. 7   Purchase $1,600 in merchandise from Travis Inc., credit terms 2/10, n/30; invoice date 12/5, freight $162.
Dec. 9   Purchase $65 in merchandise from Braden Inc., credit terms n/30; invoice date 12/8, freight $9.
Dec. 13   Purchase $2,750 in merchandise from Camille Inc., credit terms n/30; invoice date 12/12, freight $117.
Dec. 14   Purchase $162 in merchandise from Braden Inc., credit terms 2/10, n/30; invoice date 12/14, freight $33.
Dec. 19   Purchase $966 in merchandise from Derek Supply Co., credit terms 2/10, n/30; invoice date 12/19, freight $67.

Prepare journal entries to record the following transactions for a retail store.

EXERCISES

Exercise 12–1
Recording entries for
merchandise purchases

L03

Apr. 2   Purchased merchandise from Lyon Company under the following terms: $4,600 price, invoice dated April 2, credit terms of 2/15, n/60, and FOB shipping point.
3   Paid $300 for shipping charges on the April 2 purchase.
4   Returned to Lyon Company unacceptable merchandise that had an invoice price of $600.
17   Sent a check to Lyon Company for the April 2 purchase, net of the discount and the returned merchandise.
18   Purchased merchandise from Frist Corp. under the following terms: $8,500 price, invoice dated April 18, credit terms of 2/10, n/30, and FOB destination.
21   After negotiations, received from Frist a $1,100 allowance on the April 18 purchase.
28   Sent check to Frist paying for the April 18 purchase, net of the discount and allowance.

Check   April 28, Cr. Cash $7,252

Santa Fe Company purchased merchandise for resale from Mesa Company with an invoice price of $24,000 and credit terms of 3/10, n/60. The merchandise had cost Mesa $16,000. Santa Fe paid within the discount period. Prepare entries that Santa Fe Company should record for the merchandise purchase and the cash payment.

Exercise 12–2
Analyzing and recording
merchandise transactions

L03

Insert the letter for each term in the blank space beside the definition that it most closely matches.

Exercise 12–3
Applying merchandising terms

L01 L02 L03

A. Cash discount   **E.** FOB shipping point   **H.** Purchase discount
B. Credit period   **F.** Gross profit   **I.** Sales discount
C. Discount period   **G.** Merchandise inventory   **J.** Trade discount
D. FOB destination

_____ **1.** Reduction below list or catalog price that is negotiated in setting the price of goods.

_____ **2.** Reduction in a receivable or payable if it is paid within the discount period.

_____ **3.** Time period that can pass before a customer's payment is due.

_____ **4.** Difference between net sales and the cost of goods sold.

_____ **5.** Ownership of goods is transferred when the seller delivers goods to the carrier.

_____ **6.** Ownership of goods is transferred when delivered to the buyer's place of business.

_____ **7.** Goods a company owns and expects to sell to its customers.

_____ **8.** Purchaser's description of a cash discount received from a supplier of goods.

_____ **9.** Seller's description of a cash discount granted to buyers in return for early payment.

_____ **10.** Time period in which a cash discount is available.

Exercise 12-4

Recording purchase returns and allowances

(LO3)

On May 5, Baker purchases 1,500 units of merchandise from Allied Parts for $14 per unit. Baker is a retailer and purchases the units for resale. Three separate transactions *a* through *c* also occur.

a. On May 7, Baker returns 200 units because they did not fit the customer's needs.

b. On May 8, Baker discovers that 300 units are damaged but are still of some use and, therefore, keeps the units. Allied Parts sends Baker a credit memorandum for $600 to compensate for the damage.

c. On May 15, Baker discovers that 100 units are the wrong color. Baker keeps 60 of these units because Allied sends a $120 credit memorandum to compensate. However, Baker returns the remaining 40 units to Allied.

Prepare the appropriate journal entries for Baker Co. to record the May 5 purchase and each of the three separate transactions *a* through *c*.

Exercise 12-5

Analyzing and recording merchandise transactions—both buyer and seller

(LO3)

Check   (1) May 20, Cr. Cash $37,442

On May 11, Sydney Co. accepts delivery of $40,000 of merchandise it purchases for resale from Troy Corporation. With the merchandise is an invoice dated May 11, with terms of 3/10, n/90, FOB shipping point. When the goods are delivered, Sydney pays $345 to Express Shipping for delivery charges on the merchandise. On May 12, Sydney returns $1,400 of goods to Troy, who receives them one day later. On May 20, Sydney mails a check to Troy Corporation for the amount owed. Troy receives it the following day.

1. Prepare journal entries that Sydney Co. records for these transactions.

2. Prepare journal entries that Troy Corporation records for these transactions.

Exercise 12-6

Computing revenues, expenses, and income

(LO3) (LO4) (LO6)

Fill in the blanks in the following separate income statements *a* through *e*. Put net losses in parentheses.

	a	b	c	d	e
Sales	$62,000	$43,500	$46,000	$?	$25,600
Cost of goods sold					
Merchandise inventory (beginning)	8,000	17,050	7,500	8,000	4,560
Total cost of merchandise purchases	38,000	?	?	32,000	6,600
Merchandise inventory (ending)	?	(3,000)	(9,000)	(6,600)	?
Cost of goods sold	34,050	16,000	?	?	7,000
Gross profit	?	?	3,750	45,600	?
Expenses	10,000	10,650	12,150	3,600	6,000
Net income (loss)	$?	$16,850	$ (8,400)	$42,000	$?

Exercise 12-7

Preparing journal entries for inventory purchases and sales

(LO3)

Journalize the following merchandising transactions for Chilton Systems.

1. On November 1, Chilton Systems purchases merchandise for $1,500 on credit with terms of 2/5, n/30, FOB shipping point; invoice dated November 1.

2. On November 5, Chilton Systems pays cash for the November 1 purchase.

3. On November 7, Chilton Systems discovers and returns $200 of defective merchandise purchased on November 1 for a cash refund.

4. On November 10, Chilton Systems pays $90 cash for transportation costs with the November 1 purchase.

5. On November 13, Chilton Systems sells merchandise for $1,600 on credit. The cost of the merchandise is $800.

6. On November 16, the customer returns merchandise from the November 13 transaction. The returned items sell for $300 and cost $150.

Ziegler Inc. has the following cash disbursements in April.

Exercise 12-8
Cash disbursements journal

(LO3)

Apr. 9 Issued check no. 210 to Kitt Corp. to buy store supplies for $650.
Apr. 17 Issued check no. 211 for $1,400 to pay off a note payable to City Bank.
Apr. 20 Purchased merchandise for $4,500 on credit from Lite, terms 2/10, net 30.
Apr. 28 Issued check no. 212 to Lite to pay the amount due for the purchase of April 20, less the discount.

Prepare headings for a cash disbursements journal like the one in Exhibit 12.13. Journalize the April transactions that should be recorded in the cash disbursements journal.

Prepare journal entries to record the following merchandising transactions of Blink Company.

PROBLEM SET A

Problem 12-1A
Preparing journal entries for merchandising activities

(LO3)

July 1 Purchased merchandise from Boden Company for $6,000 under credit terms of 1/15, n/30, FOB shipping point, invoice dated July 1.
   3 Paid $125 cash for freight charges on the purchase of July 1.
   9 Purchased merchandise from Leight Co. for $2,200 under credit terms of 2/15, n/60, FOB destination, invoice dated July 9.
   11 Received a $200 credit memorandum from Leight Co. for the return of part of the merchandise purchased on July 9.
   16 Paid the balance due to Boden Company within the discount period.
   24 Paid Leight Co. the balance due within the discount period.

Check July 16, Cr. Cash $5,940
July 24, Cr. Cash $1,960

Prepare journal entries to record the following merchandising transactions of Sheng Company.

Problem 12-2A
Preparing journal entries for merchandising activities

(LO3)

Aug. 1 Purchased merchandise from Arotek Company for $7,500 under credit terms of 1/10, n/30, invoice dated August 1.
   8 Purchased merchandise from Waters Corporation for $5,400 under credit terms of 1/10, n/45, FOB shipping point, invoice dated August 8. The invoice showed that at Sheng's request, Waters paid the $140 shipping charges and added that amount to the bill. (*Recall:* Discounts are not applied to freight and shipping charges.)
   12 After negotiations with Waters Corporation concerning problems with the merchandise purchased on August 8, Sheng received a credit memorandum from Waters granting a price reduction of $700.
   18 Paid the amount due Waters Corporation for the August 8 purchase less the price reduction granted.
   30 Paid Arotek Company the amount due from the August 1 purchase.

Check Aug. 18, Cr. Cash $4,793

Valley Company's adjusted trial balance on August 31, 2008, its fiscal year-end, follows. (Also, merchandise inventory was $41,000 on August 31, 2008.)

Problem 12-3A
Computing merchandising amounts

(LO1) (LO3) (LO6)

	Debit	Credit
Merchandise inventory, August 31, 2007	$ 25,400	
Other (noninventory) assets	130,400	
Total liabilities		$ 25,000
K. Valley, Capital		104,550
K. Valley, Withdrawals	8,000	
Sales		225,600
Sales discounts	2,250	
Sales returns and allowances	12,000	
Purchases	92,000	
Purchase discounts		2,000
Purchase returns and allowances		4,500
Transportation-In	4,600	
Sales salaries expense	32,000	
Rent expense—Selling space	8,000	
Store supplies expense	1,500	
Advertising expense	13,000	
Office salaries expense	28,500	
Rent expense—Office space	3,600	
Office supplies expense	400	
Totals	$361,650	$361,650

Required

1. Compute the company's net sales for the year.

Check (2) Merchandise available for
sale, $115,500
        (3) Gross profit, $136,850

2. Compute the company's total cost of merchandise available for sale.
3. Compute gross profit.
4. Compute net income.

Problem 12–4A

Purchases journal and accounts payable subsidiary ledger

(L04) (L05)

Gomez Corp. has the following credit purchase transactions in the month of October.

Oct. 4   Purchased merchandise from Benjamin Inc. under the following terms: $950 price; invoice date 10/2, credit terms n/30, freight $62.

      7   Purchased merchandise from Rachel Inc. under the following terms: $1,350, invoice date 10/5, credit terms 2/10, n/30; freight $92.

      9   Purchased merchandise from Bethany Co. under the following terms: $725, invoice date 10/8, credit terms n/30, freight $65.

     13   Purchased merchandise from Benjamin Inc. under the following terms: $1,350, invoice date 10/12, credit terms n/30, freight $117.

     14   Purchased merchandise from Matthew Inc. under the following terms: $657, invoice date 10/14, credit terms 2/10, n/30; freight $23.

Required

1. Account for these purchases in a purchases journal using Accounts Payable (acct. #207), Purchases (acct. #502) and Transportation-In (acct. #503). The purchases journal page is page 4. Include the invoice date and credit terms.

2. Post these accounts to the general ledger (including the references).

3. Post these accounts to the accounts payable subsidiary ledger.

PROBLEM SET B

Problem 12–1B

Preparing journal entries for merchandising activities

(L03)

Prepare journal entries to record the following merchandising transactions of Yarvelle Company.

May 2   Purchased merchandise from Havel Co. for $10,000 under credit terms of 1/15, n/30, FOB shipping point, invoice dated May 2.

      5   Paid $250 cash for freight charges on the purchase of May 2.

     10   Purchased merchandise from Duke Co. for $3,650 under credit terms of 2/15, n/60, FOB destination, invoice dated May 10.

     12   Received a $400 credit memorandum from Duke Co. for the return of part of the merchandise purchased on May 10.

     17   Paid the balance due to Havel Co. within the discount period.

     25   Paid Duke Co. the balance due within the discount period.

Check May 25, Cr. Cash $3,185

Problem 12–2B

Preparing journal entries for merchandising activities

(L03)

Prepare journal entries to record the following merchandising transactions of Mason Company.

July 3   Purchased merchandise from OLB Corp. for $15,000 under credit terms of 1/10, n/30, FOB destination, invoice dated July 3.

     10   Purchased merchandise from Rupert Corporation for $14,200 under credit terms of 1/10, n/45, FOB shipping point, invoice dated July 10. The invoice showed that at Mason's request, Rupert paid the $500 shipping charges and added that amount to the bill. (*Recall:* Discounts are not applied to freight and shipping charges.)

     14   After negotiations with Rupert Corporation concerning problems with the merchandise purchased on July 10, Mason received a credit memorandum from Rupert granting a price reduction of $2,000.

     20   Paid the amount due Rupert Corporation for the July 10 purchase less the price reduction granted.

     31   Paid OLB Corp. the amount due from the July 3 purchase.

Check July 20, Cr. Cash, $12,578
        July 31, Cr. Cash, $15,000

Barkley Company's adjusted trial balance on March 31, 2008, its fiscal year-end, follows.

Problem 12-3B
Computing merchandising amounts

(LO1) (LO3) (LO6)

	Debit	Credit
Merchandise inventory, March 31, 2007	$ 37,500	
Other (noninventory) assets	202,600	
Total liabilities		$ 42,500
C. Barkley, Capital		164,425
C. Barkley, Withdrawals	3,000	
Sales		332,650
Sales discounts	5,875	
Sales returns and allowances	20,000	
Purchases	138,500	
Purchase discounts		2,950
Purchase returns and allowances		6,700
Transportation-In	5,750	
Sales salaries expense	44,500	
Rent expense—Selling space	16,000	
Store supplies expense	3,850	
Advertising expense	26,000	
Office salaries expense	40,750	
Rent expense—Office space	3,800	
Office supplies expense	1,100	
Totals	$549,225	$549,225

On March 31, 2008, merchandise inventory was $56,500.

Required

1. Calculate the company's net sales for the year.
2. Calculate the company's total cost of merchandise available for sale.
3. Compute gross profit.
4. Compute net income.

Check (2) Merchandise available for sale, $134,600;

(3) Gross profit, $191,175

(4) Net income, $55,175

Johnson Corp. has the following credit purchase transactions in the month of January.

Problem 12-4B
Purchases journal and accounts payable subsidiary ledger

(LO4) (LO5)

Jan. 5 Purchased merchandise from Bethany Inc. under the following terms: $725, invoice date 1/4, credit terms 2/10, n/30; freight $65.

9 Purchased merchandise from Daniel Inc. under the following terms: $1,650, invoice date 1/8, credit terms n/30, freight $109.

14 Purchased merchandise from David Co. under the following terms: $673, invoice date 1/12, credit terms n/30; freight $57.

22 Purchased merchandise from Bethany Inc. under the following terms: $675, invoice date 1/21, credit terms 2/10, n/30; freight $123.

28 Purchased merchandise from Jessica Inc. under the following terms: $553, invoice date 1/28, credit terms 2/10, n/30; freight $52.

Required

1. Account for these purchases in a purchases journal using Accounts Payable (acct. #207), Purchases (acct. #502), and Transportation-In (acct. #503). The purchases journal page is page 3. Include the invoice date and credit terms.
2. Post these accounts to the general ledger (including the references).
3. Post these accounts to the accounts payable subsidiary ledger.

SERIAL PROBLEM

Success Systems

(This serial problem began in Chapter 1 and continues through most of the book. If previous chapter segments were not completed, the serial problem can begin at this point. It is helpful, but not necessary, that you use the Working Papers that accompany the book.)

SP 12 Adriana Lopez created Success Systems on October 1, 2007. The company has been successful, and its list of customers has grown. To accommodate the growth, the accounting system is modified to set up separate accounts for each customer. The following chart of accounts includes the account number used for each account and any balance as of December 31, 2007. These balances are taken from SP 5. Lopez decided to add a fourth digit with a decimal point to the 106 account number that had been used for the single Accounts Receivable account. This modification allows the company to continue using the existing chart of accounts. For simplicity, ignore payroll taxes and sales taxes in this problem.

No.	Account Title	Dr.	Cr.
101	Cash	$80,260	
106.1	Alex's Engineering Co.	0	
106.2	Wildcat Services	0	
106.3	Easy Leasing	0	
106.4	Clark Co.	2,300	
106.5	Chang Corp.	0	
106.6	Gomez Co.	3,500	
106.7	Delta Co.	0	
106.8	KC, Inc.	0	
106.9	Dream, Inc.	0	
119	Merchandise inventory	0	
126	Computer supplies	775	
128	Prepaid insurance	1,800	
131	Prepaid rent	875	
163	Office equipment	10,000	
164	Accumulated depreciation—Office equipment		625
167	Computer equipment	25,000	
168	Accumulated depreciation—Computer equipment		1,250
201	Accounts payable		2,100

No.	Account Title	Dr.	Cr.
210	Wages payable		600
236	Unearned computer services revenue		2,500
301	A. Lopez, Capital		117,435
302	A. Lopez, Withdrawals	0	
403	Computer services revenue		0
413	Sales		0
414	Sales returns and allowances	0	
415	Sales discounts	0	
505	Purchases	0	
506	Purchase returns and allowances		0
507	Purchase discounts		0
508	Transportation-In	0	
612	Depreciation expense—Office equipment	0	
613	Depreciation expense—Computer equipment	0	
623	Wages expense	0	
637	Insurance expense	0	
640	Rent expense	0	
652	Computer supplies expense	0	
655	Advertising expense	0	
676	Mileage expense	0	
677	Miscellaneous expenses	0	
684	Repairs expense—Computer	0	

In response to requests from customers, Lopez will begin selling computer software. The company will extend credit terms of 1/10, n/30, FOB shipping point, to all customers who purchase this merchandise. However, no cash discount is available on consulting fees. Additional accounts (Nos. 119, 413, 414, 415, 505, 506, 507, and 508) are added to its general ledger to accommodate the company's new merchandising activities. All revenue and expense accounts have zero balances as of January 1, 2008. Its transactions for January through March follow:

Jan. 4   Paid cash to Michelle Jones for five days' work at the rate of $150 per day. Four of the five days relate to wages payable that were accrued in the prior year.

5   Adriana Lopez invested an additional $10,000 cash in the business.

7   Purchased $5,700 of merchandise from Kansas Corp. with terms of 1/10, n/30, FOB shipping point, invoice dated January 7.

9   Received $3,500 cash from Gomez Co. as full payment on its account.

11   Completed a five-day project for Alex's Engineering Co. and billed it $6,500, which is the total price of $9,000 less the advance payment of $2,500. (*Hint:* Debit Unearned Computer Services Revenue for $2,500.)

Check Jan. 11, Dr. Unearned Computer Services Revenue $2,500

13   Sold merchandise with a retail value of $6,000 to Chang Corp., invoice dated January 13.
15   Paid $400 cash for freight charges on the merchandise purchased on January 7.
16   Received $5,600 cash from Delta Co. for computer services provided.
17   Paid Kansas Corp. for the invoice dated January 7, net of the discount.
20   Chang Corp. returned $500 of defective merchandise from its invoice dated January 13. The returned merchandise is discarded. (The policy of Success Systems is to not adjust its accounts for returned merchandise.)
22   Received the balance due from Chang Corp., net of both the discount and the credit for the returned merchandise.
24   Returned defective merchandise to Kansas Corp. and accepted a credit against future purchases. The defective merchandise invoice cost, net of the discount, was $496.
26   Purchased $9,500 of merchandise from Kansas Corp. with terms of 1/10, n/30, FOB destination, invoice dated January 26.
26   Sold merchandise for $4,700 on credit to KC, Inc., invoice dated January 26.
29   Received a $496 credit memorandum from Kansas Corp. concerning the merchandise returned on January 24.
31   Paid cash to Michelle Jones for 10 days' work at $150 per day.
Feb. 1   Paid $2,625 cash to Summit Mall for another three months' rent in advance. (Debit Prepaid Rent, an asset.)
3   Paid Kansas Corp. for the balance due, net of the cash discount, less the $496 amount in the credit memorandum.
5   Paid $800 cash to the local newspaper for an advertising insert in today's paper.
11   Received the balance due from Alex's Engineering Co. for fees billed on January 11.
15   Adriana Lopez withdrew $5,200 cash for personal use.
23   Sold merchandise for $3,800 on credit to Delta Co., invoice dated February 23.
26   Paid cash to Michelle Jones for eight days' work at $150 per day.
27   Reimbursed Adriana Lopez for business automobile mileage (1,000 miles at $0.32 per mile).
Mar. 8   Purchased $3,250 of computer supplies from Cain Office Products on credit, invoice dated March 8.
9   Received the balance due from Delta Co. for merchandise sold on February 23.
11   Paid $1,200 cash for minor repairs to the company's computer.
16   Received $6,250 cash from Dream, Inc., for computing services provided.
19   Paid the full amount due to Cain Office Products, including amounts created on December 15 (of $2,100) and March 8.
24   Billed Easy Leasing for $11,000 of computing services provided.
25   Sold merchandise for $3,900 on credit to Wildcat Services, invoice dated March 25.
30   Sold merchandise for $2,500 on credit to Clark Company, invoice dated March 30.
31   Reimbursed Adriana Lopez for business automobile mileage (600 miles at $0.32 per mile).

The following additional facts are available for preparing adjustments on March 31 prior to financial statement preparation:

a. The March 31 amount of computer supplies still available totals $1,950.

b. Three more months have expired since the company purchased its annual insurance policy at a $2,400 cost for 12 months of coverage.

c. Michelle Jones has not been paid for seven days of work at the rate of $150 per day.

d. Three months have passed since any prepaid rent has been transferred to expense. The monthly rent expense is $875.

e. Depreciation on the computer equipment for January 1 through March 31 is $1,250.

f. Depreciation on the office equipment for January 1 through March 31 is $625.

Required

1. Prepare journal entries to record each of the January through March transactions.

2. Post the journal entries in part 1 to the accounts in the company's general ledger. (*Note:* Begin with the ledger's post-closing adjusted balances as of December 31, 2007.)

3. Prepare a partial work sheet consisting of the first six columns (similar to the one shown in Exhibit 6B.1) that includes the unadjusted trial balance, the March 31 adjusting journal entries (*a*) through (*f*), and the adjusted trial balance. Do not prepare closing entries and do not journalize the adjustments or post them to the ledger. Recall that adjustments (*a*)–(*f*) are discussed in Chapter 5.

Check   (2) Ending balances: Cash, $87,266; Sales, $20,900;

(3) Unadj. totals, $182,060; Adj. totals, $184,985;

BEYOND THE NUMBERS

REPORTING IN ACTION

(LO1) (LO3)

BTN 12-1 Refer to Best Buy's financial statements in Appendix A to answer the following.

Required

1. Assume that the amounts reported for inventories and cost of sales reflect items purchased in a form ready for resale. Compute the net cost of goods purchased for the fiscal year ended February 26, 2005.
2. Best Buy includes freight costs in cost of goods sold. List three such costs, using information in footnote 1.

COMPARATIVE ANALYSIS

(LO6)

BTN 12-2 Key comparative figures ($ millions) for both Best Buy and Circuit City follow.

Key Figures	Best Buy		Circuit City	
	Current Year	Prior Year	Current Year	Prior Year
Revenues (net sales)	$27,433	$24,548	$10,472	$9,857
Cost of sales	20,938	18,677	7,904	7,573

Required

1. Compute the dollar amount of gross margin and the gross margin ratio for the two years shown for both companies.
2. Which company earns more in gross margin for each dollar of net sales? How does each company compare to the industry average of 29%?
3. Did the gross margin ratio improve or decline for these companies?

ETHICS CHALLENGE

(LO3)

BTN 12-3 Review the "You Call It" on page 285, which illustrates an ethical challenge associated with purchase discounts.

Required

1. In your view, is the company currently abusing its suppliers' cash discount policy? Explain.
2. Is it appropriate to indicate that the late payments are due to computer or mail problems? Explain.
3. Assume you feel uncomfortable with your company taking the suppliers' cash discounts. What steps could you take to remedy the situation?

TAKING IT TO THE NET

(LO6)

BTN 12-4 Access the SEC's EDGAR database (www.sec.gov) and obtain the April 29, 2005, filing of its fiscal 2005 10-K report (for year ended January 29, 2005) for J. Crew Group, Inc.

Required

Prepare a table that reports the gross margin ratios for J. Crew using the revenues and cost of goods sold data from J. Crew's income statement for each of its most recent four years. Analyze and comment on the trend in its gross margin ratio.

TEAMWORK IN ACTION

(LO1) (LO6)

BTN 12-5 Official Brands' general ledger and supplementary records at the end of its current period reveal the following.

Sales	$600,000	Merchandise inventory (beginning of period)	$ 98,000
Sales returns	20,000	Invoice cost of merchandise purchases	360,000
Sales discounts	13,000	Purchase discounts received	9,000
Cost of transportation-in	22,000	Purchase returns and allowances	11,000
Operating expenses	50,000	Merchandise inventory (end of period)	84,000

Required

1. *Each* member of the team is to assume responsibility for computing *one* of the following items. You are not to duplicate your teammates' work. Get any necessary amounts to compute your item from the appropriate teammate. Each member is to explain his or her computation to the team in preparation for reporting to the class.

In teams of four, assign the same student *a* and *e*. Rotate teams for reporting on a different computation and the analysis in step 3.

   a. Net sales
   b. Total cost of merchandise purchases
   c. Cost of goods sold
   d. Gross profit
   e. Net income

2. Check your net income with the instructor. If correct, proceed to step 3.

3. Assume that a physical inventory count finds that actual ending inventory is $76,000. Discuss how this affects previously computed amounts in step 1.

BTN 12-6   Refer to the opening feature about CoCaLo. Assume that Renee Pepys Lowe estimates current annual sales at approximately $10 million and reports the following income statement.

ENTREPRENEURS IN BUSINESS
(L03)

COCALO	
Income Statement	
For Year Ended January 31, 2007	
Net sales	$10,000,000
Cost of sales	6,100,000
Expenses (other than cost of sales)	2,000,000
Net income	$ 1,900,000

CoCaLo sells to various retailers, ranging from small shops to large chains such as Target. Assume that Renee Pepys Lowe currently offers credit terms of 1/15, n/60, and ships FOB destination. To improve her cash flow, Lowe is considering changing her credit terms to 3/10, n/30. In addition, she proposes to change her shipping terms to FOB shipping point. She expects that the increase in discount rate will increase her net sales by 9%, but her gross margin ratio (and ratio of cost of sales divided by net sales) is expected to remain unchanged. She also expects that her delivery expenses will be zero under this proposal; thus, her expenses other than cost of sales are expected to increase only 6%.

Required

1. Prepare a forecasted income statement for the year ended January 31, 2008, based on the proposal.

2. Based on the forecasted income statement alone (from part 1), do you recommend CoCaLo implement the new sales policies? Explain.

3. What else should Lowe consider before she decides whether or not to implement the new policies? Explain.

ANSWERS TO MULTIPLE CHOICE QUIZ

1. c; Gross profit = $550,000 − $193,000 = $357,000
2. d; ($4,500 − $250) × (100% − 2%) = $4,165
3. b.

4. e.
5. a; Gross margin ratio = ($675,000 − $459,000)/$675,000 = 32%

A Look Back

Chapter 12 considered the accounting for merchandise purchases and inventory. We also explained the use of the purchases journal and the accounts payable subsidiary ledger.

A Look at This Chapter

Chapter 13 provides an overview of the accrual basis of accounting. We present additional adjustments needed to match expenses with revenues. We also review the trial balance work sheet.

A Look Ahead

In Chapter 14 we explain closing procedures necessary for the accounting system. We also describe how to classify income statements and balance sheets.

Chapter **13**

Accrual Accounting Overview

LEARNING OBJECTIVES

 LO 1 Describe the importance of periodic reporting and the periodicity assumption.

 LO 2 Explain accrual accounting and how it improves financial statements.

LO 3 Identify the types of accounting adjustments and their purpose.

LO 4 Explain how accounting adjustments link to financial statements.

 LO 5 Describe the alternatives in accounting for prepayments.

"Never give up on your entrepreneurial dream"
—Tony Lee

Master of the Ring

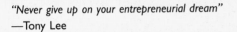

MASSILLON, OH—Tony Lee dreamed of attending college and one day owning a business. But he set his dream aside to join the Army and serve in the Gulf War fresh out of high school. Soon after Tony returned home, he and his girlfriend had a baby girl and Tony needed a job. He found work as a janitor at Eaton Corporation, a manufacturer of steel rings.

While cleaning restrooms and sweeping floors, Tony hoped a machine job would come his way at Eaton. After one year, Tony got a chance to run a machine making steel rings. But Tony's determination drove him to learn how to operate every machine in the factory. Afterward, he set his sights on handling customer complaints, buying raw materials, and preparing and interpreting accounting reports.

Tony still dreamed of attending college but could not afford it. So he instead spent many nights studying accounting at the local library. He learned how accounting tracks business activities. He learned about accrual accounting, special journals, general ledgers, and systems technology.

When Eaton announced its closing in 2003, Tony wasted no time. Using his knowledge of factory operations and accounting, he prepared a buyout proposal. He projected accounting results and identified changes necessary for the company to survive. Tony then wrote a detailed business plan, analyzed competitors, and arranged for potential financing. Tony even sold his beloved motorcycle and took a second mortgage on his family's home to resuscitate the company.

Within two months, Tony and six other investors owned the ring manufacturer—renamed **Ring Masters (Ring-Masters.net)**. Says one investor, "Tony knew the product, knew the customer, and had a tremendous amount of loyalty from the employees."

Today, Ring Masters produces over 200,000 steel rings every day. Sales are up nearly 20% to around $3 million annually, and Tony hopes to double that within five years.

[Sources: *Ring Masters Website*, January 2007; *Stark Development Board Website*, July 2005; *The Plain Dealer*, July 2005; *Inc.*, April 2005]

Financial statements reflect revenues when earned and expenses when incurred. This is known as *accrual accounting*. This chapter explains how and why accounts are adjusted so that financial statements at the end of the reporting period reflect the effects of all transactions. We also illustrate adjusting entries and show how they are reflected in a 10-column work sheet.

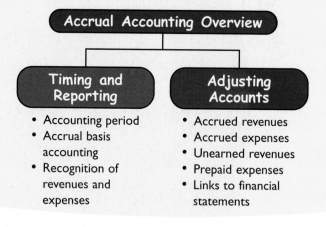

Accrual Accounting Overview

Timing and Reporting
- Accounting period
- Accrual basis accounting
- Recognition of revenues and expenses

Adjusting Accounts
- Accrued revenues
- Accrued expenses
- Unearned revenues
- Prepaid expenses
- Links to financial statements

Timing and Reporting

Regular, or periodic, reporting is an important part of the accounting process. This section describes the impact on the accounting process of periodic reporting.

The Accounting Period

LO1 Describe the importance of periodic reporting and the periodicity assumption.

"Best Buy announces earnings per share of . . ."

The value of information is often linked to its timeliness. Useful information must reach decision makers frequently and promptly. To provide timely information, accounting systems prepare reports at regular intervals. The **periodicity assumption** is that an organization's activities can be divided into specific time periods such as a month, a three-month quarter, a six-month interval, or a year. Exhibit 13.1 shows various **accounting,** or *reporting,* **periods.** Most organizations use a year as their primary accounting period. Reports covering a one-year period are known as **annual financial statements.** Many organizations also prepare **interim financial statements** covering one, three, or six months of activity.

Exhibit 13.1

Accounting Periods

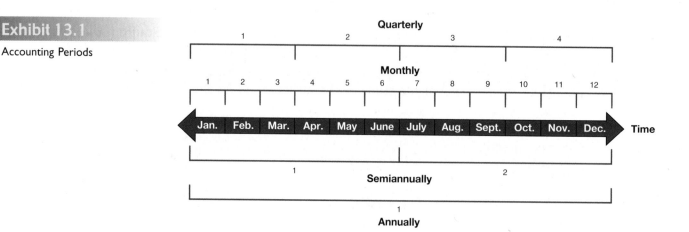

The annual reporting period is not always a calendar year ending on December 31. An organization can adopt a **fiscal year** consisting of any 12 consecutive months. It is also acceptable to adopt an annual reporting period of 52 weeks. For example, Gap's fiscal year consistently ends the final week of January or the first week of February each year.

Companies with little seasonal variation in sales often choose the calendar year as their fiscal year. For example, the financial statements of **Marvel Enterprises** (the company that controls characters such as Spider-Man, X-Men, and Shang-Chi) reflect a fiscal year that ends on December 31. Companies experiencing seasonal variations in sales often choose a **natural business year** end, which is when sales activities are at their lowest level for the year. The natural business year for retailers such as Wal-Mart, Target, and Staples usually ends around January 31, after the holiday season.

Accrual Basis Accounting

After external transactions and events are recorded, several accounts still need adjustment before their balances appear in financial statements. This need arises because internal transactions and events remain unrecorded. **Accrual basis accounting** uses the adjusting process to recognize revenues when earned and expenses when incurred (matched with revenues). Sometimes cash is received before (or after) the revenue is earned. Likewise, sometimes cash is paid before an expense is incurred.

LO2 Explain accrual accounting and how it improves financial statements.

As an example, consider SuperSub, a submarine sandwich shop. In order to pay lower rent, SuperSub paid rent of $24,000 in advance for 24 months beginning on December 1, 2007. Accrual accounting requires that $1,000 of rent expense be reported on December's income statement. Another $12,000 of rent expense is reported in year 2008 and the remaining $11,000 is reported as rent expense in the first 11 months of 2009. Exhibit 13.2 illustrates this allocation of rent cost across these three years. The accrual basis balance sheet reports any unexpired rent as a Prepaid Rent asset.

Exhibit 13.2

Accrual Basis Accounting for Allocating Prepaid Rent to Expense

Transaction: Purchase 24 months' rent beginning December 2007

Rent Expense 2007			
Jan	Feb	Mar	Apr
$0	$0	$0	$0
May	June	July	Aug
$0	$0	$0	$0
Sept	Oct	Nov	Dec
$0	$0	$0	$1,000

Rent Expense 2008			
Jan	Feb	Mar	Apr
$1,000	$1,000	$1,000	$1,000
May	June	July	Aug
$1,000	$1,000	$1,000	$1,000
Sept	Oct	Nov	Dec
$1,000	$1,000	$1,000	$1,000

Rent Expense 2009			
Jan	Feb	Mar	Apr
$1,000	$1,000	$1,000	$1,000
May	June	July	Aug
$1,000	$1,000	$1,000	$1,000
Sept	Oct	Nov	Dec
$1,000	$1,000	$1,000	$0

Recognizing Revenues and Expenses

We use the periodicity assumption to divide a company's activities into specific time periods, but not all activities are complete when financial statements are prepared. Thus, adjustments often are required to get correct account balances.

We rely on two principles in the adjusting process: revenue recognition and matching. The **revenue recognition principle** requires that revenue be recorded when earned. Most companies earn revenue when they provide services and products to customers. A major goal of the adjusting process is to have revenue recognized (reported) in the time period when it is earned.

The **matching principle** aims to record expenses in the same accounting period as the revenues that are earned as a result of these expenses. This matching of expenses with the revenue benefits is a major part of the adjusting process.

Matching expenses with revenues often requires us to predict certain events. When we use financial statements, we must understand that they require estimates and therefore include measures that are not always precise. Walt Disney's annual report explains that its production costs

> Recording expense early overstates current-period expense and understates current-period income; recording it late understates current-period expense and overstates current-period income.

from movies, such as *Pirates of the Caribbean,* are matched to revenues based on a ratio of current revenues from the movie divided by its predicted total revenues.

HOW YOU DOIN'?   Answers—p. 322

1. Describe a company's annual reporting period.
2. Why do companies prepare interim financial statements?
3. What two accounting principles most directly drive the adjusting process?
4. If your company pays a $4,800 premium on April 1, 2007, for two years' insurance coverage, how much insurance expense is reported in 2008 using cash basis accounting? Using accrual basis accounting?

Adjusting Accounts

LO3 Identify the types of accounting adjustments and their purpose.

In Chapter 5, we discussed some adjustments needed for both the income statement accounts (revenue or expense) and the balance sheet accounts (asset or liability) to obtain their correct balances. In this section, we suggest a framework for considering the types of adjustments that must be made at the end of the reporting period. We also introduce some new adjustments.

Framework for Adjustments

Adjustments are necessary for transactions that extend over more than one accounting period. It is helpful to group adjustments by the timing of cash receipt or cash payment in relation to the recognition of the related revenues or expenses. Exhibit 13.3 identifies types of adjustments.

Exhibit 13.3

Types of Adjustments

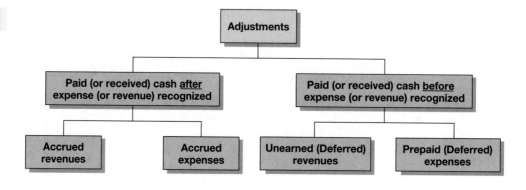

The left side of this exhibit shows accrued revenues and accrued expenses, which reflect transactions when cash is paid or received *after* a related expense or revenue is recognized. The right side of this exhibit shows unearned revenues and prepaid expenses (including prepaid rent and depreciation), which reflect transactions when cash is paid or received *before* a related expense or revenue is recognized. They are also called *deferrals* because the recognition of an expense (or revenue) is *deferred* until after the related cash is paid (or received).

Adjusting entries are necessary for each of these so that revenues, expenses, assets, and liabilities are correctly reported. It is helpful to remember that each adjusting entry affects one or more income statement accounts *and* one or more balance sheet accounts. Adjusting entries never affect the Cash account. Adjusting entries are posted to general ledger accounts just like other general journal entries.

Accrued Revenues

Accrued revenues are also called *accrued assets.*

The term **accrued revenues** refers to revenues earned in a period that are both unrecorded and not yet received in cash (or other assets) at the end of the period. An example is a technician who bills customers only when the job is done. If one-third of a job is complete by the end of a period, then the technician must record one-third of the expected billing as revenue in that period—even though there is no billing or collection. The adjusting entries for accrued revenues increase assets and increase revenues as shown in Exhibit 13.4. Accrued revenues commonly arise from services, products, interest, and rent. We use service fees to show how to adjust for accrued revenues.

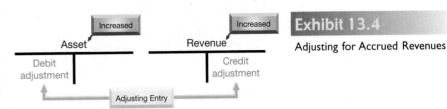

Exhibit 13.4

Adjusting for Accrued Revenues

Accrued Services Revenue Accrued revenues are not recorded until adjusting entries are made at the end of the accounting period. These accrued revenues are earned but unrecorded because either the buyer has not yet paid for them or the seller has not yet billed the buyer. SuperSub, a submarine sandwich shop, provides an example. SuperSub has received an agreement to cater a New Year's Eve party for a group of anesthesiologists for a fixed fee of $1,800. SuperSub caters the party and then later bills for its sandwiches. The revenue recognition principle suggests that since the goods have been provided, that revenue should be recognized on SuperSub's December income statement. The balance sheet also must report that the group of anesthesiologists owes SuperSub $1,800. The year-end adjusting entry to account for accrued sales revenue is

	Adjustment (a)		
Dec. 31	Accounts Receivable	1800 00	
	Sales Revenue		1800 00
	To record accrued revenue.		

$$Assets = Liabilities + Equity$$
$$+1,800 \qquad\qquad +1,800$$

Accounts Receivable		106
Dec. 12	4,000	
Adj. (a)	1,800	
Balance	5,800	

Sales Revenue		403
Dec. 12		7,200
25		1,600
29		250
Adj. (a)		1,800
Balance		10,850

Accounts receivable are reported on the year-end balance sheet at $5,800, and the $10,850 of sales revenue is reported on the income statement. *Not* making the adjustment would understate (1) both sales revenue and net income by $1,800 in the December income statement and (2) both accounts receivable (assets) and equity by $1,800 on the December 31 balance sheet.

Allowance for Doubtful Accounts When a company sells its products or services on credit, it expects that some customers will not pay what they promised. The accounts of these customers are *uncollectible accounts* or *bad debts*. The total amount of uncollectible accounts is a cost of selling on credit. The matching principle requires expenses to be reported in the same accounting period as the sales they helped produce. To match bad debts expense with the sales it produces, a company must estimate future uncollectibles.

There are several ways to estimate the expense for uncollectibles. These will be covered in detail in Chapter 15. SuperSub uses the *percentage of accounts receivable* method and, based on past experience, estimates that 5% of accounts receivable will be uncollectible. At the end of December, SuperSub's accounts receivable balance is $5,800. This implies that SuperSub expects not to collect $290 of its

YOU CALL IT   Answer—p. 322

Loan Officer The owner of an electronics store applies for a business loan. The store's financial statements reveal large increases in current-year revenues and income. Analysis shows that these increases are due to a promotion that lets consumers buy now and pay nothing until January 1 of next year. The store recorded these sales as accrued revenue. Does your analysis raise any concerns?

accounts receivable (.05 × $5,800). Assuming SuperSub's beginning balance in the Allowance for Doubtful Accounts was zero, the adjusting entry to record this estimated expense is

Assets = Liabilities + Equity
−290   −290

		Adjustment (b)		
Dec.	31	Bad Debts Expense	2 9 0 00	
		Allowance for Doubtful Accounts		2 9 0 00
		To record estimated bad debts.		

Credit approval is usually not assigned to the selling dept. because its goal is to increase sales, and it may approve customers at the cost of increased bad debts. Instead, approval is assigned to a separate credit-granting or administrative dept.

The estimated bad debts expense of $290 is reported on the income statement (as either a selling expense or an administrative expense). The **Allowance for Doubtful Accounts** is a contra asset account. A contra account is used instead of reducing accounts receivable directly because at the time of the adjusting entry, the company does not know which customers will not pay. SuperSub's account balances (in T-account form) for Bad Debts Expense and its Allowance for Doubtful Accounts are as shown in Exhibit 13.5.

Exhibit 13.5

General Ledger Balances after Bad Debts Adjusting Entry

Bad Debts Expense		
Adj. (b)	290	

Allowance for Doubtful Accounts		
	Adj. (b)	290

Accrued Expenses

Accrued expenses refer to costs that are incurred in a period but are both unpaid and unrecorded at the end of the period. Accrued expenses must be reported on the income statement of the period when incurred. Adjusting entries for recording accrued expenses involve increasing expenses and increasing liabilities as shown in

Exhibit 13.6

Adjusting for Accrued Expenses

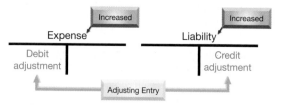

Exhibit 13.6. This adjustment recognizes expenses incurred in a period but not yet paid. Common examples of accrued expenses are salaries, interest, rent, and taxes. We use salaries and payroll taxes to show how to adjust accounts for accrued expenses.

Accrued expenses are also called *accrued liabilities.*

Accrued Salaries   At SuperSub, full-time employees are paid twice a month, on the 15th and on the last day of the month. Since they are paid on December 31, no adjusting entries are required. However, to deal with the big catering orders around the new year, SuperSub hired some part-time employees. Through December 31, 2007, the part-time employees had earned $610 in salaries. Since they will not be paid until January 4, an adjusting entry should be made to reflect the proper amount of expense in the December 2007 income statement. The adjusting entry is

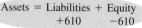

Assets = Liabilities + Equity
+610   −610

		Adjustment (c)		
Dec.	31	Salaries Expense	6 1 0 00	
		Salaries Payable		6 1 0 00
		To record part-time employees salary to Dec. 31.		

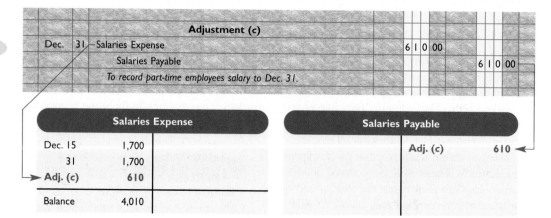

Salaries Expense		
Dec. 15	1,700	
31	1,700	
Adj. (c)	610	
Balance	4,010	

Salaries Payable		
	Adj. (c)	610

Salaries expense of $4,010 is reported on the December income statement and $610 of salaries payable (liability) is reported in the balance sheet. *Not* making the adjustment (1) understates salaries expense and overstates net income by $610 in the December income statement and (2) understates salaries payable (liabilities) and overstates equity by $610 on the December 31 balance sheet.

Accrued Payroll Taxes   Payroll taxes are owed after salaries are paid. However, to properly match expenses to the correct period, we make an adjusting entry to accrue payroll taxes in the same period that the salaries are expensed. SuperSub's full-time employees' payroll taxes have already been recorded in December 2007, when the payroll was paid. (In the example below we assume taxes for full-time employees have been sent to the taxing authority; refer to Chapter 10 for details.) However, the company must accrue payroll taxes for the part-time employees that worked in December. The entire $610 of accrued salaries are subject to the employer's share of social security and Medicare taxes (as discussed in Chapter 10) as well as federal and state unemployment taxes. Likewise, the entire $610 in accrued salaries is subject to unemployment taxes. The unemployment tax rates for SuperSub is 0.8% for federal and 5.4% for state. Assuming none of SuperSub's part-time employees' annual income is above the maximum amount for Social Security ($94,200 in 2006), SuperSub computes accrued payroll taxes as:

Social Security tax	$610	×	6.2%	=	$37.82
Medicare tax	$610	×	1.45%	=	8.85
Federal unemployment tax	$610	×	0.8%	=	4.88
State unemployment tax	$610	×	5.4%	=	32.94
Total accrued payroll taxes					$84.49

The adjusting journal entry to reflect the accrued payroll taxes for part-time employees is

Adjustment (d)		
Dec. 31 Payroll Tax Expense	84 49	
Medicare Tax Payable		8 85
Federal Unemployment Tax Payable		4 88
Social Security Tax Payable		37 82
State Unemployment Tax Payable		32 94
To accrue payroll taxes for part-time employees.		

Assets = Liabilities + Equity
+84.49   −8.85
                      −4.88
                      −37.82
                      −32.94

Payroll Tax Expense			
Dec. 15	235.00		
31	235.00		
Adj. (d)	84.49		
Balance	554.49		

Social Security Tax Payable			
		Adj. (d)	37.82
			37.82

Medicare Tax Payable			
		Adj. (d)	8.85
		Balance	8.85

Federal Unemployment Tax Payable			
		Adj. (d)	4.88
		Balance	4.88

State Unemployment Tax Payable			
		Adj. (d)	32.94
		Balance	32.94

Unearned (Deferred) Revenues

The term **unearned revenues** refers to cash received in advance of providing products and services. Unearned revenues, also called *deferred revenues,* are liabilities. When cash is received in advance, an obligation to provide products or services is accepted. As products or services are provided, the unearned revenues become *earned* revenues. Adjusting entries for unearned revenues involve increasing revenues and decreasing unearned revenues, as shown in Exhibit 13.7.

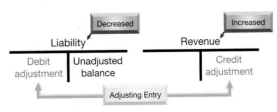

Decreased		Increased
Liability		Revenue
Debit adjustment	Unadjusted balance	Credit adjustment
	Adjusting Entry	

Exhibit 13.7

Adjusting for Unearned Revenues

To *defer* is to postpone. We postpone reporting amounts received as revenues until they are earned.

An example of unearned revenues is from **The New York Times Company**, which reports unexpired (unearned) newspaper subscriptions of nearly $80 million: "Proceeds from . . . subscriptions are deferred at the time of sale and are recognized in earnings on a pro rata basis over the terms of the subscriptions." Unearned revenues are nearly 10% of the current liabilities for the Times. Another example comes from the **Boston Celtics**. When the Celtics receive cash from advance ticket sales and broadcast fees, they record it in an unearned revenue account called *Deferred Game Revenues.* The Celtics recognize this unearned revenue with adjusting entries on a game-by-game basis. Since the NBA regular season begins in October and ends in April, revenue recognition is mainly limited to this period. For a recent season, the Celtics' quarterly revenues were $0 million for July–September; $34 million for October–December; $48 million for January–March; and $17 million for April–June.

SuperSub has unearned revenues. It agreed on December 1 to provide catered lunches once a week for the local Lions Club for the next 10 weeks. On that same day, the Lions Club paid SuperSub the $3,000 fee covering the entire 10-week period. The entry to record the cash received in advance is

Assets = Liabilities + Equity
+3,000   +3,000

Dec.	1	Cash	3 0 0 0 00	
		Unearned Sales Revenue		3 0 0 0 00
		Received advance payment for catering.		

This advance payment increases cash and creates an obligation to cater the lunches for the next 10 weeks. As time passes, SuperSub will earn revenue by catering lunches. By December 31, it has provided four weeks of lunches and earned 4/10 of the $3,000 unearned revenue. This amounts to $1,200 ($3,000 × 4/10). The revenue recognition principle implies that $1,200 of the advance payment be reported as revenue on the December income statement. The adjusting entry to reduce the liability account and recognize earned revenue, along with T-account postings, is

Assets = Liabilities + Equity
        −1,200   +1,200

Adjustment (e)				
Dec.	31	Unearned Sales Revenue	1 2 0 0 00	
		Sales Revenue		1 2 0 0 00
		To record earned revenue that was received in		
		advance ($3,000 × 4/10).		

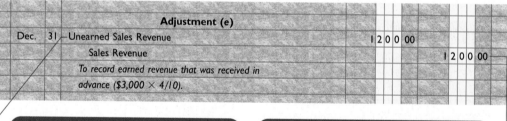

Unearned Sales Revenue					Sales Revenue		
Adj. (e)	1,200	Dec. 26	3,000		Dec. 5		7,200
					12		1,600
		Balance	2,750		29		250
					Adj. (a)		1,800
					Adj. (e)		1,200
					Balance		12,050

The adjusting entry transfers $1,200 from unearned revenue (a liability account) to a revenue account. *Not* making the adjustment (1) understates revenue and net income by $1,200 in the December income statement and (2) overstates unearned revenue and understates equity by $1,200 on the December 31 balance sheet.

Accounting for unearned revenues is crucial to many companies. For example, the **National Retail Federation** reports that gift card sales, which are unearned revenues for sellers, are approaching $20 billion annually. Gift cards are now the top-selling holiday gift. (An alternate method of accounting for unearned revenues is presented in Appendix 13A.)

Prepaid (Deferred) Expenses

Prepaid expenses refer to items *paid for* in advance of receiving their benefits. Prepaid expenses are assets. When these assets are used, their costs become expenses. Adjusting entries for prepaids increase expenses and decrease assets as shown in the T-accounts of Exhibit 13.8. Such adjustments reflect transactions and events that use up prepaid expenses (including passage of time).

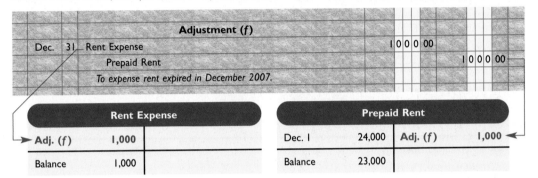

Exhibit 13.8

Adjusting for Prepaid Expenses

Prepaid Rent   On December 1, 2007, SuperSub paid $24,000 for 24 months' rent. The asset account Prepaid Rent was debited for $24,000. On December 31, 2007, one month of rent had expired. An adjustment reflecting one month's rent of $1,000 ($24,000 × 1/24) should be recorded. The adjusting journal entry is

		Adjustment (f)		
Dec.	31	Rent Expense	1 0 0 0 00	
		Prepaid Rent		1 0 0 0 00
		To expense rent expired in December 2007.		

Assets = Liabilities + Equity
−1,000   −1,000

Rent Expense				Prepaid Rent			
Adj. (f)	1,000			Dec. 1	24,000	Adj. (f)	1,000
Balance	1,000			Balance	23,000		

The balances in the accounts now reflect the rent expense for the period and the remaining prepaid rent at the end of the period.

Supplies   On December 1, 2007, SuperSub had $3,000 of supplies available. On December 31, 2007, $1,800 worth of supplies remained, suggesting that $1,200 of supplies had been used up during December. The adjustment reflecting the supplies used is

		Adjustment (g)		
Dec.	31	Supplies Expense	1 2 0 0 00	
		Supplies		1 2 0 0 00
		To expense supplies used in December 2007.		

Assets = Liabilities + Equity
−1,200   −1,200

Supplies Expense				Supplies			
Adj. (g)	1,200			Dec.1 bal.	3,000	Adj. (g)	1,200
Balance	1,200			Balance	1,800		

The balances in the accounts now reflect the supplies expense for the period and the supplies remaining at the end of the period.

Prepaid Insurance   On December 1, 2007, SuperSub paid $1,800 for 18 months of insurance coverage. The asset account Prepaid Insurance was debited for $1,800. On December 31, 2007, one month of insurance had expired. The adjustment reflecting one month's coverage of insurance of $100 ($1,800 × 1/18) is

		Adjustment (h)		
Dec.	31	Insurance Expense	1 0 0 00	
		Prepaid Insurance		1 0 0 00
		To expense insurance expired in December 2007.		

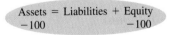

Assets = Liabilities + Equity
−100   −100

Insurance Expense				Prepaid Insurance			
Adj. (h)	100			Dec. 1	1,800	Adj. (h)	100
Balance	100			Balance	1,700		

The balances in the accounts now reflect the insurance expense for the period and the remaining prepaid insurance at the end of the period.

Depreciation   On December 1, 2007, SuperSub purchased $18,000 of equipment to use in its submarine shop. As SuperSub uses the equipment, depreciation expense is recorded to allocate the costs of using the equipment over its useful life. The useful life of SuperSub's equipment is 36 months. The depreciation expense per month is $500 ($18,000/36). The adjusting journal entry for December is

Assets = Liabilities + Equity
−500   −500

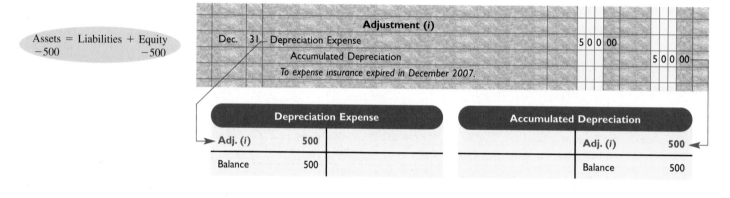

The balances in the accounts now reflect the depreciation expense for the period and the accumulated depreciation on the equipment. The contra account Accumulated Depreciation is used instead of directly crediting the Equipment account.

Links to Financial Statements

LO4 Explain how accounting adjustments link to financial statements.

The process of adjusting accounts is intended to bring an asset or liability account balance to its correct amount. It also updates a related expense or revenue account. These adjustments are necessary for transactions and events that extend over more than one period.

Exhibit 13.9 summarizes the four types of transactions requiring adjustment. Understanding this exhibit is important to understanding the adjusting process and its importance to financial statements. Remember that each adjusting entry affects one or more income statement accounts *and* one or more balance sheet accounts (but not cash).

Exhibit 13.9

Summary of Adjustments and Financial Statement Links

	BEFORE Adjusting		
Category	**Balance Sheet**	**Income Statement**	**Adjusting Entry**
Prepaid expenses†	Asset overstated	Expense understated	Dr. Expense
	Equity overstated		Cr. Asset*
Unearned revenues†	Liability overstated	Revenue understated	Dr. Liability
	Equity understated		Cr. Revenue
Accrued expenses	Liability understated	Expense understated	Dr. Expense
	Equity overstated		Cr. Liability
Accrued revenues	Asset understated	Revenue understated	Dr. Asset
	Equity understated		Cr. Revenue

* For depreciation, the credit is to Accumulated Depreciation (contra asset).

† Exhibit 13.9 assumes that Prepaid Expenses are initially recorded as assets and that Unearned Revenues are initially recorded as liabilities.

Information about some adjustments is not always available until several days or even weeks after the period-end. This means that some adjusting and closing entries are recorded later than, but dated as of, the last day of the period. One example is a company that receives a utility bill on January 10 for costs incurred for the month of December. When it receives the bill, the company records the expense and the payable as of December 31. Other examples include long-distance phone usage and costs of many service billings. The December income statement reflects these additional expenses incurred, and the December 31 balance sheet includes these payables, although the amounts were not actually known on December 31.

Work Sheet

To summarize our SuperSub example, Exhibit 13.10 contains a partial work sheet for SuperSub for the year ended December 31, 2007. To make sure we have adequately captured all of the adjustments, we must confirm that the debits equal the credits in the adjustments column. In the case of SuperSub, both the adjustments debits and credits total $6,784.49.

In Chapter 14, we use the **adjusted trial balance** columns to help prepare financial statements.

> ### YOU CALL IT
> Answer—p. 322
>
> **Financial Officer**   At year-end, the president instructs you, the financial officer, not to record accrued expenses until next year because they will not be paid until then. The president also directs you to record in current-year sales a recent purchase order from a customer that requires merchandise to be delivered two weeks after the year-end. Your company would report a net income instead of a net loss if you carry out these instructions. What do you do?

Exhibit 13.10

Partial Work Sheet

SUPERSUB
Work Sheet
Year Ended December 31, 2007

Description	Unadjusted Trial Balance Debit	Unadjusted Trial Balance Credit	Adjustments Debit	Adjustments Credit	Adjusted Trial Balance Debit	Adjusted Trial Balance Credit
Cash	4 0 0 0 00				4 0 0 0 00	
Accounts receivable	4 0 0 0 00		(a) 1 8 0 0 00		5 8 0 0 00	
Allowance for doubtful accounts		0		(b) 2 9 0 00		2 9 0 00
Merchandise inventory	2 2 0 0 00				2 2 0 0 00	
Prepaid insurance	1 8 0 0 00			(h) 1 0 0 00	1 7 0 0 00	
Prepaid rent	24 0 0 0 00			(f) 1 0 0 0 00	23 0 0 0 00	
Supplies	3 0 0 0 00			(g) 1 2 0 0 00	1 8 0 0 00	
Store equipment	18 0 0 0 00				18 0 0 0 00	
Accumulated depreciation—Store equipment		0		(i) 5 0 0 00		5 0 0 00
Social Security tax payable		0		(d) 3 7 82		3 7 82
Medicare tax payable		0		(d) 8 85		8 85
Federal unemployment tax payable		0		(d) 4 88		4 88
State unemployment tax payable		0		(d) 3 2 94		3 2 94
Salaries payable		0		(c) 6 1 0 00		6 1 0 00
Unearned revenue		3 0 0 0 00	(e) 1 2 0 0 00			1 8 0 0 00
Polly Guthrie, Capital		52 7 4 5 00				52 7 4 5 00
Polly Guthrie, Withdrawals	1 0 0 0 00				1 0 0 0 00	
Income summary		0				
Sales		9 0 5 0 00		(a) 1 8 0 0 00 (e) 1 2 0 0 00		12 0 5 0 00
Purchases	3 0 0 0 00				3 0 0 0 00	
Transportation-in	5 0 00				5 0 00	
Purchase returns and allowances		5 0 00				5 0 00
Purchase discounts		7 5 00				7 5 00
Salaries expense	3 4 0 0 00		(c) 6 1 0 00		4 0 1 0 00	
Uncollectible accounts expense			(b) 2 9 0 00		2 9 0 00	
Depreciation expense—Store equipment			(i) 5 0 0 00		5 0 0 00	
Rent expense			(f) 1 0 0 0 00		1 0 0 0 00	
Insurance expense			(h) 1 0 0 00		1 0 0 00	
Payroll tax expense	4 7 0 00		(d) 8 4 49		5 5 4 49	
Supplies expense			(g) 1 2 0 0 00		1 2 0 0 00	
Totals	64 9 2 0 00	64 9 2 0 00	6 7 8 4 49	6 7 8 4 49	68 2 0 4 49	68 2 0 4 49

Answers—p. 322

HOW YOU DOIN'?

5. If an adjusting entry for accrued revenues of $200 at year-end is omitted, what is this error's effect on the year-end income statement and balance sheet?

6. Describe how an accrued revenue arises. Give an example.

Demonstration Problem

The following information relates to Joel's Alarm Services on December 31, 2007. The company, which uses the calendar year as its annual reporting period, initially records prepaid and unearned items in balance sheet accounts (assets and liabilities, respectively).

a. The company's weekly payroll is $8,750, paid each Friday for a five-day workweek. Assume December 31, 2007, falls on a Monday, but the employees will not be paid their wages until Friday, January 4, 2008. (For simplicity, ignore payroll taxes for this problem).

b. Eighteen months earlier, on July 1, 2006, the company purchased equipment that cost $20,000. Its useful life is predicted to be five years, at which time the equipment is expected to be worthless (zero salvage value).

c. On October 1, 2007, the company agreed to work on a new housing development. The company is paid $120,000 on October 1 in advance of future installation of alarm systems in 24 new homes. That amount was credited to the Unearned Services Revenue account. Between October 1 and December 31, work on 20 homes was completed.

d. On September 1, 2007, the company purchased a 12-month insurance policy for $2,400. The transaction was recorded with a $2,400 debit to Prepaid Insurance.

e. On December 29, 2007, the company completed a $7,000 alarm installation service that has not been billed and not recorded as of December 31, 2007.

Required

1. Prepare any necessary adjusting entries on December 31, 2007, in relation to transactions and events *a* through *e*.

2. Prepare T-accounts for the accounts affected by adjusting entries, and post the adjusting entries. Determine the adjusted balances for the Unearned Revenue and the Prepaid Insurance accounts.

3. Complete the following table and determine the amounts and effects of your adjusting entries on the year 2007 income statement and the December 31, 2007, balance sheet. Use up (down) arrows to indicate an increase (decrease) in the Effect columns.

Entry	Amount in the Entry	Effect on Net Income	Effect on Total Assets	Effect on Total Liabilities	Effect on Total Equity

Planning the Solution

• Analyze each situation to determine which accounts need to be updated with an adjustment.

• Calculate the amount of each adjustment and prepare the necessary journal entries.

• Show the amount of each adjustment in the designated accounts, determine the adjusted balance, and identify the balance sheet classification of the account.

• Determine each entry's effect on net income for the year and on total assets, total liabilities, and total equity at the end of the year.

Solution to Demonstration Problem

1. Adjusting journal entries.

(a)	Dec.	31	Wages Expense	1 7 5 0 00	
			Wages Payable		1 7 5 0 00
			To accrue wages for the last day of the year		
			($8,750 × 1/5).		
(b)	Dec.	31	Depreciation Expense—Equipment	4 0 0 0 00	
			Accumulated Depreciation—Equipment		4 0 0 0 00
			To record depreciation expense for the year		
			($20,000/5 years = $4,000 per year).		
(c)	Dec.	31	Unearned Services Revenue	100 0 0 0 00	
			Services Revenue		100 0 0 0 00
			To recognize services revenue earned		
			($120,000 × 20/24).		
(d)	Dec.	31	Insurance Expense	8 0 0 00	
			Prepaid Insurance		8 0 0 00
			To adjust for expired portion of insurance		
			($2,400 × 4/12).		
(e)	Dec.	31	Accounts Receivable	7 0 0 0 00	
			Services Revenue		7 0 0 0 00
			To accrue services revenue earned.		

2. T-accounts for adjusting journal entries *a* through *e*.

Wages Expense			Wages Payable		
(a)	1,750			(a)	1,750

Depreciation Expense—Equipment			Accumulated Depreciation—Equipment		
(b)	4,000			(b)	4,000

Unearned Revenue			Services Revenue		
		Unadj. Bal. 120,000		(c)	100,000
(c)	100,000			(e)	7,000
		Adj. Bal. 20,000		Adj. Bal.	107,000

Insurance Expense			Prepaid Insurance		
(d)	800		Unadj. Bal.	2,400	
					(d) 800

Accounts Receivable				
(e)	7,000		Adj. Bal. 1,600	

3. Financial statement effects of adjusting journal entries.

Entry	Amount in the Entry	Effect on Net Income	Effect on Total Assets	Effect on Total Liabilities	Effect on Total Equity
a	$ 1,750	$ 1,750 ↓	No effect	$ 1,750 ↑	$ 1,750 ↓
b	4,000	4,000 ↓	$4,000 ↓	No effect	4,000 ↓
c	100,000	100,000 ↑	No effect	$100,000 ↓	100,000 ↑
d	800	800 ↓	$ 800 ↓	No effect	800 ↓
e	7,000	7,000 ↑	$7,000 ↑	No effect	7,000 ↑

APPENDIX

13A Alternative Accounting for Prepayments

This appendix explains an alternative in accounting for prepaid expenses and unearned revenues.

Recording the Prepayment of Expenses in Expense Accounts

LO5 Describe the alternatives in accounting for prepayments.

An alternative method is to record *all* prepaid expenses with debits to expense accounts. If any prepaids remain unused or unexpired at the end of an accounting period, then adjusting entries must transfer the cost of the unused portions from expense accounts to prepaid expense (asset) accounts. This alternative method is acceptable. The financial statements are identical under either method, but the adjusting entries are different. To illustrate the differences between these two methods, let's look at SuperSub's cash payment of December 1 for 18 months of insurance coverage beginning on December 1. SuperSub's recorded that payment with a debit to an asset account, but it could have recorded a debit to an expense account. These alternatives are shown in Exhibit 13A.1.

Exhibit 13A.1

Alternative Initial Entries for Prepaid Expenses

			Payment Recorded as Asset	Payment Recorded as Expense
Dec. 1	Prepaid Insurance		1,800	
	Cash			1,800	
Dec. 1	Insurance Expense			1,800
	Cash				1,800

At the end of its accounting period on December 31, insurance protection for one month has expired. This means $100 ($1,800/18) of insurance coverage expired and is an expense for December. The adjusting entry depends on how the original payment was recorded. This is shown in Exhibit 13A.2.

Exhibit 13A.2

Adjusting Entry for Prepaid Expenses for the Two Alternatives

			Payment Recorded as Asset	Payment Recorded as Expense
Dec. 31	Insurance Expense		100	
	Prepaid Insurance			100	
Dec. 31	Prepaid Insurance			1,700
	Insurance Expense				1,700

When these entries are posted to the accounts in the ledger, we can see that these two methods give identical results. The December 31 adjusted account balances in Exhibit 13A.3 show Prepaid Insurance of $1,700 and Insurance Expense of $100 for both methods.

Exhibit 13A.3

Account Balances under Two Alternatives for Recording Prepaid Expenses

Payment Recorded as Asset			
Prepaid Insurance			**128**
Dec. 1	1,800	Dec. 31	100
Balance	1,700		

Insurance Expense			**637**
Dec. 31	100		

Payment Recorded as Expense			
Prepaid Insurance			**128**
Dec. 31	1,700		

Insurance Expense			**637**
Dec. 1	1,800	Dec. 31	1,700
Balance	100		

Recording the Prepayment of Revenues in Revenue Accounts

As with prepaid expenses, an alternative method is to record *all* unearned revenues with credits to revenue accounts. If any revenues are unearned at the end of an accounting period, then adjusting entries must transfer the unearned portions from revenue accounts to unearned revenue (liability) accounts. The adjusting entries are different for these two alternatives, but the financial statements are identical. To illustrate the accounting differences between these two methods, let's look at SuperSub's December 1 receipt of $3,000 for services covering 10 weekly lunches. SuperSub's recorded this transaction with a credit to a liability account. The alternative is to record it with a credit to a revenue account, as shown in Exhibit 13A.4.

		Receipt Recorded as Liability	Receipt Recorded as Revenue
Dec. 1	Cash	3,000	
	Unearned Sales Revenue	3,000	
Dec. 1	Cash		3,000
	Sales Revenue		3,000

Exhibit 13A.4

Alternative Initial Entries for Unearned Revenues

By the end of its accounting period on December 31, SuperSub's has earned $1,200 of this revenue. This means $1,200 of the liability has been satisfied. Depending on how the initial receipt is recorded, the adjusting entry is as shown in Exhibit 13A.5.

		Receipt Recorded as Liability	Receipt Recorded as Revenue
Dec. 31	Unearned Sales Revenue	1,200	
	Sales Revenue	1,200	
Dec. 31	Sales Revenue		1,800
	Unearned Sales Revenue		1,800

Exhibit 13A.5

Adjusting Entry for Unearned Revenues for the Two Alternatives

After adjusting entries are posted, the two alternatives give identical results. The December 31 adjusted account balances in Exhibit 13A.6 show unearned revenue of $1,800 and sales revenue of $1,200 for both methods.

Receipt Recorded as Liability			
Unearned Consulting Revenue			236
Dec. 31	1,200	Dec. 1	3,000
		Balance	1,800

Consulting Revenue			403
		Dec. 31	1,800

Receipt Recorded as Revenue			
Unearned Consulting Revenue			236
		Dec. 31	1,800

Consulting Revenue			403
Dec. 31	1,800	Dec. 1	3,000
		Balance	1,200

Exhibit 13A.6

Account Balances under Two Alternatives for Recording Unearned Revenues

Summary

LO1 Describe the importance of periodic reporting and the periodicity assumption. The value of information is often linked to its timeliness. To provide timely information, accounting systems prepare periodic reports at regular intervals. The time period principle assumes that an organization's activities can be divided into specific time periods for periodic reporting.

LO2 **Explain accrual accounting and how it improves financial statements.** Accrual accounting recognizes revenue when earned and expenses when incurred—not necessarily when cash inflows and outflows occur. This information is valuable in assessing a company's financial position and performance.

LO3 **Identify the types of accounting adjustments and their purpose.** Adjustments can be grouped according to the timing of cash receipts and cash payments relative to when they are recognized as revenues or expenses as follows: prepaid expenses, unearned revenues, accrued expenses, and accrued revenues. Adjusting entries are necessary so that revenues, expenses, assets, and liabilities are correctly reported.

LO4 **Explain how accounting adjustments link to financial statements.** Accounting adjustments bring an asset or liability account balance to its correct amount. They also update related expense or revenue accounts. Every adjusting entry affects one or more income statement accounts *and* one or more balance sheet accounts. An adjusting entry never affects cash.

LO5 **Describe the alternatives in accounting for prepayments.** Debiting all prepaid expenses to expense accounts when they are purchased is acceptable. When this is done, adjusting entries must transfer any unexpired amounts from expense accounts to asset accounts. Crediting all unearned revenues to revenue accounts when cash is received is also acceptable. In this case, the adjusting entries must transfer any unearned amounts from revenue accounts to unearned revenue accounts.

Guidance Answers to **YOU CALL IT**

Loan Officer   Your concern in lending to this store arises from analysis of current-year sales. While increased revenues and income are fine, your concern is with collectibility of these promotional sales. If the owner sold products to customers with poor records of paying bills, then collectibility of these sales is low. Your analysis must assess this possibility and recognize any expected losses.

Financial Officer   Omitting accrued expenses and recognizing revenue early can mislead financial statement users. One action is to request a second meeting with the president so you can explain that accruing expenses when incurred and recognizing revenue when earned are required practices. If the president persists, you might discuss the situation with legal counsel and any auditors involved. Your ethical action might cost you this job, but the potential pitfalls for falsification of statements, reputation and personal integrity loss, and other costs are too great.

Guidance Answers to **HOW YOU DOIN'?**

1. An annual reporting (or accounting) period covers one year and refers to the preparation of annual financial statements. The annual reporting period is not always a calendar year that ends on December 31. An organization can adopt a fiscal year consisting of any consecutive 12 months or 52 weeks.

2. Interim financial statements (covering less than one year) are prepared to provide timely information to decision makers.

3. The revenue recognition principle and the matching principle lead most directly to the adjusting process.

4. No expense is reported in 2008. Under cash basis accounting, the entire $4,800 is reported as an expense in April 2007 when

the premium is paid. Under accrual accounting, $2,400 is reported as expense in 2008.

5. If the accrued revenues adjustment of $200 is not made, then both revenues and net income are understated by $200 on the current year's income statement, and both assets and equity are understated by $200 on the balance sheet.

6. An accrued revenue arises when revenue is earned but not yet received in cash. An example would be consulting work that has been performed for which payment has not yet been received.

Key Terms   mhhe.com/wildCA

Key Terms are available at the book's Website for learning and testing in an online Flashcard Format.

Accounting period (pp. 308) Length of time covered by financial statements; also called *reporting period*.

Accrual basis accounting (p. 309) Accounting system that recognizes revenues when earned and expenses when incurred; the basis for generally accepted accounting principles (GAAP).

Accrued expenses (p. 312) Costs incurred in a period that are both unpaid and unrecorded; adjusting entries for recording accrued expenses involve increasing expenses and increasing liabilities.

Accrued revenues (p. 310) Revenues earned in a period that are both unrecorded and not yet received in cash (or other assets); adjusting entries for recording accrued revenues involve increasing assets and increasing revenues.

Adjusted trial balance (p. 317) List of accounts and balances prepared after period-end adjustments are recorded and posted.

Adjusting entry (p. 310) Journal entry at the end of an accounting period to bring an asset or liability account to its proper amount and update the related expense or revenue account.

Allowance for Doubtful Accounts (p. 312) Contra asset account with a balance approximating uncollectible accounts receivable; also called *Allowance for Uncollectible Accounts*.

Annual financial statements (p. 308) Financial statements covering a one-year period; often based on a calendar year, but any consecutive 12-month (or 52-week) period is acceptable.

Fiscal year (p. 309) Consecutive 12-month (or 52-week) period chosen as the organization's annual accounting period.

Interim financial statements (p. 308) Financial statements covering periods of less than one year; usually based on one-, three-, or six-month periods.

Matching principle (p. 309) Prescribes expenses to be reported in the same period as the revenues that were earned as a result of the expenses.

Natural business year (p. 309) Twelve-month period that ends when a company's sales activities are at their lowest point.

Periodicity assumption (or principle) (p. 308) Assumption that an organization's activities can be divided into specific time periods such as months, quarters, or years.

Prepaid expenses (p. 314) Items paid for in advance of receiving their benefits; classified as assets.

Revenue recognition principle (p. 309) The principle prescribing that revenue is recognized when earned.

Unearned revenues (p. 313) Liability created when customers pay in advance for products or services; earned when the products or services are later delivered.

Multiple Choice Quiz   Answers on p. 331   mhhe.com/wildCA

Multiple Choice Quizzes A and B are available at the book's Website.

1. The accounting principle that requires revenue to be reported when earned is the
   a. Matching principle.
   b. Revenue recognition principle.
   c. Time period principle.
   d. Accrual reporting principle.
   e. Going-concern principle.

2. Adjusting entries
   a. Affect only income statement accounts.
   b. Affect only balance sheet accounts.
   c. Affect both income statement and balance sheet accounts.
   d. Affect only cash flow statement accounts.
   e. Affect only equity accounts.

3. On May 1, 2008, a two-year insurance policy was purchased for $12,000 with coverage to begin immediately. What is the amount of insurance expense that appears on the company's income statement for the year ended December 31, 2008?
   a. $2,000
   b. $4,000
   c. $6,000
   d. $10,000
   e. $12,000

4. On November 1, 2008, Stockton Co. receives $3,600 cash from Hans Co. for consulting services to be provided evenly over the period November 1, 2008, to April 30, 2009—at which time Stockton credited $3,600 to Unearned Consulting Fees. The adjusting entry on December 31, 2008 (Stockton's year-end) would include a
   a. Debit to Unearned Consulting Fees for $1,200.
   b. Debit to Unearned Consulting Fees for $2,400.
   c. Credit to Consulting Fees Earned for $2,400.
   d. Debit to Consulting Fees Earned for $1,200.
   e. Credit to Cash for $3,600.

5. Employees at Guthrie Co. worked three days at the end of 2008 and earned $5,400. They will be paid for this work at the next payroll date on January 9, 2009. What is the adjusting entry that Guthrie must make for the year ending December 31, 2008?
   a. Debit Wages Expense $5,400, Credit Prepaid Wages $5,400.
   b. Debit Wages Payable $5,400, Credit Wages Expense $5,400.
   c. Debit Prepaid Wages $5,400, Credit Wages Payable $5,400.
   d. Debit Wages Expense $5,400, Credit Wages Payable $5,400.

Superscript letter ᴬ *denotes assignments based on Appendix 13A.*

Discussion Questions

1. Why is the accrual basis of accounting generally preferred over simply using cash payments and receipts?

2. What type of business is most likely to select a fiscal year that corresponds to its natural business year instead of the calendar year?

3. What is an accrued expense and where is it reported in the financial statements?

4. What is unearned revenue and where is it reported in financial statements?

5. What is an accrued revenue? Give an example.

6. ᴬIf a company initially records prepaid expenses with debits to expense accounts, what type of account is debited in the adjusting entries for those prepaid expenses?

7. Review the balance sheet of **Best Buy** in Appendix A. Identify the liability accounts that require adjustment before annual financial statements can be prepared. What would be the effect on the income statement if these liability accounts were not adjusted?

8. Review the balance sheet of **Circuit City** in Appendix A. Identify two asset accounts requiring adjusting entries.

~~~~~~

QUICK STUDY

Classify the following adjusting entries as involving prepaid expenses (PE), unearned revenues (UR), accrued expenses (AE), or accrued revenues (AR).

QS 13-1

Identifying accounting adjustments

(LO3)

a. _____ To record revenue earned that was previously received as cash in advance.

b. _____ To record wages expense incurred but not yet paid (nor recorded).

c. _____ To record revenue earned but not yet billed (nor recorded).

d. _____ To record expiration of prepaid insurance.

e. _____ To record annual depreciation expense.

QS 13-2

Adjusting for unearned revenues

(LO3)

a. Tao receives $10,000 cash in advance for 4 months of legal services on October 1, 2008, and records it by debiting Cash and crediting Unearned Revenue both for $10,000. It is now December 31, 2008, and Tao has provided legal services as planned. What adjusting entry should Tao make to account for the work performed from October 1 through December 31, 2008?

b. In June 2008, A. Caden started a new publication called *Contest News*. Her subscribers pay $24 to receive 12 issues. With every new subscriber, Caden debits Cash and credits Unearned Subscription Revenue for the amounts received. Caden has 100 new subscribers as of July 1, 2008. She sends *Contest News* to each of these subscribers every month from July through December. Assuming no changes in subscribers, prepare the journal entry that Caden must make as of December 31, 2008, to adjust the Subscription Revenue account and the Unearned Subscription Revenue account.

QS 13-3

Preparing adjusting entries

(LO3)

During the year, Sereno Co. recorded prepayments of expenses in asset accounts, and cash receipts of unearned revenues in liability accounts. At the end of its annual accounting period, the company must make three adjusting entries: (1) accrue salaries expense, (2) adjust the Unearned Services Revenue account to recognize earned revenue, and (3) record services revenue earned for which cash will be received the following period. For each of these adjusting entries (1), (2), and (3), indicate the account from *a* through *i* to be debited and the account to be credited.

a. Prepaid Salaries   **d.** Unearned Services Revenue   **g.** Accounts Receivable

b. Cash   **e.** Salaries Expense   **h.** Accounts Payable

c. Salaries Payable   **f.** Services Revenue   **i.** Equipment

---

QS 13-4

Interpreting adjusting entries

(LO3) (LO4)

The following information is taken from Brooke Company's unadjusted and adjusted trial balances.

	Unadjusted		Adjusted	
	Debit	Credit	Debit	Credit
Prepaid insurance	$4,100		$3,700	
Interest payable		$ 0		$800

Given this information, which of the following is likely included among its adjusting entries?

a. A $400 debit to Insurance Expense and an $800 debit to Interest Payable.

b. A $400 debit to Insurance Expense and an $800 debit to Interest Expense.

c. A $400 credit to Prepaid Insurance and an $800 debit to Interest Payable.

QS 13-5

Determining effects of adjusting entries

(LO4)

In making adjusting entries at the end of its accounting period, Chao Consulting failed to record $1,600 of insurance coverage that had expired. This $1,600 cost had been initially debited to the Prepaid Insurance account. The company also failed to record accrued salaries expense of $1,000. As a result of these two oversights, the financial statements for the reporting period will [choose one] (1) understate assets by $1,600; (2) understate expenses by $2,600; (3) understate net income by $1,000; or (4) overstate liabilities by $1,000.

QS 13-6[A]

Preparing adjusting entries

(LO5)

Calvin Consulting initially records prepaid and unearned items in income statement accounts. Given Calvin Consulting's accounting practices, which of the following applies to the preparation of adjusting entries at the end of its first accounting period?

a. Earned but unbilled (and unrecorded) consulting fees are recorded with a debit to Unearned Consulting Fees and a credit to Consulting Fees Earned.

b. Unpaid salaries are recorded with a debit to Prepaid Salaries and a credit to Salaries Expense.

c. The cost of unused office supplies is recorded with a debit to Supplies Expense and a credit to Office Supplies.

d. Unearned fees (on which cash was received in advance earlier in the period) are recorded with a debit to Consulting Fees Earned and a credit to Unearned Consulting Fees.

In the blank space beside each adjusting entry, enter the letter of the explanation *A* through *F* that most closely describes the entry.

A. To record this period's depreciation expense.

B. To record accrued salaries expense.

C. To record this period's use of a prepaid expense.

D. To record accrued interest revenue.

E. To record accrued interest expense.

F. To record the earning of previously unearned income.

Exercise 13-1
Classifying adjusting entries
(LO3)

_____	1.	Interest Expense	4,702
		Interest Payable	4,702
_____	2.	Insurance Expense	1,653
		Prepaid Insurance	1,653
_____	3.	Unearned Professional Fees	19,250
		Professional Fees Earned	19,250
_____	4.	Interest Receivable	3,300
		Interest Revenue	3,300
_____	5.	Depreciation Expense	12,413
		Accumulated Depreciation	12,413
_____	6.	Salaries Expense	6,250
		Salaries Payable	6,250

Prepare adjusting journal entries for the year ended December 31, 2008, for each of these separate situations. Assume that prepaid expenses are initially recorded in asset accounts. Also assume that fees collected in advance of work are initially recorded as liabilities.

a. Depreciation on the company's equipment for 2008 is computed to be $23,000.

b. Two-thirds of the work related to $15,000 of cash received in advance was performed this period.

c. The Prepaid Insurance account had a $2,600 debit balance at December 31, 2008, before adjusting for the costs of any expired coverage. An analysis of insurance policies showed that $2,100 of coverage had expired as of December 31, 2008.

d. Wage expenses of $6,700 have been incurred but are not paid as of December 31, 2008.

Exercise 13-2
Preparing adjusting entries
(LO3)

Check (c) Dr. Insurance Expense, $2,100

For each of the following separate cases, prepare adjusting entries required of financial statements for the year ended December 31, 2008. Assume that prepaid expenses are initially recorded in asset accounts and that fees collected in advance of work are initially recorded as liabilities.

a. One-third of the work related to $15,000 cash received in advance is performed this period.

b. The company has earned (but not recorded) $1,000 of interest from investments in CDs for the year ended December 31, 2008. The interest revenue will be received on January 10, 2009.

c. The company has a bank loan and has incurred (but not recorded) interest expense of $2,500 for the year ended December 31, 2008. The company must pay the interest on January 2, 2009.

Exercise 13-3
Preparing adjusting entries
(LO3)

Check (b) Cr. Interest Revenue, $1,000

Reese Management has four part-time employees, each of whom earns $300 per day. They are normally paid on Fridays for work completed Monday through Friday of the same week. They were paid in full on Friday, December 28, 2007. The next week, the five employees worked only four days because New Year's Day was an unpaid holiday. Show (*a*) the adjusting entry that would be recorded on Monday, December 31, 2007, and (*b*) the journal entry that would be made to record payment of the employees' wages on Friday, January 4, 2008. (For simplicity, ignore payroll taxes.)

Exercise 13-4
Adjusting and paying accrued wages
(LO3)

The following three separate situations require adjusting journal entries to prepare financial statements as of April 30. For each situation, present both the April 30 adjusting entry and the subsequent entry during May to record the payment of the accrued expenses.

a. On April 1, the company retained an attorney at a flat monthly fee of $3,500. This amount is payable on the 12th of the following month.

b. An $800,000 note payable requires $8,000 of interest to be paid at the 20th day of each month. The interest was last paid on April 20 and the next payment is due on May 20. As of April 30, $2,667 of interest expense has accrued.

Exercise 13-5
Adjusting and paying accrued expenses
(LO3)

Check (b) May 20 Dr. Interest Expense, $5,333

Exercise 13-6
Analyzing and preparing adjusting entries

Following are two income statements for Alexis Co. for the year ended December 31. The left column is prepared before any adjusting entries are recorded, and the right column includes the effects of adjusting entries. The company records cash receipts and payments related to unearned and prepaid items in balance sheet accounts. Analyze the statements and prepare the eight adjusting entries that likely were recorded. (*Note:* 30% of the $7,000 adjustment for Fees Earned has been earned but not billed, and the other 70% has been earned by performing services that were paid for in advance.)

ALEXIS CO.
Income Statements
For Year Ended December 31

	Unadjusted	Adjusted
Revenues		
Fees earned	$18 000 00	$25 000 00
Commissions earned	36 500 00	36 500 00
Total revenues	$54 500 00	$61 500 00
Expenses		
Depreciation expense—Computers	0 00	1 600 00
Depreciation expense—Office furniture	0 00	1 850 00
Salaries expense	13 500 00	15 750 00
Insurance expense	0 00	1 400 00
Rent expense	3 800 00	3 800 00
Office supplies expense	0 00	580 00
Advertising expense	2 500 00	2 500 00
Utilities expense	1 245 00	1 335 00
Total expenses	21 045 00	28 815 00
Net income	$33 455 00	$32 685 00

Exercise 13-7^A

Exercise 13-7A
Adjusting for prepaids recorded as expenses and unearned revenues recorded as revenues

LO5

Ricardo Construction began operations on December 1. In setting up its accounting procedures, the company decided to debit expense accounts when it prepays its expenses and to credit revenue accounts when customers pay for services in advance. Prepare journal entries for items *a* through *d* and the adjusting entries as of its December 31 period-end for items *e* through *g*.

a. Supplies are purchased on December 1 for $2,000 cash.

b. The company prepaid its insurance premiums for $1,540 cash on December 2.

c. On December 15, the company receives an advance payment of $13,000 cash from customers for remodeling work.

d. On December 28, the company receives $3,700 cash from another customer for remodeling work to be performed in January.

e. A physical count on December 31 indicates that Ricardo has $1,840 of supplies available.

Check   (*f*) Cr. Insurance Expense, $1,200; (*g*) Dr. Remodeling Fees Earned, $11,130

f. An analysis of the insurance policies in effect on December 31 shows that $340 of insurance coverage had expired.

g. As of December 31, one remodeling project has been worked on and completed. The $5,570 fee for this project had been received in advance.

PROBLEM SET A

Problem 13-1A
Identifying adjusting entries with explanations

LO3

For each of the following entries, enter the letter of the explanation that most closely describes it in the space beside each entry. (You can use letters more than once.)

A. To record receipt of unearned revenue.

B. To record this period's earning of prior unearned revenue.

C. To record payment of an accrued expense.

D. To record receipt of an accrued revenue.

E. To record an accrued expense.

F. To record an accrued revenue.

G. To record this period's use of a prepaid expense.

H. To record payment of a prepaid expense.

I. To record this period's depreciation expense.

_____	1.	Interest Expense	1,000	
		Interest Payable		1,000
_____	2.	Depreciation Expense	4,000	
		Accumulated Depreciation		4,000
_____	3.	Unearned Professional Fees	3,000	
		Professional Fees Earned		3,000
_____	4.	Insurance Expense	4,200	
		Prepaid Insurance		4,200
_____	5.	Salaries Payable	1,400	
		Cash		1,400
_____	6.	Prepaid Rent	4,500	
		Cash		4,500
_____	7.	Salaries Expense	6,000	
		Salaries Payable		6,000
_____	8.	Interest Receivable	5,000	
		Interest Revenue		5,000
_____	9.	Cash	9,000	
		Accounts Receivable		9,000
_____	10.	Cash	7,500	
		Unearned Professional Fees		7,500
_____	11.	Cash	2,000	
		Interest Receivable		2,000
_____	12.	Rent Expense	2,000	
		Prepaid Rent		2,000

A six-column table for JKL Company follows. The first two columns contain the unadjusted trial balance for the company as of July 31, 2008. The last two columns contain the adjusted trial balance as of the same date.

Problem 13-2A

Interpreting unadjusted and adjusted trial balances, and preparing financial statements

(LO3) (LO4)

mhhe.com/wildCA

	Unadjusted Trial Balance		Adjustments		Adjusted Trial Balance	
Cash	$ 34,000				$ 34,000	
Accounts receivable	14,000				22,000	
Office supplies	16,000				2,000	
Prepaid insurance	8,540				2,960	
Office equipment	84,000				84,000	
Accum. depreciation—						
Office equip		$ 14,000				$ 20,000
Accounts payable		9,100				10,000
Interest payable		0				1,000
Salaries payable		0				7,000
Unearned consulting fees		18,000				15,000
Long-term notes payable		52,000				52,000
J. Logan, Capital		40,000				40,000
J. Logan, Withdrawals	5,000				5,000	
Consulting fees earned		123,240				134,240
Depreciation expense—						
Office equip	0				6,000	
Salaries expense	67,000				74,000	
Interest expense	1,200				2,200	
Insurance expense	0				5,580	
Rent expense	14,500				14,500	
Office supplies expense	0				14,000	
Advertising expense	12,100				13,000	
Totals	$256,340	$256,340			$279,240	$279,240

Required

Analyze the differences between the unadjusted and adjusted trial balances to determine the eight adjustments that likely were made. Show the results of your analysis by inserting these adjustment amounts in the table's two middle columns. Label each adjustment with a letter *a* through *h* and provide a short description of it at the bottom of the table.

Problem 13-3A

Preparing adjusting entries

(LO2)(LO3)

The following information is available for Drew Gooden Company. Assume that December 31 is the end of its annual accounting period.

   a. The Prepaid Insurance account shows a debit balance of $2,340, representing the cost of a three-year fire insurance policy that was purchased on October 1 of the current year.

   b. The Office Supplies account has a debit balance of $400; a year-end inventory count reveals $80 of supplies still available.

   c. On November 1 of the current year, Unearned Rent was credited for $1,500. This amount represented a prepayment received for a three-month period beginning November 1.

   d. Depreciation on office equipment is $600.

   e. Accrued salaries amount to $4,000. Payroll taxes need to be accrued on these salaries. Assume Social Security tax of 6.2%, Medicare tax of 1.45%, and federal and state unemployment tax rates of 0.8% and 5.4%, respectively.

Required

Record the December 31 adjusting entries for the transactions and events *a* through *e*.

Problem 13-4A[A]

Recording prepaid expenses and unearned revenues

(LO5)

Gomez Co. had the following transactions in the last two months of its year ended December 31.

Nov.	1	Paid $1,800 cash for future newspaper advertising.
	1	Paid $2,460 cash for 12 months of insurance through October 31 of the next year.
	30	Received $3,600 cash for future services to be provided to a customer.
Dec.	1	Paid $3,000 cash for a consultant's services to be received over the next three months.
	15	Received $7,950 cash for future services to be provided to a customer.
	31	Of the advertising paid for on November 1, $1,200 worth is not yet used.
	31	A portion of the insurance paid for on November 1 has expired. No adjustment was made in November to Prepaid Insurance.
	31	Services worth $1,500 are not yet provided to the customer who paid on November 30.
	31	One-third of the consulting services paid for on December 1 have been received.
	31	The company has performed $3,300 of services that the customer paid for on December 15.

Required

   1. Prepare entries for these transactions under the method that records prepaid expenses as assets and records unearned revenues as liabilities. Also prepare adjusting entries at the end of the year.

   2. Prepare entries for these transactions under the method that records prepaid expenses as expenses and records unearned revenues as revenues. Also prepare adjusting entries at the end of the year.

Analysis Component

   3. Explain why the alternative sets of entries in requirements 1 and 2 do not result in different financial statement amounts.

PROBLEM SET B

Problem 13-1B

Identifying adjusting entries with explanations

(LO3)

For each of the following entries, enter the letter of the explanation that most closely describes it in the space beside each entry. (You can use letters more than once.)

   A. To record payment of a prepaid expense.

   B. To record this period's use of a prepaid expense.

   C. To record this period's depreciation expense.

   D. To record receipt of unearned revenue.

   E. To record this period's earning of prior unearned revenue.

   F. To record an accrued expense.

   G. To record payment of an accrued expense.

   H. To record an accrued revenue.

   I. To record receipt of accrued revenue.

_____	1.	Interest Receivable	3,500
		Interest Revenue	3,500
_____	2.	Salaries Payable	9,000
		Cash	9,000
_____	3.	Depreciation Expense	8,000
		Accumulated Depreciation	8,000
_____	4.	Cash	9,000
		Unearned Professional Fees	9,000
_____	5.	Insurance Expense	4,000
		Prepaid Insurance	4,000
_____	6.	Interest Expense	5,000
		Interest Payable	5,000
_____	7.	Cash	1,500
		Accounts Receivable	1,500
_____	8.	Salaries Expense	7,000
		Salaries Payable	7,000
_____	9.	Cash	1,000
		Interest Receivable	1,000
_____	10.	Prepaid Rent	3,000
		Cash	3,000
_____	11.	Rent Expense	7,500
		Prepaid Rent	7,500
_____	12.	Unearned Professional Fees	6,000
		Professional Fees Earned	6,000

A six-column table for Yan Consulting Company follows. The first two columns contain the unadjusted trial balance for the company as of December 31, 2008, and the last two columns contain the adjusted trial balance as of the same date.

Problem 13–2B
Interpreting unadjusted and adjusted trial balances

(L03)

	Unadjusted Trial Balance		Adjustments		Adjusted Trial Balance	
Cash	$ 45,000				$ 45,000	
Accounts receivable	60,000				66,660	
Office supplies	40,000				17,000	
Prepaid insurance	8,200				3,600	
Office equipment	120,000				120,000	
Accumulated depreciation—						
Office equip.		$ 20,000				$ 30,000
Accounts payable		26,000				32,000
Interest payable		0				2,150
Salaries payable		0				16,000
Unearned consulting fees		40,000				27,800
Long-term notes payable		75,000				75,000
Z. Yan, Capital		80,200				80,200
Z. Yan, Withdrawals	20,000				20,000	
Consulting fees earned		234,600				253,460
Depreciation expense—						
Office equip.	0				10,000	
Salaries expense	112,000				128,000	
Interest expense	8,600				10,750	
Insurance expense	0				4,600	
Rent expense	20,000				20,000	
Office supplies expense	0				23,000	
Advertising expense	42,000				48,000	
Totals	$475,800	$475,800			$516,610	$516,610

Required

Analyze the differences between the unadjusted and adjusted trial balances to determine the eight adjustments that likely were made. Show the results of your analysis by inserting these adjustment amounts in the table's two middle columns. Label each adjustment with a letter _a_ through _h_ and provide a short description of it at the bottom of the table.

Problem 13-3B

Preparing adjusting entries

(LO2) (LO3)

The following information is available for Khalid Amin Company. Assume that December 31 is the end of the annual accounting period.

a. The Prepaid Insurance account shows a debit balance of $3,600, representing the cost of a three-year fire insurance policy that was purchased on October 1 of the current year.

b. The Office Supplies account has a debit balance of $800; a year-end inventory count reveals $90 of supplies still available.

c. On November 1 of the current year, Unearned Rent was credited for $3,300. This amount represented a prepayment received for a three-month period beginning November 1.

d. Depreciation on office equipment is $900.

e. Accrued salaries amount to $8,000. Payroll taxes need to be accrued on these salaries. Assume Social Security tax of 6.2%, Medicare tax of 1.45%, federal and state unemployment tax rates of 0.8% and 5.4%, respectively.

Required

Record the December 31 adjusting entries for the transactions and events *a* through *e*.

Problem 13-4B[A]

Recording prepaid expenses and unearned revenues

Tremor Co. had the following transactions in the last two months of its fiscal year ended May 31.

Apr.	1	Paid $2,450 cash to an accounting firm for future consulting services.
	1	Paid $3,600 cash for 12 months of insurance through March 31 of the next year.
	30	Received $8,500 cash for future services to be provided to a customer.
May	1	Paid $4,450 cash for future newspaper advertising.
	23	Received $10,450 cash for future services to be provided to a customer.
	31	Of the consulting services paid for on April 1, $2,000 worth has been received.
	31	A portion of the insurance paid for on April 1 has expired. No adjustment was made in April to Prepaid Insurance.
	31	Services worth $4,600 are not yet provided to the customer who paid on April 30.
	31	Of the advertising paid for on May 1, $2,050 worth is not yet used.
	31	The company has performed $5,500 of services that the customer paid for on May 23.

Required

1. Prepare entries for these transactions under the method that records prepaid expenses and unearned revenues in balance sheet accounts. Also prepare adjusting entries at the end of the year.

2. Prepare entries for these transactions under the method that records prepaid expenses and unearned revenues in income statement accounts. Also prepare adjusting entries at the end of the year.

Analysis Component

3. Explain why the alternative sets of entries in parts 1 and 2 do not result in different financial statement amounts.

REPORTING IN ACTION

(LO1)

BTN 13-1   Refer to **Best Buy**'s financial statements in Appendix A to answer the following.

1. Identify and write down the revenue recognition principle as explained in the chapter.

2. Research Best Buy's footnotes to discover how it applies the revenue recognition principle. Report what you discover.

COMPARATIVE ANALYSIS

(LO3)

BTN 13-2   Merchandising companies, such as **Best Buy** and **Circuit City**, sell gift cards to their customers. Best Buy and Circuit City would record these as unearned revenue. When the gift cards are redeemed, revenue is then recognized.

Required

1. Review Best Buy and Circuit City financial statements in Appendix A. Which liability account for Best Buy and for Circuit City would likely include unearned revenue?

2. Show the required journal entry to record the unearned revenue when the gift card is sold.

BTN 13-3 Recall the ethical dilemma in the "You Call It" box on page 317 that suggested delaying recognition of accrued expenses and early revenue recognition.

ETHICAL CHALLENGE

LO3 LO4

Required

1. Relying on the matching principle, discuss the rationale for revenue recognition. Explain why the delayed recognition of accrued expense and the early recognition of revenue would violate GAAP.
2. If the president insists on such accounting treatment, what would you do to remedy this ethical situation?

BTN 13-4 Merchandising companies, such as **Best Buy** and **Circuit City**, sell gift cards to their customers to generate future revenues.

TAKING IT TO THE NET

LO3

Required

Visit the Websites of Best Buy (**BestBuy.com**) and Circuit City (**CircuitCity.com**) and compare and contrast each company's gift card policies.

BTN 13-5 Four types of adjustments are described in the chapter: (1) prepaid expenses, (2) unearned revenues, (3) accrued expenses, and (4) accrued revenues.

TEAMWORK IN ACTION

LO3

Required

1. Form *learning teams* of four (or more) members. Each team member must select one of the four adjustments as an area of expertise (each team must have at least one expert in each area).
2. Form *expert teams* from the individuals who have selected the same area of expertise. Expert teams are to discuss and write a report that each expert will present to his or her learning team addressing the following:
   a. Description of the adjustment and why it's necessary.
   b. Example of a transaction or event, with dates and amounts, that requires adjustment.
   c. Adjusting entry(ies) for the example in requirement b.
   d. Status of the affected account(s) before and after the adjustment in requirement c.
   e. Effects on financial statements of not making the adjustment.
3. Each expert should return to his or her learning team. In rotation, each member should present his or her expert team's report to the learning team. Team discussion is encouraged.

BTN 13-6 Refer to the chapter's opening feature about Tony Lee and his **Ring Masters** company.

ENTREPRENEURS IN BUSINESS

LO2 LO3

Required

1. At the end of each reporting period, Tony Lee makes adjusting journal entries. Give examples of each of these types of adjusting journal entries that Tony Lee might make at his steel rings factory.
   a. Accrued revenues   c. Unearned revenues
   b. Accrued expenses   d. Prepaid expenses
2. Tony Lee hopes to double his sales from the current $3 million annually within five years. Assume that Lee's sales growth is as follows.

Year	One Year Hence	Two Years Hence	Three Years Hence	Four Years Hence	Five Years Hence
Growth in Sales	0%	20%	15%	25%	20%

Compute Lee's projected sales for each year (round to nearest dollar). If this pattern of sales growth holds, will Lee achieve his goal of doubling sales in five years?

ANSWERS TO MULTIPLE CHOICE QUIZ

1. b
2. c
3. b; Insurance expense = $12,000 × (8/24) = $4,000; adjusting entry is: *dr.* Insurance Expense for $4,000, *cr.* Prepaid Insurance for $4,000.
4. a; Consulting fees earned = $3,600 × (2/6) = $1,200; adjusting entry is: *dr.* Unearned Consulting Fee for $1,200, *cr.* Consulting Fees Earned for $1,200.
5. d

A Look Back

Chapter 13 summarized the accrual basis of accounting and described several accounting adjustments. It also completed the trial balance work sheet needed to measure net income.

A Look at This Chapter

This chapter focuses on the closing procedures necessary for an accounting system. It also describes how to format income statements and to classify balance sheets.

A Look Ahead

Chapter 15 describes how companies account for and report accounts receivable. It also explains how to account for receivables that are uncollectible.

14

Chapter

Financial Statements and the Accounting Cycle

LEARNING OBJECTIVES

LO 1 Describe how to use the adjusted trial balance to prepare financial statements.

LO 2 Prepare journal entries to close temporary accounts.

LO 3 Define and prepare multiple-step and single-step income statements.

LO 4 Explain and prepare a classified balance sheet.

LO 5 Prepare reversing entries and explain their purpose.

"We were making a unique new product . . . that had a lot of potential for growth"—Stephen Sullivan (on left is Brian Cousins)

Reaching for the Clouds

JACKSON, WY—It all started when Stephen Sullivan got a pair of pants as a gift. The pants were made of Schoeller® fabric, which is durable, lightweight, and comfortable. "I wore those pants for three years," Stephen recalls. "They reminded me of my Mom's old stretch ski pants and how much she wore them and loved them." Stephen and his friend, Brian Cousins, were working for an outdoor retailer when they devised a plan to develop and market high-performance, multisport mountain apparel called **Cloudveil (Cloudveil.com)**—Cloudveil Dome is a peak in the Tetons.

Stephen quit his day job to research outdoor apparel and learn everything about marketing and operating their new business. While Stephen bartended during evenings to survive, Brian went to work for an apparel manufacturer to learn the production and financial side of the business. "One of the smartest things we did early on was realize we didn't know everything," explains Stephen. "Then we set out to find others who did."

With their plans and dreams came financial plans. In the early stages, however, the pair admits their financial planning was not ideal. "The thinking was, 'Let's be a clothing company and go buy some sewing machines.' [We now know] that style of thinking is archaic," says Stephen. "I can't even sew!" confesses Brian.

Plans and operations soon turn to results when the financial statements are closed at the end of each accounting period. Once the classified financial statements are available, Stephen and Brian can assess which product lines are profitable and which are not. The financial statements give them the necessary information to make important decisions for products that will affect Cloudveil's future.

With careful examination of the financial statements, keen decision making, and brilliant products, the pair proclaim that attention to accounting numbers have "helped us realize solid year over year growth." This success has helped these friends pursue their tag line: *Live Close to Your Dreams.*

[Sources: *Cloudveil Website,* May 2007; *Entrepreneur,* November 2002; *Outdoor Retailer Magazine,* 2001; *Denver Post,* 2005; *Northwestern Magazine,* Fall 2004]

Once we make all necessary adjustments to the trial balance, we are ready to produce financial statements. Different financial statement formats can provide useful information to different financial statement users. We describe alternative formats for both income statements and balance sheets. We also describe the closing processes necessary to prepare for the next period's transactions.

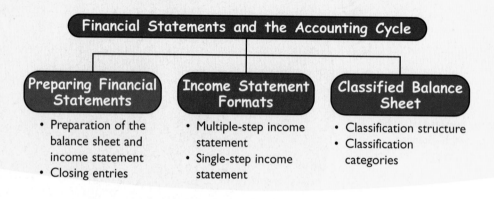

Financial Statements and the Accounting Cycle

Preparing Financial Statements	**Income Statement Formats**	**Classified Balance Sheet**
• Preparation of the balance sheet and income statement • Closing entries	• Multiple-step income statement • Single-step income statement	• Classification structure • Classification categories

Preparing Financial Statements

Using the Adjusted Trial Balance to Prepare the Balance Sheet and Income Statement

Describe how to use the adjusted trial balance to prepare financial statements.

Once the accounting adjustments are posted, we are ready to complete the work sheet by preparing the balance sheet and income statement columns. For illustration, we continue with the example of SuperSub and its adjusted trial balance (presented in Exhibit 13.10 in Chapter 13).

On the 10-column work sheet in Exhibit 14.1, we extend the account balances of its balance sheet accounts (extending from Cash to Polly Guthrie, Withdrawals) to the balance sheet columns. If the account balance is a debit in the adjusted trial balance columns, it will be a debit balance in the balance sheet column. Similarly, a balance in the credit column of the adjusted trial balance will be a credit balance in the balance sheet column. In a similar manner, we extend the account balances of the income statement accounts (extending from Sales to Supplies Expense) to the income statement columns. One item in Exhibit 14.1 warrants explanation. Even though Merchandise Inventory is a balance sheet account, debit and credit amounts are listed for it in the income statement columns of the work sheet in Exhibit 14.1. These multiple entries are part of the closing process that we discuss in the next section. The Merchandise Inventory entries will appear on the income statement as part of the cost of goods sold computation. (The accounts that enter into the cost of goods sold calculation are highlighted blue in Exhibit 14.1.)

At this point, we see that the income statement and balance sheet columns of the work sheet do not balance. The total of the income statement credit column ($14,175.00) is greater than the total of the income statement debit column ($12,904.49). The difference between these totals is $1,270.51 ($14,175.00 − $12,904.49), which is SuperSub's net income for the year ended December 31, 2007. Also, the total of the balance sheet debit column ($57,300.00) is greater than the total of the balance sheet credit column ($56,029.49). These totals also differ by the amount of net income for the year.

To balance these work sheet columns, we enter $1,270.51 in the balance sheet credit column and $1,270.51 in the income statement debit column. These amounts are entered in a new row, titled the *Net Income* row of the work sheet. The balance sheet is credited because net income increases owner's equity. Next, we compute updated balances for each of the income statement and balance sheet columns, and verify that the work sheet balances.

Exhibit 14.1

10-Column Work Sheet

SUPERSUB
Work Sheet
Year Ended December 31, 2007

Description	Unadjusted Trial Balance Debit	Credit	Adjustments Debit	Credit	Adjusted Trial Balance Debit	Credit	Income Statement Debit	Credit	Balance Sheet Debit	Credit
Cash	4,000 00				4,000 00				4,000 00	
Accounts Receivable	4,000 00		(a) 1,800 00		5,800 00				5,800 00	
Allowance for Doubtful Accounts		0 00		(b) 290 00		290 00				290 00
Merchandise Inventory	2,200 00				2,200 00		2,200 00	2,000 00	2,000 00	
Prepaid Insurance	1,800 00			(h) 100 00	1,700 00				1,700 00	
Prepaid Rent	24,000 00			(f) 1,000 00	23,000 00				23,000 00	
Supplies	3,000 00			(g) 1,200 00	1,800 00				1,800 00	
Store Equipment	18,000 00				18,000 00				18,000 00	
Accumulated Depreciation— Store Equipment		0 00		(i) 500 00		500 00				500 00
Social Security Tax Payable		0 00		(d) 37 82		37 82				37 82
Medicare Tax Payable		0 00		(d) 8 85		8 85				8 85
Federal Unemployment Tax Payable		0 00		(d) 4 88		4 88				4 88
State Unemployment Tax Payable		0 00		(d) 32 94		32 94				32 94
Salaries Payable		0 00		(c) 610 00		610 00				610 00
Unearned Revenue		3,000 00	(e) 1,200 00			1,800 00				1,800 00
Polly Guthrie, Capital		52,745 00				52,745 00				52,745 00
Polly Guthrie, Withdrawals	1,000 00				1,000 00				1,000 00	
Income Summary		0 00								
Sales		9,050 00		(a) 1,800 00 (e) 1,200 00		12,050 00		12,050 00		
Purchases	3,000 00				3,000 00		3,000 00			
Transportation-In	50 00				50 00		50 00			
Purchase Returns and Allowances		50 00				50 00		50 00		
Purchase Discounts		75 00				75 00		75 00		
Salaries Expense	3,400 00		(c) 610 00		4,010 00		4,010 00			
Uncollectible Accounts Expense			(b) 290 00		290 00		290 00			
Depreciation Expense—Store Eq.			(i) 500 00		500 00		500 00			
Rent Expense			(f) 1,000 00		1,000 00		1,000 00			
Insurance Expense			(h) 100 00		100 00		100 00			
Payroll Tax Expense	470 00		(d) 84 49		554 49		554 49			
Supplies Expense			(g) 1,200 00		1,200 00		1,200 00			
Totals	64,920 00	64,920 00	6,784 49	6,784 49	68,204 49	68,204 49	12,904 49	14,175 00	57,300 00	56,029 49
Net Income							1,270 51			1,270 51
Totals							14,175 00	14,175 00	57,300 00	57,300 00

Closing Entries

As explained in Chapter 6, there are four necessary steps to record and post the closing entries of the period.

LO2 Prepare journal entries to close temporary accounts.

1. Close revenue accounts to Income Summary
2. Close expense accounts to Income Summary
   a. Close inventory and purchases-related accounts to Income Summary to reflect the cost of goods sold (for merchandising companies)
   b. Close other expense accounts to Income Summary
3. Close the Income Summary account to the owner's capital account
4. Close the Withdrawals account to the owner's capital account

We illustrate the closing entries for SuperSub, using information from Exhibit 14.1.

1. Close revenue accounts to Income Summary

Assets = Liabilities + Owner's Equity
−12,050
+12,050

Dec.	31	Sales		12 0 5 0 00	
		Income Summary			12 0 5 0 00
		To close revenue accounts.			

2a. Close inventory and purchases-related accounts to Income Summary

For merchandisers, and as explained in Chapters 11 and 12, merchandise inventory consists of goods that a company owns and expects to sell to customers. Merchandisers who use the periodic inventory system have an additional closing entry to close their inventory and purchases-related accounts.

Under the periodic inventory method, purchases of merchandise inventory are debited to the temporary Purchases account. Since no entries have been made directly to the Merchandise Inventory account during the period, the end-of-period adjusted trial balance still reflects the beginning inventory from the unadjusted trial balance. The unadjusted and adjusted trial balances for SuperSub in Exhibit 14.1 show an inventory balance of $2,200.

A company determines the correct ending inventory by counting the remaining inventory available as of the end of the accounting period. Based on a count of inventory at December 31, 2007, SuperSub determines its ending inventory is $2,000. It must close the beginning inventory account with a credit to Merchandise Inventory. It then recognizes the ending inventory available with a debit to Merchandise Inventory. The contra-purchases accounts—Purchase Returns and Allowances, Purchase Discounts, and Transportation-In—are then closed to Income Summary. The combined journal entry is:*

Assets = Liabilities + Owner's Equity
+2,000 / −3,125
−2,200 / −50
/ −75
/ +3,000
/ +50

Dec.	31	Income Summary		3 1 2 5 00	
		Merchandise Inventory (Ending)		2 0 0 0 00	
		Purchase Returns and Allowances		5 0 00	
		Purchase Discounts		7 5 00	
		Merchandise Inventory (Beginning)			2 2 0 0 00
		Purchases			3 0 0 0 00
		Transportation-In			5 0 00
		To close inventory and purchase accounts to income summary.			

By updating Merchandise Inventory and closing Purchases, Purchase Discounts, Purchase Returns and Allowances, and Transportation-In, the periodic inventory system transfers cost of goods sold to Income Summary. The debit entry to Income Summary ($3,125) is the company's cost of goods sold for the period.

2b. Close other expense accounts to Income Summary

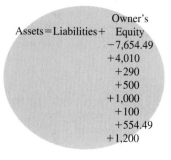

Assets = Liabilities + Owner's Equity
−7,654.49
+4,010
+290
+500
+1,000
+100
+554.49
+1,200

Dec.	31	Income Summary		7 6 5 4 49	
		Salaries Expense			4 0 1 0 00
		Uncollectible Accounts Expense			2 9 0 00
		Depreciation Expense			5 0 0 00
		Rent Expense			1 0 0 0 00
		Insurance Expense			1 0 0 00
		Payroll Tax Expense			5 5 4 49
		Supplies Expense			1 2 0 0 00
		To close expense accounts.			

---

*This approach is called the *closing entry method*. An alternative approach, the *adjusting entry method*, would not make any entries to Merchandise Inventory in the closing entries. Instead, two adjusting entries would be made. For example, using SuperSub data, the two adjusting entries would be: (1) Dr. Income Summary and Cr. Merchandise Inventory for $2,200 each and (2) Dr. Merchandise Inventory and Cr. Income Summary for $2,000 each. The first entry removes the beginning balance of Merchandise Inventory, and the second entry records the actual ending balance of Merchandise Inventory. The choice of closing entry method or adjusting entry method has no impact on financial statements.

3. Close the Income Summary account to the owner's capital account

The resulting balance in Income Summary (from steps 1 and 2), which represents the net income or net loss for the period, is closed (or transferred) to the owner's capital account. For SuperSub, the resulting balance in Income Summary is a $1,270.51 credit balance (net income). To close its Income Summary account, SuperSub must debit Income Summary for $1,270.51 and credit Polly Guthrie, Capital for $1,270.51.

Dec.	31	Income Summary	1 2 7 0 51	
		Polly Guthrie, Capital		1 2 7 0 51
		To close the Income Summary account.		

Owner's
Assets=Liabilities+ Equity
−1,270.51
+1,270.51

4. Close the Withdrawals account to the owner's capital account

The final closing entry is to transfer any withdrawals during the period to reduce the owner's capital account.

Dec.	31	Polly Guthrie, Capital	1 0 0 0 00	
		Polly Guthrie, Withdrawals		1 0 0 0 00
		To close the withdrawals account.		

Owner's
Assets = Liabilities + Equity
−1,000
+1,000

As a result of these closing entries, all of the income statement (or temporary) accounts have ending balances equal to zero.

The final optional step in the accounting cycle is to prepare reversing entries. Some companies use reversing entries in preparation for the next accounting period. Reversing entries are discussed in the appendix to this chapter.

HOW YOU DOIN'?

Answers—p. 346

1. What temporary accounts do you expect to find in a merchandising business but not in a service business?
2. Describe the closing entries normally made by a merchandising company.

Income Statement Formats

Generally accepted accounting principles do not require companies to use any one presentation format for financial statements. This section describes two common income statement formats: multiple-step and single-step.

Multiple-Step Income Statement

A **multiple-step income statement** format shows detailed computations of net sales and other costs and expenses, and reports subtotals for various classes of items. Exhibit 14.2 shows a multiple-step income statement for SuperSub. The statement has three main parts: (1) *gross profit*, determined by net sales less cost of goods sold, (2) *income from operations*, determined by gross profit less operating expenses, and (3) *net income*, determined by income from operations adjusted for nonoperating items. The gross profit section for SuperSub includes a detailed cost of goods computation. Also, SuperSub does not report any nonoperating items.

Operating expenses are classified into two sections. **Selling expenses** include the expenses of promoting sales by displaying and advertising merchandise, making sales, and delivering goods to customers. Depreciation expense on store equipment is included since this equipment is used to generate sales. **General and administrative expenses** support a company's

Define and prepare multiple-step and single-step income statements.

Exhibit 14.2

Multiple-Step Income Statement

SUPERSUB Income Statement For Year Ended December 31, 2007				
Net Sales				$12 0 5 0 00
Cost of Goods Sold				
Merchandise inventory, Beginning		$2 2 0 0 00		
Purchases	$3 0 0 0 00			
Transportation-in	5 0 00			
Less: Purchase returns and allowances	(5 0 00)			
Purchase discounts	7 5 00			
Net cost of purchases		2 9 2 5 00		
Total cost of merchandise available				
for sale		5 1 2 5 00		
Less merchandise inventory, Ending		2 0 0 0 00		
Cost of goods sold			3 1 2 5 00	
Gross profit			8 9 2 5 00	
Operating expenses				
Selling expenses				
Salaries expense	4 0 1 0 00			
Supplies expense	1 2 0 0 00			
Depreciation expense—				
Store equipment	5 0 0 00			
Total selling expenses		5 7 1 0 00		
General and administrative expenses				
Rent expense	1 0 0 0 00			
Payroll tax expense	5 5 4 49			
Uncollectible accounts expense	2 9 0 00			
Insurance expense	1 0 0 00			
Total general and				
administrative expenses		1 9 4 4 49		
Total operating expenses			7 6 5 4 49	
Net income			$1 2 7 0 51	

→ Gross profit computation

→ Income from operations computation

overall operations and include expenses related to accounting, human resource management, and financial management. These expenses are not directly related to the sales function of the business.

Nonoperating activities consist of other expenses, revenues, losses, and gains that are unrelated to a company's operations. They are reported in two sections: (1) *other revenues and gains,* which often include interest revenue, dividend revenue, rent revenue, and gains from asset disposals, and (2) *other expenses and losses,* which often include interest expense, losses from asset disposals, and casualty losses. When a company has no reportable nonoperating activities, its income from operations is simply labeled net income. A partial income statement for a company with these items might look like the following:

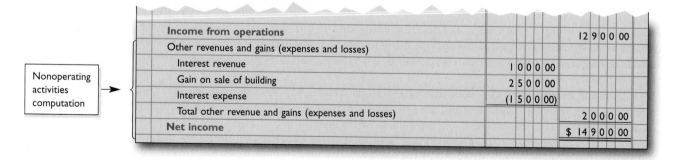

Income from operations			12 9 0 0 00
Other revenues and gains (expenses and losses)			
Interest revenue		1 0 0 0 00	
Gain on sale of building		2 5 0 0 00	
Interest expense		(1 5 0 0 00)	
Total other revenue and gains (expenses and losses)			2 0 0 0 00
Net income			$ 14 9 0 0 00

→ Nonoperating activities computation

Single-Step Income Statement

A **single-step income statement** is another widely used format. An example is shown in Exhibit 14.3 for SuperSub. It lists cost of goods sold as another expense and shows only one subtotal for total expenses. Expenses are grouped into very few, if any, categories. Many companies use formats that combine features of both the single- and multiple-step statements. Provided that income statement items are shown sensibly, management can choose the format. (In later chapters, we describe some items, such as extraordinary gains and losses, that must be reported in certain locations on the income statement.)

> Many companies report interest expense and interest revenue in separate categories after operating income and before subtracting income tax expense. As one example, see **Best Buy**'s income statement in Appendix A.

Exhibit 14.3

Single-Step Income Statement

SUPERSUB Income Statement For Year Ended December 31, 2007		
Revenues		
Net sales		$12 0 5 0 00
Expenses		
Cost of goods sold	$3 1 2 5 00	
Selling expenses	5 7 1 0 00	
General and administrative expenses	1 9 4 4 49	
Total expenses		10 7 7 9 49
Net income		$ 1 2 7 0 51

IN THE NEWS

Head Start

Incubators offer start-ups a space plus services such as management advice, office support, and financial, legal, and technical help. Studies show that nearly 90% of entrepreneurs that "hatch" from incubators (usually after two to three years) are still in business six years later—which is more than double the usual success rate.

Classified Balance Sheet

This section describes a classified balance sheet. An **unclassified balance sheet** is one whose items are broadly grouped into assets, liabilities, and equity. A **classified balance sheet** organizes assets and liabilities into important subgroups that provide more information to decision makers.

L04 Explain and prepare a classified balance sheet.

Classification Structure

A classified balance sheet has no required layout, but it usually contains the categories in Exhibit 14.4. One of the more important classifications is the separation between current and noncurrent items for both assets and liabilities. Current items are those expected to come due (either collected or owed) within one year or the company's operating cycle, whichever is longer. The **operating cycle** is the time span from when *cash is used* to acquire goods and services until *cash is received* from the sale of goods and services. "Operating" refers to company operations and "cycle" refers to the circular flow of cash used for company inputs and then cash received from its outputs. The length of a company's operating cycle depends on its

Assets	Liabilities and Equity
Current assets	Current liabilities
Noncurrent assets	Noncurrent liabilities
Long-term investments	Equity
Plant assets	
Intangible assets	

Exhibit 14.4

Typical Categories in a Classified Balance Sheet

Current is also called *short-term*, and noncurrent is also called *long-term*.

activities. For a service company, the operating cycle is the time span between (1) paying employees who perform the services and (2) receiving cash from customers. For a merchandiser selling products, the operating cycle is the time span between (1) paying suppliers for merchandise and (2) receiving cash from customers.

Most operating cycles are less than one year. This means most companies use a one-year period in deciding which assets and liabilities are current. A few companies have an operating cycle longer than one year. For instance, producers of certain beverages (wine) and products (ginseng) that require aging for several years have operating cycles longer than one year. A classified balance sheet lists current assets before noncurrent assets and current liabilities before noncurrent liabilities. This consistency in presentation allows users to quickly identify current assets that are most easily converted to cash and current liabilities that are shortly coming due. Items in current assets and current liabilities are listed in the order of how quickly they will be converted to, or paid in, cash.

Classification Categories

This section describes the most common categories in a classified balance sheet. The balance sheet for SuperSub in Exhibit 14.5 shows some of these typical categories. Its assets are classified as either current or noncurrent. Its liabilities are all classified as current. Not all companies use the same categories of assets and liabilities for their balance sheets. **K2 Inc.**'s balance sheet lists only three asset classes: current assets; property, plant, and equipment; and other assets.

YOU CALL IT

Answer—p. 345

Controller   The controller of Orvil Corporation is contemplating a balance sheet which offers few details. He reasons that this will cause less questions from the company's shareholders. Does your analysis of this situation raise any concerns?

Exhibit 14.5

Example of a Classified Balance Sheet

SUPERSUB Balance Sheet December 31, 2007		
Assets		
Current assets		
Cash		$ 4 0 0 0 00
Accounts receivable	$5 8 0 0 00	
Less: Allowance for doubtful accounts	2 9 0 00	5 5 1 0 00
Merchandise inventory		2 0 0 0 00
Prepaid expenses		
Prepaid rent	23 0 0 0 00	
Prepaid insurance	1 7 0 0 00	
Supplies	1 8 0 0 00	26 5 0 0 00
Total current assets		
Noncurrent assets		
Store equipment	18 0 0 0 00	
Less: Accumulated depreciation	5 0 0 00	17 5 0 0 00
Total assets		$55 5 1 0 00
Liabilities and Owner's Equity		
Current liabilities		
Salaries payable		$ 6 1 0 00
Social security tax payable		3 7 82
Medicare tax payable		8 85
Federal unemployment tax payable		4 88
State unemployment tax payable		3 2 94
Unearned revenue		1 8 0 0 00
Total current liabilities		$ 2 4 9 4 49
Owner's equity		
P. Guthrie, Capital		53 0 1 5 51
Total liabilities and owner's equity		$55 5 1 0 00

Current Assets   **Current assets** are cash and other resources that are expected to be sold, collected, or used within one year or the company's operating cycle, whichever is longer. Examples are cash, short-term investments, accounts receivable, short-term notes receivable, merchandise inventory, and prepaid expenses. The current assets are usually listed according to the ease with which they can be converted to cash. Contra-assets are listed in the assets section, even though they have credit balances. Prepaid expenses are usually listed last because they will not be converted to cash (instead, they are used).

> Short-term investments maturing within three months are combined with cash on both the balance sheet and cash flow statement. This combination is called *cash and cash equivalents.*

Plant Assets   Plant assets are tangible assets that are both *long lived* and *used to produce* or *sell products and services.* Examples are equipment, machinery, buildings, and land used to produce or sell products and services.

> Plant assets are also called *fixed assets; property, plant, and equipment;* or *long-lived assets.*

Noncurrent Assets

Long-Term Investments   A second major balance sheet classification is **long-term** (or *noncurrent*) **investments.** Notes receivable and investments in stocks and bonds are long-term assets when they are expected to be held for more than the longer of one year or the operating cycle. Land held for future expansion is a long-term investment because it is *not* used in operations.

Intangible Assets   **Intangible assets** are long-term resources that benefit business operations. They usually lack physical form and have uncertain benefits. Examples are patents, trademarks, copyrights, franchises, and goodwill. Their value comes from the privileges or rights granted to or held by the owner. **Huffy Corporation** reports intangible assets of $45 million, which is more than 15 percent of its total assets. Its intangibles include trademarks, patents, and licensing agreements.

Current Liabilities   **Current liabilities** are obligations due to be paid or settled within one year or the operating cycle, whichever is longer. They are usually settled by paying out current assets such as cash. Current liabilities often include accounts payable, notes payable, wages payable, taxes payable, interest payable, and unearned revenues. Also, any portion of a long-term liability due to be paid within one year or the operating cycle, whichever is longer, is a current liability. Unearned revenues are current liabilities when they will be settled by delivering products or services within one year or the operating cycle, whichever is longer. Current liabilities are reported in the order of those to be settled first.

> Many financial ratios are distorted if accounts are not classified correctly. We must be especially careful when analyzing accounts whose balances are separated into short and long term.

Long-Term Liabilities   **Long-term liabilities** are obligations *not* due within one year or the operating cycle, whichever is longer. Notes payable, mortgages payable, bonds payable, and lease obligations are common long-term liabilities. If a company has both short- and long-term items in any of these categories, they are commonly reported in both sections of the classified balance sheet. For example, assume a company owes $20,000 on a note payable, $2,000 of which is due next year. The company would include $2,000 for Notes Payable in the current liabilities section and $18,000 for Notes Payable in the noncurrent liabilities section.

> Many companies report two or more subgroups for long-term liabilities. See the balance sheets in Appendix A for examples.

Equity   Equity is the owner's claim on assets. For a proprietorship, this claim is reported in the equity section with an owner's capital account. (For a partnership, the equity section reports a capital account for each partner. For a corporation, the equity section is divided into two main subsections, common stock and retained earnings.)

HOW YOU DOIN'?

Answers—p. 346

3. Classify the following assets as (1) current assets, (2) plant assets, or (3) intangible assets: (a) land used in operations, (b) office supplies, (c) receivables from customers due in 10 months, (d) insurance protection for the next nine months, (e) trucks used to provide services to customers, (f) trademarks.

4. Cite two examples of assets classified as investments on the balance sheet.

5. Explain the operating cycle for a service company.

Demonstration Problem

Presented below is the adjusted trial balance for Worker Products Company as of December 31, 2008. On December 31, 2008, an inventory count reveals merchandise inventory of $36,000.

WORKER PRODUCTS COMPANY Adjusted Trial Balance December 31, 2008	Debit	Credit
Cash	$ 9 4 0 0 00	
Accounts receivable	25 0 0 0 00	
Merchandise inventory, December 31, 2007	24 0 0 0 00	
Office supplies	9 0 0 00	
Store equipment	75 0 0 0 00	
Accumulated depreciation—store equipment		$ 22 0 0 0 00
Office equipment	60 0 0 0 00	
Accumulated depreciation—office equipment		15 0 0 0 00
Accounts payable		42 0 0 0 00
Notes payable		10 0 0 0 00
F. Worker, Capital		110 7 0 0 00
F. Worker, Withdrawals	48 0 0 0 00	
Sales		325 0 0 0 00
Sales discounts	6 0 0 0 00	
Sales returns and allowances	16 5 0 0 00	
Purchases	210 0 0 0 00	
Purchase discounts		2 5 0 0 00
Purchase returns and allowances		1 5 0 0 00
Transportation-in	1 0 0 0 00	
Sales salaries expense	32 5 0 0 00	
Depreciation expense—store equipment	11 0 0 0 00	
Depreciation expense—office equipment	7 5 0 0 00	
Office supplies expense	1 3 0 0 00	
Interest expense	6 0 0 00	
Totals	$528 7 0 0 00	$528 7 0 0 00

Required

1. Prepare a multiple-step income statement in good form.

2. Prepare the necessary closing entries.

Planning the Solution

• Classify each income statement item as either a component of (1) gross profit, (2) income from operations, or (3) net income.

• Use Exhibit 14.2 as a guide for the format of a multiple-step income statement.

• Follow the four steps for recording the closing entries, including

 • Close revenue accounts

 • Close expense accounts

 • Close income summary accounts

 • Close withdrawal accounts.

Solution to Demonstration Problem

1. Multiple-step income statement

WORKER PRODUCTS COMPANY
Income Statement
For the Year Ended December 31, 2008

Sales			$325 000 00
Less: Sales discounts		$ 6 000 00	
Sales returns and allowances		16 500 00	22 500 00
Net sales			$302 500 00
Merchandise Inventory, 12/31/07		24 000 00	
Purchases	210 000 00		
Transportation-in	1 000 00		
Less: Purchase discounts	(2 500 00)		
Purchase returns and allowances	(1 500 00)		
Net purchases		207 000 00	
Merchandise available for sale		231 000 00	
Less: Merchandise inventory, 12/31/08		(36 000 00)	
Cost of goods sold			195 000 00
Gross profit			107 500 00
Operating expenses			
Selling expenses			
Sales salaries expense		32 500 00	
Depreciation expense—store equipment		11 000 00	
Total selling expenses		43 500 00	
General and administrative expenses			
Depreciation expense—office equipment		7 500 00	
Office supplies expense		1 300 00	
Total general and administrative expenses		8 800 00	
Total operating expenses			52 300 00
Income from operations			55 200 00
Other expenses			
Interest expense			6 00 00
Net income			$ 54 600 00

2. Closing journal entries

Dec.	31	Sales	325 000 00	
		Sales Discounts		6 000 00
		Sales Returns and Allowances		16 500 00
		Income Summary		302 500 00
Dec.	31	Income Summary	195 000 00	
		Merchandise Inventory (Ending)	36 000 00	
		Purchase Returns and Allowances	1 500 00	
		Purchase Discounts	2 500 00	
		Merchandise Inventory (Beginning)		24 000 00
		Purchases		210 000 00
		Transportation-In		1 000 00
Dec.	31	Income Summary	52 900 00	
		Sales Salaries Expense		32 500 00
		Depreciation Expense—Store Equipment		11 000 00
		Depreciation Expense—Office Equipment		7 500 00
		Office Supplies Expense		1 300 00
		Interest Expense		6 00 00
Dec.	31	Income Summary	54 600 00	
		F. Worker, Capital		54 600 00
Dec.	31	F. Worker, Capital	48 000 00	
		F. Worker, Withdrawals		48 000 00

Reversing Entries

Reversing entries are optional. They are recorded in response to accrued assets and accrued liabilities that were created by adjusting entries at the end of a reporting period. The purpose of reversing entries is to simplify a company's recordkeeping. Exhibit 14A.1 shows an example of FastForward's (a company

Exhibit 14A.1

Reversing Entries for an Accrued Expense

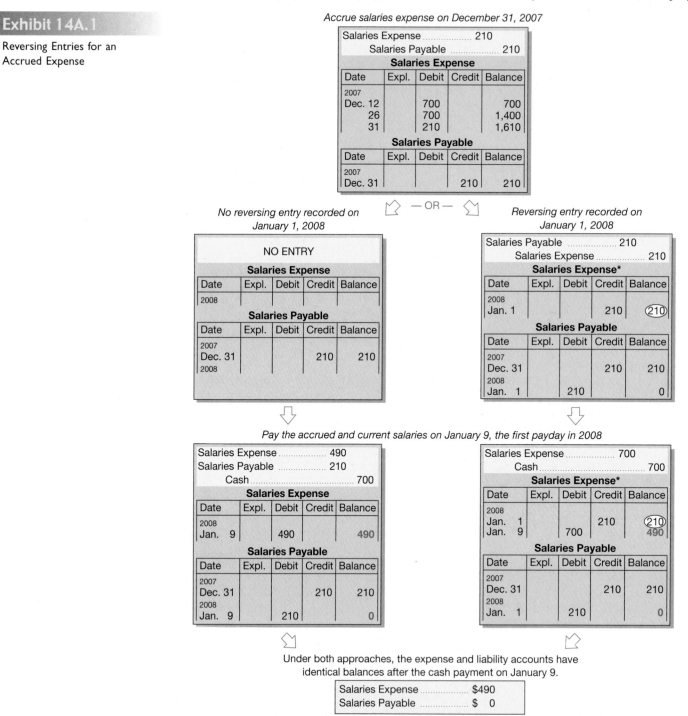

*Circled numbers in the *Balance* column indicate abnormal balances.

whose transactions we examined in detail in Chapters 2 through 6) reversing entries. The top of the exhibit shows the adjusting entry FastForward recorded on December 31 for its employee's earned but unpaid salary. We explained this entry in Chapter 5. The entry recorded three days' salary of $210, which increased December's total salary expense to $1,610. The entry also recognized a liability of $210. The expense is reported on December's income statement. The expense account is then closed. The ledger on January 1, 2008, shows a $210 liability and a zero balance in the Salaries Expense account. At this point, the choice is made between using or not using reversing entries.

> As a general rule, adjusting entries that create new asset or liability accounts are likely candidates for reversing.

Accounting *without* Reversing Entries

The path down the left side of Exhibit 14A.1 is described in the chapter. To summarize here, when the next payday occurs on January 9, we record payment with a compound entry that debits both the expense and liability accounts and credits Cash. Posting that entry creates a $490 balance in the expense account and reduces the liability account balance to zero because the payable has been settled. The disadvantage of this approach is the slightly more complex entry required on January 9. Paying the accrued liability means that this entry differs from the routine entries made on all other paydays. To construct the proper entry on January 9, we must recall the effect of the December 31 adjusting entry. Reversing entries overcome this disadvantage.

Accounting *with* Reversing Entries

LO5 Prepare reversing entries and explain their purpose.

The right side of Exhibit 14A.1 shows how reversing entries can be helpful. *A reversing entry is the exact opposite of an adjusting entry.* For FastForward, the Salaries Payable liability account is debited for $210, meaning that this account now has a zero balance after the entry is posted. The Salaries Payable account temporarily understates the liability, but this is not a problem since financial statements are not prepared before the liability is settled on January 9. The credit to the Salaries Expense account is unusual because it gives the account an *abnormal credit balance*. We highlight an abnormal balance by circling it. Because of the reversing entry, the January 9 entry to record payment is straightforward. This entry debits the Salaries Expense account and credits Cash for the full $700 paid. It is the same as all other entries made to record 10 days' salary for the employee. Notice that after the payment entry is posted, the Salaries Expense account has a $490 balance that reflects seven days' salary of $70 per day (see the lower right side of Exhibit 14A.1). The zero balance in the Salaries Payable account is now correct. The lower section of Exhibit 14A.1 shows that the expense and liability accounts have exactly the same balances whether reversing entries are used or not. This means that both approaches yield identical results.

Summary

LO1 **Describe how to use the adjusted trial balance to prepare the financial statements.** Once the adjustments are made, the adjusted trial balance is ready for preparation of financial statements. We extend the balance sheet accounts to the balance sheet columns and the income statement accounts to the income statement columns. These columns are then used as a basis for financial statements.

LO2 **Prepare journal entries to close temporary accounts.** Closing entries involve four steps: (1) close credit balances in revenue (and gain) accounts to Income Summary, (2) close debit balances in expense (and loss) accounts to Income Summary, (3) close Income Summary to the capital account, and (4) close withdrawals account to owner's capital.

LO3 **Define and prepare multiple-step and single-step income statements.** Multiple-step income statements include

greater detail for sales and expenses than do single-step income statements. They also show details of net sales and report expenses in categories reflecting different activities.

LO4 **Explain and prepare a classified balance sheet.** Classified balance sheets report assets and liabilities in two categories: current and noncurrent. Noncurrent assets often include long-term investments, plant assets, and intangible assets. Owner's equity for proprietorships (and partnerships) reports the capital account balance. A corporation separates equity into common stock and retained earnings.

LO5 **Prepare reversing entries and explain their purpose.** Reversing entries are an optional step. They are applied to accrued expenses and revenues. The purpose of reversing entries is to simplify subsequent journal entries. Financial statements are unaffected by the choice to use or not use reversing entries.

Guidance Answer to YOU CALL IT

Controller The balance sheet is meant to provide the company's financial position as of a certain point in time. If the balance sheet provides very little detail as to the asset, liability, and equity accounts,

it will not be useful to the shareholders. The controller should be encouraged to provide sufficient detail to assist the shareholders (and other financial statement users) in making sound financial decisions.

1. Purchase (of goods), Purchase Discounts, Purchase Returns and Allowances, and Cost of Goods Sold.

2. Four closing entries: (1) close revenue accounts to Income Summary, (2) close expense accounts to Income Summary, (3) close Income Summary to owner's capital, and (4) close withdrawals account to owner's capital.

3. Current assets: (*b*), (*c*), (*d*). Plant assets: (*a*), (*e*). Item (*f*) is an intangible asset.

4. Investment in common stock, investment in bonds, and land held for future expansion.

5. For a service company, the operating cycle is the usual time between (1) paying employees who do the services and (2) receiving cash from customers for services provided.

Key Terms   mhhe.com/wildCA

Key Terms are available at the book's Website for learning and testing in an online Flashcard Format.

Classified balance sheet (p. 339) Balance sheet that presents assets and liabilities in relevant subgroups, including current and noncurrent classifications.

Current assets (p. 341) Cash and other assets expected to be sold, collected, or used within one year or the company's operating cycle, whichever is longer.

Current liabilities (p. 341) Obligations due to be paid or settled within one year or the company's operating cycle, whichever is longer.

General and administrative expenses (p. 337) Expenses that support the operating activities of a business.

Intangible assets (p. 341) Long-term assets (resources) used to produce or sell products or services; usually lack physical form and have uncertain benefits.

Long-term investments (p. 341) Long-term assets not used in operating activities such as notes receivable and investments in stocks and bonds.

Long-term liabilities (p. 341) Obligations not due to be paid within one year or the operating cycle, whichever is longer.

Multiple-step income statement (p. 337) Income statement format that shows subtotals between sales and net income, categorizes expenses, and often reports the details of net sales and expenses.

Operating cycle (p. 339) Normal time between paying cash for merchandise or employee services and receiving cash from customers.

Reversing entries (p. 344) Optional entries recorded at the beginning of a period that prepare the accounts for the usual journal entries as if adjusting entries had not occurred in the prior period.

Selling expenses (p. 337) Expenses of promoting sales, such as displaying and advertising merchandise, making sales, and delivering goods to customers.

Single-step income statement (p. 339) Income statement format that includes cost of goods sold as an expense and shows only one subtotal for total expenses.

Unclassified balance sheet (p. 339) Balance sheet that broadly groups assets, liabilities, and equity accounts.

Multiple Choice Quiz   Answers on p. 357   mhhe.com/wildCA

Multiple Choice Quizzes A and B are available at the book's Website.

1. A company has $550,000 in net sales and $123,000 in gross profit. Its cost of goods sold equals
  a. $427,000   **d.** $123,000
  b. $673,000   **e.** ($123,000)
  c. $550,000

2. J. Awn, the proprietor of Awn Services, withdrew $8,700 from the business during the current year. The entry to close the withdrawals account at the end of the year is

a.	J. Awn, Withdrawals	8,700	
	Cash		8,700
b.	J. Awn, Capital	8,700	
	J. Awn, Withdrawals		8,700
c.	J. Awn, Withdrawals	8,700	
	J. Awn, Capital		8,700
d.	J. Awn, Capital	8,700	
	Salary Expense		8,700
e.	Income Summary	8,700	
	J. Awn, Capital		8,700

3. An income statement that includes cost of goods sold as another expense and shows only one subtotal for total expenses is a

  a. Balanced income statement.
  b. Single-step income statement.
  c. Multiple-step income statement.
  d. Combined income statement.
  e. Simplified income statement.

4. A classified balance sheet
  a. Measures a company's ability to pay its bills on time.
  b. Organizes assets and liabilities into important subgroups.
  c. Presents revenues, expenses, and net income.
  d. Reports operating, investing, and financing activities.
  e. Reports the effect of profit and withdrawals on owner's capital.

5. A company shows a $600 balance in Prepaid Insurance in the Unadjusted Trial Balance columns of the work sheet. The Adjustments columns show expired insurance of $200. This adjusting entry results in
  a. $200 less in net income.
  b. $200 more in net income.
  c. $200 difference between the debit and credit columns of the Unadjusted Trial Balance.
  d. $200 of prepaid insurance.
  e. An error in the financial statements.

Superscript letter ^A *denotes assignments based on Appendix 14A.*

Discussion Questions

1. What is a company's operating cycle?

2. What classes of assets and liabilities are shown on a typical classified balance sheet?

3. How is unearned revenue classified on the balance sheet?

4. What are the characteristics of plant assets?

5. What is the difference between the single-step and multiple-step income statement formats?

6.^AHow do reversing entries simplify recordkeeping?

7.^AIf a company recorded accrued salaries expense of $500 at the end of its fiscal year, what reversing entry could be made? When would it be made?

8. Refer to the balance sheet for **Best Buy** in Appendix A. What five noncurrent asset categories are used on its classified balance sheet?

9. Refer to **Circuit City**'s balance sheet in Appendix A. Identify the accounts listed as current liabilities.

The following are common categories on a classified balance sheet.

A. Current assets   **D.** Intangible assets

B. Long-term investments   **E.** Current liabilities

C. Plant assets   **F.** Long-term liabilities

For each of the following items, select the letter that identifies the balance sheet category where the item typically would appear. Some letters are used more than once.

_____ **1.** Land not currently used in operations

_____ **2.** Notes payable (due in three years)

_____ **3.** Accounts receivable

_____ **4.** Trademarks

_____ **5.** Accounts payable

_____ **6.** Store equipment

_____ **7.** Wages payable

_____ **8.** Cash

QUICK STUDY

QS 14-1
Classifying balance sheet items
(LO4)

List the following steps in preparing a work sheet in their proper order by writing numbers 1–5 in the blank spaces provided.

a. _____ Total the statement columns, compute net income (loss), and complete work sheet.

b. _____ Extend adjusted balances to appropriate financial statement columns.

c. _____ Prepare an unadjusted trial balance on the work sheet.

d. _____ Prepare an adjusted trial balance on the work sheet.

e. _____ Enter adjustments data on the work sheet.

QS 14-2
Ordering work sheet steps
(LO1)(LO2)

Match the following terms **A** through **J** with the appropriate definitions 1 through 10.

A. Plant assets   **F.** Closing entries

B. Owner's capital   **G.** Current liabilities

C. Classified balance sheet   **H.** Long-term investments

D. Intangible assets   **I.** Current assets

E. Current ratio   **J.** Unclassified balance sheet

_____ **1.** The owner's claim on the assets of a company.

_____ **2.** Tangible long-lived assets used to produce or sell products or services.

_____ **3.** Cash or other assets that are expected to be sold, collected, or used within one year or the company's operating cycle, whichever is longer.

_____ **4.** Entries recorded at the end of each accounting period to transfer end-of-period balances in revenue, expense, and withdrawals accounts to the permanent owner's capital account.

_____ **5.** Long-term assets used to produce or sell products or services; these assets usually lack physical form and their benefits are uncertain.

_____ **6.** Assets such as notes receivable or investments in stocks which are held for the longer of one year or the operating cycle of the company.

_____ **7.** A balance sheet that organizes the assets and liabilities into important subgroups.

_____ **8.** Obligations that are due to be paid or settled within one year or the operating cycle of a business, whichever is longer.

QS 14-3
Balance sheet classifications
(LO4)

_____ **9.** A balance sheet that broadly groups assets, liabilities, and equity items.

_____ **10.** A ratio that is used to help evaluate a company's ability to pay its short-term obligations, calculated by dividing current assets by current liabilities.

QS 14-4
Income statement terms
(LO3)

Match the following terms **A** through **E** with the appropriate definitions 1 through 5.

A. Merchandise inventory   **D.** Multiple-step income statement
B. Single-step income statement   **E.** General and administrative expenses
C. Selling expenses

_____ **1.** An income statement format that shows only one subtotal for total expenses.

_____ **2.** Products a company owns and intends to sell.

_____ **3.** Expenses that support overall operations and includes expenses related to accounting, human resource management, and financial management.

_____ **4.** An income statement format that shows detailed computations of net sales and other costs and expenses, and reports subtotals for various classes of items.

_____ **5.** The expenses of promoting sales by displaying and advertising merchandise, making sales, and delivering goods to customers.

QS 14-5^A
Reversing entries
(LO5)

On December 31, 2007, Yates Co. prepared an adjusting entry for $12,000 of earned but unrecorded management fees. On January 16, 2008, Yates received $26,700 cash in management fees, which included the accrued fees earned in 2007. Assuming the company uses reversing entries, prepare the January 1, 2008, reversing entry and the January 16, 2008, cash receipt entry.

EXERCISES

Exercise 14-1
Preparing the financial statements
(LO1) (LO2)

Use the following adjusted trial balance of Jones Trucking Company to prepare the (1) single-step income statement and (2) statement of owner's equity, for the year ended December 31, 2008. The K. Jones, Capital account balance is $185,000 at December 31, 2007.

Account Title	Debit	Credit
Cash	$ 18,000	
Accounts receivable	17,500	
Office supplies	3,000	
Trucks	172,000	
Accumulated depreciation—Trucks		$ 36,000
Land	85,000	
Accounts payable		12,000
Interest payable		4,000
Long-term notes payable		53,000
K. Jones, Capital		185,000
K. Jones, Withdrawals	20,000	
Trucking fees earned		130,000
Depreciation expense—Trucks	23,500	
Salaries expense	61,000	
Office supplies expense	8,000	
Repairs expense—Trucks	12,000	
Totals	$420,000	$420,000

Exercise 14-2
Preparing a classified balance sheet
(LO4)

Check   Total assets, $259,500;
K. Jones, Capital, $190,500

Use the information in the adjusted trial balance reported in Exercise 14-1 to prepare Jones Trucking Company's classified balance sheet as of December 31, 2008.

Exercise 14-3
Computing the current ratio

Use the information in the adjusted trial balance reported in Exercise 14-1 to compute the current ratio as of the balance sheet date. Interpret the current ratio for Jones Trucking Company. Assume that the industry average for the current ratio is 1.5. (*Hint:* The current ratio was introduced in Chapter 6. The current ratio is current assets divided by current liabilities.)

Listed below are a number of accounts. Use the table to classify each account. Indicate whether it is a temporary or permanent account (T or P), whether it is included in the income statement or balance sheet (IS or BS), whether it is closed at the end of the accounting period, and if so, how it is closed (Dr. or Cr. entry). The first one is done as an example.

Exercise 14-4

(L01) (L02)

Account	Permanent (P) or Temporary (T)	Income Statement (IS) or Balance Sheet (BS)	Closed (C) or Not Closed (NC)	Closed with a Debit (Dr) or Credit (CR)
a. Accounts payable	P	BS	NC	—
b. Accounts receivable				
c. Accumulated depreciation—equipment				
d. Advertising expense				
e. Cash				
f. Unearned revenues				
g. Depreciation expense—equipment				
h. Owner, withdrawals				
i. Equipment				
j. Insurance expense				
k. Interest expense				
l. Miscellaneous expense				
m. Notes payable				
n. Office supplies				
o. Office supplies expense				
p. Prepaid insurance				
q. Rent expense				
r. Owner, capital				
s. Salaries expense				
t. Salaries payable				
u. Revenue				

Based on the adjusted trial balance shown below, prepare a classified balance sheet for Focus Package Delivery as of December 31.

Exercise 14-5

Preparing classified balance sheets

(L04)

FOCUS PACKAGE DELIVERY
Adjusted Trial Balance
December 31

	Debit	Credit
Cash	$ 18 2 0 0 00	
Accounts receivable	34 2 0 0 00	
Supplies	2 1 0 0 00	
Long-term investments	25 0 0 0 00	
Delivery equipment	45 0 0 0 00	
Accumulated depreciation—delivery equipment		$ 11 0 8 0 00
Intangible assets	16 0 0 0 00	
Accounts payable		16 2 0 0 00
Wages payable		4 1 2 0 00
Long-term notes payable*		20 0 0 0 00
K. Ferman, capital		40 4 0 0 00
K. Ferman, withdrawals	15 0 0 0 00	
Delivery fees earned		145 0 0 0 00
Rent expense	8 0 0 0 00	
Wages expense	62 0 0 0 00	
Supplies expense	2 5 0 0 00	
Depreciation expense—delivery equipment	4 0 5 0 00	
Interest expense	1 0 0 0 00	
Utilities expense	3 7 5 0 00	
Totals	$236 8 0 0 00	$236 8 0 0 00

* $2,000 of the long-term note payable is due during the next year.

Exercise 14-6
Preparing closing entries

(LO2) (LO3)

Fill in the blanks (*a*) through (*g*) for the Hendricks Company for each of the income statements for 2007, 2008, and 2009. Prepare the closing entry to close the inventory and purchases-related accounts at the end of each year.

HENDRICKS COMPANY Income Statements For the Years Ended December 31	2007		2008		2009	
Sales	$7 5 0 0 00		$10 0 0 0 00	(f)		
Cost of goods sold						
Merchandise inventory (beginning)	(a)		3 7 5 00		7 5 0 00	
Total cost of merchandise purchases	2 4 0 0 00		3 6 2 5 00		$4 8 7 5 00	
Merchandise inventory (ending)	(b)		7 5 0 00		6 2 5 00	
Cost of goods sold	2 7 7 0 00	(d)			5 0 0 0 00	
Gross profit	(c)		6 7 5 0 00		5 2 0 0 00	
Operating expenses	3 7 5 0 00		3 7 5 0 00	(g)		
Net income	$ 9 8 0 00	(e)			$2 5 0 0 00	

Exercise 14-7[A]
Preparing reversing entries

(LO5)

The following two events occurred for Trey Co. on October 31, 2008, the end of its fiscal year.

a. Trey rents a building from its owner for $2,800 per month. By a prearrangement, the company delayed paying October's rent until November 5. On this date, the company paid the rent for both October and November.

b. Trey rents space in a building it owns to a tenant for $850 per month. By prearrangement, the tenant delayed paying the October rent until November 8. On this date, the tenant paid the rent for both October and November.

Required

1. Prepare adjusting entries that Trey must record for these events as of October 31.

2. Assuming Trey does *not* use reversing entries, prepare journal entries to record Trey's payment of rent on November 5 and the collection of rent on November 8 from Trey's tenant.

3. Assuming that Trey uses reversing entries, prepare reversing entries on November 1 and the journal entries to record Trey's payment of rent on November 5 and the collection of rent on November 8 from Trey's tenant.

Exercise 14-8[A]
Preparing reversing entries

(LO5)

Hawk Company records prepaid assets and unearned revenues in balance sheet accounts. The following information was used to prepare adjusting entries for Hawk Company as of August 31, the end of the company's fiscal year.

a. The company has earned $6,000 in unrecorded service fees.

b. The expired portion of prepaid insurance is $3,700.

c. The company has earned $2,900 of its Unearned Service Fees account balance.

d. Depreciation expense for office equipment is $3,300.

e. Employees have earned but have not been paid salaries of $3,400.

Prepare any necessary reversing entries for the accounting adjustments *a* through *e* assuming that Hawk uses reversing entries in its accounting system.

PROBLEM SET A

Problem 14-1A
Determining balance sheet classifications

(LO4)

In the blank space beside each numbered balance sheet item, enter the letter of its balance sheet classification. If the item should not appear on the balance sheet, enter a *Z* in the blank.

A. Current assets   **D.** Intangible assets   **F.** Long-term liabilities
B. Long-term investments   **E.** Current liabilities   **G.** Equity
C. Plant assets

_____ **1.** Long-term investment in stock   _____ **4.** Interest receivable
_____ **2.** Depreciation expense—Building   _____ **5.** Taxes payable
_____ **3.** Prepaid rent   _____ **6.** Automobiles

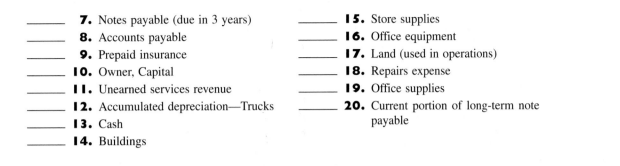

_____ **7.** Notes payable (due in 3 years)   _____ **15.** Store supplies

_____ **8.** Accounts payable   _____ **16.** Office equipment

_____ **9.** Prepaid insurance   _____ **17.** Land (used in operations)

_____ **10.** Owner, Capital   _____ **18.** Repairs expense

_____ **11.** Unearned services revenue   _____ **19.** Office supplies

_____ **12.** Accumulated depreciation—Trucks   _____ **20.** Current portion of long-term note

_____ **13.** Cash   payable

_____ **14.** Buildings

Cacuango Company's adjusted trial balance on August 31, 2008, its fiscal year-end, follows.

Problem 14-2A
Computing merchandising amounts and formatting income statements

	Debit	Credit
Merchandise inventory, August 31, 2007	$ 41,000	
Other (noninventory) assets	130,400	
Total liabilities		$ 25,000
C. Cacuango, Capital		104,550
C. Cacuango, Withdrawals	8,000	
Sales		225,600
Sales discounts	2,250	
Sales returns and allowances	12,000	
Purchases	92,000	
Purchase discounts		2,000
Purchase returns and allowances		4,500
Transportation-in	4,600	
Sales salaries expense	32,000	
Rent expense—Selling space	8,000	
Store supplies expense	1,500	
Advertising expense	13,000	
Office salaries expense	28,500	
Rent expense—Office space	3,600	
Office supplies expense	400	
Totals	$361,650	$361,650

On August 31, 2008, merchandise inventory was $41,000.

Required

1. Compute the company's net sales for the year.

2. Compute the company's total cost of net purchases for the year.

3. Prepare a multiple-step income statement that includes separate categories for selling expenses and for general and administrative expenses.

4. Prepare a single-step income statement that includes these expense categories: cost of goods sold, selling expenses, and general and administrative expenses.

Check (2) $90,100

(3) Gross profit, $136,850; Net income, $49,850

(4) Total expenses, $161,500

Use the data for Cacuango Company in Problem 14-2A to complete the following requirements.

Required

Prepare closing entries as of August 31, 2008.

Problem 14-3A
Preparing closing entries

Check $49,850 Dr. to close Income Summary

Problem 14-4A^A

Preparing adjusting, reversing, and next period entries

(LO5)

The following six-column table for Hawkeye Ranges includes the unadjusted trial balance as of December 31, 2008.

	HAWKEYE RANGES December 31, 2008						
	Unadjusted Trial Balance		Adjustments		Adjusted Trial Balance		
Account Title	**Dr.**	**Cr.**	**Dr.**	**Cr.**	**Dr.**	**Cr.**	
Cash	$ 14 0 0 0 00						
Accounts receivable	0 00						
Supplies	6 5 0 0 00						
Equipment	135 0 0 0 00						
Accumulated depreciation—Equipment		$ 30 0 0 0 00					
Interest payable		0 00					
Salaries payable		0 00					
Unearned member fees		15 0 0 0 00					
Notes payable		75 0 0 0 00					
P. Hawkeye, Capital		50 2 5 0 00					
P. Hawkeye, Withdrawals	21 1 2 5 00						
Member fees earned		42 0 0 0 00					
Depreciation expense—Equipment	0 00						
Salaries expense	30 0 0 0 00						
Interest expense	5 6 2 5 00						
Supplies expense	0 00						
Totals	$212 2 5 0 00	$212 2 5 0 00					

Required

1. Complete the six-column table by entering adjusting entries that reflect the following information.
    a. As of December 31, 2008, employees had earned $1,200 of unpaid and unrecorded salaries. The next payday is January 4, at which time $1,500 of salaries will be paid.
    b. The cost of supplies still available at December 31, 2008, is $3,000.
    c. The notes payable requires an interest payment to be made every three months. The amount of unrecorded accrued interest at December 31, 2008, is $1,875. The next interest payment, at an amount of $2,250, is due on January 15, 2009.
    d. Analysis of the unearned member fees account shows $5,800 remaining unearned at December 31, 2008.
    e. In addition to the member fees included in the revenue account balance, the company has earned another $9,300 in unrecorded fees that will be collected on January 31, 2009. The company is also expected to collect $10,000 on that same day for new fees earned in January 2009.
    f. Depreciation expense for the year is $15,000.

2. Prepare an adjusted trial balance as of December 31, 2008.

3. Prepare reversing journal entries to reverse the effects of the December 31, 2008, adjusting entries that involve accruals.

4. Prepare journal entries to record the cash payments and cash collections described for January. Assume reversing entries were made.

Check (1) Adjusted trial balance totals, $239,625

In the blank space beside each numbered balance sheet item, enter the letter of its balance sheet classification. If the item should not appear on the balance sheet, enter a Z in the blank.

A. Current assets
B. Long-term investments
C. Plant assets
D. Intangible assets

E. Current liabilities
F. Long-term liabilities
G. Equity

_____ **1.** Commissions earned
_____ **2.** Interest receivable
_____ **3.** Long-term investment in stock
_____ **4.** Prepaid insurance
_____ **5.** Machinery
_____ **6.** Notes payable (due in 15 years)
_____ **7.** Copyrights
_____ **8.** Current portion of long-term note payable
_____ **9.** Accumulated depreciation—Trucks
_____ **10.** Office equipment

_____ **11.** Rent receivable
_____ **12.** Salaries payable
_____ **13.** Income taxes payable
_____ **14.** Owner, Capital
_____ **15.** Office supplies
_____ **16.** Interest payable
_____ **17.** Rent revenue
_____ **18.** Notes receivable (due in 120 days)
_____ **19.** Land (used in operations)
_____ **20.** Depreciation expense—Trucks

White Company's adjusted trial balance on March 31, 2008, its fiscal year-end, follows.

	Debit	Credit
Merchandise inventory, March 31, 2007	$ 37,500	
Other (noninventory) assets	202,600	
Total liabilities		$ 42,500
J. White, Capital		164,425
J. White, Withdrawals	3,000	
Sales		332,650
Sales discounts	5,875	
Sales returns and allowances	20,000	
Purchases	138,500	
Purchase discounts		2,950
Purchase returns and allowances		6,700
Transportation-in	5,750	
Sales salaries expense	44,500	
Rent expense—Selling space	16,000	
Store supplies expense	3,850	
Advertising expense	26,000	
Office salaries expense	40,750	
Rent expense—Office space	3,800	
Office supplies expense	1,100	
Totals	$549,225	$549,225

On March 31, 2008, merchandise inventory was $56,500.

Required

1. Calculate the company's net sales for the year.
2. Calculate the company's total cost of net purchases for the year.
3. Prepare a multiple-step income statement that includes separate categories for selling expenses and for general and administrative expenses.
4. Prepare a single-step income statement that includes these expense categories: cost of goods sold, selling expenses, and general and administrative expenses.

Problem 14-3B

Preparing closing entries

(LO1) (LO2)

Check $55,175 Dr. to close Income Summary

Use the data for White Company in Problem 14-2B to complete the following requirements:

Required

Prepare closing entries as of March 31, 2008.

Problem 14-4B[A]

Preparing adjusting, reversing, and next period entries

(LO5)

The following six-column table for Solutions Co. includes the unadjusted trial balance as of December 31, 2008.

	SOLUTIONS CO. December 31, 2008					
	Unadjusted Trial Balance		**Adjustments**		**Adjusted Trial Balance**	
Account Title	**Dr.**	**Cr.**	**Dr.**	**Cr.**	**Dr.**	**Cr.**
Cash	$ 10 0 0 0 00					
Accounts receivable	0 00					
Supplies	7 6 0 0 00					
Machinery	50 0 0 0 00					
Accumulated depreciation—Machinery		$ 20 0 0 0 00				
Interest payable		0 00				
Salaries payable		0 00				
Unearned rental fees		7 2 0 0 00				
Notes payable		30 0 0 0 00				
G. Clay, Capital		14 2 0 0 00				
G. Clay, Withdrawals	9 5 0 0 00					
Rental fees earned		32 4 5 0 00				
Depreciation expense—Machinery	0 00					
Salaries expense	24 5 0 0 00					
Interest expense	2 2 5 0 00					
Supplies expense	0 00					
Totals	$103 8 5 0 00	$103 8 5 0 00				

Required

1. Complete the six-column table by entering adjusting journal entries that reflect the following information:

   a. As of December 31, 2008, employees had earned $400 of unpaid and unrecorded wages. The next payday is January 4, at which time $1,200 in wages will be paid.

   b. The cost of supplies still available at December 31, 2008, is $3,450.

   c. The notes payable requires an interest payment to be made every three months. The amount of unrecorded accrued interest at December 31, 2008, is $800. The next interest payment, at an amount of $900, is due on January 15, 2009.

   d. Analysis of the unearned rental fees shows that $3,200 remains unearned at December 31, 2008.

   e. In addition to the machinery rental fees included in the revenue account balance, the company has earned another $2,450 in unrecorded fees that will be collected on January 31, 2009. The company is also expected to collect $5,400 on that same day for new fees earned in January 2009.

Check (1) Adjusted trial balance totals, $111,300

   f. Depreciation expense for the year is $3,800.

2. Prepare an adjusted trial balance as of December 31, 2008.

3. Prepare reversing journal entries to reverse the effects of the adjusting entries that involve accruals.

4. Prepare journal entries to record the cash payments and cash collections described for January. Assume reversing entries were made.

(This serial problem began in Chapter 1 and continues through most of the book. If previous chapter segments were not completed, the serial problem can begin at this point. It is helpful, but not necessary, that you use the Working Papers that accompany the book.)

SERIAL PROBLEM

Success Systems

SP 14   The March 31, 2008, adjusted trial balance of Success Systems (reflecting its transactions from October 2007 through March of 2008) follows. The March 31, 2008, amount of merchandise available totals $680. For simplicity, we ignore payroll taxes and sales taxes in this problem.

No.	Account Title	Debit	Credit
101	Cash	$ 87,266	
106.1	Alex's Engineering Co.	0	
106.2	Wildcat Services	3,900	
106.3	Easy Leasing	11,000	
106.4	Clark Co.	4,800	
106.5	Chang Corporation	0	
106.6	Gomez Co.	0	
106.7	Delta Co.	0	
106.8	KC, Inc.	4,700	
106.9	Dream, Inc.	0	
119	Merchandise inventory	0	
126	Computer supplies	1,950	
128	Prepaid insurance	1,200	
131	Prepaid rent	875	
163	Office equipment	10,000	
164	Accumulated depreciation—Office equipment		$ 1,250
167	Computer equipment	25,000	
168	Accumulated depreciation—Computer equip.		2,500
201	Accounts payable		0
210	Wages payable		1,050
236	Unearned computer services revenue		0
301	A. Lopez, Capital		127,435
302	A. Lopez, Withdrawals	5,200	
403	Computer services revenue		31,850
413	Sales		20,900
414	Sales returns and allow.	500	
415	Sales discounts	55	
505	Purchases	15,200	
506	Purchase returns and allowances		496
507	Purchase discounts		152
508	Transportation-in	400	
612	Depreciation expense—Office equipment	625	
613	Depreciation expense—Computer equipment	1,250	
623	Wages expense	3,900	
637	Insurance expense	600	
640	Rent expense	2,625	
652	Computer supplies expense	2,075	
655	Advertising expense	800	
676	Mileage expense	512	
677	Miscellaneous expenses	0	
684	Repairs expense—Computer	1,200	
	Totals	$185,633	$185,633

Check (2) Net income, $24,336
       (3) A, Lopez, Capital
           (3/31/08), $146,571
       (4) Total assets, $147,621

Required

1. Record the necessary closing entries at March 31, 2008.
2. Prepare a single-step income statement for the three months ended March 31, 2008.
3. Prepare a statement of owner's equity for the three months ended March 31, 2008.
4. Prepare a classified balance sheet as of March 31, 2008.

BEYOND THE NUMBERS

REPORTING IN ACTION
(LO3)

BEST BUY

BTN 14–1 Refer to Best Buy's financial statements in Appendix A to answer the following.

Required

1. In its first footnote, Best Buy lists the primary costs classified in both costs of goods sold and selling, general, and administrative expenses. Give some examples of the primary costs included in each category.

Fast Forward

2. Access Best Buy's annual report for fiscal years ending after February 26, 2005, at its Website (BestBuy.com) or the SEC's EDGAR database (www.SEC.gov). Have these primary costs changed in each of these categories in the fiscal years ending after February 26, 2005? Explain.

COMPARATIVE ANALYSIS
(LO4)

BEST BUY

circuit CITY

BTN 14–2 Access the classified financial statements for Best Buy and Circuit City in Appendix A.

Required

1. Compare and contrast the assets section on the balance sheet for both Best Buy and Circuit City. How are they different? How are they similar?

2. Best Buy provides more detail for its property, plant, and equipment than Circuit City does. How is that information helpful to the financial statement user?

3. Circuit City provides more detail of its current assets than Best Buy does. What specific additional information provided by Circuit City would prove useful to the financial statement user?

ETHICS CHALLENGE
(LO2)

BTN 14–3 Erica Gray, CPA, is a sole practitioner. She has been practicing as an auditor for 10 years. Recently a long-standing audit client asked Gray to design and implement an integrated computer-based accounting information system. The fees associated with this additional engagement with the client are very attractive. However, Gray wonders if she can remain objective on subsequent audits in her evaluation of the client's accounting system and its records if she was responsible for its design and implementation. Gray knows that professional auditing standards require her to remain independent in fact and appearance from her auditing clients.

Required

1. What do you believe auditing standards are mainly concerned with when they require independence in fact? In appearance?

2. Why is it important that auditors remain independent of their clients?

3. Do you think Gray can accept this engagement and remain independent? Justify your response.

TEAMWORK IN ACTION
(LO1) (LO2)

BTN 14–4 The unadjusted trial balance and information for the accounting adjustments of Noseworthy Investigators follow. Each team member involved in this project is to assume one of the four responsibilities listed. After completing each of these responsibilities, the team should work together to prove the accounting equation utilizing information from teammates (1 and 4). If your equation does not balance, you are to work as a team to resolve the error. The team's goal is to complete the task as quickly and accurately as possible.

NOSEWORTHY INVESTIGATORS
Unadjusted Trial Balance

Account Title	Debit	Credit
Cash	$16,000	
Supplies	12,000	
Prepaid insurance	3,000	
Equipment	25,000	
Accumulated depreciation—Equipment		$ 7,000
Accounts payable		3,000
D. Noseworthy, Capital		34,000
D. Noseworthy, Withdrawals	6,000	
Investigation fees earned		33,000
Rent expense	15,000	
Totals	$77,000	$77,000

Additional Year-End Information

a. Insurance that expired in the current period amounts to $2,200.

b. Equipment depreciation for the period is $4,000.

c. Unused supplies total $5,000 at period-end.

d. Services in the amount of $800 have been provided but have not been billed or collected.

Responsibilities for Individual Team Members

1. Determine the accounts and adjusted balances to be extended to the balance sheet columns of the work sheet for Noseworthy. Also determine total assets and total liabilities.

2. Determine the adjusted revenue account balance and prepare the entry to close this account.

3. Determine the adjusted account balances for expenses and prepare the entry to close these accounts.

4. Prepare T-accounts for both D. Noseworthy, Capital (reflecting the unadjusted trial balance amount) and Income Summary. Prepare the third and fourth closing entries. Ask teammates assigned to parts 2 and 3 for the postings for Income Summary. Obtain amounts to complete the third closing entry and post both the third and fourth closing entries. Provide the team with the ending capital account balance.

5. The entire team should prove the accounting equation using post-closing balances.

BTN 14-5   Review this chapter's opening feature involving Cloudveil. Cloudveil currently produces high-performance, multisport mountain apparel. Assume that Stephen Sullivan and Brian Cousins are considering producing a new line of apparel for high-altitude camping. They plan on meeting with a financial institution for potential funding and have been asked by its loan officers for their financial statements.

ENTREPRENEURS IN BUSINESS

Required

1. What type of financial statement information will the loan officers consider?

2. What information on the classified balance sheet would help the loan officers assess whether Cloudveil will be able to repay its loans?

ANSWERS TO MULTIPLE CHOICE QUIZ

1. a; $550,000 − $123,000 = $427,000

2. b

3. b

4. b

5. a

Appendix

Financial Statement Information

This appendix includes financial information for (1) **Best Buy** and (2) **Circuit City**. This information is taken from their annual 10-K reports filed with the SEC. An **annual report** is a summary of a company's financial results for the year along with its current financial condition and future plans. This report is directed to external users of financial information, but it also affects the actions and decisions of internal users.

A company uses an annual report to showcase itself and its products. Many annual reports include attractive photos, diagrams, and illustrations related to the company. The primary objective of annual reports, however, is the *financial section,* which communicates much information about a company, with most data drawn from the accounting information system. The layout of an annual report's financial section is fairly established and typically includes the following:

- Letter to Shareholders
- Financial History and Highlights
- Management Discussion and Analysis
- Management's Report on Financial Statements and on Internal Controls
- Report of Independent Accountants (Auditor's Report) and on Internal Controls
- Financial Statements
- Notes to Financial Statements
- List of Directors and Officers

This appendix provides the financial statements for Best Buy (plus selected notes) and Circuit City. The appendix is organized as follows:

- **Best Buy A-2** through **A-18** ■ **Circuit City A-19** through **A-23**

Many assignments at the end of each chapter refer to information in this appendix. We encourage readers to spend time with these assignments; they are especially useful in showing the relevance and diversity of financial accounting and reporting.

> *Special note:* The SEC maintains the EDGAR (**E**lectronic **D**ata **G**athering, **A**nalysis, and **R**etrieval) database at www.sec.gov. The **Form 10-K** is the annual report form for most companies. It provides electronically accessible information. The **Form 10-KSB** is the annual report form filed by "small businesses." It requires slightly less information than the Form 10-K. One of these forms must be filed within 90 days after the company's fiscal year-end. (Forms 10-K405, 10-KT, 10-KT405, and 10-KSB405 are slight variations of the usual form due to certain regulations or rules.)

Financial Report

Selected Financial Data

The following table presents our selected financial data. Certain prior-year amounts have been reclassified to conform to the current-year presentation. All fiscal years presented reflect the classification of Musicland's financial results as discontinued operations.

Five-Year Financial Highlights

$ in millions, except per share amounts

Fiscal Year	2005	2004	2003	2002	2001
Consolidated Statements of Earnings Data					
Revenue	$27,433	$24,548	$20,943	$17,711	$15,189
Operating income	1,442	1,304	1,010	908	611
Earnings from continuing operations	934	800	622	570	401
Loss from discontinued operations, net of tax	—	(29)	(441)	—	(5)
Gain (loss) on disposal of discontinued operations, net of tax	50	(66)	—	—	—
Cumulative effect of change in accounting principles, net of tax	—	—	(82)	—	—
Net earnings	984	705	99	570	396
Per Share Data					
Continuing operations	$2.79	$2.41	$1.90	$1.77	$1.26
Discontinued operations	—	(0.09)	(1.34)	—	(0.02)
Gain (loss) on disposal of discontinued operations	0.15	(0.20)	—	—	—
Cumulative effect of accounting changes	—	—	(0.25)	—	—
Net earnings	2.94	2.13	0.31	1.77	1.24
Cash dividends declared and paid	0.42	0.40	—	—	—
Common stock price:					
High	62.20	62.70	53.75	51.47	59.25
Low	43.87	25.55	16.99	22.42	14.00
Operating Statistics					
Comparable store sales change	4.3%	7.1%	2.4%	1.9%	4.9%
Gross profit rate	23.7%	23.9%	23.6%	20.0%	18.5%
Selling, general and administrative expense rate	18.4%	18.6%	18.8%	14.9%	14.5%
Operating income rate	5.3%	5.3%	4.8%	5.1%	4.0%
Year-End Data					
Current ratio	1.4	1.3	1.3	1.2	1.1
Total assets	$10,294	$8,652	$7,694	$7,367	$4,840
Long-term debt, including current portion	600	850	834	820	296
Total shareholders' equity	4,449	3,422	2,730	2,521	1,822
Number of stores					
U.S. Best Buy stores	668	608	548	481	419
Magnolia Audio Video stores	20	22	19	13	13
International stores	144	127	112	95	—
Total retail square footage (000s)					
U.S. Best Buy stores	28,260	26,421	24,243	21,599	19,010
Magnolia Audio Video stores	194	218	189	133	133
International stores	3,139	2,800	2,375	1,923	—

Fiscal 2001 included 53 weeks. All other periods presented included 52 weeks.

BEST BUY

Consolidated Balance Sheets

$ in millions, except per share amounts

Assets	February 26, 2005	February 28, 2004
Current Assets		
Cash and cash equivalents	$ 470	$ 245
Short-term investments	2,878	2,355
Receivables	375	343
Merchandise inventories	2,851	2,607
Other current assets	329	174
Total current assets	6,903	5,724
Property and Equipment		
Land and buildings	506	484
Leasehold improvements	1,139	861
Fixtures and equipment	2,458	2,151
Property under master and capital lease	89	78
	4,192	3,574
Less accumulated depreciation	1,728	1,330
Net property and equipment	2,464	2,244
Goodwill	513	477
Tradename	40	37
Long-Term Investments	148	—
Other Assets	226	170
Total Assets	$10,294	$8,652
Liabilities and Shareholders' Equity		
Current Liabilities		
Accounts payable	$ 2,824	$2,460
Unredeemed gift card liabilities	410	300
Accrued compensation and related expenses	234	269
Accrued liabilities	844	724
Accrued income taxes	575	380
Current portion of long-term debt	72	368
Total current liabilities	4,959	4,501
Long-Term Liabilities	358	247
Long-Term Debt	528	482
Shareholders' Equity		
Preferred stock, $1.00 par value: Authorized — 400,000 shares; Issued and outstanding — none	—	—
Common stock, $.10 par value: Authorized — 1 billion shares; Issued and outstanding — 328,342,000 and 324,648,000 shares, respectively	33	32
Additional paid-in capital	952	836
Retained earnings	3,315	2,468
Accumulated other comprehensive income	149	86
Total shareholders' equity	4,449	3,422
Total Liabilities and Shareholders' Equity	$10,294	$8,652

See Notes to Consolidated Financial Statements.

Consolidated Statements of Earnings
$ in millions, except per share amounts

For the Fiscal Years Ended	February 26, 2005	February 28, 2004	March 1, 2003
Revenue	$27,433	$24,548	$20,943
Cost of goods sold	20,938	18,677	15,998
Gross profit	6,495	5,871	4,945
Selling, general and administrative expenses	5,053	4,567	3,935
Operating income	1,442	1,304	1,010
Net interest income (expense)	1	(8)	4
Earnings from continuing operations before income tax expense	1,443	1,296	1,014
Income tax expense	509	496	392
Earnings from continuing operations	934	800	622
Loss from discontinued operations (Note 2), net of $17 and $119 tax	—	(29)	(441)
Gain (loss) on disposal of discontinued operations (Note 2)	50	(66)	—
Cumulative effect of change in accounting principle for goodwill (Note 1), net of $24 tax	—	—	(40)
Cumulative effect of change in accounting principle for vendor allowances (Note 1), net of $26 tax	—	—	(42)
Net earnings	$ 984	$ 705	$ 99
Basic earnings (loss) per share:			
Continuing operations	$ 2.87	$ 2.47	$ 1.93
Discontinued operations	—	(0.09)	(1.37)
Gain (loss) on disposal of discontinued operations	0.15	(0.20)	—
Cumulative effect of accounting changes	—	—	(0.25)
Basic earnings per share	$ 3.02	$ 2.18	$ 0.31
Diluted earnings (loss) per share:[1]			
Continuing operations	$ 2.79	$ 2.41	$ 1.90
Discontinued operations	—	(0.09)	(1.34)
Gain (loss) on disposal of discontinued operations	0.15	(0.20)	—
Cumulative effect of accounting changes	—	—	(0.25)
Diluted earnings per share	$ 2.94	$ 2.13	$ 0.31
Basic weighted average common shares outstanding (in millions)	325.9	323.3	321.1
Diluted weighted average common shares outstanding (in millions)[1]	336.6	333.9	330.7

[1]   The calculation of diluted earnings per share assumes the conversion of our convertible debentures due in 2022 into 5.8 million shares of common stock and adds back related after-tax interest expense of $6.5 for all periods presented.

See Notes to Consolidated Financial Statements.

BEST BUY

Consolidated Statements of Changes in Shareholders' Equity

$ and shares in millions

	Common Shares	Common Stock	Additional Paid-In Capital	Retained Earnings	Accumulated Other Comprehensive Income (Loss)	Total
Balances at March 2, 2002	**319**	**$31**	**$ 702**	**$1,794**	**$ (6)**	**$2,521**
Net earnings	—	—	—	99	—	99
Other comprehensive income (loss), net of tax:						
Foreign currency translation adjustments	—	—	—	—	34	34
Other	—	—	—	—	(1)	(1)
Total comprehensive income						132
Stock options exercised	3	1	43	—	—	44
Tax benefit from stock options exercised	—	—	33	—	—	33
Balances at March 1, 2003	**322**	**32**	**778**	**1,893**	**27**	**2,730**
Net earnings	—	—	—	705	—	705
Foreign currency translation adjustments	—	—	—	—	59	59
Total comprehensive income						764
Stock options exercised	5	—	114	—	—	114
Tax benefit from stock options exercised	—	—	41	—	—	41
Vesting of restricted stock awards	—	—	3	—	—	3
Common stock dividends, $0.40 per share	—	—	—	(130)	—	(130)
Repurchase of common stock	(2)	—	(100)	—	—	(100)
Balances at February 28, 2004	**325**	**32**	**836**	**2,468**	**86**	**3,422**
Net earnings	—	—	—	984	—	984
Other comprehensive income, net of tax:						
Foreign currency translation adjustments	—	—	—	—	59	59
Other	—	—	—	—	4	4
Total comprehensive income						1,047
Stock options exercised	6	1	219	—	—	220
Tax benefit from stock options exercised and employee stock purchase plan	—	—	60	—	—	60
Issuance of common stock under employee stock purchase plan	1	—	36	—	—	36
Vesting of restricted stock awards	—	—	1	—	—	1
Common stock dividends, $0.42 per share	—	—	—	(137)	—	(137)
Repurchase of common stock	(4)	—	(200)	—	—	(200)
Balances at February 26, 2005	**328**	**$33**	**$ 952**	**$3,315**	**$149**	**$4,449**

See Notes to Consolidated Financial Statements.

BEST BUY

Consolidated Statements of Cash Flows

$ in millions

For the Fiscal Years Ended	February 26, 2005	February 28, 2004	March 1, 2003
Operating Activities			
Net earnings	$ 984	$ 705	$ 99
(Gain) loss from and disposal of discontinued operations, net of tax	(50)	95	441
Cumulative effect of change in accounting principles, net of tax	—	—	82
Earnings from continuing operations	934	800	622
Adjustments to reconcile earnings from continuing operations to total cash provided by operating activities from continuing operations:			
Depreciation	459	385	310
Asset impairment charges	22	22	11
Deferred income taxes	(28)	(14)	(37)
Other	23	16	15
Changes in operating assets and liabilities, net of acquired assets and liabilities:			
Receivables	(30)	(27)	(89)
Merchandise inventories	(240)	(507)	(256)
Other assets	(190)	(25)	(21)
Accounts payable	347	272	(5)
Other liabilities	243	250	117
Accrued income taxes	301	197	111
Total cash provided by operating activities from continuing operations	1,841	1,369	778
Investing Activities			
Additions to property and equipment	(502)	(545)	(725)
Purchases of available-for-sale securities	(7,789)	(2,989)	(1,844)
Sales of available-for-sale securities	7,118	2,175	1,610
Other, net	7	1	49
Total cash used in investing activities from continuing operations	(1,166)	(1,358)	(910)
Financing Activities			
Long-term debt payments	(371)	(17)	(13)
Issuance of common stock under employee stock purchase plan and for the exercise of stock options	256	114	40
Repurchase of common stock	(200)	(100)	—
Dividends paid	(137)	(130)	—
Net proceeds from issuance of long-term debt	—	—	18
Other, net	(7)	46	(15)
Total cash (used in) provided by financing activities from continuing operations	(459)	(87)	30
Effect of Exchange Rate Changes on Cash	9	1	—
Net Cash Used in Discontinued Operations	—	(53)	(79)
Increase (Decrease) in Cash and Cash Equivalents	225	(128)	(181)
Cash and Cash Equivalents at Beginning of Year	245	373	554
Cash and Cash Equivalents at End of Year	$ 470	$ 245	$ 373
Supplemental Disclosure of Cash Flow Information			
Income tax paid	$ 241	$ 306	$ 283
Interest paid	35	22	24
Capital and financing lease obligations incurred	117	26	—

See Notes to Consolidated Financial Statements.

BEST BUY

Best Buy

<u>SELECTED</u> Notes to Consolidated Financial Statements

$ in millions, except per share amounts

1.   Summary of Significant Accounting Policies

Description of Business

Best Buy Co., Inc. is a specialty retailer of consumer electronics, home-office products, entertainment software, appliances and related services.

We operate two reportable segments: Domestic and International. The Domestic segment is comprised of U.S. Best Buy and Magnolia Audio Video operations. At February 26, 2005, we operated 668 U.S. Best Buy stores in 48 states and the District of Columbia. At February 26, 2005, we operated 20 Magnolia Audio Video stores in California, Washington and Oregon. The International segment is comprised of Future Shop and Best Buy operations in Canada. At February 26, 2005, we operated 114 Future Shop stores throughout all Canadian provinces and 30 Canadian Best Buy stores in Ontario, Alberta, British Columbia, Manitoba and Saskatchewan. Future Shop and Canadian Best Buy stores offer products and services similar to those offered by U.S. Best Buy stores except that Canadian Best Buy stores do not sell appliances.

In support of our retail store operations, we also operate Geek Squad, a computer repair and service provider, and Web sites for each of our brands (BestBuy.com, BestBuyCanada.ca, FutureShop.ca, MagnoliaAV.com and GeekSquad.com).

Fiscal Year

Our fiscal year ends on the Saturday nearest the end of February. Fiscal 2005, 2004 and 2003 each included 52 weeks.

Cash and Cash Equivalents

Cash primarily consists of cash on hand and bank deposits. Cash equivalents primarily consist of money market accounts and other highly liquid investments with an original maturity of three months or less when purchased. We carry these investments at cost, which approximates market value. The amount of cash equivalents at February 26, 2005, and February 28, 2004, was $156 and $73, respectively, and the weighted average interest rates were 2.9% and 0.9%, respectively.

Outstanding checks in excess of funds on deposit totaled $393 and $351 at February 26, 2005, and February 28, 2004, respectively, and are reflected as current liabilities.

Merchandise Inventories

Merchandise inventories are recorded at the lower of average cost or market. In-bound freight-related costs from our vendors are included as part of the net cost of merchandise inventories. Also included in the cost of inventory are certain vendor allowances that are not a reimbursement of specific, incremental and identifiable costs to promote a vendor's products. Other costs associated with acquiring, storing and transporting merchandise inventories to our retail stores are expensed as incurred and included in cost of goods sold.

Our inventory loss reserve represents anticipated physical inventory losses (e.g., theft) that have occurred since the last physical inventory date. Independent physical inventory counts are taken on a regular basis to ensure that the inventory reported in our consolidated financial statements is accurately stated. During the interim period between physical inventory counts, we reserve for anticipated physical inventory losses on a location-by-location basis.

Property and Equipment

Property and equipment are recorded at cost. We compute depreciation using the straight-line method over the estimated useful lives of the assets. Leasehold improvements are depreciated over the shorter of their estimated useful lives or the period from the date the assets are placed in service to the end of the initial lease

$ in millions, except per share amounts

term. Accelerated depreciation methods are generally used for income tax purposes.

Repairs and maintenance costs are charged directly to expense as incurred. Major renewals or replacements that substantially extend the useful life of an asset are capitalized and depreciated.

Estimated useful lives by major asset category are as follows:

Asset	Life (in years)
Buildings	30-40
Leasehold improvements	10-25
Fixtures and equipment	3-15
Property under master and capital lease	3-35

Goodwill and Intangible Assets

Goodwill

Goodwill is the excess of the purchase price over the fair value of identifiable net assets acquired in business combinations accounted for under the purchase method. Effective March 3, 2002, we adopted SFAS No. 142, *Goodwill and Other Intangible Assets,* which eliminated the systematic amortization of goodwill. This Statement also requires that we review goodwill for impairment at adoption and at least annually thereafter.

During the fourth quarter of fiscal 2005, we completed our annual impairment testing of our goodwill and tradename, using the same valuation techniques as described above, and determined there was no impairment.

Tradename

We have an indefinite-lived intangible asset related to our Future Shop tradename that totaled $40 and $37 at February 26, 2005, and February 28, 2004, respectively, which is included in the International segment. The change in the indefinite-lived intangible asset balance from February 28, 2004, was the result of fluctuations in foreign currency exchange rates.

Lease Rights

Lease rights, representing costs incurred to acquire the lease of a specific commercial property, are recorded at cost and are amortized to rent expense over the remaining lease term, which ranges up to 16 years, beginning with the date we take possession of the property.

The gross cost and accumulated amortization of lease rights were $27 and $29; and $9 and $6, respectively, at February 26, 2005, and February 28, 2004, respectively. Lease rights amortization was $4, $4 and $2 for fiscal 2005, 2004 and 2003, respectively. Current lease rights amortization is expected to be approximately $3 for each of the next five fiscal years.

Income Taxes

We account for income taxes under the liability method. Under this method, deferred tax assets and liabilities are recognized for the estimated future tax consequences attributable to differences between the financial statement carrying amounts of existing assets and liabilities and their respective tax bases, and operating loss and tax credit carryforwards. Deferred tax assets and liabilities are measured using enacted income tax rates in effect for the year in which those temporary differences are expected to be recovered or settled. The effect on deferred tax assets and liabilities of a change in income tax rates is recognized in our statement of earnings in the period that includes the enactment date. A valuation allowance is recorded to reduce the carrying amounts of deferred tax assets if it is more likely than not that such assets will not be realized.

Long-Term Liabilities

The major components of long-term liabilities at February 26, 2005, and February 28, 2004, included deferred compensation plan liabilities, long-term rent-related liabilities, deferred income taxes and advances received under vendor alliance programs.

Foreign Currency

Foreign currency denominated assets and liabilities are translated into U.S. dollars using the exchange rates in effect at the balance sheet date. Results of operations and cash flows are translated using the average exchange rates throughout the period. The effect of exchange rate

$ in millions, except per share amounts

fluctuations on translation of assets and liabilities is included as a component of shareholders' equity in accumulated other comprehensive income. Gains and losses from foreign currency transactions, which are included in SG&A, have not been significant.

Revenue Recognition

We recognize revenue from the sale of merchandise at the time the customer takes possession of the merchandise. We recognize service revenue at the time the service is provided, the sales price is fixed or determinable, and collectibility is reasonably assured. Proceeds from the sale of gift cards are deferred until the customer uses the gift card to acquire merchandise or services. Amounts billed to customers for shipping and handling are included in revenue. An allowance has been established for estimated sales returns.

We sell extended service contracts on behalf of an unrelated third party. In jurisdictions where we are not deemed to be the obligor on the contract, commissions are recognized in revenue at the time of sale. In jurisdictions where we are deemed to be the obligor on

the contract, commissions are recognized in revenue ratably over the term of the service contract.

Sales Incentives

We frequently offer sales incentives that entitle our customers to receive a reduction in the price of a product or service. Sales incentives include discounts, coupons and other offers that entitle a customer to receive a reduction in the price of a product or service by submitting a claim for a refund or rebate. For sales incentives in which we are the obligor, the reduction in revenue is recognized at the time the product is sold.

We have a customer loyalty program which allows members to earn points for each purchase completed at U.S. Best Buy stores. Points earned enable members to receive a certificate that may be redeemed on future purchases at U.S. Best Buy stores. The value of points earned by our loyalty program members is included in accrued liabilities and recorded as a reduction of revenue at the time the points are earned, based on the percentage of points that are projected to be redeemed.

Costs of Goods Sold and Selling, General and Administrative Expenses

The following table illustrates the primary costs classified in each major expense category.

Cost of Goods Sold	SG&A
• Total cost of products sold including: — Freight expenses associated with moving merchandise inventories from our vendors to our distribution centers; — Vendor allowances that are not a reimbursement of specific, incremental and identifiable costs to promote a vendor's products; • Costs of services provided; • Physical inventory losses; • Markdowns; • Customer shipping and handling expenses; • Costs associated with operating our distribution network, including payroll and benefit costs, occupancy costs, and depreciation; and • Freight expenses associated with moving merchandise inventories from our distribution centers to our retail stores.	• Payroll and benefit costs for retail and corporate employees; • Occupancy costs of retail, services and corporate facilities; • Depreciation related to retail, services and corporate assets; • Advertising; • Vendor allowances that are a reimbursement of specific, incremental and identifiable costs to promote a vendor's products; • Outside service fees; • Long-lived asset impairment charges; and • Other administrative costs, such as credit card service fees, supplies, and travel and lodging.

$ in millions, except per share amounts

Advertising Costs

Advertising costs, which are included in SG&A, are expensed the first time the advertisement runs. Advertising costs consist primarily of print and television advertisements as well as promotional events. Gross advertising expenses, before expense reimbursement from vendor allowances, for fiscal 2005, 2004 and 2003 were $712, $675 and $567, respectively.

Stock-Based Compensation

We have a stock-based compensation plan that includes stock options and restricted stock. We also have an employee stock purchase plan. The table below illustrates the effect on net earnings and earnings per share as if we had applied the fair value recognition provisions of SFAS No. 123 to stock-based compensation for each of the last three fiscal years.

	2005	2004	2003
Net earnings, as reported	$ 984	$ 705	$ 99
Add: Stock-based compensation expense included in reported net earnings, net of tax[1]	(1)	5	1
Deduct: Stock-based compensation expense determined under fair value method for all awards, net of tax[2]	(60)	(101)	(85)
Net earnings, pro forma	$ 923	$ 609	$ 15
Earnings per share:			
Basic — as reported	$3.02	$2.18	$0.31
Basic — pro forma	$2.83	$1.88	$0.05
Diluted — as reported	$2.94	$2.13	$0.31
Diluted — pro forma	$2.80	$1.88	$0.05

[1] Amounts represent the after-tax compensation costs for restricted stock awards.

[2] In the fourth quarter of fiscal 2005, we increased our expected participant stock option forfeiture rate as a result of transferring to a third-party provider certain corporate employees, and the departure of certain senior executives. This higher level of expected stock option forfeitures reduced our fiscal 2005 pro forma stock-based compensation expense. Fiscal 2005 pro forma stock-based compensation expense may not be indicative of future stock-based compensation expense.

2. Discontinued Operations

In fiscal 2004, we sold our interest in Musicland. The buyer assumed all of Musicland's liabilities, including approximately $500 in lease obligations, in exchange for all of the capital stock of Musicland and paid no cash consideration. The transaction also resulted in the transfer of all of Musicland's assets, other than a distribution center in Franklin, Indiana, and selected nonoperating assets. The loss from discontinued operations for fiscal 2004 included a loss on the disposal of discontinued operations (which was primarily noncash) of $66, net of tax, related to the sale of Musicland. In connection with the sale, Musicland purchased transition support services from us for approximately one year from the date of the sale.

In accordance with SFAS No. 144, Musicland's financial results are reported separately as discontinued operations for all periods presented.

During fiscal 2003, we recorded an after-tax, noncash impairment charge of $308 for the full write-off of goodwill related to our acquisition of Musicland. In addition, we recorded an after-tax, noncash charge of $8 for the change in our method of accounting for Musicland vendor allowances. The charges are classified as cumulative effects of changes in accounting principles in discontinued operations (see Note 1, *Summary of Significant Accounting Policies*).

Also during fiscal 2003, in accordance with SFAS No. 144, we recorded a pre-tax impairment charge of $166 related to a reassessment of the carrying value of

BEST BUY

BEST BUY

$ in millions, except per share amounts

Musicland's long-lived assets. The $166 charge was recorded in loss before income taxes, in the table below. We determined fair values utilizing widely accepted valuation techniques, including discounted cash flows. We based fair values on the then-current expectations for the business in light of the then-existing retail environment and the uncertainty associated with future trends in prerecorded music products.

The financial results of Musicland, included in discontinued operations, were as follows:

For the Fiscal Years Ended	Feb. 26, 2005	Feb. 28, 2004[1]	March 1, 2003
Revenue	$—	$354	$1,727
Loss before income taxes	—	(46)	(244)
Loss before the disposal and the cumulative effect of accounting changes, net of $17 and $119 tax, respectively	—	(29)	(125)
Gain (loss) on disposal of discontinued operations[2]	50	(66)	—
Cumulative effect of change in accounting principles, net of $5 tax	—	—	(316)
Gain (loss) from discontinued operations, net of tax	$50	$ (95)	$ (441)

[1]   Fiscal 2004 includes operating results from March 2, 2003, through June 16, 2003, the date we sold our interest in Musicland.

[2]   Fiscal 2005 gain on disposal of discontinued operations represents the reversal of valuation allowances on deferred tax assets as described below. Fiscal 2004 loss on disposal of discontinued operations is net of $25 tax benefit offset by a $25 valuation allowance.

3.   Investments in Debt Securities

Our short-term and long-term investments are comprised of municipal and United States government debt securities. In accordance with SFAS No. 115, *Accounting for Certain Investments in Debt and Equity Securities,* and based on our ability to market and sell these instruments, we classify auction-rate debt securities and other investments in debt securities as available-for-sale and carry them at amortized cost. Auction-rate debt securities are long-term bonds that are similar to short-term instruments because their interest rates are reset periodically and investments in these securities can be sold for cash on the auction date. We classify auction-rate debt securities as short-term or long-term investments based on the reset dates.

In accordance with our investment policy, we place our investments in debt securities with issuers who have high-quality credit and limit the amount of investment exposure to any one issuer. We seek to preserve principal and minimize exposure to interest-rate fluctuations by limiting default risk, market risk and reinvestment risk.

On an annual basis, we review the key characteristics of our debt securities portfolio and their classification in accordance with GAAP. If a decline in the fair value of a security is deemed by management to be other than temporary, the cost basis of the investment is written down to fair value, and the amount of the write-down is included in the determination of income.

During our annual review in the fourth quarter of fiscal 2005, we reclassified our auction-rate debt securities from cash and cash equivalents to short-term investments or long-term investments, as appropriate, for all periods presented. The amortized cost of the securities reclassified for fiscal 2004 was $2,355. The unrealized gain on the securities in conjunction with this reclassification was not significant.

We also revised the presentation in the consolidated statements of cash flows for the years ended February 28, 2004, and March 1, 2003, to reflect the gross purchases and sales of these securities as investing activities rather than as a component of cash and cash equivalents, which is consistent with the presentation for the fiscal year ended February 26, 2005.

$ in millions, except per share amounts

The carrying amount of our investments in debt securities approximated fair value of February 26, 2005, and February 28, 2004, respectively, due to the rapid turnover of our portfolio and the highly liquid nature of these investments. Therefore, there were no significant unrealized holding gains or losses.

The following table presents the amortized principal amounts, related weighted average interest rates, maturities and major security types for our investments in debt securities:

	February 26, 2005		February 28, 2004	
	Amortized Principal Amount	Weighted Average Interest Rate	Amortized Principal Amount	Weighted Average Interest Rate
Short-term investments (less than one year)	$2,878	3.22%	$2,355	1.59%
Long-term investments (one to three years)	148	3.73%	—	—
Total	$3,026		$2,355	
Municipal debt securities	$3,019		$2,355	
Debt securities issued by U.S. Treasury and other U.S. government entities	7		—	
Total	$3,026		$2,355	

4. Debt

	Feb. 26, 2005	Feb. 28, 2004
Convertible subordinated debentures, unsecured, due 2022, initial interest rate 2.25%	$402	$ 402
Convertible debentures, unsecured, due 2021, interest rate 2.75%[1]	—	353
Master lease obligations, due 2006, interest rate 5.9%	55	58
Capital lease obligations, due 2005, interest rates ranging from 5.5% to 8.0%	13	16
Financing lease obligations, due 2008 to 2022, interest rates ranging from 5.6% to 6.0%[2]	107	—
Mortgage and other debt, interest rates ranging from 1.8% to 8.9%	23	21
Total debt	600	850
Less: current portion	(72)	(368)
Total long-term debt	$528	$ 482

[1]   In June 2004, we redeemed our convertible debentures due in 2021, for $355. No gain or loss was incurred.

[2]   In fiscal 2005, we recorded $107 of financing leases as a result of our review of our lease accounting practices. See Note 7, *Leases,* for further information.

The mortgage and other debt are secured by certain property and equipment with a net book value of $98 and $97 at February 26, 2005, and February 28, 2004, respectively.

Convertible Debentures

In January 2002, we sold convertible subordinated debentures having an aggregate principal amount of $402. The proceeds from the offering, net of $6 in offering expenses, were $396. The debentures mature in 2022 and are callable at par, at our option, for cash on or after January 15, 2007.

Holders may require us to purchase all or a portion of their debentures on January 15, 2007; January 15, 2012; and January 15, 2017, at a purchase price equal

BEST BUY

$ in millions, except per share amounts

to 100% of the principal amount of the debentures plus accrued and unpaid interest up to but not including the date of purchase. We have the option to settle the purchase price in cash, stock, or a combination of cash and stock.

The debentures will be convertible into shares of our common stock at a conversion rate of 14.4927 shares per $0.001 principal amount of debentures, equivalent to an initial conversion price of $69.00 per share, if the closing price of our common stock exceeds a specified price for a specified period of time, if our credit rating falls below specified levels, if the debentures are called for redemption or if certain specified corporate transactions occur. At February 26, 2005, none of the criteria for conversion had been met. The debentures have an initial interest rate of 2.25% per annum. The interest rate may be reset, but not below 2.25% or above 3.25%, on July 15, 2006; July 15, 2011; and July 15, 2016. One of our subsidiaries has guaranteed the convertible debentures.

Credit Facilities

We have a $200 bank revolving credit facility which is guaranteed by certain of our subsidiaries. The facility expires on December 22, 2009. Borrowings under this facility are unsecured and bear interest at rates specified in the credit agreement. We also pay certain facility and agent fees. The agreement contains convenants that require us to maintain certain financial ratios.

Other

The fair value of long-term debt approximated $603 and $902 as of February 26, 2005, and February 28, 2004, respectively, based on the ask prices quoted from external sources, compared with carrying values of $600 and $850, respectively.

The future maturities of long-term debt, including master and capitalized leases, consist of the following:

Fiscal Year	
2006	$ 72
2007[1]	415
2008	14
2009	14
2010	20
Thereafter	65
	$600

[1] Holders of our debentures due in 2022 may require us to purchase all or a portion of their debentures on January 15, 2007. The table above assumes that all holders of our debentures exercise their redemption options.

5. Shareholders' Equity Stock Compensation Plans

Outstanding options were granted at exercise prices equal to the fair market value of our common stock on the date of grant and have a 10-year term. Options issued to employees generally vest over a four-year period. Options issued to our directors vest immediately upon grant.

Earnings per Share

Basic earnings per share is computed based on the weighted average number of common shares outstanding. Diluted earnings per share is computed based on the weighted average number of common shares outstanding adjusted by the number of additional shares that would have been outstanding had the potentially dilutive common shares been issued. Potentially dilutive shares of common stock include stock options, unvested restricted stock awards, shares issuable under our ESPP as well as common shares that would have resulted from the assumed conversion of our convertible debentures (see Note 4, *Debt*). Since the potentially dilutive shares related to the convertible debentures are included in the calculation, the related interest, net of tax, is added back to income from continuing operations, as the interest would not have been paid if the convertible debentures were converted to common stock.

$ in millions, except per share amounts

The following table presents a reconciliation of the numerators and denominators of basic and diluted earnings per share from continuing operations for fiscal 2005, 2004 and 2003:

	2005	2004	2003
Numerator:			
Earnings from continuing operations, basic	$ 934	$ 800	$ 622
Adjustment for assumed dilution:			
Interest on convertible debentures due in 2022, net of tax	7	6	6
Earnings from continuing operations, diluted	$ 941	$ 806	$ 628
Denominator (in millions):			
Weighted average common shares outstanding	325.9	323.3	321.1
Effect of dilutive securities:			
Shares from assumed conversion of convertible debentures	5.8	5.8	5.8
Stock options and other	4.9	4.8	3.8
Weighted average common shares outstanding, assuming dilution	336.6	333.9	330.7
Basic earnings per share — continuing operations	$ 2.87	$ 2.47	$ 1.93
Diltuted earnings per share — continuing operations	$ 2.79	$ 2.41	$ 1.90

Repurchase of Common Stock

In June 2004, our Board authorized the purchase of up to $500 of our common stock from time to time through open market purchases. The $500 share repurchase program, which became effective on June 24, 2004, terminated and replaced the $400 share repurchase program authorized by our Board in fiscal 2000.

In April 2005, our Board authorized the purchase of up to $1.5 billion of our common stock from time to time through open market purchases. This share repurchase program has no stated expiration date. The $1.5 billion share repurchase program terminated and replaced the $500 share repurchase program authorized by our Board in June 2004.

During fiscal 2005, we purchased and retired 2.3 million shares at a cost of $118 under the $500 share

repurchase program, and 1.6 million shares at a cost of $82 under the $400 share repurchase program.

Comprehensive Income

Comprehensive income is computed as net earnings plus certain other items that are recorded directly to shareholders' equity. The only significant other item included in comprehensive income is foreign currency translation adjustments. Foreign currency translation adjustments do not include a provision for income tax because earnings from foreign operations are considered to be indefinitely reinvested outside the U.S. Investment gains/losses were not significant.

$ in millions, except per share amounts

6.   Net Interest Income (Expense)

Net interest income (expense) for fiscal 2005, 2004 and 2003 was comprised of the following

	2005	2004	2003
Interest expense[1]	$(44)	$(32)	$(30)
Capitalized interest	—	1	5
Interest income	45	23	23
Net interest income (expense)	1	(8)	(2)
Interest expense allocated to discontinued operations[2]	—	—	(6)
Net interest income (expense) from continuing operations	$ 1	$ (8)	$ 4

[1]   Fiscal 2005 interest expense includes $21 of expense related to our lease accounting corrections.

[2]   We allocated interest expense to discontinued operations based upon debt that was attributable to Musicland's operation.

7.   Leases

We lease portions of our corporate facilities and conduct the majority of our retail and distribution operations from leased locations. The leases require payment of real estate taxes, insurance and common area maintenance, in addition to rent. The terms of our lease agreements generally range up to 20 years. Most of the leases contain renewal options and escalation clauses, and certain store leases require contingent rents based on specified percentages of revenue. Other leases contain covenants related to the maintenance of financial ratios.

For leases that contain predetermined fixed escalations of the minimum rent, we recognize the related rent expense on a straight-line basis from the date we take possession of the property to the end of the initial lease term. We record any difference between the straight-line rent amounts and amounts payable under the leases as part of deferred rent, in accrued liabilities or long-term liabilities, as appropriate.

Cash or lease incentives (tenant allowances) received upon entering into certain store leases are recognized on a straight-line basis as a reduction to rent from the date we take possession of the property through the end of the initial lease term. We record the unamortized portion of tenant allowances as a part of deferred rent, in accrued liabilities or long-term liabilities, as appropriate.

At February 26, 2005, and February 28, 2004, deferred rent included in accrued liabilities was approximately $11 and $3, respectively, and deferred rent included in long-term liabilities was approximately $171 and $73, respectively.

We also lease certain equipment under noncancelable operating and capital leases. Assets acquired under capital leases are depreciated over the shorter of the useful life of the asset or the initial lease term.

Rental expense for all operating leases, during the past three fiscal years, including leases of property and equipment, was as follows:

	2005	2004	2003
Net rent expense for continuing operations	$501	$468	$440

$ in millions, except per share amounts

The future minimum lease payments under our capital, financing and operating leases by fiscal year (not including contingent rentals) as of February 26, 2005, are as follows:

Fiscal Year	Capital Leases	Financing Leases	Operating Leases
2006	$ 6	$ 16	$ 541
2007	2	15	541
2008	2	15	524
2009	2	14	511
2010	2	14	486
Thereafter	1	79	3,247
Subtotal	15	153	$5,850
Less: imputed interest	(2)	(46)	
Present value of lease obligations	$13	$107	

8. Benefit Plans

We sponsor retirement savings plans for employees meeting certain age and service requirements. The plans provide for company-matching contributions, which are subject to annual approval by our Board. The total matching contributions were $14, $13 and $13 in fiscal 2005, 2004 and 2003, respectively.

9. Income Taxes

Income tax expense was comprised of the following for the past three fiscal years:

	2005	2004	2003
Current:			
Federal	$502	$456	$375
State	36	49	51
Foreign	(1)	5	3
	537	510	429
Deferred:			
Federal	(4)	(9)	(22)
State	(20)	(1)	(3)
Foreign	(4)	(4)	(12)
	(28)	(14)	(37)
Income tax expense	$509	$496	$392

Deferred taxes are the result of differences between the bases of assets and liabilities for financial reporting and income tax purposes.

10. Segments

We operate two reportable segments: Domestic and International. The Domestic segment is comprised of U.S. Best Buy and Magnolia Audio Video operations. The International segment is comprised of Future Shop and Best Buy operations in Canada. Our segments are evaluated on an operating income basis, and a stand-alone tax provision is not calculated for each segment.

The following table presents our business segment information for continuing operations.

	2005
Revenue	
Domestic	$24,616
International	2,817
Total revenue	$27,433
Operating Income	
Domestic	$ 1,393
International	49
Total operating income	1,442
Net interest income (expense)	1
Earnings from continuing operations before income tax expense	$ 1,443
Assets	
Domestic	$ 8,372
International	1,922
Total assets	$10,294

BEST BUY

$ in millions, except per share amounts

11. Contingencies and Commitments

Contingencies

We are involved in various other legal proceedings arising in the normal course of conducting business. We believe the amounts provided in our consolidated financial statements, as prescribed by GAAP, are adequate in light of the probable and estimable liabilities. The resolution of those proceedings is not expected to have a material impact on our results of operation or financial condition.

Commitments

In 2004, we engaged Accenture LLP to assist us with improving our operational capabilities and reducing our costs in the Human Resources and Information Systems areas. Our future contractual obligations to Accenture are expected to range from $124 to $235 per year through 2011, the end of the contract period. Prior to our engagement of Accenture, a significant portion of these costs were incurred as part of normal operations.

We had outstanding letters of credit for purchase obligations with a fair value of $92 as of February 26, 2005.

As of February 26, 2005, we had commitments for the purchase and construction of facilities valued at approximately $83. Also, as of February 26, 2005, we had entered into lease commitments for land and buildings for 73 future locations. These lease commitments with real estate developers provide for minimum rentals ranging from 10 to 20 years, which if consummated based on current cost estimates, will approximate $53 annually over the lease terms.

We assumed a liability for certain extended service contracts when we acquired Future Shop in fiscal 2002. We established an accrued liability for the acquired extended service contracts based on historical trends in product failure rates and the expected material and labor costs necessary to provide the services. The remaining terms of these acquired extended service contracts vary by product and extend through fiscal 2007. The estimated remaining liability for acquired extended service contracts at February 26, 2005, was $9. Subsequent to the acquisition, all new extended service contracts were sold on behalf of an unrelated third party, without recourse.

Financial Report

CONSOLIDATED BALANCE SHEETS

(Amounts in thousands except share data)	At February 28 or 29 2005	2004
ASSETS		
CURRENT ASSETS:		
Cash and cash equivalents..	$ 879,660	$ 783,471
Short-term investments	125,325	–
Accounts receivable, net of allowance for doubtful accounts of $120 and $547	172,995	170,568
Retained interests in securitized receivables	–	425,678
Merchandise inventory...	1,459,520	1,517,256
Deferred income taxes...	29,518	–
Prepaid expenses and other current assets...	18,697	22,088
TOTAL CURRENT ASSETS	2,685,715	2,919,061
Property and equipment, net..	738,802	677,107
Deferred income taxes...	73,558	88,146
Goodwill	215,884	–
Other intangible assets	31,331	–
Other assets	44,092	46,212
TOTAL ASSETS..	$3,789,382	$3,730,526
LIABILITIES AND STOCKHOLDERS' EQUITY		
CURRENT LIABILITIES:		
Accounts payable	$ 961,718	$ 833,825
Accrued expenses and other current liabilities....................................	228,966	149,605
Accrued income taxes	72,274	71,163
Deferred income taxes...	–	79,422
Current installments of long-term debt...	888	1,115
Liabilities of discontinued operations	–	3,068
TOTAL CURRENT LIABILITIES	1,263,846	1,138,198
Long-term debt, excluding current installments..................................	11,522	22,691
Accrued straight-line rent and deferred rent credits	230,426	206,784
Accrued lease termination costs	104,234	75,722
Other liabilities...	91,920	63,170
TOTAL LIABILITIES	1,701,948	1,506,565
STOCKHOLDERS' EQUITY:		
Common stock, $0.50 par value; 525,000,000 shares authorized; 188,150,383 shares issued and outstanding (203,899,395 in 2004)	94,075	101,950
Capital in excess of par value..	721,038	922,600
Retained earnings...	1,247,221	1,199,411
Accumulated other comprehensive income...	25,100	–
TOTAL STOCKHOLDERS' EQUITY	2,087,434	2,223,961
Commitments and contingent liabilities [NOTES 12, 13 AND 16]		
TOTAL LIABILITIES AND STOCKHOLDERS' EQUITY..........	$3,789,382	$3,730,526

See accompanying notes to consolidated financial statements.

CIRCUIT CITY

CONSOLIDATED STATEMENTS OF OPERATIONS

(Amounts in thousands except per share data)	2005	%	2004	%	2003	%
			Years Ended February 28 or 29			
NET SALES AND OPERATING REVENUES	$10,472,364	100.0	$9,857,057	100.0	$10,054,864	100.0
Cost of sales, buying and warehousing	7,903,641	75.5	7,573,049	76.8	7,647,992	76.1
GROSS PROFIT	2,568,723	24.5	2,284,008	23.2	2,406,872	23.9
Finance income	5,564	0.1	32,693	0.3	27,292	0.3
Selling, general and administrative expenses	2,457,032	23.5	2,277,479	23.1	2,385,310	23.7
Stock-based compensation expense	19,400	0.2	38,658	0.4	53,251	0.5
Interest expense	2,066	–	1,804	–	1,093	–
Earnings (loss) from continuing operations before income taxes	95,789	0.9	(1,240)	–	(5,490)	(0.1)
Income tax provision (benefit)	35,878	0.3	(453)	–	(181)	–
NET EARNINGS (LOSS) FROM CONTINUING OPERATIONS	59,911	0.6	(787)	–	(5,309)	(0.1)
NET EARNINGS (LOSS) FROM DISCONTINUED OPERATIONS	1,747	–	(88,482)	(0.9)	87,572	0.9
NET EARNINGS (LOSS)	$ 61,658	0.6	$ (89,269)	(0.9)	$ 82,263	0.8
Net earnings (loss) from discontinued operations attributed to:						
Circuit City common stock	$ 1,747		$ (88,482)		$ 65,264	
CarMax Group common stock	$ –		$ –		$ 22,308	
Weighted average common shares:						
Circuit City:						
Basic	193,466		205,865		207,217	
Diluted	196,227		205,865		207,217	
CarMax Group:						
Basic	–		–		37,023	
Diluted	–		–		38,646	
NET EARNINGS (LOSS) PER SHARE:						
Basic:						
Continuing operations	$ 0.31		$ –		$ (0.03)	
Discontinued operations attributed to Circuit City common stock	0.01		(0.43)		0.31	
	$ 0.32		$ (0.43)		$ 0.29	
Discontinued operations attributed to CarMax Group common stock	$ –		$ –		$ 0.60	
Diluted:						
Continuing operations	$ 0.31		$ –		$ (0.03)	
Discontinued operations attributed to Circuit City common stock	0.01		(0.43)		0.31	
	$ 0.31		$ (0.43)		$ 0.29	
Discontinued operations attributed to CarMax Group common stock	$ –		$ –		$ 0.58	

See accompanying notes to consolidated financial statements.

CIRCUIT CITY

CONSOLIDATED STATEMENTS OF STOCKHOLDERS' EQUITY AND COMPREHENSIVE INCOME

(Amounts in thousands except per share data)	Shares Outstanding Circuit City	Shares Outstanding CarMax Group	Common Stock Circuit City	Common Stock CarMax Group	Capital In Excess of Par Value	Retained Earnings	Accumulated Other Comprehensive Income	Total
BALANCE AT FEBRUARY 28, 2002	208,823	36,851	$104,411	$ 18,426	$893,537	$1,744,129	$ —	$2,760,503
Net earnings and comprehensive income	—	—	—	—	—	82,263	—	82,263
Compensation for stock options	—	—	—	—	34,637	—	—	34,637
Exercise of common stock options	311	246	156	123	5,035	—	—	5,314
Shares issued under employee stock purchase plans	457	—	229	—	7,400	—	—	7,629
Shares issued under stock incentive plans	843	—	421	—	17,207	—	—	17,628
Tax effect from stock issued	—	—	—	—	5,986	—	—	5,986
Cancellation of restricted stock	(479)	(8)	(240)	(4)	(8,081)	—	—	(8,325)
Unearned compensation restricted stock	—	—	—	—	9,830	—	—	9,830
Cash dividends — common stock ($0.07 per share)	—	—	—	—	—	(14,687)	—	(14,687)
Distribution of CarMax, Inc. common stock to stockholders	—	(37,089)	—	(18,545)	—	(536,765)	—	(555,310)
Special dividend from CarMax	—	—	—	—	—	28,400	—	28,400
BALANCE AT FEBRUARY 28, 2003	209,955	—	104,977	—	965,551	1,303,340	—	2,373,868
Net loss and comprehensive loss	—	—	—	—	—	(89,269)	—	(89,269)
Repurchases of common stock	(9,266)	—	(4,633)	—	(79,720)	—	—	(84,353)
Compensation for stock options	—	—	—	—	24,184	—	—	24,184
Exercise of common stock options	1,369	—	685	—	11,843	—	—	12,528
Shares issued under stock incentive plans	2,546	—	1,273	—	19,312	—	—	20,585
Tax effect from stock issued	—	—	—	—	(10,595)	—	—	(10,595)
Cancellation of restricted stock	(705)	—	(352)	—	(10,074)	—	—	(10,426)
Unearned compensation restricted stock	—	—	—	—	2,099	—	—	2,099
Cash dividends — common stock ($0.07 per share)	—	—	—	—	—	(14,660)	—	(14,660)
BALANCE AT FEBRUARY 29, 2004	203,899	—	101,950	—	922,600	1,199,411	—	2,223,961
Comprehensive income:								
Net earnings	—	—	—	—	—	61,658	—	61,658
Other comprehensive income, net of taxes:								
Foreign currency translation adjustment (net of deferred taxes of $13,707)	—	—	—	—	—	—	25,100	25,100
Comprehensive income								86,758
Repurchases of common stock	(19,163)	—	(9,582)	—	(250,250)	—	—	(259,832)
Compensation for stock options	—	—	—	—	18,739	—	—	18,739
Exercise of common stock options	3,489	—	1,745	—	26,761	—	—	28,506
Shares issued under stock incentive plans	723	—	361	—	7,393	—	—	7,754
Tax effect from stock issued	—	—	—	—	(1,564)	—	—	(1,564)
Cancellation of restricted stock	(798)	—	(399)	—	(6,378)	—	—	(6,777)
Shares issued in acquisition of InterTAN, Inc.	—	—	—	—	6,498	—	—	6,498
Unearned compensation restricted stock	—	—	—	—	(2,761)	—	—	(2,761)
Cash dividends — common stock ($0.07 per share)	—	—	—	—	—	(13,848)	—	(13,848)
BALANCE AT FEBRUARY 28, 2005	**188,150**	**—**	**$ 94,075**	**$ —**	**$721,038**	**$1,247,221**	**$25,100**	**$2,087,434**

See accompanying notes to consolidated financial statements.

CONSOLIDATED STATEMENTS OF CASH FLOWS

| | Years Ended February 28 or 29 | | |
	2005	2004	2005
OPERATING ACTIVITIES:			
Net earnings (loss)	$ **61,658**	$ (89,269)	$ 82,263
Adjustments to reconcile net earnings (loss) to net cash provided by (used in) operating activities of continuing operations:			
Net (earnings) loss from discontinued operations	**(1,747)**	88,482	(87,572)
Depreciation and amortization	**154,788**	197,607	159,800
Stock option expense	**18,739**	24,184	30,823
Amortization of restricted stock awards	**(434)**	13,395	20,828
(Gain) loss on dispositions of property and equipment	**(206)**	7,500	15,659
Provision for deferred income taxes	**(116,455)**	(35,618)	(18,664)
Changes in operating assets and liabilities:			
(Increase) decrease in accounts receivable, net	**(65,112)**	(30,183)	6,229
Decrease (increase) in retained interests in securitized receivables	**32,867**	(186,537)	(92,888)
Decrease (increase) in merchandise inventory	**159,278**	(107,520)	(175,493)
Decrease (increase) in prepaid expenses and other current assets	**7,148**	(3,923)	21,081
Decrease (increase) in other assets	**3,925**	12,553	(26,181)
Increase (decrease) in accounts payable	**101,991**	(85,727)	(58,041)
Increase (decrease) in accrued expenses and other current liabilities, and accrued income taxes	**36,008**	50,577	(48,069)
Increase in other long-term liabilities	**63,549**	18,966	7,116
NET CASH PROVIDED BY (USED IN) OPERATING ACTIVITIES OF CONTINUING OPERATIONS	**455,879**	(125,513)	(163,109)
INVESTING ACTIVITIES:			
Proceeds from the sale of the private-label operation	**475,857**	–	–
Acquisitions, net of cash acquired of $30,615	**(268,774)**	–	–
Purchases of property and equipment	**(269,166)**	(175,769)	(150,757)
Proceeds from sales of property and equipment	**106,369**	40,427	59,888
Purchases of investment securities	**(125,325)**	–	–
NET CASH USED IN INVESTING ACTIVITIES OF CONTINUING OPERATIONS	**(81,039)**	(135,342)	(90,869)
FINANCING ACTIVITIES:			
Payments on short-term debt	**(1,853)**	–	(397)
Principal payments on long-term debt	**(28,008)**	(1,458)	(24,865)
Repurchases of common stock	**(259,832)**	(84,353)	–
Issuances of Circuit City common stock, net	**27,156**	11,391	8,901
Issuances of CarMax Group common stock, net	–	–	298
Dividends paid	**(13,848)**	(14,660)	(14,687)
NET CASH USED IN FINANCING ACTIVITIES OF CONTINUING OPERATIONS	**(276,385)**	(89,080)	(30,750)
CASH (USED IN) PROVIDED BY DISCONTINUED OPERATIONS:			
BANKCARD OPERATION	**(4,282)**	248,736	(94,533)
CARMAX OPERATION	–	–	26,185
DIVX OPERATION	–	–	(10,500)
EFFECT OF EXCHANGE RATE CHANGES ON CASH	**2,016**	–	–
Increase (decrease) in cash and cash equivalents	**96,189**	(101,199)	(363,576)
Cash and cash equivalents at beginning of year	**783,471**	884,670	1,248,246
CASH AND CASH EQUIVALENTS AT END OF YEAR	$ **879,660**	$ 783,471	$ 884,670

See accompanying notes to consolidated financial statements.

Appendix B

Accounting Principles

LEARNING OBJECTIVES

LO 1 Describe a rules-based and a principles-based approach toward accounting standards.

LO 2 Define the primary objective of financial reporting.

LO 3 Discuss qualitative characteristics of useful accounting information.

LO 4 Describe assumptions underlying useful accounting information.

LO 5 Explain principles of useful accounting information.

LO 6 Describe constraints on useful accounting information.

For accounting information to be useful, it must possess certain qualitative characteristics. The purpose of this appendix is to provide a conceptual framework for accounting principles that are desirable for accounting information.

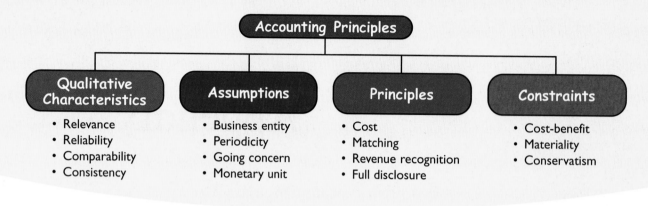

Rules–Based versus Principles–Based Accounting

LO1 Describe a rules-based and a principles-based approach toward accounting standards.

U.S. accounting practices are often viewed as *rules-based* (as mentioned in Chapter 1). This means that companies are required to apply technical, specific, and detailed rules in preparing financial statements and reports. A *principles-based* approach is sometimes argued as preferable. A principles-based system would develop and apply broad, fundamental concepts for accounting. Companies would have more flexibility in preparing principles-based financial statements to meet the intent of the accounting principle rather than just the specific accounting rule.

For example, a broad accounting principle might be that a company must report all debt it might have to repay. Certain executives of **Enron** were able to mislead investors by not reporting some of its debt. While many of Enron's reports technically followed rules-based standards, the reports failed to adequately disclose all of its debts. As another example, a broad principle might be that a company must report all of its building leases that it is contractually obligated to pay as a liability on its balance sheet. Executives of many retail companies (such as **Wal-Mart** and **Payless Shoe Source**) follow the rules-based standards of accounting for leases. Their balance sheets generally fail to comprehensively report all of the leases that each company is required to pay. In both instances, while the rules are technically followed, the accounting has not achieved the intent of the standards.

Sarbanes-Oxley Act and Principles-Based Accounting

As a result of the Enron scandal and other abuses of rules-based accounting practices, the **Sarbanes-Oxley Act** requires the **Securities and Exchange Commission,** the government group that establishes financial reporting requirements, to study the feasibility of shifting to a more "principles-based" approach. The **Financial Accounting Standards Board,** the private group that sets standards for accounting practice, has also proposed changes designed to create a more principles-based approach to accounting standards. Many accounting experts believe that a change to principles-based standards will force companies preparing financial statements to focus on the intent of accounting standards rather than just technical compliance with the rules. On the other side of the debate, some accounting experts worry that a shift to principles-based standards will lead to lawsuits as shareholders and companies fight over the true intent of the standards.

A principles-based system requires a sound conceptual framework. To more fully understand the principles-based approach, the existing conceptual framework of accounting principles is presented in this appendix.

Objectives of Financial Reporting

LO2 Define the primary objective of financial reporting.

External financial statements users, such as investors and creditors, use accounting information in financial reports to make decisions (such as whether to buy or sell a stock or extend a loan). To help in decisions, accounting reports must possess useful information.

The primary objective of financial reporting is to provide useful economic information to assist decision makers. There are many elements of accounting information. Exhibit B.1 provides a pyramid detailing the framework of qualitative characteristics, assumptions, principles, and constraints for providing useful accounting information.

Exhibit B.1

Elements of Useful Accounting Information

The objective of financial reporting is to provide useful accounting information to decision makers.

Qualitative Characteristics of Accounting Information
To be useful to decision makers, accounting information must be:

1. Relevant
a. Predictive Value (helps with forecasts)
b. Feedback Value (corrects or confirms forecasts)
c. Timely (available when needed)

2. Reliable
a. Verifiable (can be verified by an independent party)
b. Representational Faithfulness (reports what happened)
c. Neutrality (information is not biased)

3. Comparable
(Different companies use similar accounting principles and methods)

4. Consistency
(Same company uses the same accounting principles and methods each year)

Assumptions	**Principles**	**Constraints**
1. Business entity (business is accounted for separately from its owner and other business entities) **2. Periodicity** (the life of a company can be divided up into smaller reportable time periods) **3. Going Concern** (entity will continue operating instead of being closed or sold) **4. Monetary Unit** (transactions expressed in monetary units)	**1. Cost** (accounting information is based on cash or equal-to-cash basis) **2. Matching** (expenses are recorded as incurred to generate revenues) **3. Revenue Recognition** (revenue recorded when earned and realizable) **4. Full Disclosure** (any information that can influence the judgment of a decision maker is reported)	**1. Cost-benefit** (benefits to accounting information users is greater than the cost to prepare it) **2. Materiality** (transactions too small to make an impact on a decision maker are recorded in the most cost-beneficial way) **3. Conservatism** (select accounting methods that are least likely to overstate assets and income)

Qualitative Characteristics of Useful Accounting Information

As noted in Exhibit B.1, to be useful, accounting information must be relevant, reliable, comparable and consistent across time. Exhibit B.2 provides an illustration of these qualitative characteristics.

Relevance

To provide useful information, that information must be **relevant** to the decision maker. Information is relevant if it would make a difference in a business decision. Information is relevant when it helps users predict the future (*predictive value*) or evaluate the past (*feedback value*) and is received in time to affect their decisions (*timeliness*).

Reliability

Information is **reliable** if users can depend on it to be free from bias and error. Reliable information is *verifiable* and *faithfully represents* the substance of the underlying economic transaction. If Best Buy sold a television for $4,000, it should be reported in its sales revenue

LO3   Discuss qualitative characteristics of useful accounting information.

Exhibit B.2

Qualitative Characteristics of Useful Accounting Information

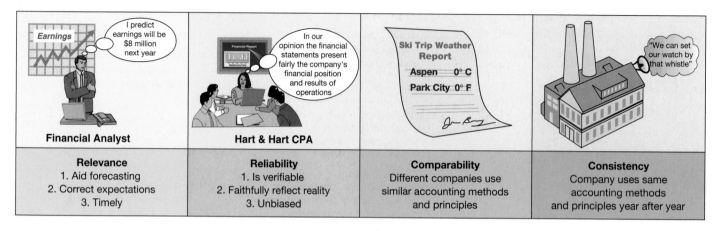

Relevance	Reliability	Comparability	Consistency
1. Aid forecasting 2. Correct expectations 3. Timely	1. Is verifiable 2. Faithfully reflect reality 3. Unbiased	Different companies use similar accounting methods and principles	Company uses same accounting methods and principles year after year

as $4,000. Reliable accounting information is neutral, or free from bias. In other words, accounting information should not be designed to lead accounting information users to accept or reject any specific decision alternative.

Comparability

Information is **comparable** if it helps uses to identify differences and similarities between companies. Comparability is possible only if companies follow similar accounting methods and practices. However, even if all companies uniformly follow the same accounting practices, comparable reports do not result if the practices are not appropriate. For example, comparable information would not be provided if all companies were to ignore the useful lives of their assets and depreciate all assets over two years.

Comparability is often harder for cross-country comparisons. Suppose we want to make an investment in an automobile manufacturer such as Daimler Chrysler, a German company, or Toyota, a Japanese company. Since these countries have their own set of accounting rules and methods, a direct comparison will be difficult. The **International Accounting Standards Board** has been established to help harmonize accounting practices across countries.

Consistency

Accounting information users generally look at multiple time periods of a company's financial statements to see if there are any noticeable trends. To make this comparison over multiple periods, the same accounting principles and methods should be used in each period. Otherwise, it is hard to know if changes over time are due to real fundamental changes in financial performance or are simply because the company changed the way it accounted for certain items. Applying the same accounting information methods and practices over time is known as **consistency.**

Underlying Accounting Assumptions

LO4 Describe assumptions underlying useful accounting information.

Four assumptions underlie the overall objective of providing useful information to decision makers. These are the business entity assumption, the periodicity assumption, the going concern assumption and the monetary unit assumption.

Business Entity Assumption

The **business entity assumption** means that a business is accounted for separately from other business entities, including its owner. The reason for this principle is that separate information about each business is necessary for good decisions. A business entity can take one of three legal forms: *proprietorship, partnership,* or *corporation.*

Abuse of the business entity assumption was a main culprit in the collapse of **Enron.**

1. A **sole proprietorship,** or simply **proprietorship,** is a business owned by one person. No special legal requirements must be met to start a proprietorship. It is a separate entity for accounting purposes, but it is *not* a separate legal entity from its owner. This means, for example, that a court can order an owner to sell personal belongings to pay a proprietorship's debt. This *unlimited liability* of a proprietorship is a disadvantage. However, an advantage is that a proprietorship's income is not subject to a business income tax but is instead reported and taxed on the owner's personal income tax return. Business characteristics are summarized in Exhibit B.3.

Characteristic	Proprietorship	Partnership	Corporation
Business entity	yes	yes	yes
Legal entity	no	no	yes
Limited liability	no*	no*	yes
Unlimited life	no	no	yes
Business taxed	no	no	yes
One owner allowed	yes	no	yes

Exhibit B.3

Characteristics of Businesses

* Proprietorships and partnerships that are set up as LLCs provide limited liability.

2. A **partnership** is a business owned by two or more people, called *partners*. Like a proprietorship, no special legal requirements must be met in starting a partnership. The only requirement is an agreement between partners to run a business together. The agreement can be either oral or written and usually indicates how income and losses are to be shared. A partnership, like a proprietorship, is *not* legally separate from its owners. This means that each partner's share of profits is reported and taxed on that partner's tax return. It also means *unlimited liability* for its partners. However, at least three types of partnerships limit liability. A *limited partnership* (*LP*) includes a general partner(s) with unlimited liability and a limited partner(s) with liability restricted to the amount invested. A *limited liability partnership* (*LLP*) restricts partners' liabilities to their own acts and the acts of individuals under their control. This protects an innocent partner from the negligence of another partner, yet all partners remain responsible for partnership debts. A *limited liability company* (*LLC*), offers the limited liability of a corporation and the tax treatment of a partnership (and proprietorship). Most proprietorships and partnerships are now organized as LLCs.

 IN THE NEWS

Smaller Is Better

Entrepreneurship is key to modern business and economic success. U.S. small businesses:

- Total about 25 million and employ more than half of the U.S. workforce.
- Provide 60% to 80% of new jobs annually and pay about 50% of total U.S. payroll.
- Employ about 40% of high tech workers (such as engineers and scientists).
- Appeal to 65% of young people who desire to launch their own business.

3. A **corporation** is a business legally separate from its owners, meaning it is responsible for its own acts and its own debts. Separate legal status means that a corporation can conduct business with the rights, duties, and responsibilities of a person. A corporation acts through its managers, who are its legal agents. Separate legal status also means that its owners, who are called **shareholders** (or **stockholders**), are not personally liable for corporate acts and debts. This limited liability is its main advantage. A main disadvantage is what's called *double taxation*—meaning that (1) the corporation's income is taxed and (2) any distribution of income to the corporation's owners through dividends is taxed as part of the owners' personal income, usually at the 15% rate.

YOU CALL IT   Answer—p. B-9

Entrepreneur   You and a friend develop a new design for in-line skates that improves speed and performance by 25% to 40%. You plan to form a business to manufacture and market these skates. You and your friend want to minimize taxes, but your prime concern is potential lawsuits from individuals who might be injured on these skates. What form of organization do you set up?

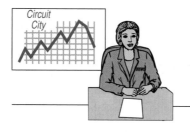

"Circuit City announces earnings per share of . . ."

Periodicity Assumption

A component of providing relevant and useful information is that it must be timely. Useful information must reach decision makers frequently and promptly. To provide timely information, accounting systems prepare reports at regular intervals. This results in an accounting process impacted by the periodicity (or time period) principle. The **periodicity assumption** is that an organization's activities can be divided into specific time periods such as a month, a three-month quarter, a six-month interval, or a year.

Going-Concern Assumption

The **going-concern assumption** means that accounting information reflects an assumption that the business will continue operating instead of being closed or sold. This implies, for example, that a factory facility is reported at cost instead of, say, liquidation values that assume immediate, involuntary closure.

IN THE NEWS

For currency conversion:
www.xe.com

Principles and Scruples

Auditors, directors, and lawyers are using principles to improve accounting reports. Examples include loan restatements at Countrywide, financial restatements at Delphi, accounting reviews at Echostar, and expense adjustments at Electronic Data Systems. Principles-based accounting has led accounting firms to drop clients deemed too risky.

Monetary Unit Assumption

The **monetary unit assumption** means that we can express transactions and events in monetary, or money, units. Money is the common denominator in business. Examples of monetary units are the dollar in the United States, Canada, Australia, and Singapore; the pound sterling in the United Kingdom; and the peso in Mexico, the Philippines, and Chile. The monetary unit assumption also means that financial statement amounts are typically not adjusted for the effects of inflation.

HOW YOU DOIN'?   Answers—p. B-9

1. Why is it important to have comparable accounting methods between companies?
2. Why is the business entity principle important?
3. What are the three basic forms of business organization?
4. Identify the owners of corporations and the terminology for ownership units.

Accounting Principles

LO5 Explain principles of useful accounting information.

Accounting relies on four key principles (as illustrated in Exhibit B.1): cost, matching, revenue recognition, and full disclosure.

Cost Principle

The cost principle is also called the *historical cost principle.*

The **cost principle** means that accounting information is based on actual cost. Cost is measured on a cash or equal-to-cash basis. This means if cash is given for a service, the transaction's cost is measured as the amount of cash paid. If something besides cash is exchanged (such as a car traded for a truck), the transaction's cost is measured as the cash value of what is given up or received. The cost principle emphasizes reliability, and information based on cost is considered objective. To illustrate, suppose a company pays $5,000 for equipment. The cost principle requires that this purchase be recorded at a cost of $5,000. It makes no difference if the owner thinks this equipment is worth $7,000.

Matching Principle

The **matching principle** prescribes that expenses be reported in the same period and on the same income statement as the revenues that were earned as a result of those expenses. To illustrate, suppose a business provides traffic consulting services to a municipal client. All of the expenses (consultant labor, computer use, copies, travel, presentation preparation, use of office space) incurred to complete those consulting services should be recorded in the same period as the consulting services.

Sometimes, it is difficult to match each expense with its related revenue. There are three general guidelines that are used in applying the matching principle (with examples):

Guideline	Example
• Cause and effect	Expenses directly incurred to generate revenue such as consultant labor
• Systematic and rational allocation	Depreciation of office equipment and office space
• Immediate recognition of some costs with uncertain future benefits	Advertising, salary of consultant's supervisor

Revenue Recognition Principle

Revenue (sales) is the amount received from selling products and services. The **revenue recognition principle** provides guidance on when a company must recognize revenue. To *recognize* revenue means to record it. If revenue is recognized too early, a company would look more profitable than it is. If revenue is recognized too late, a company would look less profitable than it is. The following three concepts are important to revenue recognition. (1) *Revenue is recognized when earned*. The earnings process is normally complete when services are performed or a seller transfers ownership of products to the buyer. (2) *Proceeds from selling products and services need not be in cash*. A common noncash proceed received by a seller is a customer's promise to pay at a future date, called *credit sales*. (3) *Revenue is measured by the cash received plus the cash value of any other items received*.

When a bookstore sells a textbook on credit is its earnings process complete? *Answer:* The bookstore can record sales for these books minus an amount expected for book returns.

IN THE NEWS

Revenues for the New England Patriots football team include ticket sales, television and cable broadcasts, radio rights, concessions, and advertising. Revenues from ticket sales are earned when the Patriots play each game. Advance ticket sales are not revenues; instead, they represent a liability until the Patriots play the game for which the ticket was sold.

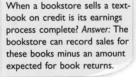

Full Disclosure Principle

Companies have many choices on what information to report. The **full disclosure principle** requires that all accounting information important enough to affect a decision be presented. Such accounting information may be disclosed in the financial statements, footnotes to the financial statements, or as supplementary information. There is always the possibility that too much information or too much detail will overwhelm the user. Therefore, companies try to be clear but concise.

Accounting Constraints

All of the assumptions and principles discussed thus far help accountants provide useful information to decision makers. However, providing all of this quality information can be too costly to the company. There is a balance between providing sufficient information to the decision maker without being too costly to the company preparing the accounting information. There are three constraints to providing useful information to the decision maker: cost-benefit, materiality, and conservatism.

 Describe constraints on useful accounting information.

Cost-Benefit

The benefit to decision makers of receiving accounting information must be worth the cost of providing it. The **cost-benefit** trade-off suggests that information will only be provided if the benefits to users outweigh the costs of preparing and disclosing it.

However, the costs and benefits are not always easy to compute. Moreover, the costs are usually borne by the company, and the benefits are received by a diverse set of decision makers across the world. Still, it is useful to try to carefully consider the costs and benefits before producing or requiring the disclosure of additional accounting information.

Materiality

Materiality asks the question: Is the item big enough to make an impact on the decision maker? If the item is not big enough to make a difference, then **generally accepted accounting principles (GAAP)** do not have to be followed. To illustrate, if Circuit City makes a $10 mistake in recording an expense when its overall expenses are $10 billion, the $10 error is most likely not a material item and GAAP need not be followed.

Conservatism

Conservatism suggests that when faced with two equally plausible accounting method choices (or estimates), the company should choose the accounting method (or estimate) that is least likely to overstate assets and income or to understate liabilities and expenses. Managers are generally optimistic, and this constraint offsets that optimism to help present a more conservative view of a company's financial position. The general concept can be summarized in this way: if in doubt, recognize all losses but do not recognize any gains.

A common example of conservatism is in the valuation of inventory. Inventories are usually recorded at their cost. However, if the market value of the inventory falls below its cost, conservatism requires that inventories be written down to the market value. To illustrate, consider a company that sells computer systems. Due to the quick technology advances and declining prices of new computer hardware, if a computer does not sell relatively quickly, the market value can fall below the cost to manufacture and sell it. Due to conservatism, the computer is written down to its market value.

HOW YOU DOIN'? Answers—p. B-9

5. Why is the revenue recognition principle important?

6. Do you think a $10 million error would be material in a $100 million sales company?

Summary

LO1 **Describe a rules-based and a principles-based approach toward accounting standards.** The rules-based approach implies that companies are required to apply technical, specific, and detailed rules in preparing financial statements and reports. The principles-based approach develops and applies broad, over-arching, and fundamental concepts for accounting.

LO2 **Define the primary objective of financial reporting.** The primary objective of accounting is to provide useful economic information to assist decision makers to make decisions.

LO3 **Discuss qualitative characteristics of useful accounting information.** The qualitative characteristics of useful accounting information are that the information must be relevant, reliable, comparable and consistent. Information is relevant if it would make a difference in a decision. Reliable information is information that can be depended on. Companies can be compared to each other if they use the same accounting methods and principles.

Consistency is met when firms apply the same accounting methods and principles year after year.

LO4 **Describe assumptions underlying useful accounting information.** There are several underlying assumptions to support the overall objective of providing useful information to decision makers including the business entity assumption, the periodicity assumption, the going concern assumption, and the monetary unit assumption.

LO5 **Explain principles of useful accounting information.** Accounting principles help make accounting information useful to decision makers. They include the cost, revenue recognition, matching, and full disclosure principles.

LO6 **Describe constraints on useful accounting information.** There are three constraints to providing useful information to decision makers. The benefits must be greater than the costs, the item must be material, and the accounting choices must be conservative.

Guidance Answers to *YOU CALL IT*

Entrepreneur   You should probably form the business as a corporation if potential lawsuits are of prime concern. The corporate form of organization protects your personal property from lawsuits directed at the business and places only the corporation's resources at risk. A downside of the corporate form is double taxation: The corporation must pay taxes on its income, and you normally must pay taxes on any money distributed to you from the business (even though the corporation already paid taxes on this money). You should also examine the ethical and socially responsible aspects of starting a business in which you anticipate injuries to others. Formation as an LLC or S corp. should also be explored.

Guidance Answers to *HOW YOU DOIN'?*

1. Comparable accounting information provides a similar measuring stick for both companies to assess their relative financial performance. If companies have different accounting methods, there is no way to compare them. It would be like comparing apples to oranges.

2. Users desire information about the performance of a specific entity. If information is mixed between two or more entities, its usefulness decreases.

3. The three basic forms of business organization are sole proprietorships, partnerships, and corporations.

4. Owners of corporations are called *shareholders* (or *stockholders*). Corporate ownership is divided into units called *shares* (or *stock*).

   The most basic of corporate shares is common stock (or capital stock).

5. The revenue recognition principle gives guidelines of when to recognize (record) revenue. This is important; for example, if revenue is recognized too early, the financial statements report revenue sooner than it should and the business looks more profitable than it is. The reverse is also true.

6. Yes, this would be considered to be a material item since it represents 10% of the firm's sales, suggesting it would make a difference on a decision maker's decisions.

Key Terms

mhhe.com/wildCA

Key Terms are available at the book's Website for learning and testing in an online Flashcard Format.

Business entity assumption (p. B-4) Concept that assumes a business will be accounted for separately from its owner(s) and any other entity.

Comparability (p. B-4) A qualitative characteristic of accounting information suggesting that information is more useful if it can be related to an industry or competitor benchmark.

Conservatism (p. B-8) Concept that prescribes use of the less optimistic estimate when two estimates are about equally likely.

Consistency (p. B-4) A qualitative characteristic of accounting information that prescribes use of the same accounting method(s) and practice(s) over time so that financial statements are comparable across periods.

Corporation (p. B-5) Business that is a separate legal entity under state or federal laws with owners called *shareholders* or *stockholders*.

Cost-benefit (p. B-8) A constraint of useful accounting information prescribing that information will only be provided if the benefits to users outweigh the costs of preparation.

Cost principle (p. B-6) Accounting principle that prescribes financial statement information to be based on actual costs incurred in business transactions.

Financial Accounting Standards Board (FASB) (p. B-2) Independent group of full-time members responsible for setting accounting rules.

Full disclosure principle (p. B-7) Principle that prescribes financial statements (including notes) to report all relevant information about an entity's operations and financial condition.

Generally Accepted Accounting Principles (GAAP) (p. B-8) Rules that specify acceptable accounting practices.

Going-concern assumption (p. B-6) Concept that prescribes financial statements to reflect the assumption that the business will continue operating indefinitely.

International Accounting Standards Board (IASB) (p. B-4) Group that identifies preferred accounting practices and encourages global acceptance; issues International Financial Reporting Standards (IFRS).

Materiality (p. B-8) Prescribes that accounting for items that markedly impact financial statements, and any inferences drawn from them, adhere to GAAP.

Monetary unit assumption (p. B-6) Concept that assumes transactions and events can be expressed in money units.

Partnership (p. B-5) Unincorporated association of two or more persons to pursue a business for profit as co-owners.

Periodicity assumption (p. B-6) The life of a company can be divided up into smaller, reportable time periods.

Proprietorship (p. B-5) Business owned by one person that is not organized as a corporation.

Relevance (p. B-3) A qualitative characteristic of accounting information that prescribes that information be useful, understandable, timely, and pertinent for decision making.

Reliability (p. B-3) The principle that information is verifiable and faithfully represents the substance of the underlying economic transaction.

Revenue recognition principle (p. B-7) The principle prescribing that revenue is recognized when earned.

Sarbanes–Oxley Act (p. B-2) Created the *Public Company Accounting Oversight Board,* regulates analyst conflicts, imposes corporate governance requirements, enhances accounting and control disclosures, impacts insider transactions and executive loans, establishes new types of criminal conduct, and expands penalties for violations of federal securities laws.

Securities and Exchange Commission (SEC) (p. B-2) Federal agency Congress has charged to set reporting rules for organizations that sell ownership shares to the public.

Shareholders (p. B-5) Owners of a corporation; also called *stockholders*.

Sole proprietorship (p. B-5) Business owned by one person that is not organized as a corporation; also called *proprietorship*.

Stockholders (p. B-5) Owners of a corporation.

Multiple Choice Quiz   Answers on p. B-14   mhhe.com/wildCA

Multiple Choice Quizzes A and B are available at the book's Website.

1. The principle that prescribes that a business be accounted for separately and distinctly from its owner or owners is known as the:
   a. Matching principle.
   b. Business entity assumption.
   c. Going-concern assumption.
   d. Revenue recognition principle.
   e. Cost principle.

2. The rule that prescribes financial statements reflect the assumption that the business will continue operating instead of being closed or sold, unless evidence shows that it will not continue, is the:
   a. Going-concern assumption.
   b. Business entity assumption.
   c. Matching principle.
   d. Cost Principle.
   e. Monetary unit assumption.

3. To include the personal assets and transactions of a business's owner in the records and reports of the business would conflict with the:
   a. Matching principle.
   b. Realization principle.

   c. Business entity assumption.
   d. Going-concern assumption.
   e. Revenue recognition principle.

4. The accounting principle that prescribes accounting information be based on actual cost and requires assets and services to be recorded initially at the cash or cash-equivalent amount given in exchange, is the:
   a. Accounting equation.
   b. Cost principle.
   c. Going-concern assumption.
   d. Revenue recognition principle.
   e. Business entity assumption.

5. The qualitative characteristic of reliability:
   a. Means that information is supported by independent, unbiased evidence.
   b. Means that information can be based on what the preparer thinks is true.
   c. Means that financial statements should contain information that is optimistic.
   d. Means that a business may not reorganize revenue until cash is received.
   e. All of the above.

Discussion Questions

1. Describe the four key qualitative characteristics of useful accounting information.

2. Why is the business entity assumption important?

3. Why is the matching principle important?

4. What are the three basic forms of business organization?

5. What does the reliability characteristic imply for information reported in financial statements?

6. A business reports its own office stationery on the balance sheet at its $400 cost, although it cannot be sold for more than

$10 as scrap paper. Which accounting principle(s) justifies this treatment?

7. What is **Best Buy**'s revenue recognition policy (as detailed in the footnotes [page A-10])? **BEST BUY**

8. By examining **Circuit City**'s financial statements in Appendix A, what evidence is there that they used the matching principle?

QUICK STUDY

QS B-1

Identifying characteristics of accounting information

L03

Identify the following characteristics of useful accounting information as being a component of either Relevant (R) or Reliable (L). (*Hint:* Refer to Exhibit B.1.)

1. Timeliness

2. Verifiable

3. Representational Faithfulness

4. Predictive Value

5. Feedback Value

6. Neutrality

Fill in the blanks with appropriate accounting terminology.

1. Accounting information is _____ if different companies use similar accounting principles.

2. Information is _____ if it would make a difference in a business decision.

3. Accounting information is _____ if the same company uses the same accounting methods year after year.

4. Information is reliable if users can depend on it to be free from _____ and error.

QS B-2
Terminology of the characteristics of accounting information
(LO3)

Identify the appropriate assumption underlying useful accounting information for each description 1 through 4.

1. Hancock Hats reports its sales on a monthly basis.

2. Joann Hancock, owner of Hancock Hats, keeps the accounting records of her business separate from her personal accounts.

3. Hancock Hats reports its financial statements assuming it will continue to be in business for the foreseeable future.

4. Hancock Hats expresses its financial statements using the U.S. dollar.

QS B-3
Assumptions underlying useful accounting information
(LO4)

Identify the appropriate accounting principle for each description 1 through 4.

1. Callahan's Castles records expenses incurred to produce revenues in the accounting period.

2. Callahan's Castles discloses all information about pension expenses that can influence the decision maker.

3. Callahan's Castles records sales on its toy castles when they are delivered to the customer.

4. Callahan's Castles records its computer equipment at its acquisition cost.

QS B-4
Principles of useful accounting information
(LO5)

Fill in the blanks with appropriate accounting terminology.

1. _____ suggests that transactions that are too small to make an impact on a decision maker are recorded in the most cost beneficial way.

2. Conservatism suggests that accounting methods be selected that are least likely to _____ assets and income.

3. The _____-benefit constraint suggests that the benefits to receiving accounting information than the costs to prepare it.

QS B-5
Constraints of useful accounting information
(LO6)

Identify which general accounting principle best describes each of the following practices.

a. In December 2006, Chavez Landscaping received a customer's order and cash prepayment to install sod at a new house that would not be ready for installation until March 2007. Chavez should record the revenue from the customer order in March 2007, not in December 2006.

b. If $51,000 cash is paid to buy land, the land is reported on the buyer's balance sheet at $51,000.

c. Jo Keene owns both Sailing Passions and Dockside Supplies. In preparing financial statements for Dockside Supplies, Keene makes sure that the expense transactions of Sailing Passions are kept separate from Dockside's statements.

EXERCISES

Exercise B-1
Identifying accounting principles or assumptions
(LO4) (LO5)

The following describe several different business organizations. Determine whether the description refers to a sole proprietorship, partnership, or corporation.

a. Ownership of Zander Company is divided into 1,000 shares of stock.

b. Wallingford is owned by Trent Malone, who is personally liable for the company's debts.

c. Elijah Fong and Ava Logan own Financial Services, a financial services provider. Neither Fong nor Logan has personal responsibility for the debts of Financial Services.

d. Dylan Bailey and Emma Kayley own Speedy Packages, a courier service. Both are personally liable for the debts of the business.

e. IBC Services does not have separate legal existence apart from the one person who owns it.

f. Physio Products does not pay income taxes and has one owner.

g. Aaliyah Services pays its own income taxes and has two owners.

Exercise B-2
Distinguishing business organizations
(LO4)

Match each of the numbered descriptions with the principle it best reflects. Indicate your answer by writing the letter for the appropriate principle in the blank space next to each description.

A. Cost principle

B. Business entity principle

Exercise B-3
Identifying accounting principles
(LO4) (LO5)

    C. Revenue recognition principle

    D. Going-concern principle

_____ **1.** Financial statements reflect the assumption that the business continues operating.

_____ **2.** Every business is accounted for separately from its owner or owners.

_____ **3.** Revenue is recorded only when the earnings process is complete.

_____ **4.** Information is based on actual costs incurred in transactions.

Exercise B-4

Identifying accounting principles and assumptions

(L04) (L05)

You are reviewing the accounting records of Cathy's Antiques, owned by Cathy Miller. You have uncovered the following situations. Cite the appropriate accounting principle or assumption and suggest an action for each separate item.

1. In August, a check for $500 was written to Wee Day Care Center; this amount represents child care for her son Brandon.

2. Cathy plans a Going Out of Business Sale for May, since she will be closing her business for a month-long vacation in June. She plans to reopen July 1 and will continue operating Cathy's Antiques indefinitely.

3. Cathy received a shipment of pine furniture from Quebec, Canada; the invoice was stated in Canadian dollars.

4. Joseph Clark paid $1,500 for a dining table; the amount was recorded as revenue. The table will be delivered to Mr. Clark in six weeks.

Exercise B-5

Identifying accounting principles and assumptions

(L03) (L04) (L05)

Match each of the numbered transactions to the accounting terms A through F applicable to recording and reporting them.

A. Business entity assumption

B. Reliability

C. Cost principle

D. Going-concern assumption

E. Monetary unit assumption

F. Revenue recognition principle

_____ **1.** An insurance company receives insurance premiums for six future months' worth of coverage.

_____ **2.** A building is for sale at $480,000; an appraisal is given for $450,000.

_____ **3.** Helen Cho, a sole proprietor, pays for her daughter's preschool out of business funds.

_____ **4.** Mayan Imports receives a shipment from Mexico; the invoice is stated in pesos.

_____ **5.** To make the balance sheet look better, Helen Cho added several thousand dollars to the Equipment account that she believed was undervalued.

Exercise B-6

Identifying qualitative characteristics

(L03)

Fill in the blanks with the appropriate accounting terms or phrases.

1. _____ means that a company applies the same concept year after year.

2. For information to be relevant, it should have predictive or feedback _____, and it must be presented in a _____ manner.

3. _____ is the quality of information that suggests it can be depended on to represent reality, be verifiable and not be biased.

4. _____ means that two companies can be assessed relative to each other.

Exercise B-7

Identifying constraints of providing useful information

(L06)

1. Pagnozzi Properties is trying to decide if it needs to install a new accounting system to keep track of every detailed construction cost. The cost of the system will be $20,000 and the benefits are uncertain.

2. Gary Peters makes a $20 mistake when accounting for travel expenses. He has a question of whether this mistake needs to be corrected since it is relatively small.

3. Manuel Sanchez wants to know which accounting choice to make when accounting for consulting expenses at the end of the year. He decides that when in doubt, it would be better to understate rather than overstate net income.

In each case 1 through 3, identify the constraint that each of these statements addresses.

1. Inventory is reported at market value when cost is lower.

2. Computers costing less than $1,000 are immediately expensed even though their useful life is three years.

3. The auditors of Dietrich Co. found an error of $50 in its financial statements and decide to restate their financial statements; Dietrich has sales revenue of $15 million.

4. To appropriately account for the pension liability, Ziebart Co. installs an abnormally expensive system to track employees, their health, and their pension status. Ziebart argues that this system is necessary to comply with accounting guidelines.

Indicate the accounting constraint, if any, that is violated by each practice.

Exercise B-8
Identifying constraints violated

(LO6)

Target Corporation follows accounting rules in reporting its lease obligations. However, the vast majority of their store leases are not reported as liabilities on their balance sheet. Similar to other retail establishments, Target structures their leases to avoid reporting their leases on the balance sheet.

1. Why does Target Corp. wish to avoid reporting its store leases on the balance sheet?

2. Would a principles-based approach continue to allow Target Corp. to avoid reporting its store leases on the balance sheet?

3. Which qualitative characteristic(s) of accounting information is violated when Target Corp. avoids reporting its store leases on the balance sheet?

Exercise B-9
Rules-based vs. principles-based accounting

(LO1) (LO3)

Identify the accounting assumption, principle, or constraint that best describes the accounting practices at Ben Wallace Company.

1. Land is valued at its original purchase price rather than its appraised value.

2. Ben Wallace Company issues financial statements every three months.

3. Expenses are allocated to the appropriate revenues each accounting period.

4. All relevant financial information is disclosed in the financial reports.

5. Personal computers costing less than $1,000 are expensed in the current period even though their useful life is three years.

6. The CEO's personal business records are kept separate from the company's records.

7. The U.S. dollar is the unit of currency used in financial reports.

PROBLEM SET A

Problem B-1A
Identify accounting assumptions, principles, or constraints

(LO4) (LO5) (LO6)

Presented below are transactions that occurred during 2008.

1. Susan Scholz, the president of Lake of the Ozarks cabin properties, buys a computer for personal use and charges it to her company's expense account.

2. In preparation of its financial statements, Ettredge Inc. omitted information about its method of accounting for accounts receivable.

3. To make its profits look better, Shanghai Automotive booked sales before its cars were shipped.

4. Jose Martinez reports all of its assets and liabilities at liquidation value, even though the company does not expect to go out of business in the foreseeable future.

5. Tom Hapgood writes up his inventory on the balance sheet since its market value is higher than its cost.

Problem B-2A
Identifying assumptions, principles, or constraints violated

(LO4) (LO5) (LO6)

Required

For each of the above transactions, identify the assumption, principle, or constraint that has been violated.

Identify the accounting assumption, principle, or constraint that best describes the accounting practices at Steve Hill Company.

1. Financial statements are prepared each year.

2. Market value changes after an asset's purchase are not recorded in the accounts.

3. Notes and supplementary information are included with the financial statements.

4. The factory is not reported at liquidation value. (Do not use the cost principle.)

5. Manufactured toys are not recorded as revenues until they have been sold and shipped.

6. Requires that generally accepted accounting principles be followed for all material items.

PROBLEM SET B

Problem B-1B
Identify accounting assumptions, principles, or constraints

(LO4) (LO5) (LO6)

Problem B-2B

Identifying assumptions, principles, or constraints violated

Danny Manning and Larry Brown are accountants for the Engineering Institute. They disagree over the following transactions that occurred during 2008. Larry disagrees with Danny on each of the transactions below.

1. The Engineering Institute finds a bargain for a commercial-grade plotter and pays $3,000. Danny argues that if they had bought it from the dealer, they would have paid $4,000. Danny suggests they record the plotter for $4,000.

2. Timothy West, president of the Engineering Institute, used his company expense account to purchase a new BMW for his personal use. Danny argues that since the president is also the owner of the Engineering Institute, it really does not matter who paid for it.

3. Depreciation for the year was $114,000. Danny argues that since net income is expected to be lower in the current fiscal year, they should just charge it as an expense next year.

4. Danny suggests that the Engineering Institute value its equipment on its balance sheet at its liquidation value, which is $50,000 less than cost.

5. The Engineering Institute signed a lease on its offices for the next five years. A lease liability is not included on the company's balance sheet. Danny doesn't think such information needs to be disclosed.

Required

For each of the above transactions, identify why Larry disagrees. Also identify the assumption, principle, or constraint that has been violated.

~~~~~~

ANSWERS TO MULTIPLE CHOICE QUIZ

1. b   **4.** b
2. a   **5.** a
3. c

Glossary

Accelerated depreciation method Method that produces larger depreciation charges in the early years of an asset's life and smaller charges in its later years.

Account Record within an accounting system in which increases and decreases are entered and stored in a specific asset, liability, equity, revenue, or expense. *(pp. 19 & 44)*

Account balance Difference between total debits and total credits (including the beginning balance) for an account. *(p. 47)*

Accounting Information and measurement system that identifies, records, and communicates relevant information about a company's business activities. *(p. 4)*

Accounting cycle Recurring steps performed each accounting period, starting with analyzing transactions and continuing through the post-closing trial balance (or reversing entries). *(p. 126)*

Accounting equation Equality involving a company's assets, liabilities, and equity; Assets = Liabilities + Equity; also called *balance sheet equation.* *(p. 18)*

Accounting period Length of time covered by financial statements; also called *reporting period. (p. 308)*

Accounts payable ledger Subsidiary ledger listing individual creditor (supplier) accounts. *(p. 289)*

Accounts receivable Amounts due from customers for credit sales; backed by the customer's general credit standing.

Accounts receivable ledger Subsidiary ledger listing individual customer accounts. *(p. 263)*

Accrual basis accounting Accounting system that recognizes revenues when earned and expenses when incurred; the basis for GAAP. *(p. 309)*

Accrued expenses Costs incurred in a period that are both unpaid and unrecorded; adjusting entries for recording accrued expenses involve increasing expenses and increasing liabilities. *(pp. 104 & 312)*

Accrued revenues Revenues earned in a period that are both unrecorded and not yet received in cash (or other assets); adjusting entries for recording accrued revenues involve increasing assets and increasing revenues. *(p. 310)*

Acid-test ratio Ratio used to assess a company's ability to settle its current debts with its most liquid assets; defined as quick assets (cash, short-term investments, and current receivables) divided by current liabilities. *(p. 266)*

Adjusted trial balance List of accounts and balances prepared after period-end adjustments are recorded and posted. *(pp. 106 & 317)*

Adjusting entry Journal entry at the end of an accounting period to bring an asset or liability account to its proper amount and update the related expense or revenue account. *(pp. 100 & 310)*

Aging of accounts receivable Process of classifying accounts receivable by how long they are past due for purposes of estimating uncollectible accounts.

Allowance for Doubtful Accounts Contra asset account with a balance approximating uncollectible accounts receivable; also called *Allowance for Uncollectible Accounts. (p. 312)*

Allowance method Procedure that (a) estimates and matches bad debts expense with its sales for the period and/or (b) reports accounts receivable at estimated realizable value.

Amortization Process of allocating the cost of an intangible asset to expense over its estimated useful life.

Annual financial statements Financial statements covering a one-year period; often based on a calendar year, but any consecutive 12-month (or 52-week) period is acceptable. *(p. 308)*

Appropriated retained earnings Retained earnings separately reported to inform stockholders of funding needs.

Assets Resources a business owns or controls that are expected to provide current and future benefits to the business. *(p. 18)*

Authorized depository A bank that can accept payroll deposits from its own checking account customers. *(p. 230)*

Authorized stock Total amount of stock that a corporation's charter authorizes it to issue.

Average cost See *weighted average.*

Avoidable expense Expense (or cost) that is relevant for decision making; expense that is not incurred if a department, product, or service is eliminated.

Bad debts Accounts of customers who do not pay what they have promised to pay; an expense of selling on credit; also called *uncollectible accounts.*

Balance column account Account with debit and credit columns for recording entries and another column for showing the balance of the account after each entry. *(p. 80)*

Balance sheet Financial statement that lists types and dollar amounts of assets, liabilities, and equity at a specific date. *(p. 24)*

Bank reconciliation Report that explains the difference between the book (company) balance of cash and the cash balance reported on the bank statement. *(p. 181)*

Bank statement Bank report on the depositor's beginning and ending cash balances, and a listing of its changes, for a period. *(p. 180)*

Basic earnings per share Net income less any preferred dividends and then divided by weighted-average common shares outstanding.

Betterments Expenditures to make a plant asset more efficient or productive; also called *improvements.*

Bond Written promise to pay the bond's par (or face) value and interest at a stated contract rate; often issued in denominations of $1,000.

Bond indenture Contract between the bond issuer and the bondholders; identifies the parties' rights and obligations.

Book value Asset's acquisition costs less its accumulated depreciation (or depletion, or amortization); also sometimes used synonymously as the *carrying value* of an account. *(p. 104)*

Book value per common share Recorded amount of equity applicable to common shares divided by the number of common shares outstanding.

Book value per preferred share Equity applicable to preferred shares (equals its call price [or par value if it is not callable] plus any cumulative dividends in arrears) divided by the number of preferred shares outstanding.

Break-even point Output level at which sales equals fixed plus variable costs; where income equals zero.

Budget Formal statement of future plans, usually expressed in monetary terms.

Budget report Report comparing actual results to planned objectives; sometimes used as a progress report.

Budgetary control Management use of budgets to monitor and control company operations.

Business entity assumption Concept that assumes a business will be accounted for separately from its owner(s) and any other entity. *(p. B-4)*

Call price Amount that must be paid to call and retire a callable preferred stock or a callable bond.

Callable bonds Bonds that give the issuer the option to retire them at a stated amount prior to maturity.

Callable preferred stock Preferred stock that the issuing corporation, at its option, may retire by paying the call price plus any dividends in arrears.

Canceled checks Checks that the bank has paid and deducted from the depositor's account. *(p. 181)*

Capital expenditures Additional costs of plant assets that provide material benefits extending beyond the current period; also called *balance sheet expenditures.*

Capital stock General term referring to a corporation's stock used in obtaining capital (owner financing).

Carrying value of bonds Net amount at which bonds are reported on the balance sheet; equals the par value of the bonds less any unamortized discount or plus any unamortized premium; also called *carrying amount* or *book value.*

Cash Includes currency, coins, and amounts on deposit in bank checking or savings accounts. *(p. 174)*

Cash discount Reduction in the price of merchandise granted by a seller to a buyer when payment is made within the discount period. *(p. 259)*

Cash equivalents Short-term, investment assets that are readily convertible to a known cash amount or sufficiently close to their maturity date (usually within 90 days) so that market value is not sensitive to interest rate changes.

Cash flow on total assets Ratio of operating cash flows to average total assets; not sensitive to income recognition and measurement; partly reflects earnings quality.

Cash Over and Short Income statement account used to record cash overages and cash shortages arising from errors in cash receipts or payments. *(p. 175)*

Change in an accounting estimate Change in an accounting estimate that results from new information, subsequent developments, or improved judgment that impacts current and future periods.

Chart of accounts List of accounts used by a company; includes an identification number for each account. *(p. 78)*

Check Document signed by a depositor instructing the bank to pay a specified amount to a designated recipient. *(p. 179)*

Check register Another name for a cash disbursements journal when the journal has a column for check numbers. *(p. 166)*

Circular E IRS federal income tax withholding tables. *(p. 204)*

Classified balance sheet Balance sheet that presents assets and liabilities in relevant subgroups, including current and noncurrent classifications. *(p. 339)*

Clock card Source document used to record the number of hours an employee works and to determine the total labor cost for each pay period.

Closing entries Entries recorded at the end of each accounting period to transfer end-of-period balances in revenue, gain, expense, loss, and withdrawal (dividend for a corporation) accounts to the capital account (to retained earnings for a corporation). *(p. 130)*

Closing process Necessary end-of-period steps to prepare the accounts for recording the transactions of the next period. *(p. 130)*

Columnar journal Journal with more than one column. *(p. 263)*

Common stock Corporation's basic ownership share; also generically called *capital stock.*

Common-size financial statement Statement that expresses each amount as a percent of a base amount. In the balance sheet, total assets is usually the base and is expressed as 100%. In the income statement, net sales is usually the base.

Comparability A qualitative characteristic of accounting information suggesting that information is more useful if it can be related to an industry or competitor benchmark. *(p. B-4)*

Comparative financial statement Statement with data for two or more successive periods placed in side-by-side columns, often with changes shown in dollar amounts and percents.

Complex capital structure Capital structure that includes outstanding rights or options to purchase common stock, or securities that are convertible into common stock.

Conservatism principle Principle that prescribes the less optimistic estimate when two estimates are about equally likely. *(p. B-8)*

Consistency principle Principle that prescribes use of the same accounting method(s) over time so that financial statements are comparable across periods. *(p. B-4)*

Continuous improvement Concept requiring every manager and employee continually to look to improve operations.

Contra account Account linked with another account and having an opposite normal balance; reported as a subtraction from the other account's balance. *(p. 103)*

Contract rate Interest rate specified in a bond indenture (or note); multiplied by the par value to determine the interest paid each period; also called *coupon rate, stated rate,* or *nominal rate.*

Contribution margin per unit Amount that the sale of one unit contributes toward recovering fixed costs and earning profit; defined as sales price per unit minus variable expense per unit.

Contribution margin ratio Product's contribution margin divided by its sale price.

Control Process of monitoring planning decisions and evaluating the organization's activities and employees.

Controllable costs Costs that a manager has the power to control or at least strongly influence.

Controlling account General ledger account, the balance of which (after posting) equals the sum of the balances in its related subsidiary ledger. *(p. 264)*

Conversion costs Expenditures incurred in converting raw materials to finished goods; includes direct labor costs and overhead costs.

Convertible bonds Bonds that bondholders can exchange for a set number of the issuer's shares.

Convertible preferred stock Preferred stock with an option to exchange it for common stock at a specified rate.

Copyright Right giving the owner the exclusive privilege to publish and sell musical, literary, or artistic work during the creator's life plus 70 years.

Corporation Business that is a separate legal entity under state or federal laws with owners called *shareholders* or *stockholders. (p. B-5)*

Cost All normal and reasonable expenditures necessary to get an asset in place and ready for its intended use.

Cost accounting system Accounting system for manufacturing activities based on the perpetual inventory system.

Cost-benefit A constraint of useful accounting information prescribing that information will only be provided if the benefits to users outweigh the costs of preparation. *(p. B-8)*

Cost center Department that incurs costs but generates no revenues; common example is the accounting or legal department.

Cost object Product, process, department, or customer to which costs are assigned.

Cost of goods sold Cost of inventory sold to customers during a period; also called *cost of sales. (p. 280)*

Cost principle Accounting principle that prescribes financial statement information to be based on actual costs incurred in business transactions. *(p. B-6)*

Cost variance Difference between the actual incurred cost and the standard cost.

Cost-volume-profit (CVP) analysis Planning method that includes predicting the volume of activity, the costs incurred, sales earned, and profits received.

Credit Recorded on the right side; an entry that decreases asset and expense accounts, and increases liability, revenue, and most equity accounts; abbreviated Cr. *(p. 46)*

Credit memorandum Notification that the sender has credited the recipient's account in the sender's records. *(p. 261)*

Credit period Time period that can pass before a customer's payment is due. *(pp. 259 & 284)*

Credit terms Description of the amounts and timing of payments that a buyer (debtor) agrees to make in the future. *(p. 259 & 283)*

Creditors Individuals or organizations entitled to receive payments. *(p. 45)*

Current assets Cash and other assets expected to be sold, collected, or used within one year or the company's operating cycle, whichever is longer. *(pp. 134 & 341)*

Current liabilities Obligations due to be paid or settled within one year or the company's operating cycle, whichever is longer. *(pp. 134 & 341)*

Current ratio Ratio used to evaluate a company's ability to pay its short-term obligations, calculated by dividing current assets by current liabilities. *(p. 135)*

Customer orientation Company position that its managers and employees be in tune with the changing wants and needs of consumers.

Cycle efficiency (CE) A measure of production efficiency, which is defined as value-added (process) time divided by total cycle time.

Cycle time (CT) A measure of the time to produce a product or service, which is the sum of process time, inspection time, move time, and wait time; also called *throughput time.*

Date of declaration Date the directors vote to pay a dividend.

Date of payment Date the corporation makes the dividend payment.

Date of record Date directors specify for identifying stockholders to receive dividends.

Days' sales in inventory Estimate of number of days needed to convert inventory into receivables or cash; equals ending inventory divided by cost of goods sold and then multiplied by 365; also called *days' stock on hand.*

Days' sales uncollected Measure of the liquidity of receivables computed by dividing the current balance of receivables by the annual credit (or net) sales and then multiplying by 365; also called *days' sales in receivables.* *(p. 185)*

Debit Recorded on the left side; an entry that increases asset and expense accounts, and decreases liability, revenue, and most equity accounts; abbreviated Dr. *(p. 46)*

Debit memorandum Notification that the sender has debited the recipient's account in the sender's records. *(p. 285)*

Debt ratio Ratio of total liabilities to total assets; used to reflect risk associated with a company's debts. *(p. 58)*

Debt-to-equity ratio Defined as total liabilities divided by total equity; shows the proportion of a company financed by non-owners (creditors) in comparison with that financed by owners.

Declining-balance method Method that determines depreciation charge for the period by multiplying a depreciation rate (often twice the straight-line rate) by the asset's beginning-period book value.

Departmental accounting system Accounting system that provides information useful in evaluating the profitability or cost effectiveness of a department.

Departmental contribution to overhead Amount by which a department's revenues exceed its direct expenses.

Depletion Process of allocating the cost of natural resources to periods when they are consumed and sold.

Deposit ticket Lists items such as currency, coins, and checks deposited and their corresponding dollar amounts. *(p. 179)*

Deposits in transit Deposits recorded by the company but not yet recorded by its bank. *(p. 182)*

Depreciation Expense created by allocating the cost of plant and equipment to periods in which they are used; represents the expense of using the asset. *(p. 103)*

Diluted earnings per share Earnings per share calculation that requires dilutive securities be added to the denominator of the basic EPS calculation.

Dilutive securities Securities having the potential to increase common shares outstanding; examples are options, rights, convertible bonds, and convertible preferred stock.

Direct costs Costs incurred for the benefit of one specific cost object.

Direct expenses Expenses traced to a specific department (object) that are incurred for the sole benefit of that department.

Direct labor Efforts of employees who physically convert materials to finished product.

Direct labor costs Wages and salaries for direct labor that are separately and readily traced through the production process to finished goods.

Direct material Raw material that physically becomes part of the product and is clearly identified with specific products or batches of product.

Direct material costs Expenditures for direct material that are separately and readily traced through the production process to finished goods.

Direct method Presentation of net cash from operating activities for the statement of cash flows that lists major operating cash receipts less major operating cash payments.

Direct write-off method Method that records the loss from an uncollectible account receivable at the time it is determined to be uncollectible; no attempt is made to estimate bad debts.

Discount on bonds payable Difference between a bond's par value and its lower issue price or carrying value; occurs when the contract rate is less than the market rate.

Discount period Time period in which a cash discount is available and the buyer can make a reduced payment. *(pp. 259 & 284)*

Dividend in arrears Unpaid dividend on cumulative preferred stock; must be paid before any regular dividends on preferred stock and before any dividends on common stock.

Dividend yield Ratio of the annual amount of cash dividends distributed to common shareholders relative to the common stock's market value (price).

Double-entry accounting Accounting system in which each transaction affects at least two accounts and has at least one debit and one credit. *(p. 47)*

Earnings per share (EPS) Amount of income earned by each share of a company's outstanding common stock; also called *net income per share.*

Effective interest method Allocates interest expense over the bond life to yield a constant rate of interest; interest expense for a period is found by multiplying the balance of the liability at the beginning of the period by the bond market rate at issuance; also called *interest method.*

Efficiency Company's productivity in using its assets; usually measured relative to how much revenue a certain level of assets generates.

Efficiency variance Difference between the actual quantity of an input and the standard quantity of that input.

Electronic funds transfer (EFT) Use of electronic communication to transfer cash from one party to another. *(p. 180)*

Employee Someone whose work is under the direction of an employer. *(p. 202)*

Employee benefits Additional compensation paid to or on behalf of employees, such as premiums for medical, dental, life, and disability insurance, and contributions to pension plans. *(p. 207)*

Employee earnings records Record of an employee's net pay, gross pay, deductions, and year-to-date payroll information. *(p. 211)*

Employee's Withholding Allowance Certificate (Form W-4) A form which shows an employee's withholding allowances. *(p. 202)*

Employer identification number (EIN) A number issued by the federal government that uniquely identifies a business. *(p. 228)*

Employer Quarterly Unemployment Tax Report A report filed with the state that shows an employer's uneployment taxes owed. *(p. 237)*

EOM Abbreviation for *end of month;* used to describe credit terms for credit transactions. *(p. 259)*

Equity Owner's claim on the assets of a business; equals the residual interest in an entity's assets after deducting liabilities; also called *net assets.* *(p. 18)*

Equity ratio Portion of total assets provided by equity, computed as total equity divided by total assets.

Ethics Codes of conduct by which actions are judged as right or wrong, fair or unfair, honest or dishonest. *(p. 8)*

Expanded accounting equation Assets = Liabilities + Equity; Equity equals [Owner capital − Owner withdrawals + Revenues − Expenses] for a noncorporation; Equity equals [Contributed capital + Retained earnings + Revenues − Expenses] for a corporation where dividends are subtracted from retained earnings. *(p. 19)*

Expenses Outflows or using up of assets as part of operations of a business to generate sales. *(p. 19)*

External transactions Exchanges of economic value between one entity and another entity. *(p. 19)*

External users Persons using accounting information who are not directly involved in running the organization. *(p. 5)*

Extraordinary repairs Major repairs that extend the useful life of a plant asset beyond prior expectations; treated as a capital expenditure.

Factory overhead Factory activities supporting the production process that are not direct material or direct labor; also called *overhead* and *manufacturing overhead*.

Factory overhead costs Expenditures for factory overhead that cannot be separately or readily traced to finished goods; also called *overhead costs*.

Favorable variance Difference in actual revenues or expenses from the budgeted amount that contributes to a higher income.

Federal depository bank Bank authorized to accept deposits of amounts payable to the federal government. *(p. 230)*

Federal Insurance Contributions Act (FICA) Taxes Taxes assessed on both employers and employees; for Social Security and Medicare programs. *(pp. 203 & 228)*

Federal Reserve Bank A bank that can accept payroll deposits from any business. *(p. 230)*

Federal Unemployment Taxes (FUTA) Payroll taxes on employers assessed by the federal government to support its unemployment insurance program. *(p. 228)*

Financial accounting Area of accounting mainly aimed at serving external users. *(p. 5)*

Financial Accounting Standards Board (FASB) Independent group of full-time members responsible for setting accounting rules. *(pp. 9 & B-2)*

Financial reporting Process of communicating information relevant to investors, creditors, and others in making investment, credit, and business decisions.

Financial statement analysis Application of analytical tools to general-purpose financial statements and related data for making business decisions.

Financing activities Transactions with owners and creditors that include obtaining cash from issuing debt, repaying amounts borrowed, and obtaining cash from or distributing cash to owners.

Finished goods inventory Account that controls the finished goods files, which acts as a subsidiary ledger (of the Inventory account) in which the costs of finished goods that are ready for sale are recorded.

First-in, first-out (FIFO) Method to assign cost to inventory that assumes items are sold in the order acquired; earliest items purchased are the first sold.

Fiscal year Consecutive 12-month (or 52-week) period chosen as the organization's annual accounting period. *(p. 309)*

Fixed budget Planning budget based on a single predicted amount of volume; unsuitable for evaluations if the actual volume differs from predicted volume.

Fixed budget performance report Report that compares actual revenues and costs with fixed budgeted amounts and identifies the differences as favorable or unfavorable variances.

Fixed cost Cost that does not change with changes in the volume of activity.

Flexible budget Budget prepared (using actual volume) once a period is complete that helps managers evaluate past performance; uses fixed and variable costs in determining total costs.

Flexible budget performance report Report that compares actual revenues and costs with their variable budgeted amounts based on actual sales volume (or other level of activity) and identifies the differences as variances.

FOB Abbreviation for *free on board;* the point when ownership of goods passes to the buyer; *FOB shipping point* (or *factory*) means the buyer pays shipping costs and accepts ownership of goods when the seller transfers goods to carrier; *FOB destination* means the seller pays shipping costs and buyer accepts ownership of goods at the buyer's place of business. *(p. 285)*

Form 940 IRS form used to report an employer's federal unemployment taxes (FUTA) on an annual filing basis. *(p. 237)*

Form 940-EZ The Employer's Annual Federal Unemployment Tax Return. This shows the amount of FUTA tax the employer owes for the year. *(p. 237)*

Form 941 IRS form filed to report FICA taxes owed and remitted. *(p. 232)*

Form 8109 A preprinted Federal Tax Deposit Coupon. It is used when an employer deposits money into a federal depository bank. *(p. 231)*

Form 8109-B A Federal Tax Deposit Coupon used by new businesses or when the business does not have a supply of preprinted Forms 8109. *(p. 231)*

Form SS-4 An Internal Revenue Service form filed by a busuiness in order to receive an employer identification number. *(p. 228)*

Form W-2 Annual report by an employer to each employee showing the employee's wages subject to FICA and federal income taxes along with amounts withheld. *(p. 234)*

Form W-3 The Transmittal of Wage and Tax Statements form. This form reports the total wages and tax withholding information for all the employer's employees for the year. *(p. 235)*

Form W-4 Withholding allowance certificate, filed with the employer, identifying the number of withholding allowances claimed.

Franchises Privileges granted by a company or government to sell a product or service under specified conditions.

Full disclosure principle Principle that prescribes financial statements (including notes) to report all relevant information about an entity's operations and financial condition. *(p. B-7)*

General accounting system Accounting system for manufacturing activities based on the *periodic* inventory system.

General and administrative expenses Expenses that support the operating activities of a business. *(p. 337)*

General journal All-purpose journal for recording the debits and credits of transactions and events. *(pp. 79 & 262)*

General partner Partner who assumes unlimited liability for the debts of the partnership; responsible for partnership management.

General partnership Partnership in which all partners have mutual agency and unlimited liability for partnership debts.

Generally accepted accounting principles (GAAP) Rules that specify acceptable accounting practices. *(pp. 9 & B-8)*

General-purpose financial statements Statements published periodically for use by a variety of interested parties; includes the income statement, balance sheet, statement of owner's equity (or statement of retained earnings for a corporation), statement of cash flows, and notes to these statements.

Going-concern assumption Concept that prescribes financial statements to reflect the assumption that the business will continue operating indefinitely. *(p. B-6)*

Goods in process inventory Account in which costs are accumulated for products that are in the process of being produced but are not yet complete; also called *work in process inventory.*

Goodwill Amount by which a company's (or a segment's) value exceeds the value of its individual assets less its liabilities.

Gross margin (See *gross profit.*) *(p. 280)*

Gross margin ratio Gross margin (net sales minus cost of goods sold) divided by net sales; also called *gross profit ratio. (p. 291)*

Gross pay Total compensation earned by an employee. *(p. 202)*

Gross profit Net sales minus cost of goods sold; also called *gross margin.* *(p. 280)*

Gross profit method Procedure to estimate inventory when the past gross profit rate is used to estimate cost of goods sold, which is then subtracted from the cost of goods available for sale.

Horizontal analysis Comparison of a company's financial condition and performance across time.

Impairment Diminishment of an asset value.

Income (See *net income.*)

Income statement Financial statement that subtracts expenses from revenues to yield a net income or loss over a specified period of time; also includes any gains or losses. *(p. 24)*

Income Summary Temporary account used only in the closing process to which the balances of revenue and expense accounts (including any gains or losses) are transferred; its balance is transferred to the capital account (or retained earnings for a corporation). *(p. 130)*

Incremental cost Additional cost incurred only if a company pursues a specific course of action.

Indefinite useful life Asset life that is not limited by legal, regulatory, contractual, competitive, economic, or other factors.

Independent contractor Someone who does a job for an employer, but decides how to do the work. *(p. 202)*

Indirect costs Costs incurred for the benefit of more than one cost object.

Indirect expenses Expenses incurred for the joint benefit of more than one department (or cost object).

Indirect labor Efforts of production employees who do not work specifically on converting direct materials into finished products and who are not clearly identified with specific units or batches of product.

Indirect labor costs Labor costs that cannot be physically traced to production of a product or service; included as part of overhead.

Indirect material Material used to support the production process but not clearly identified with products or batches of product.

Indirect method Presentation that reports net income and then adjusts it by adding and subtracting items to yield net cash from operating activities on the statement of cash flows.

Individual employee earnings records Records that summarize each employee's earnings, deductions, and net pay during each calendar year. *(p. 211)*

Installment note Liability requiring a series of periodic payments to the lender.

Intangible assets Long-term assets (resources) used to produce or sell products or services; usually lack physical form and have uncertain benefits. *(p. 341)*

Interest Charge for using money (or other assets) loaned from one entity to another.

Interim financial statements Financial statements covering periods of less than one year; usually based on one-, three-, or six-month periods. *(p. 308)*

Internal controls or **Internal control system** All policies and procedures used to protect assets, ensure reliable accounting, promote efficient operations, and urge adherence to company policies. *(p. 157)*

Internal transactions Activities within an organization that can affect the accounting equation. *(p. 19)*

Internal users Persons using accounting information who are directly involved in managing the organization. *(p. 6)*

International Accounting Standards Board (IASB) Group that identifies preferred accounting practices and encourages global acceptance; issues International Financial Reporting Standards (IFRS). *(pp. 9 & B-4)*

Inventory Goods a company owns and expects to sell in its normal operations. *(p. 281)*

Inventory turnover Number of times a company's average inventory is sold during a period; computed by dividing cost of goods sold by average inventory; also called *merchandise turnover.*

Investing activities Transactions that involve purchasing and selling of long-term assets; includes making and collecting notes receivable and investments in other than cash equivalents.

Investment center Center of which a manager is responsible for revenues, costs, and asset investments.

Investment center return on total assets Center net income divided by average total assets for the center.

Invoice Itemized record of goods prepared by the vendor that lists the customer's name, items sold, sales prices, and terms of sale. *(pp. 164 & 282)*

Invoice approval Document containing a checklist of steps necessary for approving the recording and payment of an invoice; also called *check authorization. (p. 164)*

Job Production of a customized product or service.

Job cost sheet Separate record maintained for each job.

Job lot Production of more than one unit of a customized product or service.

Job order cost accounting system Cost accounting system to determine the cost of producing each job or job lot.

Job order production Production of special-order products; also called *customized production.*

Joint cost Cost incurred to produce or purchase two or more products at the same time.

Journal Record in which transactions are entered before they are posted to ledger accounts; also called *book of original entry. (p. 78)*

Journalizing Process of recording transactions in a journal. *(p. 78)*

Just-in-time (JIT) manufacturing Process of acquiring or producing inventory only when needed.

Land improvements Assets that increase the benefits of land, have a limited useful life, and are depreciated.

Large stock dividend Stock dividend that is more than 25% of the previously outstanding shares.

Last-in, first-out (LIFO) Method to assign cost to inventory that assumes costs for the most recent items purchased are sold first and charged to cost of goods sold.

Lean business model Practice of eliminating waste while meeting customer needs and yielding positive company returns.

Lease Contract specifying the rental of property.

Leasehold Rights the lessor grants to the lessee under the terms of a lease.

Leasehold improvements Alterations or improvements to leased property such as partitions and storefronts.

Ledger Record containing all accounts (with amounts) for a business; also called *general ledger. (pp. 44 & 80)*

Lessee Party to a lease who secures the right to possess and use the property from another party (the lessor).

Lessor Party to a lease who grants another party (the lessee) the right to possess and use its property.

Liabilities Creditors' claims on an organization's assets; involves a probable future payment of assets, products, or services that a company is obligated to make due to past transactions or events. *(p. 18)*

Licenses (See *franchises.*)

Limited liability company Organization form that combines select features of a corporation and a limited partnership; provides limited liability to its members (owners), is free of business tax, and allows members to actively participate in management.

Limited liability partnership Partnership in which a partner is not personally liable for malpractice or negligence unless that partner is responsible for providing the service that resulted in the claim.

Limited partners Partners who have no personal liability for partnership debts beyond the amounts they invested in the partnership.

Limited partnership Partnership that has two classes of partners, limited partners and general partners.

Liquid assets Resources such as cash that are easily converted into other assets or used to pay for goods, services, or liabilities. *(p. 174)*

Liquidating cash dividend Distribution of assets that returns part of the original investment to stockholders; deducted from contributed capital accounts.

Liquidity Availability of resources to meet short-term cash requirements. *(p. 174)*

List price Catalog (full) price of an item before any trade discount is deducted. *(p. 282)*

Long-term investments Long-term assets not used in operating activities such as notes receivable and investments in stocks and bonds. *(p. 341)*

Long-term liabilities Obligations not due to be paid within one year or the operating cycle, whichever is longer. *(p. 341)*

Look-back rule A rule used to classify business as monthly or semiweekly depositors. *(p. 230)*

Lower of cost or market (LCM) Required method to report inventory at market replacement cost when that market cost is lower than recorded cost.

Maker of the note Entity who signs a note and promises to pay it at maturity.

Managerial accounting Area of accounting mainly aimed at serving the decision-making needs of internal users; also called *management accounting. (p. 6)*

Manufacturing statement Report that summarizes the types and amounts of costs incurred in a company's production process for a period; also called *cost of goods manufacturing statement.*

Margin of safety Excess of expected sales over the level of break-even sales.

Market prospects Expectations (both good and bad) about a company's future performance as assessed by users and other interested parties.

Market rate Interest rate that borrowers are willing to pay and lenders are willing to accept for a specific lending agreement given the borrowers' risk level.

Market value per share Price at which stock is bought or sold.

Matching principle Prescribes expenses to be reported in the same period as the revenues that were earned as a result of the expenses. *(p. 309)*

Materiality Prescribes that accounting for items that markedly impact financial statements, and any inferences drawn from them, adhere to GAAP. *(p. B-8)*

Materials ledger card Perpetual record updated each time units are purchased or issued for production use.

Materials requisition Source document production managers use to request materials for production; used to assign materials costs to specific jobs or overhead.

Maturity date of a note Date when a note's principal and interest are due.

Merchandise (See *merchandise inventory.*) *(p. 258)*

Merchandise inventory Goods that a company owns and expects to sell to customers; also called *merchandise* or *inventory. (p. 281)*

Merchandiser Entity that earns net income by buying and selling merchandise. *(pp. 258 & 280)*

Merit rating Rating assigned to an employer by a state based on the employer's record of employment. *(p. 228)*

Minimum legal capital Amount of assets defined by law that stockholders must (potentially) invest in a corporation; usually defined as par value of the stock; intended to protect creditors.

Mixed cost Cost that behaves like a combination of fixed and variable costs.

Modified Accelerated Cost Recovery System (MACRS) Depreciation system required by federal income tax law.

Monitary unit assumption Concept that assumes transactions and events can be expressed in money units. *(p. B-6)*

Mortgage Legal loan agreement that protects a lender by giving the lender the right to be paid from the cash proceeds from the sale of a borrower's assets identified in the mortgage.

Multiple-step income statement Income statement format that shows subtotals between sales and net income, categorizes expenses, and often reports the details of net sales and expenses. *(p. 337)*

Mutual agency Legal relationship among partners whereby each partner is an agent of the partnership and is able to bind the partnership to contracts within the scope of the partnership's business.

Natural business year Twelve-month period that ends when a company's sales activities are at their lowest point. *(p. 309)*

Natural resources Assets physically consumed when used; examples are timber, mineral deposits, and oil and gas fields; also called *wasting assets*.

Net income Amount earned after subtracting all expenses necessary for and matched with sales for a period; also called *income, profit,* or *earnings*. *(p. 19)*

Net loss Excess of expenses over revenues for a period. *(p. 19)*

Net pay Gross pay less all deductions; also called *take-home pay*. *(p. 207)*

Net purchases Net cost of merchandise purchased; computed as Purchases minus Purchase Discounts, minus Purchase Returns and Allowances, plus Transportation-In. *(p. 286)*

Net realizable value Expected selling price (value) of an item minus the cost of making the sale.

Noncumulative preferred stock Preferred stock on which the right to receive dividends is lost for any period when dividends are not declared.

Nonparticipating preferred stock Preferred stock on which dividends are limited to a maximum amount each year.

No-par value stock Stock class that has not been assigned a par (or stated) value by the corporate charter.

Non-value-added time The portion of cycle time that is not directed at producing a product or service; equals the sum of inspection time, move time, and wait time.

Off-balance-sheet financing Acquisition of assets by agreeing to liabilities not reported on the balance sheet.

Operating activities Activities that involve the production or purchase of merchandise and the sale of goods or services to customers, including expenditures related to administering the business.

Operating cycle Normal time between paying cash for merchandise or employee services and receiving cash from customers. *(p. 339)*

Operating leases Short-term (or cancelable) leases in which the lessor retains risks and rewards of ownership.

Opportunity cost Potential benefit lost by choosing a specific action from two or more alternatives.

Ordinary repairs Repairs to keep a plant asset in normal, good operating condition; treated as a revenue expenditure and immediately expensed.

Organization expenses (costs) Costs such as legal fees and promoter fees to bring an entity into existence.

Out-of-pocket cost Cost incurred or avoided as a result of management's decisions.

Outstanding checks Checks written and recorded by the depositor but not yet paid by the bank at the bank statement date. *(p. 182)*

Overapplied overhead Amount by which the overhead applied to production in a period using the predetermined overhead rate exceeds the actual overhead incurred in a period.

Overhead cost variance Difference between the total overhead cost applied to products and the total overhead cost actually incurred.

Owner, capital Account showing the owner's claim on company assets; equals owner investments plus net income (or less net losses) minus owner withdrawals since the company's inception; also referred to as *equity*. *(pp. 19 & 46)*

Owner investment Assets put into the business by the owner. *(p. 19)*

Owner withdrawals (See *withdrawals*.) *(pp. 19 & 46)*

Paid-in capital (See *contributed capital*.)

Paid-in capital in excess of par value Amount received from issuance of stock that is in excess of the stock's par value.

Par value Value assigned a share of stock by the corporate charter when the stock is authorized.

Par value of a bond Amount the bond issuer agrees to pay at maturity and the amount on which cash interest payments are based; also called *face amount* or *face value* of a bond.

Par value stock Class of stock assigned a par value by the corporate charter.

Participating preferred stock Preferred stock that shares with common stockholders any dividends paid in excess of the percent stated on preferred stock.

Partner return on equity Partner net income divided by average partner equity for the period.

Partnership Unincorporated association of two or more persons to pursue a business for profit as co-owners. *(p. B-5)*

Partnership contract Agreement among partners that sets terms under which the affairs of the partnership are conducted; also called *articles of partnership*.

Partnership liquidation Dissolution of a partnership by (1) selling noncash assets and allocating any gain or loss according to partners' income-and-loss ratio, (2) paying liabilities, and (3) distributing any remaining cash according to partners' capital balances.

Patent Exclusive right granted to its owner to produce and sell an item or to use a process for 17 years.

Payee of the note Entity to whom a note is made payable.

Payroll bank account Bank account used solely for paying employees; each pay period an amount equal to the total employees' net pay is deposited in it and the payroll checks are drawn on it. *(p. 210)*

Payroll deductions Amounts withheld from an employee's gross pay; also called *withholdings*. *(p. 204)*

Payroll register Record for a pay period that shows the pay period dates, regular and overtime hours worked, gross pay, net pay, and deductions. *(p. 208)*

Period costs Expenditures identified more with a time period than with finished products costs; includes selling and general administrative expenses.

Periodic inventory system Method that records the cost of inventory purchased but does not continuously track the quantity available or sold to customers; records are updated at the end of each period to reflect the physical count and costs of goods available.

Periodicity assumption (or principle) Assumption that an organization's activities can be divided into specific time periods such as months, quarters, or years. *(pp. 308 & B-6)*

Permanent accounts Accounts that reflect activities related to one or more future periods; balance sheet accounts whose balances are not closed; also called *real accounts*. *(p. 130)*

Perpetual inventory system Method that maintains continuous records of the cost of inventory available and the cost of goods sold.

Petty cash Small amount of cash in a fund to pay minor expenses; accounted for using an imprest system. *(p. 176)*

Planning Process of setting goals and preparing to achieve them.

Plant assets Tangible long-lived assets used to produce or sell products and services; also called *property, plant and equipment (PP&E)* or *fixed assets*. *(p. 103)*

Post-closing trial balance List of permanent accounts and their balances from the ledger after all closing entries are journalized and posted. *(p. 133)*

Posting Process of transferring journal entry information to the ledger; computerized systems automate this process. *(p. 79)*

Posting reference (PR) column A column in journals in which individual ledger account numbers are entered when entries are posted to those ledger accounts. *(p. 80)*

Predetermined overhead rate Rate established prior to the beginning of a period that relates estimated overhead to another variable, such as estimated direct labor, and is used to assign overhead cost to production.

Preemptive right Stockholders' right to maintain their proportionate interest in a corporation with any additional shares issued.

Preferred stock Stock with a priority status over common stockholders in one or more ways, such as paying dividends or distributing assets.

Premium on bonds Difference between a bond's par value and its higher carrying value; occurs when the contract rate is higher than the market rate; also called *bond premium*.

Premium on stock (See *contributed capital in excess of par value*.)

Prepaid expenses Items paid for in advance of receiving their benefits; classified as assets. *(pp. 101 & 314)*

Price-earnings (PE) ratio Ratio of a company's current market value per share to its earnings per share; also called *price-to-earnings*.

Price variance Difference between actual and budgeted revenue or cost caused by the difference between the actual price per unit and the budgeted price per unit.

Prime costs Expenditures directly identified with the production of finished goods; include direct materials costs and direct labor costs.

Principal of a note Amount that the signer of a note agrees to pay back when it matures, not including interest.

Principles of internal control Principles prescribing management to establish responsibility, maintain records, insure assets, separate recordkeeping from custody of assets, divide responsibility for related transactions, apply technological controls, and perform reviews. *(p. 157)*

Prior period adjustment Correction of an error in a prior year that is reported in the statement of retained earnings (or statement of stockholders' equity) net of any income tax effects.

Product costs Costs that are capitalized as inventory because they produce benefits expected to have future value; include direct materials, direct labor, and overhead.

Profit center Business unit that incurs costs and generates revenues.

Profit margin Ratio of a company's net income to its net sales; the percent of income in each dollar of revenue; also called *net profit margin*. *(p. 108)*

Profitability Company's ability to generate an adequate return on invested capital.

Promissory note (or note) Written promise to pay a specified amount either on demand or at a definite future date; is a *note receivable* for the lender but a *note payable* for the lendee.

Proprietorship Business owned by one person that is not organized as a corporation. *(p. B-5)*

Proxy Legal document giving a stockholder's agent the power to exercise the stockholder's voting rights.

Purchase discount Term used by a purchaser to describe a cash discount granted to the purchaser for paying within the discount period. *(p. 283)*

Purchase order Document used by the purchasing department to place an order with a seller (vendor). *(pp. 163 & 282)*

Purchase requisition Document listing merchandise needed by a department and requesting it be purchased. *(pp. 163 & 281)*

Purchases journal Journal normally used to record all purchases on credit. *(p. 289)*

Quantity variance Difference between actual and budgeted revenue or cost caused by the difference between the actual number of units and the budgeted number of units.

Ratio analysis Determination of key relations between financial statement items as reflected in numerical measures.

Raw materials inventory Goods a company acquires to use in making products.

Realizable value Expected proceeds from converting an asset into cash.

Receiving report Form used to report that ordered goods are received and to describe their quantity and condition. *(pp. 164 & 282)*

Recordkeeping Part of accounting that involves recording transactions and events, either manually or electronically; also called *bookkeeping. (p. 4)*

Relevance A qualitative characteristic of accounting information that prescribes that information be useful, understandable, timely and pertinent for decision making. *(p. B-3)*

Relevant benefits Additional or incremental revenue generated by selecting a particular course of action over another.

Reliability The principle that information is verifiable and faithfully represents the substance of the underlying economic transaction. *(p. B-3)*

Responsibility accounting budget Report of expected costs and expenses under a manager's control.

Responsibility accounting performance report Responsibility report that compares actual costs and expenses for a department with budgeted amounts.

Responsibility accounting system System that provides information that management can use to evaluate the performance of a department's manager.

Restricted retained earnings Retained earnings not available for dividends because of legal or contractual limitations.

Retailer Intermediary that buys products from manufacturers or wholesalers and sells them to consumers. *(p. 258)*

Retained earnings Cumulative income less cumulative losses and dividends.

Retained earnings deficit Debit (abnormal) balance in Retained Earnings; occurs when cumulative losses and dividends exceed cumulative income; also called *accumulated deficit.*

Return on assets (See *return on total assets*) *(p. 26)*

Revenue expenditures Expenditures reported on the current income statement as an expense because they do not provide benefits in future periods.

Revenue recognition principle The principle prescribing that revenue is recognized when earned. *(pp. 309 & B-7)*

Revenues Gross increase in equity from a company's business activities that earn income; also called *sales. (p. 19)*

Reverse stock split Occurs when a corporation calls in its stock and replaces each share with less than one new share; increases both market value per share and any par or stated value per share.

Reversing entries Optional entries recorded at the beginning of a period that prepare the accounts for the usual journal entries as if adjusting entries had not occurred in the prior period. *(p. 344)*

S corporation Corporation that meets special tax qualifications so as to be treated like a partnership for income tax purposes.

Sales discount Term used by a seller to describe a cash discount granted to buyers who pay within the discount period. *(p. 259)*

Sales journal Journal normally used to record sales of goods on credit. *(p. 262)*

Sales mix Ratio of sales volumes for the various products sold by a company.

Sales-per-employee ratio Net sales divided by the average number of employees; it is a measure of employee productivity. *(p. 212)*

Salvage value Estimate of amount to be recovered at the end of an asset's useful life; also called *residual value* or *scrap value.*

Sarbanes–Oxley Act Created the *Public Company Accounting Oversight Board,* regulates analyst conflicts, imposes corporate governance requirements, enhances accounting and control disclosures, impacts insider transactions and executive loans, establishes new types of criminal conduct, and expands penalties for violations of federal securities laws. *(p. B-2)*

Schedule of accounts payable List of the balances of all accounts in the accounts payable ledger and their total. *(p. 290)*

Schedule of accounts receivable List of the balances for all accounts in the accounts receivable ledger and their total. *(p. 266)*

Secured bonds Bonds that have specific assets of the issuer pledged as collateral.

Securities and Exchange Commission (SEC) Federal agency Congress has charged to set reporting rules for organizations that sell ownership shares to the public. *(pp. 9 & B-2)*

Self-employment tax Social Security and Medicare taxes for persons who operate their own businesses. *(p. 203)*

Selling expenses Expenses of promoting sales, such as displaying and advertising merchandise, making sales, and delivering goods to customers. *(p. 337)*

Serial bonds Bonds consisting of separate amounts that mature at different dates.

Shareholders Owners of a corporation; also called *stockholders. (p. B-5)*

Signature card Includes the signatures of each person authorized to sign checks on the bank account. *(p. 179)*

Simple capital structure Capital structure that consists of only common stock and nonconvertible preferred stock; consists of no dilutive securities.

Single-step income statement Income statement format that includes cost of goods sold as an expense and shows only one subtotal for total expenses. *(p. 339)*

Small stock dividend Stock dividend that is 25% or less of a corporation's previously outstanding shares.

Sole proprietorship Business owned by one person that is not organized as a corporation; also called *proprietorship. (p. B-5)*

Solvency Company's long-run financial viability and its ability to cover long-term obligations.

Source documents Source of information for accounting entries that can be in either paper or electronic form; also called *business papers. (p. 76)*

Special journal Any journal used for recording and posting transactions of a similar type. *(p. 262)*

Specific identification Method to assign cost to inventory when the purchase cost of each item in inventory is identified and used to compute cost of inventory.

Spending variance Difference between the actual price of an item and its standard price.

Standard costs Costs that should be incurred under normal conditions to produce a product or component or to perform a service.

State unemployment taxes (SUTA) State payroll taxes on employers to support its unemployment programs. *(p. 228)*

Stated value stock No-par stock assigned a stated value per share; this amount is recorded in the stock account when the stock is issued.

Statement of cash flows A financial statement that lists cash inflows (receipts) and cash outflows (payments) during a period; arranged by operating, investing, and financing.

Statement of owner's equity Report of changes in equity over a period; adjusted for increases (owner investment and net income) and for decreases (withdrawals and net loss). *(p. 24)*

Statement of partners' equity Financial statement that shows total capital balances at the beginning of the period, any additional investment by partners, the income or loss of the period, the partners' withdrawals, and the partners' ending capital balances; also called *statement of partners' capital*.

Statement of retained earnings Report of changes in retained earnings over a period; adjusted for increases (net income), for decreases (dividends and net loss), and for any prior period adjustment.

Statement of stockholders' equity Financial statement that lists the beginning and ending balances of each major equity account and describes all changes in those accounts.

Stock dividend Corporation's distribution of its own stock to its stockholders without the receipt of any payment.

Stock split Occurs when a corporation calls in its stock and replaces each share with more than one new share; decreases both the market value per share and any par or stated value per share.

Stockholders Owners of a corporation. *(p. B-5)*

Stockholders' equity A corporation's equity; also called *shareholders' equity* or *corporate capital*.

Straight-line depreciation Method that allocates an equal portion of the depreciable cost of plant asset (cost minus salvage) to each accounting period in its useful life. *(p. 103)*

Straight-line bond amortization Method allocating an equal amount of bond interest expense to each period of the bond life.

Subsidiary ledger List of individual sub-accounts and amounts with a common characteristic; linked to a controlling account in the general ledger. *(p. 263)*

Sunk cost Cost already incurred and cannot be avoided or changed.

T-account Tool used to show the effects of transactions and events on individual accounts. *(p. 46)*

Target cost Maximum allowable cost for a product or service; defined as expected selling price less the desired profit.

Temporary accounts Accounts used to record revenues, expenses, and withdrawals (dividends for a corporation); they are closed at the end of each period; also called *nominal accounts*. *(p. 130)*

Term bonds Bonds scheduled for payment (maturity) at a single specified date.

Time ticket Source document used to report the time an employee spent working on a job or on overhead activities and then to determine the amount of direct labor to charge to the job or the amount of indirect labor to charge to overhead.

Total asset turnover Measure of a company's ability to use its assets to generate sales; computed by dividing net sales by average total assets.

Total quality management (TQM) Concept calling for all managers and employees at all stages of operations to strive toward higher standards and reduce number of defects.

Trade discount Reduction from a list or catalog price that can vary for wholesalers, retailers, and consumers. *(p. 283)*

Trademark or **Trade (Brand) name** Symbol, name, phrase, or jingle identified with a company, product, or service.

Transportation-In Freight costs paid by the buyer. *(p. 282)*

Treasury stock Corporation's own stock that it reacquired and still holds.

Trial balance List of accounts and their balances at a point in time; total debit balances equal total credit balances. *(p. 55)*

Unadjusted trial balance List of accounts and balances prepared before accounting adjustments are recorded and posted. *(p. 106)*

Unavoidable expense Expense (or cost) that is not relevant for business decisions; an expense that would continue even if a department, product, or service is eliminated.

Unclassified balance sheet Balance sheet that broadly groups assets, liabilities, and equity accounts. *(p. 339)*

Uncontrollable costs Costs that a manager does not have the power to determine or strongly influence.

Underapplied overhead Amount by which overhead incurred in a period exceeds the overhead applied to that period's production using the predetermined overhead rate.

Unearned revenue Liability created when customers pay in advance for products or services; earned when the products or services are later delivered. *(pp. 45 & 313)*

Unfavorable variance Difference in revenues or costs, when the actual amount is compared to the budgeted amount, that contributes to a lower income.

Units-of-production depreciation Method that charges a varying amount to depreciation expense for each period of an asset's useful life depending on its usage.

Unlimited liability Legal relationship among general partners that makes each of them responsible for partnership debts if the other partners are unable to pay their shares.

Unsecured bonds Bonds backed only by the issuer's credit standing; almost always riskier than secured bonds; also called *debentures*.

Useful life Length of time an asset will be productively used in the operations of a business; also called *service life*.

Value-added time The portion of cycle time that is directed at producing a product or service; equals process time.

Value chain Sequential activities that add value to an entity's products or services; includes design, production, marketing, distribution, and service.

Variable cost Cost that changes in proportion to changes in the activity output volume.

Variance analysis Process of examining differences between actual and budgeted revenues or costs and describing them in terms of price and quantity differences.

Vendee Buyer of goods or services. *(p. 164)*

Vendor Seller of goods or services. *(pp. 163 & 282)*

Vertical analysis Evaluation of each financial statement item or group of items in terms of a specific base amount.

Voucher Internal file used to store documents and information to control cash disbursements and to ensure that a transaction is properly authorized and recorded. *(p. 161)*

Voucher register Journal (referred to as *book of original entry*) in which all vouchers are recorded after they have been approved. *(p. 166)*

Voucher system Procedures and approvals designed to control cash disbursements and acceptance of obligations. *(p. 161)*

Wage bracket withholding table Table of the amounts of income tax withheld from employees' wages. *(p. 204)*

Weighted average Method to assign inventory cost to sales; the cost of available-for-sale units is divided by the number of units available to determine per unit cost prior to each sale that is then multiplied by the units sold to yield the cost of that sale.

Wholesaler Intermediary that buys products from manufacturers or other wholesalers and sells them to retailers or other wholesalers. *(p. 258)*

Withdrawals Payment of cash or other assets from a proprietorship or partnership to its owner or owners.

Withholding allowance This determines the amount of federal income taxes to withhold from an employee's pay. *(p. 202)*

Workers' compensation insurance An insurance program that provides benefits to workers who are injured on the job. *(p. 229)*

Work sheet Spreadsheet used to draft an unadjusted trial balance, adjusting entries, adjusted trial balance, and financial statements. *(pp. 100 & 126)*

Working capital Current assets minus current liabilities at a point in time.

Working papers Analyses and other informal reports prepared by accountants and managers when organizing information for formal reports and financial statements. *(p. 100)*

Workplace fraud The deliberate misuse of an employer's assets for an employee's personal gain. *(p. 156)*

Credits

Page 3 Courtesy of LoveSac Corporation

Page 6 AP Images/Louis Lanzano

Page 17 Daniel Berehulak/Getty Images

Page 19 AP Images/Douglas C. Pizac

Page 43 Warren Brown, CakeLove

Page 46 ©Mike Segar/Reuters/CORBIS

Page 56 ©PhotoLink/Getty Images

Page 75 ©Erika Dufair photography, Courtesy of Vosges Haut-Chocolat

Page 78 ©NBAE 2005. Victor Baldizon/Getty Images

Page 99 Courtesy of Alienware® Corporation

Page 125 Courtesy of Betty Rides

Page 155 Chipper Hatter

Page 158 ©Alfred Pasieka/Photo Researchers, Inc.

Page 173 Courtesy of Moe's Southwest Grill

Page 175 Photodisc/Getty Images

Page 176 ©Alan Majchrowicz/Getty Images

Page 201 Courtesy of YoungSong Martin

Page 227 Courtesy of 1-800-GOT-JUNK?

Page 257 Courtesy of Life is good®

Page 260 AP Images/Mark Duncan

Page 279 Courtesy of CoCaLo, Inc.

Page 286 ©Tim de Waele/CORBIS

Page 307 Courtesy of Tony Lee

Page 309 ©2005 Marvel/CORBIS

Page 310 ©Walt Disney Co./Courtesy Everett Collection

Page 333 David Gonzales/Courtesy of Cloudveil Mountain Works.

Page 339 ©BARRY RUNK/STAN/Grant Heilman Photography

Index

Note: Page numbers followed by *n* indicate footnotes; underlined entries are URLs.

Chart of Accounts

Following is a typical chart of accounts. Each company has its own unique accounts and numbering system.

Assets

Current Assets

101 Cash
102 Petty cash
103 Cash equivalents
104 Short-term investments
105 Market adjustment, _____ securities (S-T)
106 Accounts receivable
107 Allowance for doubtful accounts
108 Legal fees receivable
109 Interest receivable
110 Rent receivable
111 Notes receivable
119 Merchandise inventory
120 _____ inventory
121 _____ inventory
124 Office supplies
125 Store supplies
126 _____ supplies
128 Prepaid insurance
129 Prepaid interest
131 Prepaid rent
132 Raw materials inventory
133 Goods in process inventory, _____
134 Goods in process inventory, _____
135 Finished goods inventory

Long-Term Investments

141 Long-term investments
142 Market adjustment, _____ securities (L-T)
144 Investment in _____
145 Bond sinking fund

Plant Assets

151 Automobiles
152 Accumulated depreciation—Automobiles
153 Trucks
154 Accumulated depreciation—Trucks
155 Boats
156 Accumulated depreciation—Boats
157 Professional library
158 Accumulated depreciation—Professional library
159 Law library
160 Accumulated depreciation—Law library
161 Furniture
162 Accumulated depreciation—Furniture
163 Office equipment
164 Accumulated depreciation—Office equipment
165 Store equipment
166 Accumulated depreciation—Store equipment
167 _____ equipment

168 Accumulated depreciation—_____ equipment
169 Machinery
170 Accumulated depreciation—Machinery
173 Building _____
174 Accumulated depreciation—Building _____
175 Building _____
176 Accumulated depreciation—Building _____
179 Land improvements _____
180 Accumulated depreciation—Land improvements _____
181 Land improvements _____
182 Accumulated depreciation—Land improvements _____
183 Land

Natural Resources

185 Mineral deposit
186 Accumulated depletion—Mineral deposit

Intangible Assets

191 Patents
192 Leasehold
193 Franchise
194 Copyrights
195 Leasehold improvements
196 Licenses
197 Accumulated amortization—_____

Liabilities

Current Liabilities

201 Accounts payable
202 Insurance payable
203 Interest payable
204 Legal fees payable
207 Office salaries payable
208 Rent payable
209 Salaries payable
210 Wages payable
211 Accrued payroll payable
214 Estimated warranty liability
215 Income taxes payable
216 Common dividend payable
217 Preferred dividend payable
218 State unemployment taxes payable
219 Employee federal income taxes payable
221 Employee medical insurance payable
222 Employee retirement program payable
223 Employee union dues payable
224 Federal unemployment taxes payable
225 FICA taxes payable
226 Estimated vacation pay liability

Unearned Revenues

230 Unearned consulting fees
231 Unearned legal fees
232 Unearned property management fees
233 Unearned _____ fees
234 Unearned _____ fees
235 Unearned janitorial revenue
236 Unearned _____ revenue
238 Unearned rent

Notes Payable

240 Short-term notes payable
241 Discount on short-term notes payable
245 Notes payable
251 Long-term notes payable
252 Discount on long-term notes payable

Long-Term Liabilities

253 Long-term lease liability
255 Bonds payable
256 Discount on bonds payable
257 Premium on bonds payable
258 Deferred income tax liability

Equity

Owner's Equity

301 _____, Capital
302 _____, Withdrawals
303 _____, Capital
304 _____, Withdrawals
305 _____, Capital
306 _____, Withdrawals

Paid-In Capital

307 Common stock, $ _____ par value
308 Common stock, no-par value
309 Common stock, $ _____ stated value
310 Common stock dividend distributable
311 Paid-in capital in excess of par value, Common stock
312 Paid-in capital in excess of stated value, No-par common stock
313 Paid-in capital from retirement of common stock
314 Paid-in capital, Treasury stock
315 Preferred stock
316 Paid-in capital in excess of par value, Preferred stock

Retained Earnings

318 Retained earnings
319 Cash dividends (or Dividends)
320 Stock dividends

Other Equity Accounts

321 Treasury stock, Common
322 Unrealized gain—Equity
323 Unrealized loss—Equity

Revenues

401 _____ fees earned
402 _____ fees earned
403 _____ services revenue
404 _____ services revenue
405 Commissions earned
406 Rent revenue (or Rent earned)
407 Dividends revenue (or Dividend earned)
408 Earnings from investment in _____
409 Interest revenue (or Interest earned)
410 Sinking fund earnings
413 Sales
414 Sales returns and allowances
415 Sales discounts

Cost of Sales

Cost of Goods Sold

502 Cost of goods sold
505 Purchases
506 Purchases returns and allowances
507 Purchases discounts
508 Transportation-in

Manufacturing

520 Raw materials purchases
521 Transportation-in on raw materials
530 Factory payroll
531 Direct labor
540 Factory overhead
541 Indirect materials
542 Indirect labor
543 Factory insurance expired
544 Factory supervision
545 Factory supplies used
546 Factory utilities
547 Miscellaneous production costs
548 Property taxes on factory building
549 Property taxes on factory equipment
550 Rent on factory building
551 Repairs, factory equipment
552 Small tools written off
560 Depreciation of factory equipment
561 Depreciation of factory building

Standard Cost Variance

580 Direct material quantity variance
581 Direct material price variance
582 Direct labor quantity variance
583 Direct labor price variance
584 Factory overhead cost variance

Expenses

Amortization, Depletion, and Depreciation

601 Amortization expense—_____
602 Amortization expense—_____
603 Depletion expense—_____
604 Depreciation expense—Boats
605 Depreciation expense—Automobiles
606 Depreciation expense—Building _____
607 Depreciation expense—Building _____
608 Depreciation expense—Land improvements _____
609 Depreciation expense—Land improvements _____
610 Depreciation expense—Law library
611 Depreciation expense—Trucks
612 Depreciation expense—_____ equipment
613 Depreciation expense—_____ equipment
614 Depreciation expense—_____
615 Depreciation expense—_____

Employee-Related Expenses

620 Office salaries expense
621 Sales salaries expense
622 Salaries expense
623 _____ wages expense
624 Employees' benefits expense
625 Payroll taxes expense

Financial Expenses

630 Cash over and short
631 Discounts lost
632 Factoring fee expense
633 Interest expense

Insurance Expenses

635 Insurance expense—Delivery equipment
636 Insurance expense—Office equipment
637 Insurance expense—_____

Rental Expenses

640 Rent expense
641 Rent expense—Office space
642 Rent expense—Selling space
643 Press rental expense
644 Truck rental expense
645 _____ rental expense

Supplies Expenses

650 Office supplies expense
651 Store supplies expense
652 _____ supplies expense
653 _____ supplies expense

Miscellaneous Expenses

655 Advertising expense
656 Bad debts expense
657 Blueprinting expense
658 Boat expense
659 Collection expense
661 Concessions expense
662 Credit card expense
663 Delivery expense
664 Dumping expense
667 Equipment expense
668 Food and drinks expense
671 Gas and oil expense
672 General and administrative expense
673 Janitorial expense
674 Legal fees expense
676 Mileage expense
677 Miscellaneous expenses
678 Mower and tools expense
679 Operating expense
680 Organization expense
681 Permits expense
682 Postage expense
683 Property taxes expense
684 Repairs expense—_____
685 Repairs expense—_____
687 Selling expense
688 Telephone expense
689 Travel and entertainment expense
690 Utilities expense
691 Warranty expense
695 Income taxes expense

Gains and Losses

701 Gain on retirement of bonds
702 Gain on sale of machinery
703 Gain on sale of investments
704 Gain on sale of trucks
705 Gain on _____
706 Foreign exchange gain or loss
801 Loss on disposal of machinery
802 Loss on exchange of equipment
803 Loss on exchange of _____
804 Loss on sale of notes
805 Loss on retirement of bonds
806 Loss on sale of investments
807 Loss on sale of machinery
808 Loss on _____
809 Unrealized gain—Income
810 Unrealized loss—Income

Clearing Accounts

901 Income summary
902 Manufacturing summary

A. K. A.

The same financial statement sometimes receives different titles. Below are some of the more common aliases.*

Balance Sheet	Statement of Financial Position
	Statement of Financial Condition
Income Statement	Statement of Income
	Operating Statement
	Statement of Operations
	Statement of Operating Activity
	Earnings Statement
	Statement of Earnings
	Profit and Loss (P&L) Statement
Statement of Cash Flows	Statement of Cash Flow
	Cash Flows Statement
	Statement of Changes in Cash Position
	Statement of Changes in Financial Position
Statement of Owner's Equity	Statement of Changes in Owner's Equity
	Statement of Changes in Owner's Capital
	Statement of Shareholders' Equity[†]
	Statement of Changes in Shareholders' Equity[†]
	Statement of Stockholders' Equity and Comprehensive Income[†]
	Statement of Changes in Capital Accounts[†]

* The term **Consolidated** often precedes or follows these statement titles to reflect the combination of different entities, such as a parent company and its subsidiaries.
[†]Corporation only.

We thank Dr. Louella Moore from Arkansas State University for suggesting this listing.